ROBERT KENNEDY AND HIS TIMES

Volume II

Arthur M. Schlesinger, Jr.

ROBERT KENNEDY
AND HIS TIMES

Illustrated with Photographs

Volume II

HOUGHTON MIFFLIN COMPANY   BOSTON

Acknowledgments

I AM DEEPLY GRATEFUL to Jean Kennedy Smith and John Douglas for their careful reading of the manuscript. Though I did not adopt all their suggestions, their contribution to a clearer and more accurate text has been indispensable. I equally thank and absolve other friends who took time from overcrowded lives to read, correct and improve portions of the book—George W. Ball, Richard Boone, William Bundy, William B. Cannon, Ramsey Clark, Archibald C. Cox, Frederick W. Flott, Michael V. Forrestal, Richard Goodwin, David Hackett, Barbara Wendell Kerr, Mieczyslaw Maneli, Burke Marshall, Clark Mollenhoff, Lloyd Ohlin, Joseph L. Rauh, Jr., Pierre Salinger, Stephen C. Schlesinger, Frederick A. O. Schwarz, Jr., John Seigenthaler, Stephen E. Smith.

Obviously the book could not have been written had it not been for the great generosity of Ethel Kennedy in permitting me unrestricted access to the papers of Robert F. Kennedy. I am also greatly indebted to the Kennedy family for letting me see the collection of family papers herein designated as the Hyannis Port Papers as well as the papers of Joseph P. Kennedy and Stephen Smith in New York. All these collections will go in due course to the Kennedy Library in Boston. Like all students of the recent political history of the United States, I have benefited immeasurably from the ready and expert cooperation of the directors and staffs of the presidential libraries —especially of Dan H. Fenn, Jr., John F. Stewart, William W. Moss, Joan-Ellen Marci and so many others at the Kennedy Library, which houses the papers of John F. Kennedy, Frank Mankiewicz, Burke Marshall, Theodore C. Sorensen and William vanden Heuvel as well as the transcripts produced in the John F. Kennedy and Robert F. Kennedy Oral History Programs; and also of archivists at the Lyndon B. Johnson Library in Austin, Texas, and the Herbert Hoover

Library in West Branch, Iowa. Selections from Robert Kennedy's FBI files, made available to me under the Freedom of Information Act, are designated in the notes as "RFK/FBI/FOIA release." I thank Jules Feiffer, Mary Bailey Gimbel, Richard Goodwin, David Hackett, Thomas Johnston, Patricia Kennedy Lawford, Allard Lowenstein, William Manchester, Mieczyslaw Maneli, John Bartlow Martin, Barrett Prettyman, Jr., Abba Schwartz, James Stevenson, William C. Sullivan, Felicia Warburg, James Wechsler and Theodore H. White for their kindness in making personal papers available to me; A. J. P. Taylor and the Beaverbrook Foundation for sending me copies of the correspondence between Joseph P. Kennedy and Lord Beaverbrook from the Beaverbrook Papers; the late Herman Kahn and the Yale University Library for facilitating my consultation of the papers of Walter Lippmann and Chester Bowles; and John C. Broderick and the Manuscript Division of the Library of Congress for the papers of James M. Landis and Hugo Black.

I stand in particular debt to the oral history interviewers who have done so much to enrich and amplify the record of the time: Anthony Lewis, William Manchester, John Bartlow Martin and John Stewart for their interviews with Robert Kennedy; the host of volunteers who conducted interviews for the Kennedy Library after the death of John F. Kennedy; and the expert corps of Kennedy Library professionals who have interviewed close associates of both John and Robert Kennedy—notably Roberta Greene and L. J. Hackman, who between them conducted more than sixty interviews, and to many others. Jean Stein generously allowed me to see the oral history interviews she undertook for her invaluable book, edited in collaboration with George Plimpton, *American Journey* (New York, 1970). I thank especially the innumerable interviewees who kindly permitted me to quote from their transcripts as well as many other persons, cited in the notes, who allowed me to interview them directly.

At Houghton Mifflin, Richard McAdoo watched the book stretch out in time and length with exemplary patience, and Helena Bentz Dorrance prepared the manuscript for the printer with exemplary thoroughness. I must also thank Luise Erdmann for reading the proofs and Julia Stair for an excellent index.

Once again I rejoice to express my unlimited gratitude to Gretchen Stewart and to Mary Chiffriller for the devoted and meticulous care they expended on typing several drafts of the manuscript, collating texts, checking references, getting the manuscript to the publisher and meanwhile keeping a busy office in a semblance of order. President

Harold Proshansky and the Graduate School of the City University of New York, especially the efficient librarians, were helpful at all times. Above all, I thank Alexandra Emmet Schlesinger, who not only read the manuscript with fastidious and unerring eye but suffered and sustained the author during the throes of composition; and I thank our children still at home, Robert Emmet Kennedy Schlesinger and Peter Cushing Allan, for putting up with it all.

ARTHUR M. SCHLESINGER, JR.

Contents

Volume II

ROBERT KENNEDY
AND HIS TIMES

The Cuban Connection: II

THE DAILY LIFE of an Attorney General went on. The missiles of October were an interruption, framed between Ole Miss in September, the housing order in November, the preparation for the Georgia county-unit case in December. Still Robert Kennedy could not completely disengage from Cuba. There remained Operation Mongoose. There remained the Bay of Pigs prisoners.

I

The crisis finished Mongoose. "We had a terrible experience," Robert Kennedy recalled in 1964. CIA's Task Force W was "going to send sixty people into Cuba right during the missile crisis." One of them sent word to the Attorney General that they did not mind going but wanted to make sure he thought it worthwhile. "I checked into it, and nobody knew about it. . . . The CIA didn't and the top officials didn't." The ineffable William K. Harvey, it developed, had conceived on his own the project of dispatching ten commando teams to Cuba. Three had already departed. Kennedy called a meeting at the Pentagon. As Harvey later put it, the Attorney General took "a great deal of exception." "I was furious," Kennedy remembered, "because I said you were dealing with people's lives . . . and then you're going to go off with a half-assed operation such as this. . . . I've never seen [Harvey] since."[1]

On October 30 the Executive Committee canceled all "sabotage or militant operations during negotiations with Soviets" and sent General Lansdale to Florida to make sure that Task Force W obeyed.[2] Shortly thereafter both Mongoose and the Special Group (Augmented) were abolished. The CIA, taking care of its own, made Harvey station chief in Rome, where he was soon sodden with drink.

Lansdale moved on to other matters, then retired in the autumn of 1963. Rip Robertson went off to Vietnam.

Asked for his retrospective assessment, Maxwell Taylor said Mongoose "didn't work well at all."[3] Lansdale thought it worse than that. CIA's mindless hit-and-run tactics, he said, far from creating a political movement against the regime, stiffened the "national resolve" behind Castro.[4] The effects beyond Cuba were no better. Had sabotage been more successful, the result could have been only to increase Cuba's economic dependence on the Soviet Union. The secret war, not unreasonably seen by Castro as preparation for a new and better invasion, intensified the Cuban desire for Soviet protection.

The program Robert Kennedy and Lansdale had intended was different from the program CIA carried out. But the political base for their anti-Castro uprising simply did not exist inside Cuba, nor did the CIA wish to create such a base. The Bay of Pigs ought to have made it sufficiently clear how covert action degenerated as directives passed from immaculate conference rooms at CIA headquarters to embattled officers in the field and from there to war lovers behind the lines. Lansdale tried to control Harvey; but a Lansdale in Washington implied a Harvey in Miami, as a Harvey implied a Rip Robertson, and a Rip Robertson implied a Ramón Orozco, grinning as he brought his two severed ears back from Cuba.

The problem was why they had not called off Mongoose long before. The answer perhaps was a driven sense in the administration that someone ought to be doing *something* to make life difficult for Castro. Mongoose was poorly conceived and wretchedly executed. It deserved greatly to fail. It was Robert Kennedy's most conspicuous folly.

II

Mongoose had always weighed less on Robert Kennedy's mind than his other Cuban commitment of 1962: the Bay of Pigs prisoners.

Castro had given his list of drugs and medicines—ten thousand items, specified in detail—to the unflagging James Donovan in mid-October, two days before the world knew of the Soviet missiles. The crisis behind him, Castro was almost madder at the Russians than at the Americans. He was looking for a way to reestablish himself as an independent actor on the world scene. He needed the medical supplies. And he had no easy alternative for the prisoners. "You can't shoot them," Donovan had said in his frank, semikidding way.

"Maybe you could have done that at one time, but you can't do it now. . . . If you want to get rid of them, if you're going to sell them, you've got to sell them to me. There's no world market for prisoners."[5]

In mid-November, Castro let Alvaro Sanchez of the Cuban Families Committee visit the prisons. Appalled, Sanchez rushed back to the United States. "I'm a cattleman, Mr. Attorney General," Sanchez told Robert Kennedy on November 24, "and these men look like animals who are going to die." He could tell, he said, by looking at the back of their necks. "If you are going to rescue these men, this is the time because if you wait you will be liberating corpses." Kennedy said, "You are right. I think this is the moment." "We put them there," he told Edwin Guthman, "and we're going to get them out— by Christmas!" Guthman said it was not possible. "We will," Kennedy said.[6] This meant, under the terms of the Castro-Donovan agreement, that within a month Castro would have to receive 20 percent of the items on his list and acceptable guarantees for the delivery of the rest within six to nine months; also the $2.9 million owed for the sick and wounded prisoners sent to the United States the previous April.

There followed a classic Robert Kennedy operation. Nicholas Katzenbach, who had spent two years himself in a prisoner-of-war camp, became coordinator; Louis Oberdorfer of the Tax Division, field commander. Several Washington lawyers were enlisted: John Nolan to work with Donovan; Barrett Prettyman to solve the transportation problems; John Douglas as a general trouble-shooter. (All three joined the Department in 1963.) Mitchell Rogovin of the Internal Revenue Service handed down quick rulings on the tax deductibility of corporate contributions. Lawrence Houston of the CIA operated indistinctly in the background.

"None of us knew anything about any of the problems," Joseph Dolan said later. "Nobody knew anything about transportation, drugs, or baby food." Dolan, tying up loose ends at Ole Miss, was summoned back to Washington by Oberdorfer. He arrived to find a meeting in progress.

> Oberdorfer looked up and said to me, "Bob has a project going; we are going to try to get the Cuban prisoners out." I said, "Oh, damn." Everybody looked at me in a surprised way. I sat down and was there for about a minute when all of a sudden I said, "Oh." Lou said, "What is the matter?" I said, "You mean we are going to negotiate?" . . . I really thought that with Bob Kennedy we were going to get something going with some

boats and we were going down to get the prisoners out. I had just returned from Oxford, Mississippi, and expected anything.[7]

The first problem was the drug industry—under congressional investigation for price markups and other sharp practices, filled with self-pity over what it regarded as bureaucratic persecution, distrustful of the Kennedy administration, even less fond of Castro and not disposed to do favors for either by donating drugs to ransom prisoners. Speaking with uncommon eloquence before industry leaders, the Attorney General argued the American responsibility for brave men who, at American instigation, had risked their lives for freedom and now, unless freed themselves, would die miserably in Castro's jails. His presentation, according to Oberdorfer, "had a tremendous impact on those businessmen. They came back to my office with red eyes . . . and they really got busy."[8]

The Attorney General had to tread a difficult line. Many of the sixty-three companies that made donations were under antitrust or Federal Trade Commission investigation.* He repeatedly said that cooperation would bring no favors, refusal no reprisals. In fact, the drug industry made no great sacrifice. Tax rulings based on wholesale prices produced windfall profits for some companies because of the high markups. A few companies even tried to unload inventories of obsolescent items. And, as Lloyd Cutler, the counsel for the Pharmaceutical Manufacturers Association, said after it was all over:

> The action of the drug industry in responding to the Attorney General's request was not followed by any visible change in the attitude or policies of any division in the Department of Justice. . . . Both antitrust and criminal prosecutions have been just as vigorous, and their legislative attitude is essentially the same and not entirely what we ourselves would think was the correct government policy.[9]

Supplies rapidly accumulated. So did problems. The Pentagon, for example, worried about items of alleged military value on Castro's list, such as retractable steel rulers. The Attorney General said tersely, "Are they bombs?" and they stayed in.[10] The biggest problem was getting the goods to Havana by Christmas. "Experts in the field," said Barrett Prettyman, "told us flatly that this operation was impossible—$11 million worth of goods could not be solicited from all over the country, prepared for shipment, transported by rail, air and truck, reloaded at a common point for transporting by sea and air, and unloaded in Cuba, all within less than two weeks"—and especially in

* At the time, thirteen firms were actually defendants in antitrust actions, twelve in FTC actions (Victor Navasky, *Kennedy Justice* [New York, 1971], 338, 453–457).

the Christmas season.[11] But they all charged ahead. Prettyman has left a description of Oberdorfer's headquarters:

> . . . constant calls (often with four or five people waiting for each of us on incoming lines), a steady barrage of incoming and outgoing memoranda and files, quick and pointed conferences between from two to a dozen persons, sandwiches and coffee snatched at odd moments, the influx of businessmen, railroad men, airline executives, shippers and government personnel, the large donations chart that was changed and watched and worried over, the sudden appearance of the Attorney General with words of advice and some hurried decisions, the tension when a big donation hung in the balance, the irritation at red tape and confusion, the relief when a donor or a shipment developed out of nowhere, the laughter when a company tried to unload an absurd product, the concern when the direct line to Donovan remained silent too long.[12]

On December 18, Donovan flew to Havana, where Nolan and Prettyman soon joined him. Nolan: Donovan and Castro had established a "very cordial, bantering" relationship; "Castro, I think, regarded Jim as kind of a character, a role that Donovan played to the hilt."[13] Prettyman: Castro "leaped at the chance to take a group of us to Hemingway's home," a wild ride with two cars abreast along narrow country roads.[14] The drug shipments were arriving, but, with all the jollity, a difficulty remained: the ransom left unpaid for the April prisoner release. After half the remaining prisoners had been loaded into planes, the Cubans made it clear that this was it until they received the $2.9 million.

Robert Kennedy turned to Cardinal Cushing of Boston, a sponsor for the Cuban Families Committee. "I remembered a talk I had with Jack about the Bay of Pigs prisoners," Cushing said later. "It was the first time I ever saw tears in his eyes."[15] Such a reaction from the least sentimental Kennedy impressed the highly sentimental cardinal, who raised $1 million in a few hours from Latin American friends ("I promised them it would be repaid within three months and it was").[16] General Lucius Clay, another committee sponsor, valiantly raised the rest on his personal note. Word flashed to Havana. The last members of the Brigade boarded the planes.

It was now the day before Christmas. In Miami wives and children waited in a tumult of emotion and relief. When the last of 1113 prisoners had disembarked, Donovan called Katzenbach in Washington, and Katzenbach called Kennedy at Hickory Hill, where he was surrounded by his children on Christmas Eve: "Bob, they are all in; it's over." Katzenbach added in his ironic way, "Bob, I don't think I will come in tomorrow." "Why not?" said Kennedy. "No reason at all,

Bob," said Katzenbach. "I'm just not coming in." "All right, you
guys," said Kennedy, "what about Hoffa?" He was being ironic too,
but, reflected Dolan, this was the essence of Robert Kennedy: "always on to the next hill, on to the next hill, on to the next hill."[17]

III

Four days after Christmas John Kennedy went to the Orange Bowl in
Miami and addressed the reunited Bay of Pigs Brigade. Rusk and
Bundy advised against his going. So did O'Donnell, who said: "It will
look as though you're planning to back them in another invasion of
Cuba." But Robert encouraged him, believing, O'Donnell thought,
that the appearance "would ease the President's sense of guilt."[18] In
the emotion of the day, Kennedy made a promise, not in the script,
that the Brigade's battle flag would be returned "in a free Havana."[19]
The exiles, taking this as O'Donnell had feared, chanted *"Guerra!
Guerra! Guerra!"*[20] Actually Kennedy's script was designed to signal
Havana that Washington's objection was to Cuba's external alliances
and aspirations, not to its revolution. "We support the right of every
free people," he also said, "to transform the economic and political
institutions of society so that they may serve the welfare of all." Both
the Brigade and Castro received the wrong message.

In Washington the Executive Committee, now diminished in size
and rebaptized the Standing Group, wrestled with Cuba policy. Its
members were McNamara, McCone, Bundy, Sorensen and Robert
Kennedy. The administration was no closer to an answer to Castro
than in earlier years. On one extreme was Bundy, who proposed on
January 4, 1963, an exploration of the possibility of communicating
with Castro. Thereafter what Bundy called in April the "gradual development of some form of accommodation with Castro" became a
standard item in lists of policy alternatives.[21] On the other extreme
was the Defense Department, which, as Sterling Cottrell of State reported to Bundy late in January, still favored "increasing degrees of
political, economic, psychological and military pressures" to bring
about "the overthrow of the Castro-Communist regime." If anti-
Castro groups in Cuba requested assistance, Defense thought the
United States "should be in a position to respond with open military
support . . . up to the full range of military forces."[22] The Pentagon
felt more than ever, as one of State's Cuban specialists put it, that "we
had missed the big bus" in not invading Cuba during the missile
crisis.[23]

As for Robert Kennedy, he was particularly worried by Castro's own secret war against Latin America, especially when the Cubans in February organized a guerrilla front against Betancourt in Venezuela. On March 14, following what he evidently found a most unsatisfactory NSC meeting, he sent his brother a testy memorandum urging new efforts to counter Cuban-trained operatives in South America. As for Cuba itself,

> John McCone spoke at the meeting today about revolt amongst the military. He described the possibilities in rather optimistic terms. What is the basis for that appraisal? What can and should we do to increase the likelihood of this kind of action? . . . Do we have evidence of any break amongst the top Cuban leaders and if so, is the CIA or USIA attempting to cultivate that feeling? I would not like it said a year from now that we could have had this internal breakup in Cuba but we just did not set the stage for it.[24]

The President, as usual, felt less tragically about Cuba. Though he did tell Bundy to send his brother's questions to CIA, he did not respond directly to the Attorney General, who wrote him plaintively nearly two weeks later: "Did you feel there was any merit to my last memo? . . . In any case, is there anything further on this matter?"[25]

IV

Most of the 200,000 Cuban refugees in the United States were hard-working, law-abiding people, happy at the chance of a new life in a land of relative political and intellectual freedom.* A minority were violent men, consumed with a single hope and a single hatred, living for the day when they could return to Havana with Fidel Castro's head on a pike. Embittered by the peaceful resolution of the missile crisis, the anti-Castro zealots were now determined to force the administration into action against its will—by rumors and raids and exile manipulation of American domestic politics. "European embassies," wrote the English ambassador to Havana, "began to be plagued . . . with anonymous phone calls and letters and mysterious visitors bringing with them sketches and plans of caves all over the country where the Cuban Government was alleged to have hidden away a proportion of their stock of rockets. . . . It seemed 90 percent certain to most of us that this was another attempt by would-be counter-revolu-

---

* Of these refugees, 153,634 entered legally from January 1961 to the missile crisis; 29,962 from the missile crisis to November 1965; others arrived "illegally" on boats and rafts (L. D. Bender, *The Politics of Hostility: Castro's Revolution and United States Policy* [Hato Rey, Puerto Rico, 1975], 118).

tionaries to bring about a United States invasion in a last desperate gamble to bring down the Castro regime."[26] The rumors raced on to Miami and thence to the United States Senate.

On January 31, 1963, the indefatigable Kenneth Keating declared that the Soviet Union had cunningly filled Cuban caves with nuclear missiles. Soon Keating shifted his target to the Soviet soldiers still in Cuba. Richard Nixon denounced Kennedy's Cuban policy—"we have goofed an invasion, paid tribute to Castro for the prisoners, then given the Soviets squatters' rights in our backyard"—and demanded a "command decision" to get the Russians out.[27] John Kennedy muttered privately that 17,000 Soviet troops in Cuba were not so bad compared to 27,000 American troops in Turkey, but added wearily, "It isn't wise politically, to understand Khrushchev's problems in quite this way."[28] It wasn't wise politically because the visible pressure was all for drastic action. In April, when James Reston of the *New York Times* wrote in some detail about the "subversive war" conducted by the American government against Cuba,* no one in Congress or the press saw this as a matter for investigation or criticism.

Actually, by the time Reston wrote, the secret war was almost at an end. The exile raids had become too much. Under such designations as Alpha 66 and Commandos L-66, daring men in small fast boats, setting out from the Bahamian keys, sometimes from Florida itself, had been landing saboteurs in Cuba and firing torpedoes at Cuban ships; even, as on March 18 and again on March 26–27, at Soviet ships. These raids, John Kennedy told Marquis Childs, the columnist, "made everything worse."[29] The NSC met gloomily on the subject at the end of March. Robert Kennedy noted:

> McCone presentation—Gave facts & then said felt less criticism by newspapers & Congress if we do not stand down the raids.
>
> Rusk: If these raids are going to be carried out we have to accept responsibility—better if they are going to be done that we do it. . . .
>
> Decided to proceed & work up plan to prevent attacks from continuing.[30]

The next day the administration announced it would "take every step necessary" to stop raids from the United States. As the CIA station chief in Miami recalled it, "The whole apparatus of government, Coast Guard, Customs, Immigration and Naturalization, FBI, CIA, were working together to try to keep these operations from going to

---

* James Reston, "Kennedy and His Critics on Cuba," *New York Times,* April 21, 1963. The Reston column proves that the "secret war" was not much of a secret.

Cuba."[31] The FBI entered exile camps and seized caches of dynamite and bomb casings. A number of Cubans were indicted. Early in April, Kennedy terminated CIA financial support for Miro Cardona and the Cuban Revolutionary Council. The Standing Group meanwhile decided that the CIA sabotage program was "not worth the effort expended on it." On April 3, Bundy informed a Cuba meeting that no further sabotage operations were under way.[32] When Robert Kennedy brought up the subject again the next month, Bundy ordered another review and then told the Attorney General: "The sum and substance of it is that useful organized sabotage is still very hard to get. . . . Proposals which do more good than harm are rare."[33]

V

Early in April 1963, Donovan and Nolan had returned to Havana to wrap up the prisoner exchange negotiations. This time Castro took them to the Bay of Pigs and delivered an amiable battlefield lecture. To demonstrate the impassability of the area beyond the beachhead, he strode several paces into the salt marsh until mud oozed to the top of his boots. They lunched on a boat in the bay and spent the sun-drenched afternoon fishing and skin-diving, guided by a Russian PT boat.[34]

Donovan's mission now was to secure the release of a number of Americans, including CIA men, from Cuban prisons. (When this was first broached to him, Donovan had said, "Jesus Christ, I've already done the loaves and the fishes, and now they want me to walk on the water.")[35] Castro asked about future United States policy. Donovan pointed to the restrictions placed on exile groups but added that the prisoners remained "a stumbling block." Castro pursued the question. "His ideal government, he emphasized, was not to be Soviet oriented." He asked how diplomatic ties might be resumed. Donovan replied: the way porcupines make love—very carefully. At a minimum Donovan thought there must be assurances that Cuba would leave other Latin countries alone. Later, Dr. René Vallejo, Castro's intimate friend and personal physician, who had interned in Boston and served with the U.S. Army in the war,[36] took Donovan aside and said that Fidel "wanted to officially establish such relationships . . . even though certain Communist officials in the Cuban government were unalterably opposed."*

---

* This account of the Castro-Donovan talks is drawn from Donovan's debriefing by M. C. Miskovsky of the CIA and Miskovsky's memorandum of April 13, 1963, to

Donovan considered Castro "a most intelligent, shrewd and relatively stable political leader."[37] "Throughout the prisoner exchange negotiations," Nolan reported to Robert Kennedy, "he had been both reasonable and reliable and has not been difficult to deal with."[38] "Our impressions," Nolan said later, "would not square with the commonly accepted image. . . . Castro was never irrational, never drunk, never dirty." "What do you think?" Robert Kennedy asked. "Can we do business with that fellow?"[39]

Donovan's efforts secured the release of nearly 10,000 Cubans and Americans from Cuban detention by July 4.[40] After Donovan's visit and on his recommendation,[41] Castro gave Lisa Howard of the American Broadcasting Company ten hours of interview in late April. She concluded that Castro was "looking for a way to reach a rapprochement," probably for economic reasons. The "U.S. limitations on exile raids," Castro had said, were "a proper step toward accommodation." Che Guevara and Raul Castro, Lisa Howard thought, opposed accommodation; Vallejo and Raul Roa, the foreign minister, favored it. Castro himself, Howard felt, was ready to discuss rapprochement "with proper progressive spokesmen." He indicated, however, "that if a rapprochement was wanted President John F. Kennedy would have to make the first move."*

John McCone. Donovan later wrote of Castro: "A handsome man and witty conversationalist, he little resembles the caricature which we see in the United States. His grooming in personal life is impeccable" (James B. Donovan, *Challenges* [New York, 1967], 100–101).

* CIA debriefing of Lisa Howard, May 1, 1963, RFK Papers. This had not always been Che Guevara's position. On August 17, 1961, after the Punta del Este conference, he had held a conversation in Montevideo with Richard Goodwin. He then said, as Goodwin reported to President Kennedy, "that they didn't want an understanding with the United States, because they knew that was impossible. They would like a *modus vivendi*—at least an interim *modus vivendi*. . . . He thought we should put forth such a formula because we had public opinion to worry about whereas he could accept anything without worrying about public opinion. I said nothing, and he waited and then said . . . (1) That they could not give back the expropriated properties . . . but they could pay for them in trade. [Payment for expropriated properties, Goodwin said later, was "the thing that meant least to JFK." Che's idea that it was of primary importance revealed his own Marxist dogmatism about democratic leaders.] (2) They could agree not to make any political alliance with the East—although this would not affect their natural sympathies. (3) They would have free elections—but only after a period of institutionalizing the revolution had been completed. . . . This included the establishment of a one-party system. (4) Of course, they would not attack Guantanamo. . . . (5) He indicated, very obliquely and with evident reluctance because of the company in which we were talking, that they could also discuss the activities of the Cuban revolution in other countries. . . . He said they could discuss no formula that would mean giving up the type of society to which they were dedicated." He also thanked Goodwin for the Bay of Pigs: "It had been a great political victory for them

But a few days after his talks with Lisa Howard, Castro was on his way to the Soviet Union. Returning after five weeks in a glow of enthusiasm, he did his best to dispel the anti-Soviet doubts he had himself fostered after the missile crisis. The collapse of the 1963 sugar crop made him more dependent than ever on Soviet aid. On the other hand, he may have also come back impressed by Khrushchev's post-crisis desire for détente.

The American government was no less vacillating. When the Standing Group met in Washington at the end of May, bafflement prevailed. McCone argued for sabotage in order to "create a situation . . . in which it would be possible to subvert military leaders to the point of their acting to overthrow Castro." McNamara questioned the utility of sabotage and preferred overt economic pressures. The Attorney General, ever the activist, said the United States "must do something against Castro, even though we do not believe our actions would bring him down."[42] On June 3 the Special Group recommended the exploration of "various possibilities of establishing channels of communication to Castro." The American government appeared, like Castro, to be facing in two directions. For on June 19 the Special Group suddenly approved a new sabotage program directed at major segments of the Cuban economy.[43]

VI

The June 19 decision meant the resurrection, in a highly qualified way, of the secret war. The object was no longer to overthrow the regime; only to "nourish a spirit of resistance and disaffection which could lead to significant defections and other byproducts of unrest."[44] The new campaign, while less ambitious than Mongoose, seems, after the failure of Mongoose, even more pointless. Given the imperfect documentation, one must surmise what lay behind the June revival:

—enabled them to consolidate—and transformed them from an aggrieved little country to an equal" (Goodwin to JFK, August 22, 1961, Schlesinger Papers).

Perhaps Guevara was following instructions from Castro, rationalizing this ("an interim *modus vivendi*") as a Leninist tactic in the tradition of Brest-Litovsk, or perhaps he was less radical then than he became by 1963. There was no follow-up in Washington because, as Goodwin reminded me in 1977, the timing and psychology were wrong. It was too soon after the Bay of Pigs humiliation. More important, Betancourt, Haya de la Torre, Frei and the democratic left in Latin America would have been appalled. A modus vivendi would have legitimized a Marxist regime in the hemisphere and therefore given a color of legitimacy to Communist actions against democratic regimes in Venezuela and elsewhere (Richard Goodwin, in interview by author, June 11, 1977).

the desire to divert Castro from Venezuela, where his secret war against Betancourt was building to a climax; a desire also to intensify his economic stringencies; beyond this, a relief from frustration, a feeling that Castro deserved harassment, a hope that what the White House saw as no more than "pinpricks"[45] would, without interrupting détente, reassure Latin American governments, Cuban exiles, Republican critics and the CIA that the administration was not faltering in its opposition to Castro.

The imperfect record also makes it hard to discover what had actually been going on since Mongoose. When Desmond FitzGerald, who had replaced Harvey as the CIA's man for Cuba, was asked by the Special Group on June 19 whether the Cubans might retaliate, he replied that they always had this capability "but that they have not retaliated to date, in spite of a number of publicized exile raids." The phrase "exile raids" implied that the Agency had been doing nothing itself. Certainly the Special Group, according to the Church committee, had authorized "little, if any," CIA sabotage in the first six months of 1963.[46] But had CIA been up to its old tricks? Had it indeed been responsible for the March attacks on Soviet shipping—the attacks the President and the National Security Council had blamed on Alpha 66 and Commandos L-66? Captain Bradley Earl Ayers, a paratrooper assigned to CIA, recalled General Victor Krulak, the JCS counterinsurgency specialist, telling him in the spring of 1963 that the operations attributed to exile groups were mostly "planned and conducted under the supervision of the CIA . . . from bases in southern Florida." When Ayers himself went to southern Florida to train Cuban commando units, he learned that "customarily, either by prearrangement through exile operatives or because of their own wish to capitalize on the political impact of such incidents, one of the splinter, independent Cuban exile groups, such as Alpha 66, would publicly take credit for the [CIA] raids."[47] Despite the death of Mongoose and the lack of Special Group authorization, CIA / Miami evidently continued, under exile cover, to wage its private war against Castro. "When the target diminishes," as James Angleton, CIA's counterespionage chief, said later, "it's very difficult for a bureaucracy to adjust. What do you do with your personnel? We owed a deep obligation to the men in Miami."[48] It was easier to crank up a large clandestine operation than to wind it down.

The FBI continued raiding exile camps after June 19,[49] but perhaps these were camps not under CIA control. CIA / Miami, according to Ayers, meanwhile received orders to "increase the effectiveness and frequency of hit-and-run raids by exile commando groups."* Robert Kennedy thought Desmond FitzGerald an improvement over the detested Harvey. Sabotage was "better organized than it had been before and was having quite an effect." What kind of projects? asked John Bartlow Martin. Kennedy replied, a little inconsistently, "Well, just going in blowing up a mine . . . a bridge. Some of them ended in disaster, people were captured, tried and confessed. It wasn't very helpful." "Any direct assassination attempt on Castro?" "No." "None tried?" "No." "Contemplated?" "No."[50] Alas, Kennedy did not know all the projects FitzGerald was organizing.

Other efforts were mounted against the Castro regime from Central America. Here the record is unusually murky. At the end of June, Luis Somoza, son of the thieving Nicaraguan dictator and a former president of Nicaragua himself, asked to see the Attorney General. The State Department advised Kennedy that Somoza wanted to know the American attitude toward an anti-Castro base about to be set up in Nicaragua by Manuel Artime, the Bay of Pigs leader. "We recommend that you limit your reply to . . . general terms," State said; Kennedy might express sympathy with the exiles but no particular knowledge of Artime.[51] There was, indeed, an Artime operation and Hal Hendrix of the *Miami News* supposed it managed either by CIA or, "on a hip pocket basis," by the Attorney General himself.[52]

Somoza was soon telling Caribbean notables that he had received a "green light" from Robert Kennedy to mount anti-Castro raids from Nicaraguan bases.[53] In another month he claimed he was "leading a movement of the five Central American countries to overthrow Castro and that he had the blessing of the United States government." When a Central American repeated this remark to the State Department, the coordinator of Cuban affairs responded that Somoza had received neither a green nor even an amber light from Washington and that his claims should be treated with "extreme reserve."[54] In 1964, the Somozas alleged that Robert Kennedy and McNamara had assured them of full U.S. support for Artime. The State Department promptly cabled the American ambassador in Managua, "No high

* B. E. Ayers, *The War That Never Was* (Indianapolis, Ind., 1976), 100. Ayers also claimed that Robert Kennedy himself paid two visits to CIA installations in Florida—one after it had been decided to hit a major Cuban oil refinery (ibid., 76, 147–148). Kennedy's appointment books show no trips to Florida between April 27–28 (when he went to see his father at Palm Beach) and November 28–December 3 (at Palm Beach and Hobe Sound). He made two earlier weekend trips that year to Palm Beach: January 25–28 and March 15–18.

USG officials have made statements about USG support for Artime
such as those attributed to them," though some may have said they
considered Artime "a responsible, dedicated Cuban leader."[55]

My guess is that CIA was financing Artime,* that State disapproved and may not even have known and that Robert Kennedy, if
he knew, thought Artime a brave man who had earned an opportunity to show what he could do. But the whole episode remains
perplexing. Robert Kennedy understood so lucidly the enormity of a
Pearl Harbor air strike on a small country. It is odd that he did not
see that the same principle applied to the secret war. Still, in the May
of Birmingham and Bull Connor, in the June when George Wallace
stood in the schoolhouse door, in the summer when Medgar Evers
died and Martin Luther King dreamed, in the autumn of the civil
rights bill, Cuba was not a subject to which the Attorney General
devoted sustained attention.

VII

It deserved sustained attention. The White House saw the resumed
secret war as a way of keeping Castro off balance and neutralizing
bureaucratic discontent while deciding whether it would be possible
to risk a try at accommodation. But the CIA, under its distended
theory of authorization, saw it as a license to renew its attempts to
kill the Maximum Leader. These attempts made even less sense in
1963 than they had before. The notion of invading Cuba had been
dead for years. I suppose that, in 1961 and 1962, CIA might still
have regarded assassination as the ultimate logic of a frenetic
overthrow-Castro policy. But in 1963, with invasion absolutely excluded, with the anti-Castro policy drastically modified and with the
White House drifting toward accommodation, assassination had no
logic at all.

In the spring of 1963, moreover, the Standing Group had asked
the CIA's Intelligence Branch to assess possible developments in the
event of Castro's death. This had nothing to do with assassination
plots; estimating the consequences of the death of a national leader,
from whatever cause, was a favorite intelligence exercise, applied
indifferently to de Gaulle, Khrushchev, Salazar or Castro. The CIA

---

* It certainly was by 1964–65. See Senate Select Committee to Study Governmental
Operations with respect to Intelligence Activities (hereafter cited as Church commit-
tee), *Interim Report: Alleged Assassination Plots Involving Foreign Leaders*, 94
Cong., 1 Sess. (1975), 89–90. (Artime is referred to under the code designation B-1.)

Office of National Estimates decided that Castro's death, far from benefiting the United States, would probably mean that "his brother Raul or some other figure in the regime would, with Soviet backing and help, take over." And, if Castro were by any chance assassinated, "the U.S. would be widely charged with complicity."[56]

So far as the Church committee could discover, the Clandestine Service's assassinatory enthusiasm had lain dormant after January 1963, when its technicians failed to perfect the explosive seashell designed to blow up the Maximum Skindiver. The June 19 decision to revive the secret war now rekindled that old feeling. CIA turned to an "agent in place" in Havana—Rolando Cubela Secades, a revolutionary zealot who had killed Batista's military intelligence chief in 1956, fought beside Castro in the Escambray Mountains, seized the Presidential Palace in advance of Castro's own arrival in Havana in 1959 and in 1960 was Castro's instrument in destroying the ancient freedoms of the University of Havana. Thereafter Cubela claimed disillusionment. The Agency recruited him in 1961 and gave him the code name of Am/Lash. A heavy drinker and a psychiatric patient, Cubela was not the ideal operative; better, however, in the CIA view, than no man in Havana at all.[57]

The Agency, which had dropped contact with Cubela after the missile crisis, got in touch again. In early September he met a CIA man in São Paulo, Brazil, and said he was prepared to attempt an "inside job" against Castro's life.[58] On September 7, the very day that CIA/Washington received the report on the Brazil meeting, Castro attended a party at the Brazilian embassy in Havana. There he told Daniel Harker of the Associated Press, "Kennedy is the Batista of our time, and the most opportunistic President of all time." He warned against "terrorist plans to eliminate Cuban leaders." He said: "We are prepared to . . . answer in kind. United States leaders should think that if they assist in terrorist plans to eliminate Cuban leaders, they themselves will not be safe."[59]

The fact that Castro chose the Brazilian embassy for this interesting disquisition alarmed CIA counterespionage experts. Was he signaling his knowledge of the São Paulo meeting? Their suspicions increased when Cubela requested murder weapons and a meeting with Robert Kennedy. Was Cubela an *agent provocateur*? Even if not, was it safe, given his known instability, to bring him into direct contact with high American officials? "My disapproval of it was very strong," one counterespionage officer testified. "Des FitzGerald knew it . . . and preferred not to discuss it any more with me." Richard Helms solved the Robert Kennedy request by deciding, according to the CIA inspector general's report, that "it was not necessary to seek approval from Robert Kennedy for FitzGerald to speak in his name."[60]

It was in this period that McCone read about Sam Giancana and the CIA in the *Chicago Sun-Times* and demanded an explanation. His subordinates, on the principle of admitting only defunct operations, explained Giancana away as a historical incident. They told him nothing about Am/Lash. Nor, so far as the record shows, was anyone outside CIA—in the White House, State, Defense or Justice— told about Am/Lash.*

Presenting himself falsely as Robert Kennedy's "personal representative," Desmond FitzGerald met Cubela on October 29, 1963. Cubela asked anxiously for some means of killing Castro without being killed himself. FitzGerald claimed to have told Cubela that the United States would support a successful coup but would have "no part of an attempt on Castro's life." The case officer, who served as interpreter, did not remember any such disclaimer. In any event, when the three met again three weeks later, FitzGerald, according to the CIA record, promised Cubela "everything he needed (telescopic sight, silencer, all the money he wanted)." In addition, FitzGerald presented Cubela with a ball-point pen containing a hypodermic needle so fine that the victim would allegedly not notice its insertion. Cubela grumbled that CIA could surely produce "something more sophisticated than that." No one remembers whether he took the poison pen with him or threw it away. The meeting took place in Paris on November 22, 1963.[61]

The Agency plied Cubela with weapons and encouragement for another year and a half. In the spring of 1965, it brought him together with Manuel Artime in Central America. The two men planned to revive the Bay of Pigs formula: an exile invasion combined with the murder of Castro. But Castro, as the CIA belatedly recognized, had penetrated the operation.[62] Cubela was arrested. In 1966 he confessed plotting with Artime and begged for the firing squad. Castro interceded on his behalf. Cubela received thirty years.[63]

The Church committee found evidence of at least eight CIA at-

---

* Church committee, *Assassination Plots*, esp. 161–166, 175; Church committee, *Final Report*, bk. V, *The Investigation of the Assassination of President John F. Kennedy*, 94 Cong., 2 Sess. (1976), 27, 69. In 1966 CIA said in a memorandum to the Secretary of State, "The Agency was not involved with [Am/Lash] in a plot to assassinate Fidel Castro." Richard Helms later told the Church committee that this memorandum was "inaccurate" (*Assassination Plots*, 178).

tempts to kill Castro from 1960 through 1965. In 1975 Castro gave George McGovern a list of 24 supposed CIA attempts over the same period, some against himself, some against other Cuban leaders. Oddly there was little duplication. The CIA denied involvement in fifteen of Castro's cases. In the other nine it admitted relationships with people mentioned but not for the purpose of assassination.[64] From all this mighty effort Castro emerged unscathed. Either the CIA repeatedly bungled or else Castro knew in advance—in the Rosselli case, perhaps through Trafficante; in the Am/Lash case, perhaps through Cubela himself, either because he was a double agent (how else to explain his freedom to travel abroad?) or simply because he was emotional, suggestible and careless.

In the course of his talks with Donovan and Nolan in April 1963, Castro had got on the subject of assassination. Asked later whether Castro thought the United States government was trying to kill him, Nolan replied, "If he did, he didn't let on. . . . But we talked for, as I recall, an hour or so riding in the car about the possibility of some-body, a disaffected Cuban, shooting Castro."* In the spring Castro may not have been sure about an official American hand in the assas-sination attempts. After all, the underworld had reasons of its own to rub him out, and who would have supposed that gangsters were working for the CIA? Am/Lash was another matter. When Cubela met with what he believed to be Robert Kennedy's "personal repre-sentative," Castro may have had for the first time what seemed con-clusive evidence tying the Kennedys directly to the plots against his own life.

At this point, total murkiness takes over. In 1967 John Rosselli, now fighting deportation as well as charges of gambling fraud, dis-closed to his lawyer, Edward Morgan of Washington, his role in the CIA assassination plots. He had subsequently learned, he said, from "sources in places close to Castro," that Castro had found out about the plots and decided that, "if that was the way President Kennedy wanted it, he too could engage in the same tactics." So, Rosselli claimed, Castro "despatched teams . . . to the United States for the purpose of assassinating President Kennedy."[65] Rosselli later sug-

---

* In 1966 Castro gave Lee Lockwood a detailed account of CIA activities against Cuba but said not a word about assassination (Lockwood, *Castro's Cuba, Cuba's Fidel* [New York, 1967], 202–203). Donovan and Nolan were much impressed by Castro's security—the handling of the cars, for example, that made it impossible for any other car on the road to get into a shooting position. "They did this without ap-parent effort . . . like they'd run a lot of drills on it" (Nolan, in recorded interview by Frank DeRosa, April 25, 1967, 17, JFK Oral History Program).

gested to the columnist Jack Anderson that Castro, with Latin irony, intended to use against Kennedy the same members of the old Santos Trafficante gang in Havana that the CIA had intended to use against him.[66]

Trafficante and Rosselli were friends, at least in the fashion of the underworld. They dined together at Fort Lauderdale twelve days before Rosselli was hacked up and stuffed into the oil drum. "Authorities believe," according to the *New York Times,* "it was a member of the Trafficante organization who was able to lure Mr. Rosselli to his death."[67] Like all members of his trade, Trafficante regarded Robert Kennedy as Public Enemy Number One. No Attorney General in history had pursued the syndicates so relentlessly. There was every indication, after the Valachi testimony in the autumn of 1963, that the worst was yet to come. Trafficante, in addition, was a friend of Jimmy Hoffa's. A year before, he had discussed the President with a Cuban acquaintance. "Have you seen," the gangster said, "how his brother is hitting Hoffa, a man who is a worker, who is not a millionaire? . . . Mark my words, this man [John] Kennedy is in trouble, and he will get what is coming to him. . . . He is going to be hit."[68]

VIII

Yet it was more complicated than that. Both Castro and Kennedy had been pursuing dual policies since the missile crisis: at one moment, reaffirming impassable ideological antagonism; at the next, squinting toward accommodation.

Castro's goal was to secure independence for his country. After Khrushchev's willfulness during the crisis, he no doubt saw a need to assert Cuban sovereignty against the Soviet Union as well as against the United States. This argued for placing his country in the position where it could play one superpower off against the other. On Kennedy's side, his objection had never been to the Cuban revolution per se. It was to a Soviet-aligned Cuba, a repository for Soviet missiles, a base for the subversion of the Alliance for Progress. The rudiments of a deal were there: Cuba retaining its revolution and sovereignty but no longer a satellite or a subverter. Each leader, however, surrounded by Cold War doctrinaires in his own camp, had to proceed in stealth. Neither trusted the other. Neither disdained the other.

Asked in April 1964 about a deal with Castro, Robert Kennedy said, "We always discussed that as a possibility, and it was a question of trying to work it out."[69] His own attitude toward the Cuban revolution, for all his recurrent needling about sabotage, notably relaxed in the course of 1963. The beguiling Donovan-Nolan portrait of Castro probably impressed him. His continuing campaign to lift the travel restrictions stamped in American passports now focused on Cuba. He thought it preposterous to prosecute American students who wanted to inspect the Castro revolution. "What's wrong with that?" he said to me one day. "If I were twenty-two years old, that is certainly the place I would want to visit. . . . I think our people should go anywhere they want."[70]

The State Department objected, asking how Latin American countries could be expected to keep their citizens out of Cuba if the United States let theirs in. Katzenbach, on Kennedy's behalf, responded that their travel controls were for their own self-protection and that their security problems should not govern the rights of United States citizens to wander as they chose.[71] A memorandum from Ball to Rusk summed up the situation at the end of 1963:

> At meeting this afternoon concerning Attorney General's proposal to remove travel restrictions on Cuba, [Edwin] Martin [the assistant secretary for inter-American affairs] and others made strong presentation that removal or easing of restrictions . . . would make more difficult our policy of getting Latin Americans to maintain travel restrictions and would erode U.S. policy of isolation of Cuba in hemisphere. . . . On the other hand, there was general agreement that travel restrictions are contrary to American tradition and put U.S. in unfavorable light around the world. Accordingly our recommendation is that we give consideration to abolishing travel restrictions to all areas except Cuba.[72]

Even this, however, went too far for a cautious Secretary of State confronted by a Cold War Congress.

The summer of 1963 saw the negotiation of the limited test ban treaty in Moscow, followed by John Kennedy's unexpectedly successful western swing in defense of the treaty and then, on September 24, by its comfortable ratification in the Senate. The people, it appeared, were considerably ahead of the politicians on Cold War issues. This enlarged possibilities within the hemisphere and increased the interest of the Kennedys in what Robert described a few months later as "some tentative feelers that were put out by [Castro] which were accepted by us . . . through Bill Attwood."[73]

Attwood, a gifted journalist, formerly an editor of *Look,* was American ambassador to Guinea, on home leave to convalesce from an attack of polio. While recovering, he had been seconded to work with Adlai Stevenson at the United Nations. The Guinean ambassa-

dor to Cuba had told him that Castro, unlike the Communists around
him, disliked Cuba's satellite status and was looking for a way of escape. Attwood, who had interviewed Castro in 1959, found this reasonable. The Cuban leader had seemed, like Sekou Touré of Guinea,
sufficiently naive to be swayed by Communist advisers but too idio-
syncratic to endure Communist discipline.[74] Then, in early September, Carlos Lechuga, the Cuban ambassador to the UN, raised with
Attwood the possibility of exploratory talks.[75]

On September 18 Attwood sent the State Department a "Memorandum on Cuba." The policy of isolating Cuba, he argued, not
only intensified Castro's desire to cause trouble but froze the United
States before the world "in the unattractive posture of a big country
trying to bully a small country."

> According to neutral diplomats and others I have talked to at the UN and
> in Guinea, there is reason to believe that Castro is unhappy about his pres-
> ent dependence on the Soviet bloc; that he does not enjoy in effect being a
> satellite; that the trade embargo is hurting him—though not enough to en-
> danger his position; and that he would like to establish some official contact
> with the United States and go to some length to obtain normalization of
> relations with us—even though this would not be welcomed by most of his
> hard-core Communist entourage, such as Che Guevara.
>
> All of this may or may not be true. But it would seem that we have
> something to gain and nothing to lose by finding out whether in fact Cas-
> tro does want to talk and what concessions he would be prepared to
> make. . . .
>
> [Attwood proposed] a discreet inquiry into the possibility of neutraliz-
> ing Cuba on our terms. It is based on the assumption that, short of a
> change in regime, our principal political objectives in Cuba are:
>
> a. The evacuation of all Soviet bloc military personnel.
> b. An end to subversive activities by Cuba in Latin America.
> c. Adoption by Cuba of a policy of non-alignment.

The time and place for the inquiry, Attwood suggested, were the
current session of the UN General Assembly. As a journalist who had
interviewed Castro, he could plausibly meet Lechuga and chat about
old times. If Castro were interested, one thing might lead to another.
If Attwood were invited to go to Cuba, he would travel "as an individual but would of course report to the President before and after
the visit. . . . For the moment, all I would like is the authority to
make contact with Lechuga. We'll see what happens then."[76]

IX

This was a bold proposition for 1963. With a presidential election coming up the next year, it was a course filled with extraordinary risk. If Keating or Goldwater (or Nixon or Rockefeller), if the Cuban exiles, caught a whiff of it, there would be hell to pay. Averell Harriman, now under secretary of state for political affairs, was the first man in Washington to receive the memorandum. Responding the next day, he told Attwood that he was "adventuresome" enough to favor the plan but that, because of its political implications, Attwood should discuss it with Robert Kennedy.[77] "Bill Attwood got in touch with me," Robert Kennedy said the next year, "and I had him get in touch with Mac Bundy." The Attorney General thought the effort "worth pursuing." Bundy, who had long favored a look at accommodation, reported back to Attwood that the President was in favor of "pushing towards an opening toward Cuba" to take Castro "out of the Soviet fold and perhaps wiping out the Bay of Pigs and maybe getting back to normal."[78] Attwood talked to Lechuga. Lisa Howard, brought in because of her Cuban friendships, talked to Dr. René Vallejo. On October 31, Vallejo told Howard that Castro was ready for a meeting and that, understanding the importance of secrecy, he would send a plane to fly a designated American official to a private airport near Havana.[79] "The President gave the go-ahead," as Robert Kennedy summed it up in 1964, "and [Attwood] was to go to Havana, I don't know, December last year or January of this year and perhaps see Castro and see what could be done [to effect a] normalization of relationship."[80]

In the meantime, President Kennedy was pressing the matter on an entirely separate channel. Jean Daniel of *L'Express* was in Washington. Attwood and Ben Bradlee, both old friends of Daniel's, urged the President to see him.[81] Nothing happened. Bradlee called again, mentioning that Daniel was on his way to Havana. "Have him come tomorrow at 5:30," Kennedy said at once. They began—it was October 24—with the obligatory chat about de Gaulle. Daniel brought up Indochina. "We haven't enough time to talk about Vietnam," said Kennedy, "but I'd like to talk to you about Cuba."

He had thought about few subjects, Kennedy said, with greater care. "There is no country in the world . . . where economic colonization, humiliation and exploitation were worse than in Cuba, in part owing to my country's policies during the Batista regime. I believe that we created, built and manufactured the Castro movement out of whole cloth and without realizing it." He assured Daniel "that I have understood the Cubans. I approved the proclamation which Fidel Castro made in the Sierra Maestra. . . . I will go even further: to some extent it is as though Batista was the incarnation of a number of sins on the part of the United States. Now we shall have to pay for those sins. In the matter of the Batista regime, I am in agreement with the first Cuban revolutionaries. That is perfectly clear."

Unfortunately, Kennedy continued, it had ceased to be a purely Cuban problem. It had become a Soviet problem. Castro had betrayed his promises of the Sierra Maestra and "has agreed to be a Soviet agent in Latin America." In so doing, he had brought the world to the verge of nuclear war. The Russians understood this; "I don't know whether [Castro] realizes this, or even if he cares about it." Kennedy rose; the interview was over. Daniel detained him for two quick questions. Did the American President see an incompatibility between American liberalism and socialist collectivism? Kennedy said, "We get along very well with Tito and Sekou Touré." What about the economic blockade of Cuba? "The continuation of the blockade," Kennedy said, "depends on the continuation of subversive activities." Then: "Come and see me on your return from Cuba. Castro's reactions interest me."[82]

Daniel went on to Havana. On November 5, Bundy told Attwood that the President was more interested than the State Department in exploring the Cuban overtures. A State Department memorandum of November 7 certainly took a much harder line than the White House. "Before the United States could enter into even minimum relations with any Cuban Government," the Department opined, Havana would not only have to end political, economic and military dependency on "the Sino-Soviet bloc"* and cease its subversion within the hemisphere, but would have to "renounce Marxism-Leninism as its ideology, remove Communists from positions of influence, provide compensation for expropriated properties and restore private enterprise in manufacturing, mining, oil and distribution.[83] This insistence on repealing most of the revolution was not part of Kennedy's thinking, nor did it appear in a Bundy memorandum of November 12, prepared as guidance for Attwood. The only "flatly unacceptable" points in Castro's policy, Bundy said, were Cuba's submission to external Communist influence and his subversion directed at the rest of the hemisphere.[84]

Havana was doubtless conducting its own internal debate. Vallejo, the stout proponent of accommodation, kept calling Lisa Howard to

---

* It seems incredible, but the troubles between Moscow and Peking had evidently not come to the notice of the State Department, at least not of the American Republics Division.

promise that Attwood would be brought to Cuba secretly, that only he and Castro would meet him and that Che Guevara specifically would not be present. Vallejo added that he could not come to New York and that Attwood should await word from Lechuga.[85]

On November 18, Kennedy himself flashed a new message to Castro. Speaking before the Inter-American Press Association in Miami, he emphasized once again that the Alliance for Progress did "not dictate to any nation how to organize its economic life. Every nation is free to shape its own economic institutions in accordance with its own national needs and will." As for Cuba, a "small band of conspirators" had made it "a weapon in an effort dictated by external powers to subvert the other American republics. This, and this alone, divides us. As long as this is true, nothing is possible. Without it, everything is possible. . . . Once Cuban sovereignty has been restored we will extend the hand of friendship and assistance to a Cuba whose political and economic institutions have been shaped by the will of the Cuban people."*[86] The next day Bundy told Attwood that the President wanted to see him as soon as he had spoken to Lechuga. The President, Bundy said, would not be leaving Washington again, except for a brief trip to Dallas.[87]

X

In the meantime, Jean Daniel had been spending three fruitless weeks in Havana. He passed on word about his White House meeting. Castro declined to see him—perhaps estopped by his own hard-liners; more likely wishing to postpone bargaining until he knew the outcome of the attempt to disrupt Venezuela's December presidential election. This was the month when Castro, with great fanfare, was staging his Week of Solidarity with the Venezuelan revolution. Finally Daniel booked passage to Mexico City for November 20. At ten

---

* The CIA told Cubela that Desmond FitzGerald had helped write the speech and that the passage about the "small band of conspirators" was meant as a green light for an anti-Castro coup (Church committee, *Assassination of President Kennedy*, 20). Edward Jay Epstein repeats this CIA claim as a fact (Epstein, *Legend: The Secret World of Lee Harvey Oswald* [New York, 1978], 240). On its face the passage was obviously directed against Castro's extracontinental ties and signaled that, if these were ended, normalization was possible; it was meant in short as assistance to Attwood, not to FitzGerald. This was the signal that Richard Goodwin, the chief author of the speech, intended to convey. A search of the JFK Papers shows that Goodwin, Ralph Dungan, Bundy, Gordon Chase of Bundy's staff and I were involved in discussions about the speech. No evidence was uncovered of any contribution from FitzGerald and the CIA (W. W. Moss to author, March 30, 1978).

o'clock on the evening of the nineteenth, Castro, accompanied by Vallejo, unexpectedly came to his hotel room.

They talked till four in the morning. Daniel described his conversation with Kennedy. Castro listened, Daniel thought, with "devouring and passionate interest," stroking his beard, tugging on his paratrooper's beret, "making me the target of a thousand malicious sparks cast by his deep-sunk lively eyes." He made Daniel repeat three times Kennedy's indictment of Batista; three times also Kennedy's remark that Castro himself, in defiance of the superpowers, had almost brought the world to nuclear war. Khrushchev, Castro recalled, had called Kennedy "a capitalist with whom one could talk." Daniel felt that Castro saw Kennedy as an "intimate enemy."

"I believe Kennedy is sincere," Castro finally said. "I also believe that today the expression of this sincerity could have political significance. . . . He inherited a difficult situation. . . . I also think he is a realist." But, instead of addressing himself to the particularities of negotiation, Castro rambled on about the inequities of American policy. He blandly denied to Daniel the Cuban revolutionary role in Latin America of which he had bragged earlier that month to Herbert Matthews. He refused to discuss Cuban relations with Russia; "I find this indecent." As for relations with Washington, "We have forgotten the United States. We feel neither hatred nor resentment anymore, we simply don't think about the US." Still he could not understand why Washington would not accept Cuba as it was. "Why am I not Tito or Sekou Touré?"

He continued to ramble. Someday, he thought, there would appear in the United States a man capable of understanding the explosive reality of Latin America. "Kennedy could still be this man," he mused. "He still has the possibility of being, in the eyes of history, the greatest President of the United States, the leader who may at last understand that there can be coexistence between capitalists and socialists. . . . He would then be an even greater President than Lincoln. . . . Personally, I consider him responsible for everything, but I will say this: he has come to understand many things over the past few months; and then too, in the last analysis, I'm convinced that anyone else would be worse. . . . You can tell him that I'm willing to declare Goldwater my friend if that will guarantee Kennedy's reelection!"

Castro was in no hurry about negotiation. He supposed he had all the time in the world. He made no comment on Kennedy's Miami hints of the day before. Holding out for the Venezuelan prize, he stalled, putting off Daniel with pieties: "Since you are going to see Kennedy again, be an emissary of peace. . . . I don't want anything. I don't expect anything. But there are positive elements in what you report."[88] That was November 20. Two days later, lunching in his villa at the beach with Daniel, he heard the news from Dallas.

"Es una mala noticia," he muttered again and again; "this is bad news." To Daniel: *"Voilà,* there is the end to your mission of peace." Later: "I'll tell you one thing: at least Kennedy was an enemy to whom we had become accustomed. This is a serious matter, an extremely serious matter." In the afternoon he had a fusillade of questions about Lyndon Johnson. Finally, as if well aware that political leaders might not be able to control their intelligence agencies: "What authority does he exercise over the CIA?"[89]

The next day at the UN, Lechuga at last received instructions from Castro to begin talks with Attwood. On December 4, Attwood told me that his secret explorations were, he believed, reaching a climax; that Castro might be trying to get out from under Guevara and the Communists and strike a deal with the United States.[90] But on December 23, Bundy observed at his morning staff meeting that, because Lyndon Johnson expected to run against Nixon, he did not want to give him any openings; "i.e., he does not want to appear 'soft' on anything, especially Cuba."[91] Bundy informed Attwood that "the Cuban exercise would probably be put on ice for a while—which it was," Attwood wrote in 1967, "and where it has been ever since."[92] Castro, looking back a decade later, reflecting perhaps on an opportunity he had squandered because he overestimated his capacity to make a revolution in Venezuela, said of Kennedy, "He was one of the few men who had enough courage to question a policy and to change it. . . . We would have preferred that he continue in the presidency."[93] On balance, it must be judged unlikely that Fidel Castro was conspiring to kill the American President with whom he was striving to come to terms—and whose successor offered no promise of more favorable policies.* Of course, he might not have exercised complete authority over his own CIA.

* Donald E. Schulz also emphasizes Castro's public threats in his September interview with Daniel Harker: "If Castro were going to have Kennedy assassinated would he broadcast it to the world? . . . The demand for retaliation would have been overwhelming" ("Kennedy and the Cuban Connection," *Foreign Policy,* Spring 1977).

XI

No one can say how far these explorations might have gone. Castro was possibly prepared, even perhaps pleased, to move a Tito stride away from the Soviet Union in exchange for the resumption of trade with the United States. But he was not yet prepared in November 1963 to throw in his revolutionary hand in Latin America. Not until June 1964, after his operatives had flopped irremediably in Venezuela, did he make clear any readiness, in the words of Maurice Halperin, "to cut off all aid to revolutionary movements in Latin America, in return for a normalization of relations with the United States and the other estranged republics."[94] Nor could he be sure how violent the opposition in his own ranks might be to a policy of rapprochement—from Che Guevara, his personal Leon Trotsky; from the Communists; from his intelligence people, who, like the CIA, might have unleashed projects of their own; from allies, if he had such, in the American underworld, who had independent reasons for wishing to end the power of the Kennedys.

Kennedy also faced formidable resistance to a change in course. The State Department, apart from Harriman, was not happy with Kennedy's willingness to accept the social changes wrought by the revolution; nor, it must be supposed, did Kennedy's Miami speech of November 18 delight former owners of plantations, mines and mills for whom the "liberation" of Cuba meant primarily the restoration of lost wealth and privilege. And, though the Attwood plan was closely held, it seems inconceivable that the CIA knew nothing about it. American intelligence had Cuban UN diplomats under incessant surveillance. It followed their movements, tapped their telephone calls, read their letters, intercepted their cables. Suspecting, as it must have, that Attwood and Lechuga were doing something more than exchanging daiquiri recipes, the CIA, in pursuing the Am/Lash operation, must be convicted either of abysmal incompetence, which is by no means to be excluded, or else of a studied attempt to wreck Kennedy's search for normalization.

But the deepest rage of all against John Kennedy was among the anti-Castro *fanaticos* in the Cuban exile community. In their obsessed view normalization would complete the perfidious course begun at the Bay of Pigs and carried farther during the missile crisis. No one had a greater interest in putting the Kennedy-Castro explorations on ice than those Cubans who had committed their lives to the destruction of the Castro regime.

Robert Kennedy had stayed in touch with his friends in the Brigade. But the administration made no effort to keep the Brigade alive as an entity or to make it a political or military force.[95] Instead those of its members not recruited by CIA were offered only the opportunity to enlist in the United States Army as individuals. The Brigade leaders protested to the CIA in June that commando raids would not overthrow Castro, that the only hope was "a massive U.S. intervention." They were, Helms reported to the Attorney General, "disheartened in that they do not foresee such an invasion."[96]

Most Bay of Pigs prisoners were constrained for a season by their loyalty to the Kennedys, to whom, after all, they owed their freedom. Other exiles were less constrained. Miro Cardona resigned as chairman of the Cuban Revolutionary Council in an outburst of wild accusations against the Kennedy administration. A broadside of unknown origin told Cuban exiles in Miami that "only one development" would return them to their homeland—"if an inspired Act of God should place in the White House within weeks a Texan known to be a friend of all Latin Americans."[97] The Task Force W Cubans, trained by the CIA in clandestinity and violence, brooded darkly over what one of them, Dr. Orlando Bosch, denounced in an angry letter to the President as their betrayal by the Kennedys.[98] Thereafter the compliant ones, like Barker, Sturgis, Martinez, huddled around the CIA case officers and went down the trail of espionage, deception and dirty tricks that ended in Watergate. The crazy ones, like Orlando Bosch, became terrorists. In 1968 Bosch's exploits won him ten years in the federal penitentiary. Paroled in 1972, he went underground, resumed murderous activities of diverse sorts and in 1977 was in a Venezuelan prison charged with organizing the bombing of an Air Cubana plane and killing all seventy-three aboard. Other CIA Cubans were implicated in a wave of bombings and killings in Miami. Even the once sober Miro Cardona cried in 1973, "We are alone, absolutely alone. . . . There is only one route left to follow and we will follow it: violence."[99]

The men in Washington who in 1960 had planned the murder of Castro and the invasion of Cuba poured a stream of malignant emotion, pro-Castro and anti-Castro, into the very wellsprings of American life.

(24)

Missions to the Third World

EVER SINCE THEIR JOURNEY across Asia in 1951, John and Robert Kennedy had believed that nationalism was the most vital political emotion in the developing world. They instinctively sympathized with new nations struggling for survival; and, after Khrushchev's 1961 prediction of Communist world victory through national liberation wars, they saw the Third World as the crucial battleground between communism and democracy. As President, John Kennedy cultivated the new leaders, welcomed them to Washington and, to emphasize his personal concern, confided the Peace Corps to his brother-in-law and dispatched his brother on Third World missions.

I

Africa was a natural place to begin. The State Department had traditionally regarded Africa as a European preserve. The point of American policy, besides protecting American investments, had been to avoid actions that might offend European allies and, in the jargon of the day, "weaken NATO." John Kennedy himself had been accused of doing this when he gave his notorious speech in 1957 on Algeria. In the White House he proposed to deal with African questions on African merits.

In August 1961 the Ivory Coast celebrated its first anniversary of independence. The Attorney General headed the American delegation. He chafed under the official briefings until the State Department produced a young officer named Brandon Grove, just back from three years in the Ivory Coast. Impressed by Grove's intelligence and candor, Kennedy added him to the delegation. Once in the Ivory Coast, Kennedy bridled at the embassy schedule of official receptions and demanded to talk to students and labor leaders. "The embassy," recalled David Halberstam, who covered the trip for the *New York Times,* "felt he ran roughshod over it, pushed its members around, made unnecessary and unfair demands, and insulted the good Ivorien friends. Almost everyone else loved it."[1]

Felix Houphouët-Boigny, the astute and durable president of the new republic, seized the opportunity to give the President's brother an indoctrination in the problems of West Africa. Kwame Nkrumah of Ghana, Houphouët-Boigny warned, "had surrounded himself with sycophantic advisers who had so inflated his existing ego and messianic complex that he was now thoroughly convinced that it was his divinely ordained mission to lead all of Africa." The Russians were encouraging him in these delusions. Robert Kennedy asked whether the United States should help Ghana build the Volta Dam. Houphouët-Boigny's reply was a tepid yes.[2] The Attorney General was not convinced.

The Volta Dam propelled Robert Kennedy into one of his few sharp disagreements with his brother. His suspicions were emphatically reinforced when his old friend from Rackets Committee days, Clark Mollenhoff, returned from a year's fellowship in Africa. Muckraking as usual, Mollenhoff denounced the dam simultaneously as a capitalist plot pushed by American business interests and as a project whose main beneficiary would be the Communists.[3] In September 1961, after Nkrumah inveighed against the United States at a meeting of neutralist leaders in Belgrade, the Attorney General wrote the President: "We are limited to the amount of money we are going to spend in Africa and it would be better perhaps to spend it on our friends rather than those who have come out against us."[4]

On December 5, 1961, the National Security Council faced the decision. Robert Kennedy, an NSC regular after the Bay of Pigs, used to sit modestly along the wall with the staff people rather than at the cabinet table with the statutory members. The President resolved to go ahead. His grounds were that commitments had been made, that the dam was of long-run benefit for the people of Ghana and Africa, that it made economic sense and that, presumably, Nkrumah would not be there forever. As the discussion proceeded, John Kennedy said, "The Attorney General has not yet spoken but I can feel the cold wind of his disapproval on the back of my neck."[5]

On December 7, Robert Kennedy fired a parting shot:

I would like to state why I think such a project is not in the interests of the United States. First, I think it is very clear that Nkrumah is growing closer and closer to the Soviet Bloc. . . .

> Another strong reason . . . is the effect it will have on the other African states. Friends of ours such as the Ivory Coast, Togo, Upper Volta, have received anywhere from one to five or six million dollars in aid. Ghana which is bitterly opposed to us and playing "footsies" with the Soviet Union is receiving this amount of money with no strings attached. If I were one of these other countries I would certainly, from now on, figure the best way to get money for my country would be to play the Soviet Union off against the United States. . . .
>
> I think also, if we give this money without any strings attached it will encourage Nkrumah to be more stringent with his repressive measures. He has already placed several hundred of his opposition in jail without trial and within the last month has passed some measures which will give him dictatorial control over life and liberty.[6]

"The President finally decided to put the dam in Ghana," Robert Kennedy reflected in 1964, "and we had some spirited arguments about it . . . and I think probably looking at it in retrospect that it was the correct decision."[7] In time, Nkrumah surrendered unconditionally to his delusions of grandeur, was overthrown, fled to Guinea where he evidently infected Sekou Touré with similar delusions and died. The Volta Dam was a success.

II

Robert Kennedy saw his opposition to Nkrumah as in the interests of true African nationalism. The African Bureau found him its strongest ally in its perennial argument with the Pentagon and with the State Department's Europeanists.

Thus in the summer of 1963 a dispute erupted over impending UN votes on African issues. The Pentagon, arguing the alleged military indispensability of naval bases in the Azores and of tracking stations in South Africa, wanted to support Portugal and South Africa against black Africa. On July 1, I sent Robert Kennedy a memorandum suggesting that Defense "make a much more rigorous examination than it seems yet to have made of the alternatives to Azores and the tracking stations." This was the bitter summer of the civil rights war, and the Attorney General had more urgent matters on his mind and desk. Nevertheless (as I discovered in going through his papers) he underlined a sentence in the memorandum asking whether "these military facilities are so indispensable to us that they must determine our African policy" and scribbled a note to Angie Novello: "Have me speak to Bob M about this Wed." Ten days later McNamara sent Rusk a cost-benefit analysis discounting the supposedly decisive strategic considerations and concluding: "I believe the decisions on these issues should be based on general considerations of foreign policy. I hope that you share the views I have expressed."[8]

Angola and Mozambique were the only European colonies of consequence left in Africa. Robert Kennedy thought that their independence was both right and inevitable, that it was foolish for the United States to identify itself with Portuguese suzerainty and that the American interest lay in winning the confidence of the anticolonial leaders. Rusk considered it improper, as by the book it doubtless was, for men engaged in rebellion against NATO allies to be received officially in Washington. When Eduardo Mondlane, the head of the Mozambique Liberation Front, came to the United States, Wayne Fredericks, the deputy assistant secretary of state for African affairs, told Kennedy that Mondlane would almost certainly be the leader of an independent Mozambique (as he would have been, had he not been assassinated in 1969). Perhaps, Fredericks suggested, the Attorney General might care to meet Mondlane in a neutral spot—dinner at someone's house, for example. Kennedy said, "I will see him in the office of the Attorney General of the United States. Bring him here."[9] Kennedy helped arrange a CIA subsidy to cover Mondlane's travel and other expenses and also got CIA money for Holden Roberto in Angola—to be spent not on weapons but on aid to refugees fleeing from villages burned down by the Portuguese and on the education of promising young Angolans in European and American universities.

On November 20, 1963, Robert Kennedy wrote Bundy saying that the Standing Group simply must discuss the "policy of the United States toward the individuals and organizations which are attempting to gain independence in Mozambique, South Africa, Angola and Rhodesia. . . . I gather that we really don't have much of a policy. . . . These areas are going to be extremely important to us in the future. . . . Personally I feel if we could take steps now, either through the CIA and/or making a concentrated effort with students and intellectuals, we could head off some of the problems that are undoubtedly going to appear on the horizon in the next year or so."[10]

"I felt very strongly," he told John Bartlow Martin in April 1964, "that we should become more involved." At that point he was exercised over Zanzibar, where a "people's republic" of obscure but impassioned views had recently been established. For the last four months, he said, he had been trying "to get somebody to do something about Zanzibar. . . . Averell Harriman wrote a memorandum

. . . and George Ball wrote back and said it was foolish to waste our time, it was such a small country and added that, if God could take care of the little swallows in the skies, He could certainly take care of a little country like [Zanzibar]. . . . Imagine that!"[11]

Three days after Kennedy said this, the United Republic of Tanzania was formed, and Zanzibar became a problem for Julius Nyerere (and for God). Ball plainly had the better of that argument. Martin asked later how John Kennedy felt about involvement in Africa. Robert said, "Well, I don't know, really. I think he wanted to get involved. I don't know—I never had the discussion about that particular problem with him, but it came up before our Counterinsurgency committee as to what we would do in some of these areas and I was always in favor of becoming more involved."*

III

John Kenneth Galbraith, the ambassador to India, convalescing in a Honolulu hospital in February 1962, recorded in his journal a visit from Robert and Ethel Kennedy. "They were marvelously vital, just having gone sailing outside Pearl Harbor and tipped over their dinghy. I proposed they say they had been cut down by an enemy destroyer with stress on the fact that Bob had saved the whole crew. He could then be President."[12]

This time the Kennedys were going around the world. Edwin Reischauer, the leading American historian of Japan and newly appointed ambassador to Tokyo, had urged the Attorney General to accept an invitation to Japan, where anti-American violence had forced Eisenhower to cancel a visit in 1960. The State Department had jobs for him in Indonesia. Mayor Willy Brandt had invited him to give the Ernst Reuter Lecture at the Free University of Berlin. The Department again provided Brandon Grove as an escort. John Seigenthaler was also in the party, along with a few newspapermen, among them Anthony Lewis of the *New York Times,* Kennedy's Harvard classmate but still a rather wary acquaintance. The uninhibited and some-

---

* RFK, in interview by John Bartlow Martin, May 14, 1964, I, 5, JFK Oral History Program. He had not always felt that way. Earlier he had sensibly told a questioner at Howard University, "Do you want us to intervene all over the world? Telling this government what to do and that one what not to do? A lot of countries in Africa have one-man governments. If we protested, they'd tell us to mind our own business. We stand for democracy and we try to show people by example, but we can't go running all over the globe, telling people what to do" (Fletcher Knebel, "Bobby Kennedy: He Hates to Be Second," *Look,* May 21, 1963).

times unruly company tried Brandon Grove's Foreign Service sense of propriety. Once, when Ethel Kennedy forgot to turn off the water in their Tokyo hotel and her bath overflowed, Grove said with dignified wrath, "Some day they will learn that this is a *real world* with *real people* in it."[13]

Kennedy set forth the theme of his trip in a speech at Tokyo's Nihon University. This was, he said, the century of "the awakening of peoples in Asia and Africa and Latin America—peoples stirring from centuries of stagnation, suppression and dependency." The resources of the earth and the ingenuity of man could provide abundance for all—

> so long as we are prepared to recognize the diversity of mankind and the variety of ways in which people will seek national fulfillment. . . . We do not condemn others for their differences in economic and political structures. We understand that newer nations have not had time, even if they wished, to build institutions relying primarily on private enterprise as we have done. . . .
>
> We have no intention of trying to remake the world in our image but we have no intention either of permitting any other state to remake the world in its image. . . . We call to the young men and women of all nations of the world to join with us in a concerted attack on the evils which have so long beset mankind—poverty, illness, illiteracy, intolerance, oppression, war.[14]

He had begun at Nihon with a few sentences in what he supposed, after laborious rehearsal by Edwin Reischauer and his Japanese wife, might resemble the native tongue. "The audience thought I was speaking English and waited for the translation. Simultaneously we all realized what had happened and to everyone's relief I restarted in English."[15] The audience laughed, and all seemed well. But ominous reports were coming in from the next stop, Waseda University, where the Zengakuren, the Marxist student clubs, were on the offensive. "We . . . were told we shouldn't go," Reischauer said later, "but we decided at the last minute that it would look bad to back out."[16]

At Waseda three thousand students jammed a hall built for half that number. Several hundred had come to revile the brother of the American President. "It is possible," Kennedy began dryly, over a barrage of cries and hisses, "that there are those here today who will disagree with what I say."[17] In the front row a young man yelled hysterically—"a skinny little Japanese boy," as Seigenthaler remembered him, "tense, shouting, shouting, shouting, screaming at the top of his lungs, really red-faced; just completely wrought up emotionally."[18] After a moment, Kennedy reached out his hand and pulled his heckler to the platform. "Perhaps you could make your statement," he said, "and ask me a question and then give me an opportunity to answer." There was no question, but a ten-minute tirade. When the critic, exhausted, came to an end, Kennedy, enlightened by instant translation, commenced a reply. At this point the public address system, and every light in the house, went dead.

There followed a quarter hour of chaos. Someone from the embassy, anticipating the worst, had brought a battery-operated bullhorn. Reischauer, speaking fluent Japanese, quieted the audience. Kennedy, "without loss of temper or composure," according to the embassy report,[19] took the bullhorn and said: "We in America believe that we should have divergencies of views. We believe that everyone has the right to express himself. We believe that young people have the right to speak out."[20] After a few moments in this vein, he invited more questions from the audience, which by this time was turning in his favor. He concluded with some personal words: "My brother, the President, entered politics at a young age. Although now President, he is still young, and all those who held key positions in his campaign are young. He believes that the future of the world belongs, not just to the younger generation of my country, but to the younger generation of all countries."[21]

Someone bellowed in the rear of the hall; whether in rage or agreement, Kennedy could not tell. The interpreter explained that this was the school cheerleader, desiring to make apology. In a moment, the cheerleader was on the platform gesticulating wildly (inadvertently punching Ethel Kennedy in the pit of the stomach; "she doubled up, stood up immediately, smiled and went on," observed Seigenthaler)[22] and leading the student body in the Waseda song. The audience responded, as if at a football rally before the homecoming game. The Kennedy party, alas, learned the song—"Miyako no seihoku"—and later inflicted it mercilessly on parties at Hickory Hill.[23]

There was, said the Tokyo newspaper *Yomiuri* the next day, "no question who won." Another paper, *Sankei,* said Kennedy was "superb." "In his frankness, simplicity and courage," said a *Yomiuri* columnist, "Mr. Kennedy reminds us of [the] pioneer of old."[24] Moreover, through television, "the Japanese nation," as Reischauer said later, "saw this whole unrehearsed play, as it were, with the ranting young radical student and the calm and reasonable young political leader from America, and it made a tremendous impression. And after that, you know, it was just a smashing success."[25]

IV

Instructions had gone forth to American embassies: the Kennedys could be scheduled to the hilt, but with a minimum of official ceremony and a maximum of informal mingling with students, intellectuals, trade unionists and factory workers. "We drew him up a tremendous program," said Reischauer, "every minute occupied till 10 o'clock at night, and he wired back, 'Program looks fine. What do I do from 6 to 8 A.M.?' So we put on that, too. He skated with workers, 6 to 8 A.M."[26] The embassy, noting Kennedy's "easy rapport with laborers and union representatives," recalled the indifference shown to Japanese workers by Mikoyan a short while before. "The Attorney General, by contrast, started talking knowledgeably about working conditions and labor union activities whenever he came into speaking distance of a laborer."[27]

The combination of bluntness, humor, courtesy and charm was effective. Even the Zengakuren lost their ardor. Pickets still yelled, "Go home, Kennedy. Go home, Kennedy." "Then," Seigenthaler reported, "one of them would yell, 'Where's Ethel, Bobby?' so that we had the feeling we were even getting through to them."[28] When the party went on to Osaka, Nara and Kyoto, crowds lined country roads to watch them drive by. They slept on floors, ate snails and seaweed for breakfast and whale meat for lunch, visited ancient temples and modern plants. "When he went off the beaten track, as he did constantly," said the embassy, "it was to mingle with workers, labor union people, students or intellectuals in their own environment. The 'one of us' reaction was most pronounced among these people."[29] They met, wrote one Japanese journalist, "all classes of the people, boys and girls, workers, students, housewives, and farmers, and saw their actual conditions. . . . My impression is that Kennedy's personal magnetism was overwhelming."[30]

"The overwhelming consensus of opinion," the deputy chief of the embassy's translation services branch reported, "is that the Attorney General's 'whirlwind' visit was the most successful accomplishment by the United States in its postwar relations with Japan."[31] The visit, the embassy concluded, "commanded the attention of more people and elicited a more positive response from the Japanese public than any good will visit in Japanese history."[32]

The schedule was so crowded that Reischauer hardly had a moment alone with Kennedy. They finally reserved fifteen minutes before the group departed for Indonesia. "During those fifteen minutes," Reischauer recalled, "I outlined the Okinawa problem, what we would have to begin doing about it, and one or two other problems. . . . He had hardly gotten back to Washington before action began on all of these. . . . And if I really had something that I just had to get to the President, you know, and that we had to get to work on, I could always do it that way. . . . It was the most important channel."[33]

V

Now sixty years old, the flamboyant and vainglorious Achmed Sukarno had been active in the Indonesian independence movement before Robert Kennedy was born. In the Eisenhower years the State Department had looked on him as a sort of Communist. John Kennedy, who thought it easy to understand why Sukarno might be anti-American after what the CIA had done to him in 1958,[34] had him pegged as a clever nationalist politician and charmed him with notable success when Sukarno visited Washington in 1961.

While the Robert Kennedy party was still in Tokyo, Communists had stoned the American embassy in Djakarta and painted the city with KENNEDY GO HOME signs. Sukarno, taking no chances with the safety of his guests, installed them in the presidential palace (which Ethel plunged into darkness one evening by plugging in her hair dryer and blowing the fuses) and surrounded them by soldiers wherever they went. There was one failure of security. When Robert Kennedy spoke at the University of Indonesia, "suddenly this little wraith of a kid," as Seigenthaler described it, "a tall, slender boy, broke through the lines of people and, standing at a distance of about fifteen feet, took a full windup and let fly a piece of hard shelled fruit, which hit Bob on the end of the nose. It was thrown with full force—I mean, he looked like Bob Feller." Kennedy, Seigenthaler said, "never flinched. The only time he took a backward step was when it hit him; it knocked him back just a step. He turned around to me and said, 'Did you see that little s.o.b.?' . . . and he sort of put his eyes up in the top of his head as he said, 'Whew.'" The police grabbed the thrower, twisted both arms behind him, turned him upside down and rushed him out to a car. "We never saw or heard of him again," Seigenthaler said. "Bob told Gunawan, the Attorney General, that he hoped they wouldn't do anything to harm him."*

In the question period, students asked Kennedy insistently why the United States was not backing Indonesia in its quarrel with the Netherlands, now threatening to explode into hostilities, over the future of West New Guinea. Kennedy replied that his country had "vigorously supported Indonesia's struggle for independence" and declared his hope that these "two close friends of the United States" would be able to work out West New Guinea. The audience objected to his agnosticism. Kennedy went into one of his famous exercises in bluntness. "We have allies throughout the world," he said,

> and we don't agree with everything that they do, and they don't agree with everything we do. I don't know any of you who agree with every one of your fellow students. . . . I suppose a day doesn't go by when we don't disagree with the English on some matter or other. We are going to disagree with Indonesia, and you are going to disagree with us.
>
> But we are both democratic countries. We both should have a foundation of friendship, so that every time an incident comes up and we don't do exactly what you want us to do, you don't say, "To hell with the United States."

There was an ovation. "Strangely enough," Kennedy wrote later, "it was this answer more than any other that seemed to establish a friendly rapport."[35]

What got him into trouble that night was not West New Guinea but Texas. A student who had done his homework in American history brought up the Mexican War. "I would say," said Kennedy, "that as far as the war with Mexico—although there might be some from Texas that might disagree—I would say that we were unjustified. I don't think that this is a very bright page in American history." This response went down well in Indonesia; less well in Texas. Soon a cable arrived from Salinger: YOUR REMARKS ABOUT TEXAS APPEAR TO BE CAUSING SOME FUSS. IF YOU ARE PRESSED ON THIS MATTER, PRESIDENT SUGGESTS YOU ATTEMPT TO MAKE SOME HUMOROUS REMARK. GOOD LUCK. Later the Attorney General told the press that he had been instructed to clear any future Texas speeches with the Vice President. He noted privately, however, that most of the critics denounced him for supposed aspersions cast on the battle of the Alamo; they "did not even have the correct war."[36]

---

* John Seigenthaler, in recorded interview by R. J. Grele, February 23, 1966, 397–398, JFK Oral History Program. Bob Feller was the Cleveland Indians' pitcher, renowned for his fast ball.

Kennedy, the embassy cabled the State Department, made his "most notable impression on Indonesian students. . . . Young audiences which were initially cold or even hostile rapidly warmed to his frank, man-to-man approach, admission that not all was perfect in US, demand for grown-up approach to inevitable differences of opinion, and assurances that US did not seek to impose its system on world." Soon, when his car passed, people waved and shouted, "Hello, Kennedy." When he walked the streets, "people poured out of nearby stalls or buildings, elbowed each other aside to indulge in un-Indonesian practice of shaking hands." The embassy concluded: "No short-term visitor to Indonesia has had impact on public that Attorney General Kennedy did during February 12–18 visit."[37] The implied comparison was with Khrushchev, who in 1960 had been put off by Sukarno's "scandalous" appetite for women, was visibly bored by Javanese ritual and, when shown artisans printing fabric by hand, had said only, "They could do it faster with machines."[38]

VI

"I didn't like him from what I had heard of him," Robert Kennedy said privately of Sukarno in 1964, "and I didn't like him when I was there and I haven't liked him since." Like Khrushchev, he was offended by Sukarno's satyriasis and by the gallery of nudes that adorned the presidential palace. "I don't have respect for him. I think that he's bright. I think he's completely immoral, that he's untrustworthy. . . . I think he's a liar. I think he's got very few redeeming features. He speaks like hell, he's a demagogue. He's not a Communist. I think he's anti-white but I think he liked the President, . . . he admires the United States and I think he liked me and he liked Ethel."[39] This was indeed the case. "I like people with flame in their eyes," he told Howard Jones, the American ambassador. "He and Bobby hit it off beautifully," Jones said later.[40]

Robert Kennedy's specific mission in Djakarta was to head off war between Indonesia and the Netherlands over West New Guinea, a territory whose status was left unresolved when Indonesia became independent in 1949. Jones had long advocated a forthcoming policy on West Irian, as the Indonesians called it. He saw no future in the United States taking the losing side in a colonial war. He also warned that the Soviet Union was exploiting the issue. True enough: Moscow had already suborned several of Sukarno's generals. "Unbeknownst to him," Khrushchev said later, "some of these generals were even

Communist Party members."[41] Nevertheless Jones's recommendations found a dusty answer in Washington. "If Sukarno starts aggressing against his neighbors," Dean Rusk told Jones, "he'll find us on the other side. We learned our lesson with Hitler. The time to stop him was at the beginning." It was not, Jones wrote, till Averell Harriman took over as assistant secretary for Far Eastern affairs in November 1961 that "our recommendations from Djakarta began to receive a sympathetic hearing."[42] "It could have developed," Harriman said later, "into a very difficult situation in which the Dutch would be spending a lot of money and a lot of people would be killed . . . a conflict in which there could only be one end, namely the withdrawal of the Dutch."[43]

Kennedy's particular task was to persuade Sukarno to talk to the Dutch without preconditions. Except for Jones's indispensable counsel, he was on his own. "Your relation to the President," Bundy cabled, "will give ample authority to your own words, and the experience of men like Harriman is that in such a situation it is better not to be bound by a canned message."[44] The talks began. Kennedy, Jones reported to Washington, "stressed that as a major world statesman Sukarno must appreciate utter absurdity of permitting question of peace or war on so important an issue to turn on procedural rather than substantive point." The Indonesians had everything to gain and nothing to lose from negotiation. "In our opinion," Kennedy said, "an acceptable solution would result from talks but if this did not happen and GOI [government of Indonesia] felt it must take military action its position before world would be strengthened." The United States, he added, recognized that the territory was going to Indonesia "in some way at some time. . . . If we did not think talks had chance of success we also would not be urging them." Only there could be no preconditions; "this was a matter of prestige with Dutch and they could not be moved on this."[45]

"In my judgment," Kennedy warned Washington, "Indos will fight unless this issue is resolved, and this would be full of dire implications for the free world in Asia."[46] But Sukarno dropped his preconditions after the visit; and, when Kennedy went to Holland later in the month, he assured the Dutch that, "based on my conversations with Sukarno, Subandrio [the foreign minister] and others that I was sure they were interested in resolving this whole matter without armed conflict."[47] "It is abundantly clear," Jones wrote Kennedy in May, "that you were able to start the ball rolling toward a negotiated settlement."[48] Eventually, interminable meetings between the Dutch

and the Indonesians, with Ellsworth Bunker, a veteran American diplomat, serving as mediator, led to an agreement in August 1962
under which West New Guinea, after an interim UN administration,
would go to Indonesia. Sukarno told Jones, "It could not have been
done without your government."[49]

Critics denounced the settlement as capitulation. In 1963 Sir Robert Menzies, the Australian Prime Minister, complained bitterly to
the wife of the American ambassador about Robert Kennedy's role.
"It is not as bad as they think," Kennedy told her, "although I guess
I must accept some responsibility. I think, however, any alternative
action on our part would have brought on a war in that part of the
world which would have been no help to Australia or the United
States."[50]

On the larger arena it was a masterstroke. Moscow sent Mikoyan
to Djakarta in July 1962 in a last-minute effort to block the settlement. Khrushchev's irritated summation made the case for the Har-
riman-Jones-Kennedy policy:

> Sukarno cleverly utilized both the Soviet Union and the United States to
> achieve his goal of getting Holland to back down. . . . We felt it was
> wrong of him not to inform us of his intentions in advance. In any event,
> while continuing to support the Dutch publicly [not true], the Americans
> obviously put pressure on them behind the scenes. As a result, Holland
> submitted to the negotiations and agreed to hand over West Irian. . . .
> Since armed conflict had been avoided, our advisors who had been training
> the Indonesians were no longer needed, so they came home.[51]

VII

The novice diplomat had, in addition, a more secret mission: to
secure the release of Allen Pope, the CIA pilot who had been captured in 1958 and condemned to death in 1960. The death sentence
had not been carried out. When Sukarno visited Washington in 1961,
John Kennedy had asked for Pope's release. Sukarno said it would
happen in due course. Mrs. Pope, a comely airline stewardess, flew to
Djakarta. "She cried bitterly," Sukarno later said, "and begged me to
pardon him. When it comes to women I am weak. I cannot stand
even a strange woman's tears. Then his mother and sister visited me
and those two sobbing was more than I could bear."[52] However, he
managed to restrain his emotion. Pope remained in prison. Mrs.
Pope called on Robert Kennedy. "I was tremendously impressed with
her and then she talked about the children and the fact that the chil-

dren were fighting with one another and one child had never seen her
father. So I was really very taken up with it."[53]

He brought up Pope at their first meeting. Sukarno said he would
have to think about it. He was still thinking at their last meeting.
Kennedy concluded that he was trying to use Pope as a bargaining
counter over West New Guinea. "I explained to him that . . . he
could take Pope out and shoot him and it wouldn't affect what we did
on West New Guinea because what we were going to do on West
New Guinea was . . . in the interests of the United States and the interests of justice." There was a long pause. Then Sukarno said,
"Well, let me tell you, Mr. Attorney General, you're just going to
have to let me handle this in my own way." Kennedy said that was
fine; "but could you give me some indication so that I might tell
President Kennedy that you do have in mind standing by what you've
already told him, that you are going to let this fellow out." Another
long pause; then Sukarno: "Mr. Attorney General, you're going to
have to leave this to me to handle in my own way." Kennedy, his
voice growing testy: "Could you tell me whether you're going to
stand by your promise to the President of the United States?"
Sukarno said again he would handle the matter in his own way.

"I never really had the feeling that Bob was angry because I know
him so well," recalled Seigenthaler, "but I had the distinct impression
that Sukarno thought he was angry." Kennedy said, "Am I to go
back to the President and say you will not tell us that you'll stand by
your word?" He stood up. "I can't understand that," he said. "Everybody tells me that you're a man who stands by his word . . . and the
President of the United States believes that, and now you won't say
that. I'm his brother. He sent me here as his representative. I'm
speaking for him when I'm asking you what you're going to do about
this . . . and you won't tell me." He walked out on the balcony.

"We were sitting there in a circle," recalled Seigenthaler. "I looked
at Howard Jones, and I thought he was going to fall off his chair."
After a moment, Seigenthaler joined Kennedy. Kennedy said, "Do
you think that what I said to him is going to have any impression on
him?" Seigenthaler thought it was very definitely having an impression. Kennedy said he wanted "to make sure that when I leave here
he knows how strongly we feel about this. That kid belongs out."
Jones came onto the balcony. "Look," he said to Kennedy, "you
feel strongly about this. He also feels strongly about it. . . . I remember riding with him on a boat one time, and he showed me out
under the water where a ship had been sunk, and he said, 'That's the

work of your CIA agent Pope.' You can't leave him in there like this. You've got to go back in." Kennedy said, "Oh, I'm going back in. Don't misunderstand, Mr. Ambassador. I'm not upset at all, but I want him to know that this is a matter that holds some potential danger."

They returned to the room. Kennedy went at once to Sukarno and said, "If I have offended you by my bluntness . . . I certainly apologize for that. You've been extremely nice to me here. You've been very nice to my wife. . . . But I could not leave without saying to you what I feel about this, what my brother feels about it, and what we will continue to feel so long as Mr. Pope is in prison." Another long silence; then Sukarno: "Mr. Attorney General, you are forceful and you are young, and I am forceful and I am old. . . . I am hopeful that I can do something that will be proper. But I simply am not in a position at this time to say any more than that." Then, said Seigenthaler, they went out together where the press was waiting, "and they were like two foxes. I mean, they just smiled and shook hands."[54]

Anger, or the simulation thereof, is a not unknown diplomatic weapon. Sukarno, the old fox, saw what the young fox was up to and evidently admired his technique. Asked later whether Kennedy had been abrasive, Jones reflected, "He was a very positive guy. But abrasive? His Irish wit kept him from being abrasive. There were one or two points where . . . the discussions became very, very heated; but then they both calmed down, and their personal relations were cordial and friendly. Evidence of that was that Sukarno welcomed Bobby back two years later";[55] but that is another story.

Kennedy departed the next day. In June, four months after the visit, Sukarno sent word to Pope: "You are pardoned. But I do so silently. . . . Just go home, hide yourself, get lost, and we'll forget the whole thing."[56] "I am back in the United States a free man," Pope wrote Kennedy in July, "and for this . . . my wife and I shall always be eternally grateful."[57] He later came to Washington to express his gratitude in person—"a good-looking fellow," the Attorney General thought, ". . . the soldier of fortune type." He said he was going back to the Far East. Kennedy asked about his wife. "She's not going," Pope said. "We don't live together. We've been separated for some time."*

---

* RFK, in Martin interview, April 13, 1964, II, 37. Pope was going to work for a CIA subsidiary, Southern Air Transport (J. B. Smith, *Portrait of a Cold Warrior* [New York, 1976], 205).

VIII

On February 19, 1962, the Kennedys arrived in Calcutta. I was in India on a Food for Peace mission with George McGovern, and the Attorney General had asked me to travel with him to Berlin. Galbraith, back from Hawaii, noted in his journal that Robert "looked very tired," but that "Ethel seemed unchanged by the round-the-world campaigning. She spoke appreciatively of the art and culture of Japan, Indonesia and Bangkok with special reference to President Sukarno's collection of nude paintings." Galbraith added:

> Arthur had written a speech for Bob to give in Berlin. I had thought it all right. Bob immediately pinpointed its faults: strictly conventional praise of the bravery of Berliners, strictly conventional damnation of the Communists. On second thought, I was forced to conclude, as did Arthur, that the criticism was sound.[58]

Kennedy was evidently less of a Cold War rhetorician in 1962 than Schlesinger or even Galbraith.

On the plane to Europe Bobby was filled with reflections about his trip. What was clearest of all, he told me, was that, in countries like Japan and Indonesia, America could make contact with the youth and the intellectuals *only* as a progressive nation. "I kept asking myself," he said, "what a conservative could possibly say to these people. I could talk all the time about social welfare and trade unions and reform; but what could someone say who didn't believe in these things? Can you imagine—Barry Goldwater in Indonesia?"[59]

In Rome we lunched at Alfredo's. The press party, which by this time had fallen in love with Bobby and Ethel, sent over champagne from their neighboring table, procured an accordionist and started an impromptu dance that went on till four-thirty in the afternoon. I somehow remember through vinous mists the newspapermen bringing in a motor scooter and Ethel driving it precariously between the tables, though that may have been another occasion. The next day the Kennedys concentrated on matters spiritual, such as an audience with the Pope, while I stuck to the temporal side, meeting with Nenni, La Malfa and other political leaders and clearing the Attorney General's German speeches, now amply revised, with Washington.

Entry in my journal, February 22:

> We arrived in Berlin on a cold, blowy, snowy day. Willy Brandt, General Clay and Al Lightner (head of the US Mission in West Berlin) met us at the airport. As we got off the plane, the band played "When the Crimson in triumph flashing, mid the strains of victory." After a brief airport cere-

mony and gallant but incompetent tries at German by Bobby and Ethel, we set forth on a motorcade to the *Rathaus*. The streets were lined with cheering people, who had waited for hours in the bitter cold. It was all deeply moving until one remembered that a good many of them were cheering just as hard twenty years ago for Hitler.

Edward Kennedy joined us in Berlin. February 22 was his thirtieth birthday; also George Washington's two hundred thirtieth. Both events received due recognition at Mayor Brandt's dinner that evening. After Bobby saluted the two "notable Americans" whose birthday it was, Brandt proposed a toast to "the President, government and people of the United States." The Attorney General, responding, said, "That's the three of us—the President, that's my brother; the government, that's me; and [looking hard at Teddy] you're the people." The otherwise sensible Brandt did not appreciate Kennedy humor and wrote gravely in his memoirs that, though he admired the Kennedys, this event made him "regard the family's political expansion with disquiet."[60]

Robert Kennedy gave the Ernst Reuter Lecture that evening at the Free University. "We do not stand here in Berlin," he said, "just because we are against Communism. We stand here because we have a positive and progressive vision of the possibilities of free society." Marx's indictment of "the heartless laissez-faire capitalism of the early 19th century" now applied precisely, Kennedy suggested, to twentieth-century communism: this had become the contemporary means "of disciplining the masses, repressing consumption and denying the workers the full produce of their labor." And, by "historical paradox," it was free society that now seemed most likely "to realize Marx's old hope of the emancipation of man."[61]

The next morning Lightner assembled a group of editors, ministers and politicians for breakfast. I had never heard Robert Kennedy in a foreign policy discussion of this sort before and was considerably impressed. It was six months after the erection of the Wall. Emotions were intense in West Berlin; the temptation for visitors to respond to them was intense too. I noted: "Bobby, I thought, handled himself exceptionally well. He was frank and direct in discussion; he made no effort to gratify his audience by saying the things we all knew they so desperately wanted to hear, and instead spoke with great honesty and realism about the remoteness of German unification, the impossibility of doing much about the Wall, etc."[62]

In Bonn, Konrad Adenauer, almost half a century older than his visitor, won Robert Kennedy's heart for a moment by giving him a scrapbook about the convent that Rose Kennedy had attended in Germany nearly sixty years before; then lost ground by remarking later that, of all the world leaders he met, the one he most admired was John Foster Dulles.[63] Thence Kennedy went to The Hague to wrap up the Indonesian matter; then to Paris and de Gaulle: "He wasn't nearly as warm as Adenauer. He was cold and tough [and] opposed to meeting with the Russians."[64] On February 28, 1962, they were back in Washington—14 countries, 30,000 miles in 28 days; exhilaration, exhaustion. The wary Anthony Lewis now concluded that Robert Kennedy was "a very unusual person, a person who in a kind of tormented way was struggling to do everything on the merits, which was, I thought, all one could ask. Certainly, nothing was ever the same after that trip. I mean, he certainly became the most important person for me in the government."[65] Ethel Kennedy gave Brandon Grove a pair of cuff links: one engraved REAL WORLD, the other REAL PEOPLE.

IX

Even the Foreign Service conceded that, for all his strange hobbies, like youth and counterinsurgency, the Attorney General had peculiar skills as a propounder of home truths to world leaders. So in December 1962 he was prevailed upon to undertake a mission to Brazil. This was about the last thing he wished to do. After the Battle of Ole Miss in September, the missile crisis in October, the housing order in November, he was now in December liberating Bay of Pigs prisoners, as well as, in spare moments, preparing for his Supreme Court debut in January. But Brazil was the largest country in Latin America, and the Alliance for Progress needed its full collaboration.

In later years the Alliance for Progress was harshly criticized as, at best, a classic example of liberal good intentions overpackaged, overpromised, oversold; at worst, an "arrogant" North American effort to change Latin American countries into "mirror images" of the United States and "to make the region perpetually safe for private U.S. investment." The Alliance unquestionably had its share of illusion and error. The criticism also had its share of myth.[66]

The first myth was that the Alliance was a North American design imposed arbitrarily on Latin America. In fact, the contribution of the Kennedy administration was to give ideas long proposed by progressive Latin American economists and political leaders comprehensive form, collective endorsement and public dollars. The democratic left in Latin America embraced the Alliance. Eduardo Frei of Chile enumerated the objectives of "the Latin American revolution": destruction of the oligarchies; breaking up semifeudal estates and redistributing the land; assuring equal access to education and political power; sharing the gains of economic development; utilizing international capital for the benefit of the national economy. "These," he said, "are precisely the same objectives as those of the Alliance."[67] After John Kennedy received his astonishing welcome in the crowded streets of Bogotá in 1963, Alberto Lleras Camargo of Colombia said to him, "Do you know why these people were cheering you? It's because they think you're on their side against the oligarchs."[68]

The oligarchs, with a few distinguished exceptions, detested the Alliance. Kennedy warned them: "Those who make peaceful revolution impossible will make violent revolution inevitable."[69] They disagreed. Ellis Briggs, an American diplomat of the old school, spoke for them when he denounced the Alliance as a "blueprint for upheaval" and expressed sympathy for "hard-pressed" Latin leaders to whom Kennedy's exhortation "sounded suspiciously like the Communist Manifesto."[70]

Nor was the Alliance either fostered or applauded by American business. If the Kennedy plan had been to integrate the southern hemisphere more firmly than ever in the American corporate economy, presidential speeches stimulating and legitimizing social change in Latin America were an odd way of going about it. It did not even occur to us to invite United States businessmen to the founding meeting at Punta del Este, Uruguay, in August 1961, till the week before. Nor did we follow up on their recommendation that a permanent committee be established to promote foreign private investment.[71] A. F. Lowenthal, a discriminating critic of United States hemisphere policy, has written, "Far from reflecting big business domination of United States foreign policy, the Alliance for Progress commitment emerged in part because of the unusual (and temporary) reduction of corporate influence in the foreign policy-making process."[72]

The strongest witness against the idea that the Alliance was an instrument of Wall Street imperialism was Fidel Castro himself. "In a way," he remarked to Jean Daniel in 1963, "it was a good idea, it marked progress of a sort. Even if it can be said that it was overdue, timid, conceived on the spur of the moment, under constraint, . . . despite all that I am willing to agree that the idea in itself constituted an effort to adapt to the extraordinarily rapid course of events in Latin America."[73] This remained his view. "The goal of the Alli-

ance," he told Frank Mankiewicz a dozen years later, "was to effect
social reform which would improve the condition of the masses in
Latin America. . . . It was a politically wise concept put forth to
hold back the time of revolution, . . . a very intelligent strategy. . . . Basically one has to admit that the idea of the Alliance for
Progress was an intelligent one; however, an utopian one."[74]

Utopian because, as Castro told Herbert Matthews in 1963, "you
can put wings on a horse, but it won't fly."[75] "Kennedy's good ideas
aren't going to yield any results," Castro assured Jean Daniel. Historically the United States had been committed to the Latin oligarchs.
"Suddenly a President arrives on the scene who tries to support the
interests of another class (which has no access to the levers of
power)." What happens then? "The trusts see that their interests are
being a little compromised; . . . the Pentagon thinks the strategic
bases are in danger; the powerful oligarchies in all the Latin American countries alert their American friends; they sabotage the new policy; and in short, Kennedy has everyone against him."[76]

X

Not, in retrospect, a bad analysis. Kennedy in fact overestimated the
possibilities of peaceful revolution in Latin America—as Castro
overestimated the possibilities of violent revolution. Both Washington
and Havana underestimated the rigidity of the old structures, the in-
ertia of the masses and especially the tenacity of the oligarchs, who
simply denied that those who made peaceful revolution impossible
made violent revolution inevitable and were well used to calling out
the army to suppress either.

The Alliance for Progress required a continent of Betancourts for
success. But the progressive democratic parties had their problems.
Governor Luis Muñoz-Marin of Puerto Rico put forward an urgent
one in 1962:

> One terrible disadvantage of political parties of the Democratic Left all
> over Latin America is that they are poor, while their enemies are well-
> heeled. The totalitarian left never seems to lack for funds . . . and the to-
> talitarian right is wealthy, per se. . . . In many a country where the Alli-
> ance may be pouring in tens of *millions,* the ultimate political battle may
> be lost because the parties of the Democratic Left lack a few *thousands* of
> dollars for desperately needed, legitimate, democratic action.[77]

This at least Washington could remedy. The CIA had already
helped José Figueres and Norman Thomas establish in Costa Rica

the Institute of Political Education, which Muñoz-Marin called "perhaps the most important seed-bed for democratic leaders in Latin America."[78] With Robert Kennedy's vigorous support, the Agency passed funds to parties of the democratic left in Chile and elsewhere. Was this all so base? A decade later found it so. It seemed useful at the time—why should we not help the friends of peaceful revolution as much as the Russians and Cubans helped the friends of violent revolution?—but it established bad habits and contained an awful potentiality for abuse. The deeper trouble was the ultimate artificiality of the conditions CIA intervention sought to create. The progressive democratic leaders, while the finest people in Latin America, were falling out of touch with fresh currents in politics and with the militants of the younger generation. If they could not sustain themselves, it was vain to try to sustain them from without.

President Kennedy never pretended the Alliance would be easy. In June 1962 he warned against the expectation "that suddenly the problems of Latin America, which have been with us and with them for so many years, can suddenly be solved overnight." "We face extremely serious problems in implementing the principles of the Alliance for Progress," he said in December. ". . . It's trying to accomplish a social revolution under freedom under the greatest obstacles. . . . It's probably the most difficult assignment the United States has ever taken on."[79] The Alliance, he said again on November 18, 1963, was "a far greater task than any we have ever undertaken in our history."

He ended in 1963, as he had begun in 1961, by saying that this was no miracle to be passed in Washington; it depended in the end on the people of Latin America. "They and they alone," he had said at the start, "can mobilize their resources, enlist the energies of their people, and modify their social patterns so that all, and not just a privileged few, share in the fruits of growth."[80] It was the Latin Americans, he said on November 18, 1962, who must "modify the traditions of centuries" and undergo "the agonizing process of reshaping institutions. . . . Privilege is not easily yielded up. But until the interests of the few yield to the needs of the Nation, the promise and modernization of our society will remain a mockery."[81]

XI

Brazil was the largest nation in Latin America. It overflowed with energy, talent, resources, inequities and problems. Its role could be pivotal in the Alliance. It was in a condition of political and economic disarray.

The intelligent but mysterious Janio Quadros had resigned after a few months as President in August 1961. The Vice President, João Goulart, succeeded to the office at the price, exacted by the army and other conservative interests, of having to accept a prime minister and a quasi-parliamentary regime. Goulart, an inept pupil of the renowned Getulio Vargas, was a wealthy landowner of ostentatious populist sentiment. He was not, as some in the Pentagon and the CIA supposed, a Communist. He was rather a left-wing political boss who made deals with Communists or anyone else. An incompetent administrator, he "liked power," as Roberto Campos, the witty Brazilian ambassador to Washington, put it, "but . . . detested government."[82] Most of all he was a *gaucho,* happiest with the cowboys on his ranch.[83]

Goulart paid a visit to Kennedy in April 1962. There was not much on the agenda. Kennedy wished Brazil would do more to support the Alliance. Goulart agreed. Pressed by George Meany to bring up Communist infiltration into the Brazilian labor movement, Kennedy recalled his own experiences on the Senate Labor Committee and introduced the subject "delicately," Lincoln Gordon, now the American ambassador to Brazil, thought. Roberto Campos thought Goulart "a bit irked."[84] Congress was huffing and puffing over the expropriation of International Telephone and Telegraph properties by Goulart's radical brother-in-law, Leonel Brizola, governor of the state of Rio Grande do Sul. Harold Geneen of ITT, making an early foray into foreign policy, was urging what soon became the Hickenlooper Amendment—cutting off foreign aid to any country nationalizing American property without full and speedy compensation. Kennedy made it clear, Campos recalled, that he was not "defending the interests of big business" and saw no future for foreign ownership in fields like telephones and other utilities where "every time a rate had to be raised . . . it became a diplomatic problem." Still, Brazil must recognize that expropriation without compensation would only drive Congress to restrictive legislation. His interest, Kennedy emphasized, was "in getting some procedure that would enable us to engage in . . . frictionless nationalization"[85]—a striking change from previous American Presidents whose interest was in stopping nationalization per se.*

* I suppose it is impossible to convince the Eric Hobsbawms of this world of it, though the Harold Geneens had no problem believing it; but preventing nation-

Kennedy's purpose, Campos recognized, was "to convert Goulart
into a liberal leader of the Alliance for Progress." For a moment he
seemed to have some success. Campos thought Goulart "struck by
Kennedy's personality and liberal posture" and "pleasantly surprised" by the warmth of his reception.[86] He invited Kennedy to
come to Brazil in July. On his return, however, Goulart plunged into
a campaign for the restoration of full presidential powers. Soon he
forced the parliament to agree to a plebiscite on the question in January 1963. In view of the political uncertainty, Gordon recommended
that Kennedy postpone his visit.

Goulart did little about the Alliance, named a Brizola man as
prime minister and watched economic confusion grow. Still the *gaucho* in him responded to Kennedy's handling of the missile crisis.
"You know we have been defending Cuba's right to be free from invasion," he told Gordon, ". . . but, if they have offensive Russian

---

alization was for John Kennedy an issue of small interest. Lincoln Gordon recalled
Kennedy's reaction at a time, shortly before Goulart's visit, when an ITT subsidiary
in Porto Alegre was expropriated. A State Department official put out a statement
condemning the action and talking about the bad effects it would have on private investment and American aid. Kennedy was furious when he read this and, calling the
assistant secretary for inter-American affairs, asked, "Who is trying to undermine my
Alliance?" (Lincoln Gordon, in interview by author, October 17, 1974).

He was not greatly concerned with internal economic policies. When Jeddi Jagan,
the Marxist Prime Minister of British Guiana, argued that only "socialism" could
break the development bottlenecks in his country, Kennedy told him, "We are not engaged in a crusade to force private enterprise on parts of the world where it is not
relevant. If we are engaged in a crusade for anything, it is national independence.
That is the primary purpose of our aid. The secondary purpose is to encourage individual freedom and political freedom. But we can't always get that; and we have
often helped countries which have little personal freedom, like Yugoslavia, if they
maintain their national independence. That is the basic thing. So long as you do that,
we don't care whether you are socialist, capitalist, pragmatist or whatever" (author's
journal, October 25, 1962). The difference between Jagan and his rival Forbes
Burnham, apart from the contest between Indians and Africans within Guyana, was
not that Jagan was socialist and Burnham was not but that Jagan was pro-Soviet and
Burnham was not.

The British government supported Jagan, though Hugh Gaitskell, the leader of the
Labour opposition, preferred Burnham. The CIA grew considerably exercised over
Jagan, and the British felt—quite rightly, I think, in retrospect—that it was much ado
about nothing. The President's old friend Hugh Fraser was handling the matter as a
junior minister in the Tory government. "American policy," he said later, "was making this really far more important than it should have been because [British Guiana]
was really nothing but a mudbank" (Hugh Fraser, in recorded interview by Joe
O'Connor, September 17, 1966, 9, JFK Oral History Program). Washington finally
persuaded the British to change the electoral system to proportional representation.
This brought a coalition government under Burnham to power in 1964. As Prime
Minister of the Cooperative Republic of Guyana, Burnham subsequently pursued,
without United States retaliation, a policy of nationalization, hostility to foreign investment and neutralism.

missile bases there, that's a threat not only to the United States but to the whole western hemisphere, including us, and we are with you." When the missiles were withdrawn, he poured out two huge whiskeys and proposed to Gordon that they drink a toast. As the American ambassador formulated an innocuous speech to world peace, Goulart looked at him and smiled—"he has a very charming smile"—and said in effect, "To hell with that. Let's drink to the American victory."[87]

But Goulart's associates were more and more vocally anti-Yanqui. With political turmoil increasing, the ambassador considered a visit by President Kennedy more untimely than ever. Still he felt that something ought to be done to strengthen the personal relationship established in the spring. In late November 1962 Gordon proposed that Robert Kennedy come to Brazil and express the President's concerns. The Attorney General's reaction, Gordon recalled, was "wry—'that's a hell of a mission to ask me to take on'—but he was a good soldier."[88]

Robert Kennedy arrived in Brasília on December 17, 1962. A teasing cable from Ethel about Maya Plisetskaya greeted him: IS IT TRUE THE BOLSHOI IS IN BRASILIA? TRES INTERESSANT. KINDLY REMOVE THE MISTLETOE FROM OVER THE TOP OF YOUR HEADS. MME. GOULART DOES NOT UNDERSTAND. . . . YANKEE COME HOME.[89] He began the talks with Goulart by observing that a new government was to be formed and a new program adopted. "This could be a major turning point in relations between Brazil and the United States and in the whole future of Latin America." President Kennedy thought their meeting in the spring had laid the foundation "for the same type of cordial personal relationship that had existed between Vargas and Roosevelt." But recent developments had created "the gravest doubts." It was hard to envisage collaboration if Brazil showed no "spirit of active participation or leadership" in the Alliance and if the Brazilian government and trade unions were "systematically and resolutely anti-American." As for American business, the Attorney General himself "had struggled with some of the same companies with which the Brazilian Government was sometimes in conflict," but, while "business abuse should be combatted . . . business should be treated fairly."

The Americans, Goulart responded, had to understand the contest of "the popular classes against the old dominant elites." If the Brazilian people felt that Washington was allied with the elites, anti-Americanism was inevitable. Some in the government, he conceded, had "fixed hostility to the United States—although not toward President Kennedy"; but that was a consequence of the continuing political crisis and would change after the plebiscite. As Goulart went on and on, Kennedy scribbled a note to Gordon: "We seem to be getting no place."

Kennedy, when he got the floor after more than an hour, wondered whether Goulart really understood President Kennedy's concern. The Kennedys, after all, had their own problems with American business. Brizola mattered no more than Barry Goldwater. But "a policy to prove Brazil's independence by systematic hostility to the United States cannot be reconciled with good Brazilian-American relations." Goulart asked sharply what Kennedy had in mind. Lincoln Gordon identified government agencies where he thought there had been serious left-wing penetration. There was a moment of tension. Then everyone relaxed, and the meeting ended agreeably. Washington could be sure, Goulart said, that he would not play the Communist game. "In any showdown, there was no doubt that Brazil stood on the side of the United States."[90]

Campos later characterized the results of the meeting as "negligible, if not negative." Goulart, he thought, resented Kennedy's emphasis on Communist infiltration in his government and on the treatment of American corporations.[91] Gordon felt that Kennedy had been too casual in manner, had allowed the conversation to wander, had not seemed sufficiently in earnest—almost as if he was simply performing a chore.[92] Kennedy observed of Goulart later, "I didn't like him. He looks and acts a good deal . . . like a Brazilian Jimmy Hoffa. . . . I didn't dislike him as much as I disliked Sukarno. But . . . I didn't think he could be trusted."[93]

Actually the talks may have had some transient impact. Goulart's cabinet after the plebiscite was not bad. Its key figure, San Tiago Dantas, was intelligent and effective. Unfortunately Dantas was dying of cancer. Goulart was unpopular in Congress, and Dantas failed to get the United States assistance he hoped for. Later in the year Goulart fired his moderate ministers and headed down the Vargas-Perón road of demagogic populist nationalism.

The mission to Brazil lasted only twenty-four hours and therefore gave Kennedy no opportunity for his usual sessions with students and labor. It was less successful than the mission to Indonesia, though in the end neither Sukarno nor Goulart could be "saved"—either for the democratic or the Marxist worlds; both succumbed to fantasy and were overthrown by their own armies. The Latin American trip, however, left Robert Kennedy with a consuming interest in the Alliance for Progress as offering the most promising formula for democratic development in the Third World. "I might have gotten more involved in Latin America," he mused in 1964, ". . . in the second term, anyway."[94]

His Third World missions persuaded him not only of the folly of the slapdash, self-intoxicated, rhetorical left in the style of Nkrumah and Sukarno but, even more than before, of the hopelessness of supposing the oligarchies could stop the course of history. "Far too often, for narrow, tactical reasons," he wrote after his return, "this country has associated itself with tyrannical and unpopular regimes that had no following and no future. Over the past twenty years we have paid dearly because of support given to colonial rulers, cruel dictators or ruling cliques void of social purpose. This was one of President Kennedy's gravest concerns."[95] It was increasingly one of Robert Kennedy's strongest convictions.

(25)

The Brothers: II

THE YEAR 1961 was a damned long time ago. For perhaps the last time in their history it was possible for Americans to feel as if all the world were young and all dreams within grasp. I exaggerate of course. But many of us who came to Washington with the Kennedys did suppose that reason could serve as an instrument for social change and that we were moving in the grain of history. When the President on his first day directed Richard Goodwin to find out why the Coast Guard unit in the inaugural parade had no black faces, Goodwin called the Treasury, he said later, with "a rush of energy bordering on elation" and thought, "Why, with a telephone like this we can change the world."[1] Alas, it proved more difficult to change the world than to desegregate the Coast Guard. Euphoria crashed on the Cuban beachhead. Asked in December 1962 how experience had matched expectation, Kennedy replied: "In the first place the problems are more difficult than I had imagined they were. Secondly, there is a limitation upon the ability of the United States to solve these problems."[2] The next year he quoted Franklin Roosevelt on Lincoln—"a sad man because he couldn't get it all at once. And nobody can."[3]

I

For Robert Kennedy these years—his thirty-fifth to thirty-eighth— were fantastically crowded. Unrelenting pressure was etching lines in his face. His rumpled, sand-brown hair was now flecked with gray. Amidst the cascade of public responsibilities, the center of his life remained Hickory Hill, that graceful white mansion—the green lawn rolling down to the tennis court and swimming pool, a pandemonium of children, dogs, ponies, rabbits, cockatoos, jokes, games—where Ethel presided with inexhaustible high spirits.

Hickory Hill was the most spirited social center in Washington. It was hard to resist the raffish, unpredictable, sometimes uncontrollable Kennedy parties. One night at a dinner for the Duchess of Devonshire, with thirty guests crowded into a small dining room, Ethel, who serenely said grace before every meal, finished with a codicil: "And please, dear God, make Bobby buy me a bigger dining-room table." Soon there was a bigger table, in time a new wing, and the parties expanded accordingly. When weather permitted, they were held on the terrace, with the small children "standing around peeping over the hedge, barefooted, in those little nightgowns" (Theodore H. White) or watching "owl-like, with grave, proprietary eyes" (George Plimpton) from a tree house in the tall hickory. One party gave me undesired notoriety when Lee Udall, the wife of the Secretary of the Interior, pushed me fully clothed into the swimming pool as I stood on the edge, contemplating whether I should not jump in anyway to help Ethel, who had been tumbled in a few seconds before when her chair slipped from a platform suspended over the pool. André Malraux, after his exposure to Brumus, the black dog, and Meegan, the white dog, and the children in their red pajamas, was moved to break into English, a language he spoke as rarely as possible, and say, "This house is 'hellzapopping.' "[4]

Their eighth child, Christopher George, was born on Kathleen's twelfth birthday, July 4, 1963; the seventh, Kerry, was now almost four. Robert Kennedy loved children, his own and most others. Children dissolved his reticences, released his humor and his affection, brought him, one felt, more fully out of himself and therefore perhaps more fully into himself. Children in neglect, privation, distress wounded him, like an arrow into the heart. Photographs of the period show him playing with his own children on the beach in summer or in the snow in winter, walking with them hand in hand, carrying them on his shoulders, holding them pensively in his arms. He ruled by encouragement and humor rather than by strict discipline. He was a natural instructor, patient in answering their questions and in teaching them to throw and catch and swim. "There wasn't a problem that the kids didn't have," said Art Buchwald, who became a Hickory Hill familiar, "that he wouldn't interrupt whatever he was doing to solve."[5]

Physical fitness was his accompanying mania. Whenever he could, he swam, played tennis, sailed, skated, skied, pressed more or less unwilling friends into touch football. In February 1963 John Kennedy happened on a 1908 letter from Theodore Roosevelt, another physical fitness maniac, laying down the proposition that Marines ought to be able to hike fifty miles in twenty hours. The President sent the letter over to General Shoup, asking whether present-day Marines were as fit as their predecessors. "I, in turn," he added, "will ask Mr. Salinger for a report on the fitness of the White House staff."

He then told Salinger that someone from the White House—preferably one whose sacrifice would inspire millions of other out-of-shape Americans—must march the fifty miles with the Marines. The portly Salinger, who had studiously avoided all forms of exercise except cigar-smoking for twenty years, tried for several days to dodge the challenge, finally resorting to the desperate expedient of insisting on step-by-step coverage by the White House press corps. At Camp Lejeune, Marine officers went into training. Around the country athletic citizens started off on fifty-mile walks of their own. On the brink Salinger extracted a statement from the President's Council on Physical Fitness saying that only persons in appropriate physical condition should attempt the hike—a standard, he pointed out, that clearly disqualified him. Carleton Kent of the *Chicago Sun-Times* spoke for the White House press: "Thank God, the Press Secretary is a coward."

On a Friday afternoon at the Department of Justice, Robert Kennedy, who always had to test himself against everything, decided that he too would make the hike. To Edwin Guthman, Louis Oberdorfer and James Symington, who had the bad luck to be with him, he said, "You're all going with me, aren't you?" At five o'clock on Saturday morning the four, joined by David Hackett, the best athlete at Milton, met by the old Chesapeake & Ohio Canal. Their plan was to walk to, or toward, Camp David in Maryland. The thermometer stood at twenty degrees. The towpath was covered by snow and ice. As the miles passed, Hackett, Oberdorfer and Symington dropped out. A helicopter flew low; the pilot waved. "Maybe there's a national emergency and I'll have to go back," Kennedy said hopefully. It was a *Life* photographer. After thirty-five miles Guthman gave up. The Attorney General whispered, "You're lucky, your brother isn't President of the United States."[6] On he doggedly went to the finish. David Brinkley of NBC wrote him later: "As an aroused and concerned citizen, I feel it my duty to call to your attention certain pertinent facts, as follows: President Theodore Roosevelt, who is now credited with originating all this hiking and exercising therapy, died young, at sixty."[7]

II

A great sorrow marred the familial felicities of these years. On December 19, 1961, while playing golf in Palm Beach, Joseph P. Kennedy, now seventy-three years old, fell suddenly sick. His niece Ann Gargan drove him back to his house. He said brusquely, "Don't call any doctors."[8] For once his command was ignored. They rushed him to the hospital. It was an intracranial thrombosis, paralyzing his right leg, arm and face, paralyzing the hemisphere of his brain that governed his ability to speak.

He had stayed resolutely in the background from the moment his son became a presidential candidate. "My day is done," he had told the reporter Bob Considine in 1957. "Now it's their day."[9] "I don't want my enemies to be my son's enemies," he told John Seigenthaler in 1960, "or my wars to be my son's wars."[10] He had meticulously avoided public appearances in the election year, declining to speak at the banquet celebrating the twenty-fifth anniversary of the Securities and Exchange Commission,[11] even declining to attend his son's acceptance speech in Los Angeles. The proud old man practiced self-abnegation with sensitivity and grace. His pride in his children had always exceeded his pride in himself.

After the election, the ambassador said that "the saddest thing about all this" was that "Jack doesn't belong any more to just a family. . . . The family can be there. But there is not much they can do sometimes for the President of the United States."[12] After the inauguration he called Stephen Smith. "I want to help," he said, "but I don't want to be a nuisance. Can you tell me: do they want me or don't they want me?" Smith reported the conversation to Robert Kennedy, who listened carefully and thanked him.[13] Soon afterward the ambassador left for Europe. When he returned, he did not visit his son's White House. The President called him frequently at Hyannis Port and Palm Beach. "His father used to wait for the call," Charles Spalding remembers. "And it was really touching if you knew Mr. Kennedy, who was a terribly aggressive individual, the way he would hold himself in check and the way he would make his recommendations . . . in the restraint and in the manner in which he did it."[14] It was almost as if life had moved beyond him, as if his sons, who never stopped loving him and who were his life, needed him no longer.

John and Robert flew at once to Palm Beach after the stroke.

Their father developed pneumonia, pulled through, then began a long invalidism. He could not control his speech but did not know it and, since he continued to understand what was said to him, continued to speak. Only his "no" came through clearly, though sometimes it meant "yes." Most words poured out in an unintelligible garble. His family nodded as if they understood. "Thanks, Dad," the President would say, "I'll take care of it. I'll do it your way."[15]

For a time he underwent therapy at Dr. Howard Rusk's Institute of Physical Medicine and Rehabilitation in New York. Ann Gargan became his eternal companion, in perennial contention with the professional nurse, Rita Dallas, over the best mode of treatment. His wife and children enveloped him in affection. "There was never a moment," Rita Dallas later wrote,

> when the love each child felt for Mr. Kennedy was not evident. . . . Time and again I would see them stand outside his door and actually seem to screw up courage from deep inside before entering the sickroom. They went in to him with shoulders squared, but when they left his presence, they would often sag against the wall in despair. . . . Each one radiated confidence to him, and always, when his children were around, Mr. Kennedy took on a new vigor.[16]

No one among them was more attentive than Jacqueline Kennedy.

He was indomitable. "I never saw a man," said his nurse, "fight so hard to stay vital and alive. . . . He would fail and fall back, but his drive for survival invariably forced him forward again."[17] At last he came to his son's White House. Ben Bradlee saw him there in the spring of 1963. "The old man is bent all out of shape," he wrote,

> his right side paralyzed from head to toe, unable to say anything but meaningless sounds and "no, no, no, no," over and over again. But the evening was movingly gay, because the old man's gallantry shows in his eyes and his crooked smile and the steel of his left hand. And because his children involve him in their every thought and action. They talk to him all the time. They ask him "Don't you think so, Dad?" or "Isn't that right, Dad?" And before he has a chance to embarrass himself or the guests by not being able to answer, they are off on the next subject. . . . When he eats, he drools out of the right side of his mouth, but Jackie was wiping it off quickly, and by the middle of dinner there really is no embarrassment left. . . . The Kennedys are at their best . . . when they are family, and forthright and demonstrative, and they were at their best tonight.[18]

At times the frustration became too much to bear. Robert Kennedy took the brunt of it, as he had when he was a small boy so many years before. Once the presence of the President and the Attorney General stimulated the ambassador to rise from his wheelchair and try to walk without a brace. He stood erect for a moment, then commenced to stagger. "In a lightning move," reported his nurse, "Bobby grabbed his father. Mr. Kennedy tried to struggle loose and began swatting at him with his cane. . . . Even though he was ducking blows, Bobby gradually succeeded in easing the tension by starting to laugh and tease his father." The doctor intervened, persuading the old man to sit down. "He was screaming and shaking his fist at his son." Robert leaned over, kissed his father and said, "Dad, if you want to get up, give me your arm and I'll hold you till you get your balance. . . . That's what I'm here for, Dad. Just to give you a hand when you need it. You've done that for me all my life, so why can't I do the same for you now."

In summers at Hyannis Port, Rita Dallas wrote, "it hurt me whenever Mr. Kennedy treated him roughly. It seemed that he yelled at him constantly, but as time went on, I realized it was almost as though he were trying to urge him on to accomplish greater and greater things." Robert understood, never complained, cherished his father, exercised every day with him in the swimming pool. "During the years that followed, I watched Bobby strengthen his father, laughing with him, praising him, then he would swim away. His eyes would fill with tears, and a look of deep sorrow would cloud his face, but he would quickly compose himself, and begin once more doing what he could to assist him in therapy."[19] Robert himself characteristically said it was Jack who was "the best with my father because he really made him laugh and said outrageous things to him."[20] One more shadow had fallen over the Kennedy family.

III

Among strangers the Attorney General was still diffident and often uneasy. One day the clerks of the Supreme Court justices invited him to lunch. "His mastery of the questions—and you can imagine the Supreme Court law clerks were a very snotty crew—was quite, quite impressive," said Peter Edelman, Arthur Goldberg's clerk. "[But] all the time that this tough guy was answering questions . . . his hands were shaking under the table and were knotted up with one another."[21]

Shyness made Kennedy appear abrupt or preoccupied. On occasion people saw a veil fall over his eyes; they did not know where they stood with him or whether they were getting through or not. On occasion the old combativeness flared up. On occasion he seemed imperious, too ready to override people in the determination to get things done, expecting too much too easily in the way of loyalty or service. He now radiated a sense of power, derived from his own gifts and intensities as well as from his relationship to the President. I remember Marie Harriman's birthday party in April 1963. Randolph Churchill, who had come to Washington to accept his father's honorary American citizenship, was there; also Franklin D. Roosevelt, Jr., and Robert Kennedy—sons of the three great Anglo-American political dynasties of the twentieth century. "The dominating figure of the three," I noted in my journal, ". . . was Bobby, who kidded the others mercilessly."[22] Randolph Churchill described the evening in a London newspaper: "He has a wonderful gift of quick repartee, a delightful smile and a most engaging personality."* Robert Kennedy thanked him for "something nice you wrote about me," adding, "This does not happen with overwhelming frequency here in the United States so I am having your piece made into leaflets and have instructed the Air Force to take them and drop them all across this country so that people will come to realize that they have a fine fellow as Attorney General. Our U-2 pilots will also drop some in Cuba."[23]

Achievers fascinated him, whether James Baldwin or General MacArthur or Richard Daley, whether scholars or astronauts or film stars. I remember a luncheon that William Walton gave for Marlene Dietrich in September 1963:

> Bobby, with his innocent audacity, asked Marlene who was the most attractive man she had ever met. She answered promptly: "Jean Gabin," and then added that the years she had spent with him were the happiest of her life. Bobby asked why she had left him. She said, "Because he wanted to marry me." When Bobby expressed surprise, she said, "I hate marriage. It is an immoral institution. I told him that, if I stayed with him, it was because I was in love with him, and that is all that mattered." Bobby asked her whether she still saw him. She said, "No, he won't see me any more. He has married, and has grown terribly fat, and thinks he is no longer attractive, and does not want me to see him." Bobby said, "Does he still love you?" Marlene: "Of course."[24]

The same audacity brought him to Marilyn Monroe. We both met her the same night after she had sung "Happy Birthday, Mr. Presi-

---

* Randolph Churchill in *News of the World* (London), April 14, 1963. Churchill had had his ups and downs with the Kennedys, as he had had with everybody else. On September 26, 1948, the *New York Times* had published a letter from Joseph P. Kennedy attacking Winston Churchill's war memoirs on the ground of "misquotations" and other "inaccuracies." On October 17, the *Times* carried a long and characteristically truculent reply from Randolph Churchill.

dent" at a Madison Square Garden celebration of John Kennedy's forty-fifth birthday. It was May 19, 1962, at a small party given by that loyal Democrat Arthur Krim of United Artists. Adlai Stevenson wrote a friend about his "perilous encounters" that evening with Marilyn, "dressed in what she calls 'skin and beads.' I didn't see the beads! My encounters, however, were only after breaking through the strong defenses established by Robert Kennedy, who was dodging around her like a moth around the flame."[25] We were all moths around the flame that night. I wrote:

> I do not think I have seen anyone so beautiful; I was enchanted by her manner and her wit, at once so masked, so ingenuous and so penetrating. But one felt a terrible unreality about her—as if talking to someone under water. Bobby and I engaged in mock competition for her; she was most agreeable to him and pleasant to me—but then she receded into her own glittering mist.[26]

There was something at once magical and desperate about her. Robert Kennedy, with his curiosity, his sympathy, his absolute directness of response to distress, in some way got through the glittering mist as few did. He met her again at Patricia Lawford's house in Los Angeles. She called him thereafter in Washington, using an assumed name. She was very often distraught. Angie Novello talked to her more often than the Attorney General did. One feels that Robert Kennedy came to inhabit the fantasies of her last summer. She dreamily told her friend W. J. Weatherby of the *Manchester Guardian* that she might get married again; someone in politics, in Washington; no name vouchsafed. Another friend, Robert Slatzer, claims she said Robert Kennedy had promised to marry her. As Weatherby commented, "Could she possibly believe that Kennedy would ruin himself politically for her?" Given the desperation of her life, this idea, Norman Mailer suggested, perhaps became "absolutely indispensable to her need for a fantasy in which she could begin to believe." In other moods she spoke more reasonably. She once mentioned the rumors about Robert Kennedy to her masseur Ralph Roberts, with whom according to Mailer she had "a psychic communion that is obviously not ordinary." "It's not true," she said to Roberts. "I like him, but not physically."* On the weekend of August

---

* W. J. Weatherby, *Conversations with Marilyn* (New York: Ballantine reprint, 1977), 154–155, 164; Norman Mailer, *Marilyn: A Biography* (New York, 1973), 229, 232; Robert F. Slatzer, *The Life and Curious Death of Marilyn Monroe* (New York, 1974), 1, 3–4. Even by Slatzer's highly conspiratorial account, her long-distance phone bill from May 27 to August 5 amounted only to $209—not much for a Holly-

4 Kennedy was in San Francisco at a meeting of the American Bar Association. She killed herself through an overdose of sleeping pills, probably by accident, perhaps by intent, on the night of August 4. This was less than three months after they met. I doubt whether they had seen each other more than half a dozen times.

He always wanted to learn new things. "I was an orphan," said Art Buchwald, "and I was raised in foster homes, and I was in a Jewish upbringing. And he was very fascinated with this because this is something that he had never experienced. . . . He was very interested in other people's lives, particularly if they weren't Harvard, Yale or Princeton, which he knew about."[27] When he met John Glenn, the first American to enter space orbit, "he was interested," Glenn recalled, "in exactly the personal experience of what it's like. What does it feel like to be weightless? What did you think about just before the booster lit off? . . . What did the sunset look like? . . . What did you think about during reentry? . . . a thousand and one questions."[28]

He read more than ever, mostly history and biography.* He even listened to long-playing records of Shakespeare's plays while shaving in the morning. At last he was fulfilling his mother's dream of self-improvement—and perhaps exciting new maternal dreams. Rose Kennedy wrote Robert semi-jocularly from Paris in 1961:

> I think you should work hard: and become President after Jack—
>   It will be good for the country
>   And for you
>   And especially good for you know who,
>   Ever your affectionate and peripatetic mother.[29]

Returning from a fortnight of Aspen seminars in the summer of 1961, Robert and Ethel asked me whether I would organize a series of evening meetings in Washington at which heavy thinkers might remind leading members of the administration that a world of ideas existed beyond government. I stalled for a time, trusting they would forget. Not a chance; and the first Hickory Hill seminar convened on

---

wood actress (Slatzer, 141). Peter Lawford subsequently described talk of an affair with either Kennedy as "garbage" (*Star,* February 24, 1976).

* Between Christmas and Easter 1962–63, he read E. S. Creasy's *Fifteen Decisive Battles of the World;* S. F. Bemis's *John Quincy Adams and the Foundations of American Foreign Policy;* Irving Stone's *They Also Ran;* Alan Moorhead's *The White Nile;* Barbara Ward's *The Rich Nations and the Poor Nations;* Herbert Agar's *The Price of Union;* Barbara Tuchman's *The Guns of August;* Cecil Woodham-Smith's *The Great Hunger;* Paul Horgan's *Conquistadors in North American History;* and *Seven Days in May* by Fletcher Knebel and Charles Bailey (see Fletcher Knebel, "Bobby Kennedy: He Hates to Be Second," *Look,* May 21, 1963).

November 27, 1961. The lecturers ranged from Isaiah Berlin to Al Capp; the audience from McNamara and Dillon to Alice Roosevelt Longworth. Except for the summers, we managed, under the Attorney General's gentle pressure, a meeting every month or so. (Thus a note in July 1963: "I hope you are working on a schedule for our seminars starting mid-September. You said you would and if you don't I'll tell J. Edgar —— ."[30] Even Mrs. Longworth, her cynicism well honed by sixty years of life in Washington, became a devotee. "They sound rather precious," she said later, "but there was nothing precious about these lectures. It was all sorts of fun." John Kenneth Galbraith, waylaid on a visit from New Delhi to hold forth on economics, recorded his impression:

> Bobby confined his role to interrogation. But he was a very rapt and eager prosecutor of the positions; you had the feeling that if you were shabby on any important point you could pretty well count on Bobby to come in and press you on it. This was matched in some degree by the eagerness of the questioning that Ethel put. It stands in my mind as a bright, lively, and professional evening.[31]

"The most striking thing about Bob," Ramsey Clark said, "was his desire and capacity for growth."[32] "He continually embraced new things," noted the writer Peter Maas, "and he didn't reject something just because it didn't fit in with an earlier period."[33] "Most people," said Anthony Lewis, "acquire certainties as they grow older; he *lost* his. He changed—he grew—more than anyone I have known."[34]

IV

John Kennedy's close friends, as Kenneth O'Donnell perceptively noted, were all people he had met in the 1930s and 1940s. Robert kept "making close friends up until the time of his death."[35] Among his intimates Bobby was usually a competitor and sometimes a needler but essentially easy, considerate and so often unexpectedly sweet. "When I first met him," said Michael Forrestal, son of FDR's Secretary of the Navy and himself an able lawyer who had come to the White House to work on Southeast Asia, "I damned near punched him in the nose. I found him very offensive, rude and obnoxious. . . . But within about a month, after seeing a little bit more of him, I became more or less a captive of his, . . . the *most* astounding person I've ever met."[36]

It was in these years that I got to know him well. When he recruited me for the White House in 1960, we had little more than an amiable acquaintance. Nor would I—a liberal, intellectual, professor, writer, agnostic; a non-hiker, non-skier, non-touch football player, non-mountain climber, whose only athletic pleasure was indifferent tennis—have seemed especially his type.

We got along. I served some purpose in the White House in his considerably more synoptic view of the administration. He called me from time to time to ask me to look into this or that problem; no special pattern emerged. Sometimes he asked me to bring up things with his brother. I wondered why he did not call his brother directly but rarely questioned and supposed I had some minor role in a larger stratagem. When I was blocked in something I thought important, I went to him. He always listened and often acted. I found him excellent company. He was very funny in a sardonic throwaway style, and also keenly appreciative of humor in others. When a remark entertained him, he had the most engaging habit of clapping two or three times. Jocular letters arrived in one's mail. Once Senator Hugh Scott of Pennsylvania attacked me; I replied suitably. Soon I received a handwritten note:

> In connection with your letter to Senator Scott on whether you're a communist or something. You looked like a subversive with Marilyn Monroe in New York and Mark DeWolfe Howe likes you so don't expect any support from over here.
>
> Teddy's brother[37]

Underneath the teasing, one felt that he was deeply protective of friends.

"He could be at times," Kenneth O'Donnell and David Powers wrote in their book, "incredibly naive, too impressed by celebrities, too impulsive or too unrealistic. At most other times, especially when his older brother was depending on his firm support, he was wise, calm, restrained, full of courage and understanding. . . . Always he was the kindest man we ever knew."[38] Most who knew him well would warmly endorse the concluding thought. This was hardly the prevailing public idea in 1963. The impressions of the fifties—his father, the McCarthy committee, the Rackets Committee, the pursuit of Hoffa—had not died. They now received influential restatement at the hands of the writer Gore Vidal. "His obvious characteristics," Vidal wrote in *Esquire* in March 1963, "are energy, vindictiveness and a simple-mindedness about human motives which may yet bring him down. . . . He has none of his brother's human ease; or charity. . . . He would be a dangerously authoritarian-minded President."[39] A dozen years later Vidal summed up his theory of Robert

Kennedy: "really a child of Joe McCarthy, a little Torquemada."[40]

I suppose that the historian must suggest a background for Vidal's attack. Vidal was a talented man, a writer of lucid and graceful prose, an authentic wit, excellent historical novelist, adept playwright, brilliant essayist, litigious citizen, always filled with charm and malice. He and Jacqueline Kennedy both had had, in successive periods, Hugh D. Auchincloss as a stepfather. His ambition had long extended to politics. "He tells me he will one day be president of the United States," Anaïs Nin wrote in 1945; adding soon, "He is insatiable for power."[41] "I certainly wanted to be president," Vidal said in 1975. ". . . Before *The City and the Pillar* [his novel about homosexuality], I thought I had a very good crack at it."[42] He ran for Congress in 1960. Robert Kennedy came into Dutchess County to speak on his behalf but, when they met, failed to recognize him. As John English, a New York Democratic leader, later told the story, "Vidal got very uptight about it. And Kennedy was embarrassed because [Vidal] was related to Jackie and so forth, and he was really [hard] on himself for not having a better memory."[43] This no doubt introduced an early edginess into their relationship.

Nevertheless Vidal was delighted to have friends in the White House. In April 1961 he wrote an adoring piece about John Kennedy for the *London Sunday Telegraph:* "the most accessible and least ceremonious of recent Presidents . . . withdrawn, observant, icily objective in crisis. . . . His wit is pleasingly sardonic. Most important, until Kennedy it was impossible for anyone under fifty (or for an intellectual of any age) to identify himself with the President."*

On November 11, 1961, the Kennedys gave a dance at the White House for Lee Radziwill. Vidal was there. As the evening passed, he gave the strong impression of having drunk far too much. Someone, I forget who, perhaps Jacqueline Kennedy, asked me whether I would get him out of there. I enlisted Kenneth Galbraith and George Plimpton. We took Vidal back to his hotel. The next day Vidal came to see me. He often did in those days, but he later told someone that, assuming I was the White House chronicler (not in fact my job or expectation), he wanted in this case to explain particularly what had happened the night before. I noted in my journal:

> Gore Vidal got into violent fights, first with Lem Billings, then with Bobby. According to Gore, Bobby found him crouching by Jackie and steadying

* The piece appeared in the *Sunday Telegraph,* April 9, 1961. Reprinting it in 1962 in *Rocking the Boat* (Boston, 1962), 3–14, Vidal noted (282) that the Bay of Pigs had rather undercut the portrait he had drawn for the British. "Nevertheless, I take back nothing."

himself by putting his arm on her shoulder. Bobby stepped up and quietly
moved the arm. Gore then went over to Bobby and said, "Never do anything like that to me again." Bobby started to step away when Gore added,
"I have always thought that you were a god-damned impertinent son of a
bitch." At this, according to Gore, Bobby said, "Why don't you get yourself lost." Gore replied, "If that is your level of dialogue, I can only respond by saying: Drop dead." At this Bobby turned his back and went
away.[44]

Vidal's enemies delightedly embellished the story. I can testify that he
was not forcibly ejected, nor cast bodily into Pennsylvania Avenue,
nor was there any kind of major scene. Jacqueline Kennedy, however, was irritated by his behavior and resolved not to have him in
the White House again.

Vidal and Robert Kennedy were not in any event made for each
other. Vidal genuinely admired the President—"an ironist in a profession where the prize usually goes to the apparent cornball," he wrote
as late as 1967.* But he could not abide the younger brother's puri-
tanism and zeal. For his part, Robert Kennedy, I imagine, regarded
bisexuality with disapproval—he became more understanding of the
varieties of human experience in later years—and mistrusted Gore's
destructive propensities. I surmise that, as awareness of his excommunication sank in, Vidal's resentment concentrated on the Attorney
General and boiled over in *Esquire*.

Shortly after the piece came out, Robert Kennedy was in the family apartment in New York. He had invited Budd Schulberg for
breakfast along with Edwin Guthman. Just back from mass, he asked
his guests what they would like. They said bacon and eggs. "A nice
Catholic boy like me," Kennedy said, "has to cook bacon and eggs
on Friday for a couple of backsliding Jewish boys." As he prepared
the breakfast, he said, "If only Gore Vidal could see me now—the
lovable Bobby—standing over a hot stove to see that his friends get a
good nutritious start on the day." Behind the wry humor, Schulberg
said later, "I felt a real hurt, even a sense of bafflement in Bob that
his public image was so much closer to Vidal's caricature than to the
actual, intensely human being we knew."[45] Yet Robert Kennedy well
understood the function he served. "The President," he said in an interview, "has to take so much responsibility that others should move
forward to take the blame. People want someone higher to appeal

---

* Gore Vidal, "The Holy Family," *Esquire*, April 1967. I must perhaps declare an
interest, because Vidal, whose company I continue to find entertaining, if problematic,
described *A Thousand Days* in the same piece as "the best poltical novel since *Coningsby*"—though, as an admirer of *Coningsby*, I take this as a high compliment.

to. . . . It is better for ire and anger to be directed somewhere else."[46]

V

The fraternal partnership did not cover every aspect of policy. As Sorensen said later, the President "made important decisions on which the Attorney General was not his most influential adviser and may not have been consulted at all."[47] Except for poverty, Robert Kennedy was not much involved in economic issues. As civil rights increasingly absorbed his time and passion, he withdrew from foreign affairs. In April 1963, when Dobrynin handed him a hectoring Soviet paper about American foreign policy, the Attorney General told him: "I thought it was so insulting and rude . . . that I would neither accept it nor transmit its message." If the Kremlin wanted to send messages like this, deliver them formally through the State Department, "not through me."[48] Thereafter, the Attorney General dropped out of the Soviet relationship.

The President's struggle for détente continued. "One of the ironic things," the President remarked that spring to Norman Cousins of the *Saturday Review,* ". . . is that Mr. Khrushchev and I occupy approximately the same political positions inside our governments. He would like to prevent a nuclear war but is under severe pressure from his hard-line crowd, which interprets every move in that direction as appeasement. I've got similar problems. . . . The hard-liners in the Soviet Union and the United States feed on one another."[49] Each leader persevered. Kennedy's American University speech in June 1963 led to the Harriman mission to Moscow, the test ban treaty, the ratification by the Senate.

Opposition to détente persisted in both capitals. Early in October, Kennedy authorized the sale of wheat to the Soviet Union. Lyndon Johnson was unhappy. "The Vice President," John Kennedy told me on October 11, "thinks that this is the worst foreign policy mistake we have made in this administration."[50] Khrushchev had comparable troubles. While he was away from Moscow on a hunting trip in late October, the KGB arrested Professor Frederick Barghoorn of Yale as a spy. Kennedy immediately demanded Barghoorn's release. "Khrushchev returned home," said Yuri Ivanovich Nosenko of the KGB, "and he was so mad. 'Who allowed this operation? What fools have done it?' " (The fool turned out to be Brezhnev.)[51]

Robert Kennedy strongly supported the Soviet wheat deal: "I felt it was difficult to turn down the request for the purchase of food [for hungry people]. . . . Also I thought that . . . the Cold War had diminished somewhat—the problems hadn't but the cold war had."[52] Above all, his brother imparted to him the intense belief that the control of nuclear weapons was the world's supreme issue. John Kennedy, Robert said in 1964, "felt stronger about that question almost than anything else."[53] He told Robert late in 1963 that "his greatest disappointment was that he had not accomplished more on disarmament."[54]

The realities of Kennedy's policy bear little resemblance to revisionist caricature. On October 22, 1963, George Kennan, who had resigned as ambassador to Yugoslavia and from public life, wrote Kennedy: "I don't think we have seen a better standard of statesmanship in the White House in the present century."[55] Mike Mansfield, the Senate's most steadfast voice for restraint and humanity in foreign policy, had been in Congress since 1943. Asked on his retirement in 1976 to discuss the seven Presidents he had served, from Franklin Roosevelt through Gerald Ford, Mansfield described Kennedy in his laconic fashion as "the best of the lot."[56]

VI

Despite the fraternal tie, Robert suffered frustrations familiar to every cabinet member. "Far from being influenced easily by Bobby," O'Donnell thought, "the President was quick to point out an error or weakness in one of Bobby's proposals."[57] The Attorney General, though not the most faithful attendant at cabinet meetings, came to feel that the President would do better if he paid more attention to the cabinet. He wrote his brother in March 1963:

> The best minds* in Government should be utilized in finding solutions to . . . major problems. They should be available in times other than deep crisis and emergencies as is now the case. You talk to McNamara but mostly on Defense matters, you talk to Dillon but primarily on financial questions, Dave Bell on AID matters, etc. These men should be sitting down and thinking of some of the problems facing us in a broader context. I think you could get a good deal more out of what is available in Government than you are at the present time.[58]

> * ME [handwritten footnote]

More lightheartedly in November, he recalled Daniel Webster's reminder to John Tyler that William Henry Harrison's practice had been to let the cabinet make the decisions, "each member . . . and the President having but one vote." "I wonder," the Attorney General said, "if this gives you any ideas about the role that Stew [Udall], Orville [Freeman], Luther [Hodges] and John [Gronouski] and some of the rest of us should be playing at future meetings."[59]

Kidding remained the favorite Kennedy form of communication. Early in the administration, Robert noticed that "Jack had on his desk, 'Profiles in Courage' and the Bible. I asked him . . . if these were the books of the world's two great authors."[60] When *Life* described the Attorney General as the number two man in town, the older brother said darkly, "That means there's only one way for you to go, and it ain't up!"[61] Robert was delighted by a photograph showing two of his children peering from under the presidential desk; the President's inscription was: "Dear Bobby: They *told* me you had your people placed throughout the government." They talked kiddingly even about matters on which they felt seriously; and always talked in the cryptic half sentences that bespoke perfect understanding.

In 1963 Ben Bradlee asked John Kennedy why—"never mind the brother bit"—he thought Robert was so great. The President replied: "First, his high moral standards, strict personal ethics. He's a puritan, absolutely incorruptible. Then he has this terrific executive energy. We've got more guys around here with ideas. The problem is to get things done. Bobby's the best organizer I've ever seen." ("Management in Jack Kennedy's mind," Chester Bowles once commented, ". . . consisted largely of calling Bob on the telephone and saying, 'Here are ten things I want to get done.'")[62] John Kennedy added to Bradlee: "He's got compassion, a real sense of compassion. Those Cuban prisoners . . . weighed on his mind for eighteen months. . . . His loyalty comes next. It wasn't the easiest thing for him to go to [Joe] McCarthy's funeral."[63]

John Kennedy used Robert in part as Franklin Roosevelt used Eleanor—as a lightning rod, as a scout on far frontiers, as a more militant and somewhat discountable alter ego, expressing the President's own idealistic side while leaving the President room to maneuver and to mediate. At the same time, the Attorney General was John Kennedy's Harry Hopkins, Lord Root of the Matter, the man on whom the President relied for penetrating questions, for follow-up, for the protection of the presidential interest and objectives. Robert Kennedy, McNamara said, "recognized that his greatest contribution to the President would be to speak candidly, to contradict him if he felt he was wrong and to move him to the right course if he felt he was not on that course. The President never hesitated to turn down Bobby's advice, but many, many times he took it when, initially, he, the President, was in favor of an opposite course. They had an *extraordinarily* close relationship: affection, respect, admiration."[64]

I do not think Richard Goodwin overstated the case when he wrote years later that "President Kennedy's most impolitic appointment . . . also made the greatest contribution to the success and historical reputation of his Administration."[65]

VII

The relationship was closest in working hours. For the President, evenings and weekends were times of respite. Jacqueline Kennedy once told me that he preferred not to see at night people who insisted on the problems of the day.[66] He wanted distraction, a change of subject, easy conversation with old friends.

Robert understood this well enough in the abstract. Explaining Jacqueline's singular charms for his brother, he told Pearl Buck, "What husband wants to come home at night and talk to another version of himself? Jack knows she'll never greet him with 'What's new in Laos?' "[67] But in practice Robert himself often could not resist asking what was new in Laos. "Bobby got his relaxation out of talking about those things," observed Spalding. ". . . He never seemed to need any release from it at all, whereas the President obviously did."[68] For John Kennedy, at the end of a long day, Robert was often too demanding, too involved in issues, too much another version of himself. Teddy made the President laugh. Bobby was his conscience, reminding him of perplexities he wished for a moment to put aside. So Robert and Ethel were not often at the White House on purely informal occasions.

Alike in so many ways, united by so many indestructible bonds, the two brothers were still different men. John Kennedy remained, as Paul Dever had said, the Brahmin; Robert, the Puritan. In English terms, one was a Whig, the other a Radical. John Kennedy was urbane, objective, analytical, controlled, contained, masterful, a man of perspective; Robert, while very bright and increasingly reflective, was more open, exposed, emotional, subjective, intense, a man of commitment. One was a man for whom everything seemed easy; the other

a man for whom everything had been difficult. One was always graceful, the other often graceless. Meeting Robert for the first time in
1963, Roy Jenkins of England thought him "staccato, inarticulate
. . . much less rounded, much less widely informed, much less at
ease with the world of power than his brother."[69] John Kennedy,
while taking part in things, seemed, as Tom Wicker observed, almost
to watch himself take part and to criticize his own performance; Robert "lost himself in the event."[70]

John Kennedy was a life enhancer. His very presence was exhil-
arating—more so than anyone I have ever known. "It was like a lot
of flags on a ship with Jack, easy and bright," said Spalding. "Gaiety
was the key to his nature. . . . He was always the greatest, greatest
company; so bright and so restless and so determined to wring every
last minute. . . . [He] gave you that heightened sense of being."[71]
He was, Robert told John Bartlow Martin, "really an optimist . . . a
little bit like my father, always saw the bright side of things."[72] Robert himself was variable, moody; "the pendulum just swings wider for
him than it does for most people," as Lawrence O'Brien said.[73] Underneath the action and jokes there was a streak of brooding melancholy. John Kennedy, one felt, was at bottom a happy man; Robert, a
sad man.

John Kennedy seemed invulnerable; Robert, desperately vulnerable. Friends wanted to protect the younger brother; they never
thought the older brother required protection. One felt liked by John
Kennedy, needed by Robert Kennedy. Robert had the reputation for
toughness; but, as Kenneth O'Donnell said, John "was much the
toughest of the Kennedy brothers."[74] "Robert Kennedy," said Pierre
Salinger, "gave the impression of a very tough man when he was in
fact very gentle. John Kennedy, under his perfect manners, was one
of the toughest men that ever was."*

John Kennedy was a man of cerebration; "a man who mistrusted
passion," as Richard Neustadt said. Robert trusted his passions.[75]
Reason was John Kennedy's medium; experience was Robert's. Both
men deeply cared about injustice, but the President had an "intellectual understanding" of the great social problems, said Ben Bradlee; Robert "had it in his gut."[76] One attacked injustices because he
found them irrational; the other because he found them unbearable.

---

* Pierre Salinger, *Je suis un Américain* (Paris, 1975), 180. Note also Jerry Bruno:
"I always got a laugh out of the notion that it was Bobby Kennedy who was the
ruthless one while John Kennedy was nice and relaxed" (Jerry Bruno and Jeff Greenfield, *The Advance Man* [New York: Bantam reprint, 1972], 40).

The sight of people living in squalor appalled John Kennedy but, like FDR before him, he saw it from without. Robert had a growing intensity of personal identification with the victims of the social order.

John Kennedy was an ardent liberal reformer. But he was, in his own phrase, an idealist without illusions. He accepted reality. "There is always inequity in life," he observed in 1962. "Some men are killed in a war and some men are wounded, and some men never leave the country. . . . Life is unfair."[77] He was, said Neustadt, "much more resigned to the restraints of institutional life." He was also responding to a calmer time. Had he been President in the later 1960s, he might well have been as radical as his brother, though with the composure of FDR rather than with Robert's rushing passion, and very likely more effective. Robert Kennedy, in a more turbulent time, rebelled against institutional restraints. He was ready, said Neustadt, "to leap outside established institutions to get things done. . . . He could come to terms with institutions but he always hated to." He had, more than his brother, "this drive to the direct approach." His notion was that "every wrong . . . somehow . . . if you can't right it, you've got to bust in the attempt."[78]

Charles Spalding said in 1963, "Jack has traveled in that speculative area where doubt lives. Bobby does not travel there."[79] The President's mind was witty and meditative; the Attorney General's, direct and practical. Roy Wilkins of the NAACP felt that the President "invited you to commune with him. . . . I never got the impression you're communing with Robert Kennedy. You're talking to him; you're arguing with him; and you're dealing with . . . a hard, clear-thinking, determined public servant who has, in addition to a conviction, a moral concern."[80]

The differences in intellectual outlook came out in attitudes toward ultimate things. John Kennedy was a practicing but conventional Catholic. Lord Longford, an English Catholic, once remarked to Eunice Shriver that a book should be written about President Kennedy and his faith. Eunice replied, "It will be an awfully slim volume."[81] Robert's volume would have been thicker. The President's ethos was more Greek than Catholic. He took his definition of happiness from Aristotle—the full use of your powers along lines of excellence. He seemed to imply that man achieved salvation by meeting his own best standards rather than by receiving the grace of God. Life, he appeared to feel, was absurd. Its meaning was the meaning men gave it through the way they lived. There was also a Hindu touch. He had these lines inscribed on a silver beer mug he gave David Powers on his birthday in 1963:

> *There are three things which are real:*
> *God, human folly and laughter.*
> *The first two are beyond our comprehension*
> *So we must do what we can with the third.*

"No one else at the White House, then or a year later," wrote Tom Wicker, "knew that the source of those lines was Aubrey Menen's version of *The Ramayana*. I could find the words in no book of quotations. The Library of Congress was not able to tell me who wrote them. . . . But Ted Clifton, Kennedy's military aide, recalls him writing down those words one spring morning, quickly and without reference to any book. He had them by heart."[82]

Robert Kennedy began as a true believer. He acquired his perceptions of the complexity of things partly because his beloved older brother led him to broader views of society and life and partly because he himself possessed to an exceptional degree an experiencing nature. John Kennedy was a realist brilliantly disguised as a romantic; Robert Kennedy, a romantic stubbornly disguised as a realist.

(26)

Corridors of Grief

IN THE YEARS 1961 and 1962, opponents of the administration tended to separate the Kennedy brothers. Robert was the villain who persecuted steel barons and enforced racial integration. The President, as Robert wryly observed, "wasn't such a bad fellow." But in 1963, "instead of talking about Robert Kennedy, they started talking about the Kennedy brothers, which he used to point out to me frequently." The lowering atmosphere, Robert feared, foretold a mean contest for reelection. "We saw all this literature that was coming out and the letters that poured in—you know, just real hatred." In the fall Robert asked his brother "on what basis I could get out as Attorney General because I thought it was such a burden to carry in the 1964 election." The President thought this "a bad idea, because it would appear . . . that we were running out on civil rights." They decided he should stay for the time being. They would look at the situation again in the spring.[1]

I

They speculated about the probable Republican opponent. The man they yearned for was their old friend from the Rackets Committee, Barry Goldwater. "We had worked with Goldwater," Robert Kennedy said later, "and we just knew he was not a very smart man, and he's going to destroy himself. [The President] was concerned that he would destroy himself too early and not get the nomination."[2] John Kennedy told Ben Bradlee, "I really like him, and if we're licked at least it will be on the issues. At least the people will have a clear choice."* The Republican the President thought would be "the most

* Benjamin C. Bradlee, *Conversations with Kennedy* (New York, 1975), 232. Goldwater himself said later: "I looked forward to running against Jack. And we used to

difficult to beat" was Governor George Romney of Michigan. "He was always for God," Robert Kennedy said, "and he was always for [motherhood] and against big government and against big labor." The President "was very concerned that Romney was going to win [the Republican nomination], and he never discussed it with anyone, I think, other than perhaps myself." He did not mention Romney as a possible opponent lest this build him up. He mentioned Goldwater at every opportunity.[3]

The Kennedys had their own preparations to make for 1964. The Attorney General was dissatisfied with the Democratic National Committee. He thought John Bailey, the chairman, had become "almost a figurehead,"[4] and he feared, from evidence adduced by Paul Corbin, that other committee officials were misusing their party positions. There was always a family solution. Starting in the spring, Stephen Smith came to Washington several days each week to set up the campaign. Planning proceeded through the summer and early autumn. On November 13 the campaign group—the Attorney General, Smith, Theodore Sorensen, Kenneth O'Donnell, Lawrence O'Brien, John Bailey and Richard Maguire from the National Committee and Richard Scammon, director of the Census Bureau and an eminent psephologist—met with the President. "I was anxious to have it clear through the campaign," Robert Kennedy recalled, "that Steve Smith was going to be running things and people should be reporting to him. So that was one of the major purposes [of the meeting] for the President to say that."[5] The rest of the meeting was devoted to registration, the convention site (it now looked like Atlantic City), funds, films and other campaign detail.[6] They wondered how to give interest to a convention dedicated to the renomination of an incumbent. The President said that, if he and the Attorney General got into a public fight, it would make things more lively.[7]

The press soon heard about the meeting. The absence of the Vice President or any representative, the activity of the Department of Justice in the Bobby Baker case, the desire for a good story in a dull week and, perhaps, the morbid suspicions of the Vice President himself led to a burst of talk that the Kennedys were planning to dump Johnson in 1964. Johnson was chronically nervous about his prospects. In 1962 when Ted Lewis wrote lightly in the *New York Daily*

---

talk about it. We had a hell of a good idea that I think would have helped American politics. . . . We would travel together as much as possible and appear on the same platform and express our views" (Roy Reed, "The Liberals Love Barry Goldwater Now," *New York Times Magazine*, April 7, 1974).

News that Eunice Shriver was talking about a Kennedy-Kennedy ticket in 1964, Johnson had sent Walter Jenkins, his assistant, to ask O'Donnell whether this was a campaign to deny him renomination. O'Donnell protested incredulously that, if Eunice had said anything at all, it was obviously a joke. The President later suggested that his sisters reserve their jokes for less sensitive matters.[8]

The idea of dumping Johnson, the President said to Ben Bradlee on October 22, 1963, was "preposterous on the face of it. We've got to carry Texas in '64, and maybe Georgia."[9] When George Smathers mentioned it: "George, you must be the dumbest man in the world. If I drop Lyndon, it will make it look as if we have a really bad and serious scandal on our hands in the Bobby Baker case, which we haven't and that will reflect on me."[10] "There was no plan to dump Lyndon Johnson," Robert Kennedy told John Bartlow Martin the next spring. "It didn't make any sense. . . . And there was never any discussion about dropping him."[11] Nor was there anything resembling evidence for such a plan—at least until 1968 when Evelyn Lincoln, the President's secretary, in a book called *Kennedy and Johnson,* claimed to remember a conversation on November 19, 1963, in which Kennedy told her he was thinking about Governor Terry Sanford of North Carolina as his running mate; in any case, "it will not be Lyndon."[12] When I saw an advance copy of the Lincoln book in February 1968, I alerted Robert Kennedy, who was off skiing in Vermont. He said again there was never any intention to dump Johnson, adding, "Can you imagine the President ever having a talk with Evelyn about a subject like this?"* Johnson himself informed his own brother in 1963, "Jack Kennedy has personally told me that he wants me to stay on the team. Some of the people around him are bastards, but I think he's treated me all right."[13]

The ticket was definitely to be the same. The campaign theme, the President told the November meeting, was to be "peace and prosperity."[14] Looking back at the first three years, John Kennedy was dissatisfied with the amount of time he had had to give to foreign affairs, though he had seen no choice: "each day was a new crisis." "He thought a good deal more needed to be done domestically," his brother said in 1964; ". . . We really had to begin to make a major effort to deal with the unemployed and the poor in the United States," even at the cost of "several billions of dollars each year."[15]

The civil rights struggle had driven Kennedy down in the polls

---

* Author's journal, February 10, 1968. The nonexistence of any dump-Johnson plan is fully and emphatically confirmed by Stephen Smith.

from an overwhelming 76–13 approval in January 1963 to 59–28 in November. This was still a comfortable margin, however, and in a Gallup trial heat against Goldwater in October, Kennedy won easily 55–39.[16] But the President himself felt, his brother said the next spring, "that he had not gotten himself across as a person with much compassion and that people . . . didn't feel personally involved with him."[17] His doubts may have reflected a conversation with Marquis Childs, back from a trip through the south and southwest. Childs had been "startled" by the hostility toward the President. Kennedy was soft on the blacks, soft on the Commies. "From smug editorial writers to filling station attendants, I heard hatred" reminiscent of the hatred of Franklin Roosevelt a generation before. "The rich and privileged were again excoriating that son of a bitch in Washington, and not only the rich and privileged this time. It was for me a deeply disturbing phenomenon." He told Kennedy the time had come for a book like his own *They Hate Roosevelt* of 1936. "I don't believe it," the President said. "I just don't believe that's true. . . . I don't think they feel toward me the way they felt toward Roosevelt. I can't believe that." Childs had never seen him so tense. This was October 31, 1963.[18]

II

On November 20, 1963, Robert Kennedy had his thirty-eighth birthday. There was a party in his office. "All office parties are bad," said Patrick Anderson of the Committee on Juvenile Delinquency, "but this one was miserable."[19] John Douglas thought the Attorney General "glum" and "depressed."[20] After a time Robert Kennedy climbed on his desk and delivered an ironic disquisition. It was great, he said, to have achieved so much in so short a life: to have elected a President; to have become the great asset in the administration; now to have assured the President's reelection by the popularity of his policies on civil rights, Hoffa, wiretapping . . . Ramsey Clark and John Douglas walked out together wondering about the Attorney General's melancholy. He clearly thought himself a terrible political liability. Douglas said, "I guess Bob won't be here by Christmas."[21]

Robert Kennedy went on to the annual White House reception for the judiciary. These parties were attended traditionally by judges and the top people at Justice. The Attorney General had begun inviting long-time Justice employees—clerks, telephone operators, elevator operators. "There were an awful lot of people there," the Attorney

General recalled. "But it was a terrific thrill for people who'd . . . been in the Government for long periods of time and never been in the White House. . . . I stayed longer than the President or Jackie. . . . Then I don't know why I left but I went upstairs and I talked to Jackie." She was looking forward, she said, to the impending trip to Texas.

The President joined them. He was looking forward to the trip too. The political problems in Texas—an angry feud between the populist Democrats led by Senator Ralph Yarborough and the oil Democrats led by the Vice President's protégé Governor John Connally—made it the more interesting. The President, his brother thought, "liked John Connally and liked Yarborough and he's so used to people fighting and not liking each other in politics, it didn't surprise him. He always thought those things could be worked out. . . . He said how irritated he was with Lyndon Johnson who wouldn't help at all in trying to iron out any of the problems in Texas, and that he was an s.o.b. . . . because this was his state and he just wasn't available to help out or just wouldn't lift a finger to try to assist." Soon Ethel bounded up from the reception and reminded her husband that he had a birthday party of his own at Hickory Hill.[22]

It was a characteristic Hickory Hill party—large, loud, happy, with satiric toasts and heckling guests. Only Ethel departed from the prevailing mood. Instead of making her usual chaffing toast about her husband, she gravely asked the party to drink to the President of the United States. Robert Kennedy sat up talking with Gene Kelly, the actor, in the library till two-thirty in the morning. Ethel forgot to tell him about her birthday present—a sauna in the basement—till it was three and they were in bed.

III

The next day he presided over an organized crime meeting. Federal attorneys came from across the country to consider the next phase in the campaign against the syndicates. The meeting continued on Friday, November 22. Shortly after noon the Attorney General suggested a recess. He took Robert Morgenthau and the chief of Morgenthau's criminal division, Silvio Mollo, out to Hickory Hill for a swim and luncheon.

It was a sunlit day, unseasonably warm for November. The three men sat with Ethel Kennedy around a table by the swimming pool, eating clam chowder and tuna fish sandwiches. Shortly before quarter to two, the Attorney General said they had better get back. Fifty yards away workmen were painting the new wing of the house. Morgenthau abstractedly noticed one of them, a painter's hat jammed over his ears, a transistor radio in his hand, run abruptly toward the pool. He was shouting. No one understood what he said. Then a telephone extension rang across the pool. Ethel went to answer it. "She said J. Edgar Hoover was calling," Robert Kennedy remembered later, "so I thought something was wrong because he wouldn't be . . . calling me here." Suddenly Robert Morgenthau realized what the workman had cried: "They say the President is shot." On the phone Hoover said,

> "I have news for you. The President's been shot"; or "I have news for you" and I might have said, "What?" and he said, "The President's been shot." And—well, I don't know what I said—probably "Oh" or something—and I don't know whether he then—I asked him or got into whether it was serious, and I think he said, "I think it's serious." . . . He said, "I'll call you back . . . when I find out more." I don't remember anything more of that conversation.

Morgenthau saw Robert Kennedy turn away and clap his hand to his mouth. There was a look of "shock and horror" on his face. Ethel saw too and rushed to his side. For a few seconds Robert could not speak. Then he almost forced out the words: "Jack's been shot. It may be fatal."[23]

They walked dazedly back to the house. Ethel led Morgenthau and Mollo to a television set in the living room, then accompanied Robert upstairs. Morgenthau wanted to leave but felt he could not until others arrived. "I went off," Robert remembered,

> and called Kenny [O'Donnell, with the party in Dallas], I think. I never got through to him. . . . Then I talked to the Secret Service and I think I talked to Clint Hill [a Secret Service man with the party] . . . but I don't know who it was . . . in the hospital down there and they said that . . . it was very serious. And I asked if he was conscious and they said he wasn't, and I asked if they'd gotten a priest, and they said they had. . . . Then, I said, will you call me back, and he said, yes, and then he—Clint Hill called me back, and I think it was about thirty minutes after I talked to Hoover . . . and he said, "The President's dead."

Robert walked downstairs, put his head in the living room and told Morgenthau, "He's dead."

Robert Kennedy: "So then Hoover called . . . I don't remember what [his words] were. . . . He was not a very warm or sympathetic figure." William Manchester later asked him whether Hoover sounded excited. "No, not a bit. No, nor upset . . . not quite as excited as if he was reporting the fact that he found a Communist on the faculty of Howard University."* There were many calls.

> I think I called Teddy, and then John McCone called me and said, "I'll come out," and he came out. . . . I called Teddy and all my sisters, and I tried to get hold of Jean, and she wasn't there. . . . But I talked to Steve or talked to somebody to tell her to come down to Washington to stay with Jackie. . . . I talked to Sarge about trying to organize the funeral arrangements and he took charge of that and did a terrific job. I talked to Teddy and asked him to go up to tell my father and my mother. . . . I talked to my mother and we agreed to wait—not telling my father until the next morning. . . . I talked to Eunice and . . . she decided that she would go up to my mother. She's the closest really to my mother so that made sense. Jean was closest to Jackie so that made sense. . . . I had to stay here, so Teddy went up to tell my father.

John McCone arrived; the CIA was a short distance from Hickory Hill. Kennedy and McCone went out to the lawn. In a moment Lyndon Johnson was on the phone. Kennedy took the call by the pool.

> First he expressed his condolences. Then he said . . . this might be part of a worldwide plot, which I didn't understand, and he said a lot of people down here think I should be sworn in right away. Do you have any objection to it? And—well, I was sort of taken aback at the moment because it was just an hour after . . . the President had been shot and I didn't think—see what the rush was. And I thought, I suppose, at the time, at least, I thought it would be nice if the President came back to Washington—President Kennedy. . . . But I suppose that was all personal. . . . He said, who could swear me in? I said, I'd be glad to find out and I'll call you back.

He called Katzenbach, who said anyone could do it, including a district court judge. "So I called Johnson back and said anybody can."†

Dean Markham, Robert's football friend, arrived. David Hackett was soon there, and Byron White, and Edwin Guthman, and others. "How are you doing?" Kennedy said to Guthman. "I've seen better days," Guthman replied. "Don't be so gloomy," said Kennedy. "That's one thing I don't need now." "There's so much bitterness," he soon said as he paced the lawn with Guthman. "I thought they'd

* Howard University was the black university in Washington, D.C. Conceivably Hoover might have said Harvard University. In either case, it was one of Hoover's pet hates.

† In fact this discussion was supererogatory. Johnson became President on his predecessor's death, not on the administration of the oath. As Van Buren said long ago, "The Presidency under our system like the king in a monarchy, never dies" (Martin Van Buren, *Inquiry into the Origin and Course of Political Parties in the United States* [New York, 1867], 290).

get one of us, but Jack, after all he'd been through, never worried about it. . . . I thought it would be me."[24]

Ethel left to pick up the children at their schools and break the dreadful news. Robert walked back and forth between the tennis court and the swimming pool. Brumus trailed along at his heels. The children came, and he embraced them, comforting them as he had tried to comfort his friends. He told them, "He had the most wonderful life." He seemed controlled. But Ethel, noticing his eyes rimmed with red, handed him a pair of dark glasses and joined his restless walk. As the shadows lengthened, he prepared to drive to the Pentagon. From there he would go by helicopter to Andrews Field and meet his brother's body. On the elevator to McNamara's office he said to Guthman, "People just don't realize how conservative Lyndon really is. There are going to be a lot of changes."[25]

He did not want a crowd at Andrews. He told Sargent Shriver, "The last thing that Jackie, everybody wants [is] to see a lot of—I wasn't very realistic about it. . . . [Justice] Arthur Goldberg got on the phone and said that this was something more than personal, this is the President of the United States, and I think we should all go. And I said, if you want to go, go. I wasn't going to get into an argument about it. So they all came. I didn't see them, but they were all there, and it was nice."

He arrived at Andrews half an hour before the plane was due from Dallas. He took a solitary walk in the enveloping night. "There were all those people out there, and I didn't want to see any people." He sat for a few minutes in the back of an Army truck. Then he made arrangements to get on the plane without running the gantlet of television cameras. "As the plane came in, I walked around. I don't think anybody saw me, and I went up where the pilot is—the front entrance. And everybody's eyes were on the back entrance." He boarded the plane by himself, hurried past the Johnson party and hugged Jackie.

They went to Bethesda Hospital. There were so many details. The funeral home wanted to know how grand the coffin should be. "I was influenced by . . . that girl's book on [burial] expenses . . . Jessica Mitford [*The American Way of Death*]. . . . I remember making the decision based on Jessica Mitford's book. . . . I remember thinking about it afterward, about whether I was cheap or what I was, and I remembered thinking about how difficult it must be for everybody making that kind of decision." Jessica Mitford's sister, in the circularity of life and death, was the sister-in-law of Kathleen Kennedy's husband Billy Hartington.

The question arose whether the coffin should be open or closed. The casket arrived at the White House early in the morning of the twenty-third. After a brief service in the East Room, "I asked everybody to leave and I asked them to open it. . . . When I saw it, I'd made my mind up. I didn't want it open and I think I might have talked to somebody to ask them to look also." He had indeed asked McNamara to come into the East Room. "After a time," I recorded in my journal, "he came out and asked Nancy Tuckerman [Jacqueline Kennedy's social secretary] and me to go in, look at the bier and give our opinion whether the casket should be open or shut. And so I went in, with the candles fitfully burning, three priests on their knees praying in the background. . . . For a moment, I was shattered. But . . . it was too waxen, too made up. It did not really look like him. Nancy and I told this to Bobby and voted to keep the casket closed. When Bill Walton agreed, Bobby gave instructions."[26]

He spent the night in the Lincoln bedroom. Charles Spalding went with him and said, "There's a sleeping pill around somewhere." Spalding found a pill. Robert Kennedy said, "God, it's so awful. Everything was really beginning to run so well." He was still controlled. Spalding closed the door. "Then I just heard him break down. . . . I heard him sob and say, 'Why, God?' "[27]

IV

He lay fitfully for an hour or two. Soon it was daylight. He walked down the hall and came in on Jacqueline, sitting on her bed in a dressing gown, talking to the children. Young John Kennedy said that a bad man had shot his father. His older sister, Caroline, said that Daddy was too big for his coffin. Later in the morning "there was a dispute about where the President would be buried. . . . Kenny [O'Donnell] and Larry [O'Brien] and Dave Powers were all for him going to Boston, and I was for him being buried out here. . . . They were rather strong. So that made it rather difficult for me. . . . They were going either to turn the Boston Common over and build something in the middle or . . . they were going to set some other place aside . . . but I said the place . . . in Boston that he was going to be buried, where Patrick [the baby who died at birth a few months before] was buried, was unsatisfactory." In the afternoon he met Robert McNamara at Arlington Cemetery. It was raining "like hell."

They looked first at a site toward the bottom of the hill, next to Oliver Wendell Holmes. "I said that it would make a major difference if we could have it higher."28

He went to the services at the Rotunda of the Capitol. Maude Shaw, the governess, had made John wear gloves. Robert told him to take them off. In the limousine Jackie said, "Where are John's gloves?" Robert said that boys didn't wear gloves. They looked out the car's windows. "That was the first time I saw that horse"—Blackjack, the great, black, restless funeral horse. "That was what really kept your mind off it. You didn't know whether he was going to run away. . . . I was so nervous about the fellow who was holding him. . . . It was nice as you look back on it that he was so restless." He listened to the speeches. "I thought they were nice; just [Mike] Mansfield's such a nice man, liked the President so much. I didn't care much what he said. I thought . . . the repetitious business . . . was awkward. And [Chief Justice] Warren, I thought, was inappropriate, to talk about hate."29

Then the funeral. He put his PT-boat tie clip, a silver rosary Ethel had given him and a cutting of his hair into the coffin.30 I wrote in my journal, "The ceremony at Arlington, against a background of wildly twittering birds, was solemn and heartrending. De Gaulle was there, and Eisenhower, and Truman, looking shattered. Evelyn Lincoln said to me, 'The thing he hated most of all was fanatics.' The day was sunny, crisp and cold. I have never felt so depressed."31 Robert Kennedy sent a letter to each of his children and told his sisters to do likewise. He wrote his son Joe:

> On the day of the burial
> of your Godfather
> John Fitzgerald Kennedy

THE WHITE HOUSE
WASHINGTON

Nov. 24, 1963

Dear Joe,
 You are the oldest of all the male grandchildren. You have a special and particular responsibility now which I know you will fulfill.
 Remember all the things that Jack started—be kind to others that are less fortunate than we—and love our country.

> Love to you
> Daddy32

He appeared, I noted the day after Dallas, "composed, withdrawn and resolute."33 Ben Bradlee the same day saw him "clearly emerging as the strongest of the stricken."[34] Discipline and duty summoned him to the occasion. Within he was demolished. "It was much harder for him than anybody," said LeMoyne Billings, his friend of so many years. He had put "his brother's career absolutely first; and not anything about his own career whatsoever. And I think that the shock of losing what he'd built everything around . . . aside from losing the loved figure . . . was just absolutely [devastating]—he didn't know where he was. . . . Everything was just pulled out from under him."[35] They had been years of fulfillment, but of derivative fulfillment: fulfillment not of himself but of a brother and a family. Now in a crazed flash all was wiped out. *"Why, God?"*

v

Robert Kennedy was a desperately wounded man. "I just had the feeling," said John Seigenthaler, "that it was physically painful, almost as if he were on the rack or that he had a toothache or that he had a heart attack. I mean it was pain and it showed itself as being pain. . . . It was very obvious to me, almost when he got up to walk that it hurt to get up to walk." Everything he did was done through a "haze of pain."[36] "He was the most shattered man I had ever seen in my life," said Pierre Salinger. "He was virtually non-functioning. He would walk for hours by himself." Douglas Dillon offered him his house in Hobe Sound, Florida, where Robert and Ethel went with a few friends at the end of the month. They played touch football— "really vicious games," Salinger recalled. ". . . It seemed to me the way he was getting his feelings out was in, you know, knocking people down."[37]

Sardonic withdrawal seemed to distance the anguish. Seigenthaler went out to Hickory Hill after the funeral. "Obviously in pain, he opened the door and said something like this, 'Come on in, somebody shot my brother, and we're watching his funeral on television.'"[38] When Helen Keyes arrived from Boston to help with his mail, "I didn't want to see him; I just figured I'd dissolve; and I walked in and he said, 'Come in.' I said, 'All right.' And he said to me, 'Been to any good funerals lately?' Oh, I almost died, and yet once he said that it was out in the open, and, you know, we just picked up and went on from there."[39] Senator Herbert Lehman of New York died early in December. Robert Kennedy, in New York for the services, said to his Milton friend Mary Bailey Gimbel, "I don't like to let too many days go by without a funeral."[40]

Friends did their best. John Bartlow Martin, retiring as ambassador to the Dominican Republic, went to say goodbye. "How his face had aged in the years I'd known him." Martin attempted a few words of comfort. "With that odd tentative half-smile, so well known to his friends, so little to others, he murmured . . . 'Well, three years is better than nothing.' "[41] Peter Maas arrived from New York on the first day the Attorney General went out publicly—to a Christmas party arranged by Mary McGrory of the *Washington Star* for an orphanage.

> The moment he walked in the room, all these little children—screaming and playing—there was just suddenly silence. . . . Bob stepped into the middle of the room and just then a little [black] boy—I don't suppose he was more than six or seven years old—suddenly darted forward, and stopped in front of him, and said, "Your brother's dead! Your brother's dead!" . . . The adults, all of us, we just kind of turned away. . . . The little boy knew he had done something wrong, but he didn't know *what;* so he started to cry. Bobby stepped forward and picked him up, in kind of one motion, and held him very close for a moment, and he said, "That's all right. I have another brother."[42]

He gave his own annual Christmas party for poor children. A three-man clown band played by the Christmas tree in his office. The children received presents, then trooped downstairs to the auditorium for a show. Someone thought the clowns should go down too to entertain them as they waited. The chief clown told Patrick Anderson of the Juvenile Delinquency Committee that they weren't going anywhere until they had a smoke. Anderson: "Kennedy returned and spoke to me: 'The clowns should be where the children are.' Our eyes met for a long moment and it seemed, incredibly, as if he wanted my agreement. 'Yes, sir,' I said, 'they should be,' and I herded the reluctant clowns downstairs."[43]

It went on and on. He went skiing with Charles Spalding. "You almost prolong the pain not to lose the person," Spalding thought. ". . . It just hurts so bad. Then you figure, if it doesn't hurt I'll be further away from what I've lost. So it just seemed that those nights would go on forever."[44]

VI

He refused to involve himself in the problem of who had murdered his brother. He "never really wanted any investigation," Nicholas Katzenbach thought.[45] Nothing would bring John Kennedy back to life. Investigation would only protract the unbearable pain. Almost better, Robert Kennedy seemed at times to feel, to close the book. He left to Katzenbach all dealings with the Warren Commission, appointed by the new President on November 29 to ascertain the truth about Dallas.

The Chief Justice and his colleagues had perforce to depend greatly on the intelligence agencies. They did not know that the agencies had their own secret reasons to fear a thorough inquiry. If it came out that the putative killer might have had intelligence connections, domestic or foreign, that FBI agents should have had him under close surveillance, that CIA assassins might have provoked him to the terrible deed, the agencies would be in the deepest trouble. But if Lee Harvey Oswald could be portrayed as a crazed loner acting on some solitary impulse of his own, they would be in the clear.

In CIA, James J. Angleton, the counterespionage chief and CIA liaison with the Warren Commission, compiled a dragnet of names and called for information from all branches of the Agency. One name on his list was Rolando Cubela Secades. Desmond FitzGerald decided to withhold from Angleton the story of CIA's role in Cubela's plot to murder Castro. He even ordered any mention of the poison pen deleted from the report of the November 22 meeting.* Nor did Allen Dulles, a member of the Warren Commission, repair the ignorance of his colleagues. (He may not have known about Cubela, but he certainly knew about the 1960–61 assassination attempts.)

The FBI succumbed equally to the bureaucratic imperative. As Edward Jay Epstein has persuasively argued, the Bureau might well have suspected that Oswald had been involved with the KGB and actually believed he had met with a Soviet intelligence officer in Mexico City two months before Dallas. But Oswald's name was not in the FIB's voluminous Security Index. Hoover at once called for an internal inquiry into the "investigative deficiencies in the Oswald case." After reading the report, he noted despairingly that the findings "have resulted in forever destroying the Bureau as the top level investigative organization." Early in December he secretly censured

---

* My source is the informative book by Edward Jay Epstein, *Legend: The Secret World of Lee Harvey Oswald* (New York, 1968), 253–254. Epstein's source was evidently Angleton. I know no reason to doubt this particular story. But, since Angleton in his quest, necessary but maniacal, for Soviet "moles" (penetration agents burrowing their way into the adversary system) at one time thought I might be a Soviet agent in the White House (after a Soviet official in Caracas came up with the date of the Bay of Pigs landing), I may perhaps be pardoned if I do not regard him with the reverence that pervades the Epstein book.

seventeen FBI officials.[46] Externally he was desperate to avert any suspicion that the Bureau had failed. "The thing I am most concerned about," he told Walter Jenkins of the new White House, ". . . is having something issued so we can convince the public that Oswald is the real assassin." Katzenbach, no doubt reflecting Hoover, wrote Bill Moyers, another of the new President's special assistants:

1. The public must be satisfied that Oswald was the assassin; that he did not have confederates who are still at large; and that the evidence was such that he would have been convicted at trial.

2. Speculation about Oswald's motivation ought to be cut off, and we should have some basis for rebutting thought that this was a Communist conspiracy or (as the Iron Curtain press is saying) a right-wing conspiracy to blame it on the Communists.[47]

Robert Kennedy, Katzenbach said later, knew nothing about this memorandum.[48]

For reasons of bureaucratic self-preservation, the CIA and the FBI thus found themselves in the ironic position of denying any possibility of Cuban or Soviet implication. Nor did the new administration wish to think about the unthinkable problems that would arise if there were indication of international conspiracy. All the pressures in Washington were toward a quick and uncomplicated verdict. Robert Kennedy, I believe, had his own thoughts. We spent the evening of December 9 together. "I asked him, perhaps tactlessly, about Oswald. He said that there could be no serious doubt that Oswald was guilty, but there was still argument if he had done it by himself or as part of a larger plot, whether organized by Castro or by gangsters. The FBI thought he had done it by himself, but McCone thought there were two people involved in the shooting."[49]

At about the same time, Kennedy asked Walter Sheridan how Jimmy Hoffa had taken the news. "I didn't want to tell him," Sheridan said later, "but he made me tell him." Hoffa in Miami, hearing that Harold Gibbons and top Teamsters in Washington had lowered the flag over the marble palace to half-mast, "flew into a rage." He yelled at his secretary for crying. A reporter asked him about the Attorney General. Hoffa spat out: "Bobby Kennedy is just another lawyer now." A Teamster leader in Puerto Rico soon wrote Robert Kennedy that he planned to solicit donations from union brothers to "clean, beautify and supply with flowers the grave of Lee Harvey Oswald. You can rest assured contributions will be unanimous."[50]

Robert Kennedy perceived so much hatred about, so many enemies: the Teamsters; the gangsters; the pro-Castro Cubans; the anti-

Castro Cubans; the racists; the right-wing fanatics; the lonely deluded nuts mumbling to themselves in the night. I do not know whether he suspected how much vital information both the FBI and the CIA deliberately denied the Warren Commission or whether he ever read its report. But on October 30, 1966, as we talked till two-thirty in the morning in P. J. Clarke's saloon in New York City, "RFK wondered how long he could continue to avoid comment on the report. It is evident that he believes that it was a poor job and will not endorse it, but that he is unwilling to criticize it and thereby reopen the whole tragic business."[51]

The next year Jim Garrison, the New Orleans district attorney, started making sensational charges about a conspiracy. I asked Kennedy what he made of them. He thought Garrison might be onto something; NBC, he added, had sent Walter Sheridan to New Orleans to find out what Garrison had. Garrison's villain turned out to be the CIA. Kennedy said to Sheridan something like: "You know, at the time I asked McCone . . . if they had killed my brother, and I asked him in a way that he couldn't lie to me, and they hadn't."* Kennedy asked Frank Mankiewicz of his Senate staff whether he thought Garrison had anything. "And I started to tell him, and he said, 'Well, I don't think I want to know.' "[52] Kennedy told me later: "Walter Sheridan is satisfied that Garrison is a fraud."

I cannot say what his essential feeling was. He came to believe the Warren Commission had done an inadequate job; but he had no conviction—though his mind was not sealed against the idea of conspiracy—that an adequate inquiry would necessarily have reached a different conclusion. At times his view was, I believe, close to that expressed by his friend Anthony Lewis in 1975. "The search for conspiracy," Lewis wrote, "only increases the elements of morbidity and paranoia and fantasy in this country. . . . It obscures our necessary understanding, all of us, that in this life there is often tragedy without reason."[53]

VII

Tragedy without reason? But was there anything in the universe without reason? The question echoed: *"Why, God?"* For an agnostic the

---

* Walter Sheridan, in recorded interview by Roberta Greene, June 12, 1970, 19, RFK Oral History Program. In 1967 Marvin Watson of Lyndon Johnson's White House staff told Cartha DeLoach of the FBI that Johnson "was now convinced there was a plot in connection with the assassination. Watson stated the President felt that CIA had had something to do with this plot" (*Washington Post*, December 13, 1977).

murder of John Kennedy seemed one more expression of the ultimate fortuity of things. But for those who believed in a universe infused by the Almighty with pattern and purpose—as the Kennedys did— Dallas brought on a philosophical as well as an emotional crisis. Robert Kennedy in particular had to come to terms with his brother's death before he could truly resume his own existence.

In these dark weeks and months, on solitary walks across wintry fields, in long reverie at his desk in the Department of Justice, in the late afternoon before the fire in Jacqueline Kennedy's Georgetown drawing room, in his reading—now more intense than ever before, as if each next page might contain the essential clue—he was struggling with that fundamental perplexity: whether there was, after all, any sense to the universe. His faith had taught him there was. His experience now raised the searching and terrible doubt. If it were a universe of pattern, what divine purpose had the murder of a beloved brother served? An old Irish ballad haunted him.

> *Sheep without a shepherd;*
> *When the snow shuts out the sky—*
> *Oh, why did you leave us, Owen?*
> *Why did you die?*[54]

He scrawled on a yellow sheet:

The innocent suffer—how can that be possible and God be just.

and

All things are to be examined & called into question—
There are no limits set to thought.[55]

Over Easter in 1964 he went with Jacqueline, her sister and brother-in-law, the Radziwills, and Charles Spalding to Paul Mellon's house in Antigua. Jacqueline, who had been seeking her own consolation, showed him Edith Hamilton's *The Greek Way.* "I'd read it quite a lot before and I brought it with me. So I gave it to him and I remember he'd disappear. He'd be in his room an awful lot of the time . . . reading that and underlining things."[56] Edith Hamilton's small classic, then more than thirty years old, opened up for him a world of suffering and exaltation—a world in which man's destiny was to set himself against the gods and, even while knowing the futility of the quest, to press on to meet his tragic fate.

Robert Kennedy's underlinings suggest themes that spoke to his anguish. He understood with Aeschylus "the antagonism at the heart of the world," mankind fast bound to calamity, life a perilous adventure; but then "men are not made for safe havens. The fullness of life is in the hazards of life. . . . To the heroic, desperate odds fling a challenge." This was not swashbuckling defiance; rather it was the perception that the mystery of suffering underlay the knowledge of life. "Having done what men could," Thucydides had written of the brilliant youths, who, pledging the sea in wine from golden goblets, sailed to conquer Sicily and died miserably in the mines of Syracuse, "they suffered what men must." Robert Kennedy memorized the great lines from the *Agamemnon* of Aeschylus: "He who learns must suffer. And even in our sleep pain that cannot forget, falls drop by drop upon the heart, and in our own despair, against our will, comes wisdom to us by the awful grace of God."

Suffering was the common badge of humanity. Euripides wrote of "the giant agony of the world"—a world made up of a myriad of individuals, each endowed with a terrible power to suffer, an "awful sum of pain" to which no individual could be indifferent save at the price of his humanity. "Know you are bound to help all who are wronged," the mother of Theseus cried in the *Suppliants*. As John Kennedy's sense of the Greeks was colored by his own innate joy in existence, Robert's was directed by an abiding melancholy. He underscored a line from Herodotus: "Brief as life is there never yet was or will be a man who does not wish more than once to die rather than to live." In later years, at the end of an evening, he would sometimes quote the *Oedipus Tyrannus* of Sophocles:

> The long days store up many things nearer to grief than joy
> . . . Death at the last, the deliverer.
> Not to be born is past all prizing best.
> Next best by far when one has seen the light
> Is to go thither swiftly whence he came.[57]

He read much more of Edith Hamilton—*The Echo of Greece, Three Greek Plays, The Ever-Present Past* (from which he took the quotation he used so much subsequently—"to tame the savageness of man and make gentle the life of the world"). In August 1966, we were chatting in Hyannis Port. "Almost shyly, he pulled out of the briefcase . . . *Three Greek Plays*—a well-thumbed volume, with pages loose and falling out—and asked me to read two passages from 'The Trojan Women,' one describing the horrors of war, the other the importance of friendship and loyalty. They are both powerful passages and clearly had great meaning for him."[58] A scribble to Angie Novello after Richard Goodwin had sent him the Arrowsmith translation of *Thetis and Achilles:* "Angie. What other translations are there of William Arrowsmith of Greek plays."[59] "He knew the Greeks cold," recalled one of the bright young men on his Senate staff. ". . . He'd cite some play, and say, 'You know that?' We didn't at all. I think he got some delight out of that."[60]

The fact that he found primary solace in Greek impressions of character and fate did not make him less faithful a Catholic. Still, at the time of truth, Catholic writers did not give him precisely what he needed. And his tragic sense was, to use Auden's distinction, Greek rather than Christian—the tragedy of necessity rather than the tragedy of possibility; "What a pity it had to be this way," rather than, "What a pity it was this way when it might have been otherwise."[61] Next to the Greeks, he read Albert Camus most intently—*The Notebooks; Resistance, Rebellion and Death; The Myth of Sisyphus; The Plague*. His commonplace book of these years is filled with Camus:

> But sometimes in the middle of the night their wound would open afresh. And suddenly awakened, they would finger its painful edges, they would recover their suffering anew and with it the stricken face of their love.

> Smiling despair. No solution, but constantly exercising an authority over myself that I know is useless. The essential thing is not to lose oneself, and not to lose that part of oneself that lies sleeping in the world.

> We are faced with evil. I feel rather like Augustine did before becoming a Christian when he said, "I tried to find the source of evil and I got nowhere." But it is also true that I and few others know what must be done. . . . Perhaps we cannot prevent this world from being a world in which children are tortured. But we can reduce the number of tortured children. And if you believers don't help us, who else in the world can help us do this?[62]

With all he had striven for smashed in a single afternoon, he had an overwhelming sense of the fragility and contingency of life. He had never taken plans very seriously in the past. He could not believe in them at all now. "Who knows if we will be here next week?" If things were worth doing, they were not to be deferred to the precarious future: so he would protect his family, his friendships, his reading from the exactions of public affairs. At the same time he knew he was a child of fortune as well as of fatality—that he had enjoyed far more freedom and happiness than most people, far more opportunity to enlarge his choices and control his existence. This made his obligation to help all who had been wronged the more acute and poignant.

Robert Kennedy at last traveled in that speculative area where doubt lived. He returned from the dangerous journey, his faith intact,

but deepened, enriched. From Aeschylus and Camus he drew a sort
of Christian stoicism and fatalism: a conviction that man could not
escape his destiny, but that this did not relieve him of the responsibility of fulfilling his own best self. He supplemented the Greek
image of man against fate with the existentialist proposition that man,
defining himself by his choices, remakes himself each day and therefore can never rest. Life was a sequence of risks. To fail to meet them
was to destroy a part of oneself.

He made his way through the haze of pain—and in doing so
brought other sufferers insight and relief. "For the next two and a
half years," wrote Rita Dallas, his father's nurse, "Robert Kennedy
became the central focus of strength and hope for the family. . . .
Despite his own grief and loneliness, he radiated an inner strength
that I have never seen before in any other man. . . . Bobby was the
one who welded the pieces back together."[63] As his father had said
so long before, he would keep the Kennedys together, you could bet.

He was now the head of the family. With his father stricken, his
older brothers dead, he was accountable to himself. The qualities he
had so long subordinated in the interest of others—the concern under
the combativeness, the gentleness under the carapace, the idealism, at
once wistful and passionate, under the toughness—could rise freely to
the surface. He could be himself at last.

(27)

Stranger in a Strange Land

JOHN KENNEDY ALWAYS HAD a certain fondness for Lyndon Johnson. He saw his Vice President, with perhaps the merest touch of condescension, as an American original, a figure out of Mark Twain, not as a threat but as a character. The President, Ben Bradlee observed in 1963, "really likes his roguish qualities, respects him enormously as a political operator . . . and he thinks Lady Bird [Mrs. Johnson] is 'neat.'" But, with the best will in the world, the relationship between President and Vice President is doomed—a generalization almost without historical exception. For the Vice President has no serious duty save to wait around for the President to die. This is not the basis for cordial and enduring friendships. In spite of all Kennedy's indulgence for Johnson, there were times, Bradlee noted, "when LBJ's simple presence seems to bug him."[1] "Every time I came into John Kennedy's presence," said Johnson, "I felt like a goddamn raven hovering over his shoulder."[2]

I

Kennedy nevertheless appreciated the frustrations and humiliations inseparable from that most hopeless of constitutional offices. He once told Johnson, "I don't know how you're able to contain yourself."[3] He tolerated no cracks about Johnson from his staff (nor, so far as I could see, was there much inclination to make cracks, though Johnson stoutly believed otherwise). Johnson himself told Dean Rusk that "he had been better treated than any other Vice President in history and knew it."[4] "He's done much better by me," Johnson used to muse (truthfully), "than I would have done by him under the same circumstances."[5] Shortly before his death he told Bobby Baker, "Jack Kennedy always treated me fairly and considerately."[6] I once

remarked in the company of George Reedy, a Johnson special assistant in these years and afterward an astute philosopher of the Presidency, that Kennedy treated Johnson with a consideration exceedingly rare in the history of the White House. Reedy commented,
"Historically, Arthur is absolutely correct. I thought, myself, that
President Kennedy was rather generous to Vice-President Johnson.
But that didn't mean that Vice-President Johnson appreciated it in
the slightest."[7]

For Johnson was insatiable. No amount of consideration would
have been enough. He requested an office next to the President's. "I
have never heard of such a thing," said Kennedy, and gave him an
office in the Executive Office Building across the way. He nagged
Evelyn Lincoln to make sure he would be invited to all White House
meetings. Failing to find his name on the list for a private White
House dinner, he even asked Mrs. Lincoln whether there had not
been a mistake. "Tell him," said Kennedy, "that you have checked
and you found there was no mistake."[8] Johnson made it a practice to
descend on the President with personal complaints, "often," said
Kenneth O'Donnell, "about Bobby." In time Kennedy and O'Donnell
worked out a routine. "The President would first hear him out alone,
and then call me into his office and denounce me in front of Johnson
for whatever the Vice-President was beefing about. I would humbly
take the blame . . . and the Vice-President would go away somewhat
happier."[9]

Johnson was a man notably larger than life in ambitions, energies, needs and insecurities. In the Senate he had been accustomed to
the exercise of personality and power. His role was suddenly one of
self-abnegation, and he played it with impeccable public loyalty. He
had his disagreements with Kennedy, but there was never a whiff of
discord, complaint or self-pity to newspapermen or even to old
friends on the Hill. This unprecedented self-discipline exacted a
growing psychic cost. By 1963 the Vice President faded astonishingly
into the background. Evelyn Lincoln calculated that in 1961 he had
spent ten hours and nineteen minutes in private conferences with the
President, in 1963 one hour and fifty-three minutes. At meetings in
the Cabinet Room he became an almost spectral presence. As the
President's "sureness and independence increased," Mrs. Lincoln
noted, "the Vice President became more apprehensive and anxious to
please."[10] Bill Moyers, who had worked for him in the Senate and
was now deputy director of the Peace Corps, thought that his self-
confidence was trickling away. He was, said Moyers, "a man without

a purpose . . . a great horse in a very small corral." Ranching similes were irresistible. Daniel Patrick Moynihan remembered looking into the Vice President's eyes and thinking, "This is a bull castrated very late in life."[11] Ruminating on his Vice Presidency, Johnson said later: "I detested every minute of it."[12]

II

"Johnson," wrote O'Donnell, "blamed his fallen prestige on Bobby Kennedy." "His complaints against Bobby Kennedy," said Bobby Baker, "were frequent and may have bordered on the paranoic."[13] No affection contaminated the relationship between the Vice President and the Attorney General. It was a pure case of mutual dislike. "Maybe it was just a matter of chemistry," Johnson said in retrospect.[14]

Chemistry was certainly part of it. The Vice President and the Attorney General were immiscible. Johnson was seventeen years older, six inches taller, expansive in manner, coarse in language, emotions near the surface. It was southwestern exaggeration against Yankee understatement; frontier tall tales, marvelously but lengthily told, against laconic irony. Robert Kennedy, in the New England manner, liked people to keep their physical distance. Johnson, in the Texas manner, was all over everybody—always the grip on the shoulder, tug at the lapel, nudge in the ribs, squeeze of the knee. He was a crowder, who set his great face within a few inches of the object of his attention and, as the more diffident retreated, backed them across the room in the course of monologue. Robert Kennedy baffled Johnson. Johnson repelled Robert Kennedy.

One night, after a White House dance for General Gavin, they scrambled eggs in an upstairs kitchen. Johnson said, "Bobby, you do not like me. Your brother likes me. Your sister-in-law likes me. Your Daddy likes me. But *you don't like me.* Now, why? Why don't you like me?" "This went on and on for hours," said Charles Spalding, who was there, "like two kids in the sixth form. . . . Johnson kept pursuing him, saying he didn't like him. . . . It was rather persistent questioning and a little difficult for everybody. . . . He was trying to rake up this relationship and find out what it was that was rankling Bobby."[15]

Finally Johnson said, "I know why you don't like me. You think I attacked your father [at the 1960 convention]. But I never said that. Those reports were all false. . . . I never did attack your father and

I wouldn't and I always liked you and admired you. But you're angry with me and you've always been upset with me." The next morning Kennedy repeated the conversation to John Seigenthaler. "Bob hardly remembered" the attack on his father and asked Seigenthaler to look up the facts. Seigenthaler soon found the damning story in the *New York Times*. "There can't be much doubt in anybody's mind," he reported to the Attorney General, ". . . that he was vicious."[16] Later, Robert Kennedy recalled with incredulity Johnson's claim that night that he was not interested in the Presidency himself, that he had been for John Kennedy from the start, that he simply could not call off his supporters, that he had never heard anyone saying anything bad about the Kennedys. Robert Kennedy: "My experience with him since then—he lies all the time, I'm telling you. . . . He lies even when he doesn't have to lie."[17]

Still, he admired Johnson's restraint as Vice President. Ramsey Clark said he "never heard Bob Kennedy . . . say anything unkind or political about the Vice President the whole time I was there."[18] "I never heard him criticize Johnson," said Katzenbach, "in terms of any lack of loyalty to President Kennedy."[19] Robert Kennedy told me in 1965 that Johnson "was very loyal and never spoke against the President," adding, "but he wasn't very helpful at times that he might have been helpful."[20]

For Johnson, on the other hand, Robert Kennedy was nemesis. The younger brother had begun by trying to deny him the vice presidential nomination. "He repeated that to me over a period of weeks," Pierre Salinger recalled of Johnson's first months in the White House.[21] After the inauguration, said O'Donnell, Johnson felt Robert Kennedy "had taken over his rightful position as the number two man in the government."[22] The Attorney General was the man who humiliated the Vice President at the Committee on Equal Employment Opportunities; who, Johnson assured Hugh Sidey, *Time*'s White House correspondent, "bugged him all during the time he was Vice President";* who, in the autumn of 1963, Johnson believed, was fomenting the Bobby Baker case in order to deny him renomination.[23] "President Kennedy worked so hard at making a place for me, al-

---

* Hugh Sidey, "L.B.J., Hoover and Domestic Spying," *Time*, February 10, 1975. This rumor persisted, later taking the form that the Attorney General had tapped the Johnson White House. "There is absolutely no truth to the statement . . . that the White House had been wired by Robert Kennedy and the Justice Department," Ivan Sinclair of the White House staff wrote one inquirer (Sinclair to Glen Mann, September 14, 1964). "The report which you read," George Reedy wrote another, "is untrue" (Reedy to James Tilson, September 9, 1964; both letters in Johnson Papers).

ways saying nice things, gave me dignity and standing," Johnson said to Helen Thomas of United Press International after the 1968 election. "But back in the back room they were quoting Bobby, saying I was going to be taken off the ticket."[24]

Johnson may have had deeper reasons for his obsession with Robert Kennedy. In Doris Kearns's view, he had been torn in childhood between competing self-images—the masculinity demanded by his father, the intellectuality dreamed of by his mother. Despairing of satisfying both ideals, he chose masculinity and told himself that intellectuals were destined to impotence; a man had to be virile to be effective. But Robert Kennedy, it appeared, combined the qualities that Johnson had convinced himself were incompatible. Johnson, Kearns noted, liked to impose tests of manhood, of which the most notorious was bringing politicians to his ranch and insisting that they kill deer.[25] John Kennedy, filled with deep distaste, had killed his deer after the 1960 election. I never heard that Robert Kennedy killed deer at the LBJ ranch.* But Johnson imagined he had, or at least said so for the purpose of tormenting Hubert Humphrey: "Bobby Kennedy got two of them. You're not going to let Bobby get the best of you, are you?"[26] At the same time Kennedy read books, quoted poetry and was (so Johnson thought) the darling of the intellectuals.

Above all, Robert Kennedy became the outlet for the unconscious resentment Johnson felt toward the President—a resentment he would not acknowledge, for he really liked John Kennedy, but could not altogether repress. In the fall of 1963 the Vice President lunched at the *New York Post* with Dorothy Schiff, James Wechsler and Joseph Lash. To the surprise of the *Post* people, a Johnson aide set up a recording machine in the corner. Johnson, Wechsler thought, seemed in a "strange and abstracted state." He expressed great admiration for John Kennedy. When, Johnson said, the President went around the table with the question "What would you do?" he prayed Kennedy would not turn to him first. Wechsler had the impression of "a rather beaten man whose only solace was in contemplating the burdens he had escaped by failing to achieve the presidency." The talk turned to Vietnam. Johnson, explaining the degeneration of the Diem

* Nor has Jean Kennedy Smith any recollection of RFK's killing deer. He did go deer hunting at the ranch and was disgusted by Johnson's practice of shooting deer from the comfort of an elevated concrete structure. "This isn't hunting," he said on his return, "it's slaughter" (William vanden Heuvel and Milton Gwirtzman, *On His Own: Robert F. Kennedy, 1964–1968* [Garden City, N.Y., 1970], 246).

regime, said the situation was much like that in Washington—a President with a "very strong" brother. "The inescapable overtone," Wechsler thought, "was that . . . Bobby Kennedy was running things, and in view of the Vietnam analogy, . . . [it] seemed to be an extremely bitter thrust."[27] This was October 16, 1963.

III

"I am Vice President," said the first man to hold the job. "In this I am nothing, but *I may be everything*."[28] After Dallas, Lyndon Johnson was suddenly everything. For all his towering ego, his devastating instinct for the weaknesses of others, his unlimited capacity for self-pity, he was at the same time a man of brilliant intelligence, authentic social passion and deep seriousness about his new responsibilities. He was now filled with apprehension about the nation, grief for the Kennedys and a consuming determination to restore confidence in the American government in the shortest possible time.

His insistence on presidential prerogative during that ghastly flight from Dallas came, not from unseemly haste to grab the perquisites of office, but from compelling desire to calm a frantic people and reassure a shocked world. For the stricken Kennedys, however, and for Robert in particular, it was too much too soon. Stunned and despairing, they thought only of the dead President; the living President had all the future in which to establish himself. And, though Johnson comprehended, even to a degree shared, their misery and sought in his sometimes awkward way to alleviate it, his inordinate sensitivity compounded misunderstandings. He had taken the presidential oath, but, as he sourly recalled the harsh time, "for millions of Americans, I was still illegitimate, a naked man with no presidential covering, a pretender to the throne, an illegal usurper."[29]

When the plane arrived at Andrews Field and Robert Kennedy hurried by the Johnson party to Jacqueline's side, Johnson took it as a deliberate snub: "He ran [Johnson later told Jim Bishop] so that he would not have to pause and recognize the new President."[30] Perhaps some such thought contributed to Robert Kennedy's haste. But a man more secure than Johnson would have sympathized with the terrible urgency carrying him to his murdered brother's wife. Driving from Andrews Field to the Bethesda Naval Hospital, Godfrey McHugh, President Kennedy's loyal and emotional Air Force aide, described to the Attorney General the inexplicable delay before the plane took off from Dallas and the sad confusion once they were airborne. Robert Kennedy recalled: "McHugh said that Lyndon Johnson had been—and I remember the word that he used— . . . obscene. There wasn't any other word to use and it was the worst performance he'd ever witnessed."[31] Then or later Jacqueline Kennedy told Robert of John Kennedy's last comment on Lyndon Johnson. He had said on Thursday night, November 21, probably in reference to Texas politics, that Lyndon Johnson was "incapable of telling the truth."[32]

"Four or five matters," Robert Kennedy told John Bartlow Martin the next spring, ". . . arose during the period of November 22 to November 27 . . . which made me bitterer, unhappy at least, with Lyndon Johnson."[33] He had gone to the Oval Office the day after his brother died. "I wanted to make sure the desk was gotten out of there, and I wanted to make sure all his papers were out." In the outer office he encountered Evelyn Lincoln in evident distress. The new President, she said, was already in the Oval Office and had told her, "I have a meeting at 9:30 and would like you to clear your things out of your office by then so my own girls can come in." At that point Johnson appeared and asked to speak to Kennedy.

Their conversation was brief. "He said how much he needed me— 'I need you more than the President needed you.'" As Kennedy observed to William Manchester in the spring, that soon became "a familiar refrain." "I said I don't want to discuss it and . . . that it was going to take us a period of time to move out of here, and I think, maybe, can't you wait? He said, well, of course, and then he started to explain. . . . McNamara had told him he had to move in. Dean Rusk told him he had to move in because the world would fall apart. . . . He didn't want to move in and everybody told him he should move in." Manchester later asked whether these excuses were true. "I never inquired into it, and then Mac Bundy said to me afterwards it was just a mix-up." Johnson extended Evelyn Lincoln's period of grace till noon. She was out by eleven-thirty.[34]

The first cabinet meeting was scheduled for two-thirty. Kennedy: "I was upset about what had happened on the plane and [by] the fact that he came into the office. So by this time I was rather fed up with him. . . . But I went by and Mac Bundy said it was very important that I come to the cabinet meeting." He arrived late. When he entered the room, some in the cabinet rose to their feet. Johnson did not move. Robert Kennedy:

Rusk spoke sort of for the cabinet members and made a nice little statement. . . . Adlai Stevenson had written out a page and a half or two

pages which he then read on how nice Lyndon Johnson was. . . . It didn't
offend me. . . . I felt it was fine. It just struck me that he had to read the
damn thing. . . . Afterwards somebody told me . . . how impressed Lyndon Johnson was with Dean Rusk because he's the only one who spoke up
at the cabinet meeting. So I thought . . . what he wanted is declarations of
loyalty, fidelity from all of us.[35]

The meeting was spiritless and quickly adjourned. A few moments
later, Johnson told a cabinet member with "real bitterness" in his
voice (so recorded in the cabinet member's diary) that Kennedy had
deliberately arrived late in order to spoil the meeting's effect. Kennedy had told an aide, Johnson roundly asserted, "We won't go in
until he has already sat down." When Manchester later passed on this
story, Kennedy expressed amazement first, then amusement.[36]

This was Saturday. On Sunday the question arose of Johnson's first
address to Congress. He wanted to make it on Tuesday. Kennedy: "I
didn't like that. I thought we should just wait one day—at least one
day after the funeral." When Bundy reiterated that Johnson wanted
Tuesday, "I said, well, the hell with it. Why do you ask me about it?
Don't ask me about what you want done—you'll tell me what it's
going to be anyway. So go ahead and do it."[37] In the end, Johnson
waited till Wednesday. It was an excellent address, delivered with
dignity and force. I watched from Mrs. Johnson's box. Robert Kennedy "was pale, somber and inscrutable, applauding faithfully, but
face set and his lips compressed."[38]

Johnson asked Kennedy to come and see him after the address.
The meeting was brief. Again the new President attempted explanations: why the plane had been so long delayed in the departure from
Dallas; why on Rusk's and McNamara's insistence he had moved so
quickly into the Oval Office. "People around you are saying things
about me," he told Kennedy. ". . . You can't let your people talk
about me and I won't talk about you and I need you more [than your
brother did]." Kennedy later: "I didn't get into an argument about
it. . . . I don't know quite what I did say."[39]

Kennedy and Johnson did not see each other in December. On
New Year's Day Johnson wired Kennedy from the ranch:

I KNOW HOW HARD THE PAST SIX WEEKS HAVE BEEN FOR YOU. UNDER THE
MOST TRYING CIRCUMSTANCES YOUR FIRST THOUGHTS HAVE BEEN FOR YOUR
COUNTRY. YOUR BROTHER WOULD HAVE BEEN VERY PROUD OF THE STRENGTH
YOU HAVE SHOWN. AS THE NEW YEAR BEGINS, I RESOLVE TO DO MY BEST TO
FULFILL HIS TRUST IN ME. I WILL NEED YOUR COUNSEL AND SUPPORT.

LYNDON B. JOHNSON

Kennedy replied from Aspen, Colorado, two days later:

GREATLY APPRECIATE THE THOUGHTFULNESS OF YOUR TELEGRAM. I AM
LOOKING FORWARD TO VISITING YOU IN WASHINGTON AT YOUR CONVE-
NIENCE. RESPECTFULLY

ROBERT F. KENNEDY[40]

IV

No one acted more expeditiously to emphasize Robert Kennedy's
change of fortune than J. Edgar Hoover.

Hoover and Johnson had been Washington neighbors and friends
for many years. They understood each other. Shortly after the assassination, the direct line from the Attorney General that Kennedy in
another age had instructed Hoover to answer personally rang on the
director's desk. "Mr. Hoover," an FBI agent recalled, "didn't answer
it, so everyone tried to ignore it. When it finally stopped, Mr. Hoover
said, 'Put that damn thing back on Miss Gandy's desk where it belongs.' "[41] The director replaced Kennedy's friend Courtney Evans
by the obsequious Cartha DeLoach as the FBI liaison with the White
House. Walter Jenkins, a Johnson special assistant (whose brother
was an FBI agent), replaced O'Donnell as the FBI contact. The Attorney General's office was cut out of the chain. When Dolan warned
Kennedy that the Bureau was back to its old trick of dealing directly
with the White House, Kennedy smiled wryly and said, "Those people don't work for us any more."[42] He spoke to me in early December about the "revolt of the FBI," adding grimly that this was something he would gladly occupy himself with in the next eleven
months.[43]

Kennedy never forgot the coldness with which Hoover had broken
the news from Dallas. "It wasn't the way that, under the circumstances, I would have thought an individual would talk. That was one
thing. Then I knew that within a few days he was over to the White
House giving dossiers on everyone that President Kennedy had appointed, in the White House particularly . . . with the idea that President Kennedy had appointed a lot of . . . rather questionable
figures." In his talk with Johnson after the address to Congress, Kennedy had warned that the FBI was operating once again as an independent agency. "I said I thought it was a major mistake because I
thought that they should have some control over the FBI. . . . His
response was mostly that it wasn't going on and that he wanted me to
control the Department of Justice." Kennedy rejoined that they both

"knew what was going on and that . . . if I had just been appointed Attorney General, I would resign." However, if he did, "it would be considered that I was getting out for a different reason. So that wouldn't do any good; and I was going to accept that relationship through the year; and then I'd get out." Johnson repeated that "that wasn't really the situation that existed, that J. Edgar Hoover never came to him directly. But that wasn't the truth."[44]

Kennedy's friends kept him informed about the reports Hoover pressed on the President; as, for example,

> that the Attorney General's people at the Department of Justice are holding secret meetings to try to play up the Bobby Baker case "in order to cause you embarrassment so that you'll have to take the Attorney General on the ticket." . . . [Ethel Kennedy] is alleged to have said that the FBI is out there [at Hickory Hill] not checking the phones [for wiretaps] but are putting wiretaps in so Lyndon Johnson can listen.[45]

> McNamara used to tell me that Hoover used to send over all this material on me and that Lyndon Johnson would read it to him. Lyndon Johnson told me that he never received an adverse report from J. Edgar Hoover on me. One time McNamara had a dinner at Nick Katzenbach's house to talk about their children taking a bicycle ride through Cape Cod. . . . Hoover sent a report in to Lyndon Johnson that there was a meeting—I think I was supposed to have been there—at this house in which we were discussing the overthrow of Lyndon Johnson, to take the nomination from him. Or like Abba Schwartz reported to have said at some party, "We've got to get rid of Lyndon Johnson so that Robert Kennedy can become President." . . . Lyndon Johnson says that he never received such a report.[46]

While thus feeding the new President's suspicions, the director at the same time protested to him about, as Kennedy heard it, "a conspiracy, led by me, to get rid of J. Edgar Hoover."[47] Johnson's response to Kennedy's criticisms of the FBI, or so Hoover told an interviewer in 1970, was: "Stand by your guns." As for Hoover himself: "I didn't speak to Bobby Kennedy the last six months he was in office."[48] In mid-1964, Johnson, standing in the Rose Garden with Hoover beaming at his side, announced he was exempting the director indefinitely from the law requiring retirement at seventy. "The nation cannot afford to lose you," the new President grandly said. ". . . No other American, now or in our past, has served the cause of justice so faithfully and so well."[49]

V

On the late afternoon of December 13, 1963, Richard Goodwin and

I met Kennedy in his office at Justice. Earlier in the day I had found Averell Harriman "in a state of considerable distress and wrath" over the new President's rumored decision to place Thomas Mann in charge of western hemisphere affairs. Mann, assistant secretary when Kennedy took over and thereafter ambassador to Mexico, was able, hard-boiled, opinionated, a colonialist by mentality and a free enterprise zealot. He was also a Texan, though not, I believe, a particular friend of Johnson's. But they both had the Tex-Mex attitude toward Latin America, well delineated by Johnson himself soon after assuming the Presidency. "I know these Latin Americans," Johnson told a group of reporters.

> . . . They'll come right into your yard and take it over if you let them. And the next day they'll be right on your porch, barefoot and weighing one hundred and thirty pounds and they'll take that too. But if you say to 'em right at the start, "hold on, just wait a minute," they'll know they're dealing with somebody who'll stand up. And after that you can get along fine.[50]

Mann's designation, Harriman thought, would "reverse the whole direction of Latin American policy."[51] The Attorney General had also spoken with Harriman. "I don't want to see Averell Harriman get hurt, or anyone else," he now observed to Goodwin and me. "Harriman's got his faults. I've got my faults. We've all got faults. The important thing for us to do now is to stick together."

He talked on in the fading December light. "Our power will last for just eleven months. It will disappear the day of the election. After November 5th we'll all be dead." We must

> use that power in these months to the best possible advantage. . . . There are a hundred men scattered through the government who are devoted to the purposes for which we came to Washington. We must all stay in close touch and not let them pick us off one by one. I haven't the answer in detail yet, but I am sure that the fundamental principle now is collective action.

He got up, stood tensely by his desk, his hands at his side.

> Sure, I've lost a brother. Other people lose wives. . . . But that's not what's important. What's important is what we were trying to do for this country. We worked hard to get where we are, and we can't let it all go to waste. My brother barely had a chance to get started—and there is so much now to be done—for the Negroes and the unemployed and the school kids and everyone else who is not getting a decent break in our society. This is what counts. The new fellow doesn't get this. He knows all about politics and nothing about human beings. . . . I haven't talked to

him yet. I don't feel mentally or physically prepared to do so yet. When I talk to him, I am ready to be tough about what we must have.

He continued:

There are a lot of people in this town. They didn't come here just to work for John Kennedy, an individual, but for ideas, things we wanted to do. It's one thing if you've got personal reasons for leaving, like you may want to leave, Arthur. But I don't think people should run off. . . . Remember, after November 5th we're all done. We won't be wanted or needed.[52]

The next day Johnson announced Mann's appointment. It was, I wrote in my journal, "a declaration of independence, even perhaps a declaration of aggression, against the Kennedys."[53] I wrote the Attorney General:

Johnson has won the first round. He has shown his power to move in a field of special concern to the Kennedys without consulting the Kennedys. . . . We have supposed that Johnson so badly needed the Kennedy people for the election that we would retain a measure of power for eleven months. . . . We have underestimated the power of the Presidency. The President has nearly all the cards in this contest. . . . So long as he maintains an ostensibly liberal position on issues, it will be very difficult to do anything about it. . . . We are weaker—a good deal weaker—than we had supposed. He has understood that the only sanctions we have are resignation and/or revolt—and that both sanctions are meaningless, and will seem sour grapes, unless they are provoked by a really understandable issue—and this LBJ will do his best to deny us.[54]

Kennedy thought my analysis unduly pessimistic. Johnson would have to consult the Kennedy people about the Vice Presidency, he said, and we would exert some influence on the choice of Secretary of State in the next cabinet. I said it was hard to impose a deal on Presidents. Kennedy said, "It is not so hard. I will be perfectly willing to ask President Johnson what his plans are for the State Department before we decide the role we are going to play in the campaign." I said, "We will all have to play a role in the campaign, or we will be finished forever in the party." He said, "Yes, but there is a considerable difference between a nominal role and a real role. We can go through the motions or we can go all out."[55]

So the Kennedy loyalists indulged in impotent speculation. Lyndon Johnson unquestionably surmised, if he did not know, that such discussions were going on. He could hardly be blamed for resentment and mistrust. As for myself, believing the new President had the right to his own men in the White House, I had submitted my resignation the day after Dallas, received the Johnson treatment ("I need you more than President Kennedy needed you"), agreed to stay for the transition and in January 1964 resigned again. This time it was accepted with entirely understandable alacrity.

VI

Walter Sheridan asked Robert Kennedy when he was coming back to the Justice Department: "We need you, you know." Kennedy said: "I know, but I don't have the heart for it right now."[56] His world was radically altered. Jacqueline Kennedy had seen it as the end of Camelot*—a romantic fancy that I do not recall on Robert's lips and that I am sure would have provoked John Kennedy to profane disclaimer. For Robert his brother's Washington evoked rather Periclean Athens and high ideals of civic commitment—ideals he feared might now fall before a rabble of wheeler-dealers.

His friends wondered what might recall him to action. Then his old acquaintance Sukarno provided a new crisis in Southeast Asia. The formation under British sponsorship of the Federation of Malaysia in September 1963 had given deep offense to the Indonesian leader. "I have been duped and humiliated by the British," he told Ambassador Howard Jones, his face contorted with rage. "I will not take it."[57] He proclaimed the policy of Konfrontasi—confrontation—sneaked a few guerrillas into Malaysian territory and fulminated against the new state. "We'll crunch up Malaysia," he said, "and spit out the pieces."[58]

Washington, though sympathetic to Malaysia, did not want to drive Indonesia into closer connection with Peking, which after 1962 had displaced the Soviet Union as Sukarno's Communist friend. And, if the British Commonwealth went to war, the United States might be dragged in as a result of obligations under the ANZUS treaty of 1951. All this argued for American initiative in moderating the crisis. When Jones returned to see President Kennedy in mid-November 1963, he had requested authorization to say that, if Sukarno settled the Malaysian dispute, the United States would resume economic aid, now somewhat cut back, and that President Kennedy himself would visit Indonesia the next spring. Harriman, Roger Hilsman and Mi-

---

* A few days after Dallas, Jacqueline Kennedy had recalled to Theodore H. White the lyrics of the song "Camelot" written by Alan Jay Lerner, John Kennedy's boyhood friend at Choate and Harvard, for the 1960 musical show of the same name (see Theodore H. White, "For President Kennedy an Epilogue," *Life,* December 6, 1963). The image was not perhaps, on analysis, all that romantic. King Arthur's Camelot concluded in betrayal and death.

chael Forrestal backed this recommendation. The President agreed. Two days later he left for Texas.[59]

Indonesia, it thereafter developed, had been one more point of foreign policy disagreement between Kennedy and Johnson. The new President refused to sign a determination that aid to Indonesia was in the national interest. He agreed, however, to one more try at getting negotiations under way between Sukarno and Tunku Abdul Rahman, the Malaysian Prime Minister. Harriman proposed Robert Kennedy as a presidential emissary—both on the merits and in the hope that the mission might rouse him from his depression. Howard Jones thought Kennedy "ideal. . . . He had established a warm rapport with Sukarno, knew many of the people involved, was familiar with the issues, and had proved his skill in delicate negotiation."[60] In the White House Bundy cordially agreed. The new President, however, disliked the idea. Johnson, Bundy said, "felt that he had been sort of maneuvered into approving by staff people who weren't thinking about the Johnson interest."[61] Nor did Kennedy himself much want to go. After the New Year he dubiously committed himself to the trip.

The condition precedent to negotiation was a cease-fire. "[The] Tunku cannot negotiate with a pistol at his head," Forrestal wrote the Attorney General, "and it is up to Sukarno to remove the pistol."[62] Tell Sukarno, Kennedy's instructions read, that, "if the confrontation is stopped, the natural course of history . . . will inevitably lead to a gradual reduction of the British presence. Thus it is Sukarno's own policy which is producing the British reactions to which he is objecting. This pathway is bound to lead to a bloody nose for Sukarno, and when we are forced to choose sides we will not be able to choose his."[63]

Ethel accompanied him, along with Forrestal, Guthman and Peter Maas. The atmosphere on the plane across the Pacific, with Robert and Ethel answering letters of condolence, was melancholy.[64] The first talks with Sukarno were to take place in Tokyo. Kennedy, however, had an earlier stop to make. At what the American embassy called "the insistent urging of the students and faculty," he returned to Waseda University, where students had raged at him only two years before. The auditorium was packed with an enthusiastic crowd. Thousands more, standing outside in a soft rain, listened over loudspeakers. He talked about his brother: "He was not only President of one nation; he was president of young people around the world. . . . If President Kennedy's life and death and his relationship to all in our age group mean anything, it means we young people must work harder for a better life for all the people in the world." The crowd cheered wildly. Then he led the students in singing the Waseda song.[65]

He met Sukarno in Tokyo on January 16. Sukarno said, "Did you come here to threaten me?" Kennedy smiled and said, "No, I've come to help get you out of trouble."[66] Forrestal reported to Washington his impression that Sukarno had been "quite capable of reacting irrationally if the Attorney General had not knocked the idea down."[67] Their talks went surprisingly well. Responding to Kennedy's frank presentation, Sukarno said he would agree to a ceasefire if the Malaysians agreed also. Kennedy flew on to Malaysia. The Tunku protested that Sukarno would use a cease-fire to build up his guerrilla forces but eventually yielded to the Attorney General's persuasion.

On January 22 Kennedy arrived in Indonesia, where the Communists had unleashed a clamor against a cease-fire. But Sukarno kept the word he had given in Tokyo. That afternoon, looking "utterly beat," he unburdened himself to his American biographer, Cindy Adams. "I am tired. So tired," he said. ". . . I have to make a speech at the stadium where my people are waiting for me to shout again *'Ganjang Malaysia . . .* Crush Malaysia.' And I cannot. I have agreed to a cease-fire." She asked him how he liked Kennedy. "Bob is very warm," he said. "He is like his brother. I loved his brother."[68]

"He was very, very frank with Sukarno," Forrestal said later; "told him things that nobody else would have dared to say to him." Dealing with two opinionated, angry men, Sukarno and the Tunku, "he never told a lie; he never misquoted anybody; he never concealed. . . . He was always absolutely impersonal, spoke with great directness softened by humor; the truth aroused no antagonism as he delivered it."[69] "I am most grateful," the Tunku wrote Kennedy, "for everything that you have done to bring about a cease-fire. . . . You have done more than anybody else has managed to do so far."[70]

The return to Washington was an anticlimax. Instead of reporting to the new President in private, Kennedy found himself on January 28 at a mass meeting with Johnson and ranking members of the Senate Foreign Relations and Armed Services Committee. The President displayed little interest then and none thereafter in Kennedy's trip.[71] Though the conferences Kennedy had set up between the Indonesians and the Malaysians took place, the parties failed to agree on the terms in which the cease-fire should continue. He tried to follow up.

He sent messages to the Tunku and to Sukarno. His feeling grew that
the President did not, and the State Department dared not, give a
damn about his effort. The episode left him, said Guthman, with "a
bitter taste."*

VII

Still, it restored him to activity. "I hadn't wanted to go on that trip,"
Robert Kennedy told Murray Kempton, "but afterwards I was glad I
had."[72] It was, however, almost his last involvement as Attorney
General in world affairs. Johnson's first foreign crisis had erupted before the trip—over the Panama Canal Zone. No one had consulted
Kennedy. "It's really the worst matter involving an international
problem that I have not been in," he said in March. He thought it
"very badly handled."[73] He could hardly be kept out of the next crisis, however, for it involved Cuba. The available record does not
clarify Kennedy's participation in Cuban policy after Dallas, save for
an allusion in a February memorandum to "the Attorney General's
statement that there is no point in discussing courses of action . . .
until the fundamental decision is made as to whether or not it is possible for the United States to live with Castro."[74] One deduces a
desire to keep the Attwood initiative alive.

The Cuban crisis of February arose when the Coast Guard seized
four Cuban fishing boats two miles off the Florida Keys. Thomas
Mann encouraged Johnson to view the incident as a critical Soviet
"test" of the new American President. So far as Kennedy could see, it
was no more than a traffic violation. The Attorney General had what
he subsequently described as a "rather violent" argument with Mann
at a National Security Council meeting. Kennedy's demand for information to substantiate the Mann-Johnson thesis caused an adjourn-
ment. When the NSC reassembled that afternoon, McCone conceded
that "maybe the fishing vessels just arrived there. So then I said that
this whole business about the fishing vessels was foolish . . . like a

* Guthman, *We Band of Brothers* (New York, 1971), 253. Harriman and Jones
continued to argue that military aid to Malaysia would destroy what little influence
the United States had left in Indonesia. In July Johnson invited the Tunku to Washington, where they jointly announced a program of American military assistance
to Malaysia. At the National Press Club the Tunku compared Sukarno to Hitler.
Sukarno would no doubt have succumbed to irrevocable anti-Americanism anyway as
he pursued his increasingly megalomaniac course. But Johnson's July decision left
him no alternative. (Howard P. Jones, *Indonesia: The Impossible Dream* [New York,
1971], 312, 342–343; W. Averell Harriman, in recorded interview by author, June 6,
1965, 28–30, JFK Oral History Program.)

speeding, parking ticket. Why don't they just tell them to get out of there and go home? and, if you wanted to fine them a couple of hundred bucks, fine them, but the idea of locking them up and creating a major crisis about it was foolish."[75]

Kennedy prevailed on the problem of the hapless fishermen, who were fined and sent home. But Johnson still wanted his crisis. Castro, protesting the seizure of the fishing boats, had turned off the water supply to the American naval base at Guantanamo. Mann now proposed to discharge two thousand Cubans who worked on the base. They were, he said, security risks; they brought dollars into the Cuban economy; most important of all, "The only thing the South Americans understood was money and, when you took this money away from Castro, it would be a sign to the rest of the countries of Latin America that this was a new administration which was going to stand up." Latinos, Mann said, were not like North Americans. This exasperated Kennedy. "I said I thought he sounded like Barry Goldwater making a speech at the Economic Club and that this policy of the United States had gone fifty years before." If the Cuban workers were security risks, why had they not created problems during the missile crisis? "I didn't think that made any sense." He lost this one. The employees were fired. This was, Kennedy said later, "the last meeting on any substantive matter" of foreign affairs to which he was invited.[76]

He made a final gesture about Cuba in the summer. A. J. Muste, the aged pacifist, began a peace march from Quebec to Guantanamo. The White House, unduly agitated, sought an injunction to prevent Muste from getting on a boat in Florida. The letter of authorization required the signature of the Attorney General. Kennedy asked what it was all about. He was told, "The White House wants it signed." He listened with incredulity. "Let me get this straight," he said. "You mean you want me to sign that piece of paper to tell an 84 year old man he can't walk 800 miles? . . . I don't think the security of the United States is going to be endangered by an 84 year old man. I'm not going to sign that piece of paper."[77]

He remained unchallenged in his own domain. "I don't think Lyndon Johnson paid one iota of attention to the Justice Department," Katzenbach said later. "Bobby Kennedy had license to do what he wanted to do."[78] The Attorney General was at last beginning to have the heart again for Justice. His collar still seemed a little large, his cuffs a little too close to the knuckles, "not as though he had wasted," Murray Kempton thought, "but as though he had withdrawn." The office looked the same. "I have this feeling," Kennedy mused, "that I go on doing the same old things I always did. . . . A month can go by before I need to take a problem to the White House. After all even my brother never asked me about the Lands Division."[79]

He took up the threads of the past. Jimmy Hoffa went on trial in Chattanooga in January 1964 on the charge of conspiring to fix the jury in the Test Fleet case. In March he was found guilty, receiving an eight-year sentence. In April he went on trial again, this time in Chicago on charges of diverting a million dollars from the Teamster pension funds for his own use. In July he was found guilty once more. This time it was a five-year sentence.

Hoffa's downfall brought Kennedy no pleasure. "I think he lost all interest in Hoffa," Kempton said. ". . . I never heard him say anything about Hoffa that really indicated much more than boredom with the subject in the last years of his life."[80] He went to a Justice Department party after Hoffa's Chattanooga conviction but told Angie Novello that there was "nothing to celebrate."[81] Kenneth O'Donnell thought Kennedy "unhappy that he was going to jail. . . . He had enough tragedy of his own now."[82] "He didn't like the idea of Hoffa having eight years in Lewisburg," said William Hundley. "We used to talk about Jimmy on plane trips. He would say, 'How's Hoffa doing?' If he had ever become President, the first person he would have let out was Hoffa."[83]

VIII

He was through with chasing people. His brother's last wish had been a war against poverty. He now unexpectedly found himself in a position to help carry forward that wish. The Council of Economic Advisers and the Bureau of the Budget, in trying to put an antipoverty program together, had been "bewildered," as William Capron of the council said later, "by the complete disarray of the nominal professionals in the field of poverty."[84] In the search for a "unifying principle,"[85] William B. Cannon of the Bureau of the Budget bethought himself of the President's Committee on Juvenile Delinquency.

David Hackett now proposed that the antipoverty program base itself on a community-action approach, in which local institutions would coordinate federal programs within the community and be accountable to (and funded by) a single responsive instrument in Washington. Communities were to have a year to prepare their programs. By establishing a method rather than imposing substantive solutions, the community-action approach both acknowledged that no one knew how to cure poverty and guaranteed adaptability to local circumstance.

Strongly backed by the Bureau of the Budget and the Council of Economic Advisers, the community-action approach won the initial sympathy of the new President.[86] But it was vigorously opposed by the old-line departments, most of all by Labor, where Willard Wirtz and Daniel Patrick Moynihan forcefully argued that a job program ought to have first priority. Johnson, moreover, wanted visible results well before the 1964 election. "What we said," Hackett recalled, "was, 'Go stage by stage, don't rush into legislation.' But Johnson just said, 'Go.'"[87] After Dallas, the influence of Hackett and the Department of Justice group evaporated. "Few things that Robert Kennedy had touched," Moynihan wrote later, "were not thereafter viewed with suspicion, fear, and distaste by the staff of the Johnson White House, and of course most of all by the President himself."*

In December, Sorensen had given the antipoverty planners the impression that Robert Kennedy might "seriously consider heading" the war against poverty.[88] Whether or not this was so, Johnson decided, while Kennedy was in the Far East, to offer the job to Sargent Shriver. Like Johnson, Shriver wanted immediate visibility and rapid results. As for community action: "It'll never fly," he said. ". . . Where you need the money worst, you'll have the worst plans."[89] Instead he put together an eclectic program more or less combining everybody's ideas. On Kennedy's intercession Shriver reluctantly added community action, though now divested of the emphasis on advance planning.† Still, even if Hackett's guerrillas were defeated in their hope of making community action the centerpiece, so much survived from their labors of 1961–63—the national service corps, reappearing as Volunteers in Service to America (VISTA); legal aid; mental health centers; youth development projects; neighborhood services—that, as Kenneth Clark wrote in 1969, the Juvenile Delinquency Committee

---

* Moynihan, *Maximum Feasible Misunderstanding* (New York, 1969), 80. See William B. Cannon: "The assassination also meant that [the] Hackett-Kennedy group as the agent for translating irresistible social forces and ideas into action were themselves something less than irresistible political forces" ("The Dangerous Abuse of the Middle Class," ms., ch. 6, 51).

† We turned to David Hackett and Richard Boone too for help when it looked like the Community Action Program was going to be jettisoned by the Shriver group. I firmly believe that the major reason Community Action survived was because David Hackett prevailed upon Attorney General Kennedy to intercede with Mr. Shriver" (Cannon, "Dangerous Abuse," ch. 6, 44).

had in large part laid "the foundation for the national anti-poverty program."[90]

The community-action title of the Economic Opportunity Act of 1964 was, Hackett said later, "a rearguard action."[91] Its point was to vindicate popular participation against both government and the social welfare establishment. So Hackett, Cannon and Richard Boone inserted the mystic words—"maximum feasible participation of the residents of the areas"—into the law. Their belief was that "poor people themselves could render most effective help to the poor"; their hope, that in the process communities could develop their own competencies.[92]

When the bill came before Congress in the spring of 1964, the single administration witness to speak about community action was Robert Kennedy. His testimony summed up the lessons he had drawn from the Juvenile Delinquency Committee:

> The institutions which affect the poor—education, welfare, recreation, business, labor—are huge, complex structures, operating far outside their control. They plan programs *for* the poor, not *with* them. Part of the sense of helplessness and futility comes from the feeling of powerlessness to affect the operation of these organizations.
>
> The community action programs must basically change these organizations by building into the program real representation for the poor . . . giving them a real voice in their institutions.[93]

Beck and Hoffa had taught him long before how essential it was for union members to have the power to challenge hierarchies. Community action, he hoped, would give the poor a way of exerting leverage on the structures that ruled their lives. The ideal of participation remained close to his heart for the rest of his days.

IX

The racial question was more than ever Robert Kennedy's primary concern. Congress was still debating his brother's civil rights bill. In the spring of 1964 the Attorney General carried the campaign to Georgia. A black southerner could die for his country, Kennedy told them at West Georgia College; but, if his widow wanted to travel north to visit his grave at Arlington Cemetery, "she doesn't know what hotel she can stay at. She doesn't know what restaurant she can possibly stop in . . . what restrooms [she can use]. . . . And yet her husband . . . was killed for all of us." Legislation to end this "continuous insult" was, he said, "long, long overdue. . . . How would any of us like it if we were in that situation?" Questioners brought up states' rights. Mississippi and Alabama, Kennedy replied, had not dealt justly on racial matters. Negroes "are entitled to the federal government affording them some protection." His answers, wrote Eugene Patterson in the *Atlanta Constitution*, "were direct and rough-edge. . . . And the students responded to what he said with profound, rolling applause that visibly startled him." "There is only one word for Attorney General Robert Kennedy's reception at West Georgia College Tuesday," wrote Reg Murphy, the *Constitution*'s political editor: "Fantastic."[94]

The bill, however, left out one point of supreme importance to the civil rights movement—federal protection of civil rights workers. The question John Lewis had tried to ask during the March on Washington—"Which side is the federal government on?"—still echoed. Nineteen sixty-three had been bad enough. Nineteen sixty-four promised to be worse. Young people, black and white, were flocking south to work for racial justice over Freedom Summer. The Klan organized klaverns in twenty-nine Mississippi counties between February and June.[95] The national government seemed helpless before impending violence. "There is no answer," said Katzenbach bleakly, "which embraces both compassion and law."[96] "We simply can't wetnurse everybody who goes down to try to reform or reeducate the Negro population of the South," snapped J. Edgar Hoover, blaming the trouble on the "harsh approach to the Mississippi situation by the authorities here in Washington."[97]

With the administration sticking to the view that the federal system tied its hands, the movement advanced its own proposals. Federal law-enforcement agencies, Martin Luther King pointed out early in 1964, were long accustomed to "working within secret groups and obtaining effective results. . . . There is a need to know what is going on in conspiratorial racist circles. Many of the shocking bombings might have been avoided if such knowledge had been available."[98] "We need the FBI before the fact," said Bob Moses, a brave young SNCC leader after James Chaney, Michael Schwerner and Andrew Goodman disappeared in Neshoba County in June 1964. "We have them now after the fact."[99] Why, asked James Wechsler, has "the FBI so completely and totally failed to engage in any effective form of infiltration of the forces of Southern violence—the Ku Klux Klan, the White Citizens Councils, and all their front organizations?"[100]

Was not this the answer? Why should the FBI, so successful by its own account in penetrating the CPUSA and the Mafia, not now penetrate the Klan? "President Kennedy spoke to [Hoover] about that," Robert Kennedy said later, "to try to do it on the same basis."[101] In June 1964 the Attorney General formally recommended to President Johnson the use against white supremacy groups of "techniques followed . . . in the infiltration of Communist groups."[102]

What no one outside the Bureau knew was that the FBI's Intelligence Division had long since institutionalized and elaborated such techniques in a project called the Counterintelligence Program—COINTELPRO in the trade. COINTELPRO's mission was to penetrate organizations not, however, merely to find out what they were doing but to disrupt and destroy them. Its weapons were rumor, forgery, denunciation, provocation. "No holds were barred," William C. Sullivan, the assistant director in charge of the Intelligence Division, later testified. ". . . We have used [these techniques] against Soviet agents. They have used [them] against us. . . . [The same methods were] brought home against any organization against which we were targeted. This is a rough, tough business."[103]

COINTELPRO had started against the Communist party in 1956. Two years later Hoover described it to Attorney General Rogers in highly general terms as "a program designed to promote disruption" within the CPUSA. This was about as near as he came to telling any Attorney General about COINTELPRO. The very name was unknown outside the Bureau. In January 1961 Hoover informed Robert Kennedy even more generally about a "program of counterattack against the CPUSA which keeps it off balance. Our primary purpose in this program is to bring about disillusionment on the part of individual members." The only techniques mentioned were the use of informants and the exposure of Communist infiltration of other organizations.[104] When the Kennedy White House requested a formal report on "Internal Security Programs," Hoover mentioned the Bureau's "investigative programs" and said nothing at all of disruptive activities.[105] As Richard D. Cotter put it after twenty-six years' service as research chief of the Bureau's Intelligence Division, COINTELPRO demonstrated "the astonishing degree of independence the FBI had gained in the domestic security area. The Bureau was able to initiate an extensive, risky, and highly questionable operation without consulting the Attorney General. The COINTELPRO project required only the recommendation of the Assistant Director in charge of Intelligence Division and the approval of the FBI Director."[106]

In 1964 Sullivan persuaded Hoover to transfer the Klan from the General Investigative Division, where "nothing was being done," to COINTELPRO. Sullivan had seen fiery crosses burning on the hills of central Massachusetts as a boy. His father had fought the Klan in the twenties. "I had a real interest," he said later, "in breaking up the Klan."[107] The General Investigative Division, it is true, had Klan informants. Gary Thomas Rowe, Jr., for example, had been recruited in 1959. But, after the Klan COINTELPRO began in September 1964, Rowe's FBI case officers told him, "The bureau is declaring war on the Klan. You can do anything you want to get your information." Their first inspiration was that he sleep with the wives of fellow Klansmen. Their second was that he stir up personal trouble inside the Klan, spread rumors of other infidelities, for example. As for strong-arm activities, "Well, you'll have to do what you have to do. No holds barred."[108]

X

"We have penetrated the Klan very effectively," Hoover declared publicly in December 1964, ". . . particularly in the States of Alabama, Georgia and Mississippi."[109] Nine months later he reported to the Attorney General that, of the Klan's fourteen state organizations, "we have penetrated every one of them through informants and currently are operating informants in top-level positions of leadership in seven of them." In one state the top Klansman was an FBI operative. "As a result, we have been successful to date in holding Klan violence in the entire state to an absolute minimum." In another state the FBI subsidized a runaway klavern critical of the regular Klan. At one point the Bureau even considered installing an informer as the Klan's imperial wizard. In the first year of the Klan COINTELPRO, informers accounted for 70 percent of the new membership and, at the end of the year, for about one sixth of the total—2000 out of 12,000–13,000. (Never missing a chance to extract bigger appropriations, Hoover told the House Subcommittee on Appropriations ominously, "During the past year there has been a marked increase in Klan membership.")[110]

FBI infiltration led to the discovery of the bodies of Chaney, Schwerner and Goodman, the murdered civil rights workers, and the arrest of their killers. Gary Rowe ended his long masquerade by testifying against the murderers of another civil rights worker, Viola Liuzzo. Informers were responsible for numerous other convictions.[111] The Klan was soon in rout. "When we took it over," Sullivan said, "the Klan had more than fourteen thousand very active members, and when I left in 1971 it had been reduced to forty-three hundred completely disorganized and impotent individuals."[112]

Exhilarated by its triumph, the FBI extended COINTELPRO in 1967 to so-called Black Nationalist–Hate Groups, including, incongruously, the pro-integration, nonviolent SCLC, and in 1968 to New Left groups. Flagrant excesses led some civil libertarians to attack counterespionage per se as a violation of the Bill of Rights. When the Klan bombed a school bus in Michigan, the testimony of an FBI informer convicted the bombers. "My judgment," said Professor Vern Countryman, "would be that if the only way to detect that bombing is to have the FBI infiltrate political organizations, I would rather the bombing go undetected. . . . There are worse things than having people killed." Critics dwelt on the moral corruption of informing, the psychological instability of persons predisposed to inform, the tendency of informers to become *agents provocateurs,* the historical role of informers as agents of despotism.[113]

Conceivably the question was not that simple. It was, after all, possible to inform *against* despotism too. Robert Kennedy had seen this repeatedly on the Rackets Committee. He admired the courage of rank-and-file trade unionists who, at enormous risk and small benefit, "informed" against corruption and tyranny—men like Terry Malloy as written by Budd Schulberg and played by Marlon Brando in *On the Waterfront*. There was the veteran labor organizer Sam Baron, who had started out with the International Ladies' Garment Workers, fought with the Loyalists in Spain and organized Sears, Roebuck and Montgomery Ward for the Teamsters. Baron, who detested the labor racketeers, provided evidence against Hoffa. When someone called Baron a "fink" and "stool pigeon," Kennedy observed that he regarded Baron as "a citizen who was reporting information and evidence in connection with illegal activities."[114]

"Courts have countenanced the use of informers from time immemorial," Judge Learned Hand had said in sustaining the conviction of Communist leaders under the Smith Act.[115] The Supreme Court, upholding Partin's testimony against Hoffa, ruled that neither the Fourth nor Fifth Amendment limited the use of informers: "The established safeguards of the Anglo-American legal system leave the veracity of a witness to be tested by cross-examination, and the credibility of his testimony to be determined by a properly instructed jury."[116] As a practical matter, many crimes in such areas as racial violence, racketeering, and political corruption would not be solved without informers.

The court decisions, however, assumed that the work of informers was informing. But informers in organizations engaged in criminal activity, like the Klan or the mob, often behaved criminally themselves in order to maintain cover. The FBI had instructed Gary Rowe to avoid violence. Yet "to gather information," as Rowe's FBI case officer told the Church committee, "you have to be there. . . . If [Rowe] happened to be with some Klansmen and they decided to do something, he couldn't be an angel and be a good informant."[117] On FBI instructions,[118] Rowe went along on the expedition that ended in the murder of Viola Liuzzo. There is something appalling about the FBI informant riding in the Klan car on FBI orders, impotently watching, seconds before the shots, "the most awful expression [on the victim's face] . . . that God knows I have ever seen in my life."[119]

Still, Rowe's presence brought the killers to justice. King and other black leaders advocated FBI penetration of the Klan for urgent reasons. The Kennedy and Johnson administrations turned to counter-espionage as the best means of federal protection at their command. Refusal of FBI infiltration would have left civil rights workers in the deep south at the mercy of hooded terrorists. It was not necessarily a wicked choice. Burke Marshall reflected a decade later on the way the Klan was broken in a terrible time:

> It was done . . . by bribery, by payments to informers, by whatever eavesdropping was then permitted under the bureau's rules, by the sowing of suspicion among Klan members so that none knew who was an informer and who not, by infiltration and deception, and in at least one incident by the participation of a bureau informer in the planning and attempted execution of a murder.
>
> It did not appear to those involved at the time, and it does not appear to me now, that the criminal conspiracy of violence that existed in the State of Mississippi then could have been handled by less drastic measures.[120]

XI

From the start the new President had left no doubt about his vigorous support of the civil rights bill. "I knew," Lyndon Johnson told Doris Kearns, "that if I didn't get out in front on this issue, [the liberals] would get me. . . . I had to produce a civil rights bill that was even stronger than the one they'd have gotten if Kennedy had lived. Without this, I'd be dead before I could even begin."[121]

He left the day-to-day strategy to the Department of Justice. "I'll do on the bill just what you think is best," he told Robert Kennedy in January 1964. ". . . We won't do anything that you don't want to do on the legislation, and I'll do everything you want me to do in order to obtain passage." Anthony Lewis later asked how Kennedy explained Johnson's blank check. Johnson, Kennedy replied, did not see how the bill could pass the Senate. "If he said, 'Where are you going to get the votes?' as he used to say to me—well, President Kennedy used to say the same thing [in November]—you couldn't tell him where you were going to get the votes. The person who you're going to get the votes from, really, in the last analysis, was Everett Dirksen." And, if the bill failed, Johnson, Kennedy thought, did not want sole responsibility. "If he did what the Department of Justice did, said, recommended, suggested—and particularly me—then he could always say that he did what we suggested. . . . He had a particular problem being a southerner. . . . So I think that for political reasons it made a good deal of sense. Secondly, our relationship was so sensitive at the time that I think that he probably did it to pacify me."[122]

The bill, after passing the House by a better than 2–1 vote in February, fell into a Senate filibuster in March. Dirksen was more than ever the key. By late April the minority leader, no one quite knew why, appeared ready to accept the bill with minor modifications. "Whatever Dirksen and the AG agree on," Johnson said, "I am for."[123] Dirksen's collaboration brought along enough Republican votes to end the filibuster. On July 2, Johnson signed the Civil Rights Act of 1964, thereby outlawing discrimination in voting, employment, public education and public accommodations and facilities.

It was a stronger and better bill than the one the Kennedy administration had given Congress a year earlier. The signing took place with the usual nonsense in the Oval Office. The Reuther brothers noticed Robert Kennedy in the rear of the room, staring at the floor. "Surely no one," Victor Reuther thought, "had contributed more to this moment than he." Roy Reuther seized Kennedy by the arm and firmly propelled him across the room to Johnson, saying, "Mr. President, I know you have reserved a pen for your Attorney General." Johnson blandly gave Kennedy a handful of pens.[124] The Reverend Walter Fauntroy, watching the ceremony with Martin Luther King, said later, "Our enthusiasm—that of Dr. King and myself—was sort of dampened by the sadness that we saw in Bobby's eyes and the coldness with which the President obviously treated him. . . . We commented afterwards at the coldness on the part of Johnson toward Kennedy on that important day."[125]

28

The Vice Presidency

THE SCENE AT THE SIGNING of the civil rights bill was one more grim moment in a grim spring. I do not think that either man can be held responsible for the failure of the relationship. Each in his own way made an attempt. Neither in his heart wanted the attempt to succeed. The record of Johnson-Kennedy meetings shows, apart from the cabinet (which Kennedy infrequently attended), only two meetings in January, one before Kennedy left for the Far East and the other on his return; two meetings on February 7 about Cuba; a meeting on February 11 about civil rights; telephone calls on January 31, February 1, 4, 10 and 26—and then, if the compilation is complete, no further calls until April 22, no further meetings until the late spring.[1]

I

Johnson, haunted by the circumstances that had brought him to power, was both sorrowing and vulnerable. He felt an immense need, psychological as well as political, for the Kennedys. But he could not control his diverse resentments—over popular comparisons with his predecessor, over glib journalistic comment about his alleged lack of culture and polish, over the failure of the Kennedys to fall in with his plans; at bottom over their reluctance to love him. "Lyndon Johnson had come on stage before a black curtain," wrote Liz Carpenter, Lady Bird Johnson's devoted press secretary, "and the Kennedys made no move to lift the darkness for him, or for the country. He had gone to the well for them so many times. 'Lyndon would like to take all the stars in the sky and string them on a necklace for Mrs. Kennedy,' his wife said softly in the dreadful days that followed Dallas."[2] He was "bitter," recalled Pierre Salinger, who stayed on for a few distracted months as Johnson's press secretary, "about his ina-

bility to get Mrs. Kennedy to come to the White House and participate in various ceremonies. . . . He couldn't understand, after all his
kindnesses to her, why she wouldn't come down."³

Most of all he resented Robert Kennedy: "I'd given three years of
loyal service to Jack Kennedy. During all that time I'd willingly
stayed in the background. . . . Then Kennedy was killed and I became the custodian of his will. I became the President. But none of
this seemed to register with Bobby Kennedy, who acted like *he* was
the custodian of the Kennedy dream, some kind of rightful heir to the
throne."⁴ "That upstart's come too far and too fast," he told Eric
Goldman, the Princeton historian who had a short and unhappy time
in the Johnson White House. "He skipped the grades where you
learn the rules of life. He never liked me, and that's nothing compared to what I think of him."⁵ "If Bobby Kennedy's name came up
even by accident," recalled Kenneth O'Donnell, who stayed on for a
season in the White House, ". . . he'd launch into a tirade about
what a son of a bitch Bobby Kennedy was. Ninety-nine percent of the
things were untrue. And it'd get back to Bobby Kennedy, and
Bobby'd say something about Lyndon Johnson. . . . These two men
just didn't know each other; and they built up this picture of each
other which was just incredible."⁶

For Kennedy, staying in the administration at all was a major
effort. Yet he saw himself as yoked with Johnson in the execution of
a legacy and the preservation of a party. Others might go; "but if I
go," he told Murray Kempton, pausing and searching for a word, "if
I should, uh, *desert,* that would be harmful."⁷ In public he was as
meticulously loyal to Johnson as Johnson had been to John Kennedy.
But everything was different. "What makes me sad is that I see a
problem . . . and I can't do anything about it. There was this time
when if people had something and couldn't see my brother, they
could always see me and I could pick up the phone and call
him. . . . It's strange to think that you can't just pick up the
phone."⁸

Nor could he, any more than Johnson, control his resentments. If
the new President, enveloped in insecurity, was preternaturally sensitive to comparisons with his predecessor, Robert Kennedy, enveloped
in grief, was preternaturally sensitive to slights to his brother. Walter
Heller sent him a copy of a memorandum to Johnson saying that
"under your budget and tax program" the net fiscal stimulus to the
economy would be the greatest in peacetime history. Kennedy circled
"your" and scribbled in the margin: "I thought this was Pres. K. pro-

gram."[9] "I thought that an awful lot of things that were going on that President Kennedy did," he said in May, "[Johnson] was getting the credit for and wasn't saying enough about the fact that President Kennedy was responsible."[10] He encouraged others to stay—"If any one of us is in a position to keep him from blowing up Costa Rica or something," he told Richard Goodwin in March, "I guess he had better do it"[11]—but he became unhappy when they seemed to embrace the principle "the king is dead, long live the king."[12] "He really felt," McGeorge Bundy thought, "that . . . if you were fully in the Kennedy administration you had a continuing allegiance that should, in certain circumstances, be more important to you than your allegiance to the existing President. And I couldn't feel that way."[13]

For once it was not primarily the case, so familiar in politics, of the staffs egging their principals on to combat. Johnson retained Bundy, O'Donnell, O'Brien, Dungan and brought Goodwin back to the White House. His own people were first-rate. Though Eric Goldman recalls unnamed Johnson men calling Kennedy "the perfect model of the liberal fascist" and the like,[14] my own clear impression is that Johnson's top assistants liked Robert Kennedy. I know he liked them. "I think all of them are good," he told John Bartlow Martin in May. ". . . Walter Jenkins seems like a good fellow. . . . Bill Moyers is a smart fellow and an honorable man. . . . George Reedy's fine. They're all scared, of course, of Lyndon. I guess [Jack] Valenti's a nice fellow. And they've all treated me very well. . . . The people that he has immediately around him look good."[15] It was finally a situation where the two principals just could not abide each other.

But they had to go through the motions. The new President would say to O'Donnell and O'Brien that, as Kennedy rendered it, "he thought I hated him and what he could do to get me to like him, and why did I dislike him, and whether he should have me over for a drink."[16] Johnson grew Byzantine in his endeavor to establish at least a record of benevolent intent. In March I met in New York with Alex Rose of the Liberal party, an avid dabbler in the higher politics. Ostensibly we were to discuss the vice presidential situation. But the meeting had in fact been instigated by Johnson, who had charged Rose with a message for me to pass on to Kennedy. The message, I wrote Kennedy (who was away from Washington), was "in effect, that President Johnson loves you, wants to be friends with you, that the door at the White House is always open to you."[17]

After Kennedy got back to Washington, he asked Bundy to find

out whether the President wanted him to call, saying he did not wish
to stand on ceremony. Bundy, Kennedy told me, "sounded out LBJ
and told Bobby that the President did not want a call from him, that
he was quite happy with the situation as it was, that he did not want
to give [James] Reston the satisfaction of supposing that a summit
meeting between the two was the result of his column of some days
back, and that they could get together later." When I pressed Kennedy to call Johnson nonetheless, thinking at least to establish the
record on his side, he said he felt he had gone as far as he could
properly go—that, if he persisted in calling, after receiving Bundy's
message, it would look as if he were trying to curry favor; "the White
House reaction would be, 'That fellow will do anything to become
Vice President.' "[18]

In retrospect this elaborate tiptoeing among grown men seems odd.
But, though neither wanted to see the other, neither wanted the responsibility for a break. In the end nothing could have brought them
together. What made the gulf ultimately impassable was a remark
Johnson made that spring to Salinger—a remark so guileful a man
could hardly have made without intending it to get back to Kennedy.
"You know the worst thing that Johnson has said?" Kennedy said to
me. He then incredulously repeated Johnson's remark: "When I was
young in Texas, I used to know a cross-eyed boy. His eyes were
crossed, and so was his character. . . . That was God's retribution
for people who were bad and so you should be careful of cross-eyed
people because God put his mark on them. . . . Sometimes I think
that, when you remember the assassination of Trujillo and the assassination of Diem, what happened to Kennedy may have been divine
retribution."*

* Author's journal, July 23, 1964. I have combined this story as I noted it down
with a slightly more detailed version told by RFK to John Bartlow Martin; Martin
interview, April 13, 1964, II, 57–58. Johnson's divine retribution thesis found new ammunition in March 1967 when he learned for the first time of the CIA's attempts to
murder Castro (Senate Select Committee to Study Governmental Operations with respect to Intelligence Activities [Church committee] *Final Report*, bk. V, *The Investigation of the Assassination of President John F. Kennedy: Performance of the Intelligence Agencies*, 94 Cong., 2 Sess. [1976], 85–86). The Kennedy administration,
Johnson later told Leo Janos of *Time*, "had been operating a damned Murder, Inc. in
the Caribbean" (Leo Janos, "The Last Days of the President," *Atlantic Monthly*, July
1973). "Kennedy was trying to get Castro," he told Howard K. Smith of ABC, "but
Castro got to him first" (Howard K. Smith, ABC News broadcast, June 24, 1976 [see
also *Family Weekly*, September 12, 1976]). Johnson assumed that, because the CIA
had tried to murder Castro during the Kennedy administration, Kennedy must have
authorized the plots and therefore had only himself to blame for the Dallas horror.
In fact, the same reasoning convicted Johnson as well. The CIA had continued to try
to murder Castro during the first two years of Johnson's own administration; only

II

The diverse resentments came to focus in 1964 on a specific question: the Vice Presidency, vacant now, to be filled at the Democratic convention in August.* Calculations on each side were filled with uncertainty. In some moods Johnson was not even sure he wished to run. Passing periodically from self-confidence through self-pity to self-doubt, worried about his health, worried, as he confided to James Reston in the spring, that the nation was "not far enough from Appomattox" to accept him,[19] he had, in his own words, "decidedly mixed feelings about whether I wanted to seek a four-year term."[20] Salinger later declared himself "absolutely convinced that, if [Johnson] thought he could have left the field without yielding the nomination to Robert Kennedy, whom he hated, he would not have run."†

In other moods, however, Johnson was determined to run and win. To O'Donnell, who never heard him express the slightest doubt about running, he candidly defined his intention on the Vice Presidency three weeks after John Kennedy's death. "I don't want history to say I was elected to this office because I had Bobby on the ticket with me," he said. "But I'll take him if I need him."[21] This was as far as he would go toward admitting the possibility; and he was talking, of course, to a Kennedy friend. His brother Sam Houston Johnson thought that the President never "for a single moment" considered Kennedy as his running mate. "The reasons were quite obvious: a) Lyndon hated Bobby. b) Bobby hated Lyndon."[22]

As for Kennedy, he assumed Johnson would run and intermittently wondered whether he ought to seek the second place for himself. As early as December 3, 1963, Joseph Dolan told him that the Democratic National Committeewoman from Michigan and, oddly, Senator Thomas J. Dodd of Connecticut favored him for Vice President.[23] A couple of days later Kennedy asked me what I thought. "My first reaction," I noted, "was negative, though, when he asked me why, I

---

he did not know this, because the CIA did not tell him any more than it had told Kennedy (Church committee, *Investigation of the Assassination,* 86). Castro himself in a communication to Senator George McGovern claimed ten assassination plots during the Johnson Presidency (McGovern press release, July 30, 1975).

* The Twenty-fifth Amendment, empowering the President to fill a vice presidential vacancy, was not ratified until February 10, 1967.

† Salinger added, "I had the very profound impression that, the moment Lyndon became President, he regretted it" (Pierre Salinger, *Je suis un Américain* [Paris, 1975], 294–295).

found it hard to give clear reasons. I think, first, that it seems to me a little too artificial and calculated; second, that Bobby should develop his own independent political base; and third, that LBJ might well prefer Shriver on the ground that Shriver would bring along Bobby's friends without bringing along his enemies. Bobby added that he did not like the idea of taking a job which was really based on the premise of waiting around for someone to die."[24]

In January the Democratic organization in Buffalo endorsed him for Vice President. "I have received letters from all over the country approving our action," Peter Crotty, the Buffalo leader, informed Kennedy in mid-February. ". . . I don't think there is any President who would place his own election in jeopardy by ignoring the will of the country."[25] Kennedy friends thought that the New Hampshire primary in March might further affirm the country's will. William Dunfey, the New Hampshire national committeeman, encouraged a Kennedy-for-Vice-President write-in, but did so quietly, in the New Hampshire manner: "People kind of ran ads on their own and that kind of thing. . . . Once it got moving, Bob Kennedy called me once or twice, just, you know, how did I look at this thing and was it going to be something that he would get seriously embarrassed on." Dunfey told him there wasn't much he could do about it.[26]

At this point the incorrigible Paul Corbin, still hanging on at the national committee, appeared in New Hampshire. It was impossible for anyone who did not know Corbin to believe it; but, as Edwin Guthman said later, "the truth was that Corbin was acting on his own."[27] "He had a strange way about him," John Seigenthaler, who liked Corbin, said. "When he made up his mind to do something, he'd do it."[28] Dolan, who disliked Corbin, described him as "so determined to do everything that he sincerely thought was in Robert Kennedy's interest that he would sweep all else aside," including Robert Kennedy's own wishes in the matter.[29]

"Corbin in New Hampshire," said Dolan. "That's like trying to conceal Mount Everest in Manhattan Island." After ascertaining that Kennedy had not sent him, Dunfey chased him out of the state.[30] Dunfey's annoyance was nothing, however, compared to Lyndon Johnson's rage. The President had no doubt that Kennedy had sent Corbin. Sam Houston Johnson was surely registering his brother's skepticism when he wrote, "I have never in my life seen a campaign that couldn't be stopped by a candidate who didn't want it." Lyndon Johnson himself told Kennedy after a cabinet meeting that he wanted Corbin out of both New Hampshire and the national committee. According to O'Donnell, Johnson told Kennedy, "If he is such a good fellow, you pay him. He's around town knocking my head off . . . and has been for three years, and I never met the bum in my life. Why should I have him on my payroll?" Kennedy said he did not know that Corbin was in New Hampshire, adding, "He was loyal to President Kennedy. He'll be loyal to you." Johnson responded, "I know who he's loyal to. Get him out of there." Kennedy recalled it as "a bitter, mean conversation. The meanest tone that I heard anybody take. . . . I said . . . I don't want to have that kind of conversation with you."[31]

On February 10 Johnson called Kennedy to say that Corbin had been fired; he wanted no one at the committee pledged to a particular vice presidential candidate. He had sent Kennedy to Indonesia, he explained, only because he "had to keep things equal" among those under consideration for the second place. Kennedy, who thought he had been sent to Indonesia because he had proven he could negotiate with Sukarno, said curtly, "Don't ever do a favor for me again!" The conversation ended. Kennedy stared gloomily out the window for a few moments, then said to Guthman, "I'll tell you one thing, this relationship can't last much longer."[32]

As the voting day approached, it seemed that Kennedy might actually outpoll Johnson. This would have been embarrassing all around. A few days before the primary the Attorney General put out a disclaimer. Early drafts contained statements that he was not seeking the vice presidential nomination. He regularly crossed them out. The final version said simply that the President "should be free to select his own running mate" and therefore Kennedy wanted to discourage efforts on his own behalf.[33] Johnson received 29,600 votes, Kennedy 25,900.

III

"Take it! Take it!" General Douglas MacArthur told him. "He won't live. He gambled on your brother and won. You gamble on him and you'll win." Ethel and Jacqueline urged him to go ahead.[34] Political leaders besought him to signal his availability. Walter Reuther told me, as I noted at the time, that he was "waiting for Bobby to say the word—that he would not move until he knew what Bobby wanted. I mentioned Hubert's claims. Walter said that he loved Hubert but that he could not forget Los Angeles [in 1960]. 'Hubert had a secret deal with Lyndon.'"[35] In April the Gallup poll reported Kennedy the vice presidential choice of 47 percent of Democratic voters as against 18 percent for Adlai Stevenson and 10 percent for Humphrey.[36]

His own motives were indecipherable. No one could quite tell how much, or even if, he wanted the nomination; or whether he was simply demonstrating popularity and keeping options open. The argument *for* was that, as Vice President, he might assure the Kennedy outlook and constituency a role in national policy; in any event, the Vice Presidency had the political advantage, not to be prudently relinquished to someone else, of establishing its occupant as a quasi-heir apparent. The argument *against* lay in the singular stupidity of the job itself. As the historian in his circle, I should have warned far more stringently than I did that the idea was hopeless; but I had not yet studied the Vice Presidency as carefully as I would later.[37] Nonetheless, Kennedy, having observed Lyndon Johnson, well understood the impotence of the Vice Presidency. And on top of the incurable deficiencies of the office, there were the extraordinary demands that Johnson *redivivus* was bound to make on its holder. "I heard Johnson say one time," Congressman Emanuel Celler once said, "that he wanted men around him who were loyal enough to kiss his ass in Macy's window and say it smelled like a rose."[38] Johnson's 1964 aphorism on the Vice Presidency was widely repeated in Washington that spring: "Whoever he is, I want his pecker to be in my pocket."

Searching through the oral histories, one finds that Nicholas Katzenbach, McGeorge Bundy, Richard Goodwin, Robert McNamara, Donald Wilson, Joseph Alsop, Rowland Evans, Joseph Kraft, Ben Bradlee, supposed Robert Kennedy wanted the nomination. Kenneth O'Donnell, Charles Spalding and Charles Bartlett thought he did not. I was never sure either way. The most extended statement I have found by Kennedy himself came in an oral history interview with John Bartlow Martin in mid-May. The one thing Johnson did not want, Kennedy said, "is me as Vice President. . . . I think he's hysterical about how he's going to try to avoid having me. . . . I'm just trying to make up my mind what I'm going to do." If his nomination were forced on Johnson, "it would be an unpleasant relationship. I would lose all ability to ever take any independent position. . . . Johnson's explained quite clearly that it's not the Democratic party any more, it's an all-American party, and the businessmen like it. All the people who were opposed to the President like it. I don't like it very much."

Martin suggested that Kennedy, with his powerful constituency, would be in a different position from other Vice Presidents. "I don't think you can have any influence," Kennedy repeated. "Lyndon Johnson didn't have any influence. . . . He's not going to have to pay any attention to me whatsoever." Martin said Johnson would have to pay attention; he could not afford to break with the Kennedys. Kennedy responded that Johnson was "not doing anything for the Alliance for Progress and he's not paying proper attention to Panama or Brazil. . . . If I was in the United States Senate I would have raised a fuss about Panama." Martin said there were a hundred senators. Kennedy: "Yeah, but I'm not just a senator. [Suppose] I'm senator from New York and I'm head of the Kennedy wing of the Democratic party." He mused on. "I think it's possible to be Vice President. . . . But he's not going to pay any attention to me. I can't go out and speak against . . . what he's doing in South America, what he's doing in Southeast Asia, as Vice President. . . . I make one speech like that and you've broken the—" Martin, interrupting, thought he could do it quietly, short of a speech. Kennedy: "If I was Vice President and that Cuba thing came up again, for instance, I'd be running up to the Foreign Relations Committee and saying . . . why don't they [do something about it]. . . . That's a disloyal operation."

And there was Johnson himself. Charles Spalding thought the MacArthur argument just too "macabre" for Kennedy: "I mean to sit and figure out whether Johnson was going to live or not on top of everything else, that was just too morbid."[39] Johnson alive posed problems almost as morbid: "The fact," as Kennedy put it, "that he's able to eat people up, and even people who are considered rather strong figures—I mean Mac Bundy or Bob McNamara. . . . He's mean, bitter, vicious—[an] animal in many ways. . . . I think his reactions on a lot of things are correct. . . . but I think he's got this other side of him and his relationship with human beings which makes it difficult unless you want to 'kiss his behind' all the time. That's what Bob McNamara suggested to me a couple of weeks ago if I wanted to get along."[40]

IV

On June 19 he was in Hyannis Port. That night Edward Kennedy, flying to a political dinner in Springfield, Massachusetts, crashed in thunderstorms over the Connecticut Valley. The pilot and a Kennedy aide were killed. Edward Kennedy suffered horribly—damaged vertebrae in his lower back, a punctured lung, broken ribs, uncontrollable internal hemorrhaging. Robert Kennedy raced across the state by automobile to the hospital. Stirring from unconsciousness, Ted Kennedy made out his brother through the mist and said, "Is it true that you are ruthless?"[41]

In relief Robert Kennedy and Walter Sheridan left the hospital for a walk in the summer night. "We just lay down in the grass," Sheridan said later, "and he said, 'Somebody up there doesn't like me.' Then he asked me if I thought he ought to go for the Senate or go for the Vice Presidency. I told him I thought he ought to go for the Vice Presidency."[42] The next morning someone wondered whether the Kennedys now intended to retire from politics. "The Kennedys intend to stay in public life," Robert Kennedy said crisply. "Good luck is something you make and bad luck is something you endure." "Is it ever going to end for you people?" "I was just thinking out there—if my mother hadn't had any more children after her first four, she would have nothing now. . . . I guess the only reason we've survived is that there are more of us than there is trouble."[43] William Shannon later asked whether the family disasters were affecting his religious faith. "No, they do not," he said; then, with that smile, "Of course, we do occasionally think that someone up in heaven is out to lunch when he ought to be attending to business."[44]

A week later, Robert and Ethel were on their way to Berlin at Willy Brandt's invitation to dedicate a memorial to John Kennedy. Mrs. Donald Wilson, who was with them, described what they did on disembarkation: "In rapid fire order, [Kennedy] reviewed an honor guard, delivered an arrival statement, visited a school, inspected a factory, held a press conference, went to a luncheon for 300 only long enough to eat, rode in a tank, spoke to 50,000 at the dedication of the John F. Kennedy Platz, received an honorary degree, made a second major address and attended a reception and buffet dinner for 700."[45] They asked him inevitably about German reunification. "We will stand and fight for principle," he said. ". . . But we also know what war is going to bring. . . . I think the best opportunity of breaking down the artificial barriers . . . is by a greater understanding between the peoples that live in the eastern part of Europe and the Soviet Union, and those of us who live elsewhere."[46] In this spirit the Kennedy party pressed on to Poland.

The Polish government had declined to invite Kennedy, consenting only to a "nonofficial" visit. Kennedy's particular interest, as usual, was to meet the young. "Disaffection of youth," Ambassador John Moors Cabot warned Washington, "is not just headache but nightmare to Polish Communist leadership."[47] Once Kennedy arrived, the government did its best to keep his presence secret. But word got out. When the Kennedys went to mass the day after their arrival, a crowd surged around the Cabot limousine. After a moment, Kennedy lifted Ethel to the car's roof, climbed up himself and began waving. The ambassador, an able diplomat of the old school, called to a Kennedy aide: "I say there, would you tell the Attorney General that the roof is caving in."[48] "We had an awful time fixing it," he said afterward. "This is the way we always come home from mass," said Kennedy.[49]

The Poles were determined to frustrate the intruders. Bringing presents to an orphanage, Robert and Ethel discovered that the children had been spirited away. That evening Kennedy lectured Foreign Minister Adam Rapacki about the incident. "It sounds as if we took them all to Siberia," Rapacki grumbled later.[50] The next morning they went to Cracow, where another throng besieged their car in the Cloth Market Square. The Poles sang "Sto Lat"—"May you live a hundred years"—and the Kennedys sang back in hurried improvisation "When Polish Eyes Are Smiling." Asked at a press conference if he planned to run for President, he said, "No . . . I think I'll run for mayor of Cracow." An hour late in getting back for an embassy dinner, Kennedy climbed on the cartop and spoke to still another crowd in front of Cabot's residence. Finally he said, "I have to go into dinner now. Would you like to come in with me?" When they shouted yes, he pretended to consult with Cabot over the wall and then said, "The ambassador says you can't come"—a lighthearted moment that amused Kennedy more than it did Cabot.[51]

Jozef Winiewicz, the deputy foreign minister and ranking guest, was furious. "Now, Mr. Kennedy," he said sarcastically, "you've addressed the crowd outside. Why don't you get on this table and address us?"[52] "He was very agitated," Kennedy noted later, "that I had been talking frequently to groups of people." Gomulka, Winiewicz said, would never have done anything like that. Kennedy said, "Maybe that's what's wrong with Gomulka."[53] The Poles especially resented Kennedy's call on Stefan Cardinal Wyszynski. Wyszynski told Kennedy that "the best thing that had happened to the Catholic Church in Poland was that it had been deprived of its wealth. This had brought the priests and bishops much closer to the people. The government officials . . . have become the capitalists and the church has become the proletariat." Kennedy: "Without question, he is the most impressive Catholic clergyman I have ever met."[54]

The Polish newspaper *Polityka* described Kennedy as an "indefatigable" politician "resorting to tricks used in the political life of the United States, where popularity is the most important thing."[55] The ambassador too: "Frankly, I was very annoyed about the whole business. It had its good point. Kennedy was followed by huge crowds wherever he went, but he got the Polish government practically livid with some of the things he did. And he got the embassy so mad that it could scarcely sputter."[56] Still, Cabot reported the visit to Washington as an "undoubted success" though "it would be naive to underestimate anger and shock of Polish leadership."[57] Another embassy officer called it "an ill-prepared and even dangerous exercise which came off very well" largely because of Kennedy's "skill in public relations, grasp of the larger picture, and receptivity to advice" and because of his "Irish luck."[58] When Khrushchev visited Warsaw three weeks later, Cabot, noting the "pitiful" turnout on the streets in spite of vast government publicity, told the department, "The contrast to the welcome given Attorney General Kennedy was particularly striking."[59]

v

"Every day," Lyndon Johnson recalled, "as soon as I opened the paper or turned on the television there was something about Bobby Kennedy; there was some person or group talking about what a great Vice President he'd make. . . . It just didn't seem fair. I'd waited my turn. Bobby should've waited for his. But he and the Kennedy people wanted it now. . . . I simply couldn't let it happen. With Bobby on the ticket, I'd never know if I could be elected on my own."[60]

"My brother's only concern," wrote Sam Houston Johnson, "was how and when to squelch the campaign."[61] The President explored diversionary action—mollifying the Kennedys and the Catholic vote, for example, by putting Sargent Shriver on the ticket. Moyers reported to the President that Shriver was willing and that Bobby would not complain if his brother-in-law were Johnson's running mate. O'Donnell commented, "The hell he wouldn't." In due course, Shriver gave way to Eugene McCarthy in Johnson's shell game. O'Donnell said, "There's only one Catholic in the country. That's Robert Kennedy. If you're just looking for a substitute, [you're] saying we're a bunch of cattle who run around and vote for people because of their religion." Besides, was it defensible to prefer the second senator from Minnesota, however witty and estimable a man, over the first? The Kennedy people believed that, if it was not to be Bobby, the nomination should go to Hubert Humphrey.[62]

As for Kennedy, Ben Bradlee, after going with him to Kansas City in June, had no doubt he wanted the nomination and so wrote in *Newsweek*. (They visited a home for old people. Kennedy went over to a dying woman, rubbed her hand, talked softly to her. "It just brought tears to my eyes," the hard-bitten Bradlee said later. "There was absolutely no reason for him to do it. . . . It was the most poignant thing I've ever seen in my life, and I don't move easy.")[63] In *Newsweek* Bradlee also quoted Kennedy as calling himself "the last man in the world" Johnson would want—"because my name is Kennedy, because he wants a Johnson Administration with no Kennedys in it, because we travel different paths, because I suppose some businessmen would object, and because I'd cost them a few votes in the South."[64]

By the time Kennedy returned from Europe in early July, Johnson was playing a vast and enjoyable game with everybody. In mid-July he was still talking to O'Donnell and O'Brien about putting a Catholic on the ticket.[65] He sent James Rowe to sound out Humphrey and then tormented Humphrey by discussing possible candidates in his presence without mentioning him.[66] Concerned no doubt to head off an independent Kennedy movement, he assured Salinger and Galbraith that Kennedy was very much under consideration.[67]

But Goldwater's victory over Rockefeller in the California Republican primary in early June had extinguished any need Johnson might ever have felt for Kennedy. The prospective nomination of the conservative hero gave Johnson a free ride in the north, where Kennedy was strong, and created difficulties in the south and southwest, where Kennedy would be a handicap. "The antagonism through the South against Bobby Kennedy," Jack Tarver of the *Atlanta Journal* and *Constitution* wrote Johnson, "may be unreasoning and emotional but, believe me, it is real. With him on the ticket, there is serious doubt you could carry a single state south of Ohio or east of Texas." There would be no problem, Tarver added, about Humphrey or McCarthy.[68] In these months, moreover, Johnson had solidly established himself as President in his own right. By June his polls showed that no running mate, Kennedy included, would make more than 2 percent difference to his presidential vote. "Look't here," he said to his brother one night, waving a poll across his dinner coffee. "I don't need that little runt to win. I can take anybody I damn please."[69]

All this was evident enough to Kennedy. In late July I noted: "Bobby says that he feels wholly out of it, that he is certain LBJ does not want the sense of 'a cross little fellow looking over his shoulder,' etc. He was very hostile to the idea of McCarthy and seemed distinctly to prefer Hubert."[70] One night he summoned his brother, O'Donnell, O'Brien, Fred Dutton and Stephen Smith to Hickory Hill. Goldwater was going to be the nominee, he told them, and he had decided to forget about the Vice Presidency, resign from the cabinet and run for the Senate in New York. Edward Kennedy and Smith urged him to move at once. O'Donnell begged him to wait; once Kennedy was out of the running, liberal Democrats would lose their power to force Johnson to accept Humphrey. Kennedy agreed to delay his New York announcement—"one of the finest and most unselfish decisions," O'Donnell thought, "of Bobby's controversial career." As they left, he called after O'Donnell in the darkness, "When they start that 'ruthless brat' stuff, O'Donnell, you'd better be there to bleed along with me."[71]

O'Donnell set to work with Reuther and others to build support for Humphrey. On July 15 Goldwater won the Republican nomination. A few days later Johnson asked Kennedy to come to the White House. "He's going to tell me I'm not going to be Vice President," Kennedy said when he put down the phone. "I wondered when he'd get around to it."[72]

VI

The summit meeting took place on July 29 at 1 P.M. "He's going to record every word you say," O'Donnell warned Kennedy.[73] Instead of taking his visitor in the usual manner to the sofa by the fireplace, Johnson sat formally at the presidential desk. A memorandum written by Clark Clifford lay in front of him. Reading aloud, Johnson said that, in view of Goldwater's nomination and the need for a running mate with appeal to southern and border states, he had concluded "that it would be unwise for our party . . . to select you." The memorandum went on to mention Kennedy's "unique and promising future," to solicit his aid in the campaign and to raise the possibility of his succeeding Adlai Stevenson at the United Nations. According to Johnson, the discussion was "frank . . . but there was no unpleasantness." He rememembered Kennedy saying at the end: "I'm sorry that you've reached this conclusion, because I think I could have been of help to you."[74]

Kennedy dictated his own account:

I sat down in the chair next to his desk. He looked off from me to the wall and to the floor and then said, over a three-minute span, that he was thinking a good deal about the Vice Presidency but he wanted a Vice President who could help the country, help the Party, and be of assistance to him. He repeated these thoughts in different words and concluded them by saying that that person wasn't me. I said that was fine, that I would be glad to campaign for the ticket and whatever he felt was helpful I would be glad to do.

I stayed for about 45 minutes and during the course of the conversation the following points were made: first, that he thought that I had high qualifications to be President; that he wanted to work toward that end [and] although he could not commit himself definitely at that time, he wanted to help me in whatever way he could. He wanted me to know that if I wished to go around the country and speak he would never be jealous of me. . . . If I was interested in another Cabinet position or in going to Paris, London or Moscow, he would be glad to help. He could not give me a job that someone else held right now but he was sure something could be arranged. I said that I wasn't interested in any other position. He said that if he were me he would stay over in the Department of Justice. He said I had an outstanding staff. He thought I should remain there.

He said in comparison to the staff he had at the White House the group I had selected were unusually competent. The people that contributed in the White House, he said, were the group that was selected by President Kennedy. He said he really could not count on his own people—Jenkins, Valenti, Reedy. He said Bill Moyers was good but his most useful function was rewriting what other people did. I was shocked to hear him being so critical to me of people who had been so loyal to him. Just as much as anything else, it convinced me that I could not have worked closely with him. . . .

He spoke to me about running the campaign. He said not much had been done in the organizational part and asked me if I could run it from the Department of Justice. I said I had made an arrangement with my brother that I would not participate while I was Attorney General. I had done that for two reasons: Number 1, because I felt an Attorney General should be above active political life, and secondly, because I had thought, coming just out of the campaign, I would be doing nothing else once I got started. Therefore, I said, I was reluctant to take on both of these jobs. . . .

I then brought up the subject of Bobby Baker. I said that we had an active case and we had to make a judgment how to proceed. I said I felt he should be advised and I would like to have someone's outside judgment on what we proposed to do. I suggested Jim Rowe. He countered that with Abe Fortas and Clark Clifford. I said I didn't think Abe Fortas would be proper because he had been Bobby Baker's lawyer. He said these are the two people in his judgment on whom he really relied.

He brought up the Fred Korth case. He said he was against President Kennedy's action in dismissing Fred Korth. I said I knew that because I was on the other side. But Clark Clifford was also for retaining Korth but after· reviewing the material (and also, incidentally, arguing with us at the Department of Justice) he came to the conclusion that Korth should be relieved. He said Clark finally convinced him of this also.

He then talked approximately 10 or 15 minutes about the fact that Bobby Baker got into all this difficulty after he, Lyndon, had left the Senate. . . . He said God must have been watching over him because he did not have financial dealings with Bobby. He could very well have done so because if Bobby had asked him to loan him $10,000 for the purchase of some stock he certainly would have done so.* He said the only business deal that he had had with Bobby Baker was in connection with the purchase of some insurance. The insurance company then placed $1500 (I think that was the figure) worth of advertising with his television station. He said this really didn't mean anything because the competitor company was willing to place twice as much. He said Bobby Baker went with power and when he left the Senate he latched on to other people. In any case, he said, if there was any corruption in this case it was the Republicans.

He then spent 10 or 15 minutes citing to me the facts in those cases. [Libelous material deleted.] It was obvious . . . that he was receiving detailed reports from the FBI on the activities of several of the Congressmen and Senators. . . . Incidentally, the whole conversation with Johnson was recorded. I saw the buttons on while I was sitting talking to him and later on in a conversation with Kenny and Larry he inadvertently and virtually admitted as much.[75]

Both principals were calm when they parted;[76] both, I suspect, relieved. Kennedy seemed in excellent humor when he got back to his office. He told his associates what had happened. There was a painful silence. "Aw, what the hell," Kennedy finally said with a laugh, "let's go form our own country."[77] Johnson, his creative imagination already at work, informed O'Donnell that Kennedy had offered to manage his campaign. O'Donnell, who had lunched with Kennedy directly after the meeting, said Kennedy had told him just the opposite.[78] One wondered whether Johnson's offer was not repayment, conscious or unconscious, for Kennedy's suggestion in the heat of Los Angeles four years before that Johnson forgo the Vice Presidency and become chairman of the national committee.

A question remained. "The fact that I had not volunteered to say that I would withdraw," Kennedy noted, "was obviously going to cause him some difficulty. How he could say that he had gotten rid of me was his greatest problem."[79] Johnson did not want to take public

---

* According to Baker, he did ask Johnson for a loan. Johnson thereupon called Senator Robert Kerr and said, "*Our* boy Bobby's in trouble and he needs *your* help." "I got nothing directly from Lyndon Johnson," Baker wrote later. ". . . LBJ simply was not a man to share" (Bobby Baker with Larry King, *Wheeling and Dealing: Confessions of a Capitol Hill Operator* [New York, 1978], 67–68).

responsibility for vetoing Kennedy. His solution was to direct Bundy to get Kennedy to announce that he had withdrawn on his own. The President used Bundy partly because Bundy had served from time to time as a liaison with Kennedy, partly as a brutal and characteristic Johnson loyalty test. Kennedy vigorously rejected the proposal, telling Bundy "first, it wasn't true; secondly . . . a large part of the reason that I was at all interested in the Vice Presidency was because of the interest of others. If I suddenly withdraw my name without discussing it with them it would be impossible for them to understand. Mac disagreed and said this would be very helpful to Johnson and helpful to me." Bundy honestly believed this; Kennedy as honestly believed that Bundy's intervention was an act of inexplicable disloyalty.[80] For a moment an old association became embittered. (A month later Kennedy wrote Bundy: "These have been a difficult nine months for all of us. But I wanted you to know, as I am sure you must, that you were a great help to my brother, made a major difference for him, and for your friendship to me, which, even with the misunderstandings, I know was genuine, I am most grateful.")[81]

The day after the Bundy effort, Johnson "told Kenny that he had to put out a statement by six o'clock that afternoon saying I was out but what about a statement from me saying that I had asked my name to be withdrawn. Kenny said he couldn't see how I could say that. Then he said, then why doesn't the Attorney General make up a statement? . . . I made the point that he could put out any statement that he wanted as long as it was in accordance with the facts."[82] That evening Johnson announced that he was excluding from consideration all cabinet members and all who met regularly with the cabinet—the last clause disposing of Adlai Stevenson.

The day following, Johnson had Tom Wicker of the *New York Times,* Edward T. Folliard of the *Washington Post* and Douglas Kiker of the *New York Herald Tribune* to luncheon. He provided an elaborate and caustic account of the Kennedy meeting. He had watched Kennedy, he said, "like a hawk watching chickens," and claimed that Kennedy had given a vast gulp at the bad news, "his Adam's apple going up and down like a Yo-yo." Johnson, who had an unexpected gift for mimicry, thereupon rendered his impression of the Kennedy gulp, "like a fat fish," his admiring brother said, "pulling in a mouthful of air." Within forty-eight hours, word of Johnson's table talk was all over Washington.[83] When Kennedy protested, Johnson denied he had discussed their meeting with anyone. Kennedy said the President could not be telling the truth. Johnson said he would check his schedule to see whether there might have been some conversation he had forgotten. "He tells so many lies," Kennedy noted on August 6, "that he convinces himself after a while he's telling the truth. He just doesn't recognize truth or falsehood."[84]

I spent that weekend at Hyannis Port. Kennedy was, I thought, "very matter-of-fact" about the Johnson meeting and "quite funny" about the subsequent stages. He set forth a number of possible comments if reporters asked about the exclusion of the cabinet: "I am sorry that I had to take so many nice fellows down with me" or "It seems to me premature to stop the vice presidential boom for Dean Rusk" or "I swear to the best of my knowledge I am not now and have never been a member of the cabinet on the ground that it might tend to eliminate me."[85]

VII

For Johnson the crisis was still not over. "He was afraid," Clark Clifford said later, "that at the convention in Atlantic City, because they had planned a tribute to John F. Kennedy and that Bobby was to deliver the tribute, that he might very well stampede the convention and end up being . . . the vice presidential nominee. . . . We talked about it at very considerable length."[86]

The tribute to the fallen President was originally scheduled for Tuesday night. Johnson had it moved back to Thursday, by which time the nominations would be completed. He took other precautions, the most extraordinary of which was to send Cartha DeLoach and an FBI team of thirty snoops and wiretappers to Atlantic City. The ostensible purpose was to gather intelligence "concerning matters of strife, violence, etc." The real purpose, according to William Sullivan of the FBI, was to gather political information useful to President Johnson, "particularly in bottling up Robert Kennedy—that is, in reporting on the activities of Bobby Kennedy."*[87] The FBI's senior resident agent in Atlantic City later confirmed to the Watergate Committee that "Robert Kennedy's activities were of special interest,

* See also William C. Sullivan to J. Edgar Hoover, October 6, 1971: "I saw clearly at last that the FBI, always presented to the American public as non-political . . . was just the contrary. It was immersed in politics and even went so far as to conduct purely political investigations and inquiries. At times it seemed that when we were not asked to perform politically we sought opportunities to do so. I was so concerned about this under Mr. Johnson's administration that I wrote you a letter . . . and urged that the FBI not be used politically." I thank Mr. Sullivan for making this letter available to me.

including his contacts with [Martin Luther] King."[88] DeLoach instructed him, the agent testified, that the presence of the FBI squad was not to be disclosed to the Secret Service and especially not to the Attorney General.[89]

When Bill Barry of the Bureau drove Kennedy, as he customarily did, to the airport in New York, Kennedy asked him to come along to Atlantic City. "Ethel's pregnant and I have nobody in Atlantic City, and I really want you to go." Although Atlantic City lay outside his division, Barry went nevertheless. On arrival DeLoach told him, "There's some thought that Attorney General Kennedy might try to stampede the convention. . . . If he does that and he's got an FBI agent by his side, the President will not be too happy with the FBI organization, so you're to immediately leave Atlantic City."[90]

"By means of informant coverage, by the use of various confidential techniques, by infiltration of key groups through use of undercover agents, and through utilization of agents using appropriate cover as reporters," DeLoach later boasted to his superiors, "we were able to keep the White House fully apprised of all major developments during the Convention's course." The "confidential techniques" included tapping Dr. King's hotel room and bugging the SNCC and CORE headquarters. "We disseminated 44 pages of intelligence data to Walter Jenkins," DeLoach continued. ". . . I kept Jenkins and Moyers constantly advised by telephone of minute to minute developments." When Moyers sent a letter of thanks, DeLoach replied, "Dear 'Bishop': . . . I'm certainly glad that we were able to come through with vital tidbits from time to time which were of assistance to you and Walter." Johnson ordered Jenkins to tell Hoover that "the job the Bureau had done in Atlantic City was one of the finest the President had ever seen."[91]

This unprecedented effort—no previous chief executive had ever used the FBI at a party convention—was hardly necessary. Kennedy had no intention of storming the convention. It is true that his appearance excited the emotions of delegates and the dreams of friends. "The applause hit like thunder," said John Seigenthaler after Kennedy's visit to the West Virginia delegation. ". . . I knew that the electricity was there, and it could have been put together." People around him discussed a coup, "but he really didn't want to do it." He was there to thank Democrats for supporting his brother, not to win them for himself. "If something had happened, that would have been fine, but it had to happen in the heart of Lyndon Johnson."[92]

The heart of Lyndon Johnson remained, understandably enough, obdurate. With no signs of a Kennedy insurrection, Johnson sustained his vice presidential tease to the end. On the second day of the convention, he summoned Humphrey—along, improbably, with Thomas J. Dodd—to Washington. After keeping poor Humphrey waiting in a limousine outside the south entrance to the White House, Johnson finally relented and had him in. "Most Presidents and Vice Presidents," he told Humphrey, "just don't hit it off. . . . This is like a marriage with no chance of divorce. I need complete and unswerving loyalty. . . . Do you think that you're that man?" "I think I am," replied Humphrey, hopeful and guileless.[93] "If you didn't know that I had you picked a month ago," Johnson cruelly concluded, "maybe you haven't got brains enough to be the Vice President."[94]

Robert Kennedy was glad about Humphrey. But his mind was on other matters. On Thursday night he was to introduce a film about his brother. Seigenthaler accompanied him to the auditorium. They were led through the darkness into a small dressing room under the platform. Kennedy said, "Would you check on the program? We can't hear anything back here. . . . I think Lyndon may just have put us back here with orders to forget us. They'll probably let us out day after tomorrow." He pulled out his manuscript and started reading it once again. Jackie, he told Seigenthaler, had given him a quotation from *Romeo and Juliet*. (Had either consciously noted the thrust of the last line? I never knew.)

Soon they were taken to a runway behind the platform where other dignitaries had already assembled. "He was really sort of a bastard at the family reunion," Seigenthaler thought. "Nobody was enthusiastic about coming and saying 'hello.' Lyndon had picked the whole goddamn platform. . . . [James A.] Farley, for once in his life, was decent and tried to make small conversation." Kennedy looked through his manuscript again, took out a pencil, made small changes. Finally Senator Henry Jackson, who was presiding, motioned him to the rostrum. "When Scoop introduced him, it hit. I mean, it really hit. . . . It just went on and on and on."[95]

I stood on the floor in the midst of the thunderous ovation. I had never seen anything like it. Ordinarily an organ in the background controls the pandemonium of a convention. This time they stopped the organ after a moment or so. But the demonstration roared on, reaching a new intensity every time that Robert Kennedy, standing with a wistful half-smile on his face, tried to bring it to an end. As Kennedy once more raised his hand to still the uproar, Jackson whispered to him, "Let it go on. . . . Just let them do it, Bob. . . . Let them get it out of their system."[96]

He repressed his tears. Many in the audience did not. He seemed slight, almost frail, as the crowd screamed itself hoarse. It went on for twenty-two minutes. Finally he began to speak. At the end, the quotation:

> When he shall die
> Take him and cut him out in little stars
> And he will make the face of heaven so fine
> That all the world will be in love with night,
> And pay no worship to the garish sun.

29

To the Senate

ON AUGUST 22, 1964, two days before the Atlantic City convention, Robert Kennedy announced his candidacy for the Democratic senatorial nomination in New York. "I think," he had scribbled to a newspaperman a few days before, "I shall respond to the spontaneous draft of my brother-in-law."[1] The possibility had been in his mind since early spring. The New York residential requirement was nominal, and Stephen Smith had begun quiet contingency preparations for Robert's entry. Then, after Edward Kennedy's plane crash in June, Robert briefly considered leaving politics altogether. His reception later that month in Europe persuaded him he could not thus abandon John Kennedy's legacy.

I

At the end of July Averell Harriman, David Hackett and I were at Hyannis Port for the weekend. The most recent New York poll had shown Kennedy leading Kenneth Keating, the Republican incumbent, by a healthy 52 to 35 percent and running significantly ahead of the Democratic alternatives—Adlai Stevenson, Robert F. Wagner, serving his third term as mayor of New York City, and Samuel Stratton, an upstate congressman.[2]

The Senate plainly tempted him. "He has a great desire," I noted,

to be independent of Johnson and the administration and to have his own base. . . . He thinks that he might be able to organize a bloc of New Frontier senators—Joe Tydings, George McGovern, Birch Bayh, Pierre Salinger [recently appointed to fill a Senate vacancy from California] and some others—and have some impact on the administration. But he is quite clear in his mind that he does not want to go into New York unless there is a summons by a broad and significant group within the party. Averell is prepared to lead the way on this. The real question is Alex Rose and the Liberals.[3]

Rose was my assignment. We had breakfast a couple of days later at his usual table in the old Astor Hotel on Times Square. Kennedy had problems, Rose said: mistrust among reform Democrats; prejudice among middle-class Jews; concern among the regulars that a pro-Kennedy movement would have an anti-Johnson thrust. So long as Stevenson was in the picture, Rose added, he could not commit himself to Kennedy. After a long talk, he gave me to understand in his sibylline fashion that he thought he might manage to bring the Liberal party around.[4] Harriman, Stephen Smith and Jack English, the Democratic leader in Nassau County, were meanwhile tackling the regulars. (One county leader told English: "I'll be for Kennedy if you give me one promise: if Corbin doesn't come into the state.")[5] Ronnie Eldridge and Albert Blumenthal, West Side reform leaders, along with William Haddad and others, were working on the reform Democrats.

Wagner turned out to be more of a question than Rose. The mayor was not a candidate himself, but he was the top Democratic office-holder, and, as Harriman reported to Johnson, did not wish "any other stars in the orbit."[6] His preferred candidate was Stevenson, whom he saw as an elder statesman, not as a competitor for party leadership. He was resistant to Kennedy. But Kennedy regarded Wagner's blessing as indispensable. The newcomer had to appear to be responding to an invitation, not conducting an invasion.

Stevenson turned out not to be a candidate either. He watched developments with rueful malice. "Bobby is mad to run now," he wrote a friend on August 10, "and Steve Smith is making unctuous calls daily about getting together. 'He doesn't want to do anything if I'm interested' etc. Bob Wagner is holding out but the K's have unleashed the mafia. . . . The avarice of the K's really makes me sick. I'd almost like to do it to challenge him."[7] But "almost" was not a challenge. Lacking a candidate, Wagner endorsed Kennedy. Kennedy's nomination was now certain. A trail of bitterness remained. In mid-August Stevenson happily cited "the rising protest against the Kennedy invasion from the Liberal Party, the Roosevelt-Lehman Reform groups, Labor, et al. . . . Of course, he can get the nomination, but winning is another matter what with the widespread disaffection."[8]

II

Kenneth Keating was a silver-haired, pink-faced gentleman of sixty-four. A rather conservative congressman from Rochester in the 1950s, he had as senator after 1958 gained a vaguely liberal reputation, enhanced now by his refusal to back Barry Goldwater. His benign appearance, ingratiating personality and passable record made him a tough opponent, especially for a contender vulnerable on grounds of carpetbagging.

In fact, Robert Kennedy was less a carpetbagger than his older brother had been in Massachusetts in 1946. He had lived in New York from a few months after his birth till 1942, indeed, had lived nowhere longer. Except for schools and summers, he had really never lived in Massachusetts. But he had always voted in Hyannis Port and was indelibly identified with his brother's state. Still New York had historically been hospitable to carpetbaggers. Its first senator, Rufus King, had begun by representing Massachusetts in the Continental Congress—a point I tried, as an historian, to make during the campaign to absolutely no effect. Stevenson would have been a carpetbagger. Of the two senators succeeding to Robert Kennedy's seat, the first lived in Connecticut, the second in Massachusetts.*

The carpetbagger problem at first gave rise to jocularity. Ethel suggested as his campaign slogan: "There is only so much you can do for Massachusetts."[9] A reporter, explaining he could not accompany Kennedy on an upstate tour, said, "I'm going to be in Boston, of all places." "Never heard of it," said Kennedy.[10] The novelist Richard Condon proposed that Kennedy meet the issue by ending his speeches, "Ich bin ein New Yorker."[11] It was more serious than that. What gave the carpetbagger charge its edge was the idea that the invasion of New York was one more expression of Kennedy's well-advertised ruthlessness—a power grab by a madly ambitious, arrogant, opportunistic, primitive and dangerous young man, the son of Joe Kennedy, the aide of Joe McCarthy, the confrere of J. Edgar Hoover, the oppressor of Jimmy Hoffa, who stopped at nothing to advance himself and now was cynically using New York as a launching pad for the Presidency.

The *New York Times* denounced "The Kennedy Blitzkrieg" in a

* James Buckley and Daniel Patrick Moynihan. In 1972, in addition, the Democrats nominated Ramsey Clark, who had spent most of his life in Texas. In none of these campaigns was carpetbaggerism an issue.

series of editorials. "Does the *Times* think," Francis Biddle finally wrote the paper, "Mr. Kennedy should seek office with more gentility, affording that pleasant touch of hypocrisy which is still highly prized by many 'respectable' citizens?" Roosevelt's Attorney General concluded: "As Attorney General [Kennedy] has furthered civil liberties for Negroes more than any of his predecessors, enforcing the law up to the hilt, but always with a cool and wise judgment."[12] This was to small avail. Kennedy's actual role in Washington—his contributions, for example, to the Cuban missile crisis or his real relations with J. Edgar Hoover—was hardly known in New York, and disbelieved in anti-Kennedy circles when described.

Gore Vidal and Lisa Howard organized a Democrats for Keating Committee. Other liberals—I. F. Stone, Carey McWilliams of the *Nation,* James Baldwin, Richard Hofstadter, Paul Newman, Joseph Mankiewicz, Barbara Tuchman, Nat Hentoff[13]—forgot Keating's ignoble part on such matters as wiretapping, the restriction of passports and the introduction of bills to reverse civil liberties decisions by the Supreme Court, not to mention those Soviet nuclear missiles cunningly stowed away in Cuban caves, and joined the anti-Kennedy crusade. In due course the *Times* endorsed Keating, explaining mystically that Kennedy aroused "an uneasiness that is no less real because it is elusive and difficult to define."[14] "At least," said Kennedy, "they can never say I got my job through the *New York Times.*"* As the barrage intensified, he started to decline in the polls. "It's a strange state you fellows brought me into," Kennedy told one supporter. "I haven't made my first campaign speech, and I'm already losing ground."[15]

Under Stephen Smith's direction the organization began to take shape. Justin Feldman of New York worked with John Nolan on scheduling. Two eager young lawyers, Adam Walinsky and Peter Edelman, resigned from the Justice Department and inserted themselves into the campaign. Bill Barry spent his vacation from the FBI traveling with the candidate in the last fortnight. (Later, four days before his sixth child was born, Hoover ordered him to Mobile, Alabama. Barry resigned from the Bureau.) Paul Corbin installed himself in a hotel across the river in New Jersey until he demanded so many telephones that they ejected him, suspecting he was a bookie. Thereafter he secreted himself in an apartment in New

---

* The reference was to a series in which the *Times* touted its want ads by portraying people who claimed they had gotten their jobs through the *New York Times* (Gerald Gardner, *Robert Kennedy in New York* [New York, 1965], 12).

York.[16] Ethel Kennedy was pregnant again but traveled with her husband and even on occasion nerved herself to make speeches.

At the start, enthusiasm, especially among the young, was unrestrained. "If I had my way," Kennedy would say to the screaming kids, "I'd lower the voting age to six." The week after Labor Day he concluded an upstate tour by flying to the placid little town of Glens Falls. Due at eight in the evening, he arrived at one in the morning. "Do you think anybody waited?" he asked before disembarking. To his astonishment a band struck up, and a thousand people surged around the plane. "Here we are, five hours late," he told them. "That's the smooth, hard-driving, well-oiled Kennedy machine for you." As they drove into town, men, women and children in pajamas and bathrobes waved and cheered along the road. Four thousand people, a quarter of the population, were patiently waiting in the town square. Kennedy told them: "I'd like to make my very first commitment of the campaign. I promise that, win or lose, the day after the election I'm coming back to Glens Falls!"[17]

He entertained audiences with local allusions. "The Catskills," he said, "were immortalized by Washington Irving. He wrote of a man who fell asleep and awoke in another era. The only other area that can boast such a man is Phoenix, Arizona." He begged the attention of Johnson City and its shoe industry for two reasons: "First of all, eight small children need a lot of shoes. And second, I'm the one who popularized those fifty-mile hikes."[18] But he felt he knew the real reason that the crowds were pouring out and quoted John Kennedy in every speech. "They're for him," he told Guthman, "—they're for him."[19] Soon he sank into melancholy memories. County chairmen found him moody and uncommunicative. His staff thought him unwontedly irascible. "He hated himself, in my view, for being here," Justin Feldman thought. ". . . He was being purely and simply President Kennedy's brother, and he just wasn't coming through."[20] One day Corbin, observing that he was retracing his brother's 1960 schedule, called him and said, "Get out of this mysticism. Get out of your daze. . . . God damn, Bob, be yourself. Get hold of yourself. You're real. Your brother's dead."[21]

Kennedy had decided that a frontal attack on Keating would only accentuate the impression of a ruthless young tough out to mug a kindly old man. But he continued to drop in the polls. "I was appalled," John Douglas wrote him in early October, "to learn you said yesterday that Keating's voting record is good. Every time you make a statement like that you are cutting your own throat. Keating's voting record is not good."[22] Douglas enumerated the areas. Kennedy irritably called it a "snotty" letter. If he questioned Keating's record, he responded it would look like "a personal vendetta." "In other words," said Douglas, "he thought that if he went after Keating on a perfectly valid basis, that somehow people would view it as a personal attack."[23] The "ruthless" charge had bitten deep.

On October 5 in Rochester, Richard M. Nixon, righteously denouncing what he called "a cloud of corruption" over the Johnson White House, forecast a big Keating victory.[24] On October 6, John F. Kraft, the Kennedy pollster, reported that "it ain't good" in New York City; on October 8, that Keating was leading 51–49 statewide while Johnson led Goldwater 60–40.[25] The same day Samuel Lubell, the master diagnostician of the American voter, wrote in the *New York World-Telegram:* "Robert Kennedy is running well behind. . . . Keating's lead mainly reflects a heavy break against Kennedy among normally Democratic voters in New York City. . . . In some New York City precincts a third or more of the voters going for President Johnson say, 'I'll split my ticket' on the Senate race."[26]

III

Buoyed by the sympathy flowing to underdogs, Keating had been conducting a careful campaign. But his chief political adviser was Herbert Brownell, an aggressive veteran of political wars. As Kennedy fell in the polls, Brownell smelled an opportunity to administer the coup de grâce. He urged his candidate to go hard after traditional Democratic groups now breaking from Kennedy: the blacks; the Italians; above all, the Jews.

Keating had an excellent civil rights record and solid relations with black leadership. In a speech prepared for the state NAACP convention on October 2, he accused Kennedy of having run out on the civil rights movement: "He abandoned his post at the Department of Justice with an unfinished task before him." Charles Evers, who had taken his brother Medgar's place as head of the NAACP in Mississippi, addressed the convention the same day. The state NAACP president, as Evers fumed at Keating, sent him a note: "I know Bobby's your man, but not here." "God, I was so mad," Evers said later. "I just bit my tongue." When his time came to speak, Evers threw away his text. "You're fortunate to have a man of Kennedy's caliber even visit New York, much less running for Senator," Evers told the audience. Turning to Keating: "Bobby Kennedy means more to us in Mississippi than any white man I know, including yourself, Senator." The NAACP officials refused to speak to Evers when he finished.[27] But his intervention averted an NAACP endorsement. "We in Mississippi cannot vote for [Kennedy]," Evers wrote in the *New York Post* later in the month, "but we sure can urge you to vote for this man who . . . has done more for the Negroes not only in Mississippi but throughout this country, than any other single individual."[28]

Bidding for the Italian vote, Keating accused Kennedy of smearing all Italian Americans by unveiling Joe Valachi and of doing so in order to divert attention from the crimes of Bobby Baker. Mario Biaggi, a police lieutenant and president of the Grand Council of Columbia Associations, denounced the Valachi hearing as a "one-man show produced, staged, directed and prompted" by Kennedy.[29] "He's a crumb," an Italian barber observed of Kennedy to a *Times* reporter. "He made every Italian look like a gangster."[30]

The major Republican effort, however, was directed at the Jews. Kennedy, William Haddad warned Stephen Smith, was "in trouble with the Jewish community. . . . Underlying this problem is a great uneasiness, an unsureness, a fear, as one person put it, of the tough Irish kid that beat him up on the way to school each day."[31] As for Keating, he "goes around with a yarmulke in his pocket," one rabbi told Neil Sheehan of the *Times,* "and every time you can put three Jews together he's there to give a speech."[32] At the end of September, Keating, striking hard for the Jewish vote, accused Kennedy of having made a deal with a "huge Nazi cartel . . . the chemical arsenal for Nazi Germany" when the Justice Department settled the case of the General Aniline and Film Corporation in 1963.[33]

The case, left over from the Second World War, involved the claim of a Swiss corporation to the assets of General Aniline, a company seized as enemy property in 1942. It was a singular case for Keating of all people to bring up, for Keating himself had introduced the bill permitting the sale of General Aniline. "I am gratified," he had told the Senate on March 4, 1963, "that as a result of the General Aniline & Film sale bill we have moved very close to the day when this company can become part of the mainstream of our free enterprise system."[34] He had been "fully informed as to everything that was going on," said William Orrick, who had handled the settlement, "and I say that because I did it. . . . He just lied in the campaign."[35]

Kennedy was outraged. "The charge that I made a deal with Nazis can't help but have an adverse effect on how Jewish people feel

about me," he told a press conference. ". . . If this kind of charge
were true, I wouldn't deserve to be elected to any public office. The
charge isn't true. . . . I lost my brother and brother-in-law to the
Germans. The idea that I would turn over money to the Nazis is ridiculous."[36] "I expected this campaign to be on a higher level," he
ruminated to James Stevenson of the *New Yorker.* "I found myself
being charged with making deals with Nazis and running out on
Negroes and being anti-Italian and being a crook, covering up for
Bobby Baker, and I just didn't expect it would be as bad as that."[37]
But the General Aniline fiasco both hurt Keating and legitimized a
shift in Kennedy's tactics. "It gives you the justification for attacking
him for a change," Professor Richard Neustadt told him.[38] "If he
hadn't attacked me," Kennedy said later, "I would have had a hell of
a time."[39]

IV

Free at last, Kennedy in October struck back on the issues between
Keating and himself. Old friends deployed on his behalf: not only
Charles Evers and others among the blacks, but Harry Golden from
North Carolina in Jewish neighborhoods, while Galbraith, Rauh,
Neustadt, Adam Yarmolinsky and I spoke evening after evening to
disaffected liberals. I could not forget that four years earlier I had
found the same people in the same mistrustful mood when I campaigned for John Kennedy. Now they mourned him and mistrusted
his brother.

Norman Mailer came unexpectedly to our assistance. Mailer had
never been a fan of Robert Kennedy's. The dead President had been
"the existential hero"; "Bobby!—the Irish equivalent of Roy Cohn
on the good old McCarthy team; Bobby!—with the face of a Wid-
mark gunsel, that prep-school arrogance which makes good manual
laborers think of smashing a fist through a wall; Bobby!—" etc., etc.
But Keating, with his face "like the plastic dough children play with,"
seemed even worse. As between "a neutron" and "an active principle," Mailer announced for the active principle. Besides, "I have
affection for Bobby Kennedy. I think something came into him with
the death of his brother. . . . Something compassionate, something
witty, had come into his face. Something of sinew." Besides, "I think
Bobby Kennedy may be the only liberal about, early or late, who
could be a popular general in a defense against the future powers of

the Right Wing."[40] Like all of Mailer's political journalism, it was
brilliant and rather dotty. It helped.

Most important, Kennedy was beginning to find himself as a campaigner. He still read prepared speeches in a monotone but was increasingly effective in extemporaneous delivery. He stumped the state
morning to night five or six days a week. When he called, as he regularly did, on his father, he was, Rita Dallas noted, "red-eyed from
lack of sleep, and hoarse from hours of speechmaking." The old man
gave him indecipherable words of counsel. "I'll make changes, Dad,"
Bobby would say. "You know I'll make changes. Millions of people
need help. My God, they need help."[41]

In mid-October his advertising blitz began. Kennedy mistrusted the
Madison Avenue magicians. They showed him a brochure with a
photograph in which he was displayed shaking hands with a labor
leader. Kennedy frowned. "What's wrong with this one?" he was
asked. "That fellow's in jail," Kennedy said. As for television, the
aim, he was told, "will be to present you as a warm, sincere individual." Kennedy said, "You going to use a double?"[42] The experts were
puzzled how to project him on the tiny screen. He stiffened in the studio. Clips of the candidate surrounded by apparently demented teen-
agers did not give the desired impression of statesmanship. But he
was forceful and persuasive dealing with questions. His strongest television piece emerged from a session with antagonistic students at Columbia.[43]

He also finally agreed to take advantage of the fact that Johnson
was heading for a landslide in New York. Steve Smith's new posters
read: "Get on the Johnson-Humphrey-Kennedy Team." In mid-October Johnson and Kennedy campaigned together for two days from
Buffalo to Brooklyn. Both played their roles to the hilt. "You don't
often find a man," said Johnson, "who has the understanding, the
heart and the compassion that Bobby Kennedy has." Johnson, said
Kennedy, was "already one of the great Presidents of the United
States."[44] Underneath, older feelings persisted. Richard Wade, who
was running the Kennedy campaign in northwestern New York,
thought "it drove Johnson crazy" to see hands outstretched to shake
the senatorial candidate's hand and not his own. Then "Johnson
would get up on the platform, put his arm around him and say, 'this
is ma boy, I want you to elect ma boy,' you know, six feet four and
. . . you could see the whites of Bobby's knuckles."[45] At the end of
two crowded days, Kennedy asked Johnson whether he had enjoyed
it. Johnson looked at him earnestly and said, "Of all the things in

life, this is what I most enjoy." Kennedy, telling me this, added incredulously, "Imagine saying that, of all the things in life, this is what you like most."[46]

On October 19 the *Daily News* poll showed Kennedy leading by 59.5 percent to 37.3.[47] Blacks and Puerto Ricans were flocking to him; Jews and Italians were coming back.[48] Keating, increasingly frantic, assailed this "self-seeking outsider" who was conducting "the most arrogant campaign New York State has ever witnessed" and was "temperamentally and intellectually unfit" for the Senate.[49] ("He's on to you," said Steve Smith.)[50] Keating then filed a complaint with the Fair Campaign Practices Committee over Kennedy's claim in a Syracuse speech on October 20 that Keating had "ridiculed" the test ban treaty.

Kennedy had been wrong. A speechwriter, revising a draft from the research staff, had sharpened a considerably more qualified statement portraying Keating's early misgivings about the test ban. In the end, Keating had voted for the treaty's ratification. The FCPC executive director sent Kennedy a letter accusing him of "dishonest and unfair distortion" if not "deliberate and cynical misrepresentation." The Keating staff then leaked the FCPC letter to the *Herald Tribune*. Brownell said that Kennedy had been caught "red-handed with a spectacular distortion." Kennedy, indignant over what he regarded as unwarranted overkill, submitted documentation of Keating's test ban equivocations and personally telephoned members of the FCPC board of directors. Ralph McGill of the *Atlanta Constitution* and others resigned. The FCPC withdrew its letter, saying it "should not have been written, and any accusations in it were necessarily unfair to Mr. Kennedy at that stage." The issue evaporated almost as quickly as it had arisen.[51]

In September, Keating, when he was running behind, had proposed a debate. Kennedy, after evading the challenge, accepted it in early October when *he* was behind. Keating then stalled. Now, behind again, he revived the challenge. It was once more Kennedy's turn to stall. He saw no advantage in debating Keating. "He looks like your grandfather," Kennedy would say, "and there's no way you can win it." At the end of October, Keating bought a half-hour of prime television time and called on Kennedy to appear with him. Harry Golden urged Kennedy to do it. Kennedy said, "Harry, you've got white hair, you debate Keating."[52] With Javits at his side, Keating arranged to debate an empty chair marked "Robert F. Kennedy"—the symbol, he said, of Kennedy's "ruthless contempt" for New York voters.

This was an ancient device. Kennedy, the innovator, suddenly resolved to fill the chair. "I was sure I would get in," he said later. "I
couldn't think of any way they could keep me out." When he arrived
without warning just before the telecast, studio guards turned him
back. He vigorously protested his exclusion to newspapermen. Keating meanwhile fled the reporters, leaving twin photographs for next
day's papers—Keating threatening his empty chair; Kennedy looking
in frustration at a sign PLEASE KEEP OUT. Kennedy told an audience
later that night, "There was Javits and Keating on television really
giving it to this empty chair. . . . They kicked that chair all over the
room. And there was I outside trying to get in."[53]

He won by 719,693 votes, greatly helped by Johnson, who carried
the state by 2.7 million. Kennedy neglected the President in his victory statement. Far away in Texas, Johnson said, and repeated, "I
wonder why he doesn't mention me?"[54] Bill Barry congratulated the
senator-elect in the midst of election night pandemonium. "If my
brother was alive," Kennedy said, "I wouldn't be here. I'd rather have
it that way."[55] He quoted Tennyson to the cheering campaign
workers:

> Come my friends,
> 'Tis not too late to seek a newer world.

He had an hour's sleep and next morning took the plane to Glens
Falls.

V

On January 4, 1965, Robert Kennedy was sworn in as the junior senator from New York. Edward Kennedy, leaning heavily on a cane,
his smashed back enclosed in a steel brace, gaunt after months in the
hospital, took the oath with him.* Not since 1803 had two brothers—
Dwight Foster of Massachusetts and Theodore Foster of Rhode
Island—served together in the Senate.† That evening the Women's

---

* Edward Kennedy's election to the Senate in 1962 was to complete an unfinished
term. In 1964 he was elected for the full term.
† Robert was, of course, the third Kennedy brother in the Senate in five years. The
Kennedys were still behind the Washburn brothers, three of whom served together in
the 34th, 35th and 36th Congresses representing three different states while a fourth
later represented still another state both in the House and Senate. These were Israel
Washburn, 32nd–36th Congresses from Massachusetts; E. B. Washburn, 33rd–41st
Congresses from Illinois; C. C. Washburn, 34th–36th and 40th–41st Congresses from
Wisconsin; and W. D. Washburn, 46th–48th Congresses and later senator
(1889–1895) from Minnesota.

National Press Club threw its annual soiree for new senators. "First of all," said Robert Kennedy, when presented to the audience, "I want to say how delighted I am to be here representing the great state of . . . ah . . . ah . . ."—a long wait while he made a show of searching through his notes. Having ascertained the name of the state, he concluded: "I have absolutely no presidential ambitions, and neither does my wife—Ethel Bird."*

His Senate office was small in comparison to the cavernous chamber he had occupied at Justice. The indispensable Angie Novello came along as executive secretary. When Edwin Guthman left in April to resume his newspaper career, Wes Barthelmes, a former paratrooper and reporter who had been working for Congresswoman Edith Green, became press secretary. Guthman gave Barthelmes a single piece of advice, "You've got to learn to read the pauses, these long silences."[56] Joseph Dolan, as administrative assistant, knew how to read the silences. Underneath his close-mouthed Irish manner, he was, Barthelmes noted, "a well-disguised intellectual."[57] Dolan and Kennedy communicated in a monosyllabic style that baffled the rest of the staff. Frank Mankiewicz, who replaced an exhausted Barthelmes as press secretary after a year, recalled them grunting and snorting at each other: "This guy . . ." "No, not this fellow because you remember . . ." "Oh yes, that other guy, that's right . . ." "I never was quite sure what they were talking about," Mankiewicz said, "but they seemed to know."[58]

The legislative assistants, Adam Walinsky and Peter Edelman, were in their late twenties. Walinsky had gone to Yale Law School, Edelman to Harvard; Walinksy had clerked for a judge in the Court of Appeals, Edelman for Arthur Goldberg on the Supreme Court; both had been junior attorneys at Justice, who, when they forced their way into the senatorial campaign, brought fresh ideas and enthusiasm at a midpoint of fatigue. They were one of those teams, like Tom Corcoran and Ben Cohen in the New Deal, that materialize around secure patrician reformers. Only a secure man could absorb so much needling brilliance without feeling threatened thereby; only a reformer would wish it. Like Corcoran and Cohen, both did everything, but each inclined to his specialty: Walinsky writing speeches,

---

* *Washington Post*, January 5, 1965. Like most contemporary politicians, Kennedy often called on professionals for jokes in speeches. The always helpful Alan King provided the "ah . . . ah . . . ah" gag; but, according to King, it was the Ethel-bird joke "which just broke up the place. That was his own" (Alan King, in recorded interview by Jean Stein, May 1970, 2, Stein Papers).

Edelman drafting bills; one the eloquent salesman, the other the careful researcher; one ostentatiously arrogant, the other deceptively gentle; both passionate, obstinate, hero-worshiping, exasperating, engaging. Kennedy listened to them, argued with them, learned from them. The sixties were breaking open, and they, far more than his New Frontier friends, could tell him what it was all about. He valued their testimony and could handle their indignation. When Walinsky kept putting things in speeches that Kennedy did not wish to say: "Now, Adam, get that out. That's yours, not mine. I don't want that." "Adam," said Mankiewicz, "had a marvelous relationship with him because he was always pushing him. And that's what he wanted."[59]

It was an exceptionally busy office. The mail averaged twelve hundred letters a day. At the start he intended to live within the official allowance, but by the end, in order to keep abreast of business, he was adding a hundred thousand dollars of his own for salaries.[60] As at Justice, the staff had great discretion. "He didn't spend a lot of time telling you the fourteen steps to follow," Walinsky recalled. ". . . He just sort of indicated that he thought something should be done in an area and then he expected you to grab hold and go do it. And then maybe a week or so later . . . he'd say, 'Well, where is it?' or 'How are we doing on that?' "[61] Once Walinsky failed to produce a poverty speech. "He was rather upset about it, but all he said was, 'You know, I thought that was a very important speech, and I'd really like to do well with it.' And so I said, 'I'm sorry.' He said, 'Thank you.' That was the strongest it ever got. I mean he was not one for chewing people out."[62]

Nor was he effusive in praise, but, as Barthelmes said, his assistants "were mature enough to feel that they were just working for someone who felt everyone was responsible and grown up." The compensation came in his confidence in them. "He always gave me," Barthelmes said, "an extra sense of dimension of myself." And he excited because of the feeling—again Barthelmes—that he carried "a hidden agenda with him. There were always many, many, many, many things to be done, and you were part of it."[63] "He was a very secret man," said Walinsky, ". . . terribly sensitive to people's feelings," but conveying "a certain kind of sadness and a certain sense of loss all the time. . . . There were things he carried around in his head that were unimaginable, things that he just had to live with all by himself."[64]

VI

Robert and Ethel liked New York. They took an apartment high in United Nations Plaza with a startling view of the East River and delighted in the gaieties, the theater, ballet, restaurants, museums, of the most spirited of cities. Walking in New York was fun, Robert Kennedy said, because "everybody's always in such a hurry to get home they don't see me."[65] Unlike most Upper East Siders, he systematically acquainted himself with the darker corners of the metropolis, the ghettos of Harlem and Bedford-Stuyvesant, the joyless stretches of the Bronx and Queens, the decaying housing projects, rat-infested tenements, garbage-strewn alleys, desperate prisons.

From his apartment he could see two huge Consolidated Edison stacks belching smoke into the air across the East River; it infuriated him that no one was doing anything about it. He wished he could swim in the river; but, as he observed of the Hudson, "the water's so bad here, if you fell in, you'd dissolve."[66] He liked the great state rolling out beyond the metropolis, the tranquil villages and the rippling lakes, liked, as he once put it, "the sense of rootedness and the fundamental decency, to be found in our small towns and farms."[67] "He loves travelling around New York," I noted after a talk with him in 1965, "and says that he would really like some day to become governor; 'there is so much that can be done for that state.'"[68] He was surprisingly popular upstate; indeed had done better there, relative to previous Democratic candidates, than in the city. He methodically visited mayors, city councils and regional development groups in places that had never seen a Democratic senator. He worried about the poisoning of Lake Erie, the pulpwood scum on Lake Champlain, the wetlands of Long Island, the preservation of parks and forests.

He worried even more about the preservation of people. In the summer of 1965 he received distraught letters from parents with children in state institutions for the mentally retarded. He made unannounced visits and was appalled. Children, he said, "just rock back and forth. They grunt and gibber and soil themselves. They struggle and quarrel—though great doses of tranquilizers usually keep them quiet and passive. . . . There are no civil liberties for those put in the cells of Willowbrook—living amidst brutality and human excrement and intestinal disease."[69]

The senior senator, Jacob Javits, shared many of these concerns, but their relations began in mutual suspicion. Javits, a sensitive and talented man too liberal for his party, was sometimes driven to bouts of equivocation in order to maintain Republican credentials. He had, in addition, minor vanities, especially on the question of newspaper publicity. The two offices engaged for a time in adolescent competition over which senator was doing more for New York. The principals went on television together. Riding back to his office afterward, Kennedy told Barthelmes, "Javits is so facile. He's computerized for knowledge. . . . I never want to do that again"—which, Barthelmes said later, "was about the nearest one ever got . . . to a reprimand." A few moments later Javits's press secretary phoned Barthelmes and said, "Javits just bitched and bitched at me all the way back. . . . He said, 'Don't ever put me on with Kennedy again. He's glamorous. . . . They won't remember what I said.' "[70]

Kennedy had a certain sympathy for Javits. "It's awfully hard for him, me coming into the whole thing here and sort of upstaging him," he said to Edelman. ". . . If I were in his shoes, I wouldn't like me either."[71] In his first legislative initiative, Kennedy introduced an amendment extending the Appalachia bill to cover thirteen upstate New York counties. Javits, unconsulted, was furious. "I thought it was very rude," he said later, ". . . and would have embarrassed me politically if it were strictly his and not mine also. And I told him so in unmeasured terms and not without heat. And he appreciated that and said that he could understand it perfectly . . . and that he would try to make it clear that we were together in it."[72] Soon they agreed to make joint announcements of federal projects—an unusual arrangement when the senators were from different parties.

Kennedy came to appreciate Javits's solid qualities—his acute intelligence, his breadth of informed interest, the genuine conscientiousness underneath his sensitivities. They became collaborators and in the end friends. I remember chatting with Kennedy in 1967 about Javits's reelection contest in 1968. "I don't regard the defeat of Jack Javits," he said, "as one of the more momentous issues facing the nation." Looking back on Kennedy, Javits said in 1973, "He wanted to conserve human values wherever he found them. . . . He was passionately devoted to whatever was a vivid life expression. . . . His, essentially, was a life force as a senator and as a man."[73]

VII

After his election Robert had visited his brother Edward in the Boston hospital. A photographer asked him to step back a little; "you're casting a shadow on Ted." Ted said promptly, "It'll be the same in Washington."[74]

But in the Senate it was Ted who knew the ropes, who was amiable, courteous and popular, whose return after his accident was greeted by other senators with genuine pleasure as compared to the visible skepticism with which they received the former Attorney General. Edward did his best to instruct his older brother. They called each other "Robbie" and "Eddie" and teased back and forth endlessly. They sat together on the Labor and Public Welfare Committee. At hearings senators asked questions in order of seniority, and Robert was almost at the bottom of the list. Early on, he whispered impatiently to his brother, "Is this the way I become a good senator—sitting here and waiting my turn?" "Yes," Edward said. Robert had an engagement in New York. "How many hours do I have to sit here to be a good senator?" "As long as necessary, Robbie."[75] If Robert in his zeal went on too long before the committee, a note from Edward: "You just lost Lister [Hill, the chairman]—stop talking and let's vote, or you'll lose all the others too."[76] Another member said he would help vote out one of Robert's bills if Robert accepted an invitation to speak in his state. "Is this what you have to do to get votes?" he asked his brother. "You're learning, Robbie," said Ted.[77] When pressing a bill, he would ask Ted, "What should I do now? You know how to handle these fellows. . . . You're the likable one."[78] A scribbled note, Robbie to Eddie, transmitted on the floor:

> All I want to know—when I shake my head from side to side and you nod your head up and down. Does this mean I will vote no and you agree? Obviously not. In other words when I wanted to vote no I should have nodded my head up and down—you would have shaken your head from side to side—then I would have known just how to vote.[79]

They consulted constantly, occasionally differing on inconsequential matters, but, for all the playful competition to top the other, Robert remained the head of the family.

Kennedy's daily chums were the three freshmen with whom he shared a new fifth row, installed in the back of the chamber to accommodate Democratic gains in the Goldwater election—Walter

Mondale of Minnesota, Fred Harris of Oklahoma, Joseph Tydings of Maryland. Young, liberal and irreverent, the four vastly entertained themselves by sotto voce comment on the scene before them. Kennedy had, of course, old friends in the rows ahead—George McGovern, whom he once described to me as "the most decent man in the Senate," adding in hyperbolic afterthought, "the *only* decent man in the Senate"; Frank Church from Rackets Committee days; Birch Bayh, who had crashed with his brother in the Connecticut Valley; Claiborne Pell, whom he had known from Newport.

"I had not thought at first that I would like Robert Kennedy," said Fred Harris, who had been reared in the populist faith that "rich people were *never* happy and seldom good." But Kennedy "*was* about as impressive a person as I ever met." Harris was drawn to him by his earnestness, his commitment, his "insatiable" curiosity about things, people and issues.[80] McGovern too was struck anew by his continued "hunger to learn" and by his ready cooperation. "I never asked Bob Kennedy in my life for anything that I thought was very important where he failed to follow through."[81] A certain moodiness persisted, however. "One day we would crack jokes for an hour," recalled one of his back-bench colleagues; "the next day he'd chop you off. . . . The next day [after that] your relationship would be just as though it never happened. I'm not sure that he realized how some people were hurt by that."[82]

With conservative senators, some at least, he kept up affable banter. McClellan, of course, was an old patron, though for various reasons—especially the crusty Arkansan's dislike of Robert McNamara—their friendship had somewhat soured; Fred Harris accurately described it as "the remnant of what one would suspect might have been a stronger one—of a kind of father-son relationship."[83] Eastland, though always an opponent, remained a friend. When Kennedy published *To Seek a Newer World* in 1967, he inscribed a copy for the old Confederate: "It is still not too late. Repent now!"[84] Kennedy shared with the aged Harry Byrd an enthusiasm for dogs and the Virginia countryside. Thus a handwritten note in the summer of 1965: "I was sorry to hear that you were not feeling well. We need you back here to keep a check on us young liberals who will get away with everything without you to keep an eye on us."[85] Even a 1966 telegram to George Murphy, the right-wing movie actor who had beaten Pierre Salinger in California: WE ARE APPROPRIATING BILLIONS OF DOLLARS FOR SOCIAL PROGRAMS WHILE YOU ARE OUT OF THE CITY. WE NEED YOU BACK HERE TO PUT US ON THE RIGHT TRACK.[86]

A few, like Edward Long of Missouri, whom he regarded as the Teamsters' senator, and Carl Curtis of Nebraska, whom he had detested since the Rackets Committee, he could not abide. Ralph Nader, beginning his career as consumer ombudsman, tried to testify, over Curtis's interruptions, about the dangers in automobiles. Kennedy challenged Curtis:

> KENNEDY. First, you admit you haven't read the book [*Unsafe at Any Speed*]; and, secondly, you haven't heard his testimony. Why don't you listen to his testimony and then criticize?
> CURTIS. I have no objection to hearing his testimony, but when he loses me with . . .
> KENNEDY. With big words?[87]

He had hoped for the Foreign Relations Committee, but was too low in the seniority ladder. In addition to Labor and Public Welfare, he went on Government Operations, where a decade earlier he had been a subcommittee counsel, and on the District of Columbia Committee. The committees offered ample scope for his concerns with education, civil rights, welfare, poverty, juvenile delinquency. He was generally accounted a more effective senator than his older brother but much less a "senator's senator" than his younger brother. Critics found too much sudden, isolated attack in his performance, too many eye-catching amendments, too little detailed follow-through.[88] "I would call him a first-act politician," said Senator Eugene McCarthy. "You know it's easy to write the first act. And it's relatively easy to write the third act. Lyndon Johnson was a good third-act man. . . . But it's the second act that is toughest to write. In Congress, that's where the drudgery and hard work come."* Edward Kennedy was a good second-act man.

Robert Kennedy's manner was also on occasion more brusque than senatorial tradition approved. "He was intense, he was furious about the issues and he was rather well prepared," said Fred Harris. Sometimes "he would almost be too mean."[89] His candor, said Tydings, "made him very unpopular among many of his colleagues." The Senate had its courtly idiom of disagreement. "Bobby didn't take the trouble to polish his phraseology very often. To me it was a plus rather than a minus. . . . Many people interpreted it as being blunt and rough and harsh."[90]

---

* Dick Schaap, *R.F.K.* (New York: Signet reprint, 1967), 117. Schaap does not identify the source of the quotation. I assume it to have been McCarthy in view of the conclusion of his poem "Lament of an Aging Politician": "I have left Act I, for involution / and Act II. There mired in complexity / I cannot write Act III."

But he was a personality. Whether he was in a committee room or on the Senate floor, observed David Burke, his younger brother's chief aide, "you always had the feeling that Robert was ready to explode. Something was going to happen. Watch out! There was always tension, electricity around him."[91] The Senate generally accepted him as sui generis. "When he went after something," said Javits, "he went after it with perseverance and doggedness, and again that quality of aloneness, but of distinction and of passion. . . . He was a very effective speaker . . . and rough-and-tumble debater." Asked whether any of their colleagues hated Kennedy, Javits said, "They feared him. They thought he was a dangerous opponent, or they had a certain reverence about him and his history, or they were fascinated by the loner aspect of him and his boldness and something of a touch of arrogance because of his boldness. But I was not conscious of anybody hating him."[92] One senator complained to a committee chairman that Kennedy was getting preferential treatment for a freshman. "Oh, no," was the reply. "I treat him the same way I'd treat any future President."[93]

VIII

Late in his first session he found himself drawn into a piece of unfinished family business. This was the problem John Kennedy had so long postponed, the only thing his father had ever asked of him, the appointment of the old retainer Francis X. Morrissey to the federal district court in Massachusetts. Morrissey's qualifications were no more apparent in 1965 than they had been in 1961. But, with their father hopelessly disabled, his last request hung on his sons' consciences. Lyndon Johnson seemed surprisingly cooperative. "Before I leave the Department of Justice," Robert Kennedy wrote him on the eve of his resignation, "I want to express to you my appreciation for your statement that, at an appropriate time, you would give sympathetic consideration to Frank Morrissey for appointment to the United States District Court. . . . He bears an excellent reputation as to character and integrity, has judicial temperament, and is, I believe, worthy of appointment."[94] Perhaps, in a spirit of filial piety, Robert Kennedy persuaded himself of this. But Johnson must have noted that the Attorney General had not fought for the appointment himself.

Edward Kennedy now took the initiative. Morrissey and his wife, he explained later, were "very insistent." He added, "My father was sick, . . . and I simply felt it was something that had to be put forward."[95] At least for the family record: he may not have supposed Johnson would act on his request. Then, with what can only be assumed as unrestrained internal glee, Johnson sent Morrissey's name to the Senate. Robert Kennedy was dumbfounded. "I don't believe it," he told Milton Gwirtzman of his brother's staff. "Johnson's just nominated Frank Morrissey."[96] Johnson's theory was plain enough. The Kennedys would suffer the obloquy for the nomination; further, it would place them under obligation to him while at the same time exposing their own pious pretensions. Taking no chances, the President called J. Edgar Hoover and directed him to make the most complete investigation of Morrissey; "I don't want him to get that judgeship."[97]

The nomination was greeted with universal disapproval. The *New York Herald Tribune* called it "nauseous." In Boston Judge Charles Wyzanski, who was presiding judge of the district bench, the *Boston Globe* and the respectable bar denounced it.[98] Faced with a fight, Edward Kennedy set out to win it. He was also exasperated by what seemed to him establishment snobbery toward a poor Irish lad who had not been able to afford an Ivy League law school. For a time he appeared to be succeeding. The Judiciary Committee, if with nearly half its members abstaining, sent the nomination to the floor. But Morrissey's own testimony had shown troubling discrepancies in his account of his legal education—discrepancies soon widened by the investigative reporting of the *Boston Globe*. Senator Dirksen now resolved to make Morrissey a major issue. Senator Tydings, a Kennedy friend but also a guardian of the judiciary, told the Kennedys he would have to vote against confirmation.

Tydings's defection on top of Dirksen's opposition doomed Morrissey. Tydings was plainly right on the principle. But the Kennedys, especially Robert, were bitter. "They could understand my not voting for him," Tydings said later, "but they couldn't understand my actually opposing him."[99] Tydings, after all, was a Hickory Hill familiar. Robert Kennedy had made him a federal attorney and helped him become a senator. He had violated the Kennedy loyalty system.

In his way Morrissey was violating it too—by insisting on the fight in face of the mounting embarrassment he was causing his patrons. It had been mainly Edward's problem so far, but Robert now became more involved. After counting the votes, the brothers saw they could not win and decided to send the nomination back to the Judiciary Committee. Gwirtzman asked, "How about your commitment to

Frank Morrissey?" Robert Kennedy said, "I think we've more than fulfilled our commitment to Frank Morrissey."[100] On October 21, 1965, in an emotional speech, Edward Kennedy defended Morrissey but at the same time moved the nomination's recommitment. A few weeks later Morrissey asked that his name be withdrawn. The only winner in this fracas was Lyndon Johnson.*

IX

The Morrissey episode was typical of the relations between Johnson and Robert Kennedy in 1965. Neither wished an open break. When either sought to embarrass the other, it was done under the cloak of solicitude. Mostly each wanted to keep out of the other's way. They indulged in public praise and private propitiation.

Dear Mr. President,
    You were most courteous to me today at the signing of the Voting Bill—
    I wanted you to know how much I appreciate your thoughtfulness.
                                        Respectfully,
                                        Bob Kennedy
                                        [August 17, 1965]

Dear Bob:
    Lady Bird and I join in congratulating you on this, your first birthday in Congress. We hope that this and every day that follows will bring you happiness. . . .
                                        [November 20, 1965]

Dear Bob:
    The celebration of Christmas is a holy time, a time of renewal and hope. It is a time for families and friends, neighbors and colleagues to join in the goodness of God. . . . I could not let this Christmas pass without telling you that Mrs. Johnson, my daughters, and I ask God's blessings on you and yours.
                                        [December 20, 1965][101]

Johnson took due precautions within the frame of the armed truce. He saw Kennedy as his only rival within the party and naturally wanted to weaken him as much as possible short of open provocation. He began by insisting on his old friend Edwin Weisl for New

* Also the *Boston Globe,* which received a Pulitzer Prize for its work. Robert Kennedy was at the fiftieth anniversary dinner, where the award was made. When the *Globe* was announced, "those sitting close to Bobby's front-and-center table could not resist stealing furtive looks to catch his reaction. As the scroll was being handed over, Bobby bowed his head, turned toward his dinner companion and, with a boyish grin, winked broadly" (Penn Kimball, *Bobby Kennedy and the New Politics* [Englewood Cliffs, N.J., 1968], 139).

York's national committeeman. He did this without consulting Kennedy, who soon rejoiced to discover that Weisl was not even a registered Democrat. Still Weisl rather than Kennedy controlled federal appointments in New York. "Lyndon Johnson did not extend the courtesy of advice and consent to Robert Kennedy," said Dolan. ". . . They used to whiz them by us all the time."[102] Kennedy sponsorship was in fact a handicap. When, for example, Walter Mansfield was up for a district judgeship, Ramsey Clark, as Attorney General, reassured Marvin Watson, Johnson's political operative, with Weisl's denial that Mansfield "was in any way close to Senator Kennedy."[103] The administration actually favored Javits over Kennedy. "The White House was not too anxious to build him up," Javits recalled in considerable understatement, "and we had many indications of that. . . . I think the White House was rather interested in dealing with me all they could."[104] In his determination to weaken the New York party, Johnson even repudiated an agreement made by John Kennedy under which half the Democratic money raised in New York was returned to the state. "You don't seem to understand," Johnson said coldly when Robert Kennedy reminded him of the agreement. "That was a different President."[105]

Johnson was equally concerned with blocking a Kennedy fifth column in Washington. Vice President Humphrey's right-hand man wrote Marvin Watson about an ambassadorial nomination, mysteriously delayed: "He is a Johnson man. He is *not* a Kennedy man. . . . Once again, if anyone has informed you that Rivkin is an RFK man, you were wrongly informed."* When Roger Wilkins was named director of the Community Relations Service, he wanted his commission to read "from New York" so that Kennedy would introduce him to the Senate committee passing on his nomination. The White House insisted on "from the District of Columbia." Johnson, Wilkins said, "just didn't want Bob Kennedy up there getting the credit. . . . The President was really annoyed at my swearing in and he wouldn't talk to me! Just wouldn't talk to me! . . . Never responded to anything I said to him. Nothing! Just gave me the silent treatment. . . . The President later sent a message to me through [Thurgood Marshall, now Solicitor General]. It said, you'd better get on the straight and narrow."[106]

Johnson could do nothing—nor did he try to do anything—about

* William Connell to Marvin Watson, June 2, 1965. William Rivkin, an able Chicago lawyer, had served as ambassador to Luxembourg in the Kennedy administration. He had close ties to Humphrey and warm relations with Robert Kennedy.

McNamara, Harriman, Goodwin and others with an established Kennedy relationship. But his own people knew the eyes of Texas were on them if they spent the evening at Hickory Hill. Moyers and Valenti were particular offenders. Nor were senators exempt. Once, when Fred Harris and his wife were at Hyannis Port, the phone rang during dinner. Ethel, answering, said, "It's President Johnson for you, Fred. He's found you, and you're in big trouble now." Johnson chatted inconsequentially with Harris: "He had wanted nothing in particular," Harris reflected, "except, I figured, to let me know he knew where I was." Later Johnson informed Harris through an Oklahoma oil magnate that "he could do a lot more for you if you weren't so close to those Kennedys."[107]

X

Kennedy took care to respect the armed truce. He was well aware of the widespread impression that he regarded the White House as Kennedy property and Johnson as a usurper. He read every week that he was, in the words of hostile columnists, "high-handed, ruthless, power-grabbing and consumed by an inordinate White House ambition."[108] He recognized that the press was building the Johnson-Kennedy "feud" as the great human drama of Washington.

Nothing inhibited Kennedy more than the conviction that policy disagreements with Johnson would be inexorably attributed to a personal vendetta. "A lot of what Kennedy said honestly in those days," Walter Mondale recalled, "was dismissed by the press on the grounds that it was politically motivated, that he was trying to get Johnson."[109] "He would hold back in regard to criticism of the President," said Fred Harris. ". . . He was afraid that that would appear to be political . . . that he was speaking out against Johnson out of either personal political ambition or unreasonable animosity."[110] "I think he bent over backwards," said O'Donnell, "to try to give the President whatever benefit there was."[111]

He was circumspect even with his closest senatorial colleagues and his own staff. "I never found Bob Kennedy badmouthing Johnson," said George McGovern.[112] "I don't ever recall the Senator talking in personal terms of the President," said his first press secretary. ". . . I heard him rebuke Walinsky for saying something about 'Lyndon' rather uncomplimentary. You know, it was just simply, 'OK, Adam, that's enough. That'll be enough of that.' So he didn't tolerate it."[113] Before the spring of 1967, said his second press secretary, "I never heard him say anything derogatory about the President."[114] But circumspection did not destroy his feelings. He saw Johnson more than ever as a formidable but flawed man, powerful and dangerous. The President, he confided to Barrett Prettyman, "does not know how to use people's talents, to find the very best in them and put the best to work. But more than any other man, he knows how to ferret out and use people's weaknesses."*

He vigorously supported Johnson's Great Society. Privately he resented the popular explanations of Johnson's legislative success. The Goldwater debacle in 1964 had given Johnson nearly 40 new Democrats in the House. This made him the first Democratic President since Roosevelt before 1938 with a working progressive majority in Congress. The result was the dazzling legislative record of 1965–66. The newspapers ascribed the result not to parliamentary arithmetic but to presidential genius and contrasted his accomplishments with his predecessor's failures.† Such comment wounded Kennedy. Congressman Donald Riegle of Michigan, watching Kennedy when the President addressed joint sessions of Congress, recalled that he "seldom clapped; he just seemed to smolder."[115]

He thanked heaven every day, he told me, that the Vice Presidency had fallen through; "it would have been a miserable and hopeless relationship, and nothing but trouble could have come from it."[116] The new life was certainly not boring. "Since you left home," he wrote Anthony Lewis, now head of the *New York Times*'s London bureau,

> I have become a beloved figure. The *New York Times,* the liberals in New York City, ~~Lyndon Johnson~~ all like me. . . . There have been a few black clouds overhead on occasion. Last week at various hearings on mini-

* Handwritten notes, September 1965, Prettyman Papers. Johnson once said to Nancy Dickerson, "I'm just like a fox: I can see the jugular in any man and go for it. . . . I keep myself on a leash, just as you would an animal" (Nancy Dickerson, *Among Those Present* [New York: Ballantine reprint, 1976], 177).

† Johnson did work harder than John Kennedy at congressional cajolery, bargaining and arm-twisting. But, when Johnson lost 48 Democratic House seats in the 1966 election, he found himself, despite his alleged wizardry, in the same condition of stalemate that had thwarted Kennedy and, indeed, every Democratic President since 1938. Had the sequence been different, had Johnson been elected to the Presidency in 1960 with Kennedy as his Vice President, and had Johnson then offered the 87th Congress the same program actually offered by Kennedy, the probability is that he would have had no more success than Kennedy—perhaps even less because he appealed less effectively to public opinion. And, if Johnson had died in 1963 and Kennedy had beaten Goldwater by a large margin in 1964, then Kennedy would have had those extra votes in the House of Representatives, and the pundits of the press would have contrasted his cool management of Congress with the frenetic and bumbling efforts of his predecessor. In the end, arithmetic is decisive.

mum wage, migrant workers and car safety I had slight altercations with
the President of the National Association of Manufacturers—the head of
the Chamber of Commerce—the head of the Farm Bureau—the President
of the G.M. [General Motors] Corporation ($500,000 salary), the chair-
man of the board of GM ($650,000 or perhaps it is vice versa) and the
President of the Chrysler Corporation.[117]

"I didn't really want to be a Senator," Kennedy told an English journalist in 1967, "but I like it more than I expected to."[118]

30

The Foreign Policy Breach:
Latin America

ROBERT KENNEDY'S FIRST POLICY disagreements with the Johnson administration arose in foreign affairs. He watched the evolution of Latin American policy with alarm. The snuffing out of negotiations with Castro, the Thomas Mann appointment and the controversies over Panama and Cuba were followed in April 1964 by a generals' coup against the Goulart regime in Brazil. Kennedy had no use for Goulart. But he thought that Johnson embraced the new military dictatorship with unbecoming alacrity. He was still in the cabinet, however, if now shut out of foreign policy, and he held his peace.

I

The Alliance for Progress, in the hands of Johnson and Mann, was undergoing a basic transformation—so much so that the historian must talk of two Alliances for Progress. Another program by the same name now struggled on after the political and social components of Kennedy's Alliance—i.e., its heart—had been removed. With the coming of Mann, wrote William D. Rogers, who stayed on as the Alliance's deputy administrator till 1965, "a more dramatic shift in tone and style of U.S. Alliance leadership would have been difficult to imagine."[1]

Mann took over at a propitious time for eviscerating the Alliance. In 1961–63 the fear of Castro had given urgency and legitimacy to pressure from Washington for social change. When this fear diminished—as it had after the missile crisis and after the success of counterinsurgency in Venezuela—interest in social change diminished too. This encouraged Mann to liquidate two of the three goals of Kennedy's Alliance—structural reform and political democratization—and to convert much of what remained into an instrumentality for

North American corporations. "Not until Tom Mann came back in 1964," said Alphonse de Rosso of Standard Oil of New Jersey, "did the business community feel that it was 'in' again with the United States government."[2] So Mann suspended virtually all aid to Peru in an effort to force the democratic, pro-Alliance Belaunde government to come to terms with the International Petroleum Company, a Standard Oil of New Jersey subsidiary.

John Kennedy, said Teodoro Moscoso, the Alliance's first chief in February 1965, had "stood for change—revolutionary change—and he said so even when it hurt in exalted places. . . . Do we remember [now] that there is a revolution going on?"[3] "The Alliance for Progress is dead," wrote the caustic Mexican Victor Alba. "What is left is a bureaucratic structure, mountains of mimeographed paper, a sarcastic smile on the lips of the oligarchs, and pangs of guilt on the part of the politicians of the left who did not take advantage of the Alliance and make it theirs."[4] "The Alliance for Progress, deprived of its leader," wrote Juscelino Kubitschek of Brazil, whose Operation Pan America had been one of the Alliance's inspirations, "foundered on a series of acronyms as useless as they were pompous."[5] The "vitality and spirit" with which John Kennedy had imbued the Alliance, said Juan Bosch of the Dominican Republic, "died with him in Dallas."[6]

II

In the Senate, Robert Kennedy continued to watch in silence. As usual, he doubted that criticism of Johnson would be received on its merits. Then, on April 24, 1965, came an uprising in the Dominican Republic. The target was the ineffectual authoritarian regime installed by the Dominican military in September 1963 after the overthrow of Bosch's ineffectual democratic regime. The rebels were a mixed group of Boschists, disgruntled officers and romantic leftists. A panic-stricken American ambassador in Santo Domingo sent out hysterical cables about bloodbaths and the capture of the revolt by the Communists. An inexperienced CIA director in Washington, seven hours in office and zealous to prove his anti-Communist credentials, relayed unverified messages from secret operatives in Santo Domingo about decapitations in the streets and provided dubious lists of the Dominican Communists who were supposedly taking everything over. Johnson sent in 22,000 American troops. He did this with minimal attention to the Organization of American States, an institution of which he once said, "It couldn't pour piss out of a boot if the instructions were written on the heel."[7]

I was in Buffalo at the end of a lecture tour on April 30 when Bill Moyers tracked me down and asked me to come at once to Washington. On my arrival, Moyers said that Harriman and Moscoso had gone to various capitals in Latin America to explain the United States intervention; would I do the same in Costa Rica and other Central American countries? Briefed to the teeth by the CIA and foolishly believing its absurd reports, I agreed to go. Then I discovered that Romulo Betancourt was in Washington. I strongly urged on Moyers and Bundy that Johnson call in Betancourt at once. Johnson refused, though in a rambling television speech the next day he erroneously cited Betancourt as a supporter of American intervention.

Since no one in the White House, given their master's attitude, would talk to Betancourt, I decided to see him myself. Ever since Trujillo had sent his thugs to kill Betancourt, the Venezuelans had maintained a top-flight intelligence operation in the Dominican Republic. To my astonishment, I found Venezuelan intelligence entirely skeptical of the CIA thesis. Betancourt told me he had every confidence that the United States could work with the non-Communist leaders among the rebels and swiftly isolate the few Communists.[8] I begged off the Central American mission.

I had several talks during this time with Kennedy. He thought the American military intervention an "outrage" and asked me to put something on paper for him. On May 6 he warned the Senate that the determination to stop Communist revolution in the hemisphere "must not be construed as opposition to popular uprisings against injustice and oppression just because the targets of such popular uprisings say they are Communist-inspired." He criticized the policy of driving "the genuine democrats in the Dominican revolution into association with the Communists by blanket characterizations and condemnations" and called for assurances to "all honest Dominican democrats, including those who took part in the revolution," of a future role in their country. In no case, he added, should the United States "act on our own without regard to our friends and allies in the Organization of American states." Some might dismiss the OAS as weak. "One way to make it stronger is to use it."[9]

The Dominican affair provoked bitter criticism throughout Latin America. In the United States, apprehension spilled over to Johnson's foreign policy in general. "When I consider what the administration did in the Dominican Republic," Adlai Stevenson told me—it was our last talk before he died in July—"I begin to wonder if we know what we are doing in Vietnam." Reluctant as he was to praise John Kennedy, Stevenson nonetheless contrasted Johnson's impulsive and extreme reaction with the methodical exploration of alternatives during the missile crisis.[10] One began to wonder whether Johnson understood the uses of power. John Kennedy had always tried to match threat and response. Johnson, it appeared, was the aficionado of overkill in foreign as well as in personal relations. In any event, the Dominican intervention irretrievably shattered his foreign policy consensus.

III

On June 23, 1965, Robert Kennedy made his formal maiden speech in the Senate. He chose the subject that had most consumed his brother in the last year of his life—the spread of nuclear weapons. This, "not Vietnam, or the Dominican Republic," Kennedy said, was "the most vital issue now facing this Nation and the world." Should nuclear weapons become generally available, the planet would be at the mercy of irresponsible military commanders, internal dissidents, anonymous madmen. Every passing crisis "might well become the last crisis for all mankind." He called on the American government to extend the test ban treaty of 1963 to underground tests and to seek a new treaty covering nonproliferation. Both superpowers must set an example to mankind by cutting back their own nuclear forces or, at the minimum, by freezing these forces at their present level. He also said that "we should vigorously pursue negotiations on this subject with China," then regarded as the most fanatic of Marxist states.[11]

Seventeen senators rose to praise his remarks. The White House restrained its enthusiasm. The speech, though not expressly critical of the administration, was filled with somber quotations from John F. Kennedy about nuclear proliferation and carried the inescapable implication that Johnson was not doing enough to stop it. Johnson was so annoyed that he struck the disarmament proposals from his own pending address to the United Nations lest someone think he was following Robert Kennedy's lead.[12]

The nuclear proliferation speech deepened mutual suspicions over foreign policy. But Latin America especially nagged at Kennedy. He had been there only once—the overnight mission to Goulart in 1962—since the jaunt with Lem Billings after his discharge from the

Navy in 1946. Receiving an invitation to speak in Brazil, he decided to take advantage of the November recess and revisit the subcontinent. In September Jack Valenti asked Johnson for guidance about the Kennedy trip. Jack Hood Vaughn had become assistant secretary for inter-American affairs when in 1965 Mann was promoted to the more powerful job of under secretary for economic affairs; and Bundy had proposed that he brief Kennedy. "Vaughn's question to me," Valenti wrote the President: "Should he discourage Kennedy from going to Argentina, Chile and Venezuela? And what kind of briefing should he give Kennedy?"[13]

Johnson's answer can be safely surmised. When Kennedy arrived for the briefing, he and Walinsky were placed on one side of a long table. The State Department people all sat on the other side. It had the aspect of an adversary proceeding from the start. Vaughn, ordinarily affable, was in an extraordinarily aggressive mood. "The only thing I could think of," said Frank Mankiewicz, who represented the Peace Corps at the briefing, "was that someone had given him orders to be just as hostile and bitter as he could." Kennedy began by wondering what he should say about the Dominican intervention. Vaughn said, "In the first place, nobody will ask you about it because they don't care about that issue. No one asks about that any more." Kennedy said, "Well, you and I don't talk to the same Latins because that's all they ever ask me." He offered to bet that it would be one of his first three questions in Latin America. Vaughn took the bet, adding, "If they *do* ask you, you can always tell them what your brother said about Cuba." "At that," noted Walinsky, ". . . that look comes over Robert Kennedy's face. . . . Those eyes would just go dead flat cold. I mean it was enough to wither tree branches a hundred miles away." Kennedy said frigidly, "What in particular were you suggesting?" Vaughn, after fumbling a moment, mentioned the statement that the United States would not tolerate communism in the western hemisphere. Robert Kennedy said softly, "I just hope you're not using anything that President Kennedy ever said to justify what you did in the Dominican Republic . . . because you know I opposed that."

Despite the withering look, Vaughn persisted in referring to President Kennedy as "your brother." At one point he said that the United States was in trouble in Peru because "your brother" had suspended relations after the military coup in 1963; "we'll never do that again while I'm Assistant Secretary." Kennedy said he thought it was a good thing to have done. Mankiewicz, who had been Peace Corps director in Peru at the time, agreed. The talk turned to the International Petroleum Company dispute. Kennedy questioned the punitive suspension of aid to a democratic regime. "Why," he asked, "should the [American] government get into a contest between the Peruvian government and a private American oil company?" Vaughn defended the oil company.

They moved on. Kennedy said, "What can I say in Brazil, where they've outlawed political parties and closed down the congress and are denying people their rights and so forth?" A Brazil desk officer read off a prepared statement in departmentese expressing regret that a great power had seen fit to curtail certain freedoms temporarily, etc. Kennedy cut him off, saying, "I don't talk like that." Vaughn said, "Well, why don't you just say nothing?" Kennedy said, "Are you kidding?"

"Well, Mr. Vaughn," Kennedy summed up, "let me get this straight. You're saying that what the Alliance for Progress has come down to is that if you have a military takeover, outlaw political parties, close down the congress, put your political opponents in jail, and take away the basic freedoms of the people, you can get all the American aid you want. But, if you mess around with an American oil company, we'll cut you off without a penny. Is that right? Is that what the Alliance for Progress comes down to?" Vaughn said, "That's about the size of it."[14]

IV

The Kennedy party left Miami for Lima on November 10, 1965. Ethel and Angie Novello came along, as did Walinsky, Richard Goodwin, John Seigenthaler, Thomas Johnston, head of Kennedy's New York City office, and assorted friends and reporters. William and Jean vanden Heuvel joined the group in Peru.

The embassy in Lima had wanted Kennedy to go to bullfights, American-owned factories and a white-tie reception for the King of Belgium. "Robert F. Kennedy doesn't even own a white tie," John Nolan, who scheduled the trip, had told them.[15] They now evaded the embassy cordon. Kennedy's first meeting, with university students, struck the keynote. "The responsibility of our time," he told them, "is nothing less than a revolution"—a revolution that would be "peaceful if we are wise enough; humane if we care enough; successful if we are fortunate enough. But a revolution will come whether we will it or not. We can affect its character; we cannot alter its inevitability."[16] The third question from the audience dealt with the Dominican Republic. Kennedy cabled Vaughn: YOU LOSE THE BET.

The questioners went on about American imperialism. Kennedy said that there had been too much American aid to right-wing regimes but pointed out that left-wing countries—Yugoslavia, Poland, Ghana—had received aid too. It was too easy to make the Yankees the universal alibi. "You are the Peruvian leaders of the future. If you think the Alliance for Progress is imperialistic, then don't join it. . . . You have to decide what is in your interests. If you object to American aid, have the courage to say so. But you are not going to solve your problems by blaming the United States and avoiding your own personal responsibility to do something about them."[17]

This theme was on his mind when he met a group of Peruvian intellectuals at the house of the artist Fernando Seizlo. It reminded Tom Johnston of a meeting of reform Democrats on the West Side of Manhattan. To Kennedy's irritation, they showed no concern about their own problems—the *barriadas* of Lima or the desperately poor Andean Indians—but complained endlessly about American imperialism and the International Petroleum Company. Kennedy finally said, "Well, why don't you just go ahead and nationalize the damn thing. I mean nothing's going to happen. . . . The United States government isn't going to send destroyers or anything like that. Why don't you just do it?" They were appalled; the Rockefellers ran United States policy; the Rockefellers wouldn't permit it. "Oh, come on," said Kennedy. "In our country we eat Rockefellers for breakfast."[18] A thoughtful guest had hidden a tape recorder under a couch, and a few days later a popular Peruvian magazine put the Rockefeller crack in a headline. A reporter in Buenos Aires asked Kennedy later whether it was true that he had breakfast every morning with the Rockefellers.[19]

At Cuzco a crowd of two thousand burst through a barbed-wire fence to greet him. Kennedy cut his right cheek in the melee but declined a tetanus shot and wore a ripped suit for the rest of the day. He talked to Indians and Peace Corps volunteers and on November 13 flew to Chile, to be inundated by more crowds and more headlines. His old friend Ralph Dungan was now American ambassador. They relaxed in Dungan's residence for a few hours. It was the first day on the trip, someone noted, that Kennedy had failed to visit a slum.[20]

He had luncheon and a meeting of minds the next day with Eduardo Frei, the Christian Democratic President of Chile and, along with Betancourt, the emblem of the Latin American democratic left. The day after, he went to Concepción, Chile's third largest city and a center of Communist enthusiasm. Marxist students at the university threatened a mass protest. A delegation called at his hotel. "Will you disrupt the meeting if I come?" he asked. The student leader said, "We do not condemn you personally, but as a representative of a government whose hands are stained with blood. If it was up to me, I would not let you speak."

"You describe me with blood all over my hands," Kennedy responded. "I haven't eaten you up since I have been here. I haven't had a marine stick a bayonet in you. . . . The greatest indictment of your position is that you won't let me speak. I think it is a self-confession of the error of your position." He proposed a deal: "I would speak, one of your people would speak, and then I will answer questions. If I don't answer the questions satisfactorily, then, hell, your position is much stronger. Aren't you confident? You don't sound it."[21]

After the students left, Seigenthaler and vanden Heuvel advised Kennedy not to go. Universities were off limits to police by Latin American tradition, and the rector could not guarantee Kennedy's safety. Then two Christian Democratic students knocked on the door. "If you don't come," one said, "it will be a great victory for the Communists." This made up Kennedy's mind. That night he entered a gymnasium packed with students screaming "Kennedy–paredón" ("to the wall") and throwing eggs and garbage. "It was really a frightening goddamned thing," said Martin Arnold of the *New York Times*.[22] Eggs splattered over vanden Heuvel and others, but Kennedy walked along, never looking back, and was untouched. "If these kids are going to be young revolutionaries," he muttered to Seigenthaler, "they're going to have to improve their aim."[23]

He tried to make himself heard from the platform. After a moment he challenged the Marxists to debate; "Will you test your ideas before the students of this university?" Even as they shouted "Kennedy–paredón," some had leaned across the rails to shake his hand; and now he went toward them and shook hands with the Marxist leader he had met in the afternoon. Another student spat in his face. The leader grabbed the spitter by his shirt and pulled him away. The pandemonium continued. Finally Kennedy left to a thunderous ovation. They went to bed well after midnight. At 4:00 A.M. vanden Heuvel roused the party: "Come on, the senator wants to go to the coal mines."[24]

The miners' union was solidly Communist. The embassy had kept the mine off Kennedy's schedule, and mine officials now begged him not to go down the shaft. He went anyway. "All these coal miners were wild to see him," said Arnold. "It was a miserable dank place with water dropping off and dust coming in. A terrible place! We went to the end of the shaft. It was a mile or two out into the ocean."[25] "If I worked in this mine," Kennedy told an American reporter, "I'd be a Communist too."[26]

He flew the next morning to Argentina for a frenzied forty-eight hours. Over a thousand people awaited him at the airport.[27] Harry Hopkins's son Robert, a Buenos Aires businessman, wrote me later: "Even some of the most fanatic nationalists were won over by his enthusiasm, his desire to understand Argentine problems, his frank answers to provocative questions, his concept of U.S. policy towards Latin America and by his youth. By going straight to the people, he created a surge of pro-U.S. sentiment. . . . If he were an Argentine, he could be elected President of Argentina tomorrow."[28]

On November 20 they left for Brazil. It was his fortieth birthday. Ethel had arranged a party at the São Paulo house of Mildred Sage, who was handling the Brazil schedule. There were the usual birthday poems, skits and jokes. Displaying a toy airplane, Ethel explained that it was a U-2 sent by Lyndon Johnson to report on Bobby's activities. Someone began pulling the ends of party favors to make them explode. The series of quick bangs suddenly sounded like shots. Kennedy sunk his head in his hands and said, "Oh, no. . . . Please don't."[29] On November 22, two years after Dallas, they went to mass in Bahía—"that gorgeous church with all the gold over it in that poor little town," Angie Novello remembered it; ". . . and then the first place he headed for was the *barriada* . . . and all the mud"[30]— mud and open sewers and steaming heat and a stench so vile that it drove the Brazilian security police to refuge in their car. He gathered barefoot children around him in a forlorn community center named for John Kennedy. "President Kennedy was most fond of children," he said. "Can I ask you to do a favor for him? Stay in school, study hard, study as long as you can, and then work for your city and Brazil."[31] On the plane north he sat by himself, his head buried in his arms.[32]

More than a hundred thousand people turned out later in the day in Natal. Exhilarated, he leaped to the top of the truck and shouted to the crowd: "Every child an education! Every family adequate housing! Every man a job!" They spent the night at Recife, in the heart of the horribly poor northeast, and the next morning walked the sugar cane fields where cutters worked for less than a dollar a day. Discovering that the wage was below the legal level, Kennedy became a zealous advocate of the Brazilian minimum wage law. "You're breeding your own destruction," he told a landowner, ". . . if you don't pay people a decent wage."[33] At a university, they asked him about civil rights. Politely challenging the Brazilian myth of racial equality, Kennedy said, "I don't see many dark-skinned faces in this audience."[34]

The party had reached Brazil in a state of exhaustion. Kennedy sent John Nolan a cable: NEXT TIME I SCHEDULE YOU.[35] Some of his entourage appeared petulant and highhanded. They did not like the military regime anyway and were not minding their manners. Mildred Sage found Kennedy himself, however weary, entirely cooperative. He was always considerate in the *favelas* and sugar fields. Fatigue showed when he encountered the establishment. He lectured business leaders, argued angrily with Roberto Campos at the American embassy and harassed Castello Branco, the military President, about the minimum wage. Fatigue showed in other ways. Sitting in a café in front of a Rio hotel on November 24, he heard the crackle of shots. He jumped from his seat, then realized it was the backfire of a car. "Sooner or later," he told Mildred Sage. "Sooner or later."[36]

Goodwin advocated a weekend in the jungle for relaxation. They flew to Manaus, deep in the interior, where they made their way up the Amazon in a paddle-wheel steamboat. Determined to go even farther, Kennedy boarded an ancient single-engine seaplane. Kissing Ethel goodbye, he said, "I must be crazy to get on this thing." An interlude of reckless adventure and misadventure culminated in a dash down foaming rapids in a dugout canoe and swims in piranha-infested waters. "Piranhas," Kennedy said philosophically, "have never been known to bite a U.S. senator."[37] There followed two busy days in Caracas. At the end of the month they were back in Washington.

V

An unsigned report to Lyndon Johnson from an American in Latin America speculated that Kennedy's trip was meant to launch his campaign for the Presidency.

> Without actually saying so, he disassociated himself from the Johnson Administration. He portrays himself as the complete liberal. His inference was that Johnson is an old-guard imperialist whose administration is una-

ware of South American problems. . . . Embassy aides in the countries he visited shuddered at some of the things he said and did. Nevertheless they waited on him hand and foot. . . . The newsmen traveling with him from the New York Times, Herald-Tribune, etc., appeared to be under his spell. . . . Americans closest to the scene . . . resented the way he and the group acted. They were cocky and overbearing and made themselves as much at home as if they were in Massachusetts.[38]

One of the accompanying newspapermen, evidently not fully under Kennedy's spell, described the trip in the *Saturday Evening Post* under the title "The Compulsive Candidate" with the subtitle: "Robert Kennedy Runs for President Every Day."[39] Many found it hard to explain his intervention in the domestic problems of Latin America on other grounds. The theory that he had gone south in order to dish Lyndon Johnson was one more expression of the reductionism that so exasperated Kennedy in these years. In fact, Martin Arnold said, "he did a good job for President Johnson, really, in the sense that he used to tell these people that Lyndon Johnson had come from the soil and that he would understand their type of problems. He was very good that way, even though the two men obviously hated each other."[40] When Castello Branco of Brazil, after enduring Kennedy's complaints about the poverty in the northeast, inquired into the purpose of his trip, Kennedy answered slowly that his only political ambition was reelection to the Senate; Johnson would be the Democratic candidate in 1968. "My brother," he finally said, "cared enormously about Latin America. So I came to get myself educated."[41]

The sense of legacy was the essential reason. His hope was to remind the Latin Americans that there was more to the United States than the International Petroleum Company. In this he was successful. Kennedy, wrote Paulo de Castro in *Correio da Manha* of Rio, was

the other face of America, the liberal face, which believes in democracy and does not profess the dogma of the West's salvation through the militaristic state, by interventions and the eternity of the oligarchies. . . . Robert Kennedy came to revive the message of liberal revolution that made the United States an exemplary nation, a revolution forgotten by those that today intend to transform a great democratic country into a protector of tyrannies.[42]

Kennedy believed in the American liberal revolution. He felt an obligation to do what one man could to help defenseless people in other parts of the world. He was doing this as an individual, not as a government. He did not in the end suppose it could be done by governments; certainly not by intervention in the Dominican fashion. After all, as Walinsky said, he was "a man who had had several years of experience in trying to affect conditions in a place like Mississippi but not to do it simply by moving in the fiat of the federal government." His idea was to help awaken the people and enlighten the oligarchies in the hope that countries might be moved to solve their own problems. It was a quixotic venture uncommon in history, a premonition perhaps of the world society someday to come. The Latin American trip, the response of the students, the outpouring of crowds, strengthened the feeling that it might be possible to rouse other countries to humanize their policies. "You may think that's a great act of hubris," said Walinsky, "but, indeed, he had the potential to do it and to some degree he probably did."[43]

He hoped even more to humanize the policy of his own country. The big problem, he said on *Meet the Press* the week after his return, was the impression in Latin America that "business determines the internal policy of the United States." The related problem was indiscriminate anticommunism. "If all we do . . . is to associate ourselves with those forces which are against subversion and against Communism . . . then I think it is self-defeating and will be catastrophic."[44] Such talk was not always appreciated. "What we need to preach in Latin America to those young radicals," said one business leader, "is an acceptance of the free-enterprise system and a respect for property rights. And we can't do it if Bobby Kennedy is going down there and upsetting everything we've been saying."[45]

He set to work on a speech designed to recall the Alliance to its original purposes. Walinsky was the main draftsman. Frank Mankiewicz helped too; and, when Barthelmes left the Kennedy office in the spring of 1966, Mankiewicz replaced him. Son of the Herman Mankiewicz who had written *Citizen Kane* and nephew of Joseph L. Mankiewicz, author and director of other notable films, he sprang from an alert and witty tradition and quickly became an intimate. ("Don't worry about Mankiewicz's finances," Bill Moyers wrote Kennedy from the White House. "I have arranged [for] CIA to pay half his salary since he will be working for me part-time.")[46]

Kennedy gave the speech in the Senate on May 9 and 10, 1966. There could be, he said, "no preservation of the status quo in Latin America." The Alliance had been "a pledge of revolutionary change." It proposed an end to the "closed society, a society which reserves all wealth and power and privilege for the same classes, the same families, which have held that wealth and power for the last 300 years." Reform ought to be "a condition of full participation in the Alliance. . . . Aid should not be withheld to force special advantages for U.S. business." As for the threat of communism, "Batista, not Castro," Kennedy said, "was the major cause of communism in Latin America. . . . If we allow communism to carry the banner of reform, then the ignored and the dispossessed, the insulted and injured, will turn to it as the only way out of their misery." He summed up: "There is a revolution now going on down there, and we must identify ourselves with that revolution."[47]

Nothing could have been further from the mood of Washington in the middle sixties with a Latin American policy responsive to American corporations and a President increasingly obsessed with the war in Indochina.

(31)

Vietnam Legacy

WHEN JOHN AND ROBERT KENNEDY visited Vietnam in 1951, they had been greatly "impressed," Robert recalled in 1964, by "the toughness of the French soldiers. A lot of them were Foreign Legion and paratroopers . . . and they had several hundreds of thousands and they were beaten."[1] The memory had abided. "We saw the position the French were in," Robert told Daniel Ellsberg in 1967, "and saw what they were trying to do to the Indochinese. And my brother was determined early that we would never get into that position."[2]

I

The Geneva agreement of 1954 ended the First Indochina War. The French departed. In 1955 South Vietnam became an independent republic. The new leader in Saigon was Ngo Dinh Diem, a robust nationalist opposed to the French and Ho Chi Minh's Communists alike and sponsored in the United States by such exemplary men as William O. Douglas and Mike Mansfield. Having argued for Vietnamese nationhood, John Kennedy felt a responsibility for the new nation. "This is our offspring," he said in 1956, "—we cannot abandon it." Still, much remained to be done "in a country where concepts of free enterprise and capitalism are meaningless, where poverty and hunger are not enemies across the 17th parallel but enemies within their midst. . . . What we must offer them is a revolution—a political, economic and social revolution far superior to anything the Communists can offer."[3]

When Kennedy came to office in 1961, no revolution had been offered or undertaken. Diem had emerged as a rigid and unpopular despot. The American involvement had deepened, at least rhetorically. "The loss of South Viet-Nam," Eisenhower said in a 1959 speech, "would set in motion a crumbling process that could, as it progressed, have grave consequences for us."[4] The wary general did not, however, enlarge the American military mission in Saigon beyond the 685 advisers permitted under the Geneva agreement. His South Asian worries were directed elsewhere. In his pre-inaugural briefing of Kennedy, he ignored Vietnam and called Laos the "present key to the entire area," adding, according to Clark Clifford's record of the meeting, that "he considered Laos of such importance that if it reached the stage where we could not persuade others to act with us, then he would be willing, *'as a last desperate hope, to intervene unilaterally.'*"[5] Even more than his advice to Kennedy to plunge ahead on the Bay of Pigs, this warlike exhortation strikes a peculiar note. It is hard to believe that the canny Eisenhower would himself ever have gone it alone with American troops in Laos.

Whatever Eisenhower's motives, Kennedy had no desire to follow his advice. But he had no desire either to be denounced by the national military hero. He therefore enlisted Eisenhower's wartime friend Harold Macmillan to argue the case against intervention. "As I understand it," the British Prime Minister wrote fraternally to the former President,

> President Kennedy is under considerable pressure about "appeasement" in Laos. . . . I should however be very sorry if our two countries became involved in an open-ended commitment on this dangerous and unprofitable terrain. So I would hope that in anything which you felt it necessary to say about Laos you would not encourage those who think that a military solution in Laos is the only way of stopping the Communists in that area.[6]

The Bay of Pigs finally destroyed any possibility of military intervention in Laos. "I don't think that there is any question," Robert Kennedy noted in June,

> that if it hadn't been for Cuba, we would have sent troops to Laos. We probably would have had them destroyed. Jack has said so himself. . . . It was after Cuba that he began inquiring intimately into the situation in Laos. It was then that he found out that the Communists could send five men into Laos for every one that we sent in. That they could destroy the airports and therefore cut off our people after getting only a thousand or several thousand into Laos and that the only way really that we could win in Laos was drop the atomic bomb. . . . Therefore, in order to preserve Laos, for instance, we had to be prepared to engage in a major atomic war both with China and with Russia.[7]

After hearing the generals pursue their scenario to its apocalyptic conclusion, the President instructed Averell Harriman to negotiate the neutralization of Laos with the Russians. A year later, Harriman

told me that the President's policy was still being "systematically sab-
otaged" within the government by the military and the CIA. "They
want to prove that a neutral solution is impossible," he said, "and
that the only course is to turn Laos into an American bastion."[8] But
Harriman was tougher and shrewder than the opposition and had
Kennedy's full support. Though the neutralization accord worked out
at Geneva in July 1962 did not stop the fighting, it succeeded at least
in removing Laos from the area of great-power conflict.

II

The problem remained, as Robert Kennedy described it in 1961, of
"what we were going to do with South Viet Nam which [unlike
Laos] was willing to fight and protect itself."[9] Diem had an army of
150,000, a Civil Guard of 68,000 and a Self-Defense Corps of
40,000—more than 250,000 men in arms against an estimated 12,000
Viet Cong.* "Free world forces," the *New York Times* advised the
administration in early April, ". . . still have a chance in South Vietnam, and every effort should be made to save the situation."[10]

The President now made a de facto deal with the national security
establishment: if it went along with neutralization in Laos, he would
do something for resistance in South Vietnam. The Pentagon called
for the immediate dispatch of 3600 combat troops.[11] Kennedy, com-
promising, sent a hundred military advisers and four hundred Green
Berets. "Even so small an increase," recalled Roswell Gilpatric, head
of the Vietnam task force, "was greeted by the President with a great
deal of impatience. He showed at the very outset an aversion to sending more people out there."[12]

In late April Kennedy discovered an unexpected ally—General
Douglas MacArthur, who assured him that it would indeed be a
"mistake" to fight in Southeast Asia. "He thinks," the President dictated in a rare *aide-mémoire,* "our line should be Japan, Formosa
and the Philippines. . . . He said that the 'chickens are coming
home to roost' from Eisenhower's years and I live in the chicken
coop."† Soon Kennedy brought MacArthur to Washington to lunch

---

* "A Program of Action to Prevent Communist Domination of South Vietnam,"
May 6, 1961, Senate Foreign Relations Committee staff study, "Vietnam Commitments, 1961," 92 Cong., 2 Sess. (1972), 15–16. Substantially the same figures were
given to John Kenneth Galbraith when he was briefed by the Saigon embassy, November 19, 1961 (Galbraith, *Ambassador's Diary* [Boston, 1969], 261).

† JFK, memorandum of conversation, April 28, 1961, JFK Papers. It may be well
to mention the discussion Kennedy held a few weeks later with another mystical general. Charles de Gaulle claimed in his memoirs that Kennedy "made no secret of the
fact that the United States were planning to intervene" in Indochina and ignored de

with a group of bellicose legislators. "He said," noted the Attorney General, who was also invited, "that we would be foolish to fight on the Asiatic continent and that the future of Southeast Asia should be determined at the diplomatic table."[13] Alexis Johnson of the State Department, present too, thought MacArthur's argument "not correct and not rational. . . . Nevertheless it made a very deep impression on the President. . . . I think that for the rest of the time he was in office this view of General MacArthur's . . . tended to dominate very much the thinking of President Kennedy with respect to Southeast Asia."[14] It made, said Maxwell Taylor, "a hell of an impression on the President . . . so that whenever he'd get this military advice from the Joint Chiefs or from me or anyone else, he'd say, 'Well, now, you gentlemen, you go back and convince General MacArthur, then I'll be convinced.' But none of us undertook the task."[15]

III

In the spring of the Bay of Pigs and the summer of Berlin, Vietnam was a minor concern. For Robert Kennedy it remained so until August 1963. But because he later had to struggle with his brother's Vietnam legacy, it is essential to understand what that legacy was.

The Pentagon kept up its clamor for combat units. American troops, the President observed to Arthur Krock in October 1961, had no business on the Asian mainland; moreover, the United States should not interfere "in civil disturbances created by guerrillas." He was stalling the military, he said, by sending Maxwell Taylor and

---

Gaulle's prediction that "you will sink step by step into a bottomless military and political quagmire, however much you spend in men and money" (de Gaulle, *Memoirs of Hope: Renewal and Endeavor* [New York, 1971], 255–256).

In fact, their discussion concentrated on Laos, not on Vietnam. De Gaulle strongly supported Kennedy's proposal of a neutral government under Souvanna Phouma. The discussion of intervention arose when Kennedy said that the threat of intervention might be necessary to get Moscow to agree to neutralization. De Gaulle said more generally that Southeast Asia did not offer a good terrain for western troops or western politics, and advocated the neutralization of the entire area (see the account, based on the memoranda of conversations, in Arthur M. Schlesinger, Jr., *A Thousand Days* [Boston, 1965], 351). Ambassador James Gavin, who was present, later wrote that he was "startled" to read de Gaulle's account and that it "bore little relationship to what had been said. It all may have been on President de Gaulle's mind at the time, but it certainly was not what he said" (Gavin, reviewing David Halberstam's *The Best and the Brightest, Harper's,* December 1972).

It might be noted that on other occasions de Gaulle found it hard to resist the temptation to improve the record. Ambassador Bohlen never heard de Gaulle say, "I am not interested by anything you propose," when they met after Nassau on January 4, 1963, but the phrase appeared in de Gaulle's own minutes of the conversation (see Robert Kleiman, *Atlantic Crisis* [New York, 1964], 22).

Walt Rostow to look at South Vietnam.[16] Taylor had backed neutralization in Laos. No doubt Kennedy supposed him to be, along with
MacArthur, Matthew B. Ridgway and James Gavin, a charter
member of the Army's "never again" club on the question of an
American expeditionary force in Asia. Rostow, the high priest of
counterinsurgency, would presumably oppose the use of conventional
force in a guerrilla war. Kennedy instructed Taylor to "bear in mind"
that responsibility for "the independence of South Vietnam rests with
the people and government of that country" and that, while the military problem was important, "political, social, and economic elements are equally significant."[17]

"The last thing he wanted," Taylor said later, "was to put in our
ground forces. And I knew that. I had the same feeling he had on the
subject. But all the way, starting with CINCPAC [headquarters of
the commander-in-chief for the Pacific], the feeling was that we'd
better get something into South Vietnam."[18] Within a week Taylor
recommended that 8000 American combat troops be dispatched at
once; "I do not believe that our program to save SVN [South Viet-
nam] will succeed without it." If infiltration continued from the
north, the time might come "when we must declare our intentions to
attack the source of guerrilla aggression." Above all, the United
States must make a formal and total commitment to prevent the fall
of South Vietnam to communism.[19]

Reflecting on the reception of his report, Taylor said later, "I don't
recall anyone who was strongly against, except one man and that was
the President. The President just didn't want to be convinced that
this was the right thing to do. . . . It was really the President's personal conviction that U.S. ground troops shouldn't go in."[20] Kennedy
told me sardonically, "The troops will march in; the crowds will
cheer; and in four days everyone will have forgotten. Then we will be
told that we have to send in more troops. It is like taking a drink.
The effect wears off, and you have to take another."[21]

He also discussed his misgivings with Galbraith, directing him to
stop in Saigon on his way back to his post in New Delhi and give the
other side (which Galbraith brilliantly did). But what course to follow? "There are limits," he told Galbraith, "to the number of defeats
I can defend in one twelve-month period. I've had the Bay of Pigs
and pulling out of Laos, and I can't accept a third."[22] Once again, as
in the spring, he compromised, rejecting combat units while accepting
another increase in military and economic assistance to Diem. But
he insisted, as William Bundy of the Defense Department later wrote,
on "a stiffer and more *quid pro quo* political program than the '*first*

support him, *then* help him to reform' approach of the Taylor-Rostow report."[23] And he absolutely declined in the National Security Action Memorandum of November 15 to make the total commitment to save Vietnam his advisers thought so essential. Nor did he suppose that limited assistance would weaken his control of the situation. When George Ball warned that it would finally lead to 300,000 American troops on the Asian mainland, Kennedy said, "You're crazy as hell; it can't happen"—not so long as he was President.[24]

He was under fire that autumn from Republicans of the "why not victory?" school. The collective security press, led by the *New York Times,* was also in arms. Kennedy feared that, if Congress and the newspapers learned the Pentagon wanted to send ground troops, his own hand might be forced. Accordingly, the White House disingenuously let the impression seep out that Taylor opposed combat units. Though the policy disagreement was thus concealed, the subsequent increase in military assistance was not. On December 11, 1961, the *Times* reported the arrival of two U.S. Army helicopter companies in Saigon—"the first direct military support by the United States for South Vietnam's war against Communist guerrilla forces."[25] On December 20 the *Times* told of uniformed American advisers "operating in battle areas with South Vietnamese forces" and, though not in combat, authorized to fire back if fired on.[26] No newspaper, no member of Congress, raised questions.

Three days before Christmas, Specialist Fourth Class James Thomas Davis of Livingston, Tennessee, became the first American soldier to die in Vietnam.

IV

The *Times,* denouncing Communist "aggression" in Vietnam, had said grimly, "The present situation is one that brooks no further stalling."[27] All the same, Kennedy was determined to stall. But his compromises, minor as they seemed at the time, were storing up trouble for the future. The establishment in February 1962 of the Military Assistance Command Vietnam under General Paul Harkins gave the Pentagon a new stake in the war. The *quid pro quo* stipulations on reform fell by the wayside. Reporters soon described American helicopters ferrying South Vietnamese troops to the front and American pilots strafing Viet Cong territory. By the end of 1962, twenty Americans had lost their lives in battle.[28] Neither Congress nor the press questioned the deepening involvement. All this encouraged the campaign for American combat units. "It is fashionable in some quarters," General Earle G. Wheeler, a later chairman of the JCS, declared publicly in November 1962, "to say that the problems in Southeast Asia are primarily political and economic rather than military. I do not agree. The essence of the problem is military."[29]

The "quarters" in disagreement with General Wheeler were led by Averell Harriman, now assistant secretary of state for Far Eastern affairs, Roger Hilsman, also of State, and Michael Forrestal in the White House. While accepting the strategic importance of South Vietnam, these men saw the problem as one of civil war rather than external aggression. The remedy, they believed, had to be at least as much political and economic as military. "The basic question of the whole war," Hilsman and Forrestal reported to Kennedy after a trip to South Vietnam in January 1963, was "the attitude of the villagers." The folk in the countryside would remain apathetic "or even become pro-Communist if the government does not show concern for their welfare."[30]

Harriman and his allies advocated a combination of counterinsurgency—guerrillas had to be fought by guerrillas—with political and social reform. The introduction of American troops, they believed, would hand the nationalist issue altogether to the Viet Cong. It would also strengthen Diem's authoritarianism at the expense of the reforms essential for his survival. "In wartime," General Harkins opined, "you have to have someone who is as strong . . . as Diem was—a more or less benevolent dictator."[31] The Harriman group felt on the contrary that Diem was lost unless he relaxed his despotism and broadened his base.

The critique was persuasive. Alas, the remedy was not. "Diem will not reform," Galbraith wrote Kennedy after his visit to Saigon. ". . . He cannot. It is politically naive to expect it. He senses that he cannot let power go because he would be thrown out."[32] The very idea of democratization was unintelligible to Diem, reared to believe, as he once put it, that the "sovereign" was "the mediator between the people and heaven" and therefore entitled to "sacred respect."[33] The oriental mandarin regarded reform talk as typical American simplemindedness. He was right.

As for counterinsurgency, it was never really tried in Vietnam.* Taylor and Rostow, for all their counterinsurgency enthusiasm in Washington, roared home from Saigon dreaming of big battalions.

---

* It is sometimes said that Vietnam was used as the "proving ground" of counterinsurgency. That is a myth. Counterinsurgency doctrine contributed to the "pacification" program of 1967–68; but this was as a supplement to, not as a substitute for, a military strategy resting on large units, high technology and attrition.

Edward G. Lansdale, the one American with counterinsurgency experience in South Asia, accompanied their mission. But Taylor gave him the task of assessing the feasibility of building a fence along the northern frontier—a concept Lansdale considered preposterous.[34] Thereafter, though State repeatedly recommended Lansdale's assignment to Vietnam, the Pentagon as repeatedly vetoed him.[35]

The theory that Saigon's guerrillas should fight Hanoi's guerrillas foundered on the Pentagon's irrepressible instinct, as Forrestal put it, "to turn the war into a conventional and American enterprise."[36] The Special Forces were sent to remote regions to help peripheral groups like the Montagnards. At the end of 1963 there were only 100 Green Berets left in South Vietnam.* Hilsman had great hopes that a network of fortified "strategic hamlets" could cut the Viet Cong off from the food and manpower in the villages. Diem handed the strategic hamlet program over to his creepy brother Ngo Dinh Nhu, who used it as a means of police control. Hilsman, after an inspection, pronounced it "a fraud, a sham."[37]

The military establishment pressed throughout for victory through large units, firepower and attrition. This was the opposite of counterinsurgency. The Counterinsurgency Group, wrote Charles Maechling, Jr., its staff director, never "dreamed that we would attempt to win over the peasantry of Vietnam by burning their villages, strafing them with rockets and machine guns, and then indiscriminately slaughtering the survivors."[38] The dissenters were wholly convincing in their objections to the high-technology war. Their own vision of a counterinsurgency alternative was, however, fantasy.

v

John Kennedy, I believe, belonged to neither school. He thought and said (privately) in 1961 that the United States had been "overcommitted" in Southeast Asia. Still, we were there, and he was willing to give restricted aid to a South Vietnamese government prepared to rally its own people and fight its own war. Diem, if he used the aid well, had the numerical superiority to put down the Viet Cong. It seemed a chance worth taking. But aid was to be restricted. "Resistance was encountered from the President at every stage," Gilpatric said later, "as this total amount of U.S. personnel deployment increased."[39]

Kennedy had no intention of dispatching American ground forces

* This sounds improbable, but it is so stated in Enclosure A of JCS to Special Group (CI), February 14, 1964, RFK Papers.

to save South Vietnam. Nor did he accept the Truman-Eisenhower-Pentagon view that a President had inherent authority to send an expeditionary force into battle. If combat troops "in the generally understood sense of the word"—units, not advisers—were required in Vietnam, he told a press conference in March 1962, that would be "a basic change . . . which calls for a constitutional decision, [and] of course I would go to the Congress."[40] As for counterinsurgency, if he believed it had any chance of licking the Viet Cong, he would surely have pushed it harder than he did. Lansdale, not Harkins, would have been in command in Saigon.

As against both win-the-war factions, Kennedy, I believe, was vaguely searching for a nonmilitary solution—vaguely because Vietnam was still a side show. In April 1962 Galbraith proposed that the United States offer "phased withdrawal" (there were then about 2000 troops in Vietnam) as an element in a larger deal with the Soviet Union, which in return might get Hanoi to call off the Viet Cong. Kennedy asked Defense for comment. After sneers at the idea of a "political solution," the chairman of the JCS, General Lyman Lemnitzer, denounced Galbraith for wishing the United States "to seek disengagement from what is now a well-known commitment to take a forthright stand against Communism in Southeast Asia."[41]

For the Chiefs the commitment may have been "well-known." But they had thus far failed in their efforts to force it on the President. A few days later a George Ball speech stimulated the militant Marguerite Higgins to lead her *Herald Tribune* story: "American retreat or withdrawal from South Viet-Nam is unthinkable, according to Mr. Ball. The American commitment, moreover, is now irrevocable." Ball, making a case, as lawyers do for clients—privately he opposed American involvement—portrayed the possible downfall of South Vietnam as "a loss of tragic significance to the security of free world interests in the whole of Asia and the South Pacific." Kennedy, disturbed, asked Bundy how Ball's disquisition had slipped by. The speech, Bundy informed the President, had "a tone and content that we would not have cleared, simply from the point of view of maintaining a chance of political settlement."[42]

In July 1962, despite the Joint Chiefs' excommunication of Galbraith, Kennedy instructed McNamara to start planning for the phased withdrawal of American military personnel from Vietnam. The assumption was that South Vietnamese troops would take up the slack as their capabilities improved under American training. The target date for complete disengagement was the end of 1965. After several tries, the military produced an acceptable plan in May 1963.[43]

The generals saw the withdrawal plan as a means of putting pressure on Diem to accelerate the training of Vietnamese troops. Kennedy, however, saw it at the very least as a means of setting a limit to demands from the national-security bureaucracy for escalation. He also saw it as the reserve plan for extrication. "McNamara indicated to me," said Gilpatric, "that this was part of a plan the President asked him to develop to unwind the whole thing." John McNaughton, assistant secretary of defense for international affairs, told Daniel Ellsberg, a young Pentagon hawk, in 1964 "that Robert McNamara had told him of an understanding with President Kennedy that they would close out Vietnam by '65, whether it was in good shape or bad."[44]

VI

Kennedy's growing misgivings were soon reinforced by the man with whom he had originally met Diem—Mike Mansfield. Mansfield, who had served forty years before with the Marines in the Far East and thirty years before as a professor of Far Eastern history, was no novice in the area. At Kennedy's request he visited South Vietnam in November 1962.

Back in Washington, Mansfield warned the Senate Foreign Relations Committee that the United States was nearing "the point at which the conflict in Viet Nam could become of greater concern and greater responsibility to the United States than it is to the Government and people of south Viet Nam." If the South Vietnamese would not do more, Mansfield said, the United States should "reduce its commitment or abandon it entirely."[45] In private Mansfield told Kennedy he was wrong to keep on sending advisers; far better to pull out the Americans and let the South Vietnamese stand on their own feet. Kennedy, challenged on his policy of small concessions, was annoyed. "I got angry with Mike for disagreeing with our policy so completely," he said afterward to Kenneth O'Donnell, "and I got angry with myself because I found myself agreeing with him."[46]

He was beginning to sense that small concessions were leading him into a trap. "Kennedy assumed that the war was going well in 1961 and 1962," wrote Henry Brandon, the well-informed Washington correspondent of the *London Sunday Times,* "but at the end of 1962, in a conversation with Roswell Gilpatric, he talked in a restless and

impatient way about how the U.S. had been sucked into Vietnam little by little."[47] Still, if the South Vietnamese were to have a run for
their—and our—money, how could he go public about withdrawal?
Nothing would so quickly undermine Diem, or, for that matter, so
surely create trouble on the Hill, in the press, including the *New
York Times* and the *Washington Post,* and among the voters.

No doubt he felt he had to play the hand a little longer. Asked
about the Mansfield report, he told his press conference on March 6,
1963, that the fall of Southeast Asia would inevitably affect "the security of India" and "begin to run perhaps all the way toward the
Middle East." July 17: "For us to withdraw . . . would mean a collapse not only of South Vietnam, but Southeast Asia. So we are going
to stay there." September 2: "I don't agree with those who say we
should withdraw. That would be a great mistake."[48] There were other
such statements.

Did he really believe them? Or was it all patter intended to give
Diem his chance and to keep the Pentagon and Congress quiet on the
assumption that, if Diem's incapacity to win on his own became in-
contestable, the United States would have plenty of time to change
course? But his public statements, while they improved morale in
Saigon, also misled Americans about the national stake in Vietnam
and thereby narrowed choices in Washington. Instead of controlling
the situation, the situation was beginning to control him. He grew
uncharacteristically snappish about pessimistic newspaper dispatches
from Saigon, not, I believe, because he thought they would lead to
demands for withdrawal—that was not the national mood in 1963, or
for long years after—but because they might lead to demands for
escalation. In midsummer, according to the Louis Harris poll, Americans agreed by a 2–1 margin that, "if the Communist threat to South
grew worse," they would favor sending U.S. troops "on a large
scale."[49] Kennedy also felt that press criticism decreased any possibility, slim as it might be, that Diem could pull it off.

The evidence suggests that, underneath his uncertainties, withdrawal, which had begun for him in 1962 as a precaution, was turning in 1963 into a preference. He asked his good friend Lester Pearson what the United States should do. The Canadian Prime Minister
said frankly, "Get out." Kennedy said with equal frankness, "That's
a stupid answer. Everybody knows that. The question is: How do we
get out?"[50] He now told Mansfield he had been right about total
withdrawal. "But I can't do it," he said, "until 1965—after I'm reelected." Otherwise the Republicans might beat him in 1964 over the
"loss" of Indochina as they had beaten the Democrats in 1952 over

the "loss" of China.* When Mansfield left, Kennedy remarked to O'Donnell, who had been present, "If I tried to pull out completely now from Vietnam, we would have another Joe McCarthy red scare on our hands, but I can do it after I'm reelected. So we had better make damned sure that I *am* reelected."[51] Kennedy "felt we had made an error," Mansfield told the columnist Jack Anderson in 1970. "He was going to order a gradual withdrawal. . . . [He] had definitely and unequivocally made that decision . . . but he never had the chance to put the plan into effect."[52]

Kennedy had said all along that the United States could not win the war for the South Vietnamese. After two years of intensified American aid, he was starting to conclude that they could not win it for themselves. He commenced to prepare the American people for the idea that the United States must limit its involvement. "In the final analysis," he said on television on September 2, 1963, "it is their war. They are the ones who have to win it or lose it. We can help them, we can give them equipment, we can send our men out there as advisers, but they have to win it, the people of Viet-Nam."[53]

VII

The late summer of 1963: Kennedy still playing out his public hand while secretly wondering how to get out; his two schools of advisers, united in perceiving an American responsibility to win the war but bitterly antagonistic to each other. The issue between them was now the survival of the Diem regime itself.

The Pentagon backed Diem more fervently than ever. The Harriman group had reached the conclusion that Diem and more immediately his brother Nhu and the serpentine Madame Nhu were disasters. In the new ambassador to Saigon, Henry Cabot Lodge, who replaced the complaisant Frederick Nolting, the anti-Diem school at last had a purposeful, even highhanded, ally in Saigon. Everyone knows the story of the cable of August 24, drafted by Harriman, Hilsman and Forrestal and cleared loosely around town on a summer weekend, authorizing Lodge to tell a camarilla of anti-Diem generals

* Some later condemned this political calculation as immoral. Daniel Ellsberg in his *Rolling Stone* interview (December 6, 1973) thus charged Kennedy with "a willingness to keep on bombing the Vietnamese for a couple of more years in order to get through the election." In fact, there was little bombing in the Kennedy years. In any event, would it have been better to have lost in 1964 to a presidential candidate who agreed with General Curtis LeMay that North Vietnam should be bombed back to the Stone Age? The American people in these years were not of notably dovish spirit.

that, if they overthrew Diem, the United States would recognize their new regime. The impact in Saigon was negligible. The generals did nothing. But the impact in Washington was shattering. The President, who was at Hyannis Port, thought the cable, in the words of Robert Kennedy, "had been approved by McNamara and Maxwell Taylor and everybody else, which it had not. . . . I became much more intimately involved in it then."[54]

Up to this point the Attorney General had had little to do with Vietnam. In February 1962, he had stopped over for two hours in Saigon on his way from Indonesia to Siam. He did not leave the heavily guarded airport but held forth boldly on the war. "We are going to win in Viet-Nam," he said. "We will remain here until we do win." A British correspondent noted that there had been American casualties; "do the American people understand and approve of what is going on?" "I think the American people understand and fully support this struggle," Robert Kennedy replied. ". . . I think the United States will do what is necessary to help a country that is trying to repel aggression with its own blood, tears and sweat."[55]

He accepted the party line as imparted to him by McNamara and Taylor. After a meeting of the Counterinsurgency Group in November 1962, Forrestal sent him a worried memorandum:

> I became concerned about the kind of information you seem to be getting on South Vietnam. Both Averell and I feel that the war is not going as well out there as one might be led to believe. . . . The reports we get indicate that the political problem is growing relatively worse. There has been very little indication to date that Diem's Government has been able to follow up the military operations with the type of social and economic programs which would convince the people whose security has been assured that they are better off with Diem than with the Viet Cong.[56]

Thereafter the Harriman group kept him abreast of its doubts. But in the spring and summer of 1963 the struggle for racial justice left the Attorney General little time for anything else.

Now American policy in Vietnam was in crisis, and John Kennedy wanted his brother at his side. The President thought the August 24 cable impulsive and precipitate. "He's always said that it was a major mistake on his part," Robert Kennedy recalled the next year. ". . . The result is we started down a road that we never really recovered from." John Kennedy became "very unhappy" with Harriman—so much so that Robert, noting that Harriman "put on about ten years during that period . . . because he was so discouraged," asked his brother "if he couldn't rehabilitate him by just being nice to him . . . because he's a very valuable figure."[57]

The day after the coup cable, Robert Kennedy talked to McNamara and Maxwell Taylor. "Nobody really knew what our policy was; it hadn't been discussed, as everything else had been discussed since the Bay of Pigs, in full detail before we did anything—nothing like that had been done before the decision made on Diem and so by Tuesday we were trying to pull away from that policy."[58] Stormy meetings followed. Harriman, Ball, Hilsman, Forrestal, said that the United States "must decide now to go through to a successful overthrow."[59] Taylor, McNamara, McCone, Lyndon Johnson, strongly opposed a coup. Nolting was brought in on August 27 to give the case for Diem. Gilpatric could not remember when anyone in the presence of a President "took the tongue-lashing that Nolting did from Harriman. And I don't think it would have been tolerated by the President from anybody else."[60] "The government split in two," recalled Robert Kennedy. "It was the only time really, in three years, the government was broken in two in a very disturbing war."[61] "My God!" John Kennedy said one day to Charles Bartlett. "My government's coming apart!"[62]

The Attorney General attended meeting after meeting. "He was beginning," said Forrestal, "to have serious doubts about the *whole* effort. . . . Was the United States capable of achieving even the limited objectives that we then had in Vietnam? Did the United States have the resources, the men and the thinking to have anything useful really to do in a country that was as politically unstable as South Vietnam was? Was it not possible that we had overestimated our own resources and underestimated the problem in South Vietnam? . . . He began forcing people to take a harder look at what it was we were doing there."[63] At the NSC meeting on September 6 Robert Kennedy said that the fundamental issue was what we thought we were doing in Vietnam. "The first question was whether a Communist take-over could be successfully resisted with any government. If it could not, now was the time to get out of Vietnam entirely, rather than waiting."[64] The question hovered for a moment, then died away, a hopelessly alien thought in a field of unexamined assumptions and entrenched convictions.

VIII

In Saigon Lodge was determined to overthrow Diem. THERE IS NO TURNING BACK, he had cabled Washington on August 29.[65] On September 11: TIME HAS ARRIVED FOR THE US TO USE WHAT EFFECTIVE SANCTIONS IT HAS TO BRING ABOUT THE FALL OF THE EXISTING GOV-

ERNMENT AND THE INSTALLATION OF ANOTHER.[66] He had no doubt in his mind and ample Brahmin confidence in his judgment. The American newspapermen said cheerfully: "Our mandarin is going to beat their mandarin."

"The individual that forced our position really at the time of Vietnam," Robert Kennedy said in 1965, "was Henry Cabot Lodge. . . . The President would send out messages and he would never really answer them. . . . My impression was Henry Cabot Lodge didn't pay much attention because he wanted a coup. . . . It was an impossible situation." So impossible indeed that, according to Robert Kennedy, the President decided to call Lodge home in November "and discussed with me in detail how he could be fired, because he wouldn't communicate in any way with us." The Attorney General, who had questioned Lodge's appointment, was not surprised. Robert Kennedy had warned his brother, he later recalled, "that Henry Cabot Lodge in Vietnam would cause him a lot of difficulty in six months, and I brought that up, and he said it was terrific about me because I could always remember when I was right. And he said, do you remember when you were in favor of a tax increase [during the Berlin crisis in 1961]? and that would have had a very adverse effect, and that's when you weren't right."[67]

Lodge was a strong man with the bit between his teeth. On the other hand, his Washington instructions were hardly clear or firm—a reflection both of the continuing quarrel in Washington and of the President's own uncertainties. In the television interview on September 2 the President himself had said that, if Diem did not make changes in personnel and policy, his chances of winning the war would not be good. Thereafter he signed cables laying down a checklist of reforms to which Diem would not conceivably accede—from the exile of the Nhus to a free press and free elections.[68] All this could be interpreted as support for a coup. Robert Kennedy said, however, that the President "was against getting rid of [Diem] until you knew what was going to come along and whether the government that was going to replace it had any stability and in fact [whether it] would be a successful coup."[69] Reflecting the next spring, Robert said,

Diem was corrupt and a bad leader and it would have been better if we didn't have him. But we inherited him. He came with the job. So what do you do? . . . It's better if you don't have him but you have to have somebody that can win the war, and who is that? . . . It's bad policy to get into for us to run a coup out there and replace somebody we don't like with somebody we do because it would just make every other country nervous as can be that we were running coups in and out.[70]

Here Robert Kennedy adopted the win-the-war perspective shared by supporters as well as by opponents of the coup. But, if John Kennedy had withdrawal in mind, there was all the more reason to take care. For a coup encouraged by Washington would drag the United States ever more irrevocably into responsibility for the fate of South Vietnam. And disengagement was increasingly, I believe, the presidential purpose. "By the autumn of 1963," wrote Henry Brandon, "he seemed sick of it, and frequently asked how to be rid of the commitment."[71]

At the end of September the President dispatched McNamara and Taylor on one more reconnaissance. "The question at the top of McNamara's mind," according to William Bundy, the mission's staff director, was: "Could the U.S. look forward . . . to the withdrawal of at least the bulk of its military advisors by the end of 1965? The insistence on this question shows the degree to which the planning of May [for phased withdrawal] had survived intervening events."[72] On his return McNamara answered the question in the affirmative, recommending in addition the immediate withdrawal of 1000 advisers by the end of 1963. "This is a Vietnamese war," his report said, "and the country and the war must, in the end, be run *solely* by the Vietnamese."[73]

This was the first application of Kennedy's phased withdrawal plan. Taylor went along as a way of bringing pressure on Diem.[74] The political school, however, regarded the recall of 1000 advisers with consternation. William Sullivan, the State Department representative on the McNamara-Taylor mission, threatened a minority report. The sentence about troop withdrawal was deleted. The mission then met with the President. At one point Kennedy took McNamara and Taylor into the Oval Office. When they returned, McNamara directed that the statement be restored. There was much "expostulation," Forrestal recalled. Kennedy listened impatiently, turned on his heel and left the room. The statement remained.[75]

Chester Cooper of McGeorge Bundy's staff, much agitated, rushed to Bundy, who was closeted with his brother. Troop withdrawal, Cooper said, would destroy any credibility the McNamara-Taylor mission could have had. "Both Bundys agreed, but Bill had little elbow room. Finally, in utter exasperation, Bill said, 'Look, I'm under instructions!'" McGeorge Bundy called McNamara but could

not persuade him to change his mind. "McNamara seems to have
been trapped too," Cooper concluded; "the sentence may have been
worked out privately with Kennedy, and therefore imbedded in
concrete."* Cooper's suspicion is persuasive. When McNamara left the
White House to announce the start of troop withdrawal to the press,
Kennedy called after him, "And tell them that means all the helicopter pilots too."[76]

Kennedy was equally insistent on preserving flexibility in declara-
tory policy. McNamara and Taylor had recommended that the withdrawal announcement affirm "the *overriding objective* of denying this
country to Communism and of suppressing the Viet Cong insur-
gency." Kennedy had fought off a total commitment for three years
and was not about to capitulate now. Instead the statement said
mildly that it remained American policy, "in South Viet-Nam as in
other parts of the world, to support the efforts of the people of that
country to defeat aggression."†

If the South Vietnamese could not win their war for themselves,
the United States had to lay the foundation for disengagement. The
President called an all-agency conference in Honolulu to consider, as
he somewhat confusedly told his press conference on November 14,
"how we can intensify the struggle, how we can bring Americans out
of there. Now, that is our object, to bring Americans home."[77] On
November 20 the conference accepted a speed-up of the withdrawal
plan.[78] Kennedy had trapped himself long enough and was looking
for the way out.

IX

Did he have an escape route? O'Donnell once inquired how he could
pull out without damaging American prestige. "Easy," Kennedy re-

---

* Chester Cooper, *The Lost Crusade: America in Vietnam* (New York, 1970),
215–216. William Bundy: "I have no recollection of either episode or attitude, but
my notes do make clear that the sentence was regarded as settled all through the day,
after the meeting between McNamara and the President in the morning" (Bundy ms.
on U.S. policy in East Asia during the Kennedy-Johnson years, ch. 9). Bundy in retrospect finds it hard to resolve the contradiction between the report's political pessimism and its withdrawal proposal. No doubt the answer lies in Kennedy's private determination to begin, at whatever cost, a strategy of extrication.

† See the McNamara-Taylor recommendation and the White House statement
(*Pentagon Papers*, vol. 2, 188, 753, emphasis added). The Pentagon statement would
have had Kennedy "adhere to the overriding objective . . ."; but, since Kennedy had
steadily vetoed persistent Pentagon attempts to slip by an unconditional commitment,
there was nothing for him to adhere to; nor did he. The White House statement said
only, "We will adhere to our policy of working with the people and Government of
South Viet-Nam to deny this country to communism . . ." (also Peter Dale Scott in
The Pentagon Papers, Senator Gravel Edition [Boston, 1971], vol. 5, 215–216).

plied. "Put a government in there that will ask us to leave."[79] "We would withdraw the troops," he told his press conference in May 1963, ". . . any time the government of South Vietnam would suggest it."[80] "Remember Laos," he said to Hilsman, making it "abundantly clear," Hilsman later wrote, that if the Saigon government proved incapable of reform, "his intention was to negotiate a settlement along the lines of the 1962 Geneva accord on Laos."[81] His brother, Robert Kennedy told Ellsberg in 1967, would have arranged "a Laotian type solution, some form of coalition government with people who would ask us to leave."[82]

The irony is that Diem and Nhu, without Kennedy's knowledge, were engaged in secret negotiations that could have resulted in somewhat the situation Kennedy had in mind. The Ngo brothers were, in their anachronistic fashion, authentic Vietnamese nationalists. They were reluctant about American troops and resistant to American interference. "Those who knew Diem best," Robert Shaplen of the *New Yorker* wrote after twenty years in Vietnam, "feel that neither he nor Nhu would ever have invited or allowed 550,000 American soldiers to fight in their country and to permit the devastation caused by air attacks."[83] Diem may also have felt, as Bui Kien Thanh has suggested, that massive American intervention would provoke massive Chinese intervention and deliver Vietnam to its historic enemy.[84] In May 1963 Nhu proposed publicly that the United States start withdrawing its troops. In the summer he told Forrestal in his "hooded" way that the United States did not understand Vietnam; "sooner or later we Vietnamese will settle our differences between us."[85] "Even during the most ferocious battle," Nhu said to Mieczyslaw Maneli, the Polish member of the International Control Commission established in 1954 to supervise the Geneva agreement, "the Vietnamese never forget who is a Vietnamese and who is a foreigner."[86]

Maneli was a political scientist rather than a career diplomat, a survivor of Auschwitz and Maidanek, an admirer of Kennedy, with whom he had discussed Vietnam in Poland in 1959.* In the spring of 1963 Roger Lalouette, the French ambassador in Saigon, asked Maneli to serve as an intermediary between the Ngo brothers and Hanoi. De Gaulle's interest was plain enough—to show up the blundering Americans, to rescue the west from a hopeless predicament, to restore French influence in Indochina. "The next step," Maneli re-

* I thank Dr. Maneli for permitting me to read his account of this meeting in an unpublished paper, "Encounters with John F. Kennedy and Discussions on 'Democratic Socialism,' Polish Policy, and Vietnam," 4–11.

ported to Warsaw in May, "will be neutralization. . . . In this way Vietnam, in addition to neutral Cambodia and Laos, will again become a pearl in the 'grandeur of France.' "[87]

Maneli shuttled between Saigon and Hanoi.* He pressed Ho Chi Minh and Phan Van Dong, the North Vietnamese Premier, about their peace terms. They replied that Hanoi would settle for a coalition government in a neutralized South Vietnam. "I asked," recalled Maneli, "if such a government could be headed by Mr. Diem. In the summer of 1963 the answer was finally yes." The North Vietnamese added that, if the Americans withdrew, Hanoi would give the south guarantees, including perhaps American participation in a supervisory process.[88]

As American pressure mounted against the Diem regime, Hanoi refrained from exploiting the confusion as by a new Viet Cong offensive. Maneli cabled Warsaw on July 10: "This is certainly because it wishes [Diem and Nhu] to survive for a time yet—long enough to come to an agreement with them behind the Americans' backs." A month later Maneli concluded that there was "a supersecret agreement between Diem-Nhu and Hanoi" and that Hanoi and the National Liberation Front "at the first opportunity will back Diem against the Americans." "In conversation with me and with my deputy in Hanoi," the "Vietnamese comrades" spoke of the possibility of an alliance with Diem-Nhu against the Americans "plainly and without fuss."[89]

On August 29 de Gaulle publicly offered French assistance in transforming the two Vietnams into a unified state, free of all foreign influences. Lodge's evident desire to overturn Diem worried the French. "Only Diem," Lalouette told Maneli, "can conclude peace. . . . If Diem and Nhu are removed, all our plans designed to end the fighting and bring about agreement with the North will come to naught. . . . Any other government will be even more dependent on the Americans, will be obedient to them in all things, and so there will be no chance for peace."[90] Nhu himself encouraged Maneli to carry on. Maneli could not tell how serious the brothers were. "They were carrying on such a complicated and many-sided game that one could not be certain about the direction in which they were head-

---

* He was not, he believed, the only channel. The North Vietnamese used him, he thought, "as an additional link to reinforce the dialogue they were having with Saigon through other contacts" (Stanley Karnow, "Lost Chance in Vietnam," *New Republic,* February 2, 1974). Nhu may also have been holding talks with NLF representatives, as stated in Bui Kien Thanh, "Mandarins of Vietnam," *International History Magazine,* January 1974.

ing."[91] Nhu may well have been trying to blackmail the Americans into stopping their campaign against him by the threat of a deal with Hanoi, trying at the same time to see whether such a deal offered the Ngos a better prospect for survival. "He was," Maneli said later, "playing on many instruments at the same time."[92]

His hints about treating with Hanoi were not, according to William Bundy, "taken seriously in either Saigon or Washington."[93] For the pro-Diem faction, the idea of a Diem-Ho deal so flagrantly violated the theory of Diem as a last-ditch anti-Communist that it did not seem worthy of a moment's credit. The anti-Diem faction was quite willing to believe that Nhu and de Gaulle were up to some deviltry. But this only made it the more hostile to the notion of a deal. The State Department was already furious at de Gaulle for European reasons. James M. Gavin, who had served two years as ambassador to Paris, remembered a State Department officer calling de Gaulle "a bastard who is out to get us."[94] He was meddling in Indochina, it was supposed, in order to make sure that the United States could not succeed where France had failed. Neutralization, moreover, was dismissed as a prelude to communization. Even Kennedy, while observing that "anything General de Gaulle says should be listened to, and we listened," added, "It doesn't do us any good to say, 'Well, why don't we all just go home and leave the world to those who are our enemies.'"[95] The anti-Diem group saw the secret negotiations, if true, not as an opportunity for extrication but as a threat to victory. On August 30 a Hilsman memorandum suggested that, if Diem were in fact negotiating with Ho, Washington should "encourage the generals to move promptly with a coup."*

No one knew then whether the explorations had any reality. (No one knows now.) Later Madame Nhu informed a visitor that "the two brothers had sought to negotiate an end to the conflict, and that it was to prevent this that the coup was carried out. She declared emphatically that Mr. Kennedy had activated the brothers in this effort to achieve peace; he had no part in fomenting the coup."[96]

---

* Hilsman to Rusk, August 30, 1963, JFK Papers. The memorandum, Hilsman informs me, was a response to a request by Rusk that the Far Eastern Division list anti-American moves Diem might make and the whole range of *possible* responses. It should be noted that a document in the RFK Papers entitled "South Vietnam: An Action Plan," with no date or source but, from internal evidence, September 1963 and very likely also from Hilsman, listed as an American response to Nhu-Diem tactics: if "we have sufficient hard evidence of GVN negotiations with any Communists, consider going to Moscow directly. Sound out the Soviets in a secret demarche as to the possibility of a neutralization of all Vietnam on the basis of a change of leadership in South Vietnam."

Conceivably Kennedy's October insistence on starting the troop withdrawal in December could have been taken by Diem and Nhu as encouragement to seek a negotiated peace. But I found no evidence that Kennedy was ever adequately informed on the matter. The deal did not seem real enough to have been a major factor in American attitudes toward a coup.

It was a tricky business at best. Washington would have been hard put to save Diem from the generals in any case; nor was there any guarantee that Diem, once assured of American support, would have negotiated an end to the war. Had he done so, a Diem-Ho deal followed by an American withdrawal would not have been applauded in the United States of 1963. "Fortunately," as the *New York Times* pontificated after the coup, "the new Vietnamese rulers are dedicated anti-Communists who reject any idea of neutralism and pledge to stand with the free world. It is significant that one of their charges against Mr. Nhu is that he tried to make a deal with Communist North Vietnam along the lines hinted at by President de Gaulle."[97]

This was the national mood. Still, a Diem-Ho deal could have been the means of an American exit from Vietnam in 1963, though the life expectancy of a Diem government in Saigon would have been minimal thereafter. An opportunity of some sort was perhaps missed in the autumn of 1963. Whether it might have been seized later, if Kennedy had never gone to Dallas, is another question. De Gaulle was scheduled to visit Washington in February 1964. Talking to Gavin in late October 1963, with Vietnam the dominant problem on his mind, Kennedy said, rather happily, Gavin thought, "I am going to see the General in the next few months, and I think that we will be able to get something done together."[98]

x

In Saigon a new group of dissident generals was planning a serious coup. Lodge maintained contact with the conspirators through the CIA. The National Security Council met on October 29. Robert Kennedy thought the situation no different from August, when the generals talked big and did nothing. "To support a coup," he told the group, "would be putting the future of Vietnam and in fact all of Southeast Asia in the hands of one man not now known to us. A failure of a coup risks so much. The reports we have are very thin." The President observed that, since the pro-Diem and anti-Diem forces appeared about equal, any attempt to engineer a coup would be silly.[99]

But Lodge responded to a cautionary cable: "Do not think we have the power to delay or discourage a coup. [General] Don has made it clear many times that this is a Vietnamese affair."[100] When the coup began two days later, Lodge did his best to assure the personal safety of Diem and Nhu. They refused his assistance and were killed. (Lodge did succeed in flying Nhu's children to Bangkok. The escort officer was Frederick Flott, with whom Robert Kennedy had traveled around the Soviet Union eight years before.)[101] When the President heard about Diem's murder, he leaped to his feet and, as Taylor recalled it, "rushed from the room with a look of shock and dismay on his face which I had never seen before."[102] I had not seen Kennedy so depressed since the Bay of Pigs. He said that Diem had fought for his country for twenty years and that it should not have ended like this.[103]

"I believe prospects of victory are much improved," an unrepentant and elated Lodge cabled on November 6.

> . . . The coup was a Vietnamese and a popular affair, which we could neither manage nor stop after it got started and which we could only have influenced with great difficulty. But it is equally certain that the ground in which the coup seed grew into a robust plant was prepared by us and that the coup would not have happened [as] it did without our preparation. . . .
>
> All this may be a useful lesson in the use of US power. . . . Perhaps the USG has here evolved a way of not being everywhere saddled with responsibility for autocratic governments simply because they are anti-Communist—a course which can eventually lead many people to believe that the foreign communist autocracy which they don't know is preferable to the local autocracy which they do know. . . .
>
> The prospects now are for a shorter war.[104]

Kennedy disagreed. "Just before his death," according to Henry Brandon, "he gave Mike Forrestal, in private conversation, odds of a hundred-to-one that the U.S. could not win. But he also knew that he could not get out of Vietnam before the elections in November, 1964, without inviting his own political eclipse."[105] He still supposed he had plenty of time for maneuver. He told Forrestal, "I want to start a complete and very profound review of how we got into this country, what we thought we were doing and what we now think we can do. . . . I even want to think about whether or not we should be there."[106] Wayne Morse, one of the few senatorial critics of the involvement, saw him in mid-November. Kennedy said, "Wayne, I want you to know you're absolutely right in your criticism of my Vietnam policy. Keep this in mind. I'm in the midst of an intensive study which substantiates your position on Vietnam."[107] "The facts that he envisaged a troop withdrawal and that he spoke often of the necessity of ending American participation in the war lest it become a swamp into which the United States sinks more and more," said Pierre Salinger, "prove, in my judgment, that he was on the right track at the time of his death."[108]

Of course he should have asked the searching questions long before. He should have realized the cumulative momentum of the policy of small concessions. When Kennedy became President, there were 685 American military advisers in Vietnam. In October 1963 there were 16,732. This was a formidable escalation. Still, Kennedy sent many fewer troops to Vietnam than Khrushchev sent to Cuba in 1962 or Johnson to the Dominican Republic in 1965.* The total number of American soldiers killed in Vietnam as a result of hostile action from the beginning of 1961 to the end of 1963 was only 73[109]—73 too many, but still inconsiderable compared to the tragedy to come. The process was hardly irreversible. Troops, once sent, could be withdrawn, as they were in Cuba and the Dominican Republic, as Kennedy already planned to do in Vietnam.

Kennedy had proved his manhood in the Solomon Islands and did not have to prove it again. He was a prudent executive, not inclined to heavy investments in lost causes. His whole Presidency was marked precisely by his capacity to *refuse* escalation—as in Laos, the Bay of Pigs, the Berlin Wall, the missile crisis. "Having discussed military affairs with him often and in detail for fifteen years," wrote General Gavin, "I know he was totally opposed to the introduction of combat troops in Southeast Asia."[110] After Dallas, Ho Chi Minh said thoughtfully to Maneli that Kennedy would perhaps have contributed to an early end of the war; "his death creates new problems."[111] Kennedy's failure lay in the hopelessly divided legacy he left on November 22, 1963.

* And indeed only 2000 more than Eisenhower sent to Lebanon in 1958.

(32)

The Breach Widens:
Vietnam

How to recapture the way enlightened Americans thought about Vietnam in 1964? Take the vivid book, *The Making of a Quagmire*, written that year by David Halberstam of the *New York Times*, the best and brightest of correspondents. Halberstam was a penetrating critic of the American performance in Vietnam. Yet he did not doubt the premise. Vietnam, he wrote, "is perhaps one of only five or six nations in the world that is truly vital to U.S. interests." Neutralization? "Out of the question": it would only postpone a Communist victory. Withdrawal? It would mean "a drab, lifeless and controlled society for a people who deserve better. . . . Throughout the world the enemies of the West will be encouraged to try insurgencies like the one in Vietnam. . . . We would dishonor ourselves and our allies by pulling out." Americanization of the war? "We should think and prepare for a long, long time before going in with our own troops." We were caught in a quagmire and probably would not learn the lesson in time to save Vietnam. "Perhaps at this moment we are gaining the knowledge necessary to deal with a situation in Thailand, or Angola, or a small republic in South America—some country where it is not yet too late."*

* David Halberstam, *The Making of a Quagmire* (New York, 1965), 315, 317, 319. Note might also be taken of Senator Fulbright's famous "Old Myths and New Realities" speech of March 25, 1964, in which he opposed both a negotiated settlement and the commitment of American troops and called on the United States "to support the South Vietnamese Government by the most effective means available" and "continue to meet its obligations and fulfill its commitments with respect to Vietnam" (Jules Davids, ed., *Documents on American Foreign Relations 1964* [New York, 1965], 29).

I

"We shall continue," the new President said. But Kennedy's Vietnam legacy was dual and contradictory. He had left on the public record the impression of a major national stake in the defense of South Vietnam against communism. He had left steadily enlarging programs of military and economic assistance. He had left national security advisers who for three years had been urging an American expeditionary force and a total commitment to the salvation of South Vietnam. On the other hand, he had consistently refused to send such a force or to make such a commitment. He had left a formal plan, processed successfully through the Pentagon, for the withdrawal of American advisers by the end of 1965. He had left a public campaign, belatedly begun, to instill the idea that American involvement must be limited in a war that only the South Vietnamese could win. And he had left private opposition, repeatedly and emphatically stated, to the dispatch of American ground forces.

Did Kennedy lead the country ineluctably into catastrophe in Southeast Asia? He had not made things easy for his successor. But it is not sufficient to say that Lyndon Johnson was carrying forward Kennedy's policies. The question remains: which of Kennedy's policies? Continuity was an ambiguous command. The new President could choose the continuity of deepening involvement. Or he could choose the continuity of absolute limitations—no combat troops, no heavy bombing—and planned withdrawal by 1965. Each alternative bore the Kennedy stamp. The decision was now Johnson's.

It was Johnson's of course within the framework of public illusion to which Kennedy had made significant contributions. A generation of superpowership had persuaded most Americans that they had the power and the responsibility to work their will around the planet. The strength of this national mood constrained Kennedy to defer disengagement till after the 1964 election. But the mood did not constrain Johnson. He vigorously agreed with it. He had memorized the copybook lesson of the 1930s. Appeasement, he was sure, was an invitation to aggression. In May 1961 Kennedy had sent him to Vietnam. "The basic decision in Southeast Asia is here," Johnson reported on his return. "We must decide whether to help these countries to the best of our ability or throw in the towel in the area and pull back our defenses to San Francisco."[1]

He was a stout supporter of Diem, whom in 1961 he had hailed as the "Winston Churchill" of Southeast Asia. A week after the coup scare of August 1963, he told McNamara and Rusk that "he had never really seen a genuine alternative to Diem . . . that from both a practical and a political viewpoint, it would be a disaster to pull out; that we should stop playing cops and robbers and get back to . . . winning the war."[2] He watched subsequent developments with resentful disapproval. On the day after Kennedy's funeral, Johnson, showing Hubert Humphrey a portrait of Diem hanging in the hallway of his house, said, "We had a hand in killing him. Now it's happening here."[3]

On November 24 the new President convened a small group to meet with Lodge, just in from Saigon. Robert Kennedy was not invited. Johnson told them, "I am not going to lose Vietnam. I am not going to be the President who saw Southeast Asia go the way China went."[4] Afterward he mused to Bill Moyers, "They'll think with Kennedy dead we've lost heart. So they'll think we're yellow and don't mean what we say. . . . The Chinese. The fellas in the Kremlin. They'll be taking the measure of us. . . . I'm not going to let Vietnam go the way of China. I told them to go back and tell those generals in Saigon that Lyndon Johnson intends to stand by our word."[5] Two days later National Security Action Memorandum 273 declared: "It *remains* the *central objective* of the United States in South Vietnam to assist the people and Government of that country to *win* their contest against the *externally directed* and supported communist conspiracy."[6] Here, represented as the continuation of existing policy, were both the total commitment Kennedy had always refused and the diagnosis of the conflict that Kennedy, who had described it in July 1963 as a "civil war which has gone on for ten years,"[7] had never quite accepted.

While reannouncing the December troop withdrawal, NSAM 273 also emphasized that American military programs "should be maintained at levels as high as those in the time of the Diem regime."[8] This nullified Kennedy's extrication intent. One thousand men were nominally withdrawn in December. It was, in the words of the Pentagon history, "essentially an accounting exercise" and achieved no reduction in American strength.[9] Reducing American strength was the last thing Johnson wished to do. "The President," Rusk cabled Lodge, eyes only, on December 6, "has expressed his deep concern that our effort in Viet-Nam be stepped up to highest pitch."[10] On New Year's Day Johnson pledged the Saigon government "the fullest measure of support . . . in achieving victory." "By implication," the *New York*

Times commented, "the message erased the previous date for with-drawing the bulk of United States forces by the end of 1965."[11] The erasure was made explicit and final, in full Pentagonese, on March 27, 1964.[12]

Johnson's New Year's Day bouquet also denounced neutralism; "only . . . another name for a Communist take over." De Gaulle meanwhile pressed his campaign. Reports flowed into Washington, according to William Bundy, that the post-Diem junta was "sympa-thetic to the French position."* Hanoi, Mieczyslaw Maneli later attested, thought it might come to terms with the junta.[13] Then John-son's worries were unexpectedly eliminated by a second coup on Jan-uary 30, 1964. General Khanh, the new leader, explained that the junta had been guilty of "paving the way for neutralism and thus selling out the country."[14] This, Maneli said, not the overthrow of Diem, was the "real coup."†

"At all levels concerned with Indochina," recalled William Bundy, Johnson's "personal force and imprint were felt much more strongly, right from the start, than JFK had been at any past times except for May and November of 1961 and September/October of 1963."[15]

II

Robert Kennedy's involvement in Vietnam had been strictly limited before Dallas. John Kennedy had not even found an occasion to dis-cuss his deeper doubts and intentions with his brother; there always must have seemed a world of time to do that later. Robert's own un-derstanding of his brother's position, as he expounded it to John Bartlow Martin in the spring of 1964, was that John Kennedy felt "we should win the war" because the loss of Vietnam would mean the fall of the rest of Southeast Asia; that there had been no consid-eration given to pulling out and at the same time no disposition to go further in; here Robert Kennedy cited MacArthur, adding, "we couldn't win the war for them and they had to win the war for them-

---

* William Bundy, ms. on U.S. policy in East Asia during the Kennedy-Johnson years, ch. 12. According to Mieczyslaw Maneli, "the most realistic and responsible generals considered the possibility of neutralizing Vietnam with the active cooperation of France" (Maneli, "Encounters with John F. Kennedy and Discussions on 'Demo-cratic Socialism,' Polish Policy, and Vietnam," unpub., 30).

† Maneli, in interview by author, June 22, 1977. Maneli's conclusion was that nei-ther of the immediate superpowers—America or China—wanted the war to end. The Soviet Union alone, fearing a Hanoi victory would mean either a Chinese dependency or an Asian Titoism, was in favor of negotiated peace but in this period had limited influence in Hanoi.

selves." Martin persisted: if the South Vietnamese were about to lose, would John Kennedy have sent ground forces? "Well," said Robert Kennedy, "we'd face that when we came to it."[16]

After Dallas, his involvement in Vietnam was nonexistent. Vietnam did not come up when he went to Indonesia and Malaysia in January 1964. It was not on his mind in succeeding months. The fundamental questions he had tried to raise the previous September signified an instinct to get to the root of the matter on his brother's behalf rather than a conclusion of his own that the United States should get out. Insofar as Robert followed Vietnam policy in early 1964, he probably noted that Johnson stayed within the Kennedy guidelines—no combat troops, no heavy bombing—and assumed he was doing what had to be done.

In June he began to focus on Vietnam again. One finds a flurry of Vietnam papers in his files—a CIA document doubting an immediate domino effect from the fall of Vietnam; a memorandum Mansfield had written to Johnson, restating his old doubts and saying that, if the President planned to pursue the war, he had better make a more persuasive case.[17] By this time Lodge had signaled a desire to be relieved; and on June 11 Kennedy sent a handwritten note to Johnson:

Dear Mr. President:

I just wanted to make sure you understood that if you wished me to go to Viet Nam in any capacity I would be glad to go. It is obviously the most important problem facing the United States and if you felt I could help I am at your service.

I have talked to both Bob and Mac about this and I believe they know my feelings. I realize some of the other complications but I am sure that if you reached the conclusion that this was the right thing to do then between us both or us all we could work it out satisfactorily.

In any case I wished you to know my feelings on this matter.

Respectfully,
Bob[18]

I have never been sure why he wrote this letter—probably for reasons no more complicated than old-fashioned patriotism. Johnson declined the offer. "I would be accusing myself for the rest of my life," he told Valenti, "if something happened to him out there. He could do the job. He could do it damn well, but I can't trust the security there and someone or some group might want to do him in. I couldn't live with that."[19] Evidently he thought a Vietnamese might want to avenge the murder of Diem.

There was yet no evidence of Kennedy dissent. Vietnam was not an issue in the fall election. Asked for his "exact position" by the students at Columbia, he responded with considerable inexactitude that he had no easy solution, that we should continue, but that he remembered the French in 1951, that the political and social effort was vital and that "we're not going to win that war unless the government has the support of the people. That, in my judgment, is the key to success."[20]

Johnson had no easy solution either. But he escalated the rhetoric, introducing the proposition in March 1964 that Vietnam was the crucial "test case" for Communist strategy[21] and thereafter the proposition, also unknown in the Kennedy years, that the SEATO treaty obligated the United States to intervene with full force in Southeast Asia. The gates of escape were not, however, completely shut. At the end of 1964, according to Chester Cooper, the careful participant-historian of the period, "the get-out option was by no means academic. President Johnson was still pausing warily, still undecided as to which path to follow." In early February, Cooper accompanied Bundy to Saigon. After several days, Cooper wrote later, " 'getting out' still seemed to be possible."[22] Then on February 7 the Viet Cong swarmed over the airfield at Pleiku, killing American soldiers. Johnson now made the decision to Americanize the war.

American bombers went for the first time to North Vietnam. American combat units went for the first time to South Vietnam. "Their war," as Kennedy had called it, was becoming "our war." The Washington atmosphere changed radically. "It is important for the public to realize," the former staff director of the Counterinsurgency Group wrote in 1970 (his italics), "that President Kennedy and his brother *regarded Vietnam as a massive source of vexation and concern but not as intrinsically important in itself—only as a counter in a larger game.* As civilized, well-educated Americans they were totally devoid of the obsessive attitudes that characterized President Johnson under the influence of the 'hard-liners.' "[23]

The bombing of North Vietnam disturbed Robert Kennedy. "Late in April," Lyndon Johnson recorded, "Bobby Kennedy came to see me" to urge a bombing pause. It would do no harm, Kennedy said. Maybe something useful would come of it. The President assured him, as Presidents do, that the idea was under consideration.[24] Almost at once, however, Johnson asked Congress for a supplemental $700 million for Vietnam, explaining that this was no "routine appropriation" but a vote of confidence in the whole policy. Kennedy was furious. The appropriation, as he told me, was not necessary;

ample funds were already available. What Johnson plainly wanted was congressional approval for further escalation. Still, it would be hard to vote against the request without seeming to let down the boys at the front. "Bobby," I noted in my journal, "was none the less very much inclined to vote against the resolution." This was also the week of the Dominican intervention; and my speech for him touched on Vietnam as well. When Burke Marshall and I discussed the draft with him, "we both said he had to vote for the resolution but should accompany his vote by a clear statement of what he was voting for."[25] His instinct was obviously a good deal sounder than his advisers' advice. To their eternal honor, Wayne Morse, Ernest Gruening and Gaylord Nelson voted no.

In his speech on May 6, 1965, Kennedy discussed three possible courses in Vietnam. Withdrawal would mean "a repudiation of commitments undertaken and confirmed by three administrations" and would "gravely—perhaps irreparably—weaken the democratic position in Asia." Escalation would mean "the commitment to Vietnam of hundreds of thousands of American troops" and "might easily lead to nuclear warfare." There remained the course of negotiation. "This, I take it, is the policy of the administration, the policy we are endorsing today." He was voting for the resolution, he said, in the understanding that it was no "blank check" for wider war but rather the necessary prelude for negotiations. We had erred in seeing Vietnam "as purely a military problem. . . . I believe that our efforts for peace should continue with the same intensity as our efforts in the military field."[26]

III

American involvement deepened. So did Kennedy's apprehension. He accepted an invitation to give the commencement address at the International Police Academy in July. The academy, AID's contribution to the counterinsurgency program, was a part of Kennedy's past. He thought now to suggest how the Americanization of the war was departing from the theory of counterinsurgency. Adam Walinsky worked with him on the speech, but Walinsky, as he said later, was not yet on fire about Vietnam. It was Kennedy's "own initiative. Nobody pushed him to do it."[27]

The war, Kennedy said, was ultimately a contest for the allegiance of men. "The essence of successful counterinsurgency is not to kill, but to bring the insurgent back into the national life." Destruction was no solution. "Air attacks by a government on its own villages are likely to be far more dangerous and costly to the people than is the individual and selective terrorism of an insurgent movement." The history of the last twenty years, Kennedy said, had demonstrated "beyond doubt that our approach to revolutionary war must be political—political first, political last, political always. Victory in a revolutionary war is won not by escalation, but by de-escalation."[28]

The text, released before delivery, caused great perturbation in the White House. It could only be read as an indictment of Johnson's new course. Also, framed as it was by quotations from John F. Kennedy, it contained more than a hint that Johnson had abandoned his predecessor's policies. "It will be another Kennedy vs. Johnson issue," Marvin Watson wrote darkly to the President, adding that government agencies like the Police Academy ought to be instructed to notify the White House "as to who they intend to invite to make speeches."[29] Fearful AID representatives implored Kennedy to add on delivery a passage conceding a military dimension to the problem and to drop the line about deescalation. But the original text was already in the newspapers.

The Police Academy speech had almost an elegiac quality. Counterinsurgency might have done it once, Kennedy seemed to say, but its day had passed. Yet his reluctance to force the issue with Johnson showed the fear of misunderstanding that inhibited him throughout his senatorial years. "He was worried," said Fred Harris, "that people would say that he was just trying to make political capital out of criticizing Johnson."[30] The worry was warranted. Most of the press, as Bill Moyers said later, interpreted his criticism of the Vietnam policy "as a political move on his part rather than a genuine unfolding of his own ideas about Vietnam."[31]

His ideas were plainly unfolding. Walinsky, increasingly seized by the problem, fed Kennedy's concern, stuffing the senatorial briefcase with memoranda, *I. F. Stone's Weekly,* books by Bernard Fall and other incendiary documents. Joseph Kraft, the columnist, interested Kennedy in the case of Gustave Hertz, an AID official kidnapped by the Viet Cong. The National Liberation Front, as the Viet Cong were formally known, had a diplomatic outpost in Algeria. Kraft took Kennedy to Cherif Guellal, the Algerian ambassador, who asked Ben Bella, the Algerian chief of state, to intercede with the NLF and soon went to Algiers himself to press the negotiation.

The NLF agreed to exchange Hertz for one of their own men under sentence of death in Saigon. The NLF representative told

Guellal, "We are doing it because of President Ben Bella's intervention; and we know Senator Kennedy and . . . the contribution of his late brother to Algeria's struggle for independence." It was Guellal's impression that the NLF saw an opportunity to open larger contact with the Americans. Once the exchange was made, they would release Hertz—personally to Senator Kennedy in Algiers if he wished. Kennedy took the proposal to Maxwell Taylor, who rejected it on the ground that the arrangement would upset the Saigon government. Kennedy, Guellal thought, was "upset" and "bitter." Hertz died a Viet Cong prisoner.[32]

The effort, Kraft later suggested, made Kennedy understand that the Viet Cong were not roving bands of terrorists but truly a National Liberation Front with a political structure and legitimacy of its own. If counterinsurgency were dead, then negotiations with the NLF might offer the best exit from Vietnam.[33] Guellal thought that the "persistency and consistency" with which Kennedy pursued the Hertz matter was "because he saw there was a possibility, an opening" that might lead to broader negotiations.[34]

The administration preferred victory. The *Time* cover story on October 29, 1965, was entitled "The Turning Point in Viet Nam." "Today," the house dithyrambist wrote, "South Viet Nam throbs with a pride and power, above all an *esprit* scarcely credible against the summer's somber vista. . . . The remarkable turnabout in the war is the result of one of the swiftest, biggest military buildups in the history of warfare. . . . All of free Asia . . . stands to be ultimately strengthened by the extraordinary—and still burgeoning—commitment of the lives and talent and treasure of America."[35]

Kennedy did not share the euphoria. Professor Eugene Genovese, a Rutgers historian, said that he hoped the Viet Cong would win. Patriots demanded Genovese's dismissal. Kennedy defended his right to heresy. Richard Nixon, denouncing Kennedy, said that a Viet Cong victory "would mean ultimately the destruction of freedom of speech for all time not only in Asia but in the United States as well."[36] But the agitation against the war was spreading. It was the year of teach-ins, the first antiwar turbulence on the campuses, the first bonfires of draft cards. Early in November, Kennedy defended the demonstrations in a press conference at the University of Southern California: "I don't think you can ever discuss these matters enough." As for draft cards,

RFK. If a person feels that strongly and wants to . . . burn his draft card. . . . I don't agree with it personally but I think that obviously

[is] the way [chosen by] somebody that feels very strongly about this
matter. . . .

PRESS.   What about giving blood to the North Vietnamese?

RFK.   I think that's a good idea.

PRESS.   Is that going too far?

RFK.   If we've given all the blood that is needed to the South Vietnamese.
I'm in favor of giving [to] anybody who needs blood. I'm in favor of
them having blood.

PRESS.   Even to the North Vietnamese?

RFK.   Yes.[37]

This caused particular excitement. "If you feel strongly enough for
the enemy to give him a pint of your blood every ninety days or so,"
asked the *New York Daily News,* "then why not go the whole hog?
Why not light out for the enemy country and join its armed forces?
Bobby Kennedy is young, strong and virile, and financially able to
provide for his wife and children while he is away at war."[38] The
Chicago Tribune ran a cartoon showing Kennedy standing on a flag-
draped coffin labeled AMERICAN CASUALTIES IN VIETNAM while carrying a placard reading: "I am willing to give my blood to the Communist enemy in Vietnam."[39] It was, said his old friend Barry
Goldwater, "closer to treason than to academic freedom. . . . It's
appalling to me that the press of the nation hasn't jumped down his
throat."[40] Much of it did.

This did not deter him. He lashed out with a sort of reckless im-
pulsiveness on other subjects. "That was the really endearing thing
about him," Walinsky said. ". . . No matter how hard he would try
and protect himself . . . the things that got him in trouble were the
things that were just basically right and decent; they would come out
time and time again in these impromptu comments."[41] Thus in January 1966: "We have spoken out against inhuman slaughters perpe-
trated by the Nazis and the Communists. But will we speak out also
against the inhuman slaughter in Indonesia, where over 100,000 alleged Communists have been not perpetrators, but victims?"[42] No
other American politician condemned the Indonesian massacre. In the
same month the Defense Department denied burial in Arlington
Cemetery to the American Communist leader Robert Thompson.
Thompson had gone to jail under the Smith Act in 1949. He had also
won the Distinguished Service Cross for heroism in New Guinea in
1943. Kennedy, again alone, denounced the action on the floor of the
Senate. "To hate and harry the sinner to his grave," he said, quoting
a newspaper editorial, "is hardly in the American tradition."[43] He
told me later, his reference obvious, "I don't think anyone now

buried in Arlington would object to having Thompson buried there, so I don't see why all these living people are objecting."[44]

IV

In mid-November 1965, Amintore Fanfani, the Italian foreign minister, relayed to President Johnson four points for negotiation given to a special Italian mission to Hanoi. Rusk took a fortnight to acknowledge Fanfani's report and then, after various cavils, asked Fanfani to check back with Hanoi for clarification. In the meantime, Fanfani received a new message: if Hanoi or Haiphong were bombed, this would kill negotiations. Kennedy was one of those shown this message.[45] On December 15, before Hanoi responded to Rusk's inquiry, Johnson ordered the bombing of Haiphong.

On December 19 there was a party at Hickory Hill. My son Stephen's notes record Kennedy's mood:

RFK said: "Why didn't we accept the Fanfani message positively, agreeing to the four points and offering our own interpretation of what the four points meant—plus some points of our own. . . . Then the onus would be on Hanoi to refuse. This would make us look good whether the offer was real or not. But to dismiss it out of hand is disastrous. We lose all credibility. How could the State Department wait for two weeks? How could they? Why was the State Department message so bad? If we had acted that way in the Cuban crisis we might have had war. If, on Friday night, we had asked the Soviet government for an explanation of their message instead of just agreeing to our own interpretation of it, it might have been chaos.

"I don't believe in pulling out the troops. We've got to show China we mean to stop them. If we can hold them for about 20 years, maybe they will change the way Russia has. The next 30 days will be critical in Vietnam. With the casualty lists growing, the decision to send more troops will be critical. We may have reached the point of no return once that decision has been made. I'm upset over our policy in Vietnam. I don't think we've shown an open approach. I really think Johnson wants negotiations. Ball, Harriman, McNamara too. But Rusk is against them. Fifty percent of the government is probably for them; fifty percent against them. We're in a stalemate.

"I'd like to speak out more on Vietnam. I have talked again and again on my desire for negotiations. But if I broke with the administration it might be disastrous for the country. I'd have accepted the four points two years ago—at least a year ago. I told LBJ that the last time I saw him." . . .

He said that if we had accepted the four points a year ago, or even last week, in a short while, possibly 14 days, a Gallup Poll would show most of the American people favoring it. Asked how he knew, RFK said: "I feel it in my gut." He also felt that China would not get involved in Viet-nam.[46]

Hanoi had made it clear that talks were out so long as American planes were bombing North Vietnam. McNamara, the most ardent supporter of negotiations in the cabinet, had argued since early November for a bombing pause. Johnson was skeptical. The Joint Chiefs of Staff were violently opposed.[47] So were Cabot Lodge, who had returned to Saigon as ambassador, and General William Westmoreland, the new commander in Vietnam. So were Clark Clifford and Abe Fortas, Johnson's closest unofficial advisers. But Ball supported the pause, and Rusk and Bundy dropped their earlier opposition. On December 18, Johnson, still skeptical, decided to give it a try. The pause began with a Christmas truce and ran through the month of January 1966.

About this time McNamara asked me to arrange a private meeting with New Frontier friends. Galbraith, Richard Goodwin, who had by now left the Johnson White House, and Carl Kaysen dined at my house in Georgetown on January 6. McNamara told us that he did not regard a military solution as possible. His objective, he said, was "withdrawal with honor." I noted, "He seemed deeply oppressed and concerned at the prospect of indefinite escalation. Our impression was that he feared the resumption of bombing might well put us on the slippery slide."[48] The generals were clamoring for resumption; and Kennedy, hoping to stiffen the President against the rising pressure, sent Johnson a copy of Bruce Catton's *Never Call Retreat* with a handwritten note:

> I thought it might give you some comfort to look back at another President, Abraham Lincoln, and some of the identical problems and situations that he faced that you are now meeting. I refer you to pp. 56–63 and 371–381. . . . In closing let me say how impressed I have been with the most recent efforts to find a peaceful solution to Viet Nam.[49]

Johnson replied on January 27 (the letter was written by Valenti):

> Your warm letter arrived at an appropriate time. It was one of those hours when I felt alone, prayerfully alone.
>
> I remembered so well how President Kennedy had to face, by himself, the agony of the Cuba missile crisis. I read the paragraph in Catton's book that you had marked, and then I went to a meeting in the Cabinet Room with the Congressional leaders of both parties. I read them that passage where Lincoln told a friend that all the responsibilities of the administration "belong to that unhappy wretch called Abraham Lincoln." I knew exactly how Lincoln felt.[50]

Four days later Johnson resumed the bombing.

"Bob," George McGovern wrote Kennedy, "I do hope you will continue to raise questions about Vietnam. Your voice is one of the very few that is powerful enough to help steer us away from catastrophe."[51] On January 31 Kennedy arose in the Senate. "If we regard bombing as the answer in Vietnam," he said,

—we are headed straight for disaster. In the past, bombing has not proved a decisive weapon against a rural economy—or against a guerrilla army. And the temptation will now be to argue that if limited bombing does not produce a solution, that further bombing, more extended military action, is the answer. The danger is that the decision to resume may become the first in a series of steps on a road from which there is no turning back—a road which leads to catastrophe for all mankind.[52]

v

On February 4 the Senate Foreign Relations Committee opened public hearings on Vietnam. Kennedy watched with avid attention and mounting frustration. No one seemed to have thought through the detail of a negotiated settlement. He tried to think it through himself and concluded that the price of settlement was taking the National Liberation Front into the political process. When this point did not emerge before the Foreign Relations Committee, he decided to make it on his own.

He put out his statement on February 19 before going off to ski in Vermont. Each side, he observed, had its irreducible demand. The United States was insisting that South Vietnam should not be turned over to the North. North Vietnam was insisting that South Vietnam should not be a hostile state dedicated to the extermination of Communists. *"A negotiated settlement means that each side must concede matters that are important in order to preserve positions that are essential."* The United States had to recognize that many people in South Vietnam wanted change. "There are three things you can do with such groups: kill or repress them, turn the country over to them, or admit them to a share of power and responsibility." The first two meant a continuation of the war. The last was "at the heart of the hope for a negotiated settlement."[53]

Kennedy meant that the NLF should be admitted to a share in the political process, not necessarily to a place in the government. His statement mentioned "a compromise government" as only one of the possible forms acceptance of the NLF might take. But his language was imprecise, and he was immediately denounced as the advocate of coalition with the Communists. Vice President Humphrey led the counterattack from the far Pacific, where he was touting the war for the administration. "I don't believe in writing a prescription for the ills of Vietnam that includes a dose of arsenic," the old druggist said. "It would be something like putting a fox in the chicken coop."[54] Humphrey later wrote that his doubts about escalation early in 1965 had resulted in exclusion for months from the Vietnam policy councils. On this 1966 tour, he said, he was converted by brainwashing in Saigon, by confidential pleas from Asian leaders (including Indira Gandhi) that the Americans stay in Vietnam and by his own intense desire to be restored to presidential favor.*

In Washington, the day after the statement, George Ball on *Issues and Answers* and McGeorge Bundy on *Meet the Press* assailed Kennedy. To Kennedy's particular irritation, Bundy quoted John Kennedy in opposition to united front governments. Actually, Bundy had planned to quote Robert himself, but Johnson, in one of his flashes of solicitude, warned him not to do so if he valued his friendship with the senator.[55] "I would have obviously appreciated a call," Kennedy wrote Bundy (in a paragraph he deleted after further consideration), "before you dealt with [my position] and me on Sunday afternoon. Perhaps a call would not have taken any more time than for someone to look up the quote of President Kennedy to use against my position."[56] Later he made the point about advance notice over the telephone. Bundy said that Kennedy might equally have called before he took out against the administration. Kennedy replied that he had in fact discussed the statement with Moyers the day before he put it out.[57]

The uproar was general. John Connally sent word to Johnson that he understood Kennedy to have been "the motivating force behind the Senate hearings and the Saturday statement was only his climax."[58] The *Chicago Tribune* entitled its editorial "Ho Chi Kennedy."[59] Kennedy defended his position on the *Today Show*. Murray Kempton, who accompanied him to the studio, was struck by his "concentrated attempt to be his brother's interior, to talk not as John Kennedy did on the platform, but as he seems to have in private mo-

---

* Hubert Humphrey, *The Education of a Public Man* (New York, 1976), ch. 32, esp. 320–324, 337. George McGovern, however, describes a talk with Humphrey about Vietnam in the spring of 1965—"the first real argument Hubert and I had had in a decade as neighbors and friends. He replied heatedly that he believed in the policy —that we had to stop the Communists in Vietnam or they would take all of Asia. . . . If I heard others say he wasn't with the President all the way . . . it wasn't true" (McGovern, *Grassroots* [New York, 1978], 105).

ments of crisis. . . . The most reckless and romantic of the Kennedys was deliberately reshaping himself according to his memory of the coolest and most detached of them." They went out afterward for coffee. The counterman asked Kennedy to autograph the morning's *Daily News* cartoon—a picture of a scrawny Kennedy holding a giant hatchet emblazoned APPEASE VIET CONG. "You want me to autograph *this?*" Kennedy laughed and did so. A White House telephone lineman introduced himself. "We miss him," he said. "You ought to come over and see us." "Do I dare?" said Kennedy.[60]

There was now concern in the White House that the counterattack might go too far. Maxwell Taylor saw no serious divergence, assuming that Kennedy had not implied the establishment of a coalition government in advance of free elections. If the people of South Vietnam themselves brought the fox into the chicken coop, Taylor agreed, the administration would abide by the result. Moyers, who was laboring to keep Johnson and Kennedy together, made this point in a Tuesday press briefing, adding that NLF participation in an interim government would be negotiable. Kennedy accepted the compromise.[61] Two days later, Johnson defended his Vietnam course at a Freedom House dinner. The old New Dealer David Lilienthal noted Kennedy "chewing at a cigar, looking sullen and cynical as Johnson recited all the answers to his critics. . . . 'I have heard all this hokum a thousand times' written on his face."[62]

On February 27 Kennedy appeared on *Face the Nation*. I had been away from Washington during the hullabaloo but was now back, and he asked me to join Fred Dutton in running through questions before the show. Impersonating an interrogator, I challenged him about John Kennedy's responsibility for the trouble we were in in Vietnam. He thought a moment and said, "Well, I don't know what would be best: to say that he didn't spend much time thinking about Vietnam; or to say that he did and messed it up." Then, in a sudden, surprising gesture, he thrust out his hand to the sky and said, "Which, brother, which?"[63] In a short while he told the television audience that statements "that we will never deal with assassins or murderers make it difficult for [the other side] to believe that they are being asked to come to the negotiating table for anything other than to surrender."[64]

An hour after *Face the Nation*, Humphrey, now back from the Pacific, appeared on *Issues and Answers*. Kennedy and Humphrey had become good friends. When a letter from the mayor of Mobile,

Alabama, was misdelivered to Kennedy's office in January, Kennedy had sent it along to the Vice President with a joking note:

> This was sent [to] and opened in our office by mistake. It is not part of any ruthless scheme to open and read all your mail before it goes to your office.
>
> However I am somewhat shocked and surprised at the close working and social relationships you are establishing with some people.
>
> Needless to say I shall breathe no word about any of this to Clarence Mitchell or Martin Luther King or anyone like that.[65]

On Humphrey's return three days before, Kennedy had sent another note: "Welcome home. I was taking care of everything back here while you were away. Perhaps you heard. As a matter of fact I felt a little like the fox in the chicken house myself."[66] Kennedy genuinely liked Humphrey and admired his intelligence while still finding him weak; not to be relied on, he said in 1964, to "stand fast on something that's important . . . you know, he just wobbles away."[67] The liking was perhaps one-sided. The unrelenting Humphrey treasured his resentments of 1960. "I never quite forgave him for that period," Humphrey wrote as late as 1976.*

At any event we all now watched Humphrey on the tiny screen. The NLF, he vigorously said, "engage in assassination, murder, pillage, conquest, and I can't for the life of me see why the United States of America would want to propose that such an outfit be made part of any government."[68] "It was a new and different Hubert," I noted sadly as an ancient Humphrey fan, "—hard-faced, except for some unctuous smiles, and uncharacteristically coarse in language; he sounded like Tom Dodd. His trouble, I fear, is that he cannot say something publicly without deeply believing it privately; and when, as now, he has no choice in his public utterances, he whips up a fervency of private belief. I fear also that someone has persuaded him that this is the issue on which he can knock out RFK." Kennedy himself "was both so irritated and upset by Hubert's performance that, after a few minutes, he went silently away."[69]

For a few weeks Kennedy continued to argue the case for a negotiated settlement. The public remained confused. "I made some mis-

---

* Humphrey, *Education*, 374. See also Isabelle Shelton: "I asked him, not long ago, if he still was resentful about that election, and he said he didn't want to talk about it. 'They're all gone now,' he said sadly, meaning Jack and Bobby Kennedy. Then he stood silent for a long minute, lost in thought. . . . Finally he said quietly, a little tight-lipped: 'I haven't changed my mind' " (Shelton, "Memories of Hubert Humphrey," *Washington Star*, January 22, 1978).

takes in handling it," Kennedy said later. "I think it was unpopular politically. But I would do it all over again if I had to."[70]

VI

Kennedy brooded about Vietnam but said less in public. The announcement in April 1966 of "no sanctuary" for planes attacking American aircraft from Chinese bases provoked him to rise again in the Senate and warn against escalation.[71] Mostly the old fear that disagreement would be ascribed to a personal vendetta held him back. He took the usual Kennedy refuge and made jokes. "It isn't true that President Johnson and I didn't get along during the time I was Attorney General and he was Vice President," he would say. "We began the Kennedy administration with the best of relations, close, friendly, cordial—and then, as we were leaving the inaugural stand. . . ." Or: "President Johnson and I are very courteous and correct in our correspondence these days. I address my letters to him at the White House and he writes to me at the Senate Office Building. Sometimes he only uses the initials."[72]

One day in the late spring Galbraith, Goodwin and I lunched in New York. "It would be terrible," Goodwin said, "if, when the nuclear bombs begin to drop on Peking or Washington, we had to reflect that all we did in the summer of 1966 was to rest comfortably on one or another beach." Johnson, Goodwin said, was a man possessed, wholly impervious to argument. The only thing he understood was political opposition. We decided to do what little we could to stir public opinion. Goodwin soon wrote his book *Triumph or Tragedy: Reflections on Vietnam*. Galbraith wrote *How to Control the Military*. I wrote *The Bitter Heritage*. We also discussed the formation of a national committee against the widening of the war.

When we raised this latter idea with Kennedy on July 20, he seemed skeptical. A mass movement against escalation, he said, "would have to tie itself to an issue or to a man. The issue of widening the war is too complicated and ambiguous. LBJ could always justify each specific step on the ground that it was necessary to save the lives of American troops and that it would shorten the war. As for tying it to a man—" Here he paused. The polls were already showing him the leader of the Democratic opposition. Goodwin observed that the more an anti-escalation movement seemed a pro-Kennedy movement, the less likely it would be that Johnson would respond to it. Kennedy listened carefully but said nothing.[73]

The next weekend I resumed the discussion with Galbraith and George McGovern at Galbraith's farm in Vermont. "By now," I noted, "I had begun to think for the first time of the possibility of RFK's going for the nomination in 1968." The polls suggested he could win the primaries. He had kept up his relations with the city bosses like Daley of Chicago. When we talked about this in Vermont, McGovern said he was all for it. He added that he thought Johnson had a "great yellow streak" and might conceivably be bluffed out of running again.[74]

A fortnight later I was at Hyannis Port. I did not bring up 1968, but we talked about the establishment of a Vietnam information center in Washington. Kennedy said at once, "I can think of three things right off that such a center could do." One was the problem of Vietnamese elections—"the standards we should demand that they meet." Second, defoliation: "so far as I can tell, this hurts the ordinary people in Vietnam without seriously hurting the Viet Cong, but again we don't know nearly enough about it. Third, there is the question of our turning prisoners over to the South Vietnamese and becoming accomplices in torture. This is wrong in itself, and it is also bad policy, because we can never hope to get them to come over to us if all they can expect is to be tortured."[75]

Publicly he remained silent. In September Dr. Benjamin Spock urged him to open up the fight for negotiation. You are, Spock wrote, "the only person who could lead the country back to peace and decency." Kennedy asked Goodwin to "go see him on my behalf" and tell him "that I would like to see him some time after [the November] election."[76] In October, I. F. Stone scornfully entitled an article "While Others Dodge the Draft, Bobby Dodges the War."[77]

VII

"I knew from the start," Lyndon Johnson told Doris Kearns in 1970, "that I was bound to be crucified either way I moved. If I left the woman I really loved—the Great Society—in order to get involved with that bitch of a war on the other side of the world, then I would lose everything at home. . . . And I knew that if we let Communist aggression succeed in taking over South Vietnam . . . that would shatter my Presidency, kill my administration, and damage our democracy."[78]

He was a man of titanic gyrations of mood and temper. In Vietnam meetings he was controlled and reasonable. George Ball, the

most persevering critic of the war among his advisers, found him un-
failingly courteous. But Ball, as George Reedy said, was the "official
dissenter," whose arguments were "welcomed because they prove for
the record that decision was preceded by controversy."[79] In private,
as the Vietnam debate grew more bitter, the President became driven,
irascible, inflamed by wild suspicions. Chester Bowles, on home
leave from India where he was now ambassador, met with him in the
summer of 1966. "Literally half our time together was taken up by
almost paranoiac references to Bobby Kennedy, Wayne Morse, Bill
Fulbright and others." Bowles saw "a man headed for deep trouble,
with the probability of an increasing obsession with his 'enemies.' "[80]
White House aides, Doris Kearns wrote, "were frightened by what
seemed to them signs of paranoia." The President would enter into a
compulsive monologue, punctuated by irrelevant laughs:

> Two or three intellectuals started it all you know. They produced all the
> doubt. . . . And it spread and it spread. . . . Then Bobby began taking it
> up as his cause and with Martin Luther King on his payroll he went
> around stirring up the Negroes. . . . Then the Communists stepped in.
> They control the three major networks, you know, and the forty major
> outlets of communication. Walter Lippmann is a communist and so is
> Teddy White. It's all in the FBI reports. . . . Isn't it funny that I always
> received a piece of advice from my top advisers right after each of them
> had been in contact with someone in the Communist world? And isn't it
> funny that you could always find Dobrynin's car in front of Reston's house
> the night before Reston delivered a blast on Vietnam?[81]

It was hard to make out. Was this merely an eccentric mode of relaxation? Or did he really believe what he was saying? If the latter,
Goodwin and Moyers wondered what could be done. They thought of
asking for psychiatric investigation. But, as Goodwin said, he would
just talk calmly and rationally to a panel of psychiatrists, "and everyone would think we were the ones who were crazy."[82]

The original Johnson White House began to break up. Walter
Jenkins cracked under the strain in October 1964. Reedy left in July
1965, thereafter to write in *The Twilight of the Presidency* the classic
account of the way the isolations of power withdrew Presidents from
reality. Goodwin left in September 1965, Bundy in February 1966,
Valenti in May. Moyers stayed on till December 1966. Then he left.
He told me, "You know, Arthur, I would not be leaving if I thought
I could do any good by staying."[83] He told Frank Mankiewicz, "I
thought I could make him more like me, but I've found in the last
several months that I'm becoming more like him; so I got out."[84]

Johnson's obsessions centered more than ever on Kennedy. Had there been no escalation in Vietnam,

> there would be Robert Kennedy out in front leading the fight against me, telling everyone that I had betrayed John Kennedy's commitment to South Vietnam. That I had let a democracy fall into the hands of the Communists. That I was a coward. An unmanly man. A man without a spine. Oh, I could see it coming all right. Every night when I fell asleep I would see myself tied to the ground in the middle of a long, open space. In the distance, I could hear the voices of thousands of people. They were all shouting at me and running toward me: "Coward! Traitor! Weakling!"

The language, Doris Kearns noted, betrayed unconscious concerns— "coward," "unmanly," "without a spine"—along with his envy for Kennedy, whose manliness no one questioned. The sense of Kennedy as "the enemy," she believed, only hardened his determination not to change course in Vietnam.[85]

33

The Breach Widens:
South Africa, New York

THE KENNEDY CHALLENGE seemed to be acquiring global proportions. Robert Kennedy had already carried his campaign, as the exasperated White House saw it, to Latin America. He was meddling in Vietnam. Now he was proposing to move on to Africa. In the autumn of 1965 the anti-apartheid National Union of South African Students (NUSAS) invited him to speak at its annual Day of Affirmation. As Attorney General, Kennedy had supported independence movements in black Africa. He well remembered John Kennedy's concern that South Africa's racist policies "would create a bitterness and hostility that could not be contained within the country's own borders."[1] Wayne Fredericks, still deputy assistant secretary of state for African affairs, urged him to go; South African liberals needed all the encouragement the outside world could give.[2] He accepted the invitation.

I

"Bar Kennedy!" William Loeb begged the South African government from his New Hampshire eyrie. "Bobby Kennedy is the most vicious and most dangerous leader in the United States today. It would make no more sense to us for South Africa to admit Bobby Kennedy . . . than it would to take a viper into one's bed."[3]

It took South Africa five months to decide to admit him. When the visa finally arrived, Kennedy was unexpectedly embroiled in a New York political battle. He told Fredericks he preferred now to wait until after the fall elections. "Things are moving in South Africa," Fredericks replied. "Ian Robertson [the president of NUSAS] may not be available in November. Go now. If you postpone, it will confirm the idea that everything takes precedence over Africa, including local politics." In twenty minutes Kennedy called back: all right, he would go on schedule.[4] The week before he left, Lyndon Johnson delivered a speech on Africa, his first (and last) as President. "Cynics will wonder," observed the *New York Times,* "if the attention given to Senator Kennedy's forthcoming visit" did not explain the sudden presidential discovery of the dark continent.[5]

The South African government was even less enthusiastic than the White House. When Kennedy asked the South African embassy for advice on his itinerary, the ambassador responded that he had nothing to say, that his government disapproved of NUSAS and that no ministers would receive him.[6] A fortnight before his arrival, the government placed Ian Robertson under a "ban," excluding him from political and social life for five years. Then it denied visas to forty American newspaper and television correspondents assigned to cover the trip. South Africa, the Department of Information announced, would not allow the visit "to be transformed into a publicity stunt . . . as a build-up for a future presidential election."[7] The omens were all bad. As Thomas Johnston, who advanced the trip, put it, Kennedy was "going into a terribly explosive and delicate situation where the government was completely against him and the largest percentage of the white people were against him; and the blacks were in no position to really have any information, or be for him or against him. . . . The whole trip had the makings of one of the major disasters of his life."[8]

The party—Robert and Ethel, Angie Novello, Adam Walinsky—arrived in Johannesburg just before midnight on June 4, 1966. Johnston, who met them, found Kennedy unwontedly on edge.[9] But more than fifteen hundred people jammed the airport. Hecklers shouted "Chuck him out" and "Yankee go home." They were outroared by the enthusiasts. Kennedy made his way through a screaming crowd, his cuff links torn from his sleeves in the process, and climbed on top of the automobile waiting outside.[10] The reception was at once reassuring and disturbing. It showed both the hunger for a liberal voice and the emotionalism of the family argument into which he was entering.

He spent the next day in Pretoria. The Prime Minister, Dr. Hendrik Verwoerd, declined to see him or to permit other ministers to do so. In the evening he dined with South African businessmen. They could not understand, they told him, why the United States did not embrace South Africa, which was after all the most staunchly anti-Communist of nations. Here and for the rest of his stay he tried to explain that anticommunism was not enough. "What does it mean to be against communism," he asked, "if one's own system denies the value of the individual and gives all power to the government—just as the Communists do?" The South African said, "You don't understand. We are beleaguered." Kennedy wondered who was beleaguered: his dinner companions, talking comfortably over cigars and brandy? or Alan Paton, the novelist? the banned Ian Robertson? Chief Albert Luthuli, the Zulu leader who had won the Nobel Peace Prize in 1961 and was now banished to a remote farm in the back country?[11]

The next day he flew to Cape Town, delighting in the white city glittering in the sun, then chilled as the plane swooped down over Robben Island with its political prisoners. He was two hours late, but three thousand people waited at the airport. He promptly called on Ian Robertson and gave him a copy of *Profiles in Courage,* inscribed by Jacqueline Kennedy. When he emerged from Robertson's apartment, the street was filled with people and resounded with applause.[12]

That evening was the Day of Affirmation speech. Walinsky had written a draft in Washington. Allard Lowenstein, the young liberal activist who had traveled in South Africa, thought it too cautious; you really had to go full tilt, he said. Richard Goodwin was enlisted, and the speech took shape.[13] Going over the text still once more, Kennedy set off for the University of Cape Town. It took half an hour to get through surging crowds into the hall.

He talked first about the long American struggle for racial justice. "Nations, like men, often march to the beat of different drummers, and the precise solutions of the United States can neither be dictated nor transplanted to others." Still, everyone must accept "the full human equality of all our people" and join in "a shared determination to wipe away the unnecessary sufferings of our fellow human beings." The world's cruelty, he said, could not be changed "by those who cling to a present which is already dying, who prefer the illusion of security to the excitement and danger which comes with even the most peaceful progress." For it was "a revolutionary world we live in; and thus, as I have said in Latin America and Asia, in Europe and in the United States, it is young people who must take the lead."

Let no one, he said in his most eloquent passage, be discouraged by

the belief there is nothing one man or one woman can do against the enormous array of the world's ills—against misery and ignorance, injustice and violence. . . . Few will have the greatness to bend history itself; but each of us can work to change a small portion of events, and in the total of all those acts will be written the history of this generation.

It is from numberless diverse acts of courage and belief that human history is shaped. Each time a man stands up for an ideal, or acts to improve the lot of others, or strikes out against injustice, he sends a tiny ripple of hope, and crossing each other from a million different centres of energy and daring those ripples build a current which can sweep down the mightiest walls of oppression and resistance.[14]

These lines bespoke his profoundest conviction. The next morning the *Cape Times* reprinted the entire text under a nine-column headline: 15,000 ACCLAIM CALL TO YOUTH.[15] Frank Taylor of the *London Daily Telegraph* called it "the most stirring and memorable address ever to come from a foreigner in South Africa."[16] It was Kennedy's greatest speech.

The next day he talked to Afrikaner students at Stellenbosch University. "If the blacks are not 'inferior' to the whites," he remarked in the question period, "why don't they take part in your elections? . . . Why don't you allow them to worship in your churches? What the hell would you do if you found out that God was black?" He received a surprising ovation.[17] On to Durban: DURBAN'S WILD WELCOME FOR R.F.K. was the *Cape Times* headline.[18] He dined that evening with anti-apartheid leaders: Denis Hurley, the Roman Catholic archbishop; two Zulu chiefs; and Alan Paton, whose novels he so much admired.

In the evening he addressed nearly ten thousand people at the University of Natal. "Maybe there is a black man outside this room who is brighter than anyone in this room," he said, "—the chances are that there are many." There was applause.[19] Were South Africa's policies a threat to world peace? "Not at present," he replied. "But if the situation continues as it is, South Africa will place itself in that position, and I do believe that if it continues there will be a crisis."[20] Afterward, on the way back to the hotel, he encountered a group of Africans, and they sang "We Shall Overcome" together.[21]

II

At the beginning, said Walinsky, "his only crowds were the students. . . . But then somewhere as the thing started to get across . . . there were just thousands of ordinary citizens . . . not just Englishmen but Afrikaners coming out there into the streets to cheer and to listen and to shout . . . pulling at him and tugging at him and cheering him and it was really fantastic."[22] "By the end of the third day," said Tom Johnston, "as we moved from Cape Town to Durban, you began to sense this really great change; there were so many, many more people and instead of standing there passive, sort of hostile, why they were like a campaign that begins terribly slowly and then moves to this climax, all condensed into four and a half days!"[23]

The government sensed the change too and acceded to his request to visit Chief Luthuli. He left by helicopter before dawn the next day for Luthuli's farm. "A most impressive man, with a marvelously lined but kind face," Kennedy scribbled in his travel notes. "What did one notice first? The white goatee, perhaps, so familiar in his pictures, but then quickly the smile which lit up his whole presence, the eyes which danced and sparkled, and then, when he talked of the future of his country, of his people, of the relationship between the races, [became] intense and hurt and hard, all at once." "What are they doing to my countrymen, to my country?" Luthuli asked his visitor. "Can't they see that men of all races can work together—and that the alternative is a terrible disaster for us all?"[24]

They spent the last day in Johannesburg. There was a tour of Soweto, the steaming ghetto where half a million blacks lived behind wire fences, passing in and out with identity cards. People swarmed around his car, shouting "Master, Master." "Please don't use that word," Kennedy asked in embarrassment.[25] He made speeches from the roof of the automobile, from the steps of the Catholic cathedral, from a chair in the middle of a school playground. Later the inhabitants papered their shacks with Kennedy photographs cut from the newspapers.

That evening at the University of Witwatersrand he addressed the charge that blacks were too barbarous to be entrusted with power. "It was not the black man of Africa," he said, "who invented and used poison gas and the atomic bomb, who sent six million men and women and children to the gas ovens, and used their bodies as fertilizer." Their common humanity bound white and black inextricably together. Hope lay in "the most fragile and the most powerful of human gifts—the gift of reason. Thus those who cut themselves off from ideas and clashing convictions . . . encourage the forces of violence and passion which are the only alternatives to reason."[26]

Government displeasure did not relent. "This little snip," said one deputy minister, "thinks he can tell us what to do. . . . The next thing NUSAS will invite Nkrumah here and make him its chairman. . . . We are growing militarily stronger every day and we could eat any other African state for breakfast. Kennedy can threaten us as much as he likes, but we will show the world that our policy is the only one for South Africa."[27] After Kennedy departed, *Die Transvaler,* a paper close to the government, sourly offered "deepest sympathy for the American people if Senator Kennedy becomes their future President."[28]

Yet public attacks were rare during an astonishing week. Kennedy, through tact, directness and simplicity, came over to a surprising degree not as meddling intruder but as honest friend, recognizing white South Africa's kinship with as well as its estrangement from the great traditions of western civilization. He departed in a mixture of pessimism and elation. As the plane took off, he said somberly, "If I lived in this country, I would gather up everything I have and get out now." Then, wryly: "If we stayed another two days, we could have taken over the country." It was well to leave, he decided, before he began to have more influence than he wanted to have.[29]

"What caused all that almost frantic enthusiasm?" Anthony Delius wrote in the *Cape Times* after Kennedy's departure.

> . . . What, in fact, made the senator a kind of third political force in the country in less than a week? . . . Perhaps the most attractive and compelling feature of Senator Kennedy's speeches . . . was the insistence that he and all South Africans he spoke to belonged to the same world. . . . There was a common humanity, he insisted, which went beyond all superficial differences of race and culture. And among all there might be people with extraordinary capabilities—"Why, among the black schoolchildren I saw today there might be an Einstein—or a Dr. Verwoerd." . . .
> With him a great shaft of outer daylight was let into the air-conditioned comfort and concrete corridors of the bastion that nearly everybody believed, or feared, or hoped was shut tight against such natural illumination.[30]

The *Rand Daily Mail:*

> Senator Robert Kennedy's visit is the best thing that has happened to South Africa for years. It is as if a window has been flung open and a gust of fresh air has swept into a room in which the atmosphere has become stale and foetid. Suddenly it is possible to breathe again without feeling choked. . . .
> This younger Kennedy . . . has taken the youth of the country by storm through his message of confident, unashamed idealism. That is what so many of the young people of South Africa have been yearning for—some sort of clear and unequivocal endorsement that the hopes and ideals that all decent youngsters feel are indeed part and parcel of the great traditions of the contemporary world and not, as they are being told so often, something alien, unwholesome or worse. . . .
> The effects of Senator Kennedy's visit will be felt for a long time to come. . . . And so, as he and Mrs. Kennedy fly off today, we say to them:

Thank you a thousand times for what you have done for us. Come back again. You have a place in our hearts.[31]

"Even in remote areas such as South West Africa," the American embassy soon reported, "the Kennedy speeches were passed from hand to hand in the African townships."[32] The visit, Alan Paton said, could only be described as a phenomenon. "These long waits, this excitement, those outstretched hands, what are they but the signs of a hunger and a thirst, greater than we imagined? And who better able to satisfy them than our visitor?" Kennedy was "like a fresh wind from the wider world." But it would be a mistake, Paton added soberly, "to imagine that the Kennedy visit has made our world anew. . . . He can't fight our battles for us, and it is we who have to live our particular South African tomorrow."[33]

This was for Kennedy himself the ultimate frustration. "I remember one student who spoke at a meeting," he said after his return. "It was very easy for me to go there and speak of principles, and then leave, but that young man was going to stay."[34] He promised to return the next year,[35] but the government made it clear he would never receive another visa.[36] There was, in the end, an awful justice in the verdict of the *Cape Argus:* "Like a meteor, Mr. Kennedy has flashed across the South African sky, and has gone. . . . South Africa remains as it was."[37]

III

The rest of the African trip—Tanzania, Kenya, Ethiopia—was an anticlimax. The black leaders gave him the kind of reception usually accorded visiting chiefs of state. He found Nyerere lucid and forceful; Kenyatta, who gravely toasted the President of the United States, John F. Kennedy, seemed ancient, bemused and out of it; Haile Selassie had presence and dignity but appeared a relic of another age.[38] In Dar es Salaam, Kennedy met with Eduardo Mondlane, still fighting for a free Mozambique. Mondlane's account of the guerrilla war against the Portuguese gave the Americans a chastening sense of how the Vietnam War must look to the Viet Cong.[39] (Mondlane was assassinated in 1969. His movement continued the fight and won full independence in 1975.)

They went on to Rome, where Kennedy saw the Pope. "I told him how important it was the church take a clear position—how effective Bishop Hurley was—how cruel the system was." Black Africans were turning against Christianity, Kennedy said, because, as one had told him, "the Christian God hates the Negroes." He found the Pope "impressive though frequently as I was making a point he would make one of his own that was not completely pertinent." When Kennedy was discussing South Africa, the Pope said, " 'We took an interest in African art in North Africa' as if this were a satisfactory response. Nonetheless impressive—& sensitive too. Urged me to continue talking on the moral aspects of [the] problem." His Holiness was also "very concerned about Viet Nam. Appeared solution must come from God." He thought the International Control Commission could be helpful in opening a dialogue between the North and South. "Urged that US cease opposition to China's entry into the UN." Kennedy observed "how harmful internally the war had been in US. [The Pope] said US leaders should keep pounding away at fact that they were interested in peaceful solutions."[40]

There was an intoxication about these trips. But Kennedy well understood their limits. Chester Bowles soon invited him to India. Kennedy sent the letter on to Galbraith with a note: "What do you think? To tell the truth I don't feel much like going off to India in November. I would like to start seeing the developed world like Paris."[41] When talk arose about an autumn journey to eastern Europe, Walinsky sent him an alarmed memorandum saying it's too much, you can't top it, there are too many things to be done in New York. The memo came back with a note in Kennedy's squiggly handwriting: "Adam, I'm not going anywhere this fall. I shall be hand in hand with you while we walk through the ghettoes of New York."[42]

There were indeed things to be done in New York. The trouble Kennedy was encountering in South Africa, wrote Joseph Kraft while he was still away, "is apt to look like child's play when he comes home. For by taking sides in an obscure New York judicial primary, he has set in motion a titanic struggle among the elemental forces of New York politics."[43] On his return on a rainy June afternoon, he opened his press conference by saying, to the delight of the New York reporters, "Everybody in Africa was very interested in Sam Silverman."[44]

IV

Sam Silverman represented Robert Kennedy's most serious foray thus far into New York Democratic politics. It was an impulsive venture. He well remembered his father's warning to his older brother a decade before that local politics was an "endless morass." John Kennedy, apart from one or two lapses, had heeded that warning. "It didn't make a great deal of sense to get into all those . . . fights in a state," the younger Kennedy mused in 1967, "because after a period of time it sucked away all your strength."[45] Nor did he need headlines about ruthless Bobby Kennedy trying to take over the New York party.

He was, in addition, as his perceptive friend John Burns, the state chairman, said, "bored" with politics.[46] His candid correspondent Fred Dutton had pleaded with him in vain to attend to "dull political proprieties" as his brother had.[47] The clubhouse politicians, Kennedy told Richard Goodwin, were not interested in issues; he was not interested in communion breakfasts and county dinners. They felt he neglected them. "I don't suppose I'm the jolliest fellow to have around."[48] Actually, the professionals felt not just neglected but rejected and threatened. "There aren't ten politicians in the whole state I like and trust," he told Jack Newfield of the *Village Voice*.[49] He concealed this feeling inadequately from the rest. "In Massachusetts they steal," he used to say, "but here they steal and lie too."[50]

On the other hand, he was, except for the comptroller, Arthur Levitt, the only Democratic official elected statewide in what had become almost the personal fief of Governor Nelson Rockefeller. This imposed an obligation to try and lead his party out of captivity. He felt an obligation too to the public-spirited young men and women whom the Kennedys had made a business of encouraging to enter politics. He wanted to restore the traditions of Smith, Roosevelt and Lehman, to raise the quality of candidates, to make the party an instrument of progressive government. And he of course wanted to secure his base against the depredations of Lyndon Johnson, who was still withholding patronage and by 1966 would have liked to sneak the state party (and the 1968 delegation to the presidential convention) away from Kennedy. In June, Marvin Watson reported to Johnson discussions with Mike Prendergast, whom Robert Kennedy had driven from the state chairmanship in 1961, about "ways in which your Administration can properly recognize the Democratic Party machinery there and therefore take away the separate organization which Senator Kennedy is planning."[51]

Finding the regulars hopeless, Kennedy was in fact turning increasingly to the reform Democrats and the Liberals. But, except for his West Side friends, like Ronnie Eldridge, the reformers seemed to him to be divided between opportunists trying to get into the organization and emotionalists with what James Wechsler of the *Post* called an "insistent and possibly incurable" will to lose.[52] As for the Liberals, he admired Alex Rose's talents in political maneuver but did not warm to him as a person.

Two weeks before departing for Africa, Kennedy had a drink with Rose. The idea was to renew relations; neither had anything in particular to discuss. "He's not the easiest fellow in the world to talk to, you know," as Rose said later; so, to keep things going, he showed Kennedy a Wechsler column in the afternoon paper about a special election for the surrogate court to be held in June. J. Raymond Jones, the Manhattan Democratic leader and a power in Harlem, had made a deal with the Republican county leader by which Arthur Klein, the candidate of the Democratic organization, would get Republican endorsement in exchange for Democratic endorsement of a Republican candidate for the state supreme court. Wechsler reprinted excerpts from a twenty-year-old wiretap showing that Klein, wittingly or not, had once nominated a judicial candidate selected by the mobster Frank Costello. As Kennedy read the column, Rose recalled, "I could see his face change." "Can we do something about this?" Kennedy asked. "You can," said Rose. Kennedy: "Do you think we can win?" Rose: "You can't ever lose if you do the right thing—you know what I mean?" The astute Liberal leader threw in the thought that John Lindsay, the dashing Republican congressman elected mayor the previous November, believed nothing could be done.[53]

Kennedy's face changed for several reasons, of which only one was disgust over the intrusion of the underworld into politics. The surrogate court was a scandal. Its function was the probating of wills, in the course of which favored lawyers received large fees out of the estates of deceased citizens. The reform of the surrogate court was a way of protecting poor people who often saw inheritances draining away in surrogate fees. It was also a way of denying the party organizations their most lucrative source of patronage. And it was a way to consolidate his own relations with the Liberals and the reformers; a way to dish Ray Jones, whom Kennedy regarded as an unedifying practitioner of the old politics and who had, in addition, worked for Johnson in Los Angeles in 1960; a way, as Kennedy said, to "stick it to John Lindsay,"[54] who had shunned the fight. He asked Stephen Smith and William vanden Heuvel to come up with a candidate. They proposed Samuel Silverman.

V

Silverman, a justice of the state supreme court, had been a partner in Paul, Weiss, Rifkind, Wharton and Garrison, the city's leading liberal law firm. He had participated in Robert Oppenheimer's defense against security charges brought by the Atomic Energy Commission. He had the highest respect of his profession. Hearing the report on his qualities, Kennedy said, *"Habemus papem."*[55]

He then telephoned Silverman. New York, Kennedy said, was filled with gifted Democrats who ought to be involved in public affairs. If Silverman would stand for surrogate, this would be an example to others. He added, "We both run certain risks in this." Silverman, who was happy on the supreme court, said he saw the risks Kennedy ran, but the only risk he could see for himself was that he might be elected. Kennedy said he would talk to the reform leaders and, unless they were willing to get off their asses and work, it wasn't worth doing. Silverman finally remarked that he couldn't say no to Kennedy.[56]

On May 22, a few days before leaving for Africa, Kennedy met with the reform leaders. It was, as Jack Newfield described it, "Kennedy at his evangelical best, and the reformers at their nitpicking worst." They were almost resentful to find him urging them on to the barricades. After two hours of bickering, Kennedy said quietly, "I had always been under the impression that you people really were interested in doing something [about judicial reform]. And now that I see that you're not really, I think that I have to reconsider before I ask Judge Silverman to make the commitment that he's willing to make." He started to leave the room. "It all pulled them together," Ronnie Eldridge recalled. "It was like a parent talking to the children."[57] The reformers agreed to join the battle.

Tammany and the old clubs were stoutly behind Arthur Klein. Ray Jones was fighting for political survival, and Kennedy feared that in his desperation he might raise the race issue. "It won't be bad, my being in Africa," he said as he departed, "if, you know, the Jones thing comes up."[58] It came up all right. One statement signed by Harlem district leaders charged that Kennedy's intervention was "aimed solely at J. Raymond Jones, because he is a Negro."[59] Kennedy responded by getting James Meredith and James Farmer to endorse Silverman.

Turning the campaign over to Stephen Smith, who described it as "two unknowns running against each other for a job nobody understood,"[60] Kennedy went off to Africa. Now he was back to find the campaign well organized but uphill. There were ten days to go. He flew to New York from Washington every afternoon to tour the city with Sam Silverman.

It was a rollicking few days. I accompanied the Kennedy motorcade on one suffocatingly hot June evening. At each street-corner rally Silverman would make four crisp points about the surrogate court, and James Farmer would boom away, and then Kennedy would speak. "Don't die in the city of New York," he exhorted his audiences. "Don't die—if you want to leave anything to your wife and children." Pointing to Silverman, "He is an honest man, he will protect you." He liked to tease the children in the crowd. "You all know, of course, what the surrogate is." They would cry, "Yes," and he would call back, "Some in this neighborhood don't tell the truth, I'm afraid. . . . OK, how many of you are going to go home tonight and tell your mothers and fathers to vote for Judge Silverman?" All hands shot up. "Let's go over it again. What are you going to tell your mothers and fathers when you go home?" "Vote," the children cried. "And vote for whom?" "Kennedy!" He would put his hands to his head in mock pain and say, "No, no. I don't think you have the right idea," and the marimba band would strike up and the motorcade move on to the next rally.[61]

There was always the vein of melancholy. Kennedy sat, as he customarily did, in the front seat of the car to the right of the driver. Someone called from another car that his door was not fully closed. As he slammed the door shut, he said, "I wonder what proportion of voters in New York would have thought it a good idea to warn me about this."[62] Silverman found him altogether different from what he had expected—"thoughtful and gentle. . . . I never saw any of the, you know, the ruthless reputation. . . . He'd ask what I'd think and so on, and never attempted to impose his will."[63]

Silverman won easily, even almost carrying Harlem. Kennedy at the victory party: "I well remember that Sunday when I called him to see if he would run. And he said in a ruthless kind of way, 'Just you remember, Mr. Kennedy, Silvermans don't finish second!'" Kennedy introduced the campaign manager—"a beloved figure who is replacing me on the American horizon, ruthless, mean Stephen Smith."[64] Murray Kempton titled his column for the *Post* "Kennedy Regnant," adding, "The editors of the *New York Times* have a contempt for the motives of the junior Senator from New York quite as excessive as the respect they entertain for those of its senior Senator; quite naturally then there was no mention of Robert Kennedy in the *Times* editorial celebrating the newest of our annual deliverances from the bosses."*

VI

"Kennedy Regnant"—the momentum of the Silverman triumph led to the next step in the revival of the party: the nomination of a candidate for governor against Nelson Rockefeller. The regulars had gathered behind Frank O'Connor, a pleasant and unassuming Irishman of the pre-Kennedy school who had been district attorney in Queens and was now president of the New York city council. Kennedy liked him well enough but hardly considered him a model of the new spirit with which he hoped to infuse the party, a feeling that O'Connor, a realist, accepted.

Among other aspirants, Franklin Roosevelt, Jr., had claims on Kennedy's support. John Kennedy had planned to make Roosevelt Secretary of Commerce so that he could build himself up for the New York governorship.[65] But Roosevelt was unpopular with the organization, and Kennedy, though he retained a fondness for him over the years, did not see him as an ideal candidate either. His preference was Eugene Nickerson, county executive of Nassau County, able, informed, honorable, with a tested appeal to the suburbs. Nickerson was little known upstate, however, and not a stirring campaigner. Then the Silverman victory gave Kennedy a moment of maximum influence. Many thought he could now dictate the nomination. O'Connor thought so.[66] Nickerson thought so.[67] The newspapers ran stories about his ruthlessness and predicted he would name the candidate.

Stuck with the reputation, he might as well have been ruthless. Instead he hesitated, vacillated and blew the opportunity. When Jack English, Nickerson's main backer, pressed for an endorsement, Kennedy replied, "If I do that, isn't it going to be boss rule?"[68] "He decided finally," said John Burns, "that he was not going to get himself into that kind of a position where he was going to force Nickerson or

---

* *New York Post,* June 30, 1966. Kennedy followed up his victory by proposing in the New York State Constitutional Convention in 1967 the merger of the surrogate court with the state supreme court and the establishment of a state office of public guardian. The politicians successfully defended the old system. Silverman served with distinction on the surrogate court and reformed everything within his power but, bored and frustrated, resigned in 1971 and returned to the state supreme court.

anyone else on the party."[69] If Nickerson were clearly a great candidate and O'Connor clearly hopeless, Kennedy told me at the end of July, he would come out for Nickerson; but the gap was not quite that large. "I am weak with the Irish," he added, "and, if I come out for Nickerson, I will get into a lot of trouble there."[70]

English, making a last try, warned Kennedy that O'Connor, if victorious, would back Humphrey for the presidential succession.[71] O'Connor was indeed a friend of Humphrey's and, when asked in 1970 whether the administration had been courting him, replied, "No question about it." "Bob Kennedy—I know now for a fact—" O'Connor said, "believed that I was completely in the Humphrey-Johnson camp, which was not true, but I can understand it, and I don't resent it."[72] At the time, he went down to Hickory Hill and told Kennedy, "If I were you . . . and I was thinking of supporting a candidate for governor of New York, I would want to make darn sure that he was not an enemy of mine. . . . I want to tell you now I'm not out to block you."[73]

Kennedy had lost control of the situation. After O'Connor agreed to let him pick the delegation in 1968 and to keep Burns as state chairman,[74] he put out a statement saying he would abide by the wishes of the convention. The Johnson White House watched with extreme pleasure. "The tide is now on the ebb for him," wrote Henry Hall Wilson of the legislative staff, especially because of "his fiasco in the New York gubernatorial matter. His problems will be compounded if O'Connor defeats Rockefellow [sic], as now seems highly probable."[75]

The Democrats assembled in Buffalo on September 7. "It was Robert Kennedy's burden to introduce O'Connor," wrote Jack Newfield. "The senator is deeply bored by the kaleidoscopic tribalisms of New York politics. His is the mind of the curious novelist, rather than the mechanic absorbed by details; his span of concentration is brief when it becomes focused on tactical intrigues divorced from substantive issues. . . . Still, the senator knows of O'Connor's dream of becoming Hubert Humphrey's running mate in 1972. . . . In the scorebook of presidential politics, Humphrey won in Buffalo and Robert Kennedy lost." Newfield added: "But the senator is a pro, and in the last week of October will be in the streets."[76]

VII

When he arrived on the New York streets at the end of October, Newfield was with him. Three years had passed since the radical reporter had glared with hatred at the hard-faced Attorney General shouting to demonstrators before the Justice Department. The previous February Newfield had described Kennedy on a television show as an existential man, preoccupied by suffering, who could understand himself only in action and to whom Dallas had given a unique sense of the absurdity of life. Kennedy, chancing to see the show, had asked Newfield for lunch.

"I was not fully prepared for the changes," Newfield wrote. ". . . Instead of the military crew cut, his graying, ginger hair now lapped over his earlobes in the shaggy style of the alienated young. His blue eyes were now sad rather than cold, haunted rather than hostile."[77] They argued about Kennedy's performance as Attorney General—whether he had instituted enough voter registration suits and why the FBI had only taken notes when Newfield saw blacks beaten up in Mississippi. "I liked him enormously," Newfield said later. ". . . Kennedy was the first national politician I had met who had human reactions. He wasn't plastic. He wasn't programmed. . . . I felt that he was bright and that he saw the world from an angle I couldn't even imagine."* Kennedy liked Newfield enormously too. Newfield had grown up in Bedford-Stuyvesant, the only white kid on the block, helped found Students for a Democratic Society, joined SNCC, went to Mississippi and saw the world from an angle Kennedy wanted more than ever to understand.

Back in New York after speaking for liberal Democrats across the country, Kennedy first wanted to help his favorite member of the New York House delegation, Congressman Hugh Carey of Brooklyn. Shaking hands as he walked with Carey and Newfield along crowded sidewalks, he noticed a ten-year-old girl wearing glasses. He knelt down and said, "You know something? My little girl has glasses just like yours. And I love my little girl very much."[78] Lost for a moment to the world, he rubbed the back of her neck, then turned to shaking hands again. (On another occasion in Bay Ridge, when Kennedy was walking with Carey, someone shouted, "Carey, what are you doing with that Red? Are you a Commie too?" Carey shrugged and said, "That's the way they act around here.")[79]

On the way back to Manhattan to join O'Connor, Kennedy said to

* Victor S. Navasky, "Jack Newfield Talks About R.F.K.," *New Leader,* May 26, 1969; Clark Whelton, "Memoir of a Hero Who Died at Five," *Village Voice,* June 5, 1969; Jack Newfield, in recorded interview by Jean Stein, July 21, 1968, 3–5, Stein Papers. Newfield developed his thesis about Kennedy in "Bobby Kennedy: Existential Hero" (*Cavalier,* June 1963. Kennedy told Newfield he had sent a copy of the piece to his father, first ripping it out of the girlie magazine because the rest of the contents were so obscene.

Newfield, "Do you still like me, Jack?" Newfield said, "Yes, but why do you have to campaign for a guy like Carey?" "He's such a decent fellow," Kennedy said. "He works very hard and he's very bright. Whenever we meet at least he's concerned about the issues. He's not like [James] Scheuer [a reform Democrat, also in the House] who has such a great reputation, but only asks me about patronage. . . . Also, Carey has trouble with his district. He was telling me the Church was such a problem. I wonder why the kids who come out of parochial school are so conservative."[80]

O'Connor, who had proved a listless campaigner, was behind in the polls; nevertheless, after three rallies in Manhattan, he announced he was cold and tired and would call it a day. "Kennedy's face," observed Newfield, "showed he felt this was a sign of softness." Kennedy completed the schedule, then invited Newfield to his apartment in United Nations Plaza. They had a couple of drinks. Kennedy asked a little shyly whether Newfield liked poetry. Newfield said he liked Yeats and Hart Crane. Kennedy said, "Can I read you some poetry by a poet I like very much?" Newfield, anticipating a con job for the benefit of the rebel press, thought he might come up with something like Allen Ginsberg's "Howl." Instead he read Emerson's "Fame."

When he finished, Kennedy peered out the window at the barges making their way along the East River. "Look at that!" he said. "There's a ship called *World Justice,* and it's moving away from the United Nations." Then he read Emerson again, this time the "Ode Inscribed to W. H. Channing":

> But who is he that prates
> Of the culture of mankind,
> Of better arts and life?
> Go, blindworm, go,
> Behold the famous States
> Harrying Mexico
> With rifle and with knife![81]

On November 8, O'Connor went down to defeat. Robert Kennedy spent election night with a small group ranging from John Steinbeck and Yevgeny Yevtushenko, the Soviet poet, to Sam Silverman.

34

Time of Troubles

IN THE LAST MONTHS of 1966 Robert Kennedy moved dramatically ahead of Lyndon Johnson when public opinion polls asked whom Democrats and independents favored for 1968. Kennedy's "rise in political appeal," Gallup said in August ". . . has been spectacular."[1] Louis Harris concurred in November. Kennedy himself remained skeptical. The voters, he told me, probably agreed 80 percent with Johnson on the issues between them; it was just that people did not believe Johnson any longer. "He is rueful about his own vogue, which he regarded as transient."[2] He was right.

I

There had been premonitions in the summer of 1966 when Katzenbach as Attorney General told Kennedy the Justice Department was filing a brief with the Supreme Court confessing that the FBI had engaged in illegal electronic eavesdropping in 1963. Kennedy asked Katzenbach to state in the brief that the Attorney General at the time had no knowledge of the FBI's bugging habits either in the case at hand or in general. Katzenbach refused, not because he disbelieved Kennedy but because he thought the addition irrelevant.[3] Kennedy, upset, wrote his old friend: "As you know this is a damn important matter for me. I just don't want to receive a shaft—it's not deserved— and anyway I don't like them deserved or not. I'm getting too old I guess. I can't write you as many memos as J. Edgar Hoover. And there is no sense in talking about it by phone. I feel strongly about it —and I write you just that as there's not much else to say."[4]

The departmental confession initially aroused little attention. Then Senator Edward Long of Missouri, a friend of Roy Cohn and of the Teamsters, proposed an investigation of wiretapping and bugging.

"He is out to get Bobby," Bill Moyers told Goodwin one day. "Johnson is egging him on."[5] In December 1966 Hoover himself went public, firing off letters and documents to Congressman H. R. Gross of Iowa. The press covered the altercation with relish. Either Kennedy knew about the bugging, Richard Harwood wrote in the *Washington Post*, in which case his denials impeached his credibility, or else he did not know, in which case "his executive competence could be brought into question."[6] Congressman Wayne Hays sagely advised the President to "fire J. Edgar Hoover on the strength of Bobby Kennedy's statement and answer the backlash by pointing at Kennedy. . . . your best bet for getting rid of both men."[7]

Kennedy took refuge in jokes—"I also want to deny officially the rumor that J. Edgar Hoover irritated me during that period. He was no bother at all. Of course, he bugged me now and then"[8]—but he knew that damage had been done.

II

Greater damage was to come. After Dallas, Jacqueline and Robert Kennedy had resolved to spare the dead President the indignity of having a book written about his last days by Jim Bishop, whom Jacqueline thought a hack and Robert distrusted because of a pro-Hoffa series Bishop had written in 1959. They therefore approached —or, as Jacqueline later inaccurately and infelicitously put it—"hired" William Manchester to do the book.[9] (Bishop did his book anyway.) Manchester, a skilled writer and a decent but highly emotional man, had written novels, an excellent biography of Mencken and a deft and admiring sketch of John Kennedy.

On March 28, 1964, Manchester signed a contract providing that "the final text shall not be published unless and until approved" by Jacqueline and Robert Kennedy.[10] This was a fundamental error. A provision requiring family approval of the use of materials made uniquely available by the family—letters, oral history transcripts and the like—would have been proper. A provision requiring family approval of the entire text compromised Manchester's freedom as a writer and made the Kennedys responsbile for Manchester's independent research and interpretation. The Kennedys never should have proposed such a provision. Manchester never should have acceded to it. But in the aftermath of the assassination the Kennedys were in an unduly protective mood. When John Kennedy's old friend Paul Fay wrote his bouncy memoir *The Pleasure of His Company,*

Robert Kennedy landed on him as if it were the only book through which posterity would ever know his brother. He wanted Fay to cut nearly two fifths of his jocular text. Galbraith, reading the manuscript at Jacqueline's behest, thought it harmless. Fay published it with some excisions in 1966, and an old friendship lapsed.

In early 1966 Manchester, after prodigious research, turned over a long, deeply felt, greatly overwritten manuscript. Kennedy friends read it with growing dismay. They objected especially to Manchester's treatment of Johnson. The draft opened, for example, with a hunting scene in which a boorish Johnson pressed a reluctant John Kennedy to shoot a deer on the Johnson ranch. This beginning, as I wrote Manchester, had the effect "of defining the book as a conflict between New England and Texas, decency and vulgarity, Kennedy and Johnson." The portrait of Johnson "too often acquires an exaggerated symbolism—so much so that some critics may write that the unconscious argument of the book is that Johnson killed Kennedy (that is, that Johnson is an expression of the forces of violence and irrationality which ran rampant through his native state and were responsible for the tragedy of Dallas)."[11] John Seigenthaler, Edwin Guthman and Pierre Salinger all believed that Manchester's evident hostility to Johnson "would destroy the credibility of the book."[12] Evan Thomas of Harper & Row, the putative publisher, thought the manuscript in part "gratuitously and tastelessly insulting to Johnson."[13]

The Kennedy concern was not, as Manchester supposed, "anxiety over Johnson's reaction."[14] By 1966 Johnson had turned irrevocably against Robert Kennedy. It was rather the impression the manuscript left that the Kennedys had never given Johnson a fair chance. In my own case, I recommended the elimination of the mythodrama depicting Johnson as monster-usurper, but felt that Evan Thomas had gone too far in deleting strictly factual references to Johnson.* Kennedy himself acknowledged the claims of history. He observed to Manchester of one chapter that it "will injure both Johnson and me, but apparently it's factually correct and a contribution to history. I'd like you to change it, but I guess you won't."[15]

Had it not been for the wretched contract, Manchester would have been entirely right in fighting for his reading of the historical record;

---

* On April 28, 1966, after consultation with Seigenthaler in Nashville, I wrote Kennedy, "You will be under great pressure to tone down the LBJ passages in the book. Of course, everything that is petty and gratuitous should go; but I hope you will not take out anything which is an essential part of the historical record" (RFK Papers). See also William Mancheser, *Controversy* (Boston, 1976), 19.

even within his rights in fighting for his romantic mythodrama. The contract probably should have been rewritten to release the Kennedys from responsibility; but I cannot remember anyone's suggesting that. It was probably supposed that no one would believe Manchester was truly a free agent. Or, with the controversy every day more acrimonious, the Kennedys may have considered the contract their only security on a separate issue: Manchester's use of material derived from his interviews with Jacqueline Kennedy.

On this point Manchester was clearly wrong. The proposition that an oral history interview became the private property of the interviewer was indefensible. If the person interviewed lost all rights over the transcript, the oral history program, which promised so much to the historian of the future, would be dead. Manchester had no right to use material from his interviews with Mrs. Kennedy that she did not wish him to use.

III

This became the central issue. With regard to Johnson, Manchester subdued most of his mythodrama and retained most of his history. But he was unwilling to surrender personal detail that Jacqueline Kennedy, increasingly agitated, regarded as an inexcusable violation of her privacy. With *Look* poised to begin serialization, the discussions acquired the hysteric character of a malign farce. Robert Kennedy, who had other things on his mind, became increasingly weary of the business. "It was just a damned nuisance to him," Evan Thomas said. "He hated it all and wished he had nothing to do with it."[16]

But his loyalty to his sister-in-law was unconditional. At one point he impulsively wired Thomas that publication should be canceled. "It just seems to me that rather than struggling with this any longer we should take our chances with Jim Bishop."[17] This last was strong language from Robert Kennedy. When Manchester complained how difficult it all was for him, Kennedy said in amazement, "Do you think you've suffered more than Jackie and me?"[18] By December 1966 a desperate Manchester would make no more changes. "I have reached the point," he informed his agent, "where, if the integrity of my manuscript is violated, I have no wish to go on living. . . . I am ready to die for this book."[19] Jacqueline Kennedy was equally determined to expunge the personal material she found offensive. On December 16 she filed suit to prevent the book's publication. Frank

Mankiewicz said to Kennedy, "My God, I think that's a terrible mistake." Kennedy said, "Yes, it's a terrible mistake but nothing can be done about it."[20]

The press had a field day. The columnist William S. White, a Johnson intimate, wrote that the purpose of the Manchester book had been to "gut Johnson" and "that the smile or the frown of the Kennedy cult has a power over the fortunes of any kind of book that this country has never known before."[21] Editorial writers rode their high horse about the sacred cause of freedom of information. I watched it all with a certain skepticism. Fifteen months before, the press had almost unitedly risen to denounce a writer (me) for reproducing in *A Thousand Days* comment about public officials acting in their public capacities. The historical truth of the comment was not under challenge; but editorial writers then brusquely dismissed the claims of history. Now with almost equal unanimity they invoked historical truth as an absolute in order to rebuke the widow of a murdered President for guarding her grief against a writer who sought to use her confidences without her permission.

The *Washington Post,* which had not in 1965 defended historical truth as a criterion in writing about Secretaries of State, asserted sententiously in 1966, "The lives of public men—the records of their careers, the thoughts of others about them—are not the property of their families, but the property of posterity."[22] Robert Kennedy later wrote to Katharine Graham, the *Post*'s publisher, that Jacqueline was "so upset and really crushed . . . a girl who hadn't committed any great crime but who day after day was being attacked and pilloried in all kinds of sandalous ways."[23]

On December 21 *Look* agreed to remove or modify passages relating to the personal life of Jacqueline Kennedy and her children. "These paragraphs," her lawyer explained, "were the sole reasons for the initiation of her legal action."[24] The suit against Harper & Row was settled in January, the court awarding the oral history tapes to Jacqueline Kennedy. The Kennedys had won their case but, as Robert perfectly understood, at a fearful cost. The stereotype of ruthless, arrogant Bobby Kennedy, riding roughshod over everybody, had received a tremendous infusion of new life. "It's really mostly my fault," he said to Mankiewicz. ". . . There wasn't very much time anyway and I certainly didn't want to spend it on that. We'll just have to move on."[25] Murray Kempton saw him after a visit to wounded men at the Bethesda Naval Hospital. "You know," Kennedy said, "as I was standing there, I thought to myself: there are things more important than who writes a book about somebody."[26]

IV

The men he had visited were back from Vietnam, and one of the things more important was the war. But there was also new trouble, nearer home. One day, as Ethel Kennedy was riding with her children near Hickory Hill, she noticed a cadaverous horse standing miserably in a chicken coop. "It was a bag of bones," she said, "the saddest sight I've ever seen." She told her groom to bring the horse to Hickory Hill where, despite maternal care, it died five days later. The owner sued her for $30,000 as a horse thief. The trial, in January 1967, lasted a long two days, and the jury deliberated for a longer two and a half hours. Ethel began to tease Louis Oberdorfer, her lawyer, about what would happen if they lost when, to popular applause, the jury came back with an acquittal. It was the best publicity the Kennedys had all winter. Someone asked Ethel whether she would steal a starving horse again. She replied, "I don't think I could live with myself if I didn't." As for Robert Kennedy, Oberdorfer recalled him as not too greatly concerned; "he was preoccupied then with the Vietnam business."[27]

He could not escape the Vietnam business. While generally avoiding the war during the autumn campaign, he had called for an end to the bombing in a question period after a speech in California, adding that the people of South Vietnam had a right to determine their own destiny. "Personally, I don't think they want General Ky, just as it is clear they don't want the Communists." This irreverence, at a moment when Johnson was meeting the new leader of South Vietnam in Manila, scandalized the statesmen of the press. It was, said the indignant David Broder, "a hip-shooting display of verbal carelessness, worthy of Barry Goldwater."[28] Three days later at Cam Ranh Bay Johnson exhorted American troops to "come home with that coonskin on the wall." Commentators did not denounce this as hip-shooting. One forgets too quickly the mood of 1966.

In mid-December Jack Newfield pleaded with Kennedy to speak out. If another speech would do any good, Kennedy said, "I would make it tomorrow. But the last time I spoke I didn't have any influence on policy, and I was hurt politically. I'm afraid that by speaking out I just make Lyndon do the opposite. He hates me so much that if I asked for snow, he would make rain, just because it was me. But maybe I will have to say something. The bombing is getting worse all the time now."[29]

At the end of January he went to England to address the Oxford Union. Soon after arrival he received a cable from Ethel:

SUNDAY GALLUP POLL WILL SHOW . . . DEMOCRATS REPUBLICANS AND INDEPENDENTS COMBINED KENNEDY 48 JOHNSON 39 NEITHER 13. IF THIS KEEPS UP YOU JUST MAY HAVE TO DUMP OLD HUCKLEBERRY CAPONE LOVE AND KISSES AND GOOD WORK.[30]

Alas, the poll had been taken before the Manchester dénouement. In London he saw old friends. He urged them not to acquiesce in the decline of Britain. "Your history is your power. . . . You have lost faith in your future because you are forgetting how much your past has meant to all of us." As for the preoccupying issue, "Agree or disagree with America's position in Vietnam, but do it because you believe it, not to save the pound." Waiting for Prime Minister Harold Wilson, he wrote his father a letter on 10 Downing Street stationery, recalling the family's stay in London nearly thirty years before.[31]

Then to Oxford, where the first question after his address was about Vietnam. Reluctant to attack his own government beyond the twelve-mile limit, Kennedy confined himself to expressing "grave reservations" about the bombing. The next three weeks, he added, might be crucial. "There are some signs that Hanoi is reconsidering its position." He evidently had in mind the impending visit of Aleksei Kosygin, the Soviet Premier, to London. The questions went on for an hour, ranging from birth control, which he endorsed despite the deplorable example of his own family, to China. He departed to a standing ovation.[32] The next day he left for France.

The French, however much they disagreed on everything else, were united on Vietnam. De Gaulle's position, François Mitterand, the Socialist leader, told Kennedy, had "the support of the majority."[33] Couve de Murville, the foreign minister, said there would be "a Communist government in Saigon. We may not like it but it is inevitable."[34] "The United States cannot do well," André Malraux told him, "when you are involved in a matter of inner contradiction. Vietnam is against American tradition."[35] Henry Kissinger, who was in Paris, took him to see Jean Saintény, once high commissioner in northern Indochina. Saintény, recently back from Hanoi, talked about Ho Chi Minh's determination to be independent of both Moscow and Peking. Kissinger appeared to agree that further escalation would be folly and that negotiation was a possibility to be pursued.[36]

He saw de Gaulle. "As I told your brother," the general began, "the United States is involved in a wrong course in Vietnam." There could be no peace until Washington stopped bombing and declared its intention to withdraw. This would not mean communization. "South Vietnam would not permit the North . . . to run their country. Ho Chi Minh realizes this and would not attempt it." America, the general continued, had always presented the highest ideals to the world. "All of this is being destroyed by your role in Vietnam. . . . History is the force at work in Vietnam, and the United States will not prevail against it." After seventy minutes de Gaulle concluded by offering Kennedy some remarkably bad counsel. "You are a young man," he said, with "a brilliant political future. . . . I am an old man, and I have lived through many battles and wear very many scars, so listen to me closely. . . . Do not become embroiled in this difficulty in Vietnam." Those who opposed the war would be "badly hurt." When they lose their effectiveness, then it will be time for you to step in and "help your country regain its proper course."[37]

Kennedy's most important Paris talk, as it turned out, was with Étienne Manac'h, the director of Far Eastern affairs at the Quai d'Orsay. John Gunther Dean, the Vietnam expert at the Amercan embassy, went with him. Manac'h stressed Hanoi's "complete mistrust" of American peace gestures. "Recent history has shown that, as soon as President Johnson makes offers of peace, there are parallel actions of war." Manac'h felt nevertheless that Hanoi remained ready to negotiate. "The one indispensable condition . . . is a cessation of bombing."[38] This was what Kennedy got out of Manac'h, according to his own memorandum of the conversation. The talk was in French, which he understood imperfectly and which Dean translated on the run.

But Dean, better versed in both the language and the negotiating nuances, got something more specific. Up to this time Hanoi had conditioned negotiation on American acceptance of four prior points. Now Manac'h said, citing a declaration made to him by the head of the North Vietnamese mission in Paris, Hanoi was waiving its preconditions and asking only that the bombing stop. Hanoi, in short, was offering an important concession; and Manac'h evidently felt that, if he passed the message to an American diplomat in Kennedy's presence, it could not be ignored in Washington. Afterward Dean drafted a cable, showed it to Manac'h to make certain he had it right, heard Manac'h say again how important the new Hanoi position was and sent the cable off to the State Department.[39]

Kennedy went on to Bonn, where Chancellor Kiesinger told him that "the majority of people do not understand what and why the United States is doing in Vietnam"[40] and Willy Brandt, now foreign minister, said that German-American relations had "declined as a result of the Vietnam involvement."[41] There was more of the same in Rome. Fanfani complained for an hour about the sabotage of negotiations by American bombing;[42] President Saragat said that the United States had evidently lost all interest in Europe because of Vietnam, and Russia was moving into the vacuum;[43] the Pope cited "extremely reliable sources" indicating that Hanoi had changed its attitude and was somewhat more prepared for discussions.[44] Unable to find any leader on the continent who supported or even understood America's Vietnam policy, Kennedy, his own misgivings redoubled, flew back to the United States.

V

While Kennedy was still abroad, someone in the State Department showed Dean's cable to Edward Weintal, the diplomatic correspondent of *Newsweek*. Kennedy returned on Saturday, February 4. On Sunday evening the *New York Times* received an advance copy of *Newsweek* with Weintal's story about a "significant peace signal . . . unveiled for the benefit of Robert F. Kennedy for reasons best known to the enemy."[45] The Monday *Times* led with the Kennedy "peace feeler."

When Lyndon Johnson read his *Times,* he was enraged. It was another of those recurrent seasons of military optimism. On January 8, Lodge had predicted "sensational military gains."[46] Westmoreland was delivering sanguine pronouncements with imperturbable inanity. "Joe Alsop came in for an hour," Rostow reported to Johnson on January 28. ". . . He thinks we are in the process of winning the war quite rapidly. . . . I cautioned him on some of his exuberance . . . but my personal view is that he is nearer the mark than most of the analysts."[47] Why make concessions when you are ahead? The weekend of Kennedy's return Johnson hardened his negotiating position, demanding that the North stop reinforcing its troops in the South as a condition precedent to the cessation of the bombing.*

---

* The letter to this effect, dispatched by Johnson to Ho Chi Minh on February 8, was drafted and redrafted February 2–8 (David Kraslow and S. H. Loory, *The Secret Search for Peace in Vietnam* [New York: Random House, Vintage reprint, 1968], 206).

It had been infuriating enough in Johnson's view for Robert Kennedy to wander around Europe chatting with heads of state; but for him to try and force the President's hand on negotiation, at a time when the war was going so well, was final proof of malevolence. For Johnson was sure Kennedy had leaked the story to *Newsweek* in Paris—a suspicion presumably verified when the State Department, with customary efficiency, could find no Paris cable on the Kennedy-Manac'h talk. (Dean's account was later discovered to have been misfiled.)[48]

Kennedy, not having understood that Manac'h was relaying a hot tip from Hanoi, was baffled by the *Newsweek* story. He told Mankiewicz he did not have the "foggiest idea" what they were talking about.[49] In any event, the courteous thing, he thought, was to report to the President on his trip. They met Monday afternoon, February 6, the day of the *Times* story. Kennedy left no record of the meeting; Johnson published none (Kennedy was sure he had the meeting taped);[50] and the others present—Katzenbach, who had become under secretary of state, and Rostow—have held their peace, except to agree that it was most unpleasant. When he got back to his office, Kennedy described it all incredulously to Mankiewicz and Edelman, and the historian must rely on their recollections.

"The President started right in by getting mad at me for leaking the story," Kennedy told Mankiewicz. Kennedy replied that he had not leaked the story; he was not aware there had been a peace feeler and still was not sure there had been one. "I think," Kennedy said, "the leak came from someone in your State Department." "It's not *my* State Department, God damn it," Johnson said angrily. "It's *your* State Department." The President went on about the irrelevance of negotiations. "Those guys are out of their minds," Kennedy told Mankiewicz. "They think they're going to win a military victory in Vietnam by summer. They really believe it." Johnson told him that the war would be over by June or July. "I'll destroy you and every one of your dove friends [he specified Fulbright, Church and a couple of other unfortunates] in six months. You'll be dead politically in six months."

After a time Kennedy asked whether Johnson would like to know what Kennedy thought he should do. Johnson said yes, go ahead. "Say that you'll stop the bombing if they'll come to the negotiating table," Kennedy said, "and then you should be prepared to negotiate." He outlined a series of possibilities—a cease-fire in stages, an expanded International Control Commission to deter further escalation, an international presence gradually replacing American forces, a political settlement allowing all major elements in South Vietnam to participate in the choice of a government. "There just isn't a chance in hell that I will do that," Johnson said, "not the slightest chance." Kennedy and his friends, he said, were responsible for prolonging the war and for killing Americans in Vietnam. Blood was on their hands. Kennedy said, "Look, I don't have to take that from you," and started to leave.

Katzenbach and Rostow tried to compose the situation. They asked Kennedy to tell the waiting press that there had been no peace feelers. Kennedy refused, saying he did not know whether there had been peace feelers or not. "I didn't know what the hell had been said to me." He finally agreed to say that he had not brought home any feelers—true enough, since the message had been transmitted to Washington by Dean. "Well, that wasn't a very pleasant meeting," Kennedy told his aides when he was safely back on the Hill. "He was very abusive," he said later to Newfield. ". . . He was shouting and seemed very unstable. I kept thinking that if he exploded like that with me, how could he ever negotiate with Hanoi."[51]

Versions of the meeting, suitably embellished, rapidly spread about town. *Time,* rising to the occasion, announced that Kennedy had called Johnson a son of a bitch to his face, which he had not.[52] Once again Kennedy was the loser. He appeared a publicity-seeking meddler in international relations, a compounder of trouble for an overburdened President and, as always, ruthless and arrogant. A more legitimate criticism would have been of his failure to spot the negotiation feeler, but the press did not pursue this point. Kennedy, as usual when in doubt, made a joke. Speaking in March at the Gridiron banquet, he offered his own version of the session with Johnson: "We had a long serious talk about the possibilities of a cease-fire, the dangers of escalation and the prospects for negotiations. And he promised me the next time we are going to talk about Vietnam."[53]

In any case, the Manac'h message, when the State Department finally found it, made no difference. Neither did Kosygin's assurance to Harold Wilson in London in the second week of February that unconditional cessation of the bombing would bring negotiations. On February 13 Wilson and Ambassador David Bruce urged Washington to continue the brief bombing pause over Tet, the Buddhist New Year, so that Kosygin might have time to persuade Hanoi to meet Johnson's insistence on reciprocal military deescalation in exchange for a bombing halt. On February 14 Johnson ordered the resumption

of the bombing. "Peace was almost within our grasp," said Wilson.*
Johnson preferred that coonskin on the wall.

VI

The February 6 meeting marked the end of the road. Kennedy saw
no further point, Mankiewicz said, in trying "to mute his criticism of
the war."[54] He began on February 8 with a speech in Chicago about
China.

In its quest for reasons sufficiently dire to justify the growing fury
of American intervention, the administration had evolved the thesis
that the real enemy in Vietnam was China. "The threat to world
peace," as Hubert Humphrey soon said, "is militant, aggressive Asian
communism, with its headquarters in Peking. . . . The aggression
of North Vietnam is but the most current and immediate action of
militant Asian communism."[55] In Chicago Kennedy flatly rejected
"attempts to portray Viet Nam as a Chinese-inspired conflict." Vietnamese Communism on the contrary was "a native growth, with its
own revolutionary traditions and dynamism." As for Communist
China, Kennedy called for a new American policy based on "conscious and open recognition that we live in the same world." He
looked forward, he said, to the day when an American diplomat
would go to Peking bearing the instructions Secretary of State Daniel
Webster had given Caleb Cushing in 1843: to tell the people of China
"that you are a messenger of peace from the greatest power in
America to the greatest in Asia."[56]

The next step was a speech on Vietnam itself. Kennedy took care
to talk with McNamara, Taylor and Harriman to get the administration's latest thoughts. I do not know what they told him; he always
protected such confidences. McNamara by this time had lost all faith
in the efficacy of bombing. I do not imagine he gave Kennedy to understand that victory was imminent. Taylor remained a true believer.
Harriman was more complicated. His misgivings about the war were
deep but carefully buried because, I always thought, he wanted to
conclude his distinguished career by negotiating a Vietnam settlement
and feared that any hint of disloyalty would lead Johnson to give the
job to someone less determined to make negotiations succeed.

Kennedy also sought out the most extreme opponents of the war.

* There was much more to the Washington sabotage of the Wilson-Kosygin talks.
The bizarre story is well told in Chester L. Cooper, *The Lost Crusade* (New York,
1970), 350–368.

On February 13 he asked Newfield to arrange a meeting with Tom Hayden and Staughton Lynd, two articulate radicals whose book *The Other Side,* an account of a trip to Hanoi, Kennedy had recently read. The New Leftists, to Kennedy's surprise, advocated not unilateral withdrawal but an unconditional bombing halt as a preliminary to negotiations, with which Kennedy of course agreed. Kennedy said he favored a "Laos-type" solution for Vietnam. Afterward Newfield asked his friends what they had made of Kennedy. Lynd said, "Very fair-minded. Sort of detached, and not authoritarian at all. But still very much a liberal." Hayden thought him superior to "Reuther or Rauh or any of those guys" and was reminded of Mendès-France. Kennedy told Newfield that they seemed nice, bright fellows; "but I didn't think they told me everything they felt about immediate withdrawal."[57]

Goodwin, Walinsky and I set to work on drafts. Goodwin, along with Kennedy himself, had the largest hand in the result. In the meantime, public expectancy was growing. On February 17 the *Times* announced in a five-column headline: RFK SETS MAJOR SPEECH ON BOMBING. Other senators, it should be noted, were calling for a halt. The valiant Morse and Gruening had gradually been joined by Fulbright, McGovern, Nelson, Clark, Church, Javits, Eugene McCarthy and a dozen more. But Kennedy was the one who alarmed Lyndon Johnson.

The White House orchestrated a counterattack. Johnson directed Westmoreland, "in anticipation" of the Kennedy speech, to denounce a bombing pause.[58] "I don't want to pay one drop of blood," Westmoreland promptly told reporters in Saigon, "for a pig in a poke."[59] James A. Farley was exhumed to inveigh against Kennedy's "soaring ambitions." "Insulting, belittling and interfering with the office of the Presidency," Farley said, "is not the act of a mature citizen, let alone a United States Senator."[60] Johnson even dispatched Harriman to request Kennedy "in the national interest" not to encourage Hanoi and undermine the harassed President.[61]

On Sunday, February 26, Kennedy, Goodwin and I spent the afternoon in my New York apartment putting the speech in what we hoped was final shape. The Gallup poll that morning had said that only 24 percent of the country wanted a bombing halt. I had feared Kennedy might draw back. He muttered that Sorensen had advised against the speech, but that he was sure it was the right thing to do and was determined to do it regardless of consequences.[62] About this time he warned John Burns, the state chairman: "It's going to hurt me, isn't it?" Burns said it would hurt him for a while, but "I think that over a period of time you'll be proven correct." "That's the way I feel about it," Kennedy said, but "no matter whether it hurts me or whether it doesn't," he would speak anyway. ". . . Somebody has to do something about it."[63]

VII

On March 2, 1967, Robert Kennedy came down to breakfast at Hickory Hill. He had been up till three-thirty working with Goodwin, Walinsky and Mankiewicz to put the speech into final shape. Ethel greeted him: "Hail, Caesar." Kennedy said, "I spoke to Teddy last night. He said to make sure that they announce it's the Kennedy from New York." Children drifted in. Bobby Jr., the animal collector, brought along a coatimundi which suddenly attacked Ethel, sinking sharp claws and teeth into her leg. "He's biting me," she screamed. "Oh, God, he's biting me." The animal was pried away, and Ethel went off to a doctor. When she returned, her leg in bandages, she said, "If these are all the scars the Kennedys end up with by five o'clock, it'll be all right."[64]

Johnson was making his own preparations. In the course of the day, determined to deny Kennedy the headlines, he made (in the computation by vanden Heuvel and Gwirtzman)

> two unscheduled speeches in Washington, held an unscheduled news conference to announce that Russian Premier Kosygin had agreed to talk on reducing the stockpile of nuclear weapons, announced he was inviting all the nation's governors to the White House, had Senator Henry Jackson of Washington read on the floor of the Senate a predated letter from him, explaining why the bombing was necessary, and confirmed the rumor that his daughter Luci was pregnant.[65]

The headlines went to Kennedy all the same.

In the early afternoon Kennedy met with reporters. One asked about Johnson's charge that speeches like Kennedy's were a disservice to the boys overseas. "You have to balance that," Kennedy said, "against what you think does the greatest amount of good. I don't think we're going to end the war by military action." Did he think the country was more hawkish than dovish? "Yes," Kennedy said.[66]

He rose in the Senate chamber at twenty minutes to four. His speech, like all respectable anti-escalation discourse of the time, began with a brief declaration of American determination to stay in Vietnam until commitments (undefined) were fulfilled. This had to be said in order to gain a hearing for what followed. It was also said because it was still accepted by all except the New Left. "I do not agree with those who would abandon South Viet-Nam," Chester Bowles, for example, wrote privately that spring to Hubert Humphrey.[67] Those of us who hoped for a negotiated peace believed that retention of American troops in defensive enclaves was essential to give the other side an incentive to negotiate. Unilateral withdrawal, we thought, would lead, not to negotiation, but to a Communist Vietnam. In retrospect, I feel that, while we were right in our forecast of the consequences of withdrawal, the New Left was right in seeing these consequences, whatever they might be, as less ghastly than continuing the war. I wish that unilateral withdrawal rather than negotiation had been the dove objective in 1967.

But it wasn't; and it would have done even less well than "negotiation now" in a country still a good deal more hawkish than dovish. In any case, Kennedy rushed through the obligatory ritual in two sentences. Then he got down to business. He himself had been involved, he said, in "many" of the decisions that had brought the United States into Vietnam. Literally this was not true. He meant that his brother had been involved. "I can testify," he continued, "that if fault is to be found or responsibility assessed, there is enough to go around for all—including myself." As late as January 1971, according to *Facts on File,* Kennedy "was the only major official in either Democratic administration who admitted publicly to being wrong about Vietnam."[68]

The United States had sent more than 400,000 men, he continued, into the "ever-widening war." "The most powerful country the world has known now turns its strength and will upon a small and primitive land." He enjoined his countrymen to visualize the "horror" of this "distant and ferocious" conflict. War was "the vacant moment of amazed fear as a mother and child watch death by fire fall from an improbable machine sent by a country they barely comprehend." It was "the night of death destroying yesterday's promise of family and land and home." It was "a land deafened by the unending crescendo of violence, hatred, and savage fury. . . . Although the world's imperfections may call forth the act of war, righteousness cannot obscure the agony and pain those acts bring to a single child."

This horror, Kennedy said, was "not just a nation's responsibility, but yours and mine. It is we who live in abundance and send our young men out to die. It is our chemicals that scorch the children and our bombs that level the villages. We are all participants." And now we were "steadily widening the war" at just the time when opportunities for settlement appeared to lie at hand. What was the risk in exploring these opportunities? "No one is going to defeat us, or slaughter our troops, or destroy our prestige because we dare take initiatives for peace." He asked the administration to test Hanoi's sincerity by halting the bombardment of the North and saying the United States was ready to negotiate within the week. If, as the administration objected, conflicting signals came from Hanoi, why not seize on the most favorable message, as President Kennedy had done during the missile crisis? As for the idea that we must punish the North for its iniquity, "We are not in Vietnam to play the role of an avenging angel pouring death and destruction on the roads and factories and homes of a guilty land. We are there to assure the self-determination of South Vietnam. . . . Can anyone believe this Nation, with all its fantastic power and resources, will be endangered by a wise and magnanimous action toward a small and difficult adversary?"[69]

Henry Jackson, Kennedy's old friend from the McCarthy committee, the party chairman in 1960, read the Senate Johnson's letter defending the bombing. Kennedy's proposals, Jackson said, put the United States into a position of weakness. Fulbright, McGovern, Clark, Tydings, Claiborne Pell, Albert Gore, John Sherman Cooper, supported Kennedy. At the end of the long day, Kennedy returned to his office. An aide suggested that Jackson deserved a gift. "Why not send him the coatimundi?" He caught the shuttle to New York. Phil Ochs, the folk singer, who had come down to Washington to hear the speech, was with him. Kennedy remembered that Bob Dylan was supposed to have changed his name to help his career and asked Ochs whether this was so. Ochs said it was. Kennedy said, "You think it would help me if I changed mine?"[70]

VIII

The inevitable Richard Nixon said that Kennedy's speech "had the effect of prolonging the war by encouraging the enemy. . . . Johnson is right and Kennedy is wrong."[71] Johnson agreed with that. The American people, he said a few days later at a private dinner of the Democratic National Committee, would not stand for "a dishonorable settlement disguised as a bargain for popularity purposes." He went on, said William Dunfey, the national committeeman from New Hampshire, in "an unbelievable tirade," ending by reading aloud a letter to the sister of a soldier killed in Vietnam. "Your brother," the letter said, "was in South Vietnam because the threat to the Vietnamese people is, in the long run, a threat to the free world community." The letter, Johnson revealed with unconcealed relish, was signed John F. Kennedy.[72]

Undeterred, Robert Kennedy pursued his campaign to drive home the meaning of the war. Soon after his Vietnam speech, he went to the University of Oklahoma. The president gave him a cordial introduction. Kennedy said, "That's the nicest thing any president has said about me in a long time." In the question period someone asked about student deferment from the draft. Kennedy said he was against it; he could afford to send his children to college, but others couldn't, and it was unfair. "There was hissing and booing," recalled Senator Fred Harris, who had accompanied Kennedy. Kennedy said to the audience, "Let me ask you a few questions." How many favored student deferment? Resounding cheers from the students. How many favored escalation of the war? The vast majority raised their hands. "Let me ask you one other question," said Kennedy. ". . . How many of you who voted for the escalation of the war also voted for the exemption of students from the draft?" There was, said Fred Harris (who himself still backed the war), a "giant gasp"; then stunned silence; then overwhelming applause.[73] He did this in many colleges. "The poor are carrying the burden of the struggle," he would say, and call for a universal draft determined by lottery.[74] In fact, so long as the Americans dying in Vietnam came from the other side of the tracks, the respectable middle class did not mind the war. Only when the contraction of educational deferments late in 1967 exposed their own sons did community leaders begin to turn against further escalation.

The debate was growing bitter. In mid-April 1967, Joseph Rauh invited Vice President Humphrey to hear the views of long-time liberal friends. Before Rauh's dinner I visited Kennedy at Hickory Hill. He said gloomily that his Vietnam speech "had probably stiffened LBJ's determination to pursue the opposite course. Also he could not get a hearing for anything he had to say on the merits; his every action was always interpreted in terms of political maneuver." At Rauh's house an impassioned Humphrey gave us a defense of the war, at once voluble and pathetic. He talked as if the whole thing were a Chinese Communist plot. He thought a physical barrier across northern South Vietnam—the same old fence Lansdale had derided in 1961—was a great idea. "I was most depressed of all," I wrote afterward, "by the lack of the sense of the concrete human dimension of problems which had characterized the old Hubert. Not once in his long discourse did he express any dismay over the human wreckage wrought by American policy. . . . This trailing off of humanity is accompanied by an obvious delight in hobnobbing with statesmen—many mentions of the Pope, de Gaulle, Radakrishnan, etc., etc."[75]

A week later Johnson escalated the bombing. Westmoreland denounced the doves for leading the enemy to believe "he can win politically" what he could not win militarily. George McGovern responded bitingly in the Senate. Kennedy arose to praise McGovern for "one of the most courageous speeches delivered in the Senate since I became a Senator." Kennedy went on to warn that American escalation made counterescalation by our adversaries "inevitable." He condemned the policy of seeking peace "through military action which is really going to bring about the destruction of Vietnam and the people."[76]

I spoke to McGovern and Kennedy the next day.

> Both were a little melancholy, felt that the senatorial revolt could be no more than a gesture, and wondered what kind of national support they could get. Beyond that, both felt stymied by our constitutional situation. The irony is that all of us for years have been defending the presidential prerogative and regarding the Congress as a drag on policy. It is evident now that this delight in a strong Presidency was based on the fact that, up to now, all strong Presidents in American history have pursued policies of which one had approved. We are now confronted by the anomaly of a strong President using these arguments to pursue a course which so far as I can see, can lead only to disaster.[77]

McGovern and Kennedy were right to doubt their national support. In May 1967, nearly half the college students described themselves as hawks, hardly more than a third as doves.* In October, 53 percent of Americans advocated further escalation.[78] Kennedy's opposition to the war compounded his troubles. His "standing with the American people," Louis Harris had reported at the end of January, "has taken a tumble downward."[79] "The ranks of Kennedy supporters," Gallup added in May, "have steadily declined."†

He still had not figured out how to disagree with Johnson on substance without laying himself open to charges, as Joseph Kraft had warned after the 1966 election, of putting "personal interest above all other things," of acting "to divide his party."[80] In the spring of 1967 even doves like Walter Lippmann urged him not to break with

---

* The breakdown was 49–35 (G. H. Gallup, ed., *The Gallup Poll: Public Opinion 1935–1971* [New York, 1972], vol. 3, 2065).

† He had lost 11 points from the poll Ethel had cabled so cheerily to London. Johnson now led him 49–37 (*Washington Post,* May 10, 1967).

Johnson. "A Johnson-Kennedy fight for the nomination," Lippmann wrote a fortnight after Kennedy's Vietnam speech, "would split the Democrats and . . . favor, even if it did not assure, the nomination and election of a right-wing Republican, perhaps Nixon."[81] Old Kennedy hands like Joseph Dolan, Milton Gwirtzman and Fred Dutton ("I suspect that this suggestion goes strongly against your grain") begged him to make conciliatory noises about the President. And, in a way, professions of support licensed a larger measure of opposition on issues by making it harder to charge political ambition or personal resentment.

Returning in June from the London funeral of his beloved Cissy Harlech, the wife of his old friend David Ormsby-Gore, Kennedy introduced Johnson at a Democratic dinner in New York. Sorensen handed him a hyperbolic paragraph as he rushed from the airport to the Americana Hotel. Kennedy spoke about the "height" of Johnson's aim, "the breadth of his achievements, the record of his past, the promises of his future. . . . In 1964 he won the greatest popular victory in modern times, and with our help he will do so again in 1968."[82] Many of us cringed at such extravagance. "How could you say all those things?" Peter Maas asked him the next day. Kennedy replied icily, "If I hadn't said all those things, that would give Lyndon Johnson the opportunity to blame everything that was going wrong. . . . Vietnam, the cities, the race question. . . . on that son of a bitch Bobby Kennedy."[83]

So he avoided charges of ambition and party-splitting by incurring charges of inconsistency and hypocrisy. Privately he was in despair. "An indefinable sense of depression hung over him," I wrote after seeing him in April, "as if he felt cornered by circumstance and did not know how to break out."[84] He had reached the personal conclusion that Johnson was hell-bent on smashing his way to military victory, was deluded as to victory's likelihood and indifferent as to its human consequences and, worst of all, had retreated into some realm beyond the reach of reasoned argument. I dined at Hickory Hill in late May. At the end of the evening, he walked out with me into the soft spring night. Before I drove away, he said, "How can we possibly survive five more years of Lyndon Johnson? Five more years of a crazy man?"[85] But he could not see what he could do to prevent it.

(35)

Tribune of the Underclass

ROBERT KENNEDY SAW Vietnam not in abstractions but in images—a village smashed, children scorched, the mother clasping the baby while fire rained inexplicably from the sky. This compulsion to be at one with individuals in extreme situations was increasingly the key to his politics. From childhood he had, as an underdog, sympathized with underdogs; then Dallas, at once agony and liberation, had charged sympathy with almost despairing intensity. His own experience of the waste and cruelty of life gave him access to the sufferings of others. He appeared most surely himself among those whom life had left out. Even Gore Vidal once conceded: "I think he had a real affinity for the hurt people of the world: the blacks, the poor, the misunderstood young."* He kept a commonplace book in these years. The epigraph read: "None can usurp the height but those to whom the miseries of the world are a misery and will not let them rest."[1]

I

"In every arena where the poor, the black, and the uneducated suffered indignity and neglect,". Jack Valenti said, "President Johnson and Bobby Kennedy thought alike."[2] At the start Lyndon Johnson gave mighty impetus to the twin wars against poverty and racial inequality. So long as the Great Society absorbed the President, there was strong reason for Kennedy, despite differences on foreign policy, not to break with the administration.

* Gore Vidal, in recorded interview by Jean Stein, March 25, 1969, 2, Stein Papers. Mr. Vidal wrote me in 1977: "I don't recognize the quote but if I said it I said it but, perhaps, in a different context since I regarded his metamorphosis with my usual suspicion."

As the civil rights struggle moved north, poverty and racial inequality were more than ever intertwined. In 1963 Kennedy had observed that race problems were "at least temporarily . . . more easily resolved" in the south. When segregation was based on law, repeal the law, "release a valve," and the oppressed, for a time, were satisfied. "But in the North, in Chicago or Los Angeles, . . . what steps would you take to release that valve?" Here segregation had been abolished, political and legal equality affirmed, but inequality remained. "What you have to do is make over some of these cities and really take drastic action."[3]

His last act before he resigned as Attorney General was to send Johnson a memorandum entitled "Racial Violence in Urban Centers." He urged the President to tell a conference of mayors—Kennedy appended a list of cities with large black populations—how the national government would help in meeting the problems "that have created Negro frustrations and hatreds." He suggested palliatives for long hot summers; but "the basic problems of jobs, training, and housing may take more than a generation to resolve."[4] "Problems in the North," he told Anthony Lewis in December 1964, "are not easily susceptible to passage of legislation for solution. You could pass a law to permit a Negro to eat at Howard Johnson's restaurant or stay at the Hilton Hotel. But you can't pass a law that gives him enough money to permit him to eat at that restaurant or stay at that hotel. . . . That's basically the problem of the Negro in the North."[5]

Problems of course remained for the southern Negro, now in the final phase of the drive for political rights. Early in 1965 Martin Luther King began a campaign to register black voters in Selma, Alabama. When local whites responded with tear gas and bull whips, Johnson in his eloquent "We Shall Overcome" speech in March asked Congress for new voting rights legislation. "He's got some guts," Kennedy said admiringly to John Seigenthaler.[6] From all over the country, people came to Selma to march for human rights. The passage in August of the Voting Rights Act of 1965 started a far-reaching transformation of southern attitudes.

Kennedy was asked the next spring to speak both at the University of Mississippi, where four years before the good old boys had hoped to lynch James Meredith, and at the University of Alabama, where three years before George Wallace had stood (briefly) in the schoolhouse door. A Mississippi legislator of the old school compared Kennedy's visit to a murderer returning to the scene of his crime. But five thousand people crowded the Coliseum at Ole Miss to hear him. "We must," Kennedy said, "create a society in which Negroes will be as free as other Americans—free to vote, and to earn their way, and to share in the decisions of government which will shape their lives." When in the question period someone asked about Ross Barnett, Kennedy's deadpan account of Barnett's erratic behavior in 1962 produced, to his astonishment, gales of laughter. "He came there *persona non grata*," reflected Oscar Carr, a liberal Delta planter, ". . . and I have never seen a politician of any ilk, stature, office at any time in the state more wildly acclaimed."* The reception in Alabama, Kennedy told me on his return, was even more cordial.[7]

The trip confirmed his conviction that the next battle for racial justice lay in the northern city. He remarked that people already "hate my guts" for the civil rights efforts in the south; but winning southern blacks the right to public accommodations or to vote was "an easy job compared to what we face in the North."[8] He had been appalled by the tragedy of Selma. But he was also concerned when white northerners rushed off to Selma forgetting their own problems at home. "Why do they go to Selma?" he said to Richard Rovere. "Why not to 125th Street?"[9] Thousands had marched against the brutalities of Alabama, he told the National Council of Christians and Jews,

> but the many brutalities of the North receive no such attention. I have been in tenements in Harlem in the past several weeks where the smell of rats was so strong that it was difficult to stay there for five minutes, and where children slept with lights turned on their feet to discourage attacks. . . . Thousands do not flock to Harlem to protest these conditions—much less to change them.[10]

Later he said: "All these places—Harlem, Watts, Southside—are riots waiting to happen."[11]

In August 1965 violence broke out in Watts, the black ghetto in Los Angeles. Beating, looting, burning, sniping, bombing, went on for six days, leaving 34 people dead, more than 1000 injured. The Watts riot, said Dwight D. Eisenhower sternly, "did not occur in a vacuum. I believe the U.S. as a whole has been becoming atmosphered, you might say, in a policy of lawlessness." The former Presi-

---

* Oscar Carr, in recorded interview by D. J. O'Brien, May 6–7, 1969, 14, RFK Oral History Program. W. F. Minor, who had covered Mississippi politics for two decades, thought the ovation given Kennedy "had more spontaneity and unrestrained enthusiasm than any state politician has ever received" (*New Orleans Times-Picayune,* June 9, 1968). See also Mary McGrory, *Washington Star,* March 19, 1966, Robert E. Baker in *Washington Post,* March 19, 1966, and Jack Nelson in *Los Angeles Times,* March 19, 1966. The Kennedy speeches are in his papers.

dent's solution was "greater respect for law." Kennedy lashed back. "There is no point in telling Negroes to obey the law," he said. "To many Negroes the law is the enemy. In Harlem, in Bedford-Stuyvesant it has almost always been used against them."[12] Nor would new law solve the problem of the ghetto. That problem, Kennedy said in April 1966, would yield "only to other kinds of fundamental change—to the forces created by better education and better housing and better job opportunities. And it will yield only when the people of the ghetto acquire and wisely exercise political power in the community, only when they . . . establish meaningful communication with a society from which they have been excluded."[13]

II

He set out to awaken the north to its responsibilities. His own church, he told the Pope, ought to be "the foremost champion for changing this kind of difficult, poverty-stricken life." But in places like Los Angeles—he was as blunt with Popes as with anyone else—the Catholic Church "was a reactionary force and in New York it was not particularly helpful." The Pope replied laconically, "You cannot judge the Church by its representatives in Los Angeles."[14] Kennedy also reproached black civil rights leaders for their failures in the ghetto. "The army of the resentful and desperate," he said in the week of Watts, "is larger in the North than in the South, but it is an army without generals—without captains—almost without sergeants." The black middle class has "failed to extend their hand and help to their fellows on the rungs below." Demagogues "have often usurped the positions of leadership."[15]

"Religion was the language the south understood," said Andrew Young, "and there was an almost calculated avoidance of any economic questions."[16] But economics was at the heart of the northern problem. The northern black, as Martin Luther King wrote in early 1965, sought "more significant participation in government, and the restructuring of his economic life to end ghetto existence. Very different tactics will be required to achieve these disparate goals."[17] Kennedy for his part understood that King's evangelical nonviolence, deriving from the religious heritage of the old plantation, might not be so compelling in northern slums.[18] Nevertheless King had more influence than anyone else. Kennedy thought he ought to go north.

In January 1966 King came to Chicago—because, as Pat Watters, the historian of the southern civil rights movement has written, "Senator Robert Kennedy had criticized him for not giving more time to northern problems."[19] In Chicago, King encountered something new —black militants quoting not Gandhi but Frantz Fanon and contending that violence alone could bring liberation. "The only time that I have been booed," King said later, "was one night in a Chicago mass meeting by some young members of the Black Power movement."[20] He also encountered White Power in the shape of the Daley machine. His nonviolent demonstrations—the Southern Christian Leadership Conference's first and last campaign in the north—ended in grisly riots. Nonviolence appeared impotent before the despair of the ghetto, the obduracy of the white establishment and the anger of the black militants, who now claimed from King's failure further evidence that "burn, baby, burn" was the road to salvation.

King did not hold Chicago against Kennedy. Still, there remained "a strange attitude of both admiration and caution in Martin's conversation about Bobby," Andrew Young wrote the year after both men died.

> He was extremely impressed with [Kennedy's] capacity to learn, to grow, and to deal creatively in any given situation. . . . Martin tended to feel overly humble about his own accomplishments and somewhat afraid of "power" . . . and saw Bobby as a man of both moral courage and a keen sense of political timing. Martin also talked of this quality in Gandhi. It was one thing that he was always anxious about. He was clear on the moral issues, but anguished over their implementation. He admired Bobby's blend of "crusader" and realistic politician. Closely related to this was the Kennedy "efficiency mystique." "Bobby knows how to get a job done as well as talk about it."

"After the White House years," Young continued, "they met very seldom, if at all." He could remember only a casual chat during the hearings of a Senate committee.

> Perhaps this distance was dictated by the attempts to link the statements and actions of these two great statesmen through some direct financial or political alliance. Neither man could profit by such an overt relationship and both avoided any direct association. Yet they continued down parallel paths of opposition to racism, poverty and war. A distant comradarie [sic] which needed no formal tie or physical link—a genuine spiritual brotherhood which leaped across the widest chasms of our time. . . . If there is an after life, and I have no doubt there is, I am sure they are together—finally able to share the much denied love that could never be fulfilled in a world such as ours.[21]

III

Kennedy had been exploring city slums since the days of the Committee on Juvenile Delinquency and now did so more intently than ever. "I was with him one time in Brooklyn," said Pete Hamill, the writer, "and we went into some *horrible* tenement that was one of the worst I've ever seen; there was a girl with a mangled face all torn up. He said, 'What happened to her?' The Puerto Rican mother explained that the rats had bitten her face off when she was a little baby." Kennedy was outraged: how could such things continue to "happen in the richest city on earth?"[22] He wanted others to know and filled not only speeches but table talk with accounts of life in the *barriadas* of America.

Rats, filth, bad housing, bad schools, unemployment, segregation, powerlessness, alienation, hate, crime, violence, "burn, baby, burn"—all seemed interlocked in an endless chain to which no one had the key. He had rejoiced at Johnson's embrace of the antipoverty program. But, as Vietnam escalated, Johnson began to hold back domestic spending. "In 1966," John C. Donovan, the historian of the antipoverty effort, has written, "the staunchest advocate of Mr. Johnson's war on poverty was Senator Robert Kennedy. He was perhaps the most outspoken of all Senate liberals in his criticisms of the administration's budget policy." Johnson did not like it. When Kennedy persuaded the Labor Committee to increase antipoverty appropriations, the President, as Everett Dirksen reported after a visit to the White House, "fulminated like Hurricane Inez about what we were doing to his budget."[23]

In the meantime, the welfare system was beginning to buckle under the quick expansion of relief rolls. Kennedy disliked welfare. He thought it broke up families (the "man in the house" rule reduced payments for families that stayed together), destroyed self-respect and subjected the poor to a "prying" middle-class welfare bureaucracy.[24] Still, it was manifestly better than nothing. When Wilbur Mills, the powerful fiscal boss of the House, tried to freeze welfare payments in 1967, Kennedy called his bill "the most punitive measure in the history of the country," punishing "the poor because they are there and we have not been able to do anything about them."[25]

Nor did he like the idea of replacing welfare by a guaranteed minimum income. Edelman and Walinsky kept pushing this proposal.

Kennedy resisted. He simply believed, Walinsky concluded, that "in the last analysis people had to do whatever they did for themselves. . . . He did not believe in the government just taking large sums of money and handing it out to people. . . . He believed in land reform in Latin America because, you know, people ought to have land to work. And he believed devoutly and would have torn the country apart to provide jobs for everybody. . . . But he would never have proposed large scale government doles."[26]

He feared, in addition, that concentration on the guaranteed annual income would postpone the central need—"a massive effort to create new jobs—an effort that we know is the only real solution." Employment for the poor was the centerpiece of the urban program he first presented in a series of speeches in January 1966. With all the work to be done in rebuilding the country, with wretched housing, crumbling schools, ravaged parklands, "how can we pay men to sit at home? . . . The priority here is jobs. To give priority to income payments would be to admit defeat on the critical battle front."[27] Once the employment effort became effective, Kennedy favored income maintenance for unemployables. But he always disliked the phrase "guaranteed minimum income." "He never could get it through his head," said Edelman, "that he really was for it."[28]

By 1967 no one could doubt that Vietnam was swallowing up the Great Society. With the administration otherwise engaged, Kennedy moved out on his own. In July he introduced a bill calling for tax incentives to induce private enterprise to bring plants, shops and jobs into urban poverty areas. His more basic proposal, introduced in the autumn with Joseph Clark of Pennsylvania, was to make the national government itself the employer of last resort. The Kennedy-Clark bill contemplated the creation of two million new jobs through public service employment. Again the White House intervened. The bill, as Gaylord Nelson of Wisconsin reminded the Senate in 1974, was "strongly opposed . . . by the Johnson administration" and "died even in a watered-down version on the floor of the Senate."[29]

Reemployment would only establish the economic preconditions for healthier cities. There remained the gnawing political problems—powerlessness and participation. The crisis of the city, Kennedy believed, came ultimately from "the destruction of the sense, and often the fact, of community, of human dialogue, the thousand invisible strands of common experience and purpose, affection and respect which tie men to their fellows." The history of the human race, "until today," had been "the history of community." Now community was disappearing at the time when its "sustaining strength" was more than ever necessary in a world grown "impersonal and abstract."[30] The child of the ghetto was "a prisoner in an area which is not a community or even a series of communities, but a vast, gray, undifferentiated slum."[31]

The revival of community, he believed, called for something new. The slum clearance and public housing programs of the New and Fair Deals had perpetuated segregation.[32] Massive housing projects, undertaken with the most benign intent, had become "jungles—places of despair and danger for their residents, and for the cities they were designed to save."[33] New programs, even new institutions, were necessary to wipe out the ghettos, reestablish communities and move toward a multiracial society.

But which came first—community or integration? Kennedy understood the Black Power point that black families, economically and psychologically unprepared for white neighborhoods, might better develop pride in their own culture and self before they attempted the adventure of integration. Otherwise the multiracial society would be founded on the white man's values. "The violent youth of the ghetto," he told the National Catholic Conference on Interracial Justice, "is not simply protesting his condition, but making a destructive and self-defeating attempt to assert his worth and dignity as a human being—to tell us that though we may scorn his contribution, we must still respect his power. In some ways it is a cry for love."[34] Blackness, he said, "must be made a badge of pride and honor."[35]

So he was prepared to give first place to economic and moral recovery *within* the ghetto. As this was accomplished, dispersion could begin: "The building of a truly integrated society depends on the development of economic self-sufficiency and security in the communities of poverty, for only then will the residents of these areas have the wherewithal to move freely within the society."[36] And dispersion rather than long-distance busing seemed the best way to resolve the vexed problem of school integration. "My personal opinion," he said in 1964, "is that compulsory transportation of children over long distances, away from the schools in their neighborhoods, doesn't make much sense and I am against it."[37] He said this during his senatorial campaign and mostly avoided the issue thereafter. "True school integration," he said in 1966, "depends on a desegregation of residential patterns."[38]

For the revival of the ghetto he looked not only to jobs but to the ideas of community action fostered by the Committee on Juvenile

Delinquency. He proposed in 1966 the establishment of community development corporations, owned and controlled by the residents of the area, mobilizing both local talent and resources and outside capital, private as well as public. The critical element, he emphasized, "should be the full and dominant participation by the residents." Such corporations "could go far to changing perhaps in revolutionary ways our techniques for meeting urban needs."[39]

IV

Speeches and bills did not satisfy him. He wanted to get things done—and in New York City. In 1965 Thomas Johnston, the soft-spoken Kentuckian from the Yale Drama School who headed his office in the metropolis, had worked up with HARYOU, the Urban League and other organizations a program providing some five thousand summer jobs in Harlem. The program was a success, but investigations afterward revealed incompetence or worse in the handling of funds that baffled auditors from the Office of Economic Opportunity for months to come. The experience showed too—as Kenneth Clark had already discovered in HARYOU—how hard it was to get things done in a locality dominated by powerful and selfish personalities like Adam Clayton Powell and J. Raymond Jones.[40]

And Harlem, though by far the most celebrated, was not the largest black ghetto in New York City. Across the East River in central Brooklyn lay Bedford-Stuyvesant, where 450,000 people—84 percent black, 12 percent Puerto Rican—lived, more nonwhites packed together than in any ghetto in the land save for the South Side of Chicago. Where Harlem was filled with large, crumbling tenements, Bedford-Stuyvesant had streets lined with brownstones. Fifteen percent of the people owned their homes as against 2 percent in Harlem. On the other hand, as a New York University study put it in 1967, "Bedford-Stuyvesant is more depressed and impaired than Harlem—i.e., fewer unified families, more unemployment, lower incomes, less job history."[41] Unlike Harlem, it had received almost no federal aid.[42] Its decay seemed almost irreversible.

On February 4, 1966, Kennedy took a long walk through Bedford-Stuyvesant. He saw it all: burned-out buildings, brownstones in abject decay, stripped cars rusting along the streets, vacant lots overflowing with trash and garbage, a pervading stench of filth and defeat. He met with a group of community activists, led by state supreme court judge Thomas R. Jones, the leading black politician in the area. The group was irritated and cynical. One said, "You're another white guy that's out here for the day; you'll be gone and you'll never be seen again. And that's that. We've had enough of that."[43] Judge Jones said, "I'm weary of study, Senator. Weary of speeches, weary of promises that aren't kept. . . . The Negro people are angry, Senator, and, judge that I am, I'm angry, too. No one is helping us."[44]

Kennedy was irritated too. "I could be smoking a cigar down in Palm Beach," he said as they drove back to Manhattan. "I don't really have to take that. Why do I have to go out and get abused for a lot of things that I haven't done?" Then: "Get them a swimming pool." Then, after a time, "Maybe this would be a good place to try and make an effort." What kind of an effort was still obscure. "We didn't have any sort of idea," Johnston said later, "that we could do anything that was very big."[45]

The first thought was to get foundation money. The Taconic Foundation, which had helped Kennedy on the black registration drive when he was Attorney General, was interested. Soon McGeorge Bundy, now head of the Ford Foundation, was drawn in; later Mrs. Vincent Astor and the Astor Foundation were of inestimable help. But money by itself was not a solution and could even create difficulties, as it had in Harlem the previous summer. At this point there were less than a dozen black certified public accountants in the country and none in Bedford-Stuyvesant. In September, Johnston suggested the possibility of enlisting white business leaders who might provide technical and managerial advice as well as capital.

This idea appealed to Kennedy. His relations with the business community were as chilly as ever. But he had some strong business friends, notably Douglas Dillon, Thomas J. Watson of IBM and William Paley of CBS. He believed that it was useful to draw in people who had power. He enjoyed, I believe, arranging incongruous coalitions. And, with Vietnam consuming available federal money, social policy would require a larger infusion of private funds. At the same time, he recognized that he would get nowhere if business saw Bedford-Stuyvesant as a Kennedy promotion. It had to be politically beyond suspicion. So he accompanied his courtship of business leaders with an assuagement of Republican fears. Javits presented no problem. He saw at once the value of the idea, had come by now to like Kennedy and provided wholehearted cooperation. Mayor Lindsay was more uncertain. He saluted the project but suspected the projector. Lindsay and Kennedy were the most striking political figures in

New York: competitors today; rivals, it might be tomorrow, for the Presidency itself. Lindsay privately thought Kennedy a publicity-grabber. Kennedy privately thought Lindsay a lightweight. I suspect he was also a little jealous of Lindsay, who was very tall, very hand-some and filled with what girls called charm and journalists charisma. But they agreed on most things, especially on the importance of ra-cial justice, and each essentially respected the other. Mary Lindsay and Ethel Kennedy had been schoolmates. Lindsay agreed to give his support.[46]

Armed with nonpartisan credentials, Kennedy approached business leaders. He counted heavily on André Meyer of Lazard Frères, on whom Jacqueline Kennedy had come to rely for counsel. Meyer told Kennedy and Johnston he would help on one condition. Johnston stiffened, wondering what inordinate capitalist demand was about to come. "I will come in," Meyer told Kennedy, "if you will stand up in the Senate and make an even stronger speech on Vietnam than you have. Bedford-Stuyvesant will have no meaning if we don't end that terrible war."[47] Dillon, Watson, Paley, Roswell Gilpatric, J. M. Kap-lan of Welch Grape Juice, James Oates of Equitable Life Assurance and George Moore of the National City Bank came readily along. André Meyer also suggested David Lilienthal, the old New Dealer who had carried his developmental genius from the Tennessee Valley to the far corners of the planet. Kennedy met Lilienthal for a drink at the Century Club. "I can't remember ever having my impression of a man change so soon and so suddenly," Lilienthal wrote in his diary. ". . . I asked myself: Could this earnest young man possibly be the same fellow pictured by the press and TV as a cynical, ambi-tious, ruthless trickster dealing only with political issues that would 'pay off'?"[48]

A later recruit was Benno Schmidt, a managing partner in J. H. Whitney & Company. He too had heard things about Kennedy that, as he said later, "didn't give me a particularly warm feeling toward him at the outset." Schmidt said at once that he had voted for Nixon in 1960 and Keating in 1964. So much the better, said Kennedy, promising that he would "never do anything in connection with this project that you will feel inconsistent with my assurance to you that this thing is non-political and nonpartisan."[49] In time Schmidt suc-ceeded Dillon as chairman of the Bedford-Stuyvesant Development and Services Corporation, becoming as well a close friend of both Robert and Ethel Kennedy.

v

On December 10, 1966, ten months after his walk through the gloomy streets, Kennedy, with Lindsay and Javits by his side, unfolded the development plan to a thousand people gathered in the auditorium of a Bedford-Stuyvesant school. There were two separate corporations: one, representing the people of Bedford-Stuyvesant, to decide on programs; the other, composed of business leaders, to bring in outside investment and to supply managerial assistance. Franklin A. Thomas, an able black lawyer, headed the community group. John Doar was persuaded in 1967 to leave the Justice Department and run the Development and Services Corporation.

Kennedy himself continued to play an active role. Lilienthal observed him at a meeting the next spring, "looking quite handsome in spite of the fact that his tie wasn't fully pulled up, his suit was rumpled, his sox were droopy. He listened with an intentness that was almost painful, occasionally rubbing his eyes with fatigue, his knees drawn up against the edge of the table. . . . He never let his mind wander nor did he relax for a second." As he left, murmuring that he had just flown in from Washington and now had to fly back for an evening engagement, he said, "I'm a yo-yo."[50] "It was his work, his vision, energy, enthusiasm and intelligence," said John Doar, "that kept it going." "If I wasn't the United States senator," Kennedy once said to Doar, "I'd rather be working in Bedford-Stuyvesant than any place I know."[51]

Thomas and Doar, in partnership with the community, managed in the next years to combine housing and physical renovation with jobs and social services in a way that gave Bedford-Stuyvesant a new life. Revisiting the project in 1978, Michael Harrington of *The Other America* called it "a modest success—which, in the context of so many failures, is to say a remarkable success." And, as Harrington added, if even one American neighborhood had headed toward "economic and sociological hell . . . and then reversed the diastrous trend, that is important news for the nation as a whole."[52]

It was Kennedy's profound hope that Bedford-Stuyvesant would serve as a model for self-regeneration in other ghettos. He had already, with Javits's cosponsorship, amended the Economic Opportunity Act to provide for a "special impact" program intended to channel federal development aid into urban poverty areas. But once more he was having trouble with Lyndon Johnson. Although Congress funded the amendment for two years, the administration, Kennedy said in 1968, "has opposed the program and has spent most of the funds appropriated on other manpower activities."[53] In the meantime, he introduced a bill intended to create housing and jobs in poverty areas through tax incentives and low-interest loans along with safeguards for neighborhood control. Again the President balked. "The Johnson Administration," Robert Semple wrote in the *New York Times* in September 1967, "mounted a concerted attack today on a proposal by Senator Robert F. Kennedy to build more and better low cost housing in the slums through private enterprise."[54] In another month Johnson announced a program of his own, not dissimilar to Kennedy's but more limited in scope. "How can they be so petty?" Kennedy said to Jack Newfield. "I worked on my plan for six months, and we talked to everyone in the Administration in all the relevant agencies. We accepted many of their ideas and put them in our bill. Now they came out with this thing, and the first I hear about it is on television. They didn't even try to work something out together. To them it's all just politics."*

It was not just politics to the black community. No white leader was more welcome in the ghettos. Black leaders liked Kennedy's openness, his conviction that something could be done, even his occasional abruptness of challenge, proving, as it did, that he was treating them as equals. Dr. Kenneth Clark, whose dismay over Kennedy at the Baldwin meeting in 1963 had been compounded by Kennedy's surrender of HARYOU to Adam Clayton Powell in 1964, met him

---

* Jack Newfield, *Robert Kennedy* (New York, 1969), 106. Four years later a Twentieth Century Fund Task Force on Community Development Corporations, noting the "deliberate policy decisions made by both the Johnson and Nixon administrations to discourage neighborhood-controlled urban projects," called on the national government to "take immediate steps to create a national system of support for community development corporations" (Report of the Twentieth Century Fund Task Force on Community Development Corporations, *CDCs: New Hope for the Inner City* [New York, 1971], 4, 29, 30). After Kennedy's death Gaylord Nelson introduced a Community Self-Determination Act (*Congressional Record*, July 24, 1968, S9270). Senator Fred Harris observed, "This measure very closely resembles two of the late Senator Robert Kennedy's tremendously innovative bills," adding that the Bedford-Stuyvesant experiment constituted "an important precedent for this bill, and perhaps a demonstration of the likely success of some of the bill's objectives" (S9285). The bill got nowhere. In 1972 Javits and Edward Kennedy expanded the original "special impact" program by adding a new Title VII to the Economic Opportunity Act. In an address in 1974 to the Congress of Community Development Corporations, Javits described Bedford-Stuyvesant as the place "where the community economic development corporation idea . . . was born." By this time there were 34 federally funded and 75 privately funded community development corporations (*Congressional Record*, April 9, 1974, S5522).

again in 1967. This time, the longer they talked, "the more I came around to saying, 'You know, it is possible for human beings to grow. This man has grown.' I committed myself to working with him . . . something which I never dreamed that I would after the [Baldwin] thing and the HARYOU thing."55 "Bobby Kennedy," said the Reverend Channing Phillips, a Washington black leader, "had this fantastic ability to communicate hope to some pretty rejected people. No other white man had this same quality."56

VI

His concern was confined neither to cities nor to blacks. His work on the Migratory Labor Subcommittee of the Senate Labor Committee gave him a vivid understanding of the wretched conditions among itinerant farmworkers. When a witness from the American Farm Bureau, after objecting to every specific proposal for the protection of migratory labor, admitted that his group of prosperous farmers had no program of its own, Kennedy was incredulous. He brusquely told the witness, "To be opposed to a minimum wage, to be opposed to legislation which would limit the use of children . . . to be opposed to collective bargaining completely . . . to oppose all that without some alternative makes the rest of the arguments you have senseless."57

Soon afterward, in early 1966, Walter Reuther and Jack Conway came to Washington. They were fresh from Delano, California, where the National Farm Workers Association was conducting a strike of migratory grape workers and urging a national boycott against grapes picked by nonunion labor. The leader of the strike was a Mexican American named Cesar Chavez. Reuther strongly recommended that the subcommittee go to California and hold hearings on the situation in the grapefields.58 It was a poor time for Kennedy. He was trying to figure how to save the cities; he was digging his way out of the Vietnam chicken coop; and he was reluctant to leave Washington. Yet, as he told Peter Edelman, "if Walter Reuther and Jack Conway want me to do it, I suppose I'll do it."59 Conway finally said to him, "These people need you."60 On the plane out to the coast, Kennedy still wondered why he was going.61 He arrived in time for the second day of the hearings.

The local sheriff came before the committee to explain his manner of keeping the peace. He took photographs, he said, to identify potential troublemakers; he had five thousand, he bragged, in his files.

Kennedy said, "Do you take pictures of everyone in the city?" The sheriff: "Well, if he is on strike, or something like that." Kennedy asked why he had arrested forty-four of Chavez's men engaged in lawful picketing. The strikebreakers, the sheriff explained, had said, " 'If you don't get them out of here, we're going to cut their hearts out.' So rather than let them get cut, we removed the cause." George Murphy of California, another member of the subcommittee, muttered, "I think it's a shame you weren't there before the Watts riots." Kennedy said caustically, "This is the most interesting concept. . . . How can you go arrest somebody if they haven't violated the law? . . . Can I just suggest that the sheriff reconsider his procedures in connection with these matters? . . . [Can] I suggest during the luncheon period that the sheriff and district attorney read the Constitution of the United States?"[62]

By the end of the day, Kennedy had embraced Chavez and La Causa. "He shouldn't go so far," Chavez whispered to his lieutenant Dolores Huerta, "because it's only going to hurt him." "Instead of that awful feeling against politicians who don't commit themselves," Chavez recalled,

> we felt protective. He said that we had the right to form a union and that he endorsed our right, and not only endorsed us but joined us. I was amazed at how quickly he grasped the whole picture. . . . He immediately asked very pointed questions of the growers; he had a way of disintegrating their arguments by picking at the very simple questions. . . . When reporters asked him if we weren't Communists, he said, "No, they are not Communists, they're struggling for their rights." So he really helped us, . . . turned it completely around.[63]

"Robert didn't come to us and tell us what was good for us," Dolores Huerta said later. "He came to us and asked two questions . . . 'What do you want? And how can I help?' That's why we loved him."[64]

Chavez was two and a half years younger than Kennedy. His heroes were Saint Francis and Gandhi. He had been organizing Mexican Americans since 1952. The two men had in fact met in 1960, when Chavez was running a drive to register Spanish-speaking voters. The Kennedy staff thought he was going about it in the wrong way. "If he's been here for ten years," Robert had said when the problem was brought to him, "why can't he do it the way he wants to do it?"[65] Later *Time* carelessly ascribed the success of the drive to a committee of Mexican-American politicians. Chavez asked Dolores Huerta to protest to Kennedy. "So I had the copy of *Time* magazine in my hand, and I crashed in. And Bobby Kennedy was standing there; he was talking to a lot of people. I think he saw this wild-eyed looking person walking toward him, and he threw up his hands and he said, 'I know. I know.'" The story had been a mistake, he said, and he would correct it, which he did. "So we felt very good about it," said Dolores Huerta.[66]

The meeting in Delano sealed a relationship. "Something had touched a nerve in him," said Peter Edelman, who followed the problem in Kennedy's Senate office. ". . . Always after that, we helped Cesar Chavez in whatever way we could."[67] For all their differences in background, the two men were rather alike: both short, shy, familial, devout, opponents of violence, with strong veins of melancholy and fatalism. Chavez, Kennedy believed, was doing for Spanish-speaking Americans what Martin Luther King had done for black Americans: giving them new convictions of pride and solidarity.

The rural laborer became an abiding concern. Few states treated migrant workers worse than New York. In 1967 Kennedy and Javits visited a work camp upstate. The owner's sign warned: ANYONE ENTERING OR TRESPASSING WITHOUT MY PERMISSION WILL BE SHOT IF CAUGHT. This discouraged most of the party. Kennedy, head down, kept walking. He found three migrant families living in an old bus with the seats ripped out. Inside he saw six small children, their bodies covered with running sores. The stench was overpowering. Kennedy asked an ancient black woman in the bus how much she earned. She said a dollar an hour, picking celery. He made a face, shook his head and held her calloused hand for a moment. Cardboard covered the windows of the next bus, where a child played forlornly on a filthy mattress. "As Kennedy looked down at the child," reported Jack Newfield, "his hand and his head trembled in rage. He seemed like a man going through an exorcism." The owner, as billed, had a gun. "You had no right to go in there," he said. "You're just a do-gooder trying to make some headlines." Kennedy replied in a whisper, "You are something out of the 19th century. I wouldn't let an animal live in those buses." "It's like camping out," the owner said. Once back in the twentieth century, Kennedy demanded that Rockefeller investigate health conditions in the camps and called on labor leaders to organize the migrants.[68]

Rural squalor was not confined to *braceros* and bindlestiffs. Most tragic of all were the Indians. As senator from the state eighth in the country in Indian population, Kennedy visited the remnants of the once mighty Five Nations in their upstate reservations. He talked Indians with LaDonna Harris, the Indian wife of his Oklahoma colleague, and in March 1967 he addressed an organization she had founded called Oklahomans for Indian Opportunity. Answering one question, he said, at once jokingly and seriously, "I wish I had been born an Indian." "It sounded so real and also kind of wistfully funny," said Fred Harris, "that everybody laughed and applauded overwhelmingly."[69]

He learned the grim statistics. "The 'first American,'" he said, "is still the last American in terms of employment, health and education."[70] In 1967 he persuaded the Senate to set up a committee to study Indian education. He went into the schools on the reservations and asked if there were Indian teachers and whether they were teaching Indian culture and history. He looked at library shelves to see what Indians could read about their own past. At the Blackfoot reservation in Fort Hall, Idaho, they turned up only one book on Indians—*Captive of the Delawares,* its jacket showing an Indian scalping a blond child.[71] At one reservation he learned that a baby had died of starvation the same day. He said, and meant, "When that baby died, a little bit of me died too."[72]

On the day Robert Kennedy himself died, a New York Seneca, whose reservation he had visited in 1967, wrote his widow: "We loved him, too, Mrs. Kennedy. Loving a public official for an Indian is almost unheard of, as history bears out. We trusted him. Unheard of, too, for an Indian. We had faith in him."[73] Vine Deloria, Jr., the Standing Rock Sioux who wrote *Custer Died for Your Sins,* observed that Kennedy's intercession had probably discouraged federal action "because of his many political enemies and their outright rejection of causes he advocated." Still, said Deloria in a fine sentence, he was a man "who could move from world to world and never be a stranger anywhere." And Indians thought him "as great a hero as the most famous Indian war chiefs precisely because of his ruthlessness." At last, somewhere, that reputation had its advantages. "Indians," said Deloria, "saw him as a warrior, the white Crazy Horse"—the great war chief of the Oglala Sioux who did, Deloria said, what was best and what was for the people. Kennedy, Deloria concluded, "somehow validated obscure undefined feelings of Indian people which they had been unwilling to admit to themselves. Spiritually, he was an Indian!"[74]

VII

Chicanos, migrant workers, Indians—all presented aspects of the larger shame of poverty. In March 1967 the Senate Labor Committee's Subcommittee on Poverty held new hearings. One of the witnesses was Marian Wright, a twenty-seven-year-old black lawyer from South Carolina and Yale Law School, now in Mississippi for the NAACP's Legal Defense Fund. Marian Wright told the committee how mechanization and the reduction in cotton planting under the federal subsidy program had thrown thousands of blacks out of work in the Mississippi Delta. At this point Mississippi counties had shifted from the program that gave surplus food to the poor to one that required the monthly purchase of food stamps in lump sums the poor did not have. The result, Marian Wright said, was disaster.[75]

Joseph Clark, the chairman, thought the committee should go to Mississippi and see for itself. Kennedy, Javits and Murphy accompanied him. Kennedy sent Edelman down a few days in advance to get a sense of the problem. (Edelman talked particularly to Marian Wright. Fifteen months later they were married.) The committee arrived in Jackson on April 9, 1967. They dined that evening with a spectrum of Mississippians, from Oscar Carr to Charles Evers. Carr thought Kennedy "a very shy man. . . . He continually asked questions."[76] "We talked and talked," said Evers, "and he listened."[77]

The hearings took place the next day. Kennedy, as usual, was not interested in the explanations of officials. He believed, as a reporter on the trip, Nick Kotz of the *Des Moines Register,* said, that "the poor themselves made the best witnesses." Their testimony was appalling. After the hearing Kennedy told Charles Evers, "I want to see it."[78] The next day Kennedy and Clark toured the Delta. They went, said Evers, "into one of the worst places I've ever seen." Kotz described "a dark windowless shack" smelling of "mildew, sickness, and urine." "There was no ceiling hardly," said Evers; "the floor had holes in it, and a bed that looked like the color of my arm—black as my arm—propped up with some kind of bricks to keep it from falling. The odor was so bad you could hardly keep the nausea down. . . . This lady came out with hardly any clothes on, and we spoke to her and told her who he was. She just put her arms out and said 'Thank God' and then she just held his hand."

A small child sat on the floor rubbing grains of rice round and round. "His tummy was sticking way out just like he was pregnant.

Bobby looked down at the child, and then he picked him up and sat down on that dirty bed. He was rubbing the child's stomach. He said, 'My God, I didn't know this kind of thing existed. How can a country like this allow it? Maybe they just don't know.'" He tried, said Kotz, to evoke a response from the child, talking, caressing, tickling. The child never looked up, sitting as in a trance. "Tears were running down [Kennedy's] cheek," said Evers, "and he just sat there and held the little child. Roaches and rats were all over the floor. . . . Then he said, 'I'm going back to Washington to do something about this.' No other white man in America would have come into that house."[79]

"Have you ever seen anything like this before?" asked W. F. Minor of the *New Orleans Times-Picayune*. "Yes, I have," Kennedy said. "I've seen it in Southeast Asia and in Harlem."[80] Marian Wright had thought the senators were there for publicity; "and then he came," she later told Roger Wilkins, "and he did things that I wouldn't do. He went into the dirtiest, filthiest, poorest black homes . . . and he would sit with a baby who had open sores and whose belly was bloated from malnutrition, and he'd sit and touch and hold those babies. . . . I wouldn't do that! I didn't do that! But he did. . . . That's why I'm for him."[81]

VIII

The day after they got back, Kennedy and Clark went to see Orville Freeman, the Secretary of Agriculture. Freeman wondered whether conditions were really so bad as they thought.[82] The entire Clark committee then appealed to President Johnson for action to meet the Mississippi emergency: free food stamps for the neediest, cheaper stamps for the poor, investigation of the way local officials distributed federal food.[83] Johnson asked Joseph Califano, his chief assistant on domestic affairs, what it was all about. "Freeman," Califano reported back, "does not want to upset the entire program by either giving free food to these negroes in the delta or by lowering the amount of money they have to pay for food stamps until he has the food stamp program through Congress."[84] Johnson turned the committee letter over to the Office of Economic Opportunity for answer. The reply, as described by one scholar, was "defensive . . . argumentative . . . irrelevant."[85] Daniel Patrick Moynihan surmised that the White House read the committee letter "as an attack by Kennedy on Johnson."[86] "We thought they were exaggerating the extent of the hunger," Califano said later.[87]

The issue would not go away. The Field Foundation sent down a team of doctors headed by Robert Coles, a psychiatrist who combined the concerns of a sociologist with the sensitivity of a literary artist. The Coles group reported in June that children in Mississippi were "living under such primitive conditions that we found it hard to believe we were examining American children in the twentieth century."[88] Back in Washington the doctors waited on a number of officials—Freeman, John Gardner, the Secretary of Health, Education, and Welfare, others—and "pleaded with them," Coles said, to do something for the poor people of Mississippi. "We were not only given the runaround but, in all bluntness, we ourselves were getting so depressed . . . that we were ready to give up." If their efforts offended the southern conservatives on the Agriculture committees, the Johnson officials warned, there would be even less money for commodity distribution and food stamps. "The reason we didn't give up is because several of us had decided that we would go over to see Senator Kennedy." Kennedy told them: "You don't have to take that. This is the beginning, not the end. You don't have to be discouraged."[89]

Clark called a new set of hearings, where Robert Coles and his colleagues testified. In July, John Stennis, the conservative Mississippi senator, introduced an emergency food and medical bill. Clark's committee reported it out at once. The Senate passed it in ten days. But the administration remained hostile, and the Texas chairman of the House Agriculture Committee derailed the bill. In October an administration Nutrition Task Force recommended $300 million more for food programs. Johnson rejected the recommendation. In November Congress at last passed the Stennis bill. The administration stalled on its execution. "Not until April 1968," wrote Kotz, "did interdepartmental haggling finally ebb enough so that someone could begin dispensing what was supposed to be 'emergency' aid to the sick and hungry poor." Later Johnson learned that Freeman was planning to spend $145 million over the 1968 budget on food programs. "I never authorized you to do that," the President said in a rage.[90]

Even Hubert Humphrey joined the campaign. In his only known written criticism of Johnson in these years, he set forth the situation to Mrs. Arthur Krim, who was professionally concerned about the effects of malnutrition on the mental development of small children and whose husband was the Democratic party's chief fund raiser.

"There are ways the President could have helped," Humphrey wrote, ". . . in approving some of Orville Freeman's budget requests, in supporting legislation on the Hill, and suggesting administrative change—but he has not." "On at least 12 specific occasions," according to Nick Kotz, "his aides and Cabinet officers had recommended food aid reform and Lyndon Johnson had said 'no.' "[91]

The Great Society was a fading memory. Johnson even banished the phrase from his speeches. He feared to incite inflation by increasing the budget. Perhaps he also feared to incite disorder by encouraging social protest. "Beginning with the 1967 State of the Union message," Daniel Patrick Moynihan wrote in 1968, "civil-rights and poverty issues practically disappeared from Presidential pronouncements, to be replaced by disquisitions on Safe Streets and Crime Control Acts, and other euphemisms for the forcible repression of black violence."[92]

IX

The summer of 1967 was the worst yet in the ghettos. A contagion of riots, marked by arson, looting and sniping, began in the south in May, spread to the north in June and reached an awful climax in July. Twenty-six people were killed in Newark in disorders lasting from July 12 to July 17. On July 23 violence broke out in Spanish Harlem. It was continuing two days later when I had dinner with Robert and Ethel Kennedy, Pete Hamill and José Torres, the gentle (except in the ring) former world's light heavyweight champion and a respected leader of his people. After dinner we piled into Torres's car and drove through the anxious streets of East Harlem, with buildings shuttered and knots of policemen on each corner. At one point Torres stopped the car to show us a message painted in Spanish across Third Avenue: YOU CROSS THIS LINE, YOU BE DEAD.[93]

That same night the greatest violence of all exploded in Detroit, where forty-three people died in the next four days. Governor George Romney called in the National Guard. "They have lost all control in Detroit," J. Edgar Hoover told Johnson on the evening of July 24. "Harlem may break loose within thirty minutes. They plan to tear it to pieces." Later that night Johnson sent tanks and paratroopers into Detroit.[94] He explained his decision over nationwide television in a cold statement, notably lacking any acknowledgment that human despair might possibly lie behind the explosion. Even in the White House Harry McPherson, a Johnson special assistant, thought the presentation "legalistic." There was no point, McPherson protested, in criticizing everyone else, especially Congress, "unless and until we are willing to go before them in joint session and state the case for America's cities."[95]

If McPherson was unhappy over the President's speech, Kennedy was incredulous. "It's over," he told Mankiewicz. "The President is just not going to do anything more. That's it. He's through with domestic problems, with the cities. . . . He's not going to do anything. And he's the only man who can." Mankiewicz asked what Kennedy would do if he were President. Kennedy said that, first, he would ask the heads of the three television networks to produce as rapidly as possible—and run in prime time—a two-hour documentary showing what it was like to live in a ghetto.

> Let them show the sound, the feel, the hopelessness, and what it's like to think you'll never get out. Show a black teenager, told by some radio jingle to stay in school, looking at his older brother—who stayed in school—and who's out of a job. Show the Mafia pushing narcotics; put a Candid Camera team in a ghetto school and watch what a rotten system of education it really is. Film a mother staying up all night to keep the rats from her baby. . . . Then I'd ask people to watch it—and experience what it means to live in the most affluent society in history—without hope.

Next, Kennedy continued, he would put together the racial data on every major city. He would call meetings at the White House—one a day if necessary—for each city on the danger list. He would invite not only the mayors but the bankers, contractors, real estate men, union officials, ministers; "everybody knows who really has power in a city." "Gentlemen," he would say, "this is your problem, and only you can solve it. If you don't solve it, your city will fall apart in a few years, and it will be your fault." We could do it, he told Thomas Johnston, the way we did Bedford-Stuyvesant. Let the local community define its problems and plans; let the government define the available resources; let us work it out together to save the cities. But it was no use *his* saying these things, he told Mankiewicz. "When I do, it's a political speech. The President of the United States is the only man who has the pulpit. . . . If he leads—if he shows that he cares—people will give him time."[96]

Kennedy had no more indulgence than Johnson for violence. "We must make it unequivocally clear by word and deed," he said in a speech in San Francisco on August 4, "that this wanton killing and burning cannot and will not be tolerated." But repression was not the answer. "If we can spend $24 billion for the freedom and the liberty of the people in Vietnam," he said on *Meet the Press* in August, "certainly we can spend a small percentage of that for the liberty and the freedom and the future of our own people in the United States."[97]

X

"Today in America," Robert Kennedy wrote in 1967, "we are two worlds." The world of the white middle class was reasonably pleasant. "But if we try to look through the eyes of the young slum-dweller —the Negro, and the Puerto Rican, and the Mexican-American—the world is a dark and hopeless place."[98] This was his own startling capacity. "He could see things," said Cesar Chavez, "through the eyes of the poor. . . . It was like he was ours."[99] A ghetto youth told Robert Coles, "Kennedy . . . *is* on our side. We know it. He doesn't have to say a word."[100]

Coles speculated why this should be so. It was partly, he thought, that Kennedy imparted to the powerless a conviction of their own cultural dignity, of "strengths that would enable them, given the chance, to do something and be somebody." It was his absence of glibness or condescension, an "activated urgent tension within him, a seeking for expression and then finding it in the plight of other tense people." It was their sense of him as a man who had "lived with tragedy himself, felt suffering and could share that without speaking it. It was in his language. It was in his eyes. It was in a gesture. And they felt [he] could suffer with them and pick up their suffering; and yet appreciate them as equals."[101]

And it was because of his experiencing nature. When he went into Harlem or Watts, when he visited a sharecropper's cabin or an Indian reservation, these were *his* children with bloated bellies, *his* parents wasting away in dreary old age, *his* miserable hovel, *his* wretched scraps for supper. He saw it all with personal intensity, as from the inside. "I think Bobby knows precisely," a friend once said, "what it feels like to be a very old woman."[102] Those he came among perceived this and gave him unreservedly their confidence and their love. "Our first politician for the pariahs," Murray Kempton called him;[103] "our great national outsider, our lonely reproach, the natural standard held out to all rebels. That is the wound about him which speaks to children he has never seen. He will always speak to children, and he will probably always be out of power."*

* Murray Kempton, "Bob Kennedy Voyages," *New York World-Telegram,* November 26, 1965. Kempton was more accurate than the Kennedy critics who charged that

Lawrence Spivak, the *Meet the Press* impresario, asked Kennedy in August 1967 whether he thought the American people had lost faith in their leaders. "The people are terribly disturbed across this country," Kennedy replied, "as to what direction our country is moving in . . . and whether they, as individuals, mean anything . . . whether their voices are ever going to mean anything or whether business has gotten so large, labor organizations so large that they care nothing for the individual. And even our universities and our educational system. So I think there is general dissatisfaction in our country, but not just with our political leaders."

Spivak asked how he felt himself. "I am dissatisfied with our society," Kennedy said. "I suppose I am dissatisfied with our country."[104]

---

he cultivated the poor for political reasons. The psephologist Richard Scammon estimated in 1967 that the poor represented less than 12 percent of the national vote (Stewart Alsop, "Can Anyone Beat LBJ?" *Saturday Evening Post,* June 3, 1967). Many of the poor were outside the political as well as the economic community. They had no fixed place of abode or were too poor, too cynical, too apathetic, to get on the registration rolls. Beyond that, as Stewart Alsop pointed out in 1967, Kennedy's championship of the underclass was, "far too much for his own good," alienating "the middle-class and middle-aged whites who make up a majority of the voters" (Stewart Alsop, "Bobby Kennedy's Best Chance," *Saturday Evening Post,* June 3, 1967).

36

Images

HE DID NOT KNOW the answers. But, more than other politicians of the day, he knew the questions. "Kennedy is on to something," wrote the New Leftist Andrew Kopkind. "He hovers over it like a pig in the *Perigord* sniffing a truffle. It is just below the surface; he can't quite see it; he doesn't know its size or shape or worth or even what it's called. He only knows it's there, and he is going to get it. Where does he look? Among the grape-pickers on strike in central California, in Cloth Market Square in Cracow, on the Ole Miss campus, in a Senate hearing room. And always with the same single-minded, almost frightening intensity. Perhaps the young know what it is; Kennedy spends an inordinate amount of time at schools and colleges talking with them. Maybe the poor know; he studies the condition of the urban ghettos. Is it in Latin America? He'll go and see. Is it in South Africa? Get him a visa."[1]

I

He was a divided man. One half was an incorrigible romantic. "When you have chosen your part," he underlined in his Emerson's *Essays*, "abide by it, and do not weakly try to reconcile yourself with the world. . . . Adhere to your own act, and congratulate yourself if you have done something strange and extravagant, and broken the monotony of a decorous age."[2] When the mood was on him, he permitted himself revolutionary fancies. "What do you think of Che Guevara?" he once asked Roger Baldwin, the old civil libertarian. "I think he is a bandit," Baldwin said. "What do you think?" Kennedy said, "I think he is a revolutionary hero."[3] He told an English journalist that, if he had not been born rich, he would have been a revolutionary.[4] This is what Alice Roosevelt Longworth saw when she said,

"Bobby could have been a revolutionary priest."[5] No one understood practical politics better, said Richard Goodwin; "yet the imagining heart was always in the hills, leading some guerrilla army, without speeches or contaminating compromise, fighting to translate the utmost purity of intention into the power to change a nation or a world."*

If his heart was in the hills, his head was in the councils of state. In the predominant half of his nature he remained the realistic political leader. The ethic of responsibility prevailed over the ethic of ultimate ends. He wanted to be President, he believed in constitutional democracy, he abhorred violence, he could not have been a revolutionary. Still, something more than conventional politics was required. The process was plainly not working. It was not stopping the escalation of the war. It was not giving the poor a fair break or the minorities an equal opportunity. It was not dealing with rural squalor or urban decay. It appeared to be good only at keeping power arrangements as they were. Because it seemed useless for change, the poor, the minorities, the young were losing faith in it.

This was the predicament that increasingly consumed him. He was no longer, if he had ever been, a hater of people. "Of course," Murray Kempton wrote, "he knew how to hate; he hated on his father's behalf; he grew up to hate on his brother's," but the ordeals of life had "now left behind a man we recognize as having been unskilled at hating on his own."[6] "I don't think he was a hater at all," said Wes Barthelmes. "I think he had a great rage against injustice, and I think he had a rage against the impenetrability and the immovability of institutions."[7] This last was the awful question. He used to wonder, Goodwin recalled, "Could you really change the country even if you were President?"[8]

No one understood better how America was really run. "He knew," said his friend Allard Lowenstein, ". . . about worlds the rest of us didn't know about." He had mastered the textbook components of power in America—political organization, nominations, elections, legislatures, cabinets, courts, the unions, the press, television, academia. He had investigated the inner sanctums that radicals thought really controlled the system—industrialists, bankers, oil millionaires, multinational corporations, the Pentagon, the "military-

---

* Richard N. Goodwin, "A Day," *McCall's,* June 1970. The literature is full of such comments; for a further example, Warren Rogers and Stanley Tretick, "RFK," *Look,* July 9, 1968: " 'What you really are is a revolutionary,' Stanley Tretick told him once. 'You should be in the hills with Castro and Che.' . . . 'I know it,' he said."

industrial complex," the "power elite." And he had gone beyond both the textbooks and the radicals in learning about the underground streams through which so much of the actuality of American power darkly coursed: the FBI, the CIA, the racketeering unions and the mob, Hoffa, Giancana, Trafficante, the unseen forces in American life, their hidden penetration into and protection by the more visible realm—"an invisible empire," in Lowenstein's phrase, "allied to parts of an invisible government." The "enemy within" was wider and deeper than Kennedy himself had supposed a few years before. Still his book, dismissed at that time as overwrought, read later, Lowenstein observed, less as fanatic than prophetic.[9]

With all its faults, the old liberalism had at least arrayed itself against the immovable and impenetrable institutions. Kennedy had overcome most of his former scorn for liberals, even called himself a liberal on occasion and cheerfully addressed liberal groups he would have disdained a decade before. "I notice young Congressman Bill Green is here tonight," he said at an Americans for Democratic Action dinner in Philadelphia. Bill Green's father had been the cantankerous Democratic boss of Philadelphia in the days when the ADA, over his bitter opposition, helped elect Joseph Clark, Kennedy's Mississippi companion, as reform mayor. The boss's son was now a liberal congressman, supported by the ADA. "I think his father might have been shocked to see him here," Kennedy continued; then paused and added, "but *my* father might be shocked too."[10] In New York he charmingly explained his presence as the speaker at an ADA dinner by pointing at me and saying: "We fought and argued about all these issues; and he won; and here I am tonight."[11] It was a time of paradox. Adlai Stevenson and Robert Kennedy had not liked each other, but Dick Schaap concluded his 1967 book about Kennedy by suggesting that he might well end as "the Adlai Stevenson of the 1970s."[12] Eleanor Roosevelt had resisted him almost to the time of her death, but Kennedy had become, Franklin D. Roosevelt, Jr., said, "the torch-bearer of everything that my mother stood for and fought for."[13]

Yet the old liberalism had failed to beat the structures. And its distinctive institutions tended to leave out those too poor or demoralized to form organizations of their own. The programs of the New Deal, the Fair Deal, even of the New Frontier, Kennedy said in 1967, "put into effect with the finest of intentions, have been either inadequate or retrogressive."[14] At the Philadelphia ADA dinner Kennedy remarked that most of his audience, when it thought of organized labor, thought of the long struggle to establish labor's rights. "But youth looks with other eyes. They think of labor as grown sleek and bureaucratic with power . . . a force not for change but for the status quo." The university had become a "corporate bureaucracy."[15] In different ways, welfare, public housing, farm price supports, one creation after another of the old liberalism, had congealed into props of the existing order. All this further reduced the capacity of government to change things.

In September 1967 Daniel Patrick Moynihan urged the ADA to join with conservatives in protecting "the social fabric of the nation" against radical students and militant blacks. Kennedy took the opposite view. "I think," he said, "the ADA should just fold up and go out of business. They're so out of touch with things. . . . Your generation should go out and start a new ADA that isn't dependent on the unions for money and is engaged in direct action, instead of just voting on resolutions."[16] (He later observed of Moynihan, "He knows all the facts, and he's against all the solutions.")[17] Having neglected in my White House years ever to ask John Kennedy to inscribe a photograph, supposing always there was plenty of time, I did one day ask Robert. The photograph duly arrived. He had inscribed it: "With the highest regard of a fellow author, government employee, ~~liberal,~~ Harvard graduate and a friend."

Conventional politics seemed impotent before the structures. The great forces for change—the civil rights movement, the antiwar movement, the nationalist movements of the Third World—represented direct action. If new institutions of power could be built among the powerless, if the new movements could avoid violence—this was why he so greatly valued Martin Luther King and Cesar Chavez—change might come without tearing a fragile society apart. He was too much a skeptic, or an Augustinean, to be altogether optimistic. "He always conveyed," Wes Barthelmes said, ". . . a bit of, I think, sadness as he talked about particular programs. . . . He sort of conveyed the futility of most means and the uncertain glory of most ends. But I think that, if he had any commandments, one . . . would be, 'It really is a secular sin not to try.'"[18] His favorite song—one heard it so often blaring from some unseen source in his New York apartment—was "The Impossible Dream."

II

By November 1967 when Robert Kennedy had his forty-second birthday, he was the most original, enigmatic and provocative figure in midcentury American politics. A man of intense emotion, he aroused intense emotion in others. "Bobby had a psychic violence about himself," said that perceptive actress Shirley MacLaine. "Let's be violent with our minds and get this thing changed. Let's not be violent with our triggers."[19] But intellectual violence, seeking the root of the matter, could be frightening in frightened times. "He was a tortured guy," said Barthelmes, "and he was moved by the torture of others. That unsettled people."[20] Kennedy incarnated the idea of struggle and change. This moved many. It disturbed many. He gave hope to some groups in the country, generally the weak; threatened others, generally the strong. Some saw him as compassionate savior, some as ruthless opportunist, some as irresponsible demagogue plucking at the exposed nerves of the American polity—race, poverty, the war. Few were neutral, very few indifferent.

His movement beyond liberalism both fascinated and alarmed the young militants of the day. Robert Scheer, a radical journalist before he became *Playboy*'s expert on the mental lusts of Jimmy Carter, registered both reactions in an article for the New Left magazine *Ramparts* in 1967. Kennedy, he said, was "undoubtedly a very charming and alive man for a politician" but "dangerous" because he provided "the illusion of dissent without its substance. Hubert Humphrey is a bad joke to most young people, but Bobby is believable, and for that reason, much more serious. He could easily coopt prevailing dissent without delivering to it. . . . The Kennedy people have raised cooptation to an art form." After reading the *Ramparts* piece, which the author thought very tough, Kennedy merely told him he had some interesting points. "That was his whole fucking style, you know. . . . Any other politician would say, 'I want Scheer off the plane. What's a *Ramparts* guy doing on the plane?' . . . We used to have arguments all the fucking time and friendly jostling, and I never felt tense." "Also," said Scheer, "there was a certain kind of madness to him. . . . [And] I think there were certain things Kennedy believed. I think he gave a shit about Indians, for instance. . . . I thought he gave a shit about what was happening to black people"; still, at bottom, "a very orthodox political figure," in the end just another liberal.[21]

Not all liberals agreed. "Outside of Washington," Fred Dutton wrote him, "the usual old canards about you—'too zealous,' 'ruthless,' 'narrowly ambitious for just himself rather than broader purposes and impulses'—remain far more entrenched than I had thought. . . . I frankly had thought this problem was behind you and am amazed at the extent it perseveres."[22] So the kindly veteran Gerald W. Johnson of the *Baltimore Sun,* now seventy-seven, described Kennedy in the *New Republic* as "a strong and dangerous man, driven by a maniacal energy . . . as ruthless as Torquemada."[23] The stereotypes—his father, his church, McCarthy, Hoffa, never-get-mad-get-even, the relentless prosecutor, wiretapper, grudge bearer—lingered especially among the "purist liberals," as James Wechsler called them, who seemed almost to fear power and prefer defeat to victory. This "fierce anti-Robert Kennedy obsession" led Wechsler to write a series for the *Progressive* entitled "Robert F. Kennedy: A Case of Mistaken Identity." "Some published critiques of him," Wechsler said, "should bear the warning usually associated with works of fiction: they bear little resemblance to the living character."[24] Liberal schizophrenia about Kennedy was brilliantly caught in Jules Feiffer's cartoons of the "Good Bobby" and the "Bad Bobby."[25]

The leadership of organized labor liked him no more than the purist liberals did, if for opposite reasons. There were important exceptions, like Reuther and Dubinsky; but the rest, as Don Ellinger of the Machinists, another exception, put it, "just didn't like him and that was all there was to it." George Meany called him that "jitterbug." "The big hacks would come in," said Wes Barthelmes, "and he'd question them about racial discrimination in unions. They wouldn't want to talk about anything but minimum wage."[26]

The business community suspected him as much as ever, despite valiant attempts by Thomas J. Watson, Jr., Douglas Dillon, Benno Schmidt and other friends to say that he wasn't all that sinister a fellow. Not only did he dislike self-congratulatory business banquets, said John Nolan, "but he was terrible at them. . . . He felt that what they were doing wasn't very important, and that impression was conveyed."[27] One year William Orrick invited him to attend the annual Bohemian Grove Encampment—"the greatest men's party that has been invented," as Herbert Hoover described it when he invited Joseph Kennedy in 1948.[28] Here was the American tycoon at play, with campfires, rituals, drink, dirty stories, drink, practical jokes, drink. Lyndon Johnson would have had a fine time. Kennedy detested every minute of it. "He was very difficult," Orrick said later.

THESE ARE THE BOBBY TWINS. ONE IS A GOOD BOBBY.

ONE IS A BAD BOBBY.

1.

THE GOOD BOBBY IS A COURAGEOUS REFORMER.

THE BAD BOBBY MAKES DEALS.

2.

THE GOOD BOBBY SENT FEDERAL TROOPS DOWN SOUTH TO ENFORCE CIVIL RIGHTS.

THE BAD BOBBY APPOINTED RACIST JUDGES DOWN SOUTH TO ENFORCE CIVIL RIGHTS.

3.

THE GOOD BOBBY IS A FERVENT CIVIL LIBERTARIAN.

THE BAD BOBBY IS A FERVENT WIRE TAPPER.

4.

THE GOOD BOBBY IS ILL AT EASE WITH LIBERALS.

THE BAD BOBBY IS ILL AT EASE WITH GROWNUPS.

5.

IF YOU WANT ONE BOBBY TO BE YOUR PRESIDENT YOU WILL HAVE TO TAKE BOTH...

FOR BOBBIES ARE WIDELY NOTED FOR THEIR FAMILY UNITY.

6.

© 1967 Jules Feiffer 1-29

". . . He just did not enjoy that company." And the company, Orrick added, was mostly "antagonistic toward him."[29] Dillon summed it up: "The general businessman's stereotype view of Bob Kennedy was even more inaccurate than Senator Kennedy's view of the business community."[30]

The far right hated him most of all: consider Frank A. Capell's *Robert F. Kennedy, Emerging American Dictator;* on the cover, a cut of Kennedy, a shadowy Castro looming behind him. "There can be no doubt of Bobby's pro-communist bias," Capell wrote. ". . . His dictatorial and ruthless methods combined with the power to implement them bode ill for the future. . . . Americans should BEWARE."[31] At a CIA seminar for Army officers in the spring of 1968, one of them, back from Vietnam, said, "You don't realize what it's like being sold out by these antiwar bastards, Bobby Kennedy, and the rest of the thimbleheads." A CIA instructor reproduced on the blackboard a bumper sticker he had seen on the way to work: "First Ethel Now Us."[32] Westbrook Pegler, once a splendid if intemperate writer and a chum of Joseph P. Kennedy's, recorded for his old friend's son the hope that "some white patriot of the Southern tier will spatter his spoonful of brains in public premises before the snow flies."[33] Good old Clyde Tolson of the FBI's Edgar and Clyde, discussing Kennedy in the hearing of William Sullivan in 1968, said, "I hope that someone shoots and kills the son of a bitch."*

"Why do people hate me so?" Kennedy cried out to Dorothy Schiff in 1965[34] and to others from time to time later. The English journalist Margaret Laing told him she had met two people in the previous week who felt so strongly about him they wanted to hit him. "His astonishment on hearing about this was so complete that he thought he must have misunderstood." He said, "Hit me? You mean punch me? . . . No—you're kidding." He laughed in a way that was "almost a cough."[35] A reporter asked him to explain why he was thought ruthless. He paused; then said slowly, "I think that is what happens to you when you try to do things."[36] He bantered bitterly, almost obsessively, about his supposed ruthlessness. "Although he joked about the word," Theodore H. White wrote later, "it cramped his thoughts and public behavior."[37] He took from Emerson a consol-

---

* William C. Sullivan, in interview by author, July 26, 1976. When I verified this quotation with Mr. Sullivan a few weeks before his own death, he added that Tolson said this a month or two before Kennedy was shot and killed; afterward, "I have wondered what thoughts went through Mr. Tolson's mind, if any" (Sullivan to author, October 1, 1977).

ing thought for his commonplace book: "God offers to every mind its choice between truth and repose. Take which you please—you can never have both."[38]

No one quite had the answer. "I do not understand the animus against Bobby," said William Benton. "What is the conceivable explanation? Where does it come from?"[39] "Could it be," asked Kenneth Galbraith later, "that he was the least known public figure of our time?"[40] "So many people have him absolutely wrong," observed Joseph Alsop, who lamented but adored him. "They think he is cold, calculating, ruthless. Actually, he is hot-blooded, romantic, compassionate."[41] Averell Harriman said, "It was impossible for him not to tell the truth as he saw it. I think that is why some people thought he was ruthless. At times the truth is ruthless."[42]

III

In the meantime, private life went on. There were more children— Matthew Maxwell Taylor Kennedy on January 11, 1965; Douglas Harriman Kennedy on March 24, 1967; homage to Taylor, Dillon and Harriman, three impeccable members of the American establishment. Why these men, in the same years that Kennedy was in black ghettos and grapefields and Indian reservations? Did this prove political hypocrisy? social snobbery? a hope that disparate people could be united to meet common problems? or simply a man who moved from world to world?

The world of Hickory Hill was never more enjoyable. His older children were entering their teens. "I think that they'll develop their own lives," Kennedy told an interviewer.

> I talked to one of my sons about it one time and he said that he wanted, he was 12 years old, he wanted to make a contribution. And he said, "But I don't want to get involved in political life," and I said, "Well, what do you want to do?" . . . He loves animals and he said, "I want to make a contribution like Darwin and Audubon did." And so I think people work out their own lives . . . just as long as they understand that in the last analysis what is important [is] that they give something to others, and not just turn in on themselves.[43]

An overachiever himself since infancy, Kennedy was now more than ever the collector of overachievers. One never knew whom to expect at Hickory Hill—novelists, entertainers, columnists, decathlon champions, astronauts, football stars, diplomats, politicians, mountain climbers, international beauties, appearing in every age, sex, size, color. I remember the party in November 1966 to celebrate Harriman's seventy-fifth birthday. Ethel directed the guests to come in costumes commemorating an aspect of Harriman's life. Some appeared as railroad engineers in honor of the Union Pacific. Art Buchwald, remembering Harriman and the Yale crew, was a coxswain roaring jokes through a megaphone. George Plimpton came, irrelevantly, as an Arab. Kennedy himself found somewhere the distinctive style of long black overcoat and creased felt hat that Harriman had worn as wartime ambassador to Moscow. Hubert Humphrey was there (this was only a few months after the fox-in-the-chicken-coop crack, but Kennedy was not a feudist) and gave, I noted, the best toast of the evening; "he was witty, charming, relaxed and *brief*. One felt that he was quite at peace with himself and very cheerful and comfortable in the Kennedy environment."[44]

Then, in a sudden gesture, the dining room curtains were drawn back. Outside the bay windows in life-size wax replica were Roosevelt, Churchill and Stalin as at Yalta. "It was very cold," said Plimpton, "and [the Big Three] looked forlorn out there, like waifs, and awfully cold too, because of that spooky wax color. Someone had furled a scarf around Stalin's neck and Roosevelt had a beanie-type hat to make them look a bit more cheerful."[45] Odd, one reflected: fifteen years earlier Robert Kennedy, in his prize essay at Charlottesville on the iniquity of Yalta, had named Harriman as a leading villain.

There were the annual pet shows, with prizes for the longest nose, the shortest tail and other oddities, and Buchwald as chief judge and master of ceremonies. Since the Kennedys had more pets than anyone else, they won more prizes. Brumus, still monstrously in the picture, distinguished himself one year by lifting his leg and discharging on a nice old woman sitting placidly on the lawn. "Bobby went white," Buchwald recalled, "and he ran into the house. So when it came to a profile of courage in regard to Brumus, he was a coward."[46]

Correspondence of 1967: Edward Bennett Williams—once again, after the Hoffa years, a friend—to Robert Kennedy:

I have been retained by Mr. Art Buchwald to represent him in the matter of the vicious and unprovoked attack made on him Wednesday, July 25, by the large, savage, man-eating, coat-tearing black animal owned by you and responding to the name, Broomass (phonetic).

Mr. Buchwald has been ordered to take a complete rest by his physician until such time as he recovers from the traumatic neurosis from which he is suffering as a result of the attack. He will be in isolation at Vineyard

Haven, Martha's Vineyard, Massachusetts for an indefinite period at a cost of $2,000 a month.

He is concerned about the effect of exposing this ugly episode on your political future. . . . Since Broomass is black, the case is fraught with civil rights' undercurrents.[47]

So life ran along. His father was no better, but Kennedy ministered to him whenever he could, in winters at Palm Beach, in summers at Hyannis Port. There were admonitory letters from his mother: "In regard to our conversation about 'If I was . . .' as opposed to 'If I were . . .' I should like to offer the following quotations from a book of rules on grammar. . . ."[48] Or, from Rose Kennedy's secretary: "Your mother wanted you to know that the Balfour Resolution established the Jewish home in Jerusalem, but did not make it a Jewish state. She supposed that you know the difference, but some don't. If you don't, it should be explained to you."[49]

Though I left Washington in 1965, I seemed to see more of the Kennedys than ever before. In the autumn of 1966 I moved from Princeton to New York. Thereafter Angie Novello would often phone and say, "The Senator is coming up tonight and wonders whether you could meet him at such-and-such a place a little after ten." One would find a group, small or large, and talk to the early morning, the conversation shifting easily from the light to the serious, propelled by Robert's endless curiosity, irreverent wit and acerbic honesty. I went often, too, to Hyannis Port for long, lazy, sun-drenched summer days with the Kennedys or the Smiths. For all one's forebodings about the republic these were good and joyous times.

IV

He had always been a taker of risks from that day, so many years before, when he had thrown himself off the yawl into Nantucket Sound in his determination to learn to swim, and John Kennedy had said he had shown either a lot of guts or no sense at all, depending on how you looked at it. Now physical danger almost seemed a compulsion. After Dallas the Canadian government named the tallest unclimbed peak in North America, 14,000 feet high, in honor of his brother. The National Geographic Society proposed that the remaining Kennedy brothers join in the first assault on Mount Kennedy. The plane crash eliminated Edward. Robert reluctantly—he hated heights—decided in March 1965 that he would climb Mount Kennedy himself. His family could not shake his resolution. His mother's last words to

him were, "Don't slip, dear."[50] But when his father "found a picture
in the paper of Bobby in his mountain gear, he would angrily grind it
into a ball," his nurse recalled, "and throw it across the room."[51]

Kennedy was rash but not reckless. Two veterans of the successful
Mount Everest expedition of 1963, James Whittaker and Barry
Prather, came with him. Whittaker asked Kennedy what he had been
doing to get in shape for the climb. Kennedy said, "Running up and
down the stairs and hollering 'help.'" Whittaker said to himself, "Oh,
boy!" They flew north to the Yukon Territory, Kennedy reading a
book by Churchill. They saw the peak, "a magnificent mountain,"
Kennedy recorded, "lonely, stark, forbidding." The professionals
gave him a crash course in climbing. They helicoptered to a base
camp at 8700 feet; then roped themselves together, Kennedy in the
middle, and set out across glaciers and crevasses to the summit.

After two days, they saw the final cone standing vertically against
the sky. Kennedy could not see how it was humanly possible to reach
the top. Whittaker dug his ax into the steep ice ridge and began to
pull himself, almost, it seemed to Kennedy, straight up. After sixty
feet, he shouted back to Kennedy, "You're on belay. Now you climb!"
Kennedy thought to himself, "What am I doing here?" But "I
really only had one choice and went on." After some minutes Kennedy managed to join Whittaker, Prather following. "What do you
think of it?" asked Whittaker, enjoying the hundred-fifty-mile view.
"I don't want to look at anything," said Kennedy. "I just want to
stay right here." When they reached the crest, Kennedy went ahead
for the last two hundred feet. He deposited Kennedy memorabilia,
crossed himself, stood a moment in inscrutable silence and then, with
immense relief and exhilaration, made his way down.[52]

Professional climbers thought that, roped between Whittaker and
Prather, Kennedy could hardly fail, and deprecated the achieve-
ment.[53] That may have been true enough physically. Psychologically
it was a feat for a man with a terror of heights. "I didn't really enjoy
any part of it," Kennedy said later. "Henceforth I'm going to stay on
the first floor of my house."[54] He did not, of course. In winters he
skied madly down precarious slopes in Vermont or Idaho. In summers he shot rapids in western rivers. On a trip down the Colorado,
he took to diving into the rushing water. "I've done some foolish
things," said George Plimpton, who was along, "but I wouldn't do
anything as foolish as that. . . . Jim Whittaker was the first person
up Mt. Everest; a terribly brave person, but I don't think he particu-

larly wanted to jump into the water. . . . Yet here was the Senator [in] the wildest of the white water."[55]

In summers too he assembled friends and sailed along the New England coast. In September 1965, as the Kennedy schooner was buffeted by a thirty-knot wind off Long Island, a Coast Guard cutter hailed them to say that Kathleen Kennedy had received head injuries at a horse show. Kennedy, deciding that the quickest way to reach the hospital would be via the Coast Guard, plunged into ten-foot waves and, while everyone held his breath, swam fifty yards to the cutter. This at least made some sense.[56] But he was as impetuous in plunging into the chilling waters of Maine in heavy seas to save his brother's old sea jacket or his own dog Freckles.[57]

We all worried and speculated about this almost compulsive courtship of danger. No doubt the less athletic, like myself, exaggerated the hazards. John Glenn, who careened down the Salmon River with him in kayaks, said later, "I don't recall him taking what I would consider foolish risks. I think he was a pretty good judge of his own capacity on what he could do."[58] Still, as his skiing companion (and a professional) Thomas Corcoran, nephew of the old New Dealer, put it, "He obviously enjoyed approaching the brink of the impossible."[59]

"Men are often drawn to those aspects of nature which reflect their spirit," wrote Richard Goodwin, "and he loved rapids and the pounding surf, was drawn to motion and to turmoil."[60] But it was not only an affinity of temperament; it was some sort of moral necessity. James Dickey, explaining why he had written *Deliverance,* his novel of ordinary men under extreme pressure, recalled the poet John Berryman saying "that it bothered him more than anything else that a man could live in this culture all his life without knowing whether he's a coward or not."[61] Kennedy thought it necessary to know. He marked the sentence in Emerson's *Essays,* "It was a high counsel that I once heard given to a young person, 'Always do what you are afraid to do.' "[62]

Courage, Robert Kennedy wrote, was the virtue John Kennedy "most admired,"[63] the virtue that, as Robert often quoted from Churchill, was "rightly esteemed the first of human qualities because it is the quality which guarantees all others."[64] John Kennedy once read aloud from the citation for Douglas MacArthur's Distinguished Service Cross: "On a field where courage was the rule, his courage was the dominant feature." Robert Kennedy said, "I would love to have that said about me."[65] This was why he liked Glenn and Whittaker, El Cordobés and José Torres, not to mention Martin Luther King and Cesar Chavez. As Pierre Salinger said, they were all "willing to lay their lives on the line for something they believed in, whether it was flying in space, or climbing a mountain, or facing a bull."[66]

Was there more to it than this? Sometimes it almost seemed a dance with death itself. "He believed in his powers," wrote Goodwin, "but was haunted by the omens of failure; wanted much from life but tempted death, even dared it."[67] Death remained a savage presence. In September 1966 Dean Markham, his cherished friend from Harvard days, and Ethel's brother George Skakel died in a plane crash in the mountains of western Idaho. I saw Robert and Ethel soon afterward at the Smiths. The evening was spent in Irish-wake style with uproarious reminiscence of their dead friends. Jean Smith said, "We're getting pretty used to this by now." Kennedy later told Goodwin, "Hackett and I have so much experience at this thing that we're offering a regular service for funerals. . . . We pick out a cheap casket to save the widow money. You know they always cheat you on the casket. We pick passages from the Bible and do all we can to ensure an interesting and inexpensive funeral."[68] He told Sorensen more somberly, "You had better pretend you don't know me. Everyone connected with me seems jinxed."[69]

Death was never far from his mind. "Not to be born is past all prizing best." My son Stephen's notes on a dinner in New York in the autumn of 1967:

> RFK on God: "I don't know why God put us on earth. If I had my choice, I would never have lived. I had no control over it. But why should God put on earth some people who will go to the devil? I think Graham Greene's description of the defrocked priest in *The Power and the Glory* is marvelous." He asked everybody at the table whether they believed in God. I answered that I affirmed what my grandfather had said—"I do not believe in God as a corporeal being. Godliness is simply being kind and loving to people here on earth." Somebody asked RFK whether he believed in God.
>
> "Yes," he said hesitantly, "I think. But one question which really shakes me, really shakes me—if God exists, why do poor people exist? Why does a Hitler arise? I can't give an answer for that. Only faith. . . .
>
> "Yes, I do believe in an afterlife. Religion is a salve for confusion and misdirection. It gets people over the hump easier than what your grandfather said."[70]

He may not have wished to be on earth, but God had put him there, and he still believed in God, or at least believed in belief. I do

not think he was courting death. It was rather that he had an almost
insolent fatalism about life. No one understood better the terrible fortuity of existence. Men were not made for safe havens.

V

The paradoxes of Kennedy were a natural for the literary imagination. But, unlike Europe, where culture and the state share the same
capitals, politics has generally been remote from literature in the
United States. Except for an occasional Henry Adams, writers, journalists apart, have not often been stable-companions to statesmen.[71]
Franklin Roosevelt acquired grand literary friends like Archibald
MacLeish and Robert Emmet Sherwood, but this was after he became President. Most of John Kennedy's literary friends were post-
inaugural. Robert Kennedy as senator, however, sought out, interested, beguiled and sometimes repelled the writers of his day.
(The other senator of the time with comparable tastes was Eugene
McCarthy of Minnesota.)

George Plimpton was an old friend, an overachiever of impressive
versatility and the only writer Kennedy knew who kept up with him
in the melodrama of physical risk. He had been affectionately
through labor racketeering and Watts with Budd Schulberg. Art
Buchwald was an intimate of the house. Irwin Shaw was always great
fun when he made his annual descent from Switzerland. Galbraith
was a close counselor, John Bartlow Martin a loyal friend through
the years. He had a good Irish time with newspapermen like Jimmy
Breslin and Pete Hamill, who made much of the fact that they, unlike
Kennedy, had really known what it meant to be poor. Once Kennedy
and Breslin had an argument (about Lindsay), which Breslin concluded by saying, "Fuck you, Senator!" Kennedy looked at him and
said, "You know, Jimmy, I used to think being poor built up character, and then I met you."[72] He liked James Wechsler, the liberal, and
Jack Newfield, the radical, and Murray Kempton, the anarchist, because they were bright and entertaining and passionate.

In the summers Kennedy, his brother and assorted friends often
sailed from Hyannis Port to see William Styron or Art Buchwald on
Martha's Vineyard. Philip Roth, who met Kennedy on the Vineyard,
thought him "witty and charming and very engaging."[73] Styron did
not like Kennedy at first, but liked him more as the summers passed.
"Unless you include the fact that he could put people off horribly,"
Styron said later, ". . . you're not going to get an honest picture."[74]

Richard Yates, the novelist, who worked at Justice in 1963, did not like Kennedy. Nothing, even Kennedy's affinity for the wounded of the world, could appease Gore Vidal. Nor could James Baldwin, though in later years he acknowledged complexity in Kennedy,[75] ever get over that stormy session in 1963.

Truman Capote, a United Nations Plaza neighbor, was fascinated by Kennedy's power to make people jump—"meaning, if you move through a room and everything is galvanized on you and you're terribly aware of it, and people . . . move out of their way to make room for you . . . in effect, they 'jump.' I think Bobby had that power, but he rarely used it." They occasionally had drinks together. "I always felt that he was very uneasy with me and that his friendship with me was really based on my friendship with other people that he himself was fond of. . . . There was something exotic about me that he couldn't entirely accept; I mean, he was trying to accept it like a father doesn't want to accept long hair on a kid, or sideburns, but yet, he's sort of stuck with him." Walking his dog early one morning, he saw Kennedy talking sternly to two small boys. "Truman, come over here," Kennedy called. "You won't believe this. . . . I came out here to take my dog for a walk . . . and here come these two little kids smoking cigarettes." One said, "Honestly, honestly, Mr. Kennedy, I swear we'll never do it again." "It was," said Capote, "as if he was some sort of avenging angel who had fallen out of heaven upon them." Kennedy made them promise to give up cigarettes, and they ran like maniacs down the street. Then one swung around, raced back and said, "Can I have your autograph, Mr. Kennedy?"[76]

Life asked Saul Bellow to do a piece on Kennedy—an incident described in *Humboldt's Gift.* "I liked him," Bellow (as Charlie Citrine) said, ". . . perhaps against my better judgment. . . . His eyes were as blue as the void. . . . His desire was to be continually briefed . . . receiving what I said with a kind of inner glitter that did not tell me what he thought or whether he could use such facts."[77] One of the more cryptic items in the Kennedy literature was Donald Barthelme's semisatiric, doom-laden fantasy "Robert Kennedy Saved from Drowning"—a sequence of ambiguous dreamlike snapshots: "K. at His Desk"; "K. Reading the Newspaper"; "Sleeping on the Stones of Unknown Towns (Rimbaud)"; "Gallery-going"—

K. looks at the immense, rather theoretical paintings. "Well, at least we know he has a ruler." The group dissolves in laughter. People repeat the remark to one another, laughing. The artist, who has been standing behind a dealer, regards K. with hatred.

"K. Penetrated with Sadness"; "A Friend Comments: K's Aloneness."

> K. in the water. His flat black hat, his black cape, his sword are on the
> shore. He retains his mask. His hands beat the surface of the water which
> tears and rips about him. The white foam, the green depths. I throw a line,
> the coils leaping out over the surface of the water. He has missed it. No, it
> appears that he has it. His right hand (sword arm) grasps the line that I
> have thrown him. . . . I pull him out of the water. He stands now on the
> bank, gasping.
> "Thank you."*

The mask worn to the end, the enigma remaining.

Kennedy, Norman Mailer thought, was the sheriff who could have
been an outlaw. Mailer found himself "excited by precisely [Ken-
nedy's] admixture of idealism plus willingness to traffic with demons,
ogres, and overlords of corruption." Oddly Mailer, who might have
relished Kennedy most, even perhaps understood him best, met him
only once. His mouth "had no hint of the cruelty or calculation of a
politician who weighs counties, cities, and states, but was rather a
mouth ready to nip at anything which attracted its contempt or endangered its ideas." The blue of his eyes "was a milky blue like a
marble so that his eyes, while prominent, did not show the separate
steps and slopes of light some bright eyes show, but rather were gentle, indeed beautiful." Somehow "he had grown modest as he grew
older, and his wit had grown with him." Mailer was struck by the
"subtle sadness [that] had come to live in his tone of confidence.
. . . He had come into that world where people live with the recognition of tragedy, and so are often afraid of happiness."[78]

Kennedy first met James Stevenson, the *New Yorker*'s gifted writer
and cartoonist, at a Saint Patrick's Day reception Stevenson was covering for "The Talk of the Town." Stevenson was as shy as Kennedy.
"I shook his hand, and I looked at him, and he looked at me, and
neither of us said anything. We looked for a while, and then he went

---

* Donald Barthelme, "Robert Kennedy Saved from Drowning," in *Unspeakable
Practices, Unnatural Acts* (New York, 1968). The story is striking because of its precision and insight. When I asked Mr. Barthelme about the provenance, he replied: "I
never met Robert Kennedy nor did I talk to people who had. The story was begun
while I was living in Denmark in 1965. . . . The only 'true' thing in it was Kennedy's
remark about the painter. I happened to be in the gallery when he came in with a
group; I think the artist was Kenneth Noland. Kennedy made the remark quoted
about the ruler—not the newest joke in the world. The story was published in New
American Review well before the assassination. I cannot account for the concluding
impulse of the I-character to 'save' him other than by reference to John Kennedy's
death; still, a second assassination was unthinkable at that time. In sum, any precision
in the piece was the result of watching television and reading the New York Times"
(Barthelme to author, July 16, 1977).

on. . . . But I immediately thought, 'Oh, that's an interesting person,' and then he was gone into the crowd." Kennedy thought Stevenson was interesting too and began to like seeing him. Carter Burden, then working in Kennedy's New York office, used to arrange their meetings. Stevenson, Burden recalled, "never would say anything. The senator would never say anything. But he was very comfortable in his presence." Stevenson himself said later, "You could feel a kind of direct communication without the chit-chat or whatever other people do." And: "He was much more alive than many people, let alone public figures, because he was constantly absorbing, reacting, responding. . . . And, of course, he was terribly funny." And: "You had the feeling you were looking at someone who could go in any direction, and that things could be accomplished that you really didn't believe before that could be accomplished. He carried around a kind of hope with him."[79] Their mysterious communion produced for "The Talk of the Town" the most exact and delicate prose ever written about Robert Kennedy. Thus Kennedy in a car bound for Bedford-Stuyvesant:

> A taxi-driver recognizes Kennedy and yells, "Give it to 'em, Bobby!" Kennedy waves, then stares ahead again. He is deeply preoccupied now, at his most private. . . . He abandons, piece by piece, the outside world—he puts away the magazines, the cigar is forgotten, the offer of gum is unheard, and he is utterly alone. His silence is not passive; it is intense. His face, close up, is structurally hard; there is no waste, nothing left over and not put to use; everything has been enlisted in the cause, whatever it may be. His features look dug out, jammed together, scraped away. There is an impression of almost too much going on in too many directions in too little space; the nose hooks outward, the teeth protrude, the lower lip sticks forward, the hair hangs down, the ears go up and out, the chin juts, the eyelids push down, slanting toward the cheekbones, almost covering the eyes (a surprising blue). His expression is tough, but the toughness seems largely directed toward himself, inward—a contempt for self-indulgence, for weakness. The sadness in his face, by the same token, is not sentimental sadness, which would imply self-pity, but rather, at some level, a resident, melancholy bleakness.[80]

VI

Kennedy read history and biography and an occasional novel but most of all he loved poetry. Tennyson's *Ulysses* was a favorite—

> The lights begin to twinkle from the rocks:
> The long day wanes: the slow moon climbs: the deep
> Moans round with many voices. Come, my friends,
> 'Tis not too late to seek a newer world

—and provided title and epigraph for a book he published at the end of 1967. He told my son Stephen, "Richard Burton is a man's man. We recited our favorite poetry together."[81] This conjunction of ideas would have puzzled Lyndon Johnson. Kennedy was delighted once when he was able to finish a couplet that had slipped Burton's memory.[82] He invited Yevgeny Yevtushenko to his forty-second birthday party. Yevtushenko, like the rest, was mesmerized by the eyes, "two blue clots of will and anxiety. . . . They inhabit his face like two beings uninvolved in the general gaiety. Within these eyes, an exhausting hidden work transpires. . . . Like pale blue razor blades, they pierced through anyone in conversation." At the end of the evening, the two men stood alone in the hall, holding "antique crystal goblets in which tiny green sparks of champagne were dancing." Yevtushenko proposed a toast—to Robert's completion of his brother's work. He reminded Kennedy that, according to the Russian custom, the goblets must be emptied in a single gulp and smashed against the floor. Kennedy, a little embarrassed, said these were Ethel's heirlooms—"wives will be wives"—and produced instead some glasses from the kitchen. "It somewhat surprised me," Yevtushenko said, "that one could think about insignificant glasses when such a toast was being proposed, but, of course, wives will be wives." They downed the champagne and threw the glasses hard on the floor. The glasses did not break. By Russian tradition this meant the toast would not be fulfilled. "I have always been superstitious and a terrible foreboding passed through me. I looked at Robert Kennedy. He had turned pale. Probably he, too, was superstitious." I doubt it; he was more probably tired or bored. Later Yevtushenko wrote an awful poem about the Kennedy brothers.[83]

Yevtushenko was the poet whom the Soviet authorities liked sending abroad. Andrei Voznesensky was not in favor. The American Academy of Poets invited him to the United States in the spring of 1967, then received word that the authorities might not permit him to come. It was thought that Kennedy's intercession could help. I spoke to him, and he sent off a cable at once. After Voznesensky arrived, we had breakfast one morning in the New York apartment. "Voznesensky was serious, rueful and candid," I noted. ". . . Quite different from the somewhat flamboyant and exhibitionistic Yevtushenko." He and Kennedy talked about the frustrations of the young, about the Americans most read in the Soviet Union ("Salinger, Updike and Cheever," Voznesensky said), about Pasternak,

Saint-Exupéry and John Kennedy. They liked each other very much.[84]

Allen Ginsberg, the bard of the counterculture, later chatted with Kennedy about the Soviet poets. Both Americans agreed they preferred Voznesensky. Kennedy thought him the more sensitive. Ginsberg, as Peter Edelman, who was present, recalled, explained that, "when he appeared on a platform with both of them, Yevtushenko had embraced him; but Voznesensky was clearly the more open person because they had kissed deeply and soulfully. Kennedy received that with equanimity."[85] Voznesensky's later poem about Kennedy— "June '68"[86]—was decidedly better than Yevtushenko's.

Ginsberg, a sweet and obsessed man, had come to explain to Kennedy his intricate theories about drugs, the Narcotics Bureau and the Mafia. Kennedy, who already knew about the syndicates, wanted to hear Ginsberg on the relations between the flower people, for whom Ginsberg was patron saint, and the young political militants. Ginsberg thought Kennedy "quizzical. . . . I liked him. He was friendly enough, he was available, he sounded serious. . . . He asked what were the serious possibilities of alliance between 'hippy' and 'black' groups. I was unsure. I asked if he'd ever tried grass. He said 'No,' whatever that meant." Toward the end, Ginsberg asked, "What do *you* think's going to happen to the country?" Kennedy said, "It'll get worse." Ginsberg departed, then remembered something "I'd forgotten to do which was most important." At that moment Kennedy passed through the outer office. Ginsberg asked whether he had two minutes to hear the Hare Krishna mantra. Kennedy said O.K. Ginsberg pulled out a harmonium and chanted: "Hare Krishna Hare Krishna Krishna Krishna Hare Hare Hare Rama. . . ." Kennedy said, "Now what's supposed to happen?" Ginsberg said it was "a magic spell for the preservation of the planet." Kennedy said, "You ought to sing it to the guy up the street," gesturing toward the White House. "He needs it more than I do."[87]

Among poets Kennedy had the closest and most complicated relations with Robert Lowell. "We never became good friends," Lowell said later. Still they interested each other. "I have always been fascinated by poets like Wyatt and Raleigh, who were also statesmen and showed a double inspiration," Lowell wrote Kennedy in early 1967,

—the biggest of these must be Dante, who ruled Florence for a moment, and never could have written about Farinata and Manfredi without this experience. Large parts of the Commedia are almost a Ghibelline epic. Then there are those wonderful statesmen, like Lincoln and Edmund Burke, who were also great writers.

Well, I do think you are putting into practice that kind of courage and ability that your Brother so subtly praised in his *Profiles,* and know how to be brave without becoming simple-minded. What more could one ask for in my slothful, wondering profession?[88]

Lowell had given Jacqueline Kennedy a Plutarch, which Robert, the poet later discovered, borrowed and read. Lowell was not surprised. "Bobby was very conscious of the nobility and danger of pride and fate." Remembering that Thomas Johnston had begun at the Yale Drama School, Lowell once asked him where in Shakespeare he would cast Kennedy. Johnston said at once, "Henry the Fifth." Lowell said that was trite. Kennedy objected to Lowell's objection. Henry V, Lowell reminded him, had not had that fortunate a life. He had died young, leaving in France a son who was murdered and an expeditionary force that was destroyed. Kennedy took down a volume of the Histories and read aloud the deathbed speech of Henry IV, where the old King, his crown taken prematurely by young Harry, said,

> For this the foolish over-careful fathers
> Have broke their sleep with thoughts, their brains with care
> Their bones with industry;
> For this they have engrossed and piled up
> The canker'd heaps of strange-achieved gold;
> For this they have been thoughtful to invest
> Their sons with arts and martial exercises. . . .
> For what in me was purchased,
> Falls upon thee in a more fairer sort.

Then Kennedy said, "Henry the Fourth, that's my father." At first Lowell thought this a non sequitur. As he reflected, he decided it was "very profound. . . . He meant he had a very difficult career coming from this difficult but very elevated forebear who made it possible. And he really *was* cast in the role of Henry the Fifth, not altogether a desirable one . . . perhaps a doomed one."[89]

"Doom was woven in your nerves," Lowell wrote in the best poem about Robert Kennedy,

> . . . like a prince, you daily left your tower
> to walk through dirt in your best cloth. Untouched,
> alone in my Plutarchan bubble, I miss
> you, you out of Plutarch, made by hand—
> forever approaching our maturity. . . .

One was refreshed when you wisecracked through the guests,
usually somewhat woodenly, hoarsely dry,
pure Celt on the eastern seaboard. Who was worse stranded?
Is night only your torchlight wards gone black,
white wake on wave, pyre set for the fire that fell?[90]

37

The Dilemma

AUTUMN 1967: the war intensifying, the ghettos exploding, the campuses stirring, public frustration spreading, Lyndon Johnson massive and immovable in the White House. There was a turnabout again in the polls. "Senator Robert Kennedy of New York," Gallup reported at the end of September, "has made steady gains in political appeal over the last several months, while President Johnson's appeal has been fading." In July it had been 45–39 for Johnson. Now it was 51–39 for Kennedy.[1] In October Louis Harris gave it to Kennedy 52–32.[2]

I

The war: 112 Americans killed in action in 1964, 1130 in 1965, 4179 in 1966, 7482 in 1967; American forces in Vietnam growing from 23,000 at the end of 1964 to 525,000 at the end of 1967;[3] American bombers dropping more tons of explosives in Vietnam than on all fronts in the Second World War; negotiations forgotten; peace as distant as ever; Robert Lowell and Norman Mailer leading the armies of the night against the Pentagon; Robert Kennedy defending the protesters. While he thought it a "bad mistake" to shout down government officials, he could see ample reason for street demonstrations against the war. "When we talk about the violence and the people walking out and the lawlessness, there is no [other] way for people to express their point of view, and I think that is most unfortunate."[4]

Actually, while peaceniks were burning the Secretary of Defense in effigy, McNamara was in the Pentagon context a peacenik himself, resisting the importunities of the Joint Chiefs—and of the President too—to escalate the war and now the strongest advocate of negotiations within the cabinet. Henry Kissinger, who was working with McNamara on negotiations, gave me a graphic vignette of the summer of 1967, Johnson harrying McNamara in the cabinet room: "How can I hit them in the nuts? Tell me how I can hit them in the nuts."[5] In August, without clearing his testimony with the White House, McNamara told the Senate Military Affairs Committee that it was militarily pointless to keep on bombing the North. "The President was angry," recalled Major General Robert Ginsburgh, Walt Rostow's military assistant. "He decided to back the Joint Chiefs and ease McNamara out."[6]

Johnson blamed the usual suspects. "The Kennedys began pushing him harder and harder," he told Doris Kearns. "Every day Bobby would call up McNamara, telling how the war was terrible and immoral and that he had to leave. Two months before he left he felt he was a murderer and didn't know how to extricate himself. I never felt like a murderer, that's the difference. . . . After a while, the pressure got so great that Bob couldn't sleep at night. I was afraid he might have a nervous breakdown."[7]

I met Kennedy in New York in the late evening of November 29. The afternoon papers had McNamara leaving Defense to become head of the World Bank.

RFK said that Bob had *not* had any intimation that Johnson had sent his name up for the Bank. He had had a general conversation with Johnson about it last spring . . . but that was all. Then suddenly he heard, not from the President but from a leak in London, that he was on his way out. I expressed incredulity at Bob's apparent acquiescence in this. Wouldn't any self-respecting man, I asked Bobby, have his resignation on the President's desk half an hour after he heard the London bulletin? Isn't that what you would do? . . . Why does he fall in with LBJ's plan to silence him and cover everything up? Bobby listened silently and a little gloomily. He said that he thought that was what would finally happen—that Bob would not take the World Bank job and would instead quietly resign from government. Obviously this is what Bobby had been urging him to do. When we broke up around one, we got copies of the morning *Times*. The headline: MCNAMARA TAKES WORLD BANK POST. Bobby was evidently surprised and sad.[8]

We all supposed that McNamara's dismissal removed the last hope at the summit of government for restraint in the war—a supposition reinforced when Johnson soon announced a leading hawk, Clark Clifford, as the new Secretary of Defense. Only McNamara, Kissinger told me in December, had kept negotiations alive. Kissinger added that he himself had come away from Washington "with a conviction that LBJ's resistance to negotiation verges on a sort of madness."[9] Nor was madness a White House monopoly that autumn. Calling for a hand vote at a Catholic girls' college in November, Kennedy was appalled when a majority wanted more, not less, bombing. "Do you understand what that means?" he cried. ". . . It means you are voting to send people, Americans and Vietnamese, to die. . . . Don't you understand that what we are doing to the Vietnamese is not very different than what Hitler did to the Jews?"[10]

Later that month Tom Wicker asked him on *Face the Nation* whether, in light of the administration claim that the "great threat from Asian communism" made victory essential for the security of the United States, it did not follow that "perhaps we ought to do as much as needs to be done?" The United States, Kennedy replied, had originally gone into South Vietnam in order to permit the South Vietnamese to decide their own future. Plainly the South Vietnamese did not like the future held out by the Saigon regime. So we had moved on to the national security argument.

> Now we're saying we're going to fight there so that we don't have to fight in Thailand, so that we don't have to fight on the west coast of the United States, so that they won't move across the Rockies. . . . Maybe [the people of South Vietnam] don't want it, but we want it, so we're going in there and we're killing South Vietnamese, we're killing children, we're killing women, we're killing innocent people . . . because [the Communists are] 12,000 miles away and they might get to be 11,000 miles away.

He grew passionate, even eloquent.

> Do we have a right here in the United States to say that we're going to kill tens of thousands, make millions of people, as we have . . . refugees, kill women and children? . . . I very seriously question whether we have that right. . . . Those of us who stay here in the United States, we must feel it when we use napalm, when a village is destroyed and civilians are killed. This is also our responsibility. . . . The picture last week of a paratrooper holding a rifle to a woman's head, it must trouble us more than. it does. . . .
>
> We love our country for what it can be and for the justice it stands for and what we're going to mean to the next generation. It is not just the land, it is not just the mountains, it is what this country stands for. And that is what I think is being seriously undermined in Vietnam.

There was, he said, "an unhappiness and an uneasiness within the United States at the moment, and there has to be an outlet for it."[11]

II

One who perceived the need for an outlet most acutely was Allard Lowenstein, the perennially youthful activist, now thirty-eight years old, one of Eleanor Roosevelt's last protégés, a veteran of racial struggles in Mississippi and South Africa, an early opponent of the war. In the summer of 1967 Lowenstein had conceived the quixotic enterprise of organizing a movement to dump Johnson. It was, as Jack Newfield observed, rather like Castro and a handful of guerrillas in the Sierra Maestre planning to dump Batista.[12] And it could not succeed without a presidential candidate determined to end the war.

When Lowenstein began his quest for a candidate, liberals had an alternative strategy, advocated by Joseph Rauh. It was almost impossible, Rauh reasoned, to deny renomination to incumbent Presidents; no antiwar candidates were available anyway; so why not organize a fight for a peace plank at the 1968 convention? At first Robert Kennedy thought that this tactic would only make it easy for Johnson to sidetrack the doves by promising to let them help write the platform. In mid-September he seemed slightly more favorable. "If we go ahead on this," he told me, "at least it will make the year more interesting than it is likely to be otherwise." He added, as news from all over, that Jesse Unruh, the powerful organization Democrat in California, had turned against Johnson and that Mayor Daley in Chicago was "very deeply opposed" to the war, the son of his closest friend having recently been killed in Vietnam.[13]

A fortnight later I dined at Hickory Hill. Around ten-thirty that evening Lowenstein, Newfield and James Loeb came by. Lowenstein set forth in fervent language his certitude that Johnson could be beaten in the primaries. I brought up the peace plank. Lowenstein said that Johnson was more unpopular than the war. Kennedy said, "When was the last time millions of people rallied behind a plank?" Johnson, Lowenstein said, might even pull out if defeated in the early primaries. "I think Al may be right," Kennedy said. "I think Johnson might quit the night before the convention opens. I think he is a coward." Lowenstein and Newfield told Kennedy he must run. Older, cautious and wrong, Loeb and I argued that Kennedy was too precious a commodity to be expended in a doomed effort. "I would have a problem if I ran first against Johnson," Kennedy himself finally said. "People would say that I was splitting the party out of

ambition and envy. No one would believe that I was doing it because
of how I felt about Vietnam and poor people. I think Al is doing the
right thing, but I think that someone else will have to be the first to
run. It can't be me because of my relationship to Johnson."[14]

Lowenstein pursued his quest. He dashed around the country,
sought out like-minded Democrats, set up local committees, prosecuted the search for a challenger. At Kennedy's suggestion he talked
to George McGovern. McGovern said he had been urging Kennedy
since 1965 to run against Johnson. As for himself, he was up for
reelection in South Dakota and feared that his materialization as a
peace candidate against the President might defeat him for the Senate in his still hawkish state.[15] Why not talk, McGovern told Lowenstein, to senators who did not have reelection problems—Lee Metcalf
of Montana, Eugene McCarthy of Minnesota?

Later McGovern checked back with his nominees. Metcalf had
dismissed the idea out of hand: "it's ridiculous." McGovern then
said to McCarthy, "I sent some people up to talk to you, Gene,
about running against Johnson." McCarthy said, "Yeah, I talked to
them. I think I may do it." McGovern was "astounded. . . . But it
was clear then that he was going to go. There must have been other
people that had been talking to him before that I didn't know
about."[16] This surmise was correct. The previous March, Thomas
K. Finletter had given a small old-Stevensonian dinner for McCarthy
in New York. McCarthy had held the dinner table with his eloquent
denunciation of the war. "The only way to get Johnson to change,"
he had said, "would be for someone to run against him." He just
might do it himself, he added, if no one else would. The Finletter
guests offered to set up a small headquarters for him. McCarthy
seemed interested, then backed off two days later, saying, "Well,
maybe the time isn't right; play it by ear; live off the land; let's see
what happens."[17]

Now, evidently, the time was right. My journal, October 18,
1967: "George McGovern called yesterday and said, among other
things, that he thought Eugene McCarthy had about decided to go—
i.e., that he would enter the New Hampshire, Wisconsin, California
and Massachusetts primaries against Johnson." I was astounded too.
McCarthy, who had had a brilliant career in the House in the fifties,
had been a disappointing senator, especially after the frustration of
his vice presidential hopes in 1964. He was immensely intelligent and
attractive but had come to seem indolent, frivolous, cynical; also unduly responsive to the legislative requests of the Minneapolis–St.

Paul banking community. His concern about the war, though now intense, had come distinctly later than Kennedy's and far later than McGovern's.

My journal: "Bobby called a few moments later." He had led the fight in the Senate that day for the abolition of the Subversive Activities Control Board.[18] (Among those voting to keep that inane agency in existence was McCarthy.) In the course of conversation, I passed along McGovern's arresting bulletin. McGovern:

> Within minutes Kennedy got hold of me. And he said, "Is that true?" And I said, "Yes, it is." And he was just terribly distressed about it because what became clear then is that he desperately wanted to keep that option open. . . . He said, "He's going to get a lot of support. I can tell you right now, he'll run very strong in these primaries. He'll run strong in New Hampshire. . . . I'm worried about you and other people making early commitments to him because . . . it would make it hard for all of us later on if we wanted to make some other move." . . . I can't recall in the conversations I had with Bob anything that so much disturbed him as McCarthy's announcement. . . . I don't think Bob in his wildest imagination ever dreamed that McCarthy would announce. . . . I think he thought, "My God, I should have done this."[19]

By the time I saw Kennedy the next evening in New York, his agitation, if McGovern had it right, had subsided. "He seemed to feel," I noted, "that it might have some use, though he is well aware that McCarthy is not particularly friendly to him. The danger, of course, is that Gene will make himself the hero and leader of the anti-war movement and cast RFK as Johnny-come-lately. The hope is that he may increase the fluidity of the situation and draw the Johnson fire, making it possible for RFK to emerge as a less divisive candidate. We shall see."[20]

III

It was true that McCarthy and Kennedy were not particularly friendly. On the other hand, they were not at that point particularly unfriendly. The legend that the Kennedys had never forgiven McCarthy for his nomination of Adlai Stevenson in 1960 was a legend. Actually John Kennedy thought McCarthy's the best speech of the convention.[21] The two men, said O'Donnell, "were never soulmates, but the President was a very practical fellow. He saw what Gene McCarthy was up to" in 1960—a place on the national ticket— "and [felt] Gene had as much right as he had to do it."[22] Nothing was more natural than for McCarthy to strike an alliance with Johnson who, if he beat Kennedy for the nomination, would need another northern liberal Irish Catholic as his running mate.

In 1961 President Kennedy spoke at a fund-raising dinner in Minneapolis. The next morning local Democratic dignitaries proposed to accompany him to mass. "No," Kennedy said. "I only want Gene and Abigail with me because I know damn well they always go to church." Abigail McCarthy, an intelligent and strong-willed wife, later recalled, "He was interested in where F. Scott Fitzgerald had lived and he was frank about his own casual Catholicism. He teased me about the Missal I was carrying and said, 'That seems to be the thing now—Teddy carries one around that he can hardly lift.'" (When in 1964 someone showed Abigail McCarthy a photograph of their arrival with Kennedy at the church, she surprised herself by bursting into tears.)[23] Kennedy later sent McCarthy on missions abroad—to the Vatican to find out how strongly the Church really opposed the opening to the left in Italy; to Chile for an international conference of Christian Democrats. "My relations with President Kennedy during his term," McCarthy said in later years, "were all positive and friendly. . . . There was no great feud between me and Jack Kennedy."[24]

As for Robert Kennedy, he did think it odd that McCarthy should have nominated Stevenson so resoundingly when he was really—so we all supposed—for Johnson. Perhaps for that reason, but probably more because he favored Humphrey, he would have declined, if asked, to nominate McCarthy for the Vice Presidency in 1964.[25] But the two men did not know each other well, then or later. "I do not recall," said McCarthy in 1969, "that I had more than a half-dozen conversations with him."[26] Robert's scorn for McCarthy was less political or personal than senatorial. He thought McCarthy was undependable and uninvolved, too often absent when needed for a debate or a vote, too cozy on the Finance Committee with special interests. Friends of McCarthy's did not disagree.[27]

As Galbraith, who knew all three men well, put it, the Kennedys "carried their likes and dislikes very casually; they didn't allow them to interfere with life too much. . . . I think that Bobby felt very little antagonism toward Gene. . . . Personal dislike . . . was much more strongly felt by McCarthy."[28] McCarthy was "a petulant fellow anyway, as we all know," said O'Donnell, who liked McCarthy and whom McCarthy asked in December 1967 to manage his campaign, "and . . . dreamed up all these things that the President didn't like him."[29] In fact, McCarthy, like other brilliant, lonely men, looked down on practically everybody in his own profession. He admired poets but had little use for politicians.

Moreover, McCarthy and John Kennedy, men of the same age, faith, party, heritage, had been inevitable rivals from the day in 1949 when they first met in the House of Representatives. But Kennedy was rich, eastern, secular, glamorous, while Gene McCarthy was a small-town boy from the upper midwest who attended, and later taught at, a Benedictine college and spent the year in between in a monastery. McCarthy had made it on his own and, as Galbraith said, simply thought he was intellectually "better qualified than the Kennedys. He had worked harder, studied harder, was a better economist and knew more about philosophy, poetry and theology—the elements of an educated man—than did either Bobby or the President."[30] And, if he finally gave John Kennedy grudging respect for intelligence, will and imperturbability,[31] he found Robert's exercises in intellectual self-improvement comic. He found almost everything comic. He had an elegant, original, penetrating wit. Alas, he never turned it on himself.

Yet, for all this, McCarthy probably had no greater hostility for Robert Kennedy in 1967 than he had for the rest of the Senate. In March he told James Wechsler that he would be glad to support Kennedy as the strongest candidate against Johnson.[32] In the autumn, on a couple of occasions, he urged Kennedy to run. Had Kennedy told McCarthy that he would go, I have little doubt that McCarthy at this point would have supported him. Even at a later point, after McCarthy was well into New Hampshire, O'Donnell remembers Abigail McCarthy's saying, "If Bobby'd only run, we'd get out tomorrow morning."[33]

IV

His friends disagreed as to whether Bobby ought to run.

His staff thought he should. But Kennedy, while he respected them on issues, discounted them on politics. He believed them inexperienced, emotional and, like all staff people, institutionally committed to make their boss President. His older friends from the New Frontier were more skeptical. On October 8, Pierre Salinger convened a group in New York. Edward Kennedy and Stephen Smith were there. Robert was not. The general feeling, put most forcefully by Theodore Sorensen, was that Kennedy should wait for 1972. Kenneth O'Donnell, however, said that Johnson was a bully and a coward who would run away from a fight.[34] Though O'Donnell soon came privately to believe that Kennedy *should* run in 1968, he felt that only Kennedy could make the decision and that meetings about it were a waste of time.[35] This one, in any case, O'Donnell described as "just the most inconclusive bunch of crap thrown around."[36]

Richard Goodwin, who had not been at the New York meeting, soon weighed in with a long letter to Kennedy. He began, curiously, by saying that he would advise against his trying in 1968. Then the letter turned into a powerful argument for his doing so. "I have, in fact, little doubt," Goodwin wrote, "that you can beat Johnson almost everywhere; if you really run against him and for your vision of America." He disposed of the arguments against: that Kennedy would be regarded as a spoiler, hurt his own prospects, etc. "You may well be hurt more by supporting LBJ, since you will have to say a lot of things you don't believe." Nor would it be better to wait till 1972. If Johnson were reelected, he would devote all his attention to making sure Kennedy did not succeed him. When there was a tide in the affairs of men, it should be taken at the flood. "Your prospects," he concluded, "rest on your own qualities: the less true you are to them, and the more you play the [political] game, the harder it will be. People can forgive mistakes, ambition, etc., but they never get over distrust. That's the history of the Presidency in this century."[37]

That was one side. On November 3, in another long letter, Fred Dutton, an equally valued adviser, took the opposite side. *"You are not,"* Dutton began, *"as strong with a majority of the country as your upswing in the polls and particularly your topping of President Johnson might suggest."* The polls, said Dutton, proved Johnson's weakness, not Kennedy's strength. Dutton did think it *"increasingly possible—even close to probable, I believe—that LBJ will not run next year. . . ."* In domestic politics I have never thought he is a fighter at all in a personal crunch—his toughness is of the locker room or cloakroom kind. But when he gets in the ring, even when he is trying to look tough, he wants to talk things out and whine a little, not slug it out." Still, an attempt to oust an incumbent President "will emphasize—'act out'—with the public the negative qualities which they have thought they disliked about you in the past . . . ruthlessness, self-preoccupied ambition, etc." Of course, you might "decide LBJ is so dangerous and Vietnam so bad that he must be defeated and a Democratic election blocked regardless of who the GOP nominee may be. Your plunging in might be an act of conscience to some people. But it would likely also be political suicide for you."

Dutton thought Kennedy should

even public[ly] fraternize with LBJ a little. . . . You make a mistake to indulge your view of him, however accurate. . . . At times, you are almost compulsive in your decisions, dislikes, etc. You still are not as disciplined a politician as President Kennedy. . . . Appeal to the middle class much more! . . . You and some of the more idea-oriented ones around you—as Arthur Schlesinger, Dick Goodwin, Adam, Peter, etc.—seem to want to mix it up in issue fights now instead of preempting the early future. . . . Above all, keep cool for now. Timing separates the great public men from merely the good ones.[38]

I sent Kennedy almost as long a letter the same day—how distracted he must have been by these weighty documents! I had now concluded that Lowenstein had been right and I wrong in September. If you don't run, I wrote, McCarthy will; and will thereby "become the hero of countless Democrats across the country disturbed about the war. . . . If you were to enter at some later point, there might well be serious resentment on the ground that you were a Johnny-come-lately trying to cash in after brave Eugene McCarthy had done the real fighting. In other words, McCarthy might tie up enough in the way both of emotion and even of delegates to make another anti-LBJ candidacy impossible." As for the theory that Kennedy's entry would split the Democrats and elect Nixon, this prospect, I argued, contained its own cure. "I think that you could beat LBJ in the primaries," and, if this led the Republicans to nominate Nixon, "so much the better. He is the one Republican candidate who would reunite even a divided and embittered Democratic party."[39]

I pressed the case at Hickory Hill over the first weekend in November. Kennedy's feeling remained, I noted afterward, that "it would be a great mistake for him to challenge Johnson at this point—that it would be considered evidence of his ruthlessness, his ambition and of a personal vendetta." He acknowledged the risk that McCarthy might be successful enough to prevent the emergence of another antiwar candidate, "but feels he has no alternative but to wait." Perhaps "as McCarthy beats LBJ in primaries," state leaders might ask him to run in the interests of party unity. He was refurbishing his national contacts; "Joe Dolan has been working almost full time on this for the last ten days." However, he did not think that local organizations mattered much except for Daley's in Illinois; "it is possible to win anywhere by running against the organization."[40] One felt that the conviction his motives would be misunderstood was the essential obstacle. "If his name had been something else," O'Donnell said later, "I think Bobby Kennedy would have announced for President in 1967 and taken Johnson on without any question whatsoever."[41]

McCarthy, though he had about decided, still had not declared. "All I hope for," he told Joseph Kraft, "is that Bob doesn't throw stones on the track when I'm running out there alone. But I understand that, if it goes, he's going to want to come in." Kraft relayed this to Kennedy, who said of course he would throw no stones, adding, "Tell him not to run a one-issue campaign."[42] Then, toward the end of November, McCarthy called on Kennedy to say he was about to announce. The meeting was brief and not entirely comfortable. "I didn't ask him what he was going to do," McCarthy said later. "I just said, 'I'm not worried as to whether I'm a stalking horse for you,' meaning that if Bobby were to enter later on I would not say I'd been tricked. I left it open to him. He didn't give me any encouragement or discouragement. He just accepted what I'd said."*

Kennedy told me that during their seven minutes together McCarthy had neither disclosed his own campaign plans nor shown any curiosity about Kennedy's thoughts on organization or issues or New Hampshire, the first primary. "He is a very strange fellow," Kennedy said. "After all, I don't want to blow my own trumpet, but I have had a little experience running primaries. But he didn't ask a single question." Kennedy would have advised McCarthy to say that he did not expect to win in New Hampshire and that he was entering in order to give Democrats a chance to discuss the issues. "He should walk the streets in every town, without entourage or fanfare. He should not talk about Vietnam very much, since he has all the peace votes anyway. He should run against the organization, against the Democratic establishment, against the big shots." Kennedy doubted that Johnson would get more than 20,000 votes and thought McCarthy had a "good chance" of actually taking New Hampshire.[43]

It was one of those hopeless encounters where two men meet, not much liking one another, one too proud to seek advice, the other too proud to volunteer it. The meeting confirmed Kennedy's belief that McCarthy would be no more serious as a candidate than he had latterly been as a senator. As for McCarthy, when he made his formal announcement on November 30, a reporter asked whether Kennedy

---

* As reported by William H. Honan in *New York Times Magazine,* December 10, 1968; Richard T. Stout, *People* (New York, 1970), 76–77. Kennedy entered, and McCarthy in later years did suggest he had been tricked (see Eugene McCarthy, "Kennedy's Betrayal," in *The Sixties,* ed. L. K. Obst [New York, 1977], 258–260).

might not take over his movement. McCarthy said candidly, "He might. It would certainly be nothing illegal or contrary to American politics if he or someone else were to take advantage of whatever I might do. . . . There's no commitment from him to stand aside all the way."[44]

Kennedy had just scribbled a postscript in a letter to Anthony Lewis in London: "Washington is dreadful—but what to do?"[45]

V

December 10, 1967. RFK finally summoned a council of war today on 1968. It took place at a Sunday luncheon at Bill vanden Heuvel's. Present, in addition to Bobby and Bill, were Ted Kennedy, Ted Sorensen, Dick Goodwin, Fred Dutton, Pierre Salinger and myself.

The serious discussion began with my putting the case for his running in 1968. I said . . . that, if McCarthy did moderately well in the primaries, he might expose Johnson without establishing himself; that state leaders would understand that their own tickets would go down if LBJ were at the head of the ticket; and that Bobby should then emerge as a candidate, rescue the party and end the war in Vietnam. The dissension in the Democratic party, I said, would tempt the Republicans to nominate Nixon, who would be the easiest candidate to beat.

Dick Goodwin then argued a slightly different case for running at once—entering the primaries, assuming a McCarthy withdrawal, and carrying the fight through to the convention.

RFK then said that the talk up to this point had revolved around himself and the party. He did think another factor should be weighed—i.e., the country. . . . He was not sure whether the country or the world could survive five more years of Johnson. Whether or not he was sure of winning, was there not a case for trying in 1968?

Ted Kennedy and, later, Ted Sorensen put the case for waiting. Ted Kennedy's view was that LBJ is sure of reelection and that Bobby is sure of nomination in 1972. Dick suggested that LBJ, if reelected, would use all his wiles and powers to prevent RFK's nomination. (Bobby interjected, "He would die and make Hubert President rather than let me get it.") Ted felt that he would try this, but his capacity to do damage would be limited. To do anything now, Ted said, would be to jeopardize, if not destroy, Bobby's future. It would be an unpopular step within the party; but no one should underestimate the amount of sentiment (presumably Kennedy sentiment) in the country, and this would still be there in 1972.

Ted Sorensen thought it would be futile to go into the primaries and impossible to buck up the McCarthy effort without implicating the Kennedys in his failure. RFK added that, if Gene had any success, he wouldn't get out, no matter what he might be saying at this point. . . . Pierre, who said afterward that he agreed philosophically with me and politically with Ted S., questioned the inevitability of LBJ's reelection. He said that no one should underestimate the total alienation from the President, especially among the young. . . .

Bobby said that he was by no means sure he would be any stronger in 1972 than he is now. He would have been around five years longer, taken more positions, estranged more interests, gained more enemies. Perhaps he would never be stronger than he is today. Suppose he entered the six primaries and won them; would he then get the nomination? Ted Sorensen said no; LBJ would still get it. RFK rather disagreed. A series of primary victories, he said, would have an impact on other delegations and change the picture. There was then some discussion about filing dates, etc.

It seemed evident that Bobby is sorely tempted. He would in a way like to get into the fight, and he also is deeply fearful of what another Johnson term might do to the world. But he said that practically he did not suppose he would have much chance of getting the nomination, though he thought, if he did, he could beat Nixon. He added that people in whom he had confidence were strongly opposed to his doing anything, nor, so far as he could see, were many people in the party for it. So he supposed he would do nothing, and nothing would happen. He said this regretfully and fatalistically. But he said no final decisions had to be made for a few more weeks, and in the meantime everyone should keep on brooding.[46]

VI

They were brooding at the White House too. December 4, 1967, John P. Roche, political scientist, former ADA chairman, now a presidential assistant, to Lyndon Johnson: "Bobby Kennedy is sponsoring a 'War of Liberation' against you and your Administration. To date, however, he has kept it as 'Phase I'—random guerrilla attacks. And I have been convinced that he himself has not made up his mind on whether to move on to 'Phase II'—organization of Main Force Units. I still don't think he knows what he is doing. . . . At the risk of sounding ironic, I would suggest that Bobby is no *more* decisive than you are when torn by conflicting sentiments."[47]

December 7, Johnson to David Lilienthal, who had been drafting economic development plans for Vietnam: "All you hear in the papers is about how bloodthirsty we are, nothing but killing and blood—not a word about the kind of thing *you* are doing. . . . Bobby Kennedy was on three TV shows last week."[48] December 8, Joseph Califano to Johnson: "Bill Moyers called to tell me . . . that Shriver believed Bobby Kennedy was getting ready to run against you in 1968."[49] And so on, week after week, the President's men trying to divine the intentions of the prince across the water.

The President himself was sure Kennedy would run. His advisers doubted it. January 16, James Rowe to Johnson: "I know you do

not agree, but I am convinced that Bobby Kennedy has made a political judgment that he cannot take the nomination away from you."[50]
January 26, Roche to Johnson:

> He risks total *obliteration* if he goes. . . . It is almost certain disaster in 1968 and 1972 vs. a live *possibility* in 1972. . . . If he goes in 1968, he will split the Democratic Party hopelessly, virtually guaranteeing a GOP victory. And he will never be able to put the pieces together for 1972—a significant number of us would dedicate ourselves wholeheartedly to his political destruction. . . .
>
> Does he realize this? Of course he does. He is an arrogant little *schmuck* (as we say in Brooklyn), but nobody should underestimate his intelligence.[51]

VII

For Kennedy the decision posed moral as well as political questions. He deeply believed that Johnson's war, his growing neglect of poverty and racial justice and his violent personality were disasters for the republic. Was there not a case, as he had already suggested at the December war council, for running no matter whether he won or lost? Had he not said so often that an individual could make a difference? Had he not, like his brother before him, reserved the hottest place in hell for those who remained neutral in the face of injustice? Did he not regard courage as the transcendent virtue? "All of his own convictions, all of his own statements, all of his own feelings," said Thomas Johnston, "came back to really haunt him."[52] His friend Newfield wrote bluntly in the *Village Voice:*

> If Kennedy does not run in 1968, the best side of his character will die. He will kill it every time he butchers his conscience and makes a speech for Johnson next autumn. It will die every time a kid asks him, if he is so much against the Vietnam war, how come he is putting party above principle? It will die every time a stranger quotes his own words back to him on the value of courage.[53]

Newfield was prepared for expostulation on his next meeting with Kennedy. Instead Kennedy said simply, "My wife cut out your piece. She shows it to everybody." Newfield asked what he himself thought of the article. "I understand it," Kennedy replied. ". . . On some days I even agree with it. I just have to decide now whether my running can accomplish anything. . . . I don't want to drive Johnson into doing something really crazy. I don't want it to hurt the doves in the Senate who are up for reelection. I don't want it to be interpreted in the press as just part of a personal vendetta. . . . I just don't know what to do."[54]

The moral pressure was rising. A friend was quoted in *Newsweek:* "He cannot go to South Africa and stay out of New Hampshire."[55] In early January, Murray Kempton, a long-time admirer, wrote in a rather ominous way that he preferred McCarthy. "An obvious reason is that McCarthy has the guts to go. A less obvious but more significant reason is that I was not at all surprised that he would, and I'm not the least bit surprised that Kennedy wouldn't." Jules Feiffer:

> GOOD BOBBY. We're going in there and we're killing South Vietnamese, we're killing children, we're killing women. . . . we're killing innocent people because we don't want the war fought on American soil. . . .
> BAD BOBBY. I will back the Democratic candidate in 1968. I expect that will be President Johnson.
> GOOD BOBBY. I think we're going to have a difficult time explaining this to ourselves.[56]

Kennedy spoke at a college on Long Island. In the question period a student observed that the young people had come because they thought Kennedy a man of courage and integrity. "You tell us that you are in total disagreement with what the administration is doing in Vietnam, and that you feel that a great deal more important commitment should be made . . . toward the resolution of the urban problem, and yet you tell us in the next breath that it's your intention to support the incumbent President. . . . Whatever happened to the courage and the integrity?" Said Benno Schmidt, to whom Kennedy was telling the story, "That's a tough one." "I'll say it is," said Kennedy.[57]

At least they were polite on Long Island. At Brooklyn College students hoisted a placard: BOBBY KENNEDY: HAWK, DOVE OR CHICKEN? Kennedy complained to Dolan about it. Dolan thought it rather funny. "He wasn't in a mood to laugh about it. . . . He said, 'How would you like to make a speech and have somebody get up and say, "Chicken"?' . . . He was tormented by the fact that he ought to be running. And he wasn't going against his better judgment; he was going against his instincts because his judgment was not to run."[58] James Rowe warned Johnson: "He is under constant public and private attack from his own supporters and troops. The young are calling him a 'fink.' . . . The anti-Vietnam intellectuals are now turning their tongues loose on Kennedy—he is feeling the lash of their scorn."[59]

VIII

It was an argument between the two sides of his own nature—the romantic and the realist, the guerrilla in the hills and the councilor of state. The professionals—from James Rowe to Fred Dutton and Edward Kennedy—thought his entry would be an act of hara-kiri. The intellectuals who liked to pose as professionals—from John Roche to Theodore Sorensen—thought likewise. If Robert Kennedy yielded to the temptation, Joseph Alsop wrote, as Alsop's own cousin Theodore Roosevelt had yielded in 1912, "he will destroy himself. He will destroy his party. And he will bring into power, perhaps for many years to come, the extreme right wing of the Republican Party." It would be disastrous "if the most promising and most richly equipped man of his generation in American politics allows himself to be pressured into self-destruction . . . [by] pretended friends [Schlesinger and Goodwin] who are seeking to use him for their own peculiar purposes." Fortunately, Joe said, his "astute brother" Edward and his "wise adviser" Sorensen were providing counterpressures.*

Only one professional—Unruh of California—was urging him on; and this, Kennedy recognized, was for Unruh's reasons as much as for Kennedy's. Jack English was even doubtful about New York. "With an incumbent President," he observed, "these old-line leaders would go with the Presidency because somebody wrote in a book or their mother told them, 'You know the rule says you don't dump an incumbent President.' . . . I was worried that . . . he would be stymied, hurt, and embarrassed in his own state."[60]

Most disturbing of all was the lack of support from antiwar Democrats. At Kennedy's request Sorensen said to McGovern, "Look, George, this is a very serious thing you're urging Bob to do. . . . What evidence do you have that people would support him if he announced?" McGovern called Gaylord Nelson, Frank Church, Quentin Burdick of North Dakota, and several midwestern governors, including Harold Hughes of Iowa. He found, he told me, "universal reluctance to consider the possibility, and certainly no one was prepared to do anything about it." "The trouble," he added, "is that everyone seems only interested in taking care of himself. This is the at-

---

* Joseph Alsop, "Can Bob Kennedy Be Pressured into a Sacrificial Candidacy?" *Washington Post*, January 16, 1968. Alsop was an old and cherished friend of mine. The friendship was angrily interrupted by the Indochina War. In later years it has been happily restored.

mosphere Johnson has created. Every one I talked to took that view: what would this do for me? No one was ready to stick his neck out. I was very much surprised. I expected a much better reaction."[61]

Kennedy felt a particular responsibility to fellow doves up for reelection. He said to Clark, "Joe, would it murder you if I got into this thing?" "Of course not," replied Clark, always the Philadelphia gentleman; "even if it did, I would urge you to do it." But Clark would not make a commitment to support him.[62] "There weren't members of the Senate urging him," said McGovern.[63] They well knew Johnson's capacity for retaliation. "I've talked to some of my colleagues in the Senate," Kennedy told Justin Feldman in New York, "and I can't find any support." He could be responsible, he calculated, "for the loss of six Senate seats." Actually, more than six doves were up in 1968: not only McGovern and Clark, but Morse, Gruening, Fulbright, Nelson, Church. Could Kennedy require them to choose between himself and an incumbent President of their own party? "I can't do that."[64] On January 29 McGovern, Rauh and I lunched in Washington. I mentioned that the Wisconsin people, Patrick Lucey and others, did not want Kennedy to enter their primary. McGovern said, "Well, if he did, it would give Gaylord Nelson heart failure." After a detailed rundown McGovern told us, "I cannot in all conscience recommend to Bobby that he run."[65]

Moreover, Johnson *was* President. Kennedy knew the resources of the office, and he feared the desperation of the incumbent.

In the course of his ruminations he expressed a desire to consult Walter Lippmann. I took him to the Lippmann apartment for a drink on a cold January afternoon. After some chat Kennedy said rather abruptly that he had to decide about the Presidency. He set forth his concern about the war, the cities, the poor, his sense that we were drifting toward disaster, his conviction that so many things might be done. Four more years of Johnson, he said, would be a "catastrophe" for the country; so would four years of Nixon. Yet what could he do? He had no support among the politicians. And he could not see in particular how he could overcome the advantage that Johnson had through his command of foreign policy. Nothing, Kennedy thought, would restrain Johnson from manipulating the war in whatever way would help him politically—he could escalate, de-escalate, pause, bomb, stall, negotiate, as the domestic political situation required. "For example," Kennedy said to Lippmann, "suppose, in the middle of the California primary, when I am attacking him on the war, he should suddenly stop the bombing and go off to Geneva to hold talks with the North Vietnamese. What do I do then? Either I call his action phony, in which case I am lining up with Ho Chi Minh, or else I have to say that all Americans should support the President in his search for peace. In either case, I am likely to lose in California."[66] Lippmann, I noted, listened intently but "did not deliver a strong argument (as he had to me on New Year's Eve) for Bobby's running, perhaps because he was impressed by Bobby's presentation of the complexities of the situation, perhaps because he does not regard it as his job to offer advice to politicians." Finally Kennedy asked directly what he thought. Lippmann said, "Well, if you believe that Johnson's reelection would be a catastrophe for the country—and I entirely agree with you on this—then, if this comes about, the question you must live with is whether you did everything you could to avert this catastrophe." On the way to the airport afterward, Kennedy said he had washed 1972 out of his calculations. Life was wholly unpredictable. He could not make decisions now in terms of consequences four years from now.[67]

Two days later, he spent a political day in Westchester County. Returning to the city, he stopped by a cocktail party. Melina Mercouri, the Greek actress, swept down and asked him in her best histrionic style whether he wanted to go down in history as the senator who waited for a safer day. The remark struck home to the student of Edith Hamilton. Afterward Kennedy said, "My feeling now is that if one more politician, on the level of Unruh, asks me to run, I'll do it. . . . What bothers me is that I'll be at the mercy of events Johnson can manipulate to his advantage. . . . None of the doves in the Senate wants me to do it, and that plays a role. . . . The politicians who know something about it, they say it can't be put together. . . . Anyway, I'd rather run than not." He warned Jean Smith and Patricia Lawford at dinner, "This is going to cost you a lot of money."[68]

IX

But the politics of running seemed dismal. McCarthy was campaigning little and doing badly. Gallup's January sounding showed Democrats preferring Johnson over his challenger by 71–18. And, as Kennedy hovered on the brink of challenge, the polls were turning against him too. Johnson now led 52–40.[69] In late January, Louis Harris personally advised him against running.[70] "Bobby is coming to be regarded as an extremist," said Richard Scammon, who, as director of the Census Bureau, had counseled the Kennedy White House in 1963. ". . . A reputation for extremism in this country is a one-way ticket to oblivion."[71] Kennedy observed bleakly to Dorothy Schiff that he had "a lot of enemies"—business, labor, the newspapers, even most of the politicians. ("Who is for you?" she asked. He said, "The young, the minorities, the Negroes and the Puerto Ricans.")[72]

Some of us questioned the infallibility of both pols and polls. Ethel Kennedy listened disgustedly to Sorensen's enormously practical recital of the case against running and said: "Why, Ted! And after all those high-flown phrases you wrote for President Kennedy!"[73] "You can never tell what the reaction of a political leader will be until you announce," O'Donnell said, "because if you say, 'Should I run?' they'll all say no. But if you announce you are a candidate and then ask them, . . . they're put on a spot. . . . You're going to get a different answer and a decisive answer."[74] I made the same point more academically: "The tendency, with the polls and so on, is to view politics as a mechanical process. In fact, it is a chemical process. I think that his entry into the situation as a candidate would transform the situation and create new possibilities not presently foreseeable."[75] But the taciturn O'Donnell rarely offered advice to Kennedy unless directly asked; and my advice, while lavishly offered, lacked the professional imprimatur. Against the massed professional judgment only amateurs—Ethel, Jean Smith, Goodwin, Schlesinger and a rabble of enthusiasts around the country—were telling Kennedy it could be put together.

Then, on January 23, the North Koreans seized the American intelligence ship *Pueblo*. On January 25 Johnson called up 14,000 reserves. It was one of those rally-around-the-flag moments, and it renewed Kennedy's apprehension about the power foreign affairs conferred on the Presidency. "The ordeal continues," I noted when I saw him that day. "I have never seen RFK so torn about anything—I do not mean visibly torn, since he preserves his wryness and equanimity through it all, but never so obviously divided." That evening we dined with the Kennedys and the Benno Schmidts at the Caravelle. Robert went through the familiar arguments—ruthlessness, personal vendetta, no political support, lack of popularity in the country, etc. He said his brother was "the strongest opponent" of his running. "Ethel was urging him to run," Schmidt said later, ". . . and Arthur Schlesinger was articulating all the arguments in favor of Bob's running, as only Arthur can do. . . . telling him that if he got out and won two or three primaries the delegates would have to come to him."

Schmidt then articulated the arguments against Bob's running, as only Benno could do—did he have the delegates? could he get them? could he beat an incumbent President with power to control events? At one point Kennedy said, "I think if I run I will go a long way toward proving everything that everybody who doesn't like me has said about me . . . that I'm just a selfish, ambitious, little SOB that can't wait to get his hands on the White House." Ethel said, "Bob, you've got to get that idea out of your head; you're always talking as though people don't like you. People do like you, and you've got to realize that." Kennedy said, smiling, "I don't know, Ethel, sometimes in moments of depression, I get the idea that there are those around who don't like me." Benno Schmidt drove the Kennedys back to United Nations Plaza. Kennedy said, "I'm convinced that what you say is right."[76]

On January 28 he asked Goodwin and me to dine with him: "We have to settle this thing one way or another." But, when we arrived, we found him with one of his characteristic mélanges—John Glenn, Mike Nichols, Rod Steiger, George and Elizabeth Stevens, heaven knows who else. Obviously we were not about to settle anything. I imagine that he did not want to go over it all again with those he had prepared to disappoint. Two days later, he said at an off-the-record breakfast at the National Press Club, "I have told friends and supporters who are urging me to run that I would not oppose Lyndon Johnson under any conceivable circumstances." Mankiewicz, hoping to salvage something from the wreckage, persuaded him to substitute "foreseeable" for "conceivable" before releasing the statement.[77]

That appeared to be that. Bad Bobby had prevailed. Adam Walinsky gave notice. He had to do something about Johnson and the war, he told Kennedy, and, if Kennedy would not run, he was going to do it some other way.[78] Dolan said he could not vote for Johnson and requested sabbatical leave for the campaign.[79] Edelman decided to do the same thing.[80] Mankiewicz, regarding life as uncertain, put his trust in the unforeseeable. Lowenstein, thoroughly discouraged after two months with McCarthy, appeared at Kennedy's office the same day and announced, "I'm an unforeseeable circumstance." He begged Kennedy to reconsider. Kennedy, reciting his problems once again, said, "It can't be put together." Lowenstein said furiously that the honor and direction of the country were at stake. "I don't give a damn whether you think it can be put together or not. . . . We're going to do it without you, and that's too bad because you could have been President." He stalked out of the office. Kennedy followed, touched him on the shoulder: "I hope you understand I want to do it, and that I know what you're doing *should* be done; but I just can't do it." "I sniffled," Lowenstein recalled, "nodded yes, and walked out, watching him stand in the doorway in real pain."[81]

I was badly disappointed. Still, few questions seem to an historian purely moral. A political leader, as Burke pointed out long ago, differed from a moral philosopher; "the latter has only the general view of society; the former, the statesman, has a number of circumstances to combine with those general ideas, and to take into his consideration. Circumstances are infinite, are infinitely combined, are variable and transient. . . . A statesman, never losing sight of principles, is to be guided by circumstances." I felt that Kennedy had not lost sight of principles and that circumstances were changing every day. At bottom, I believed his instinct would triumph over his judgment.

But around the country antiwar activists said to hell with it and set to work for Eugene McCarthy. And in Vietnam, even while Robert Kennedy was breakfasting at the National Press Club, the Viet Cong and the North Vietnamese unleashed a surprise assault on South Vietnam, convulsing thirty provincial capitals and invading the American embassy in Saigon.

38

The Decision

THE TET OFFENSIVE changed everything. No doubt the attackers suffered grievous losses and failed in major objectives. But they destroyed what remained of Lyndon Johnson's credit with millions of Americans. "We should expect our gains of 1967," General Westmoreland had said grandly four weeks before, "to be increased manyfold in 1968."[1] Now the enemy was swarming into the very courtyard of the American embassy. Tet showed that the administration had deceived either the American people or itself about the military prospect.* It inspired the Joint Chiefs of Staff, falling back on the only remedy it knew, to request 206,000 more troops. And it led to a basic reexamination of Vietnam by the new Secretary of Defense, Clark Clifford, who turned out to be not such a hawk after all.

I

"Half a million American soldiers," Robert Kennedy told a Chicago audience on February 8, "with 700,000 Vietnamese allies, with total command of the air, total command of the sea, backed by huge resources and the most modern weapons, are unable to secure even a single city from the attacks of an enemy whose total strength is about 250,000."[2]

Adam Walinsky and I had spent the previous afternoon with him going over the speech in his New York apartment. Here and there Richard Goodwin, who had done the original draft, and Walinsky

---

* A textbook prepared and used at West Point calls it an "intelligence failure ranking with Pearl Harbor. . . . The North Vietnamese gained complete surprise" (Lieutenant Colonel Dave R. Palmer, *Readings in Current Military History* [West Point, 1969], 103). For this citation and further analysis, see H. Y. Schandler, *The Unmaking of a President* (Princeton, 1977), 74–77.

had proposed alternate passages. "He just took the toughest one each time," as Walinsky said later[3]—and added some of his own. He put in nothing, as he had done so often in the past, to preserve his relations with the administration. He did not, as in the past, come out against unilateral withdrawal. He condemned the deception, condemned the bombing, condemned the insensate destruction, rejected the Saigon regime as incompetent and corrupt and called for "a settlement which will give the Vietcong a chance to participate in the political life of the country."[4]

It was his most passionate Vietnam speech so far. It excited passions. Kennedy told me a day or so later that Joseph Alsop, his old friend and mine, had left a message with Angie Novello: "In the last twelve hours I have talked to three friends of his, none of them particular friends of Lyndon Johnson, and each said to me that, after that speech, they were compelled to regard Bobby Kennedy as a traitor to the United States." For a moment, Alsop was closer to the national mood than Kennedy. The new Gallup poll, taken before Tet had sunk in, showed 61 percent hawks as against 23 percent doves; 70 percent wanted to continue the bombing.[5] Kennedy said to me, "It's just like Hitler—not a very good comparison—but I mean the way people who think themselves good and decent become accomplices. Do you suppose that ten years from now we will all look back and wonder how the American people ever went so far with something so terrible?"[6]

Early in March, Daniel Ellsberg, still at the Pentagon, tipped him off about the JCS request for more troops.[7] On March 7 Kennedy rose in the Senate to demand that "before any further major step is taken in connection with the war in Vietnam, the Senate be consulted." Escalation, he said, had been our invariable response to difficulty in Vietnam—and had invariably failed. We had always claimed that victory was just ahead. "It was not in 1961 or 1962, when I was one of those who predicted that there was a light at the end of the tunnel. There was not in 1963 or 1964 or 1965 or 1966 or 1967, and there is not now." How could escalation save a government so hopelessly corrupt that its own people would not fight for it? For the first time in public he struck directly, and bitingly, at Johnson. "When this [corruption] was brought to the attention of the President, he replied that there is stealing in Beaumont, Texas. If there is stealing in Beaumont, Texas, it is not bringing about the death of American boys." The claim that we had to fight in Vietnam to protect our own security reminded him, he said, of the justifications the Germans and Russians made when they overran Poland and the Baltic states at the start of the Second World War. In his most intense passage he returned to the question of moral responsibility. "Are we," he cried, "like the God of the Old Testament that we can decide in Washington, D.C., what cities, what towns, what hamlets in Vietnam are going to be destroyed?"[8]

Though he did not publicly advocate unilateral withdrawal, he had privately reached the conclusion that the United States had to get out. Harriman, arguing with William Walton, a long-time opponent of the war, said, "Your friend Bobby is not for cut-and-run as you are." Walton repeated this to Kennedy. Kennedy said, "Little does he know."[9] To Rowland Evans, still a hawk, Kennedy said, "We've got to get out of Vietnam. We've got to get out of that war. It's destroying this country."[10] To Thomas Watson of IBM: "I'd get out of there in any possible way. I think it's an absolute disaster. I think it's much worse to be there than any of the shame or difficulty that one would engender internationally by moving out. And so, with whatever kind of apologies and with whatever kind of grace I could conjure up, I'd get out of there in six months with all the troops the United States has."[11]

II

Tet changed everything, for Eugene McCarthy as well as for Lyndon Johnson. In January his campaign had been desultory and ineffectual. "I came here," François Mitterand told Kennedy, "thinking that Senator McCarthy was a stalking horse for you, but now I think he is a stalking horse for President Johnson."[12] In February, McCarthy suddenly found himself the leader of a crusade.

Found himself, and made himself: at last he was in New Hampshire and on the hustings, and he displayed a formidable instinct for the national mood. He was willful, impervious to advice, scornful of associates, but he was also strong, cool, slashing and gallant. People flocked to him, most of all the antiwar young. These had been Kennedy's people. In 1966 Murray Kempton had called Kennedy "our only politician about whom the young care."[13] Now they were leaving him. "I'm going to lose them," Kennedy said to Joseph Dolan, "and I'm going to lose them forever."[14]

The transformation of McCarthy into a serious candidate made Kennedy's position even more intolerable than before. He could not endorse Johnson. His choices now were to endorse McCarthy, which he could not bring himself to do, to remain neutral, which he could not do either, or to enter himself. Within a week of the National Press Club breakfast he was once again in palpable indecision. "How Stevensonian can we all get!" I noted on February 7.[15] Kennedy, McCarthy told a reporter, is "like Enoch Arden. He won't go away from the window. He just comes back and taps on the window or scratches on the door. Every time I think he's gone to sea, he's back again the next morning."[16]

Pressures redoubled. Ethel and his sisters would not give up. Jacqueline Kennedy wrote out excerpts from William Graham Sumner's scathing anti-imperialist essay "The Conquest of the United States by Spain" and sent them to him.* Pete Hamill, finishing a novel in Ireland, sent an emotional letter: "In Watts I didn't see pictures of Malcolm X or Ron Karenga on the walls. I saw pictures of JFK. That is your obligation . . . the obligation of staying true to whatever it was that put those pictures on those walls."[17]

His own conscience nagged at him. On February 10 he published in the *New York Times* a piece on "the malaise of the spirit" in America. The roots of despair, he said, fed at a common source: the failure of abundance to bring happiness. The gross national product rising over $800 billion a year counted "air pollution and cigarette advertising and ambulances to clear our highways of carnage . . . special locks for our doors and jails for the people who break them . . . Whitman's rifle and Speck's knife and television programs which glorify violence the better to sell toys to our children." But it did not count "the health of our youth, the quality of their education or the joy of their play . . . the beauty of our poetry or the strength of our marriages, the intelligence of our public debate or the integrity of our public officials. . . . It measures everything, in short, except that which makes life worthwhile." He wrote of the "sense that as individuals we have far too little to say or do about these issues, which have swallowed the very substance of our lives." He concluded: "We seek to recapture our country. . . . And that is what the 1968 elections must really be about."[18]

Here was the platform. But where was the candidate who would recapture the country? He lingered in miserable indecision. Some advisers, like Fred Dutton, were changing their minds. Even Robert

---

* "There is not a civilized nation in the world which does not talk about its civilizing mission just as grandly as we do. . . . Each nation laughs at all the others. . . . They are all ridiculous by virtue of these pretensions, including ourselves" (Jacqueline Kennedy to RFK, n.d. [February 29, 1968], RFK Papers).

McNamara concluded that Johnson was no longer capable of objective judgment. "I think Bob has to run," he told Lawrence O'Brien at the end of February. "I don't see any other answer."[19] But the two Teds—Kennedy and Sorensen—remained in determined opposition. Robert asked Goodwin to talk to his brother. After a long evening in Boston in mid-February, Goodwin and Edward Kennedy agreed that Robert's chances of winning the nomination were about one in five. They agreed too, Goodwin reported to Robert, that "clearly all your instincts push you in this direction. If you don't do it, you won't feel good about it." Ted had said, "He usually follows his own instincts and he's done damn well." Goodwin asked what John Kennedy would have advised. "I'm not so sure about that," Ted Kennedy said, "but I know what Dad would have said. . . . Don't do it."

Then: "Jack would probably have cautioned him against it, but he might have done it himself."[20]

III

Lyndon Johnson's response to the urban riots of 1967 had been to appoint a Commission on Civil Disorders, with Governor Otto Kerner of Illinois as chairman. At the end of February 1968 the Kerner Commission submitted a powerful report. It portrayed a nation "moving toward two societies, one black, one white—separate but unequal" and proposed strong and specific action to reverse the "deepening racial division." Kennedy, skeptical when the commission was established, was impressed by its report. "The White House," as Daniel Patrick Moynihan wrote, "would not receive it."[21]

"This means," Kennedy said, "that he's not going to do anything about the war and he's not going to do anything about the cities either."[22] It was now as impossible to support Johnson at home as abroad. Kennedy was moving toward the decision. He asked Fred Dutton to see whether his brother was still opposed. "I think Bob is going to run," Edward Kennedy told Dutton resignedly, "and it's up to us to make some sense out of it." On March 5 the two Kennedys met with Dutton and Kenneth O'Donnell. "I left the meeting," said Dutton, "feeling that a decision had been made. . . . I think all four of us felt that Bob probably could not win, but that he now had to try."[23]

On March 9 he went to Iowa to speak at a dinner for Harold Hughes. He spent the late evening with Hughes and the Democratic governors of Missouri, Kansas, and North Dakota. The governors criticized Johnson and doubted whether he could carry their states. Thus obliquely encouraged—no governor promised any support—Kennedy went on to California. Cesar Chavez had been fasting in penance for violence provoked by his union's struggle for survival. Now the fast was ending, and his friends wanted Kennedy to be with him at the Mass of Thanksgiving.

John Seigenthaler accompanied him on the trip west. Seigenthaler told Kennedy he should not run. Kennedy said, "I recognize the logic of everything you say. . . . But I'd feel better if I were doing what I think ought to be done and saying what I know should be said."[24] Crowds pressed in on Kennedy as he made his way from the airport into Delano. People hugged and kissed him. "His hands were scratched," Chavez recalled, "where people were trying to touch him. . . . You could see the blood." The communion bread was passed. Kennedy shared his piece with Chavez. A television cameraman said, "Senator, this is perhaps the most ridiculous remark I've ever made in my life. Would you mind giving Cesar another piece of bread so we can get a picture." Kennedy said, "No. In fact, he should have a lot of bread now." He had rehearsed Spanish phrases for his remarks, and, said Chavez, "brought the house down. . . . Well, you can imagine Spanish with a Boston accent! . . . He looked down where I was sitting, and he said, 'Am I murdering the language?' I said, 'No. Go ahead.' It was a great day."[25]

Kennedy praised Chavez as a hero of our times; then to the crowd, "Let me say to you that violence is no answer." Chavez was too weak to speak. His speech was read for him:

> When we are really honest with ourselves, we must admit that our lives are all that really belong to us. So it is how we use our lives that determines what kind of men we are. It is my deepest belief that only by giving our lives do we find life. I am convinced that the truest act of courage, the strongest act of manliness, is to sacrifice ourselves for others in a totally nonviolent struggle for justice. To be a man is to suffer for others. God help us be men.[26]

Beautiful words. On the plane back from Delano, Kennedy said, "Yes. I'm going to do it. If I can, I've got to try to figure out a way to get Gene McCarthy out of it; but, if I can't, I'm going to do it anyway."[27]

That Sunday evening Ethel tracked me down in Cambridge, where I was dining with Galbraith. Jubilation and relief sounded in her voice. Bobby had telephoned from the coast, she said. He would definitely run if McCarthy could be persuaded to withdraw after New

Hampshire. He wanted any thoughts on how this could be brought about.[28] It was two days before the primary.

IV

He had already asked his brother to notify McCarthy of his intention. But Ted Kennedy had "decided on his own," Robert said later, "that he didn't want to tell him in the last days of the primary campaign."[29] Perhaps Ted thought it an unfair burden on a preoccupied candidate. Perhaps he feared McCarthy might somehow turn the news against his brother. In any event, Robert discovered that McCarthy had not been informed. He then called Goodwin, who had joined McCarthy's New Hampshire campaign. Goodwin, who felt sufficiently under suspicion as a Kennedy man, was a reluctant intermediary. When he finally transmitted the message on Monday, McCarthy said, "Tell him to support me. I only want one term as President. After that, he can take it over. . . . The presidency should be a one-term office. Then the power could be in the institution. It would not be so dependent upon the person."[30]

Persuading McCarthy to pull out would not be easy. Since Tet there had been a stunning rise in the intensity of his support, especially in the universities and in the liberal community. My concern was to minimize an anti-Kennedy explosion among those who, in his season of vacillation, had turned to McCarthy and were now falling in love with a new hero. I consulted Joseph Rauh, who had already endorsed McCarthy but basically thought Kennedy would make a stronger candidate and better President. If Kennedy came out for McCarthy in New Hampshire, Rauh said, this would make it easier for the pro-Kennedy people around McCarthy to urge his subsequent withdrawal. On Monday I tried this out on Kennedy, now back in Washington. "Bobby was unwilling to do this," I noted, "—partly, I think, because it would put him in an odd position with Dick Daley and other professionals, partly because he cannot bring himself to say that he would really like Eugene McCarthy to be President of the United States. So nothing happened."[31]

New Hampshire voted the next day. Kennedy, who was speaking that night in the Bronx, asked me to meet him later in the evening at "21." I went to a small dinner for Anthony Eden at Hamilton Fish Armstrong's fine old house on West Tenth Street. Bill Moyers was another guest. Afterward, Moyers drove me uptown. Johnson, he said, was by now well sealed off from reality; the White House atmosphere was "impenetrable." The President explained away all criticism as based on personal or political antagonism. Moyers used the word "paranoid." His own personal debt to Johnson was so great, he said, that it had taken him a long time to reach this conclusion and even longer to say it, but he felt that "four more years of Johnson would be ruinous for the country." He added that Johnson "flees from confrontations. He is willing to take on people like Goldwater and Nixon, to whom he feels superior. But he does not like confrontations when he does not feel superior." I asked Moyers about Kennedy. Moyers said firmly that he thought it would be a great mistake for him to go—that he could not win; that he would alienate the party; that, if he did nothing, he would be the inevitable successor.[32]

At "21," Kennedy looked subdued. McCarthy had won 42.2 percent of the New Hampshire vote and, because of oddities in the selection system, 20 of 24 delegates. "RFK," I noted, "felt that McCarthy's success had boxed him in. Obviously he could not now expect Gene to withdraw." Kennedy said, "Of course he feels that he gave me my chance to make the try, that I didn't and that he has earned the right to go ahead. I can't blame him. He has done a great job in opening the situation up." I suggested that he might endorse McCarthy on the theory that McCarthy could not conceivably get the nomination but could, with Bobby's support, show how vulnerable Johnson was. Then, when McCarthy played out his hand, he would be obliged to endorse Kennedy; and with the professionals now persuaded Johnson was a loser, the nomination would inexorably go to Kennedy. He was not impressed, citing again the hypocrisy of saying, or seeming to say, that he wanted McCarthy for President. We departed, perplexed and rather dejected. I gave him McCarthy's phone number in New Hampshire. Later they had a conversation—friendly, he told me, but not productive.[33]

The next day Kennedy scribbled a letter to Anthony Lewis in London:

The country is in such difficulty and I believe headed for even more that it almost fills one with despair. But then when I realize all of that I wonder what I should be doing. But everyone who I respect with the exception of Dick Goodwin and Arthur Schlesinger have been against my running. My basic inclination and reaction was to try, and let the future take care of itself. However the prophecies of future doom if I took this course made to me by Bob McNamara and to a less extent Bill Moyers plus the politicians' almost unanimous feeling that my running would bring about the election of Richard Nixon and many other Republican right wingers because I would so divide and split the party and that I could not possibly win—all this made me hesitate—I suppose even more than that.

But the last two days have seen Rusk before the Foreign Relations Committee, the New Hampshire primary—and in the last week it has been quite clear that Johnson is also going to do nothing about the riot panel report.

So once again what should I do.

By the time you receive this letter, both of us will know.

If I am not off in the California primary Ethel and I will be coming to Ireland at the end of May. Why don't you join us. The Irish government is dedicating a memorial to President Kennedy on his birthday May 29th—you look a little Irish and it would be good for your black soul—and maybe mine also.[34]

V

He flew to Washington. Reporters at the airport asked him what he made of New Hampshire. He said, "I am actively reassessing the possibility of whether I will run against President Johnson." In Washington he called on McCarthy. The talk, he told me that evening, had been "friendly but did not go very far." He had congratulated McCarthy on his success and told him he was reappraising his own situation. McCarthy, Kennedy said, "had accepted that, said he had a perfect right to go ahead but that he did not intend to get out himself. He then repeated the bit about serving only one term as President—this apparently is a matter of constitutional principle for him—and saying that, 'while I'm not making an offer,' RFK might be the logical successor."[35] "There wasn't very much communication," Kennedy later observed to Jack Newfield. "I told him . . . I hoped we might work together in some coordinated way. I offered to support him in Wisconsin. But he didn't respond. He just said I could do what I wanted, and he would do what he wanted. . . . I would say he was cold to us."[36] Who really could blame him? "That Bobby; he's something, isn't he?" McCarthy said to Richard Stout of *Newsweek* the next morning.[37]

In the meantime Kennedy had called a council of war at Stephen Smith's New York apartment that afternoon, presumably to assist him in the task of reassessment we had been hearing so much about. A dozen people were there when I arrived. Ted Kennedy, looking a bit unhappy, crisply set forth various alternatives—from total inaction to total participation. Sorensen proposed that Kennedy continue speaking on the issues but remain neutral as between McCarthy and Johnson. Pierre Salinger said this would make Bobby look like a political opportunist. I suggested that Kennedy enter some primaries and support McCarthy in those he did not enter. Burke Marshall felt that Kennedy had to enter all the primaries he could. He later said to Sorensen and to me: "You, Ted, don't want Bob to run against Johnson; Arthur doesn't want him to run against McCarthy. I disagree with you both."[38]

It was seven o'clock. We turned on the evening news, knowing that Robert had taped an interview earlier that day with Walter Cronkite. Discussing his reasons for reassessment, he stopped only a hairline short of a declaration. "I don't know what we are meeting about," Ted Kennedy said. "He has made all the decisions already, and we're learning about them on television." At this point I had to go off somewhere and give a speech. By the time I got back, Robert and Ethel had arrived. The evening by now was thoroughly disorganized. Even though he had all but declared, Kennedy had, I thought, "a certain air of mingled gentleness and distraction, betraying, I imagine, the deep uncertainty he feels before he jumps." Dutton and O'Donnell were especially dissatisfied. "They talk about key people in the states," O'Donnell said. "What key people? Don't they realize that the day of the organization is over? Look what McCarthy did without an organization. . . . What Bobby has to decide is who is first. Personally I think Uncle Sam is first and RFK second. Sometimes I think they reverse the order. . . . Hell, maybe it would be better to wait for 1972, when a hundred thousand Americans will be killed in Vietnam; but I don't think so. The right thing to do is for him to run and not worry about the consequences."[39] Later they went off with Salinger to Toots Shor's and drank gloomily into the night.

Kennedy asked me to take Ethel back to United Nations Plaza. He said, "Are you happy about this?" I said I was. He looked searchingly at me and said, "But you have reservations, don't you?" I said, no, I had no reservations, but he must announce his decision soon. He said he planned to do this in the next thirty-six hours. He had told Mayor Daley, he added, that he had no choice but to challenge Johnson if there were no change in the war. Daley had spoken of getting the President to appoint a commission of eminent outsiders to review Vietnam policy. Kennedy was seeing Clark Clifford about this the next morning at eleven. Until he went through that exercise, he said, he could not announce.[40]

VI

The Vietnam commission was a curious idea. Daley was an unlikely progenitor, but he disliked the war and had mentioned the idea to Kennedy in Chicago on the day in February Kennedy had blasted the Vietnam policy. Sorensen had come to the same proposal independently in March. On the Monday before the New Hampshire primary he had discussed it with the President. During the meeting in the Smith apartment on Wednesday, Sorensen, to general amusement, received a message to call the White House. Johnson, he was told, was interested and wanted a list of possible names.[41]

What Kennedy really thought of it I do not know. I suppose he would have readily traded his candidacy for a guaranteed end to American involvement in Vietnam. But it was inconceivable—or so Dutton, O'Donnell and I thought—that Johnson would surrender control over foreign policy to an outside group. We feared Kennedy was stumbling into a trap. Kennedy may have feared that too. But he could not appear to reject an overture that purported both to unify the party and move toward peace. "At the last minute Ted had boxed us in," Dolan said later. ". . . [Kennedy] gritted his teeth about it. He was clearly unhappy about it."[42] "I had a hard time convincing Bob," Sorensen said the next day, "that even a commission would have enough impact."[43]

Kennedy and Sorensen met Clifford the next morning in Washington. According to Clifford's notes, Kennedy began by saying that he regarded the Vietnam policy as "a failure, and both because of his conscience and pressure from others, he felt compelled to take action." One way to correct the policy would be for him to become a candidate; the other was to persuade Johnson to change the policy. Sorensen said that "if President Johnson would agree to make a public statement that his policy in Vietnam had proved to be in error, and that he was appointing a group of persons to . . . come up with a recommended course of action, then Senator Robert Kennedy would agree not to get into the race." Clifford said at once that Johnson could not possibly announce that his Vietnam policy was a failure. "Kennedy agreed with this and said that he felt the statement need not go that far." An announcement of a basic reevaluation of policy, by a commission consisting of persons he recommended, would suffice.*

---

* Kennedy's list, according to Clifford, was Roswell Gilpatric, Carl Kaysen, Edwin Reischauer, Mike Mansfield, John Sherman Cooper, George Aiken, Generals Lauris

Clifford brought up the short-lived Democratic revolt against Truman in 1948 and said that Kennedy's chances of taking the nomination away from Johnson were "zero." With his own Vietnam reexamination doubtless in mind, he added cryptically that, if Kennedy were counting on the war to get him the nomination, he might be "grievously disappointed" as events developed. "There were a number of factors which remained under the President's control, such as the decision when to start negotiations." And, if Kennedy somehow got the nomination, it would so divide the party as to be valueless. Kennedy replied that he had considered these points "and still felt he would have to run unless President Johnson would agree to his proposition."[44]

Returning to Capitol Hill, Kennedy decided to talk to George McGovern. At the moment McGovern was host for one in a series of periodic luncheons held by a group of liberal Democrats who had served together in the House in the 1950s—Stewart Udall, Lee Metcalf, Frank Thompson, Eugene McCarthy and himself. This time they had planned to celebrate McCarthy's success in New Hampshire. But McCarthy had not shown up; so, when Kennedy called, they invited him instead. McGovern, who had not seen Kennedy for a few weeks, was shocked. His face was "so drawn," his wrinkles were so deep; "he looked so much older."

Perhaps he had come hoping they would urge him to run. They urged him instead not to make any immediate decisions. Thompson, Metcalf and Udall said he should campaign for McCarthy in Wisconsin, the next primary. Kennedy said, "Gene McCarthy's not competent to be President"; if it were McGovern who had gone into New Hampshire, that would have been different. ("I never knew whether he would have stuck with that or not," McGovern said later. "It's very hard for people to keep commitments like that.")

Then, in "rather an impassioned way," according to Udall, Kennedy launched into an account of the situation as he saw it—the war, the racial divisions, the cities. "You could tell his mind was already made up. . . . I almost got the feeling that it was like a Greek tragedy in the sense that events themselves had been determined by fates setting the stage, and that there was really little choice left." McGovern thought him "almost oblivious to what we were saying. . . . I

Norstad and Matthew Ridgway, Kingman Brewster and himself. With the possible exceptions of Norstad and Brewster, all were on record against further escalation of the war (Clark Clifford, memorandum of conversation with Senator Robert F. Kennedy and Theodore C. Sorensen, March 14, 1968, Johnson Papers).

realized that he wasn't even communicating with us, that he was alone with his thoughts." Udall: "I could tell he really wasn't listening to what we said because he had heard the same thing from others, and the whole thing was very clear to him . . . with all the turmoil in the country and with what he felt was a need for definition of the issues and for the championing of the people who were unchampioned. . . . He was determined to follow his own convictions and to do what was true in terms of his own personality. I sensed that, if in the end he lost, he would feel he had done the right thing. . . . He was on fire."[45]

Over at the White House Clifford was discussing the Vietnam commission with Johnson, Humphrey and Abe Fortas, now on the Supreme Court. They all agreed in rejecting the proposition because, "no matter how the arrangement was handled, it would still appear to be a political deal"; because the President's other outside advisers —his own committee of Wise Men—would feel "completely ignored"; and because Johnson could not appoint Kennedy to such a commission without causing resentment on the Hill. Clifford so informed Kennedy, who asked whether it would make any difference if he himself were not a member of the group. Clifford thought, since the main objection was the appearance of a political deal, his removal from the list would make no difference.[46]

The White House promptly leaked its side of the story. Kennedy soon responded that the incident had made it "unmistakably clear to me that so long as Lyndon B. Johnson was President our Vietnam policy would consist of only more war, more troops, more killing and more senseless destruction of the country we were supposedly there to save. That night I decided to run for President."[47] In fact he had reached that decision a week or more earlier. Only a change in Vietnam policy could have canceled it.

To many, however, it looked as if he were deciding to enter only after McCarthy had shown the way in New Hampshire. For McCarthy himself it was Enoch Arden back with a vengeance. McCarthy workers sent furious telegrams and raged at him on television: ruthless Bobby all over again. On Friday morning, March 15, of the crowded week, Kennedy, musing with Jack Newfield and Haynes Johnson: "Not to run and pretend to be for McCarthy, while trying to screw him behind his back, that's what would really be ruthless. . . . I know I won't have much support. I understand I'm going in alone. . . . It is a much more natural thing for me to run than not to run. When you start acting unnaturally, you're in trouble. . . . I'm trusting my instincts now and I feel freer."[48]

VII

The same day, the evening, Hickory Hill. Vanden Heuvel and I flew down from New York on the seven o'clock shuttle. Arthur Goldberg, now ambassador to the United Nations, was on board. We talked about Kennedy. "He thought Bobby should 'tell the truth'—say he was the best candidate and go ahead."[49]

At Hickory Hill there was, inevitably, a party, scheduled earlier for other purposes—Buchwald, Hackett, Whittaker, the mountain climber, a customary mixture of Kennedy friends. Finally, around ten-thirty, Kennedy managed to pull a group of us—Sorensen, Dutton, George Stevens, Jr., Adam Walinsky and Jeff Greenfield of his senatorial staff, and Allard Lowenstein, the mystery guest—into a side room. ("I'm completely involved in the McCarthy campaign," Lowenstein had told Stevens earlier in the evening, "but," pointing at Kennedy, "that man ought to be President.")[50] In a few moments Kennedy left to take a call from Robert Lowell, who, though he had campaigned with McCarthy in New Hampshire, now wished Kennedy luck.

Both Sorensen and Walinsky had already written announcement statements. The drafts were read and haggled over. Kennedy objected to a listing of qualifications in one of the statements: "I don't like it. It sounds too much like one of those Nixon statements—I have visited 48 foreign countries and met 40 prime ministers, 28 kings, 15 foreign secretaries. . . ." Sorensen interrupted, "And two McCarthys." Walinsky and Greenfield regarded the Sorensen draft as pontifical and righteous. They complained particularly about his concluding sentence: "At stake is not simply the leadership of our party or even our country—it is our right to moral leadership on this planet." Alas, they failed to get it out. At one point I said to Sorensen, "It gives me more pleasure than I can say to see Walinsky and Greenfield look at you the way you and Goodwin looked at Galbraith and me in 1960." Fred Dutton later recalled the scene: "Arthur Schlesinger was very cool and detached; Ted Sorensen was waiting to have the final word; Adam Walinsky was his usual high-powered self."[51]

I wish I had been cool and detached. But the outraged reaction to the prospect of a Kennedy candidacy had made me more anxious than ever about conciliating the McCarthy people. Kennedy was concerned too. Indeed, as we talked, Edward Kennedy was on his way to meet McCarthy in Green Bay, Wisconsin, with a proposal for a joint Kennedy-McCarthy effort. Together Kennedy and McCarthy could obviously amass more anti-Johnson delegates than McCarthy could by himself. With the blessing of Blair Clark, McCarthy's campaign manager, Goodwin, who was still with McCarthy, had pursued the idea with Edward Kennedy. Clark then got McCarthy to agree to a meeting that night. However McCarthy, who seemed to his wife "preoccupied and depressed," told her nothing about any meeting with Ted Kennedy and went off to bed. When Abigail McCarthy learned of Kennedy's imminent arrival, she invaded her husband's room. McCarthy told her he did not want to see Ted Kennedy. He said, as she recalled it, "'I'm going to sleep,' . . . And, incredibly enough, he did."

Clark and Goodwin arrived, leaving Kennedy at a motel nearby. There followed what Abigail McCarthy called a "bitter interlude." She trusted neither Goodwin, whose attachment to the Kennedys was notorious, nor Clark, who had gone to Harvard with John Kennedy. Finally Clark said, "Abigail, either you wake Gene up or I will." McCarthy was awakened. About two in the morning Kennedy appeared. McCarthy made it clear he wished no help in Wisconsin. Kennedy started to open his briefcase and show the plan for a coordinated campaign. McCarthy would not let him take it out. He sardonically proposed that Robert Kennedy enter primaries in Louisiana, Florida and West Virginia. After forty-five minutes Kennedy left. McCarthy said to his wife, "That's the way they are. When it comes down to it, they never offer anything real."[52]

In Hickory Hill we had gone to bed around one-thirty. There was confusion as to where everyone would sleep. Kennedy said, "Well, you guys figure that out. I know where I'm sleeping." Then he looked up, with that wry smile, and said, "Well, that's ruthless. I guess I can't be ruthless any more."[53] The rest of us disposed ourselves in the bedrooms of absent children. About six I was awakened by someone hoarsely whispering, "Ted. Ted." It was Edward Kennedy looking for Sorensen. I asked how it had gone with McCarthy. He said, "Very unsatisfactory. His people had seemed to be for it, but he wouldn't go along. I think his wife was against it." He put it more succinctly to vanden Heuvel, whom he woke up next in his search: "Abigail said no." (In her memoir she denied any such role.)

An hour or so later I was awakened again—this time by Robert Kennedy, wandering in rather gloomily in pajamas. We talked about the failure of his brother's mission. He then said, "What do you think I should do?" I said that, if McCarthy would not collaborate, and if a Kennedy-McCarthy contest resulted in the election of Johnson delegates, it would take some people a long time to forgive him. He said morosely, "Well, I have to say something in three hours." I said, "Why not come out for McCarthy? Every McCarthy delegate will be a potential Kennedy delegate. He can't possibly win, so you will be the certain inheritor of his support."* He looked at me stonily and said, "I can't do that. It would be too humiliating. Kennedys don't act that way." He stayed a moment longer, then left the room.

I dressed and went downstairs to find Edward Kennedy, Sorensen and vanden Heuvel at the breakfast table. The morning sun was glinting through the French windows, and sounds of small children enlivened the house, but the atmosphere around the table was somber. Sorensen said, "Have you talked to him?" I said I had. Vanden Heuvel said, "Where is he now?" Sorensen said, "He is upstairs looking for someone else to wake up in the hope of finding someone who agrees with him." All of us thought it would be disastrous for him to go ahead. Ted Kennedy raised his arms in the air: "I just can't believe it. It is too incredible. I just can't believe that we are sitting around the table discussing anything as incredible as this." Vanden Heuvel and I proposed that, as an interim measure, he come out for McCarthy. My impression was that both Teds thought this might be preferable to his declaring for himself. Then Robert entered the room, still in his pajamas. He had heard the last part of our talk. He said, "Look, fellows, I can't do that. I can't come out for McCarthy. Let's not talk about that any more. I'm going ahead, and there is no point in talking about anything else." With that he left.

I proposed taking one more look at the situation. There must be some other course besides endorsing McCarthy or running himself. Teddy said, "No. He's made up his mind. If we discuss it any longer, it will shake his confidence and put him on the defensive. He has to be at his best at this god damned press conference. So we can't talk

---

* In an interview with the *Boston Globe* at the end of the year, McCarthy was asked what he thought would have happened if Kennedy had not gone into the primaries. McCarthy: "I think he probably would have been nominated. . . . I would have beaten Johnson in 4 or 5 primaries and he would have looked weak. And the party wouldn't have gone for me. I don't think they would have. Bobby could have come in as the unifying force, who had not challenged the president" (*Boston Globe*, December 15, 1968).

about it any more." He was right, of course. But all I could think of was a conversation seven years before in the same house when Robert Kennedy asked me to stop worrying his brother about the Bay of Pigs.

Soon he reappeared, now half-dressed. We reviewed the statement as redrafted by Sorensen in light of the Green Bay fiasco. The final text said firmly of McCarthy, "My candidacy would not be in opposition to his, but in harmony. . . . It is important now that he achieve the largest possible majorities in the Wisconsin, Pennsylvania and Massachusetts primaries. I strongly support his effort in those states and urge all my friends to give him their votes." Robert was now in excellent humor. At one point, inserting something into the statement, he said, "It doesn't make sense without that—not that anything we are doing today makes sense anyway." Later he said, "Let's put something in about healing the wounds of the country," then added, "by splitting the Democratic party into three pieces." He went upstairs to finish dressing. A barber appeared to deal with the famous hair. Ted Kennedy said, "Cut it as close as you can. Don't pay attention to anything he says. Cut off as much as you can." Little David Kennedy gravely asked me, "Is Daddy going to run for President?"

We drove into Washington. The announcement took place in the caucus room in the Old Senate Office Building, where John Kennedy at the same age had announced his candidacy eight years before. It went off well. Our spirits began to lift. He was trusting his instincts at last, and those who loved him all felt freer. All save one. A few days later, at a New York dinner party, Jacqueline Kennedy took me aside and said, "Do you know what I think will happen to Bobby?" I said no. She said, "The same thing that happened to Jack. . . . There is so much hatred in this country, and more people hate Bobby than hated Jack. . . . I've told Bobby this, but he isn't fatalistic, like me."[54]

(39)

The Journey Begins

It was a startling adventure. Except for the scene of announcement, it bore no resemblance to John Kennedy's carefully prepared quest eight years earlier. Robert Kennedy had no campaign staff, no national organization, no delegates, almost no promises of support. At the end, all the advisers around the breakfast table at Hickory Hill, even those who had favored his running, were against his going ahead at that particular moment and in that particular way. We all expected a bad reaction. For a moment it was even worse than we had anticipated.

I

"It is difficult for me," Dwight D. Eisenhower wrote an old friend, "to see a single qualification that the man has for the Presidency. I think he is shallow, vain and untrustworthy—on top of which he is indecisive."[1] An exultant Nixon thought the Democratic split gave the Republicans a "great, historic opportunity." He did not suppose Kennedy would beat the President—"Johnson could take the war away from him in a minute—and then what?"—but he twice mentioned Johnson's "poor health" to Richard Whalen, a Nixon speechwriter (and biographer of Joseph Kennedy), and said, "Bobby may kill him." If by any chance Kennedy got the nomination, "We can beat that little S.O.B."[2]

In the White House Lyndon Johnson received gratifying word from the Hill. As reported by his congressional liaison office:

SENATOR BYRD of West Virginia. Bobby-come-lately has made a mistake. I won't even listen to him. There are many who liked his brother—as Bobby will find out—but who don't like him.
SENATOR SCOOP JACKSON. I have just issued a statement expressing 100%

> support for President Johnson. . . . We may find ourselves in a 1964
> Goldwater situation if Bobby tears the party apart.
> SENATOR GRUENING. Bobby has hurt himself by his actions, even with the
> strong feeling against the war in Vietnam. . . .
> EXTRANEOUS. . . . Bobby's candidacy further complicates matters for
> those liberals running for re-election. . . . This is particularly the view
> expressed by Wayne Morse and Abe Ribicoff.[3]

Even Gruening, even Morse, the two brave originals of the anti-Vietnam fight, were unwilling in March 1968 to come out against Johnson. Legislators who took that risk paid for it. "Senator Inouye just called from Hawaii," the legislative staff advised Johnson, "to warn us that [Congresswoman] Patsy Mink this afternoon will announce her support of Bob Kennedy. . . . Dan thinks it is time we started to play hard ball with Patsy—that we cut her off the notification list of contracts, etc."[4]

Organization Democrats, like Mayor Daley, automatically rallied to the President. Harry Truman, now eighty-three years old, sent word that he was behind Johnson 100 percent and that his challengers were "a damned bunch of smart alecks."[5] In New York Frank O'Connor said that Kennedy "might well be endangering the future of the country."[6] When Kennedy marched down Fifth Avenue in the Saint Patrick's Day parade on the day of his announcement, there were shouts from the Irish crowd of "Go back to Boston, ya bum!" Harold Hughes of Iowa, so eloquently inveighing against Johnson only a few nights before, fell into a deep silence. On March 24 the *New York Times,* after a survey of state delegations, reported that Johnson appeared to have more than 65 percent of the votes at the convention.[7]

Kennedy's respectable Washington friends were dismayed. "General Maxwell Taylor pointed out at dinner one night recently," wrote Maxine Cheshire, the society reporter of the *Washington Post,* "that none of the three 'old fogies' who have sons of Senator Robert F. Kennedy named in their honor are supporting his candidacy today."[8] Harriman and Taylor were standing by Johnson, Dillon was for Rockefeller.

The angriest reaction came naturally enough from the supporters of McCarthy. Not all: some, like Galbraith, Rauh, Lowenstein, who would have been for Kennedy, felt they had gone too far with McCarthy to switch. But they understood Kennedy's problem and hoped to influence their own candidate toward a coordinated anti-Johnson campaign. Kennedy understood their problem too—after all, he had caused it—and did not press. "In politics one sees a man in many ways," Galbraith said later. "Those of us who, in its lottery, were this year supporting Eugene McCarthy had occasion to know [Kennedy's] generosity."[9] Late in March rumors spread that Lowenstein, whom McCarthy had ignored, was dropping out of the McCarthy campaign. Kennedy encountered Lowenstein on a bus taking Democrats back to New York City from a party dinner in Binghamton. They talked. Lowenstein said he was sticking with McCarthy. After he returned to his seat a note was passed to him. It read:

> For Al, who knew the lesson of Emerson and taught it to the rest of us: "They did not yet see, and thousands of young men as hopeful, now crowding to the barriers of their careers, did not yet see if a single man plant himself on his convictions and then abide, the huge world will come round to him."
>
> From his friend, Bob Kennedy.*

But these were the exceptions. Most McCarthy supporters took their cue from their leader. Asked about Kennedy's entry, McCarthy discoursed sarcastically, in the manner that rejoiced his followers, on politicians "willing to stay up on the mountain and light signal fires . . . and dance in the light of the moon, but none of them came down."[10] McCarthy students denounced Kennedy as a ruthless opportunist. McCarthy professors were outraged. Two American historians, Lee Benson and James Shenton, took out an advertisement in the *New York Times:*

> The movement that has made Senator McCarthy its symbol exemplifies rationality, courage, morality. The movement Senator Kennedy commands exemplifies irrationality, opportunism, amorality. . . . American intellectuals . . . must choose between morality and amorality, between McCarthy and Kennedy. . . .
>
> PUBLICLY. UNEQUIVOCALLY. IMMEDIATELY.†

Old newspaper friends turned violently against him. James

---

* Jack Newfield, *Robert Kennedy* (New York, 1969), 237. Kennedy did not get the quotation (from "The American Scholar") quite right. It is "for the career," not "of their careers," "the" single man "planting" himself "indomitably on his instincts, and there abide." But it was still pretty close for a tired man bumping along in a bus at three in the morning after a political dinner in Binghamton.

† *New York Times*, March 20, 1968. For an analysis of the statement by another American historian, see D. H. Fischer, *Historians' Fallacies: Toward a Logic of Historical Thought* (New York, 1970). Fischer, whose interest was not in politics but in getting historians to talk sense, concluded: "When words are used as they are by Benson and Shenton, they become meaningless. Their statement is not merely false—it is solemn and literal nonsense."

Wechsler attacked him mercilessly in the *New York Post*. "He didn't even let Gene and the young people all around him have a few moments to savor their victory," said Mary McGrory. "They were bitter and wounded by what Bobby did, and so was I."[11] Most stinging of all was Murray Kempton, characterizing Kennedy in a column entitled "Senator Kennedy, Farewell" as a coward who had come

> down from the hills to shoot the wounded. He has, in the naked display of his rage at Eugene McCarthy for having survived on the lonely road he dared not walk himself, done with a single great gesture something very few public men have ever been able to do: In one day, he managed to confirm the worst things his enemies have ever said about him. We can see him now working for Joe McCarthy, tapping the phones of tax dodgers, setting a spy on Adlai Stevenson at the UN, sending good loyal Arthur Schlesinger to fall upon William Manchester in the alleys of the American Historical Association. . . . I blame myself, not him, for all the years he fooled me.*

II

Even those of us who had anticipated an outburst were astonished by its virulence. To this historian it seemed a curious doctrine that priority in entering a political competition conferred the moral right to be the only liberal candidate. One recalled that sixteen years before a Democratic senator with stronger liberal credentials than McCarthy beat an incumbent Democratic President in New Hampshire and then went on to win every major primary. He came to the convention as the certified people's choice and led on the first two ballots. If anyone had ever "earned" the right to exclusive liberal support, one supposed, it had been Estes Kefauver in 1952. But at the convention the Democratic organization put across a candidate who had not entered a single primary. Despite Kefauver's priority, most liberals went to Adlai Stevenson without moral qualms. Now Stevensonian liberals were complaining bitterly because Kennedy had missed a single primary. It did not make much sense.

Kennedy made one last attempt to explain himself on *Meet the*

* Murray Kempton, "Senator Kennedy, Farewell," *New York Post,* March 26, 1968. On June 11, 1968, Kempton wrote: "The language of dismissal becomes horrible once you recognize the shadow of death over every public man. For I had forgotten, from being bitter about a temporary course of his, how much I liked Senator Kennedy and how much he needed to know he was liked. Now that there is in life no road at whose turning we could meet again, the memory of having forgotten that will always make me sad and indefinitely make me ashamed" ("RFK—In Sorrow and Shame," *New York Post,* June 11, 1968).

Press the day after his announcement. "I don't think there is any question," he said, "that if I had gone into the race at an earlier time that it would have been felt by the press and by others that this was a personality struggle between President Johnson and myself. . . . What Senator McCarthy showed was that there was a deep division and split within the Democratic Party and the country that had nothing to do with me." Five times he declared his intention "to cooperate in every way possible with Senator McCarthy."[12] Thereafter he dropped the subject and moved ahead. That night he flew to Kansas, where he had an old commitment to deliver the Alfred M. Landon Lecture at Kansas State University.

Conservative Kansas presumably backed the war and detested the rebel young. But, when he changed planes at Kansas City, Missouri, a cheering crowd broke through the barriers to get near him. Later that night, at Topeka, "they tore at Robert Kennedy," wrote Jimmy Breslin. "They tore the buttons from his shirt-cuffs. . . . They tore at his suit-buttons. They reached for his hair and his face. He went down the fence, hands out, his body swaying backwards so that they could not claw him in the face, and the people on the other side of the fence grabbed his hands and tried to pull him to them."[13]

The next morning, his hands trembling and his voice flat with nervousness, Kennedy gave the Landon Lecture before a crowd of fifteen thousand in the Kansas State fieldhouse in Manhattan. These were not eastern kids with long hair and beards, Breslin noted; they were "Kansas young with scrubbed faces and haircuts and ties."[14] Perhaps, Kennedy began, it had been a mistake to announce the "reassessment" of his position. "Yesterday there was a man from the Internal Revenue Service out reassessing my home." The stories about the Vietnam commission had misrepresented the differences between himself and Johnson. "The only difference was the makeup. I wanted Senators Mansfield, Fulbright and Morse, and the President, in his own inimitable way, he wanted General Westmoreland, John Wayne and Martha Raye."* Laughter; applause; then down to business.

"Every night," Kennedy said, "we watch horror on the evening news. Violence spreads inexorably across the nation, filling our streets and crippling our lives." The administration had no answer to the war—"none but the ever-expanding use of military force . . . in

---

* Jules Witcover, *85 Days: The Last Campaign of Robert Kennedy* (New York, 1969), 101. Martha Raye had probably spent more time entertaining the troops in Vietnam than anyone except Bob Hope.

a conflict where military force has failed to solve anything." He jabbed the air with clenched fist, his voice intense and controlled. "Can we ordain to ourselves the awful majesty of God—to decide what cities and villages are to be destroyed, who will live and who will die, and who will join the refugees wandering in a desert of our own creation? . . . In these next eight months," he concluded, "we are going to decide what this country will stand for—and what kind of men we are."[15] The Kansas State students, scrubbed faces and all, went wild. "The fieldhouse," wrote Jack Newfield, "sounded as though it was inside Niagara Falls; it was like a soundtrack gone haywire."[16] The reception was, if possible, even wilder in the afternoon at the University of Kansas. That evening on the plane east Kennedy said to Breslin, "You can hear the fabric ripping. If we don't get out of this war, I don't know what these young people are going to do. There's going to be no way to talk to them. It's very dangerous."[17]

Three days later he went to Alabama, where he spoke about racial justice (and where, when asked if he would accept second place on the ticket with Johnson, he replied, "I said I was for a coalition government in Saigon, not here").[18] Before March was over, he had visited sixteen states. Frenzy accompanied him everywhere. On television the tumultuous crowds frightened people for whom the pictures on the screen evoked the riots of the summer before. Reporters too were alarmed by the crush and hysteria. Some were also repelled by what they regarded as Kennedy's playing on his audiences by rhetorical excess. They had a point. He had got it into his head that the Saigon government was not drafting its eighteen-year-olds and continued saying this after Saigon had changed its policy. "When we are told to forego all dissent and division," he said at Nashville, in obvious reference to Johnson, "we must ask: who is truly dividing the country? It is not those who call for change, it is those who make present policy." That policy, Kennedy said, had driven young people to abandon their "public commitment of a few years ago for lives of disengagement and despair, turning on with drugs and turning off America." Kennedy, sniffed Richard Harwood of the *Washington Post,* "implied that the President is to blame for the alienation and drug addiction among American youth, for rebelliousness and draft resistance on American campuses, and for the 'anarchists' and rioters in American cities."[19]

Harwood was no doubt a little strong. So perhaps was Kennedy. I wrote him after his Nashville attack on Johnson, "It is a little early in the campaign for that. Let him get personal first."[20] One source of

Kennedy's belligerence was what Mankiewicz called his "free-at-last syndrome."[21] The bonds that had so long repressed his concern about the country and his contempt for its leader were thrown off. He went on to California and said in Los Angeles, before one more screaming crowd, "The national leadership is calling upon the darker impulses of the American spirit—not, perhaps, deliberately, but through its action and the example it sets." The press agitation over this phrase—unfairly blamed on Walinsky; it had actually come from material sent along by Goodwin—displayed the pomposity that on occasion afflicted even the most reasonable of newspapermen. Of course Johnson and his Vietnam policy had called upon the darker impulses of the American spirit. Who could have doubted it? The very day Kennedy announced his candidacy Lieutenant William Calley and Company C had yielded to precisely such impulses in My Lai. But the statesmen of the traveling press were outraged. Their word for Kennedy, Harwood wrote in an influential piece at the end of the month, was "demagogue."[22]

III

Harwood suggested that the crowds were deliberately fomented as part of "a strategy of revolution, of a popular uprising of such intensity and scale" that the convention would not dare turn Kennedy down.[23] There was something to that. A candidate without organization or delegates had no choice but to demonstrate irresistible popular appeal. "Our strategy," Walinsky said, "is to change the rules of nominating a President. We're going to do it a new way. In the streets."[24] "I have to win through the people," Kennedy told Helen Dudar of the *New York Post*. "Otherwise I'm not going to win."[25]

Jimmy Breslin described a day on the California trip. Kennedy talked about Vietnam. "Our brave young men are dying in the swamps of Southeast Asia," he said. "Which of them might have written a poem? Which of them might have cured cancer? Which of them might have played in a World Series or given us the gift of laughter from the stage or helped build a bridge or a university? Which of them would have taught a child to read? It is our responsibility to let these men live. . . . It is indecent if they die because of the empty vanity of their country." His listeners "shrieked," wrote Breslin. ". . . They lost control and began pushing forward. . . . It took a half hour to get Kennedy out of the place. A half hour of police pushing and the crowd pushing back and Kennedy trying to smile while they pulled his hair and scratched his face. Women screamed that their children were being crushed to death. Kennedy had to pick up a small child who fell down between policemen."[26]

It went that way all day. At the end Breslin asked where Kennedy thought he stood. "What about Daley?" "He's been very nice to me personally," Kennedy said. "And he doesn't like the war. You see, there are so many dead starting to come back, it bothers him." But it's hard for him, Kennedy continued. "He has been a politician for a long time. And party allegiance means so much to him. It's a wrenching thing for him. We'll have to win the primaries to show the pols." "If you get Daley," he was asked, "where do you stand?" Kennedy said, "Daley means the ball game."[27]

And he had to have the crowds to win the primaries. But there was, I believe, more to it than that. He had gone ahead that Saturday morning at Hickory Hill surrounded by advisers exuding gloom. He had thereafter been savagely attacked, in many cases by people he respected and liked. Now the crowds reassured and sustained him. He told one associate, "I'm beginning to feel the mood of the country and the people and what they want."[28] He did not mind the tidal wave surging over him. Let people seize his cuff links, grab his hands, reach out to touch him. "They *loved* to touch his hair for some reason," said a California advance man. "He loved it. He seemed to sort of thrive on touching people back."[29] Bill Barry, his old friend from the FBI, took leave from his job as a bank vice president to travel with Kennedy. At the beginning, looking at his own and Kennedy's bleeding hands, he said, "I wish these people would be more courteous." Kennedy said, "They're here because they care for us and want to show us." "After that," Barry said later, "I never had any trouble adjusting to crowds. I found they wanted not just to touch a celebrity; they wanted to convey their feelings to him, and he accepted it for that."[30] Alan King said, "They're going to hurt you." Kennedy said mildly, "Well, so many people hate me that I've got to give the people that love me a chance to get at me."[31]

On March 23 the Gallup poll showed Democrats preferring Kennedy to Johnson by 44–41 (and Johnson to McCarthy by 59–29).[32] After a canvass of prospective delegations, *Newsweek* concluded at the end of the month that Lyndon Johnson "may be in real danger of being dumped by his own party."[33]

IV

Johnson had not been surprised by Kennedy's announcement. He wrote grimly in his memoirs, "I had been expecting it."[34] He had always known that, as in the classic Hollywood western, there would be the inevitable walkdown through the long silent street at high noon, and Robert Kennedy would be waiting for him.

For a moment he responded with bravado. Friends urged him on. Russell Wiggins of the *Washington Post* called his attention to passages in Richard Whalen's *Founding Father* displaying Joseph Kennedy as appeaser and defeatist: like father, like son. "One shouldn't carry the analogy too far," said Harry McPherson, transmitting Wiggins's message, "but as Joe once said, 'Bobby and I think alike.' "[35] J. Edgar Hoover kept the White House informed, reporting, for example, that Kennedy had tried to call Martin Luther King before announcing his candidacy.[36] On March 17, the day after Kennedy's announcement, Johnson flew to Minneapolis, pounded the podium and shouted about the war, "Make no mistake about it . . . we are going to win." Two days later, addressing the National Foreign Policy Conference at the State Department, "We are the Number One Nation. And we are going to stay the Number One Nation."[37] But Tet had indeed changed everything. "I am shocked by the number of calls I have received today in protest against your Minneapolis speech," James Rowe wrote him. "Our people on the firing line in Wisconsin said it hurt us badly. . . . Everyone has turned into a dove."[38] It was true: Democratic leaders across the country; the press; even, on March 26, most of his own private Vietnam commission, the Wise Men, Acheson, Dillon, McGeorge Bundy, Cyrus Vance—all now abandoning the war.

On the surface an unaccustomed benignity suddenly overtook the President. He had been confiding to senior advisers since at least the previous October that he was "inclined" not to run in 1968.[39] He talked about this a good deal more now. In mid-March he asked McPherson to give three reasons why he should run. When McPherson said that no one else could get a program through Congress, Johnson said, "Wrong. Any one of 'em—Nixon, McCarthy, Kennedy—could get a program through next year better than I could. . . . Congress and I are like an old man and woman who've lived together for a hundred years. . . . We're tired of each other."[40] On March 27, he asked who Joseph Califano thought would get the nomination if he withdrew. Expecting an explosion, Califano said Kennedy. Johnson did not explode. "What's wrong with Bobby?" he said. "He's made some nasty speeches about me, but he's never had to sit here. Anyway, you seem to like his parties." Califano smiled nervously. The President continued: "Bobby would keep fighting for the Great Society programs. And when he sat in this chair he might have a different view on the war."[41]

Within, Johnson was in turmoil. He doubted the loyalty of his own government. There was, wrote his sycophantic press secretary George Christian (after Salinger, Reedy and Moyers, Johnson was taking no chances; he brought in a man who had worked for Price Daniel and John Connally in Texas), "a decidedly anti-Johnson tinge to what was called the Johnson Administration, and it was no secret to anyone."[42] It was a secret to Kennedy and McCarthy, but no matter; it was what the White House believed. On March 17 Lady Bird Johnson wrote in her diary, "I have a growing feeling of Prometheus Bound, just as though we were lying there on the rock, exposed to the vultures, and restrained from fighting back."[43]

A nightmare of paralysis had pursued Johnson since childhood. "I did not fear death so much," he later wrote, "as I feared disability. Whenever I walked through the Red Room and saw the portrait of Woodrow Wilson hanging there, I thought of him stretched out upstairs in the White House, powerless to move, with the machinery of the American government in disarray around him. And I remembered Grandmother Johnson, who had had a stroke and stayed in a wheelchair throughout my childhood, unable even to move her hands or to speak so that she could be understood."[44] Sometimes, he would dream that he was lying in his bed with his own head but with Wilson's shriveled body. Awakening in a cold sweat, he would take a flashlight, walk downstairs, touch Wilson's portrait; then, soothed, he could sleep again.[45]

Another recurrent dream went back to Grandfather Johnson's tales of cattle stampedes in the old southwest. He was alone on a vast plain, sitting in a tall, straight chair, cattle storming down on him. He tried to move but could not. "I felt that I was being chased on all sides by a giant stampede," he told Doris Kearns; ". . . I was being forced over the edge by rioting blacks, demonstrating students, marching welfare mothers, squawking professors, and hysterical reporters. And then the final straw. *The thing I feared from the first day of my Presidency was actually coming true. Robert Kennedy had openly announced his intention to reclaim the throne in the memory of his brother*. And the American people, swayed by the magic of the name, were dancing in the streets."[46]

Time was drawing short. He felt that the country would be divided and angry so long as he remained in the White House. He had, as his protégé Bobby Baker put it, a "deep fear of defeat." Lawrence O'Brien told him that McCarthy would beat him two to one in the Wisconsin primary on April 2.[47] If he waited till after Wisconsin, he would be a repudiated President, driven from public life by the voters of his own party. This was his last chance to make withdrawal appear his own decision rather than one forced upon him. At nine o'clock on the evening of March 31, Lyndon Johnson went on television ostensibly to address the nation on the war.

V

Robert Kennedy spent March 30 conducting a hearing of his Indian subcommittee in Flagstaff, Arizona. The next day he flew back to New York. He had asked Bill Barry to find him something to read. Barry came up with *Alone*, Richard E. Byrd's memoir of a winter in Antarctica. Ethel said, "That's some book for him to read! . . . How's that going to relax him—*Alone?*"[48] When the plane landed shortly before ten o'clock at La Guardia, an ashen-faced John Burns rushed aboard. "The President is not going to run," he said. "You're kidding," said Kennedy. On the way to United Nations Plaza he was sunk in reverie. Finally he said to Richard Dougherty of the *Los Angeles Times,* "I wonder if he'd have done this if I hadn't come in."[49]

The mood when I arrived at the apartment a few minutes later was total bemusement. Kennedy looked terribly tired. Soon he was on the telephone, calling leaders around the country. A telegram was dispatched to Johnson proposing a meeting. Sorensen was at work on a statement for Kennedy's press conference the next morning; so, inevitably, was Walinsky. Around two in the morning, they were both read to Kennedy, who wearily asked me to "put them together." "Like old times," I noted. "I took the first page of Ted's, agreeing with Adam that stale rhetoric about 'we want neither the peace of the slave or the grave' should go (Adam's statement, however, was filled with equally stale rhetoric about there being more which unites us than divides us), and then added a page of my own."[50]

No one becomes more sentimental than a politician rejoicing in the withdrawal of a rival. Kennedy called Johnson's action "truly magnanimous."[51] McCarthy said Johnson deserved the "honor and respect of every citizen."[52] Johnson himself was less sentimental. When Abigail McCarthy impulsively called the White House after the broadcast, she was offended by the "note of suppressed triumph" in his voice—"the voice of a man who operated in the supreme confidence that he could outmaneuver anyone."[53] On April 2 McCarthy took 56 percent of the vote in Wisconsin; Johnson received hardly more than a third. His mood changed. He said angrily to reporters, in the style of Richard Nixon, "You fellows won't have me to pick on any more. You can find someone else to flog and insult."[54]

Told of Kennedy's request for a meeting, Johnson had said, "I won't bother answering that grand-standing little runt."[55] Nevertheless, the meeting on April 3 was friendly enough. Sorensen accompanied Kennedy; Walt Rostow and Charles Murphy were with Johnson. Johnson delivered a monologue about Vietnam, the Middle East, the budget. Kennedy inquired about Johnson's intentions in the campaign. Johnson said he planned to stay out of it but would let Kennedy know if he changed his mind. The President then began talking about John Kennedy, how well they had worked together, how he had tried to continue the Kennedy policies. But he hadn't succeeded: the young were disaffected despite all he had done for education; so were the blacks, despite all he had done for civil rights. Still, "as President Kennedy looked down at him every day from then until now, he would agree that he kept the faith." Kennedy finally said, "You are a brave and dedicated man." "I don't know," recalled Sorensen, "whether it was because he found it difficult to say or whether the emotion of the situation had overcome him, but it sort of stuck in his throat, and Johnson asked him to repeat it."[56]

When they left, Humphrey, who had been waiting in an anteroom, was ushered in. Johnson told his Vice President, according to the record of the meeting, that he had withdrawn because he "simply could not function on these great issues if he were subjected every day to attacks from Nixon, McCarthy, and Robert Kennedy." He did not ask Humphrey to run, though this assumption seemed to Humphrey to underlie the conversation.[57] Humphrey said he had considered the possibility of an immediate announcement but feared it might "demean" the President's statement. Johnson said that was up to him. He would rate Humphrey as A++ as a Vice President while he would rate himself as only B+. But, if Humphrey ran, "he must do a better job than he was able to get organized in Mil-

waukee"—a spiteful allusion to the Wisconsin result, for which the
President evidently wished to hold Humphrey responsible.
Humphrey said he had been in preliminary contact with Daley, Governor Richard Hughes of New Jersey and other party leaders. "They
appear not yet to have made up their minds. He had the impression
that they were not willing to be 'blitzed.'" Johnson said cruelly that
"he thought it possible that, in the end, Daley and Hughes would go
with Kennedy."[58]

Later in the day the President relaxed with old friends, Drew
Pearson and David Karr. He was filled with self-pity. He kept talking
about his "partnership" with John Kennedy. "Then my partner died,
and I took over the partnership. I kept on the eleven cowhands [the
cabinet]. Some of the tenderfeet left me. But I kept on." He repeated
the line about John Kennedy's putative approval as he looked down
from heaven. He was bitter about Robert Kennedy, blaming him for
the Bay of Pigs. This, Johnson said, was where the credibility gap
started, not over Vietnam. He went on and on. Karr found the performance "terrifying."[59]

VI

McGovern, Dutton, O'Donnell, Vance Hartke and others had predicted that Johnson lacked the guts to stay the course. One never
quite believed them, but they were right, and now he was gone, a
giant vanishing in a puff of smoke. Kennedy and McCarthy, instead
of running against Johnson, were left to run against each other.

"It's narrowed down to Bobby and me," McCarthy told Jeremy
Larner, his speechwriter, and Jonathan Schell, another gifted young
journalist, the day after the Wisconsin primary. "So far he's run *with*
the ghost of his brother. Now we're going to make him run *against* it.
It's purely Greek: he either has to kill him or be killed by him. We'll
make him run against Jack. . . . And I'm Jack." It was a Delphic
thought. His audience was puzzled. McCarthy leaned back and
laughed. Later Schell asked, "Did you understand that?" "Half,"
said Larner, who thought it fascinating stuff from a politician. "Well,
I didn't," said Schell. Unwilling to work against Kennedy, Schell
declined McCarthy's invitation to join his staff and returned to graduate studies at Harvard. Larner kept thinking about what McCarthy
had said. "I still got only half, and there wasn't any more, then or
later."[60] McCarthy may have meant that Robert Kennedy, having
run against Lyndon Johnson's record, would be forced, with Johnson

out, to run against aspects of John Kennedy's record. But McCarthy's "and I'm Jack" is, by this interpretation, total mystification. Perhaps McCarthy meant that he had more of John Kennedy's qualities—maturity, intellectuality, urbanity, control—than Robert had. Perhaps he meant nothing at all.

With Humphrey still waiting for a nondemeaning moment to announce, the visible drama lay in the series of contests between Kennedy and McCarthy, beginning in Indiana on May 7 and ending in New York on June 18. The Kennedy organization was taking shape. Edward Kennedy was his brother's closest adviser, always resourceful, energetic and protective. Stephen Smith, Robert told me, would be campaign manager, Sorensen, campaign director, O'Donnell, director of organization. I asked what in the world the difference was between campaign manager, campaign director and director of organization. "I don't know," he said, "but I've never put much stock in titles. There'll be enough for everyone to do."[61]

Salinger and Mankiewicz had the press. Goodwin was in charge of television. He had remained with McCarthy through Wisconsin. They parted on friendly terms. "I understood his motives and his loyalties," McCarthy said later. "And Dick was above board with me about them. Goodwin is like a professional ballplayer. You could trade him . . . and he wouldn't give away your signals to the other team."[62] Fred Dutton traveled with the candidate, offering frank counsel to Kennedy and placating Adam Walinsky and Jeff Greenfield, who, like all speechwriters, were in a state of periodic disgruntlement.* Then Lawrence O'Brien, after declining to run Humphrey's campaign, resigned as Postmaster General in April to join Kennedy's, where he expected, and found, a leading role. David Hackett headed the "boiler room" operation as he had in 1960. Hackett brought in Fraser Barron from the poverty program for "grassroots development"—the organization of the poor, of blacks, Mexican Americans, white Appalachians.

"There's danger, of course," Kennedy had told me, "in just using

* Greenfield also had a draft problem. He had warned Kennedy that, if his notification arrived, he would refuse to go, supposing that Kennedy would say that, in the circumstances, he had better leave the staff. Kennedy said instead, "Well, Jeff, you know if you go to jail, I'll see that you get treated right"—after all, he had once had some influence over the prison system—"and besides, don't worry about it. A lot of the greatest men in history have begun their careers by spending time in jails" (Peter Edelman, in recorded interview by L. J. Hackman, July 15, 1969, 83, RFK Oral History Program). A Kennedy aide said to David Halberstam of Greenfield, "That kid gets his draft notice and we're the only campaign in town with a speech writer in Canada" (Halberstam, "Travels with Bobby Kennedy," *Harper's,* July 1968).

people from 1960. Politics has changed a lot in the last eight years."[63] Nevertheless, his seemed at the start the old politics of motorcades, rally speeches and political organizations. McCarthy's strength, as Goodwin said a day or two after he rejoined us, lay in his understanding of the new politics of television and the kids; Goodwin thought that the Kennedy people greatly underrated McCarthy's seriousness and his political acuity.[64] Dutton and I shared the fear that we were getting mired in the past. In early April I circulated a memorandum to that effect called "The Old Politics and the New." The post-1960 class felt this even more strongly. "The classical political wisdom which is shaping this campaign," Thomas Johnston soon wrote Kennedy, "is similar in all important essentials to the advice which said you should not run this year." Your decision to run "was made by you, on your own, acting against this advice. . . . You are at your strongest when you are most yourself. . . . The ultimate source of your political strength is your capacity to fire and shape the moral imagination of this country."[65]

Actually, the generational clash was overplayed by the press. Dutton later thought that the prevailing disorganization caused no serious troubles in the primaries.[66] I am sure he was right. Kennedy himself arrived at a unique blend of the old and the new politics—and both, in fact, were necessary in 1968. After California he intended to reorganize the campaign and place Stephen Smith in full charge. For the time being there was too much else to do.

VII

With Johnson's withdrawal, Kennedy and McCarthy had lost their most conspicuous issues: the unpopular President and, to some degree, the increasingly unpopular war, for Johnson had also on March 31 abandoned major escalation and gestured toward negotiation. McCarthy affected to take it calmly and, for all I know, did. "Bobby has to shoot straight pool now," he told reporters, thereby deflecting attention to his rival. "When he was banking his shots off Lyndon it was a different game."[67] McCarthy's jabs often hit home. One felt a certain letdown in Kennedy, though of course he was tired after his transcontinental fortnight. (I told him he should begin to pace his campaign. He bridled a little and said, "I know I look tired, but I'm all right. I know the limits of my strength very well. There is no need to worry about that.")[68] He had enjoyed the quest. Now, in two weeks, the dragon was slain. There was, for a moment, a loss of steam and of theme.

Yet a theme remained—the theme that, along with the war, had absorbed him most in the Senate. For, more than anyone else in American politics, he had become the tribune of the underclass, the leader determined "to show," as he said, "that the individual *does* count in a society where he actually appears to count less and less,"[69] determined to overcome the alienations of American society, to bind the wounds of American life. As soon as he became a candidate he had reaffirmed this theme. "We are more divided now than perhaps we have been in a hundred years," he said on March 17. The great need was "to heal the deep divisions that exist between races, between age groups and on the war."[70] Now that he and McCarthy together had moderated the Vietnam policy and driven Johnson into retirement, he was free to move ahead where McCarthy could not easily follow—toward a coalition of the poor and powerless in the battle to bring the excluded groups into the national community. "I've got every establishment in America against me," he said on April 2.[71] "I want to work for all who are not represented," he told Charles Evers. "I want to be their President."[72]

A crucial component of any coalition would be the United Auto Workers. When Roy Reuther died in January 1968, Kennedy was the only one outside the family to sit with the Reuthers at the funeral. Victor Reuther (whose wife was on the Kennedy delegation in the District of Columbia), Leonard Woodcock, Douglas Fraser, Jack Conway, Paul Schrade and other UAW leaders worked for Kennedy in Indiana, Michigan and California. Walter Reuther delayed his decision because of an old friendship with Humphrey, but Victor was sure he would have supported Kennedy in the end.[73]

Another crucial figure in any coalition of the disestablished was Martin Luther King. Though Kennedy and King had kept their distance, events were bringing them closer together. In the spring of 1967 King had decided to oppose the war. In the summer the two men began collaboration, through intermediaries, on a new drive for economic and racial justice. Chatting with Marian Wright and Peter Edelman beside the pool at Hickory Hill, Kennedy had remarked, "The only way there's going to be change is if it's more uncomfortable for the Congress not to act than it is for them to act. . . . You've got to get a whole lot of poor people who just come to Washington and stay here until . . . Congress gets really embarrassed and they have to act." The next week Marian Wright presented the idea to King at a Southern Christian Leadership Conference retreat. This was the origin of the Poor People's Campaign of 1968. The Kennedy office was now working closely with Marian Wright and the organizers.*

When Johnson pulled out, King said to Walter Fauntroy, head of the SCLC's Washington office, "He's just doing like a Baptist preacher . . . you know, trying to get a vote of confidence. He'll pull back in later. But this country's through with him." King, Fauntroy recalled, was "*very* hopeful" that Kennedy would make it. He said, "We've got to get behind Bobby now that he's in."[74] Peter Edelman, citing Marian Wright: "King was prepared to endorse him."[75] Stanley Levison, the target of the wiretaps: "He said that while he hadn't publicly decided to take any stands yet, his mind was made up. He had decided that he would support Bobby Kennedy. . . . He felt that if he'd come this far, with the greater responsibility he could become one of the outstanding presidents. . . . No question: if he had lived, he would have supported Bobby Kennedy."[76]

On April 4 Kennedy began the Indiana campaign. He was scheduled in the evening to speak in the heart of the Indianapolis ghetto. Walter Sheridan and John Lewis had set up the meeting—John Lewis, the Freedom Rider, the SNCC chairman who had asked at the March on Washington which side the federal government was on but who had "started identifying" with Kennedy in later years as "the only political leader" addressing the "real issues of the United States" and who had offered his services as soon as Kennedy announced.[77] They had decided, Sheridan recalled, to put Kennedy "not only into the black community, but into the worst section of the black community." The Indianapolis mayor thought it dangerous; but, said Sheridan, "we had no real fears that there was going to be any problem."[78] In the afternoon Kennedy spoke at Muncie, where one of the last questions had come from a young black wondering whether Kennedy's apparent belief in the good faith of white people toward minorities was justified. Kennedy had said he thought it was. A few moments later, as they boarded the plane for Indianapolis,

* Peter Edelman, in recorded interview by L. J. Hackman, August 5, 1969, 331–333, RFK Oral History Program; Nick Kotz, *Let Them Eat Promises* (New York: Doubleday, Anchor reprint, 1971), 147, 161–165. Ten years later Andrew Young said, "I think now that Dr. King's assassination was directly related to the fear that officialdom had of his bringing large numbers of poor people to the nation's capital, demanding some response from them. . . . [At the time] I didn't see the Poor People's Campaign as the threat to Washington and the Establishment that I now see it was" (as interviewed in L. K. Obst, *The Sixties* [New York, 1977], 232, 236).

Pierre Salinger telephoned that Martin Luther King had been shot in Memphis. Perhaps they had better cancel the Indianapolis rally.[79]

Kennedy, on the plane, said to John J. Lindsay of *Newsweek,* "You know, it grieves me . . . that I just told that kid this and then walk out and find that some white man has just shot their spiritual leader." Soon they arrived in Indianapolis. Worse news: King was dead. Kennedy "seemed to shrink back," Lindsay thought, "as though struck physically." He put his hands to his face: "Oh, God. When is this violence going to stop?"[80] The chief of police warned the party not to go into the ghetto; he would not be responsible for anything that might happen.[81] Kennedy sent Ethel on to the hotel but was determined to keep his rendezvous. In the automobile he sat rapt in thought. As his car entered the ghetto, the police escort left him.[82]

It was a cold, windy evening. People had been waiting in the street for an hour but were in a festive, political-rally mood. They had not heard about King. Kennedy climbed onto a flatbed truck in a parking lot under a stand of oak trees. The wind blew smoke and dust through the gleam of the spotlights.* "He was up there," said Charles Quinn, a television correspondent, "hunched in his black overcoat, his face gaunt and distressed and full of anguish."[83] He said, "I have bad news for you, for all of our fellow citizens, and people who love peace all over the world, and that is that Martin Luther King was shot and killed tonight." There was a terrible gasp from the crowd.

Robert Kennedy, speaking out of the somber silence of the ride from the airport, speaking out of aching memory, speaking out of the depth of heart and hope:

> Martin Luther King dedicated his life to love and to justice for his fellow human beings, and he died because of that effort.
>
> In this difficult day, in this difficult time for the United States, it is perhaps well to ask what kind of a nation we are and what direction we want to move in. For those of you who are black—considering the evidence there evidently is that there were white people who were responsible—you can be filled with bitterness, with hatred, and a desire for revenge. We can move in that direction as a country, in great polarization—black people amongst black, white people amongst white, filled with hatred toward one another.
>
> Or we can make an effort, as Martin Luther King did, to understand

---

* From Lindsay to author, September 10, 1977. Mr. Lindsay added that he had recently by chance driven past the scene. "The winds still stirred the same trees but the hopes both Kennedy and King stirred in those days are largely gone from the national consciousness."

and to comprehend, and to replace that violence, that stain of bloodshed that has spread across our land, with an effort to understand with compassion and love.

For those of you who are black and are tempted to be filled with hatred and distrust at the injustice of such an act, against all white people, I can only say that I feel in my own heart the same kind of feeling. I had a member of my family killed, but he was killed by a white man. But we have to make an effort in the United States, we have to make an effort to understand, to go beyond these rather difficult times.

My favorite poet was Aeschylus. He wrote: "In our sleep, pain which cannot forget falls drop by drop upon the heart until, in our own despair, against our will, comes wisdom through the awful grace of God."

What we need in the United States is not division; what we need in the United States is not hatred; what we need in the United States is not violence or lawlessness, but love and wisdom, and compassion toward one another, and a feeling of justice towards those who still suffer within our country, whether they be white or they be black. . . .

We've had difficult times in the past. We will have difficult times in the future. It is not the end of violence; it is not the end of lawlessness; it is not the end of disorder.

But the vast majority of white people and the vast majority of black people in this country want to live together, want to improve the quality of our life, and want justice for all human beings who abide in our land.

Let us dedicate ourselves to what the Greeks wrote so many years ago: to tame the savageness of man and to make gentle the life of this world.

Let us dedicate ourselves to that, and say a prayer for our country and for our people.[84]

40

The Long Day Wanes

BACK IN THE HOTEL Kennedy called Coretta King. "I'll help in any way I can," he said. She said, "I'm planning to go to Memphis in the morning to bring back Martin's body." He said, "Let me fly you there. I'll get a plane down."[1] Southern Christian Leadership Conference officials told her this was a mistake; Robert Kennedy was running for President. Coretta King was not bothered. She remembered 1960, when Martin was in prison and John Kennedy was running for President. "Although they were political figures," she said later, ". . . they were human beings first, and their humanness reached out to the needs of other people."[2]

I

John Lewis had scheduled a meeting between Kennedy and a group of black militants after the Indianapolis rally. They waited for him now, filled, Lewis recalled, with "hostility and bitterness." When Kennedy finally arrived, one said angrily that "establishment people" were all the same: "Our leader is dead tonight, and when we need you we can't find you." Kennedy responded: "Yes, you lost a friend, I lost a brother, I know how you feel. . . . You talk about the Establishment. I have to laugh. Big business is trying to defeat me because they think I am a friend of the Negro." They talked on. Departing, the black leaders pledged their support.[3]

After the meeting, Kennedy seemed overwhelmed, despondent, fatalistic. Thinking of Dallas, perhaps also of Sophocles ("Death at last, the deliverer"), he said to Jeff Greenfield that King's death was not the worst thing that ever happened. Then he said, "You know that fellow Harvey Lee Oswald, whatever his name is, set something loose in this country." The first stories after Dallas, Greenfield remembered, had so miscalled Oswald. "That's the way he remembered [the name] because obviously he never took another look at it again." Early in the morning, restlessly roaming the hotel, he found Greenfield asleep on top of his bed and threw a blanket over him. Awakening, Greenfield said, "You aren't so ruthless after all." Kennedy said, "Don't tell anybody."[4]

That night fury raged in the ghettos of America. The next morning Kennedy kept an engagement to speak at the City Club in Cleveland. The Indianapolis remarks had been entirely his own. The Cleveland speech had contributions from Sorensen, from Walinsky, from Greenfield, all writing through the dreadful night.

Violence, Kennedy said in Cleveland, "goes on and on. . . . Why? What has violence ever accomplished? What has it ever created? No martyr's cause has ever been stilled by his assassin's bullet." Yet Americans seemed to be growing inured to violence. "We calmly accept newspaper reports of civilian slaughter in far off lands. We glorify killing on movie and television screens and call it entertainment. We make it easy for men of all shades of sanity to acquire whatever weapons and ammunition they desire. . . . We honor swagger and bluster and the wielders of force." And there was not only the violence of the shot in the night. Slower but just as deadly, he said, was "the violence of institutions. . . . This is the violence that afflicts the poor, that poisons relations between men because their skin has different colors. This is a slow destruction of a child by hunger . . . the breaking of a man's spirit by denying him the chance to stand as a father and as a man among men." So much at least was clear: "Violence breeds violence, repression brings retaliation, and only a cleaning of our whole society can remove this sickness from our soul."[5]

There were riots in 110 cities; 39 people were killed, mostly black, more than 2500 injured; more than 75,000 National Guardsmen and federal troops in the streets. He flew back to Washington, a city of smoke and flame, under curfew, patrolled by troops. He walked through the black districts. "Burning wood and broken glass were all over the place," said Walter Fauntroy. ". . . The troops were on duty. A crowd gathered behind us, following Bobby Kennedy. The troops saw us coming at a distance, and they put on gas masks and got the guns at ready, waiting for this horde of blacks coming up the street. When they saw it was Bobby Kennedy, they took off their masks and let us through. They looked awfully relieved."[6]

On April 7 Martin Luther King was buried in Atlanta. Dignitaries

crowded the Ebenezer Baptist Church. Humphrey, Nixon, Rockefeller, McCarthy—all were there, all save the President himself. Afterward there was a straggling march, five miles under the fierce sun,
from the church to Morehouse College. Kennedy hung his jacket
over his shoulder and walked with shirtsleeves rolled up. "It struck
me," noted John Maguire, the civil rights fighter, "that of *all* the
celebrities there, the only two people that were *constantly* cheered
wherever they walked . . . were Sammy Davis, junior, and Robert
Kennedy."[7] Roy Jenkins, a friend from England, noted that the
Kennedy party got most of the offers of water and Coca-Cola from
the black crowd along the streets. Jenkins asked where Lyndon
Johnson was. Kennedy observed, without bravado, that lack of physical courage kept him away.[8]

Kennedy watched the crowds with disbelief: so few white faces
among them. Jimmy Breslin said, "You'd think even a few of them
would come out and just look, even for curiosity." "You'd think so,"
Kennedy said. "Then maybe this thing won't change anything at
all?" "Oh, I don't think this will mean anything," said Kennedy. He
turned to Charles Evers, walking beside him. "Do you think this will
change anything?" "Nothing," Charles Evers said. "Didn't mean
nothing when my brother was killed." "I know," Robert Kennedy
said.[9] I saw Jacqueline Kennedy after she returned from the funeral.
"Of course people feel guilty for a moment," she said. "But they
hate feeling guilty. They can't stand it for very long. Then they
turn."[10]

II

Before leaving Atlanta, hoping to restore contact at a bitter time,
Kennedy held two meetings with black notables. One was with entertainers on the principle, verified in the reception accorded Sammy
Davis, Jr., that they exerted great influence on the black community.
The meeting was a mess. Julian Bond, a young Georgia political
leader, observed it with disgust. "It became a matter of each of these
entertainers," he recalled later, "saying in what I thought was a *very*
egotistical way, how much they were doing for the movement." Bill
Cosby finally said, "This is a lot of shit! I'm going to leave"—and
left. Kennedy said little. When they broke up, he said to Bond,
"Julian, I bet you've been to a lot of meetings like this before,
haven't you?" Bond said, "Yes." Kennedy said, "I bet you don't
want to go to any more, do you?" Bond said, "No."[11]

The more serious meeting was with Martin Luther King's closest associates—Andrew Young, Ralph Abernathy, Hosea Williams, James Bevel. "There was a lot of undirected hostility in our group," Young said later. "People were just angry and bitter and grieving. . . . They decided to take it out on him." Bevel demanded to know whether Kennedy had a program for racial justice. Others joined the assault. "It was filled with profanity," said Young, "and when preachers get to cuss, they cuss good. It's kind of poetic. . . . He wasn't upset. He just handled himself very well. He refused to say he had a program. He said, 'Well, maybe we can get together and talk about that some time.' He said, 'I do have one or two ideas. But really I didn't come here to discuss politics. That would be in the worst taste.' He said, 'I just came to pay a tribute to a man that I had a lot of respect for.'"[12]

"It was very embarrassing," Young recalled, "because you got the impression . . . well, that in a way, he was more sensitive to the situation than some of us were." The atmosphere changed. Young himself had heretofore kept his distance from Kennedy. He felt it "dangerous to like people in power. . . . I had, up to that time, been refusing to admit that I'd even vote for him."[13] Now Kennedy's existence meant, as Abernathy, King's SCLC successor, said, "that white America does have someone in it who cares."[14] King's murder, recalled Williams, "left us hopeless, very desperate, dangerous men. I was so despondent and frustrated at Dr. King's death, I had to seriously ask myself . . . Can this country be saved? I guess the thing that kept us going was that maybe Bobby Kennedy would come up with some answers for the country. . . . I remember telling him he had a chance to be a prophet. But prophets get shot."[15]

III

On the plane back to Washington Kennedy sat with Nicholas Katzenbach. Their relationship had cooled during the wiretapping dispute in 1966. It had become even colder in the winter of 1967–68. Katzenbach, now under secretary of state and obliged to support the war, had questioned a Vietnam quotation Kennedy used in *To Seek a Newer World*. After vindicating his quotation, Kennedy had inquired sarcastically whether Katzenbach had noticed how "very kind and helpful" Ramsey Clark, now Attorney General, had recently been "in the renewed dispute with Hoover regarding the Department of Justice wiretapping. Such courage and integrity were appreciated."

Katzenbach replied that "our intelligence people were guilty of inexcusably bad research" on the quotation (no surprise) and took strong exception to Kennedy's concluding lines, "a crack you would resent as deeply as I do."[16] None of this seemed important now. Kennedy touched Katzenbach's knee and said, "Forget about what happened and just erase the whole thing. Nothing more will be said."[17]

The primary contest resumed. Indiana was to vote on May 7. "Hoosiers," Kennedy was warned by John Bartlow Martin, a Hoosier himself, author of the best book on Indiana and now on the campaign staff, "are phlegmatic, skeptical, hard to move, with a 'show-me' attitude."[18] The state had once been a stronghold of the Ku Klux Klan. There was trouble between white and black workers in the cities. Eugene Pulliam's far-right *Indianapolis Star,* the most popular paper, assailed Kennedy brutally in daily cartoon and editorial. State officeholders and the party leaders backed the Democratic governor Roger Branigan, who headed the administration slate as a stand-in for the yet undeclared Hubert Humphrey. Except for the UAW, organized labor was for Branigan. The campuses were for McCarthy.

The assassination of Martin Luther King and the ensuing riots had sobered the nation. Kennedy spoke, as usual, about the miseries of the underclass and the duty to reclaim the miserable for the national community. He spoke too about the dangers of violence and the need for public order. This had begun as an adaptation to Indiana conservatism. At the end of March, Martin passed on a message from Professor Richard Wade, who had been sending over campaign workers from the University of Chicago. Wade, Martin told Kennedy, "reports that student petition circulators in Hammond encountered good response in both black ghetto and [white] backlash areas and attributes it to the feeling that, although you are pro-civil rights, you also come through as a strong executive capable of controlling disorders. Maybe as Schlesinger says ruthlessness has its uses after all."[19] After King's murder, Martin urged Kennedy to say "that violence and rioting cannot be tolerated, and emphasize it; then follow by saying neither can injustice be tolerated." Kennedy nodded, saying, "I can go pretty far in that direction. That doesn't bother me."[20] After all he had been for three and a half years the chief law enforcement officer of the land.

Kennedy had made the point about public order often before, and he now made it more often in Indiana. This briefly disturbed his younger staff, causing, Fred Dutton said later, "the most explicit debate of some substance that we had in the campaign."[21] The *New York Times* reported that, under the malign influence of Martin and Goodwin (who was innocent), Kennedy was beginning to sound like George Romney on law and order. The headline was "Kennedy: Meet the Conservative," and the effect was to suggest an opportunist tailoring his politics to his audience.[22] In fact, as Martin noted, Kennedy

> never once failed to show the other side of the coin—i.e., he never denounced violence and let it go at that but instead always followed it by denouncing injustice. It was a matter of emphasis, not substance. Naturally in Negro areas he denounced injustice with great emphasis, and gave less emphasis to rioting; but he said both. At least, this was true every time I heard him speak, and I was watching for it carefully, because I knew the press would watch and I warned him to be sure and say both, and I would have picked him up quickly if he had missed a beat.[23]

Of course Kennedy wanted white as well as black votes. McCarthy also adjusted his campaign to Indiana, deleting references to "white racism" from his speeches.[24] But white voters were not led in either case to suppose that the candidates had weakened their stand on racial justice. Charles Quinn, the television correspondent, interviewed Poles and Lithuanians after Kennedy's Gary rally. "These people," Quinn concluded, "felt that Kennedy would really do what he thought was right for the black people but, at the same time, would not tolerate lawlessness and violence. The Kennedy toughness came through on that. . . . They were willing to gamble on this man, maybe, who would try to keep things within reasonable order; and at the same time, do some of the things that they knew really should be done."[25] Nor did blacks object. They were the main victims of riots, and in the end they voted overwhelmingly for Kennedy.

In retrospect the argument hardly appeared as earthshaking as it did at the time. Kennedy saw no incompatibility between racial justice and the rule of law; rather he thought that each reinforced the other and that only someone absolutely committed to equal rights could hope to stop violence in the ghetto. As for the blue-collar whites, they too felt government had forgotten them; they too were among the unrepresented. In later years, after intellectuals discovered their existence and gave them the awful name of "ethnics,"*

---

* *Ethnic* means, simply, pertaining to a religious, racial, national or linguistic group. To confine this adjective, as current writers try to do, to people from eastern Europe is a gross solecism. A WASP is just as much an "ethnic" as a Pole or a Slovak.

Kennedy's effort to keep the black and white working class at peace with each other in Indiana no longer seemed so sinister.

IV

"He always looked so alone," wrote John Bartlow Martin,

> standing up by himself on the lid of the trunk of his convertible—so alone, so vulnerable, so fragile, you feared he might break. He was thin. He did not chop the air with his hands as his brother Jack had; instead he had a little gesture with his right hand, the fist closed, the thumb sticking up a little, and he would jab with it to make a point. When he got applause, he did not smile at the crowd, pleased; instead he looked down, down at the ground or at his speech, and waited till they had finished, then went on. He could take a bland generality and deliver it with such depth of feeling that it cut like a knife. Everything he said had an edge to it.[26]

David Halberstam heard him at a women's breakfast in Terre Haute. His formal remarks were "pedestrian." But, answering questions afterward, "he starts talking about the poor in America and gets carried away: 'The poor are hidden in our society. No one sees them any more. They are a small minority in a rich country. Yet I am stunned by a lack of awareness of the rest of us toward them.' "[27] Thomas Congdon of the *Saturday Evening Post* saw him in Vincennes at the luncheon of Civitan, a businessmen's club. The complacency of the Civitans provoked him. While they chewed away on their food, he began to talk of children starving, of "*American* children, starving in *America*." Then he said: "Do you know there are more rats than people in New York City?" The Civitans thought this hilarious and broke into guffaws. "Kennedy," wrote Congdon, "went grim and with terrible deliberateness said, '*Don't . . . Laugh. . . .*' " The room fell into confused silence.[28]

He spoke at the University of Indiana Medical School. "The national system of health care," he told an unmoved audience, "has failed to meet the most urgent medical needs of millions of Americans"—the rural and urban poor, the blacks, the Indians.[29] The applause was perfunctory. A black janitor called from the balcony, "We want Kennedy." On the floor students shouted back, "No we don't." Someone asked where the money for Kennedy's health program was coming from. Looking at the incipient M.D.'s about to enter lucrative careers, he snapped, "From you." Then:

> Let me say something about the tone of these questions. I look around this room and I don't see many black faces who will become doctors. You can

talk about where the money will come from. . . . Part of civilized society is to let people go to medical school who come from ghettos. You don't see many people coming out of the ghettos or off the Indian reservations to medical school. You are the privileged ones. . . . It's our society, not just our government, that spends twice as much on pets as on the poverty program. It's the poor who carry the major burden in Vietnam. You sit here as white medical students, while black people carry the burden of the fighting in Vietnam.[30]

Afterward, shaking his head incredulously, he said to Halberstam, "They were so comfortable, so comfortable. Didn't you think they were comfortable?"[31]

Three days later in Valparaiso: "I have seen families with a dozen fatherless children trying to exist on less than $100 a month—and I have seen people in America so hungry that they search the local garbage dump for food."[32] Again the comfortable asked their questions. "You tell me something now," he told the students in the audience. "How many of you spend time over the summer, or on vacations, working in a black ghetto, or in Eastern Kentucky, or on Indian reservations?" He gave them Camus on tortured children.[33]

The campaign had quieter moments. He visited a day nursery a few steps away from James Whitcomb Riley's house in old Indianapolis. Most of the children were from broken homes. "Two little girls," wrote David Murray in the *Chicago Sun-Times,* "came up and put their heads against his waist and he put his hands on their heads. And suddenly it was hard to watch, because he had become in that moment the father they did not know. . . . You can build an image with a lot of sharpsters around you with their computers and their press releases. But lonely little children don't come up and put their heads on your lap unless you mean it."[34]

He returned always to his central theme. "He went yammering around Indiana," recalled Martin, "about the poor whites of Appalachia and the starving Indians who committed suicide on the reservations and the jobless Negroes in the distant great cities, and half the Hoosiers didn't have any idea what he was talking about; but he plodded ahead stubbornly, making them listen, maybe even making some of them care, by the sheer power of his own caring. Indiana people are not generous nor sympathetic; they are hard . . . but he must have touched something in them, pushed a button somewhere."[35]

On May 7 Kennedy received 42 percent of the Indiana vote, Branigan 31, McCarthy 27. Kennedy also beat Hubert Humphrey 62.5 percent to 37.5 the same night in the District of Columbia.

McCarthy airily observed on television that it didn't really matter who came in first, second or third. "That's not what my father told me," the watching Kennedy said. Around midnight Kennedy went out for a late dinner. He ended talking till early in the morning with two young McCarthy volunteers he found in the airport coffee shop. They told him they planned to stick with McCarthy. After a long conversation, he said, a little sadly, "You're dedicated to what you believe, and I think that's terrific."[36] "He kind of neutralized me," one of them, Taylor Branch, said afterward. "I still worked for McCarthy, but I was drawn to Kennedy because of his flair and passion for the black people."[37]

V

Humphrey had announced his candidacy on April 27—too late to qualify for Indiana but in time for the District of Columbia. He had spent the month after Johnson's withdrawal assembling his troops. Walter Mondale and Fred Harris headed his campaign committee. They had been two of Kennedy's better friends in the Senate. Mondale owed his political career to Humphrey, and Kennedy understood his position. But the Harrises had been frequent and happy guests at Hickory Hill and Hyannis Port. Kennedy felt a sadness in losing them now. Of course, Harris had earlier declared for Johnson and was, like Mondale, a hawk on Vietnam. Yet Kennedy hoped that, after Johnson's withdrawal, Harris would rally to the causes he and Kennedy had espoused—the Indians, the Kerner Commission report, of which Harris had been a leading author, the powerless in general. Instead Harris stuck with the administration. (He grew radical later and wrote admiringly—though, in the circumstances, rather patronizingly—about Kennedy in his 1977 memoir *Potomac Fever*.)

How things had changed since Humphrey had bumped along in his bus in Wisconsin eight years before! Now he had representatives of every establishment in America for him—from George Meany to Henry Ford II, from the segregationist governor of Louisiana to the black mayor of Cleveland—and all the campaign funds he needed. It was perhaps small wonder that in his declaration he chirruped about "the politics of happiness . . . the politics of joy. And that's the way it's going to be, all the way, from here on in!"[38] Many found this insensitive three weeks after the murder of Martin Luther King, with the war still racking Vietnam and clouds of violence and hatred over America. Kennedy, who liked Humphrey, was genuinely appalled.

But labor, the party regulars and the south brought Humphrey great strength. He also had a long record of service to Jewish causes, and 60 percent of American Jews lived in the climactic primary states, California and New York. McCarthy too had strong Jewish support. The Jewish community saw him, said Adam Yarmolinsky, as "the professor who gave your bright son an A, and Bobby Kennedy was the tough kid on the block who beat up your son on his way to school."[39] When Kennedy came to New York the day after Indiana, a group of rabbis waited on him. "Why do I have so much trouble with the Jews?" he asked. "I don't understand it. Nobody has been more outspoken than I have. . . . Is it because of my father when he was in England? *That was thirty years ago.*" One of his visitors said that, after the Six Day War, American Jews needed "continual reassurance" about Israel. Kennedy wearily said he would make his position clear again on the west coast.[40]

He met with his delegate slate in the New York primary. Later his friend James Stevenson came by. "He has pushed himself to the limit," Stevenson wrote for the *New Yorker,* "but he does not mention his weariness. His face is gaunt, weathered; his eyes are sunken and red. He rubs his hand over his face again, as if to tear away the exhaustion. It is not something he has sympathy with, his hand is not consoling as it drags across his face—he is simply trying to get rid of an encumbrance."[41] Stevenson felt badly, he remarked later, about asking questions. "He wouldn't give you a slick answer; and that was so awful. I'd ask a question and then I'd feel like saying, 'Never mind. Don't answer that. Don't think about it,' because he'd pull himself together and he'd sort of wring his face and try to rub away all the weariness and exhaustion, and then he'd slowly come out with an answer that he's really thinking about because he wasn't inclined to just give a pre-mixed answer to anything."[42]

On the next day Kennedy addressed the UAW convention in Atlantic City, dined with his children at Hickory Hill and slept in Lincoln, Nebraska. In between, he flew to Hyannis Port to see his father. Rita Dallas noticed the deep lines in his face and thought he could hardly drag himself out of the plane. But he ran to his father, kissed him, then drove him to the compound, laughing, talking, elaborately emphatic in his gestures. "Mr. Kennedy never took his eyes off his son. He was completely absorbed by every move, every word." At luncheon Robert said, "Dad, I'm doing it just the way you would want me to—and I'm going to win." He stayed on till his father's nap. They said goodbye, the old man holding his son's hand with tight, lingering grip.[43]

Kennedy always snapped back quickly from fatigue; and he was beginning to move with the rhythms of the campaign. Early in Indiana reporters had thought him uncomfortable on the hustings. "Kennedy's manner," wrote David Broder of the *Washington Post,* "—the nervous, self-deprecating jokes; the trembling hands on the lectern; the staccato alternations of speech and silence; the sudden shifts of mood—all seem to betray an anticipation of hostility from the crowds."[44] They thought him even worse on television—either stiff in a studio or strident before crowds; too "hot," in Marshall McLuhan's terms, for so cool a medium.

In fact what conventional judgment saw as defects may well have been strengths. His very hesitations conveyed honesty, vulnerability. "Remember Bobby on television," wrote the Yippie Abbie Hoffman, "stuttering at certain questions, leaving room for the audience to jump in and help him agonize."[45] McLuhan himself thought Kennedy marvelously effective. "Now that Bob Kennedy has left that scene," he wrote later in the year, "it is easier to see how much bigger he was than the mere candidate role he undertook to perform. His many hidden dimensions appeared less on the rostrum than in his spontaneous excursions into the ghettos and in his easy rapport with the surging generosity of young hearts. He strove to do good by stealth and blushed to find it fame. It was this (reluctant hero) quality that gave integrity and power to his TV image."[46]

Before live audiences, the shortest way to disarm a crowd and demolish a stereotype, he had discovered, was to do what he did all the time anyway: joke about himself. There had been complaint when on his first visit he spoke, in the Massachusetts manner, of "Indian-er." Returning: "It's good to be here in Indiana. . . . Indian-uh! Some fellow from Massachusetts was in this state last week and pronounced it Indian-er. That was my younger brother. He looks like me. This fall we're going to elect a President who can pronounce Indiana."[47] His stump speech was taking form: jokes—"he has an even greater knack of wry humor than his brother had," Joseph Alsop thought;[48] references to local history and politics; then a problem defined, a rush of statistics, a rising note of urgency; his right fist smashing into his left palm, "I say that's not acceptable. . . . We can do better"; finally, a quotation from Shaw that John Kennedy had used in 1963 before the Irish Parliament and that Robert now rendered as "Some men see things as they are and say 'Why?' I dream of things that never were and say, 'Why not?' "*

"The style is neither elegant nor polished," Alsop wrote; "the statements are made staccato and there are frequent repetitions; yet what comes through most strongly is a sense of deep and true concern, a feeling that this man genuinely cares very greatly."[49] Of all the candidates he spoke most directly and concretely. His language cut far more deeply than the delphic abstractions of McCarthy or Humphrey's interminable anthology of liberal cliché. "Kennedy is, in fact," Stewart Alsop wrote, "a magnificent campaigner, capable of conveying conviction—the essence of the campaigner's art—with unique force. When he describes with passionate emphasis the awful weaknesses in our rich and complacent society, and then adds his laconic signature phrase—'I don't find that satisfactory'—it is genuinely moving."[50]

As the weeks passed, he grew visibly more relaxed. His cocker spaniel Freckles was now always by his side. "If Freckles had a single admirer in the Kennedy campaign entourage," said John Douglas, a kindly man, "it was the candidate himself. . . . Most thought it to be a pest and an abomination."[51] They should have been glad he had not brought Brumus. Once someone asked Richard Tuck, the campaign wit, why he was making such an effort over Freckles. "It may look like a dog to you," Tuck said, "but it's an ambassadorship to me." Kennedy thought this very funny. If Tuck erred thereafter, he would say, "You've just lost Madrid, Tuck."[52]

The campaign was acquiring a rollicking quality, typified most of all by the ride on the Wabash Cannonball, a sunny afternoon through north central Indiana on the old Wabash line. Trains had gone out of fashion in campaigns, but everyone—candidates, reporters, local politicians—missed whistle-stopping, and small Indiana towns, clustered around their depots, were ideal settings. A banjo group played the old song "The Wabash Cannonball" at each stop. Kennedy introduced Ethel, then gave his speech. Once he forgot to conclude with Shaw, and some reporters were left behind. They asked him never to do that again. Thereafter, "as George Bernard Shaw once said . . ." became the signal for the dash to the press bus. Between stops, reporters wrote their parody "The Ruthless Can-

---

* The quotation was both inexact and out of context. It was spoken by the Serpent in *Back to Methuselah* in an effort to seduce Eve: "You see things; and you say 'Why?' But I dream things that never were; and I say 'Why not?' " JFK had it right in Dublin.

nonball," singing it to the candidate himself before the end of the day:

> Now good clean Gene McCarthy came down the other track
> A thousand Radcliffe dropouts all massed for the attack,
> But Bobby's bought the right-of-way from here back to St. Paul,
> 'Cause money is no object on The Ruthless Cannonball. . . .
>
> So here's to Ruthless Robert, may his name forever stand,
> To be feared and genuflected at by pols across the land.
> Old Ho Chi Minh is cheering, and though it may appall,
> He's whizzing to the White House on The Ruthless Cannonball.

It went on too long—seven verses—and, after a time, some in the press wondered whether irreverence had gone too far. After a moment's silence, Kennedy said at last, "As George Bernard Shaw once said . . ." "Wild laughter," noted Thomas Congdon, "partly in relief that he had taken it lightly." "As George Bernard Shaw once said," Kennedy repeated, ". . . the same to you, buddy."[53]

VI

Complacent audiences nourished his eloquence, which was why his schedulers sent him to places like the Civitan Club and the University of Indiana Medical School. Country audiences nourished his humor. The Nebraska primary came a week after Indiana. The urban Jeff Greenfield watched the farm crowds. "They'd begin by folding their arms and looking up at him as if saying, 'OK, buddy . . . Let's hear the guff.' And then he'd begin by bantering, and . . . the myth of Robert Kennedy as a ruthless, machine guy totally began to break down."[54] "I like rural people," Kennedy told the urban Newfield. ". . . They gave me a chance. They listened to me."[55]

He was about as much a master of agricultural economics as his brother had been. During one speech a gust of wind blew a small piece of paper out of his hand. "Give me that back," he said. ". . . That's my farm program."[56] "You've got to elect me," he told farmers when he whistle-stopped across the state, "because I'm the best friend the farmer has. . . . I'm already doing more for the farmer than any of them, and if you don't believe me, just look down at my breakfast table. . . . We are consuming more milk and more bread and more eggs, doing more for farm consumption—than the family of any other candidate."[57]

He loved to parody the rituals of politics. He convulsed the press by saying in a conservative Indiana town, "Make like, not war. See

how careful I am."[58] A reporter, examining the schedule in Nebraska, said it looked like an easy day ahead. "Yes," said Kennedy.
"They've fired Marat/Sade as head of scheduling."[59] "You probably
wonder," he told the crowd in the small town of Crete, Nebraska,
"why I came to Crete. When I was trying to make up my mind
whether to run for President, I discussed it with my wife and she said
I should, because then I would be able to get to Nebraska. So I
asked her why I should get to Nebraska, and she said, 'Because then
you might have a chance to visit Crete!' " The crowd cheered. Kennedy: "All those who believe that, raise your hands," which all the
kids did.[60] Arriving in one town in the midst, he was informed, of a
Slovak festival, he asked how many Slovaks there were in the crowd.
Apparently none. "Well, why are you having a Slovak festival?"
"And they were laughing," recalled Greenfield. "They were trying to
explain to him from the crowd what was going on. It was a totally
honest, open, kind of sense of community, really; and that sense really developed all through Nebraska."[61]

Underneath the chaff the theme remained. On the day before the
vote, a student at Creighton University in Omaha asked whether military service was not one way of getting young people out of the
ghettos. "Here at a Catholic university," Kennedy said indignantly,
"how can you say that we can deal with the problems of the poor by
sending them to Vietnam? . . . Look around you. How many black
faces do you see here, how many American Indians, how many Mex-
ican-Americans? . . . If you look at any regiment or division of
paratroopers in Vietnam, forty-five percent of them are black. How
can you accept this? . . . You're the most exclusive minority in the
world. Are you just going to sit on your duffs and do nothing?"[62] He
made his last Nebraska speech in the black section of Omaha. It had
begun to pour, and the absurdity of it all overcame him. "Have any
of you noticed that it's raining?" he asked. "Yes," the crowd—
surprisingly large—shouted back. "If there are silly things to do,"
Kennedy said, "then this is the silliest. It's silly for you to be standing in the rain listening to a politician. . . . As George Bernard
Shaw once said, 'Run for the buses.' "[63]

He liked Nebraska, said John Glenn, "the plain physical beauty of
the countryside and the square fields and the plow patterns," and the
greenness of the midwestern spring.[64] And he liked the farmers. "He
really felt," said Peter Edelman, "that they, in a romantic kind of
way, . . . were his kind of people." He had found "another kind of
forgotten and alienated American, another person who thought that

this system had just left him behind."[65] On May 14 he won the Nebraska primary with 51.5 percent of the vote. "The farmers," Jules
Witcover wrote, "turned out for him in droves."[66] McCarthy, still
precariously in the race, took 31 percent.

VII

Between them, Kennedy and McCarthy polled over 80 percent of the
Nebraska vote—a smashing repudiation, Kennedy said, of the John-
son-Humphrey administration. "The people want to move in a
different direction. We can't have the politics of happiness and joy
when we have so many problems in our own country."[67] But
Humphrey warily avoided the challenge. It remained a duel between
McCarthy and Kennedy.

In fact, the two men agreed on most things. Their Senate records
were comparable—Kennedy's better by ADA standards but
McCarthy's entirely respectable.* They had differed occasionally—
over federal gun control (which McCarthy opposed), over the Subversive Activities Control Board (which McCarthy supported).
McCarthy was generally bolder in his attacks on the national security
complex, continuing, as he had done since 1964, to accuse the CIA
of having "taken on the character of an invisible government answering only to itself,"[68] and now promising, if elected, to fire J. Edgar
Hoover. In foreign policy both denounced the idea of the United
States as global policeman. "The worst thing we could do," Kennedy
said in a "no more Vietnams" speech in Indiana, "would be to take
as our mission the suppression of disorder and internal upheaval everywhere it occurs."† McCarthy flavored his critique of globalism
with personal cracks at Rusk, McNamara, Rostow and other appoint-
ees of John F. Kennedy.

Though the war receded somewhat as an issue after Johnson's retreat from escalation, the killing went on, and both Kennedy and
McCarthy continued to assail the hawks. Whatever they may have
thought privately, neither came out for unilateral withdrawal.

* Averaged over three years, Kennedy's ADA rating was 98 percent; McCarthy's,
78 percent (Robert Yoakum, "Kennedy & McCarthy: A Look at Some Votes," *New
Republic,* May 11, 1968).

† He went on, in language reminiscent of his father's writings twenty years before,
to point to "the danger that in seeking universal peace, needlessly fearful of change
and disorder, we will in fact embroil ourselves and the world in a whole series of Vietnams" (RFK, speech at the University of Indiana, Bloomington, April 24, 1968,
RFK Papers).

Humphrey, as George Christian, Johnson's last press secretary, wrote, soon made "an effort to appear more dovish than he actually had been in the Johnson administration war council."[69] He did not persuade those who recalled his emotional and bitter attack on critics of the war.*

Where McCarthy and Kennedy diverged was not so much over policies as over values. Both called for national reconciliation—who did not? It was even Nixon's year for "bringing us together"—but they conceived the task in very different terms. The early primaries encouraged Kennedy in his quest for an alliance of the disestablished and unrepresented. "There has to be a new kind of coalition," he told Newfield in Indiana, "to keep the Democratic party going, and to keep the country together. . . . We have to write off the unions and the South now, and replace them with Negroes, blue-collar whites, and the kids." Poverty would be the tie that bound. "We have to convince the Negroes and poor whites that they have common interests. If we can reconcile those two hostile groups, and then add the kids, you can really turn this country around."[70] In Nebraska he added the farmers. Nor did he forget the Indians. In April he took his Indian subcommittee to South Dakota—much to the irritation of his staff who thought it a waste of precious time. He was in a campaign, Fred Dutton reminded him, and he should knock off the Injuns. Kennedy, who was saving his voice, scribbled a note: "Those of you who think you're running my campaign don't love Indians the way I do. You're a bunch of bastards."[71]

Richard Harwood of the *Washington Post* and other newspapermen began to change their minds about the clamorous crowds. Maybe there was something more to it than demagoguery. "We discovered in 1968," Harwood said later, "this deep, almost mystical bond that existed between Robert Kennedy and the Other America. It was a disquieting experience for reporters. . . . We were forced to recognize in Watts and Gary and Chimney Rock [Nebraska] that the real stake in the American political process involves not the fate of speechwriters and fund-raisers but the lives of millions of people seeking hope out of despair."[72]

He was rallying the unrepresented to recapture and reconstruct the nation, not to destroy it. Many called him a "polarizer" and scoffed at the idea of Robert Kennedy, of all people, taking on a mis-

---

* Humphrey actually suggested that those who disagreed with Johnson and himself on the war were racists—an accusation he reiterated as late as 1976 in *The Education of a Public Man* (Garden City, N.Y., 1976), 486.

sion of reconciliation. McCarthy, according to his wife, "thought that Robert Kennedy could not be a unifying figure, that by his very nature he was divisive, that he aroused fears in the suburbanite and the middle class."[73] No doubt he did. So had Franklin Roosevelt; but by confronting problems Roosevelt had carried his nation farther toward reconciliation than a less "divisive" President would have done.

"The conventional wisdom of political analysis," Richard Whalen in the Republican camp warned Nixon, "holds that Bobby Kennedy is hurt by his black following and seeming radicalism. Maybe so, but just suppose he were to say, 'I'm the *only* man who can deal with these people. I know where to draw the line. Choose me and I'll take charge.' . . . Bobby speaks plainly, you can hear *steel* in his sentences. Even people who say they hate him, if they are scared enough, will turn toward the sound of steel."* Kennedy had a unique ability, said Robert Coles, "to do the miraculous: attract the support of frightened, impoverished, desperate blacks, and their angry insistent spokesmen, and, as well, working-class white people."[74] "His greatest gift to the country," said Alexander Bickel, "would have been the respite these two groups would have granted him to seek solutions that cannot at anyone's hands come quickly."[75] Paul Cowan, a young radical who had started out for McCarthy, now saw Kennedy as "the last liberal politician who could communicate with white working class America."[76]

Thus his mission: to bridge the great schisms—between white and nonwhite, between affluent and poor, between age and youth, between the old and the new politics, between order and dissent, between the past and the future. It was an undertaking that, as Kennedy conceived it, required not only specific programs but active leadership. Kennedy had no doubt that Johnson had abused executive power in foreign affairs. But a general recession of presidential leadership, he believed, would increase the nation's impotence in the face of deep and angry national division. In the back of his mind was FDR during the depression. Only an activist Presidency and an affirmative national government, as he saw it, could pull together a divided people in a stormy time.

---

* Whalen added: "My attitude toward Kennedy had changed in the final months of his life. I didn't often agree with him, yet I had come to respect him. Once committed, he held nothing back" (R. J. Whalen, *Catch the Falling Flag* [Boston, 1972], 171–173).

VIII

McCarthy had both a different constituency and a different theory of the Presidency. In a February article in *Look* called "Why I'm Battling LBJ," he had concentrated on the war and on constitutional questions. He had said not a word about racial justice or the fate of the dispossessed. His voting record on civil rights and poverty issues was good. But his speeches, Jack Newfield thought, revealed "a pattern of psychic distance from the poor. He is certainly not anti-Negro. . . . He is just not very interested in the other America."[77]

McCarthy was ill at ease with blacks, and they with him. The journalist Seymour Hersh resigned from his staff in Wisconsin because of the candidate's reluctance to go into the ghettos. Two weeks after King's murder, McCarthy met with black leaders in Indianapolis. One said his answers were too general; "people are asking direct questions and they need direct answers." Another said, "He didn't put himself into it"; especially compared to Kennedy—that "cat was able to relax."[78] Pride no doubt played a part. Abigail McCarthy spoke of "Gene's refusal to compete emotionally with Robert Kennedy."[79] McCarthy himself said later, "There wasn't political point in it for me. I couldn't get the Negro votes away from Bobby Kennedy."[80]

The poor were not his people. His people, as his wife described them, were "academia united with the mobile society of scientists, educators, technologists and the new post-World War II college class." He appealed to the churches and the suburbs, to civic-minded businessmen and enlightened Republicans, to "the best of Middle America," Abigail McCarthy thought, "in search of a new way of expressing itself as a consensus."[81] "Their common denominator," said Norman Mailer, with unjust but illuminating exaggeration, "seemed to be found in some blank area of the soul, a species of disinfected idealism which gave the impression when among them of living in a lobotomized ward of Upper Utopia." McCarthy, Mailer wrote, "did not look nor feel like a President. . . . No, he seemed more like the dean of the finest English department in the land."[82]

McCarthy himself summed it up in a moment of frivolous candor a few days before the vote in Oregon. The polls, he told an audience in Corvallis, showed Kennedy running best "among the less intelligent and less educated people in America. And I don't mean to fault them for voting for him, but I think that you ought to bear that in mind as you go to the polls here on Tuesday."[83] His speechwriters, Jeremy Larner and Paul Gorman, protested. "Was that unfair?" McCarthy asked. "I think it was," said Paul Gorman. "But it's true," said McCarthy. They asked what that meant. "Nothing!" he laughed.[84]

The constituency was real enough, but, unlike Kennedy's, it did not readily yield a campaign theme. Larner argued that McCarthy must "identify himself with a positive vision of America. McCarthy had such a vision, but he was content to go on expressing it in underdeveloped generalizations." His staff worked up a document proposing "public participation" as the theme and specifying how governing institutions could be brought under popular control. Their candidate professed himself delighted. But, said Larner, he then "went on just as before, saying practically nothing on the new politics. . . . There never was a McCarthy campaign in Indiana and Nebraska."[85]

If anything emerged as a theme, it was a critique of the Presidency itself. Johnson, McCarthy felt, had been "eroding and weakening" the other agencies of government. He had taken the war-making power away from Congress, had diminished the Supreme Court by appointing its Chief Justice to head the commission investigating John Kennedy's assassination, had politicized the Council of Economic Advisers, had enfeebled the Democratic National Committee and the national party. The trouble was his "personalization of the Presidency at the expense of our governmental and political institutions."[86] Actually this personalization had begun, McCarthy thought, with John Kennedy. Johnson had "done it defensively as things have got more and more out of control. Jack did it almost deliberately. He . . . conveyed the impression that all power radiated from the Presidency, which is not, and cannot be, the case in America."[87]

One remedy might be to limit the Presidency to a single term. Another was presidential self-restraint. Presidents must understand, McCarthy said in the campaign, "that this country does not so much need leadership, because the potential for leadership in a free country must exist in every man and every woman."[88] He called for the decentralization of the Presidency. "Has the integrity of Congress, of the cabinet and of the military," he asked, "been impinged upon by undue extensions of the executive power?"[89] The military seemed a curious inclusion.

McCarthy, one felt, was the first liberal candidate in the century to run *against* the Presidency; doing this, moreover, in times of turbulence that seemed to call for a strong Presidency to hold the country together. His views aroused doubts even among his own devoted workers. The political scientist Barry Stavis, for example, began to fear that, under a McCarthy administration, "the federal government would lose its power to protect exploited people. . . . McCarthy would not use the president's tools to combat a raise in the price of steel, for instance, or a strike by railroad workers' unions." "With such an attitude," Stavis wondered, "could he stop the military-industrial complex? . . . Could he stop the arms and space race? Could he get southern states to accept civil rights? Could he get northern states to accept open housing and integrated education?"[90]

IX

Because Kennedy and McCarthy agreed on so many other issues, those for whom neither the underclass nor the Presidency was a dominating consideration chose between them on personal grounds. Some felt a debt to McCarthy for venturing ahead while Kennedy had lingered behind. Others felt that Kennedy would be the stronger candidate against Humphrey and Nixon. Many made up their minds on impressions of temperament and character.

McCarthy attracted people by his detachment, his serenity, his very nonchalance. Property owners did not feel threatened by him. Where Kennedy, wrote David Halberstam, had "the look of a man who intended to rock the boat," McCarthy said radical things in a temperate way.[91] He was civilized, literate, quoted other people's verse and wrote his own. He disdained the ritual of politics. He acknowledged no obligations. He made no effort to conceal boredom. He was distant, private, imperious. An aura of mystery hung around him. Richard Harwood saw in him "vague intimations of an American de Gaulle." McCarthy, Harwood wrote, was the philosopher, Kennedy the evangelist. "McCarthy speaks in generalities and Kennedy speaks in specifics. [McCarthy] dwells on himself and his moment in history; Kennedy dwells on the tragedy of the poor. McCarthy . . . 'meanders' through his campaign; Kennedy drives on like a sprinter. McCarthy soothes; Kennedy arouses."[92]

Each in his way was fastidious. McCarthy was fastidious about wooing crowds. He thought Kennedy a rabble-rouser. He did not at first wish to go to Martin Luther King's funeral; it would be a "big vulgar public spectacle."[93] When Blair Clark told him he had to go, he was, his wife wrote, "adamantly opposed to the idea of walking" over to Morehouse College. At last, she said, "Gene began to feel the simple emotion of the situation and he . . . decided to get out of the car and walk the rest of the way."[94] Kennedy was fastidious about attacking individuals. J. Edgar Hoover would not have lasted thirty seconds in his administration, but he thought it cheap for McCarthy to seek easy cheers from academic audiences by promising to fire him.

I think it fair to say that, the closer people were to them, the more they liked Kennedy and the less they liked McCarthy. "Most politicians," wrote Halberstam, "seem attractive from a distance but under closer examination they fade. . . . Kennedy was different. Under closer inspection he was far more winning."[95] As for McCarthy, wrote Theodore H. White, "all through the year, one's admiration of the man grew—and one's affection lessened."[96]

Kennedy's staff, without exception so far as I know, adored him, spoke frankly to him, were received by him as friends. Richard Harwood could find "little camaraderie between McCarthy and those who enlisted in his campaign. They are functionaries rather than partners."[97] Books written by McCarthy aides are filled with uneasiness, with retrospective doubt, not seldom with hostility. "He treated us," wrote Barry Stavis, "not as *his* staff but as the organized segment of the American people demanding his presidency. Once an infuriated staff member threatened, 'I'm going to take that presidency and ram it down his throat.' . . . Most of the staff did not like this relationship. They wanted to be part of *his* campaign, not part of a popular demand for him, and expected him to lead it and not observe it."[98] McCarthy's attitude, said Larner, was "that he was doing his supporters a favor by 'letting them use my name.' "[99]

Both Stavis and Larner commented on his resentment of criticism. "The biggest danger I foresaw with a McCarthy presidency," said Stavis, "was that if he made a mistake, it would be difficult to pressure him into correcting it. . . . His confidence and moralism might make him as hard to sway as Dean Rusk had been."[100] "Criticism was impermissible," wrote Larner, "no matter its source or its quality. . . . He could not tolerate disagreement or equality, could not, in fact, work directly and openly with others."[101] Both commented on his withdrawal behind a cozy circle of "snobs, sycophants, stooges, and clowns." Both were concerned by what Larner called "a deep-seated bitterness, never quite accounted for by immediate circumstance, a bitterness which made him down-rate individuals, even as he was calling for a national policy of generosity."[102]

A gnawing question, recalled Stavis, was "whether we really wanted Eugene McCarthy to be president."[103] Doubts troubled them at night, "but we acted, during the daytime," said Larner, "as if we were in the service of a wise and calm daddy, crudely attacked by a renegade brother who stirred up crowds with his long hair, squeaky voice, baby talk, and unfair money." They suffered and stayed. "There was finally in McCarthy's reserve, in all he left unsaid, a special air of mystery, a hint that he drew strength from a source beyond mere mortals like Kennedy and ourselves, a gift for grace that would tell him when and how to bring that strength to bear."[104]

One aide was deeply worried by McCarthy, deeply tempted by Kennedy. "But in the end," said Larner, "he stayed and suffered." The reason, the aide explained, was the one thing Kennedy could not offer. "I thought McCarthy had a secret. I thought one day the secret would explain it all."[105] Larner entitled his book *Nobody Knows*.

X

Distance magnified McCarthy's charms and Kennedy's infirmities. It was hard in later years, after McCarthy glided away as mysteriously as he had appeared, to recall the intensity of feeling on his behalf in 1968.

The rage among his supporters against Kennedy, far from subsiding, appeared to grow. Kennedy's mode of entry handed McCarthy, as Halberstam said, "the White Knight issue."[106] Then there was the underdog effect: Kennedy with his high-powered machine, personal fortune, Irish Mafia, puffed-up names from the past (Sorensen, Salinger, Schlesinger), against McCarthy with his Children's Crusade, youth and idealism, ministers and housewives, living on the land—the big battalions moving in on the guerrilla warriors.

Once Johnson had withdrawn, Kennedy replaced him as the hate object in sections of the intellectual left, at least in New York. Jack Newfield did not exaggerate when he wrote in May of "the deep hatred of Kennedy that is now so chic among liberal intellectuals."[107] I wrote about "the McCarthy hysteria" in my journal the same month: "I have never felt so much in my life the settled target of hostility. . . . I am hissed at practically every public appearance in this city. I have just been out to get the morning *Times,* and inevitably someone harangued and denounced me on Third Avenue—again a McCarthyite. I think these people are crazy."[108]

One memory sums up my impression of that embattled spring.

George Plimpton, a strong if lonely Kennedy supporter, gave a party for McCarthy friends and invited me to present the case for our candidate. The atmosphere was icy. Questions. Someone asked about birth control and abortion. In fact, Kennedy approved birth control (for others), was sympathetic to the New York abortion law and had been helpful to Albert Blumenthal in getting it through the state legislature.* I mentioned this, then asked how McCarthy stood on these questions. No one knew, or cared. McCarthy could have come out for the auto-da-fé, one felt; this crowd would still prefer him to Kennedy. I finally asked what it was specifically they had against Kennedy. Nat Hentoff, a jazz critic and a goodhearted civil libertarian, launched into an emotional discourse—Joe McCarthy, Hoffa, Manchester, the old litany. "All I can say," he concluded, "is that he seems to me someone ruthless, vindictive, relentless, like, well—like Jean Valjean in *Les Misérables*." I said that Hentoff probably meant Javert. I was denied even this trivial victory. His loyal wife said, to general applause, "That is exactly the sort of pedantry we would expect from Kennedy people."

Robert Lowell speaking on Kennedy in Oregon: "He has just bought a hundred charisma suits. A charisma suit is made of cloth and cardboard; at the touch of a feather, at the touch of the weakest admirer, it pulls apart. But under the charisma suit is an anti-charisma Bobby-suit. It is made of cloth and steel wool. It doesn't tear at all and leaves metal threads in the rash admirer for months." Lowell added he would be "dishonorable if I didn't confess that I personally like and admire Senator Kennedy. . . . Still I wish to end up with invective; it's hard to forgive Kennedy his shy, calculating delay in declaring himself, or forgive the shaggy rudeness of his final entrance. . . . We cannot forgive Senator Kennedy for trying to bury us under a pile of gold."[109]

Yet, looking into the records, I conclude that Newfield and I were overreacting to the parochial environment of Manhattan. In fact, across the country, the arts and letters divided evenly enough between the two candidates. Elizabeth Hardwick Lowell later said of Kennedy, "I felt about him that he was one of the few people in public life who had truly changed and also that this possibility of change would continue. Many people were stopped by an image of Bobby Kennedy formed in the past. But with him I felt a wish to transcend

---

* "A couple of times when I got into some trouble over the abortion law . . . he really went to bat for me" (Albert H. Blumenthal, in recorded interview by Roberta Greene, December 14, 1973, 47–48, RFK Oral History Program).

that past. And actually at the end he had transcended his earlier self, whatever that was. Anyway he had gone beyond what we imagined him to have been and done so more than anyone I can think of."[110]

Among poets McCarthy had Lowell; Kennedy had John Berryman, John Ashbery, Donald Hall, Sandra Hochman. Among novelists McCarthy had William Styron, Mary McCarthy, Wilfrid Sheed. Kennedy had Norman Mailer, James Jones, Alison Lurie, Joyce Carol Oates, Irwin Shaw, Wright Morris, Truman Capote, Budd Schulberg. (Humphrey had Ralph Ellison and James T. Farrell.) Among playwrights McCarthy had Arthur Miller; Kennedy, William Inge and Alan Jay Lerner. McCarthy had Paul Newman and Joanne Woodward; Kennedy, Lauren Bacall, Henry Fonda, Shirley MacLaine, Warren Beatty. McCarthy had Ben Shahn; Kennedy had James Wyeth and Andy Warhol. McCarthy had Jules Feiffer; Kennedy, Charles Addams. McCarthy had J. K. Galbraith, Joseph Rauh, Allard Lowenstein, Barbara Tuchman, Erich Fromm; Kennedy had Archibald Cox, Paul Samuelson, Seymour Harris, Robert Coles, James Loeb.

It was interesting how many people who had tangled with Kennedy in the past rallied to him now. John Lewis of SNCC was only one example. J. Edward Day, who as Postmaster General had had his troubles with Kennedy; G. Robert Blakey, who had criticized his explanations of wiretapping; Joseph Mankiewicz, who had opposed him for the Senate—all endorsed him. To the dismay of those who still used the battle of the book as evidence of Kennedy's ruthlessness, William Manchester came out for him, calling him "not a brute . . . genuinely humane . . . the least understood man in the presidential arena."[111] ("When I read this spring that you were giving your support to Robert Kennedy," Jacqueline Kennedy wrote him later, "—I was absolutely startled—then so touched—and much more than that. . . . I want you to know that the last time I saw Bobby alive, we spoke of that. And it meant the same to him. . . . You gave him what he was pleading for for [from] others—a wiping off of the blackboard of the past—a faith in now—and a generosity of such magnitude and sacrifice.")[112] Alexander Bickel had written in the *New Republic* in 1961 that Kennedy was unfit to be Attorney General. "I campaigned for him in California," Bickel wrote in the *New Republic* in 1968, "and it meant a great deal to me, more than any prior political commitment or than any conceivable new one. I believed he had come to know better and more deeply than anyone how dangerously we are nearing a dead end, and I believed that he above all other public men would . . . stop war and heal suffering."[113]

Kennedy's greatest disappointment was the young. He used to say wistfully that McCarthy had the A students, and he envied McCarthy their devotion. Curiously he was stronger than McCarthy with the far-out young. In December 1967 Abbie Hoffman, in an effort to unite the hippies with the New Left, founded the Youth International Party, known popularly as "Yippie!" with the intention of besieging the Democratic convention in Chicago. "Gene wasn't much," said Hoffman. "One could secretly cheer for him the way you cheer for the Mets. It's easy, knowing he can never win. But Bobby, there was the real threat. . . . *Come on,* Bobby said, *join the mystery battle against the television machine.* Participation mystique. Theater-in-the-streets. He played it to the hilt. . . . It was no contest. . . . Yippie! grew irrelevant. . . . By the end of May we had decided to disband Yippie! and cancel the Chicago festival."[114] They reinstated the festival later.

The other America was of course with him. Cesar Chavez was on his delegate slate in California. In Mississippi, Charles Evers and Oscar Carr, the enlightened planter, were co-chairmen of the Kennedy committee. "You may tell your husband," George Wiley, the fiery leader of the National Welfare Rights Organization, wrote Ethel Kennedy, "that I am personally very much in favor of his candidacy."[115] Michael Harrington, the author of *The Other America,* the heir of Norman Thomas, campaigned stoutly for him in Indiana and California. When he met the candidate, they talked about "why so many New York reformers hated Kennedy, a phenomenon that troubled and puzzled him. He told me with a sort of hurt disbelief how a peace activist in San Francisco had spit in his face and called him a fascist." Later they walked down a chilly, silent street toward Kennedy's hotel. An old black man ran up to Kennedy: "My wife's waiting back in the car and she wants to meet you." Kennedy pulled the lapels of his coat against his face and headed back in the cold wind. Harrington never saw him again. He wrote in his autobiography, "As I look back on the sixties, he was the man who actually could have changed the course of American history."[116]

Mid-April, George McGovern introducing Robert Kennedy to a crowd of five thousand who had waited an hour in the rain in Rapid City, South Dakota; a man, McGovern said, with "the absolute personal honesty of a Woodrow Wilson, the stirring passion for leadership of Andrew Jackson, and the profound acquaintance with personal tragedy of Lincoln." McGovern continued:

> You people know the affection and esteem I held for President Kennedy, but it is my carefully measured conviction that Senator Robert Kennedy, even more than our late beloved President, would now bring to the Presidency a deeper measure of experience and a more profound capacity to lead our troubled land into the light of a new day. . . . If he is elected President of the United States, he will, in my judgment, become one of the three or four greatest Presidents in our national history.*

XI

The Kennedy campaign, Charles Quinn said later, became a "huge, joyous adventure."[117] Even reporters found themselves caught up in the enterprise against all the rules of professionalism. "Quite frankly," said Tom Wicker, head of the *New York Times* Washington bureau, "Bobby Kennedy was an easy man to fall in love with," and he warned his own people against it.[118] Jules Witcover, who later wrote an excellent book about the campaign, spoke of Kennedy's "way of pulling individuals around him into his orbit, a strange disarming quality about him that somehow evoked sympathy."[119] By the time of Oregon, as Richard Harwood, initially the most hostile of all, said later, "We were getting partisan. We hadn't quite become cheerleaders but we were in danger of it."† One reporter asked to be taken off the campaign after California because he felt he could no longer be objective.[120]

Underneath the fun lay foreboding. A shadow had fallen across the happy day of the Wabash Cannonball when the train stopped at Logansport, and someone saw on top of a building, etched against the sky, a man with a gun. He turned out to be a policeman, but Thomas Congdon long remembered the "agonized" look on the face

---

* George McGovern, introduction of Robert Kennedy at Sioux Falls and Rapid City, South Dakota, April 16, 1968. Kennedy said of McGovern at Mitchell, South Dakota, on May 10: "Of all my colleagues in the United States Senate, the person who has the most feeling and does things in the most genuine way, without that affecting his life, is George McGovern. . . . That is truer of him than anyone else in the United States Senate." For full texts, see "Senator Robert Kennedy in South Dakota 1968 (A Memorial from Senator George McGovern)," (n.p., n.d. [1968]). See also George McGovern, in recorded interview by L. J. Hackman, July 16, 1970, 57–62, RFK Oral History Program.

† Richard Harwood, in recorded interview by Jean Stein, September 6, 1968, 2, Stein Papers. Ben Bradlee, Harwood's editor, had originally given Harwood this assignment because he had been so "outspokenly skeptical of Bobby" (Benjamin C. Bradlee, *Conversations with Kennedy* [New York, 1975], 22).

of Jerry Bruno, the advance man.[121] One evening a group of reporters sat around over drinks. Someone asked whether Kennedy had the stuff to go all the way. "Of course, he has the stuff to go all the way," replied John J. Lindsay of *Newsweek,* "but he's not going to go all the way. . . . Somebody is going to shoot him." There was "stunned silence" around the table. One by one, each journalist agreed. Lindsay said, "He's out there now waiting for him."[122]

Romain Gary, the French novelist, came to America that spring with his wife, the actress Jean Seberg. They lunched with Pierre Salinger after King's murder. "You know, of course," Gary said, "that your guy will be killed." Salinger froze, stared at Gary for a long moment, then said, "I live with that fear. We do what can be done, and that isn't much. He runs around like quicksilver." A month later, Gary met Kennedy himself. The novelist found Kennedy's boyishness and charm "much more apparent than the supposed ruthlessness" and singularly thought that, "when age and white hair come, he would look a bit like Cordell Hull." He said, "Somebody is going to try to kill you." Kennedy said that there were no guarantees against assassination. "You've just got to give yourself to the people and to trust them, and from then on . . . either [luck is] with you or it isn't. I am pretty sure there'll be an attempt on my life sooner or later. Not so much for political reasons. . . . Plain nuttiness, that's all."[123]

This was why Bill Barry was along. "It was not just a professional job with me," he told Jules Witcover. "It was something my life qualified me for. This would be my juggler's gift."[124] No one worked with less cooperation from his principal. Barry's main job was to get Kennedy through crowds. When the campaigning day was over, Kennedy refused protection. Barry tried surreptitious precautions, such as hiring off-duty policemen to stay in the hotel lobby. He dared not risk Kennedy's displeasure by putting them in corridors next to his room. When Kennedy learned of such extracurricular arrangements, he canceled them.

His attitude, Barry said later, "was that he was going to live his life and not be constantly fearful of what might happen. . . . He only accepted as much protection as he got because he liked me. . . . He wouldn't have had anybody if really left to his own choice." On April 11, in Lansing, Michigan, a police lieutenant notified Barry that a man with a rifle had gone into a building across from the hotel. Barry had Kennedy's car driven into the basement garage, so he could enter it without going out on the street.

When they went to the garage, Kennedy was furious. He said, "Don't ever do this again. Don't ever change whatever we're doing until you talk to me, and I don't ever want to change it because I'm not afraid of anybody. If things happen, they're going to happen."[125] (The man with the rifle turned out to be an office worker bound for a hunting weekend.) Kennedy particularly objected to police escorts in ghettos.[126] As Lieutenant Jack Eberhardt of the Los Angeles Police Department put it, Kennedy "in no uncertain terms, told us he didn't care for our assistance. He felt that we were preventing him from getting a close rapport with his followers."[127]

There were several alarms—in Cleveland, in Salt Lake City, in California. Kennedy ignored them. Reporters nerved themselves to mention the danger. He told Charles Quinn, yes, he had thought about it, but he wasn't going to change his campaign because of it. Then his eyes got a faraway look, and he said, "You know, if I'm ever elected President, I'm never going to ride in one of those God-damned cars"; he meant one of those bulletproof, bubble-top cars.[128] "If there is somebody out there who wants to get me," he told Warren Rogers, "well, doing anything in public life today is Russian roulette."[129]

In May, Bill Barry had his forty-first birthday. There was the usual Kennedy surprise party, poems, gags, joke presents, balloons, champagne. While someone read a poem, a balloon exploded with a loud bang. "It would have been a forgotten interlude," said Helen Dudar of the *New York Post,* "except for Kennedy's reaction; it was not a shellshock reflex and it almost proceeded in slow motion. The back of his hand came up toward his face, which was frowning, and he held his hand there, his head bent, for perhaps a count of ten. The party stood suspended in time for those seconds and then Kennedy came back from wherever he'd been and it resumed."[130]

Barry and Walter Sheridan continually discussed the security problem. "And we knew," said Sheridan, "that, really, there wasn't anything you could do about it because he was uncontrollable, and if you tried to protect him he'd get mad as hell."[131] Someone later asked Barry whether Kennedy was foolhardy. "I don't know whether that's a correct word," Barry said. ". . . He just didn't want to live in fear. So I think he was making a personal judgment of his own, based on his own life force."[132]

41

To Sail Beyond . . . the Western Stars,
Until I Die

IN MID-MAY Kennedy paid a flying visit to South Dakota, where Hubert Humphrey, a native son, and Eugene McCarthy, from Minnesota across the border, had also entered the primary. George McGovern, introducing him again, quoted a snatch from "The Impossible Dream." Kennedy wearily stumbled through his speech. Afterward he asked whether McGovern really thought the quest impossible. McGovern said, "No, I don't think it's impossible. I just . . . wanted the audience to understand that it's worth making the effort— whether you win or lose." Kennedy said, "Well, that's what I think." They met for breakfast in the morning. "He came in after taking his dog for a run nearby, and he looked rested and relaxed." McGovern said goodbye at the airport. "I remember that morning just being seized with a feeling of sadness. For some reason, he looked so small. Bob, at various times, appeared different sizes to me." An interesting observation; I had similar optical illusions about him. "Sometimes he seemed like a large man . . . I mean physically. At other times, he seemed very slight, small. It depended, I guess, on the angle of vision. But, as he walked away, he looked like such a frail and small person. I just had such a feeling of sadness as he got on the plane."[1]

I

South Dakota, like California, would vote on June 5; Oregon, a week earlier. Oregon: a pleasant, homogeneous, self-contained state filled with pleasant, homogeneous, self-contained people, overwhelmingly white, Protestant and middle class. Even the working class was middle class, with boats on the lakes and weekend cabins in the mountains. Oregonians were remote from problems but responsive to issues. McCarthy was the thoughtful, independent type they liked. And he had in Oregon, he said later, "a better organization than we had in any other state. It had been working for six months. . . . It was also the best financed of our efforts."* Most important of all, he had finally found the theme his campaign had lacked since Johnson's withdrawal. That theme was Robert Kennedy.

McCarthy had grown increasingly bitter toward Kennedy, conspicuously refusing to congratulate him, for example, after Indiana and again after Nebraska.[2] Even more than Kennedy's entry, his money and his presumed sense of entitlement, "the greatest disappointment," McCarthy said the following December, "was the kind of campaign the Kennedy people conducted against me," by which he meant primarily "that whole voting record thing they put out."[3] It is not clear why this should have outraged him so particularly. Voting records are sometimes hard to interpret, and McCarthy's own explanations for his "bad" votes were complicated.[4] Moreover, as Arthur Herzog, who ran McCarthy's Oregon campaign, later wrote, "The charges were, in fact, partially true."[5] Nor were his own people all that careful. Three days before the California vote, the McCarthy for President Committee, taking a full page in the *San Francisco Chronicle,* charged wildly that Kennedy had been "directly involved" in the Bay of Pigs and "in the decisions that led us to intervene in the affairs of the Dominican Republic."[6]

Nevertheless McCarthy was deeply aggrieved over an indefensibly sloppy tabulation circulated by a free-lance New York group called Citizens for Kennedy. Salinger had promptly disclaimed this leaflet on behalf of Kennedy headquarters.[7] "Had it been our attack," said Stephen Smith, "we would have done a better job."[8] Kennedy himself, Frank Mankiewicz recalled, said he saw no point in "knocking McCarthy's voting record. . . . The people who were for Gene McCarthy were not for him because of his voting record. . . . If you could show them that McCarthy had voted wrong, let's say, on every issue in the past ten years that ADA felt was important, it wouldn't bother them."[9] Nevertheless, for all the disavowals, the inaccurate McCarthy voting record bobbed up in Indiana, in Nebraska and now in Oregon and California.

McCarthy also resented Kennedy efforts to induce McCarthy stu-

* Eugene McCarthy, *The Year of the People* (Garden City, N.Y., 1969), 145. In calling it the "best financed," McCarthy explained that he meant not that the Oregon campaign had the most money but that it had the money long enough in advance to plan the spending effectively.

dents to desert through offers, as he understood it, "of more pay, educational advantages, and the like."[10] At the same time his own agents infiltrated the Kennedy campaign, though, Barry Stavis later acknowledged, "our very efficient intelligence network within the Kennedy circles yielded nothing of any particular value."[11] Thus competition debased both camps.

McCarthy was additionally angered by Kennedy's repeated public assertions of a desire to work together. This sounded generous, but, McCarthy correctly noted, "at no time in the campaign did he expressly say that he would support me . . . for the presidency."[12] The Kennedy people tried to work out joint slates in the District of Columbia, New York, Maryland and other states. McCarthy vetoed them all. He saw them as a way of channeling McCarthy delegates to Kennedy, not vice versa. His analysis was not unreasonable. I do not think that Kennedy could conceivably have brought himself to come out for McCarthy. Nor, after Indiana and Nebraska, was there any chance that McCarthy would come out for Kennedy. Despite Vietnam and the politics of joy, each, I would guess, preferred Hubert Humphrey to the other. Kennedy never indicated this publicly. McCarthy did. "My final judgment," McCarthy wrote later, "was expressed in a press interview on May 21 when I said that I could support Vice President Humphrey if he changed his position on Vietnam and *possibly* Senator Kennedy if there was a change in his campaign methods."[13]

The acceptability of a purified Humphrey alarmed the McCarthy staff. Jeremy Larner and Paul Gorman soon drafted a speech for McCarthy to give at the Cow Palace in San Francisco assailing Humphrey and Kennedy equally. On delivery, McCarthy amplified the Kennedy section. Then he read the sentences on Humphrey, Larner wrote later, "in a subdued, rapid tone. And when it came to the distinction between candidates for the war and against it, McCarthy said it in a garbled way that could not have made sense to his audience." Larner felt physically sick. He could no longer doubt "that McCarthy hated Bobby Kennedy, that on a personal level he preferred Humphrey."[14]

In Oregon McCarthy dwelt almost obsessively on Kennedy. He challenged him, repeatedly and scornfully, to debate. He criticized him for advocating federal gun control—a well-calculated criticism in a state that regarded gun ownership as one of the rights of man. With mordant and condescending wit, McCarthy ridiculed Kennedy's advisers, his astronaut, his dog. He liked to depict Kennedy himself as a spoiled child. "Bobby," he would say, "threatened to hold his breath unless the people of Oregon voted for him."[15] On the Saturday night before the vote he brought a screaming crowd at the Portland Coliseum to its feet again and again with personal sarcasm. It was his most rousing speech.[16] "The tone of mockery," Larner thought, "was sickening."[17]

II

Kennedy did not strike back. This restraint signified no affection for McCarthy, rather a desire not to antagonize McCarthy's supporters, especially the kids. He hoped to have them with him later. When he challenged anybody, it was Humphrey and his politics of joy. For the rest, he talked about the poor; he talked about jobs; he tried persiflage. None of it worked in Oregon.

He did not have a strong organization. Congresswoman Edith Green had agreed to run his campaign on condition that her bête noire David Hackett be forbidden to enter the state.[18] She had great popularity but no apparatus. On April 28, a month before the vote, the Kennedy headquarters consisted of two desks and three people.[19] The Teamsters, the strongest union in the state, had not forgotten the Rackets Committee investigations in Portland. The mayor of Portland, who had been indicted in 1959 as a result of these investigations, was, after acquittal, still mayor in 1968.*

Kennedy's personality was too intense for Oregon. His behavior offended unfathomable local sensitivities. Doing what he had done so often around the world, he yielded, for example, on May 24 to the temptation to take a dip in the Pacific. Apparently Oregonians never swam in the Pacific until August. They thought anyone who swam in May a showoff or a fool. Most damaging of all, as Kennedy muttered to Joseph Kraft, "there's nothing for me to get hold of."[20] Employment was high. Minorities—blacks, Indians, Chicanos—were 2 percent of the population. An observer watched him speak at an oscilloscope plant outside Portland. "The employees did not rise to his impassioned attack upon poverty, hunger, the ghettos and the decay of the cities. . . . Kennedy left the plant, shaking his head and declaring that these were the strangest workers he had ever met."[21] As Pierre Salinger said, "If you were going to carry on the central theme

* "No city in the U.S. regards [Robert Kennedy] with such suspicion, and in some cases with such downright enmity, as does Portland" (Paul O'Neil, "The No. 2 Man in Washington," *Life,* January 26, 1962).

of Bob's campaign which had to do with poverty and blacks and [poor] people, this subject was absolutely falling on dead ears in Oregon. They couldn't care less. I mean the black ghetto in Portland was maybe five city blocks or something."[22] "Let's face it," Kennedy told a reporter, "I appeal best to people who have problems."[23]

His most serious mistake was his refusal to debate. He even dodged McCarthy personally when their schedules accidentally brought them together at the Portland Zoo. Jeremy Larner chased after Kennedy, saw a look of "exquisite hurt" on Kennedy's face, shouted "Coward." "For five minutes, I felt exhilarated," Larner wrote later.

> It was a lot of fun, like winning a game of touch football. I didn't think about it till I saw the film on TV back at the hotel. . . . When I heard my own voice pipe Coward, I got that flash of nausea that had come before in the Cow Palace. . . . I had become in my way pretty much like everyone else on either side: a gangster in a war of two mobs in the same family. The hurt look was no cry for pity: it was the registration that something had gone terribly wrong in our fight for territory. . . . Our family could only lose, and what did I know, what did I really know, that made me so eager to beat him?[24]

III

May 28: McCarthy, 44.7 percent; Kennedy, 38.8 percent. No Kennedy had ever before lost an election, except for the Harvard Board of Overseers. As the returns came in, Kennedy's two student organizers avoided him; they thought they had let him down. He put an arm around each and said, "I'm sorry I let you down."[25] Disdaining McCarthy's example, he sent a generous telegram of congratulation to the victor. To a reporter he said that Humphrey, not McCarthy, was the real winner. "I think what [McCarthy] wanted most was to knock me off. I guess he may hate me that much." He told the gloomy crowd at the hotel that he was going to reorganize his campaign; "I have decided to send Freckles home."[26]

The next morning he flew south to California. His press conference at the Los Angeles airport concentrated on Humphrey—on the Vice President's failure "to present his views to the voters of a single state," on the irrelevance of his "politics of joy" to "the conditions which are presently transforming our cities into armed camps." As for McCarthy, Kennedy said he would be happy to debate "with him and with the Vice President, or just the two of us."[27]

Of course winning would have been far better. Still, losing proved that Kennedy was human too. He seemed thereafter less ruthless, almost an underdog. "This defeat might be a help to your campaign—instead of a bitter blow," as Janet Auchincloss, Jacqueline Kennedy's mother, perceptively wrote him. "Somehow the first defeat—or setback—makes you a more sympathetic figure—and people will admire the courageous and graceful way you acknowledged it."[28]

As in Oregon, McCarthy was well organized and financed. Kennedy's California support, ranging from Jesse Unruh to Cesar Chavez, was multifarious and sometimes discordant. Unruh wanted to keep everything as much as possible in his own hands. Jack Conway and Walter Sheridan set up a parallel campaign for labor and the minorities. In the last weeks, when Stephen Smith had taken charge in Los Angeles and John Seigenthaler in San Francisco, a measure of coherence emerged (except that Seigenthaler brought along Paul Corbin, who organized Salinas under an assumed name, claiming to be a former lieutenant commander in the Navy. Corbin assured William Orrick that he could have been elected mayor of Salinas by the time he was through.)[29] Flying squads from the east—Alexander Bickel, Michael Harrington, Roger Hilsman, Michael Forrestal, Abba Schwartz, Edwin Reischauer, Roswell Gilpatric, George Plimpton, Pat Moynihan, Harry Golden, Adam Yarmolinsky, Marietta Tree, myself, others—invaded McCarthy strongholds in the colleges and the liberal community. Cesar Chavez registered Chicanos as never before. He also went to the campuses. When hecklers shouted, "Where was Kennedy when we were in New Hampshire?" Chavez would accurately reply, "He was walking with me in Delano!"[30]

I was on the train when Kennedy whistle-stopped through the Central Valley from Fresno to Sacramento. It was a brilliant, sunny, happy day at the end of May. The crowds were big and enthusiastic. At some stops they were mostly Mexican American. I was enchanted by the mixture of banter and intensity with which he beguiled and exhorted his hearers. At times he launched into wonderful travesties of stump speeches, pointing out how much more he could do for the local product, whatever it might be, because his family consumed more of it than any other family possibly could. Then he would turn with great seriousness to poverty, racial injustice, the war in Vietnam.[31]

Late that night he met with black militants in Oakland. "This may not be a pleasant experience," he warned John Glenn. "These people have got a lot of hostility and lots of reasons for it. When they get somebody like me, they're going to take it out on me. . . . But no matter how insulting a few of them may be, they're trying to communicate what's inside them."[32] After Kennedy talked, questions began. "It was a rough, gut-cutting meeting," said Seigenthaler, who was there, "in which a handful of people stood up and blistered white society and him as a symbol of white society."[33] Willie Brown, the black state assemblyman who was presiding, tried to compose things. They called him a "technicolor nigger." The Olympic decathlon champion, Rafer Johnson, who loved Kennedy, stood up to apologize for his people. They called him an Uncle Tom. Kennedy asked him to sit down. Someone asked acidly what Kennedy really thought of black people. He said he liked some, and some he did not like; also he liked some white people and some he did not like. "Look, man," said a local figure known as Black Jesus, "I don't want to hear none of your shit. What the goddamned hell are you going to do, boy. . . . You bastards haven't did nothing for us. We wants to know, what are you going to do for us?"[34]

They drove back to San Francisco. Seigenthaler said he was sorry, after such a long day, to have exposed Kennedy to this. Kennedy said, "I'm glad I went. . . . I'll tell you why I'm glad I went. They need to know somebody who'll listen."[35] Finally, almost to himself: "after all the abuse the blacks have taken through the centuries, whites are just going to have to let them get some of these feelings out if we are all really ever going to settle down to a decent relationship."[36] It was a long journey from the meeting with James Baldwin almost exactly five years before.

The next morning, they returned to West Oakland for a ghetto rally. There were truculent shouts of "Free Huey!" from a squadron of Black Panthers. To the surprise of the Kennedy party Black Jesus was circulating cheerfully in the crowd. "I put a leaflet out that Kennedy was coming in this area," he said later, "and that I wanted him to be treated with the utmost respect." People told the Black Panthers to shush as Kennedy began to speak. When he finished, the crowd swarmed around the car, reaching out to touch him. The car could not move, so, said Black Jesus, "I walked in front of the car and raised my hand, and they parted so we could get through."[37] The Reverend Hector Lopez, a community adviser: "Then a fascinating thing took place. . . . All of a sudden some Black Panthers got out in front of the car and started shoving the people aside so the car could carry on."[38] Willie Brown looked on with amazement. "The same persons who were raising all the hell and asking all of the very nasty questions and doing all of the loud screaming . . . were the persons who were acting as his guards and . . . clearing the car from the crowds."[39]

Black Americans, Hector Lopez reflected afterward, *believed* Kennedy. "What can you call Bobby? 'the last of the great liberals'? He wouldn't have liked that. I know he wouldn't. I guess I'd have to say he was 'the last of the great believables.' "[40]

IV

It was a tumultuous campaign. Kennedy was mobbed by admirers in Watts, spat on by haters at San Francisco State. The McCarthy campaign, aided by Humphrey money,[41] was hitting hard and cleverly at him. Television and radio spots questioned his courage and integrity. His early lead in the polls began to slip. He was holding his constituency—the blacks, the Chicanos, the poor—but suburban Democrats were sharply divided. The California Democracy had been strong for Adlai Stevenson. McCarthy appealed powerfully to the old Stevenson vote.

The debate, scheduled at last for June 1 in San Francisco, promised to be decisive. The attitude in the McCarthy camp, wrote Larner, was "lofty confidence."[42] Their candidate, they were sure, was cool, articulate, quick, the more mature, the more presidential. Kennedy knew he had to show both that he could handle McCarthy intellectually and, as ever, that he was not ruthless. His staff prepared the customary black, loose-leaf books on the issues. I do not know how carefully Kennedy went through them. But he did hold morning and afternoon briefing sessions that Saturday, meanwhile staring wistfully out the window at San Francisco sparkling in the sunlight below. It was a ravishing day. Around noon he went off to Fisherman's Wharf to campaign a little and savor the air.

We met again in the afternoon. I noted: "Bobby was in excellent form, funny, ironic and very much on the ball."[43] We wondered how to define the differences between the debaters. The Presidency seemed in 1968 too abstract as an issue. Race and the city? Kennedy had long believed that the only way to achieve integration was to give blacks the economic and psychological security that would enable them to become full members of a community. If a choice had to be made, this argued for the use of public money to improve the ghetto. A McCarthy position paper had advocated the dispersal strategy. Mankiewicz said, "Just to take people who are unemployed out of the ghetto and fill Orange County with them or Marin County isn't very helpful because they can't buy those houses anyway."[44]

McCarthy too had his briefing material. Thomas Finney, Clark Clifford's law partner, who had come west to run McCarthy's California campaign, tried to get him to focus on the debate. The managers were by now furious with their candidate's personal coterie. They called them the "astrologers," because they kept second-guessing the professionals.[45] Robert Lowell was the leading astrologer. "We tried to keep Robert Lowell away from McCarthy at very crucial times," said one McCarthy aide, "because we thought he always took the edge off."[46] We were all staying—McCarthyites and Kennedyites—at the Fairmont, San Francisco's traditional hotel for Democrats. I kept running into Lowell, a friend of twenty years, in the lobby. That Saturday morning Lowell, who thought that, if McCarthy lost, his people should support Kennedy and vice versa, had gone to see Kennedy. They had a fairly unsatisfactory talk. Kennedy, in Lowell's view, was making debater's points. Lowell said, "You mustn't talk to me this way." Kennedy said mildly that he guessed there was not much more to say. Lowell said, "I wish I could think up some joke that would cheer you up, but it won't do any good." Afterward he told McCarthy, "I felt like Rudolf Hess parachuting into Scotland."[47]

To the dismay of the professionals, the astrologers slipped through Finney's cordon and reached McCarthy before the debate. They made literary jokes and read poetry. "They castrated him at this point," said Thomas Morgan, McCarthy's press man. David Garth, his television man, rejoined, "No one is ever castrated if he doesn't want to be."[48] On the way to the studio Lowell and McCarthy composed a twentieth-century version of "Ode to St. Cecilia's Day."[49]

The debate was an anticlimax. At most three serious issues emerged. The rivals murkily disagreed as to whether the National Liberation Front should be brought into a coalition government before Vietnam negotiations began (as Kennedy thought McCarthy had been saying) or simply into the South Vietnamese political process (Kennedy's 1966 position). McCarthy went into his sequence about the government officials he planned to fire. Kennedy said, "I don't want to be playing games with people's reputations." The explosive moment came over the question of the ghettos. McCarthy argued for dispersal; Kennedy, for reconstruction. McCarthy called this "practical apartheid." Kennedy said he was all in favor of moving people out of the ghettos; but, at the present time, "to take these people out, put them in suburbs where they can't afford the housing, where their children can't keep up with the schools, and where they don't have the skills for the jobs, it is just going to be catastrophic." He added, "You say you are going to take ten thousand black people and move them into Orange County."[50] This sounded, and was, demagogic. It was not so demagogic as it sounded, however, because it had been Kennedy's consistent position. Later Kennedy told Mankiewicz that he started to say Marin County, but "I forgot at the last minute whether it was Marin or Merrin County [he did not want to demonstrate ignorance of the state by mispronunciation] so I didn't use that."[51] McCarthy replied weakly, saying that he had not understood Kennedy wished to concentrate so much on the ghetto. "One could only conclude," observed the *London Sunday Times* team, "that McCarthy had not been listening to what Kennedy had been saying for several years."[52] (On Tuesday McCarthy beat Kennedy in Orange County.)

Larner watched the debate with surprise. He thought McCarthy had the best of the opening exchange on Vietnam, but "Kennedy had had the guts to get up off the floor and fight it through, while McCarthy, dazed, was taking every punch."[53] At the end McCarthy made a slight comeback. Kennedy, for some reason, did not understand there were to be sum-ups and was caught off guard, and McCarthy was at his most eloquent. The press regarded the debate as a stand-off. But a stand-off, in the context of expectations, was a Kennedy victory. "It was clear," concluded Larner, "that Kennedy could take McCarthy head-on, with no fear of his magic powers. If McCarthy had something new and different going for him in American politics, it did not show in open competition with Kennedy."[54] McCarthy himself looked grim afterward. "He flubbed it!" cried Tom Finney. "He flubbed it!"[55] A *Los Angeles Times* telephone poll showed Kennedy the victor by 2½–1. The slide toward McCarthy stopped.

V

We had a delightful dinner afterward. Hodding Carter, the old Mississippi editor, now nearly blind, joined us. I remember the marked consideration Kennedy, with so much else on his mind, showed him. Then we went on to a fund-raising gala filled with Hollywood stars. Later I took Ethel, who was carrying her eleventh child, back to the

Fairmont.* Robert went on to a party with the performers. The next day I flew east to attend a conference on Vietnam at the University of Chicago.

On Monday, June 3, Kennedy made a final dash around the state. He visited San Francisco's Chinatown, where Abba Schwartz had organized the Chinese Americans. As the car moved through cheering crowds, shots appeared to ring out. Kennedy continued to stand and wave while motioning a friend toward Ethel, who, pale and stricken, had slumped down in her seat. The shots were Chinese firecrackers. Impartially they visited the Japanese Cultural Center, where the Kennedys and Seigenthaler sang the Waseda song. Robert flew back to Los Angeles, spoke in Long Beach, went on to San Diego. By the end of the long day he was worn to the bone and near digestive collapse. He took Ethel and six children for the night to the Malibu beach house of John Frankenheimer, the film director.

He slept late. It was a sullen day. A cold fog hung over the ocean. Theodore White came out for luncheon; later Goodwin and Dutton. Kennedy played with his children on the beach; then plunged into the gray sea. For a moment his son David was caught in the undertow. Kennedy dived and brought him to the surface. The boy's forehead was bruised. When Goodwin arrived, he looked around for Kennedy. He found him by the pool, stretched out across two chairs, his lips slightly parted, motionless. Goodwin's stomach contracted with a spasm of fear. But he was sleeping, only sleeping. "God," Goodwin thought, "I suppose none of us will ever get over John Kennedy."[56]

White called CBS for its early projections. The first reports gave Kennedy 49 percent.† The candidate asked Dutton what could be done in the hours remaining to push it up to 50 percent. Then he yawned and went off for a nap. About six-thirty Frankenheimer drove him to the Hotel Ambassador. He sped furiously along the Santa Monica Freeway. "Take it easy, John," Kennedy said. "Life is too short."[57]

The polls closed earlier in South Dakota. George McGovern called in mid-evening. Kennedy had more votes, he said, than Humphrey and McCarthy, the local boys, combined. He had swept the farmers. He had swept the Indians.[58] In the Kennedy suite they

---

* Rory Elizabeth Katherine Kennedy was born on December 12, 1968.

† This turned out to be optimistic. The final result was 46.3 percent for Kennedy and 41.8 percent for McCarthy. The rest went to a Humphrey slate headed by the state attorney general.

talked about the next steps. Stephen Smith scheduled a series of meetings to work out the campaign reorganization. David Hackett had arrived from the boiler room with a breakdown of state delegations; Humphrey, 944 delegates; Kennedy, 524½; McCarthy, 204; 872 undecided. The objective by convention time was 1432½ for Kennedy, 1152½ for Humphrey.[59]

The key was McCarthy. Looking for a place to talk in the crowded suite, Kennedy finally took Goodwin into a bathroom. "I've got to get free of McCarthy," he said. "While we're fighting each other, Humphrey's running around the country picking up delegates. I don't want to stand on every street corner in New York for the next two weeks [contesting the New York primary]. I've got to spend that time going to the states, talking to delegates before it's too late. My only chance is to chase Hubert's ass all over the country. Maybe he'll fold. . . . Even if McCarthy won't get out, his people must know after tonight that I'm the only candidate against the war that can beat Humphrey."[60] Goodwin began calling the pro-Kennedy wing of the McCarthy movement—Kenneth Gailbraith, Allard Lowenstein—asking whether they did not think the time had arrived to come over. Galbraith said, "I rather [think] this might be so. But I shouldn't do it without going and seeing Gene McCarthy first."[61] Lowenstein said he would come over if Galbraith did.[62]

Old friends milled around the suite—Newfield, Hamill and Breslin, Charles Evers and John Lewis. Kennedy talked to Budd Schulberg about the Watts Writers Workshop. "You've touched a nerve," he said. ". . . This workshop idea of yours is a kind of throwback to the Federal Theater and Writers Project of the New Deal. . . . I'd like to see it on a national scale with Federal help."[63] He spoke to Daley in Chicago, who wished him good luck and hinted that, if he won in California, Illinois would support him at the convention.[64] Jesse Unruh said it was approaching midnight: time to go down to the ballroom. Kennedy looked over suggestions for his victory statement. The draft said how great the McCarthy movement was. "I'd like to say something nice about him personally," Kennedy said.[65]

Failing to find Cesar Chavez, who had gone out in search of his wife, Kennedy asked Dolores Huerta instead to escort him downstairs. Now before the cheering crowd, he thanked those who had helped him: "ruthless" Steve Smith, Chavez, Unruh, Paul Schrade of the UAW, Rafer Johnson and Roosevelt Grier, the two devoted black athletes. "I want to express my gratitude to my dog Freckles, . . . I'm not doing this in any order of importance, but I also want to thank my wife Ethel. Her patience during this whole effort was fantastic."[66]

For a moment he was serious. "Here is [California] the most urban state of any of the states of our Union, South Dakota the most rural of any of the states of our Union. We were able to win them both. I think that we can end the divisions within the United States." He congratulated McCarthy and his followers and asked them to join with him "not for myself, but for the cause and the ideas which moved you to begin this great popular movement."

"What I think is quite clear," he said, "is that we can work together in the last analysis, and that what has been going on within the United States over a period of the last three years—the division, the violence, the disenchantment with our society; the divisions, whether it's between blacks and whites, between the poor and the more affluent, or between age groups or on the war in Vietnam—is that we can start to work together. We are a great country, an unselfish country, and a compassionate country. I intend to make that my basis for running." Jeremy Larner, listening over at the McCarthy hotel, thought it "his best speech of the campaign."[67] The crowd in the ballroom cheered and cheered. Then Kennedy left the room for a press conference, taking a short cut through the kitchen.

*   *   *

I heard the California returns at Saul Bellow's apartment in Chicago. Richard Wade and Frances FitzGerald were with us. When it was evident that Kennedy had won, I went back to my hotel and tried to call him in Los Angeles, but the line was always busy. I went to sleep. The phone rang. Wade said in a choked voice, "Turn on your television. He's been shot."

On Thursday evening I stood with many others in the soft summer night at La Guardia Airport waiting for the plane, as I had waited on a November night in Washington an eon before. Ethel Kennedy, incredibly composed, told me to come to the United Nations Plaza apartment. When I arrived, she was terrifyingly solicitous of stricken friends. Her first words to me were, "You were in Chicago for a meeting, weren't you? Wasn't it on Vietnam? How did it go?" Rose Kennedy was stoically there. Jean Smith and Eunice Shriver said good night to their mother. She said, "I'm so glad all you children are home again."[68]

At the hospital in Los Angeles, Jacqueline Kennedy had told Mankiewicz: "The Church is . . . at its best only at the time of death.

The rest of the time it's often rather silly little men running around in their black suits. But the Catholic Church understands death. I'll tell you who else understands death are the black churches. I remember at the funeral of Martin Luther King. I was looking at those faces, and I realized that they know death. They see it all the time and they're ready for it . . . in the way in which a good Catholic is." Then she said, "We know death. . . . As a matter of fact, if it weren't for the children, we'd welcome it."[69]

Well before dawn Friday morning, lines began to form around St. Patrick's Cathedral. Through the night, friends of Robert Kennedy had stood honor guard by the casket. George McGovern noticed Richard Daley, his head bowed, the cords of his neck standing out, crying uncontrollably.[70] Tom Hayden, the revolutionary, a green cap from Havana sticking out of his pocket, wept silently by himself in a back pew. Jack Newfield remembered the quotation from Pascal that Camus had used in *Resistance, Rebellion and Death:* "A man does not show his greatness by being at one extremity, but rather by touching both at once."[71]

On Saturday morning came the mass at St. Patrick's, with Edward Kennedy's moving speech and the singing of "The Battle Hymn of the Republic." Then the train made its long journey south under the savage sun. I said to O'Donnell, "What marvelous crowds!" He said, "Yes, but what are they good for?" Coretta King looked at Ethel Kennedy and said—who had better earned the right to say it?—"I don't see how she has been able to go through this awful experience with such dignity."[72]

The train arrived in Washington. Night had fallen. Mourners with twinkling candles followed the coffin into Arlington Cemetery. "There was," wrote a grieving Lady Bird Johnson, "a great white moon riding high in the sky."[73] But the cemetery itself was dark and shadowed. The pallbearers, not sure where to place the coffin, walked on uncertainly in the night. Averell Harriman finally said to Stephen Smith, "Steve, do you know where you're going?" Smith said, "Well, I'm not sure." Then Smith said, "I distinctly heard a voice coming out of the coffin saying, 'Damn it. If you fellows put me down, I'll show you the way.'"

Notes

See Acknowledgments for the location of manuscript collections and also for explanations of certain abbreviations. When two or more oral history interviews were held the same day, they are designated by a roman numeral following the date.

Prologue: 1968 (*pages* 1–2)

1. Frank Church of Idaho, *Congressional Record*, July 30, 1968, S9713.
2. The UPI estimate; the Editors of United Press International and Cowles, *Assassination: Robert F. Kennedy—1925–1968*, ed. Francine Klagsbrun and D. C. Whitney (New York, 1968), 201. See also *New York Times*, June 9, 1968.

1. The Family (*pages* 3–21)

1. James Joyce, *Ulysses* (New York, 1961), 34.
2. Rose Fitzgerald Kennedy's memoir, *Times to Remember* (Garden City, N.Y., 1974), is illuminating and indispensable; the verse from a Boston paper is on 10. For the Kennedy family, and Joseph P. Kennedy in particular, there are two serious and instructive, if hostile, biographies: R. J. Whalen, *The Founding Father: The Story of Joseph P. Kennedy* (New York, 1964); and D. E. Koskoff, *Joseph P. Kennedy: A Life and Times* (Englewood Cliffs, N.J., 1974).
3. Gail Cameron, *Rose* (New York: Dell reprint, 1972), 52.
4. As told by James A. Fayne, an old Kennedy associate, to R. J. Whalen, in Whalen, *Founding Father*, 44.
5. E. K. Lindley, "Will Kennedy Run for President?" *Liberty*, May 21, 1938; Whalen, *Founding Father*, 49.
6. Whalen, *Founding Father*, 104.
7. Joe McCarthy, *The Remarkable Kennedys* (New York, 1960), 53.
8. Michael Mooney to RFK, August 10, 1966, RFK Papers.
9. RFK to Mooney, August 18, 1966, RFK Papers.
10. Whalen, *Founding Father*, 74, 61.
11. Edward M. Kennedy, ed., *The Fruitful Bough: A Tribute to Joseph P. Kennedy* (privately printed, 1965), 112.
12. Ibid., 12.

13. McCarthy, *Remarkable Kennedys*, 66.
14. E. M. Kennedy, *Fruitful Bough*, 32.
15. Joseph P. Kennedy, *I'm for Roosevelt* (New York, 1936), 3.
16. Rose Kennedy, *Times to Remember*, 195.
17. McCarthy, *Remarkable Kennedys*, 58.
18. JPK to Felix Frankfurter, December 5, 1933, JPK Papers.
19. Raymond Moley, *The First New Deal* (New York, 1966), 381.
20. JPK to JPK, Jr., May 4, 1934, JPK Papers.
21. Arthur M. Schlesinger, Jr., *The Coming of the New Deal* (Boston, 1958), 467–468.
22. Raymond Moley, *After Seven Years* (New York, 1939), 288.
23. Harold L. Ickes, *The Secret Diary . . . : The First Thousand Days, 1933–1936* (New York, 1953), 173.
24. From a memorandum written by Rose Kennedy, evidently in 1940, JPK Papers.
25. Churchill to JPK, October 12, 1935, JPK Papers.
26. JPK to Churchill, October 19, 1935, JPK Papers.
27. Press conference no. 309, July 29, 1936, in Franklin D. Roosevelt, *Complete Presidential Press Conferences* (New York, 1972), vol. 8, 34–35.
28. Arthur Krock, *Memoirs: Sixty Years on the Firing Line* (New York, 1968), 332.
29. JPK, *I'm for Roosevelt*, 3, 7, 14, 93, 102–107.
30. JPK, address before the Democratic Businessmen's League of Massachusetts, October 24, 1936, Roosevelt Papers.
31. J. P. Kennedy, "The New Deal and Business," radio speech, October 21, 1936, JPK Papers. Kennedy wrote Roosevelt, October 24, 1936, that the speech had been partly written by a French journalist.
32. *New York Times*, January 28, 1957, quoted in William V. Shannon, *The American Irish* (New York, 1963), vii. The second sentence is ordinarily given as "My children were born here," but it makes much less sense that way.
33. JPK to Joseph I. Breen, March 16, 1937, JPK Papers.
34. Mary Bailey Gimbel, in interview by author, February 19, 1975.
35. Rose Kennedy, *Times to Remember*, 79.
36. Jean Stein and George Plimpton, eds., *American Journey* (New York, 1970), 35.
37. Rose Kennedy, *Times to Remember*, 148.
38. In the privately printed memorial volume *As We Remember Joe*, ed. John F. Kennedy (Cambridge, Mass., 1945), 4.
39. JPK, *As We Remember Joe*, 43–44.
40. JPK to Robert W. Bingham, November 11, 1935, JPK Papers.
41. Rose Kennedy, *Times to Remember*, 202.
42. Ibid., 121.
43. James MacG. Burns, *John Kennedy: A Political Profile* (New York, 1960), 28.
44. Myra McPherson, " 'Losing Was Never Funny to Joseph P. Kennedy,' " *Washington Post*, November 19, 1969.
45. Rose Kennedy, *Times to Remember*, 143.
46. E. M. Kennedy, *Fruitful Bough*, 203.
47. Rose Kennedy, *Times to Remember*, 142, 144.
48. E. M. Kennedy, *Fruitful Bough*, 210–211.
49. Stein and Plimpton, *American Journey*, 35.
50. Burns, *John Kennedy*, 20.
51. Stein and Plimpton, *American Journey*, 35.
52. Charles Spalding, in recorded interview by L. J. Hackman, March 22, 1969, 70, RFK Oral History Program.
53. Felicia Warburg Roosevelt, *Doers and Dowagers* (Garden City, N.Y., 1975), 94.
54. Robert F. Kennedy, *The Pursuit of Justice* (New York: Harper & Row, Perennial Library reprint, 1964), 3.
55. Ralph Horton, Jr., in recorded interview by Joseph Dolan, June 1, 1964, 3–4, JFK Oral History Program.

56. JPK to JFK, October 10, 1934, December 5, 1934, April 29, 1935, JPK Papers.
57. Interview with Walter Cronkite, September 19, 1960, in Senate Commerce Committee, *Freedom of Communications*, pt. 3, *The Joint Appearances of Senator John F. Kennedy and Vice President Richard M. Nixon*, 87 Cong., 1 Sess. (1961), 54–55.
58. Stein and Plimpton, *American Journey*, 35.
59. Rose Kennedy, *Times to Remember*, 139.
60. K. LeMoyne Billings, in interview by author, July 8, 1975.
61. Charles Spalding, in interview by author, February 24, 1975.
62. Rose Kennedy, in recorded interview by Felicia Warburg, April 6, 1973, tape in possession of interviewer.
63. Rose Kennedy, *Times to Remember*, 162.
64. Spalding, in interview by author.
65. Rose Kennedy, *Times to Remember*, 163.
66. Jean Kennedy Smith, in interview by author, May 11, 1975.
67. Rose Kennedy to Edward Kennedy, April 18, 1945, JPK Papers.
68. Rose Kennedy to daughters-in-law, December 1, 1960, August 26, 1969, JPK Papers.
69. Rose Kennedy, *Times to Remember*, 148.
70. Charles Spalding, in recorded interview by John Stewart, March 14, 1968, 3–4, JFK Oral History Program.
71. Author's journal, March 7, 1962.
72. Franklin D. Roosevelt, Jr., in recorded interview by Jean Stein, December 9, 1969, Stein Papers.
73. "Ted Kennedy's Memories of JFK: A Conversation with Theodore Sorensen," *McCall's*, November 1973.
74. K. LeMoyne Billings, in recorded interview by Jean Stein, n.d., 13, Stein Papers.
75. E. M. Kennedy, *Fruitful Bough*, 214.
76. Stein and Plimpton, *American Journey*, 35.
77. William Manchester, *Portrait of a President* (Boston, 1962), 187.
78. JPK to JPK, Jr., May 4, 1934, JPK Papers.
79. In a memorandum, "Russia," n.d. but probably c. 1940, JPK Papers.
80. Rose Kennedy, *Times to Remember*, 172–173.
81. Ibid., 210.
82. Ibid., 173.
83. As told by Eunice Kennedy Shriver, in E. M. Kennedy, *Fruitful Bough*, 219.
84. Whalen, *Founding Father*, 171.
85. Waldrop to author, April 18, 1975.
86. As told by William vanden Heuvel in interview with author, May 1, 1975.
87. Joseph F. Dineen, *The Kennedy Family* (Boston, 1959), 110.
88. E. M. Kennedy, *Fruitful Bough*, 214.
89. Ibid., 33.
90. As told to Alexandra Emmet, c. 1961.

2. The Father (*pages* 22–42)

1. Rose Kennedy, *Times to Remember* (Garden City, N.Y., 1974), 102–103.
2. K. LeMoyne Billings, in interview by author, July 8, 1975.
3. Margaret Laing, *The Next Kennedy* (New York, 1968), 64–65.
4. RFK to JPK, April 29, 1935, JPK Papers.
5. Reproduced in the *Washington Post*, February 24, 1970.
6. Ann Geracimos, "Bobby Kennedy Was Here," *New York Herald Tribune*, October 11, 1964.
7. Camp Winona Report, n.d. [1937], JPK Papers.

8. Rose Kennedy, *Times to Remember,* 102.
9. JPK to JPK, Jr., March 2, 1937, JPK Papers.
10. Jack Newfield, *Robert Kennedy: A Memoir* (New York, 1969), 41–42.
11. R. E. Thompson and Hortense Myers, *Robert F. Kennedy: The Brother Within* (New York, 1962), 43.
12. William V. Shannon, *The Heir Apparent: Robert Kennedy and the Struggle for Power* (New York, 1967), 43.
13. D. E. Koskoff, *Joseph P. Kennedy: A Life and Times* (Englewood Cliffs, N.J., 1974), 90.
14. Manuscript of June 1937, JPK Papers.
15. R. J. Whalen, *The Founding Father: The Story of Joseph P. Kennedy* (New York, 1964), 197.
16. Robert I. Gannon, *The Cardinal Spellman Story* (New York: Pocket Books reprint, 1962), 142.
17. Kennedy is not mentioned in the biography of Ryan by F. L. Broderick, *The Right Reverend New Dealer: John A. Ryan* (New York, 1963). See also G. Q. Flynn, *American Catholics and the Roosevelt Presidency, 1932–1936* (Lexington, Ky., 1968).
18. James A. Farley, *Jim Farley's Story: The Roosevelt Years* (New York, 1948), 198.
19. Henry Morgenthau, Jr., diary, April 13, 1935, FDR Papers; Harold L. Ickes, *The Secret Diary . . . : The First Thousand Days, 1933–1936* (New York, 1953), 692.
20. Rose Kennedy, memoranda "The Roosevelts" and "A Description of the President," JPK Papers.
21. W. O. Douglas, *Go East, Young Man* (New York, 1974), 281.
22. Edward Kennedy, ed., *The Fruitful Bough: A Tribute to Joseph P. Kennedy* (privately printed, 1965), 73.
23. Farley, *Jim Farley's Story,* 114–115.
24. Arthur Krock, in recorded interview by Charles Bartlett, May 10, 1964, 3, JFK Oral History Program.
25. Rose Kennedy, memorandum, "London" [c. 1940], JPK Papers.
26. AP dispatch in *Portland Oregonian,* March 10, 1938.
27. Koskoff, *Joseph P. Kennedy,* 377.
28. George F. Kennan, *Memoirs, 1925–1950* (Boston, 1967), 91–92.
29. "From Baseball Captain to Ambassador," unsigned typescript, 14, JPK Papers.
30. Reverend J. Butterworth, "The Ambassador's Sons Help British Youth," n.d., JPK Papers; "Bobby Kennedy, 13, Proves Chip Off the Old (Diplomatic) Block," *New York Herald Tribune,* April 3, 1939.
31. *Washington Star,* November 18, 1969.
32. Nicholas Bethell, *The War Hitler Won* (Mount Kisco, N.Y.: Futura reprint, 1976), 280.
33. Edward Moore to Paul Murphy, January 24, 1939, JPK Papers.
34. Rose Kennedy, *Times to Remember,* 221.
35. Rose Kennedy to FDR, January 8, 1939, Roosevelt Papers.
36. JPK, "Experiences in London" (address at Oglethorpe University, May 24, 1941), 13, JPK Papers.
37. Koskoff, *Joseph P. Kennedy,* 158; see also J. M. Blum, *From the Morgenthau Diaries: Years of Crisis, 1928–1938* (Boston, 1959), 518.
38. Koskoff, *Joseph P. Kennedy,* 129.
39. Rose Kennedy, "Notes on Chamberlain" [c. 1940], JPK Papers.
40. Walter Lippmann to JPK, April 7, 1938, Lippmann Papers.
41. Blum, *Years of Crisis,* 518; Farley, *Jim Farley's Story,* 199.
42. J. P. Moffat, *The Moffat Papers,* ed. N. H. Hooker (Cambridge, 1956), 220–221; Koskoff, *Joseph P. Kennedy,* 158–159.
43. *New York World-Telegram,* October 25, 1938.
44. Franklin D. Roosevelt, *Public Papers . . . 1938* (New York, 1941), 564.

45. Koskoff, *Joseph P. Kennedy*, 149–150, 168.

46. JPK, "Experiences in London," 10–11.

47. JPK, "Summary of Strategic Situation," March 3, 1939, FDR Papers; cited in W. F. Kimball, *The Most Unsordid Act: Lend-Lease, 1939–1941* (Baltimore, 1969), 20–21.

48. Harold Ickes, *Secret Diary . . . : The Inside Struggle, 1936–1939* (New York, 1954), 707.

49. Joseph Alsop and Robert Kintner, *American White Paper: The Story of American Diplomacy and the Second World War* (New York, 1940), 68.

50. JPK to Rose Kennedy, n.d. [September 1939], JPK Papers.

51. Rose Kennedy to Ethel Kennedy, January 30, 1967, JPK Papers.

52. JPK to Rose Kennedy, September 24, 1939, JPK Papers.

53. RFK to his parents, n.d. [April 1942], Hyannis Port Papers.

54. RFK to Rose Kennedy, n.d., JPK Papers.

55. *Boston Record,* November 22, 1939.

56. RFK to his parents, n.d. [November 1940], Hyannis Port Papers.

57. See report card, February 21, 1941, JPK Papers.

58. RFK letter to his mother, n.d. [spring 1940], Hyannis Port Papers.

59. Reverend Gregory Borgstedt to JPK, March 8, 1940, JPK Papers.

60. Francis I. Brady, assistant headmaster, to Rose Kennedy, May 6, 1941, JPK Papers.

61. RFK to his parents, n.d. [October 1941], Hyannis Port Papers.

62. RFK to his parents, n.d. [January or February 1942], Hyannis Port Papers.

63. RFK to his parents, n.d. [November 1941], Hyannis Port Papers.

64. RFK to his parents, n.d. [January or February 1942], Hyannis Port Papers.

65. Interview with Edward M. Kennedy, February 23, 1973.

66. Whalen, *Founding Father,* 285.

67. W. L. Langer and S. E. Gleason, *The Challenge to Isolation, 1937–1940* (New York, 1952), 345.

68. Robert Murphy, *Diplomat among Warriors* (New York, 1964), 38.

69. *Spectator,* March 8, 1940; Alexander Kendrick, *Prime Time: The Life of Edward R. Murrow* (Boston, 1969), 192.

70. Raymond E. Lee, *London Journal . . . 1940–1941,* ed. James Leutze (Boston, 1971), 219, 241.

71. O. H. Bullitt, *For the President: Personal and Secret Correspondence Between Franklin D. Roosevelt and William C. Bullitt* (Boston, 1972), 437.

72. Koskoff, *Joseph P. Kennedy,* 239.

73. Bethell, *War Hitler Won,* 283, 285.

74. JPK to Rose Kennedy, March 14, 1940, JPK Papers.

75. Rose Kennedy to JPK, March 31 [1940], JPK Papers.

76. JPK to Rose Kennedy, April 26, 1940, JPK Papers.

77. Cordell Hull, *Memoirs* (New York, 1948), vol. 1, 766.

78. FDR to JPK, May 3, 1940, in Franklin D. Roosevelt, *His Personal Letters, 1928–1945,* ed. Elliott Roosevelt and Joseph P. Lash (New York, 1950), vol. 2, 1020.

79. JPK to Rose Kennedy, May 20, 1940, JPK Papers.

80. Koskoff, *Joseph P. Kennedy,* 263.

81. Rose Kennedy to JPK, letters in JPK Papers.

82. JPK to Rose Kennedy, September 10, 1940, JPK Papers.

83. Ibid.

84. Herbert Hoover, memorandum, May 15, 1945, Hoover Papers. See also Kennedy's discussion with James V. Forrestal in 1945 of Chamberlain's conviction "that America and the world Jews had forced England into the war." James V. Forrestal, *The Forrestal Diaries,* ed. Walter Millis (New York, 1951), 122.

85. JPK, draft autobiography, ch. 17, Landis Papers.

86. Koskoff, *Joseph P. Kennedy,* 166, 188.

87. [D. W. Brogan], "R.F.K.," *Times Literary Supplement,* August 1, 1968. The review was of course unsigned in that benighted period. I make this confident attribution on the basis of internal evidence.

88. FDR to JPK, August 28, 1940, in Roosevelt, *Personal Letters,* vol. 2, 1061; Koskoff, *Joseph P. Kennedy,* 268.

89. James F. Byrnes, *All in One Lifetime* (New York, 1958), 125.

90. Lee, *London Journal,* 115.

91. Krock, *Memoirs,* 335.

92. Rose Kennedy, "Visit to Washington" [c. 1941], JPK Papers.

93. Byrnes, *All in One Lifetime,* 126.

94. *Boston Globe,* November 10, 1940.

95. Charles A. Lindbergh, *Wartime Journals* (New York, 1970), 420.

96. JPK to Harvey Klemmer, August 4, 1941, JPK Papers.

97. RFK to JPK, January 18, 1941, JPK Papers.

98. RFK to Rose Kennedy, n.d. [January 1941], JPK Papers.

99. Koskoff, *Joseph P. Kennedy,* 309.

100. Kimball, *Most Unsordid Act,* 191; Koskoff, *Joseph P. Kennedy,* 309.

101. Harry Golden, "The Bobby Twins Revisited," *Esquire,* June 1965.

102. Transcript of interview with JPK by Charles Colebaugh and William Hillman of *Collier's,* November 26, 1940, JPK Papers.

103. JPK to Charles F. Adams, April 7, 1941, JPK Papers.

104. Frank Waldrop to author, April 18, 1975.

105. JPK to Adams.

106. Kennedy, "Experiences in London," passim.

107. Koskoff, *Joseph P. Kennedy,* 313–314.

108. Herbert Hoover to JPK, July 1, 1941, JPK to Hoover, July 11, 29, 1941, Hoover Papers.

109. JPK, Jr., to John T. Flynn, January 3, 1941, JPK Papers.

110. March 9, 1941; see flier in JPK Papers.

111. JPK to Landis, August 6, 1940, Landis Papers.

112. Burns, *John Kennedy,* 42.

113. John F. Kennedy, *Why England Slept* (New York: Doubleday, Dolphin reprint, 1962), 178, 184–185.

114. Joan Blair and Clay Blair, Jr., *In Search of J. F. K.* (New York, 1975), 113–144.

3. The War (*pages* 43–65)

1. RFK to his parents, n.d. [January or February 1942], Hyannis Port Papers.

2. RFK to Rose Kennedy, n.d. [spring 1942], Hyannis Port Papers.

3. Rose Kennedy to the children, January 5, 1942, JPK Papers.

4. RFK to his parents, n.d. [January 1942], Hyannis Port Papers.

5. Rose Kennedy to the children, February 2, 1942, JPK Papers.

6. Rose Kennedy to RFK, January 12, 1942, RFK Papers.

7. Mary Bailey Gimbel, in interview by author, February 19, 1975.

8. RFK to Rose Kennedy, December 7, 1942, Hyannis Port Papers.

9. RFK to JPK, n.d. [March or April 1943], Hyannis Port Papers.

10. Samuel Adams, in recorded interview by Jean Stein, May 1970, 2, Stein Papers.

11. RFK to his parents, n.d. [January 1953], Hyannis Port Papers.

12. *Dedham County Recorder,* September 10, 1943. For more on Clem Norton, see my introduction to *The Best and Last of Edwin O'Connor,* ed. Arthur M. Schlesinger, Jr. (Boston, 1970), 10.

13. RFK to JPK, December 13, 1942, Hyannis Port Papers.

14. RFK to Rose Kennedy, n.d. [September 1943], JPK Papers.

15. Patricia Kennedy Lawford, ed., *That Shining Hour* (n.p., 1969), 5.

16. RFK to JPK, n.d. [October 1943], Hyannis Port Papers.
17. Mary Bailey Gimbel, in interview by author; Jean Stein and George Plimpton, eds., *American Journey: The Times of Robert Kennedy* (New York, 1970).
18. Adams, in Stein interview, 2–4.
19. Lawford, *That Shining Hour,* 6.
20. RFK to Rose Kennedy, n.d. [early 1943], Hyannis Port Papers.
21. RFK to Rose Kennedy, n.d. [January 1944], Hyannis Port Papers.
22. JPK to Kathleen Kennedy, January 17, 1944, JPK Papers.
23. Adams, in Stein interview, 1; Mary Bailey Gimbel, in interview by Jean Stein, n.d., 2–3, Stein Papers.
24. John Knowles, *A Separate Peace* (New York, Bantam reprint, 1966), 6, 195.
25. David Hackett, in recorded interview by John Douglas, July 22, 1970, 4, RFK Oral History Program.
26. David Hackett, in interview by author, January 27, 1975.
27. Adams, in Stein interview, 1.
28. Cleveland Amory, "Curmudgeon-at-Large," *Saturday Review,* September 7, 1974.
29. Albert Norris to Rose Kennedy, January 3, 1943[4], JPK Papers.
30. Norris to author, March 6, 1975.
31. Arthur B. Perry to JPK, January 15, 1944, JPK Papers.
32. JPK to FDR, December 7, 1941, March 4, 1942, JPK Papers. See also Franklin D. Roosevelt, *His Personal Letters, 1928–1945,* ed. Elliott Roosevelt and Joseph P. Lash (New York, 1950), vol. 2, 1289–1290.
33. JPK to Beaverbrook, August 12, 1942, Beaverbrook Papers.
34. David E. Koskoff, *Joseph P. Kennedy: A Life and Times* (Englewood Cliffs, N.J., 1974), 318, 577.
35. J. P. Lash, ed., *From the Diaries of Felix Frankfurter* (New York, 1974), 238.
36. Henry A. Wallace, *The Price of Vision: The Diary . . . 1942–1946,* ed. J. M. Blum (Boston, 1973), 144.
37. JPK to Kent, March 2, 1943, JPK Papers.
38. Kennedy to Beaverbrook, August 12, 1942, Beaverbrook Papers.
39. W. V. Shannon, *The American Irish* (New York, 1963), 357.
40. Constance Casey, in interview by author, May 14, 1975. The Caseys, who were political realists, understood the problem and were in later years good friends of John and Robert Kennedy's.
41. *Boston Herald,* August 16, 1942.
42. Edward M. Kennedy, ed., *The Fruitful Bough* (n.p., 1965), 242–243.
43. Arthur Krock, *Memoirs: Sixty Years on the Firing Line* (New York, 1968), 357.
44. JPK to Frank Kent, March 2, 1943, JPK Papers.
45. JFK to his parents, May 14, 1943, JPK Papers.
46. JFK to Henry ———, n.d. [August or September 1943], JPK Papers.
47. JFK to his parents, September 12, 1943, JPK Papers.
48. JFK to his parents, n.d. [November 1943], JPK Papers.
49. Susan Mary Alsop, *To Marietta from Paris, 1945–1960* (Garden City, N.Y., 1975), 90, 92.
50. Rose Kennedy, *Times to Remember* (New York, 1974), 285.
51. JPK to Rev. Maurice S. Sheehy, October 28, 1942, JPK Papers.
52. JFK to RFK, November 21, 1942, RFK Papers. General Lewis Hershey was, of course, director of the Selective Service System.
53. JFK to RFK, postmarked January 10, 1943, JPK Papers.
54. JPK to JFK, April 22, 1943, JPK Papers.
55. JFK to JPK, n.d. [autumn 1943], JPK Papers.
56. *Boston Record,* October 12, 1943.
57. JPK, Jr., to his parents, November 9, 1943, JPK Papers.
58. JFK to RFK, November 14, 1943, in R. J. Donovan, *PT 109* (New York, 1961), 236.

59. RFK to his parents, n.d. [March 1944], Hyannis Port Papers.

60. JPK to RFK, April 6, 1944, JPK Papers.

61. RFK to JPK, Jr., n.d. [spring 1944], JPK Papers.

62. RFK to parents, n.d. [spring 1944], RFK Papers.

63. The letter was addressed to "Mr. David Draftdodger Hackett," n.d. [April 1944], Hackett Papers.

64. To "Mr. David (the Brain) Hackett," postmarked April 3, 1944, Hackett Papers.

65. To "Pvt. David Low Hackett," postmarked September 5, 1944, Hackett Papers.

66. Rose Kennedy, *Times to Remember*, 30.

67. Kathleen Kennedy to JFK, July 29 [1943], in Rose Kennedy, *Times to Remember*, 292.

68. JPK, Jr., to JPK, April 10, 1944, JPK Papers.

69. JPK to Kathleen, April 1944, in E. M. Kennedy, *Fruitful Bough*, 208.

70. JPK to Kathleen, April 27, 1944, JPK Papers.

71. John F. Kennedy, ed., *As We Remember Joe* (Cambridge, Mass., 1945), 54.

72. Wallace, *Price of Vision*, 328.

73. Jean Kennedy Smith, in interview by author, September 7, 1975.

74. JPK to Beaverbrook, May 24, 1944, Beaverbrook Papers.

75. For more on Joseph P. Kennedy, Jr., see Hank Searls, *The Lost Prince: Young Joe, The Forgotten Kennedy* (New York, 1969); and Jack Olsen, *Aphrodite: Desperate Mission* (New York, 1970).

76. JFK, *As We Remember Joe*, 5.

77. Joe McCarthy, *The Remarkable Kennedys* (New York, 1960), 106.

78. JPK to Grace Tully, August 29, 1944, in Koskoff, *Joseph P. Kennedy*, 374–375.

79. *Boston Record*, May 9, 1957.

80. JPK to Beaverbrook, October 23, 1944, Beaverbrook Papers.

81. See, e.g., R. J. Whalen, *The Founding Father: The Story of Joseph P. Kennedy* (New York, 1964), 370; and Koskoff, *Joseph P. Kennedy*, 335.

82. Rose Kennedy, *Times to Remember*, 301.

83. RFK to Hackett, postmarked January 23, 1945, Hackett Papers.

84. Joan Blair and Clay Blair, Jr., *In Search of J. F. K.* (New York, 1976), 346.

85. RFK to his parents, n.d. [January 1945], Hyannis Port Papers.

86. Kathleen to family, February 27, 1945, JPK Papers.

87. RFK to Hackett, postmarked January 26, 1945, Hackett Papers.

88. RFK to Hackett, n.d. [November 1944], Hackett Papers.

89. RFK to Hackett, postmarked January 26, 1945, Hackett Papers.

90. RFK to Hackett, postmarked March 13, 1945, Hackett Papers.

91. RFK to Hackett, postmarked April 20, 1945, Hackett Papers.

92. RFK to Hackett, postmarked May 4, 1945, Hackett Papers.

93. JPK to RFK, January 8, 1945, RFK Papers.

94. RFK to his parents, n.d. [January 1945], Hyannis Port Papers.

95. JPK to RFK, January 29, 1945, JPK Papers.

96. RFK to his parents, n.d. [January 1945], Hyannis Port Papers.

97. JPK to RFK, March 28, 1945, March 31, 1945, May 21, 1945, JPK Papers.

98. JPK to Beaverbrook, October 23, 1944, Beaverbrook Papers.

99. JPK to Kathleen, May 1, 1945, JPK Papers.

100. "This story, which Bobby's father told for the first time last week . . ." (*Newsweek*, April 1, 1957).

101. Roy M. Mundorff, Commander, USNR, To Whom It May Concern, February 1, 1945, Hyannis Port Papers.

102. RFK to his parents, February 8, 1946, Hyannis Port Papers.

103. RFK to Billings, March 10 [1946], Hyannis Port Papers.

104. RFK to his parents, February 8, 1946, Hyannis Port Papers.

105. *The Forrestal Diaries*, ed. Walter Millis (New York, 1951), 134.

106. RFK to his parents, n.d. [March 1946], Hyannis Port Papers.

107. Charles Spalding, in recorded interview by L. J. Hackman, March 22, 1969, 4, RFK Oral History Program.
108. Joseph Dolan, in recorded interview by L. J. Hackman, April 11, 1970, RFK Oral History Program.

4. The Third Son (*pages* 66–93)

1. RFK to his mother, n.d. [May 1946], Hyannis Port Papers.
2. Paul Fay, *The Pleasure of His Company* (New York, 1966), 156–157.
3. Robert Kennedy, in recorded interview by John Stewart, July 20, 1967, 6–7, JFK Oral History Program.
4. RFK, in Stewart interview, 11.
5. Ralph G. Martin and Ed Plaut, *Front Runner, Dark Horse* (New York, 1960), 141.
6. Kenneth P. O'Donnell and David F. Powers, *"Johnny, We Hardly Knew Ye"* (Boston, 1972), 67–68.
7. K. LeMoyne Billings, in interview by author, July 8, 1975.
8. William Manchester, *Portrait of a President* (Boston, 1962), 21.
9. Otis N. Minot to JPK, April 9, 1947, JPK Papers.
10. Payson S. Wild to author, September 16, 1975.
11. R. E. Thompson and Hortense Myers, *Robert F. Kennedy: The Brother Within* (New York, 1962), 76.
12. Samuel Adams, in recorded interview by Jean Stein, May 1970, 7, Stein Papers.
13. George Plimpton, in recorded interview by Jean Stein, September 4, 1968, 1, Stein Papers.
14. John Knowles, in recorded interview by Roberta Greene, July 2, 1974, 5–7, RFK Oral History Program.
15. Anthony Lewis, in recorded interview by Jean Stein, November 7, 1968, 1, Stein Papers; Lewis, in recorded interview by L. J. Hackman, July 23, 1970, RFK Oral History Program.
16. Eunice Kennedy Shriver, in recorded interview by Roberta Greene, April 29, 1971, 19–20, RFK Oral History Program; John Deedy, "Whatever Happened to Father Feeney?" *The Critic,* May–June 1973. The intercession of Cushing's successor, Humberto Cardinal Medeiros, brought about the removal of Feeney's excommunication in 1972 (*Time,* October 14, 1974).
17. Patricia Kennedy Lawford, ed., *That Shining Hour* (n.p., 1969), 17–18; George Sullivan in the *Boston Herald Traveler,* June 6, 1968; William V. Shannon, *The Heir Apparent* (New York, 1967), 44–45; Margaret Laing, *The Next Kennedy* (New York, 1968), 100.
18. William J. Brady, Jr., in recorded interview by Roberta Greene, November 5, 1974, 7, 23, RFK Oral History Program.
19. Kenneth O'Donnell, in recorded interview by Jean Stein, October 8, 1968, 7–9, Stein Papers; Jean Stein and George Plimpton, eds., *American Journey* (New York, 1970), 39.
20. Thompson and Myers, *Robert F. Kennedy,* 77.
21. Brady, in Greene interview, 30.
22. Stein and Plimpton, *American Journey,* 39.
23. Eunice Kennedy Shriver, in interview by Roberta Greene, April 29, 1971, 8–9, and January 13, 1972, 24, RFK Oral History Program.
24. O'Donnell, in Stein interview, 24.
25. George Sullivan, *Boston Herald Traveler,* June 6, 1968.
26. Thompson and Myers, *Robert F. Kennedy,* 76.
27. R. J. Whalen, *The Founding Father: The Story of Joseph P. Kennedy* (New York, 1964), 409.

28. Joseph P. Lash, ed., *From the Diaries of Felix Frankfurter* (New York, 1975), 311, 340.

29. *New York Times,* January 14, 1952.

30. W. O. Douglas, *Go East, Young Man* (New York, 1974), 200.

31. Joseph P. Kennedy, "The U.S. and the World," *Life,* March 18, 1946.

32. *Boston Sunday Advertiser,* May 25, 1947.

33. "Why Must There Be either War or the Marshall Plan?" draft article, evidently intended for *Life,* n.d. [spring 1948], JPK Papers.

34. Ibid.

35. Jefferson to Thomas Leiper, in Jefferson, *Writings,* ed. P. L. Ford (New York, 1895), vol. 9, 445–446.

36. "Why War or the Marshall Plan?"; another draft article, untitled and undated, in JPK Papers; see also J. P. Kennedy, "A Marshall Plan for the Americas," *PIC,* October 1948.

37. JPK to Beaverbrook, March 23, 1948, Beaverbrook Papers.

38. O'Donnell, in Stein interview, 2–3.

39. Ibid., 6–7. George Sullivan, the water boy, recalled Kennedy and O'Donnell "always discussing and arguing politics and their teammates eagerly joined in" (*Boston Herald Traveler,* June 6, 1968).

40. O'Donnell, in Stein interview, 4–5; Stein and Plimpton, *American Journey,* 38–39.

41. O'Donnell, in Stein interview, 4.

42. Kenneth O'Donnell, "Joseph Kennedy Felt the Generation Gap," *London Sunday Telegraph,* November 23, 1969. In *A Thousand Days: John F. Kennedy at the White House* (Boston, 1965), I describe an incident in which O'Donnell defended Franklin Roosevelt with such vigor that Mr. Kennedy, deeply angered, left the table (93). Robert Kennedy told me the story, but he evidently got the two occasions confused.

43. JPK to Beaverbrook, March 23, 1948, Beaverbrook Papers.

44. RFK's documentation is in the JPK Papers.

45. Felicia Warburg Roosevelt, *Doers and Dowagers* (Garden City, N.Y., 1975), 9.

46. RFK's handwritten diary is in the RFK Papers. A typed version in the JPK Papers has errors of transcription. Subsequent RFK quotations about the trip, not otherwise identified, are from the diary.

47. Beaverbrook to JPK, March 12, 1948, Beaverbrook Papers.

48. RFK to his parents, n.d. [March 1948], Hyannis Port Papers.

49. G. E. Georgossy to Phil Reisman, March 31, 1948, Hyannis Port Papers.

50. Rose Kennedy to RFK, April 2, 1948, Hyannis Port Papers.

51. RFK to his parents, April 6, 1948, Hyannis Port Papers.

52. Alastair Forbes, "Upper Classmates," *Times Literary Supplement,* March 26, 1976; Forbes, "Camelot Confidential," *Times Literary Supplement,* June 13, 1975.

53. RFK to Patricia Kennedy, June 5, 1948, Lawford Papers.

54. RFK to his parents, June 30, 1948, Hyannis Port Papers.

55. RFK to his parents, from Grand Hotel, Stockholm, n.d. [July 1948], RFK Papers.

56. RFK to Paul Murphy, n.d. [July 1948], JPK Papers.

57. *Boston Advertiser,* January 16, 1949.

58. Thompson and Myers, *Robert F. Kennedy,* 46–47.

59. W. H. White to RFK, April 19, 1948, JPK Papers.

60. RFK to Paul Murphy, n.d. [April 1948], and cable, June 5, 1948, JPK Papers.

61. RFK to Patricia Kennedy, June 5, 1948, Lawford Papers.

62. E. G. Spies to Paul Murphy, June 7, 1948, JPK Papers.

63. Charles Spalding, in recorded interview by L. J. Hackman, March 22, 1969, 10, RFK Oral History Program.

64. The paper is in the Charles O. Gregory Papers, University of Virginia Law Library. I am much in debt to Frances Farmer, the librarian, for her generous assistance in gathering material about Robert Kennedy's Law School career.

65. RFK, "The Reserve Powers of the Constitution," JPK Papers.
66. Robert F. Kennedy, "A Critical Analysis of the Conference at Yalta, February 4–11, 1945," 9, 16, 19, 20, 34, 37.
67. JPK, "An American Policy . . . for Americans," JPK Papers.
68. *Congressional Record,* January 1, 1951, A8378–A8379; D. E. Koskoff, *Joseph P. Kennedy* (Englewood Cliffs, N.J., 1974), 353–356.
69. Whalen, *Founding Father,* 408.
70. RFK, in recorded interview by Anthony Lewis, December 4, 1964, I, 5, JFK Oral History Program; Bunche to RFK, March 16, 1951, Barrett Prettyman Papers.
71. RFK to Colgate W. Darden, March 7, 1951, University of Virginia Archives.
72. For the Bunche incident, I am indebted to Charles O. Gregory for a letter of September 13, 1975, and to Hardy Dillard for an interview on October 20, 1975. See also Laing, *Next Kennedy,* 120–121; Victor Lasky, *Robert F. Kennedy: The Myth and the Man* (New York: Pocket Book reprint, 1971), 69.
73. Frances Farmer to author, December 2, 1975.
74. Jean Kennedy Smith, in interview by author, September 15, 1975.
75. George Skakel to JPK, December 22, 1950, JPK Papers.
76. Lester David, *Ethel: The Story of Mrs. Robert F. Kennedy* (New York: Dell reprint, 1972), 53.
77. Jean Kennedy Smith, in interview by author, May 18, 1975.
78. Rose Kennedy, *Times to Remember* (Garden City, N.Y., 1974), 109.
79. RFK to Patricia Kennedy, n.d. [spring 1950], Lawford Papers.
80. Stein and Plimpton, *American Journey,* 39–40; see also Brady, in Greene interview, 34.
81. K. LeMoyne Billings, in interview by author, July 8, 1975.
82. K. LeM. Billings, in recorded interview by Jean Stein, n.d., 15, Stein Papers.
83. Eunice Kennedy Shriver, in Greene interview, 14, 33; Patricia Kennedy Lawford, in interview by author, July 2, 1975.

5. The Brothers: I (*pages* 94–102)

1. The exact dates were: Kathleen, July 4, 1951; Joe, III, September 24, 1952; Bobby, Jr., January 17, 1954; David, June 15, 1955; Courtney, September 9, 1956.
2. RFK, "U.S. Must Deal with New Asia," *Boston Post,* September 8, 1951.
3. James M. Landis to JPK, September 7, 1951, Landis Papers.
4. RFK to JPK, October 10, 1951, Hyannis Port Papers.
5. RFK's journal is in the RFK Papers. The account of this trip is drawn also from RFK, in recorded interview by John Stewart, July 20, 1967, RFK Papers; and from author's interview with Patricia Kennedy Lawford, July 2, 1975.
6. RFK to JPK, October 10, 1951, Hyannis Port Papers.
7. RFK to JPK, n.d. [October 1951], Hyannis Port Papers.
8. Theodore C. Sorensen, *Kennedy* (New York, 1965), 34.
9. JFK, "Report on His Trip to the Middle and Far East," speech over the Mutual Broadcasting Network, November 14, 1951, JPK Papers.
10. RFK, in Stewart interview, 21.
11. JPK, "Our Foreign Policy, Its Casualties and Prospects," address before the Economic Club of Chicago and broadcast over the Mutual Broadcasting Network, December 17, 1951, 2–4, 6–7, 9, 13, JPK Papers.
12. *New York Times,* November 25, 1952; R. J. Whalen, *The Founding Father* (New York, 1964), 436.
13. Ralph G. Martin and Ed Plaut, *Front Runner, Dark Horse* (New York, 1960), 195.
14. Kenneth P. O'Donnell and David F. Powers with Joe McCarthy, *"Johnny, We Hardly Knew Ye"* (Boston, 1972), 81.
15. Jean Stein and George Plimpton, eds., *American Journey: The Times of Robert*

Kennedy (New York, 1970), 40–41; Kenneth O'Donnell, in recorded interview with Jean Stein, October 8, 1968, 12–13, Stein Papers.

16. Stein and Plimpton, *American Journey*, 40.
17. O'Donnell and Powers, *"Johnny,"* 83; Stein and Plimpton, *American Journey*, 41.
18. O'Donnell, in Stein interview, 16.
19. RFK, in Stewart interview, 30, 41–42.
20. Martin and Plaut, *Front Runner*, 176.
21. Stein and Plimpton, *American Journey*, 42.
22. O'Donnell and Powers, *"Johnny,"* 87.
23. Martin and Plaut, *Front Runner*, 165.
24. O'Donnell and Powers, *"Johnny,"* 88.
25. RFK, in Stewart interview, 29.
26. O'Donnell, in Stein interview, 15–16.
27. Lawrence F. O'Brien, *No Final Victories* (New York, 1974), 30.
28. Margaret Laing, *The Next Kennedy* (New York, 1968), 128–129.
29. K. LeMoyne Billings, in recorded interview by Jean Stein, n.d., 2, Stein Papers.
30. Burton Hersh, *The Education of Edward Kennedy: A Family Biography* (New York, 1972), 57.
31. O'Donnell, "Joseph Kennedy Felt the Generation Gap," *London Sunday Telegraph*, November 23, 1969.
32. *Boston Record,* May 9, 1957.
33. William O. Douglas, in recorded interview by John Stewart, November 9, 1967, 14, JFK Oral History Program.
34. Paul Dever to the author, c. 1953.
35. Billings, in Stein interview, 4.
36. John Seigenthaler, in an interview during the Democratic convention of 1960; Seigenthaler, in recorded interview by W. A. Geoghegan, July 1, 1964, 86, JFK Oral History Program.
37. Joe McCarthy, *The Remarkable Kennedys* (New York, 1960), 30.
38. JPK, in interview by Charles Spalding, February 24, 1975.
39. Arthur Krock, *Memoirs: Sixty Years on the Firing Line* (New York, 1968), 354.
40. Jacqueline Onassis, in interview by author, June 3, 1976.

6. The First Investigating Committee: Joe McCarthy (*pages* 103–125)

1. I have combined the stories as recalled by O'Donnell (Jean Stein and George Plimpton, eds., *American Journey: The Times of Robert Kennedy* [New York, 1970], 45) and O'Brien (Lawrence F. O'Brien, *No Final Victories* [Garden City, N.Y., 1974], 41–42).
2. Roy Cohn repeats this claim in *McCarthy* (New York, 1968); McCarthy's Marine commander, Glenn L. Todd, told Joan and Clay Blair, "I doubt that Joe met Kennedy in the South Pacific" (Joan Blair and Clay Blair, Jr., *The Search for J. F. K.* [New York, 1976], 298).
3. Jack Alexander, "The Senate's Remarkable Upstart," *Saturday Evening Post*, August 9, 1947.
4. I take this date from Cohn, *McCarthy,* 8.
5. Richard Rovere, *Senator Joe McCarthy* (London, 1960), 9.
6. JPK, in North American Newspaper Alliance interview with P. D. Garvan, May 20, 1951, Landis Papers.
7. Cohn, *McCarthy,* 47.
8. Theodore C. Sorensen, *The Kennedy Legacy* (New York, 1969), 41. In 1959 Kennedy told James MacGregor Burns that he had opposed Robert's joining the McCarthy staff (J. MacG. Burns, *John Kennedy: A Political Profile* [New York, 1960], 152). Kenneth O'Donnell wrote, "Jack had been strongly opposed to

Bobby joining McCarthy's staff" (Kenneth P. O'Donnell and David F. Powers, *"Johnny, We Hardly Knew Ye"* [Boston, 1972], 111).

9. Cohn, *McCarthy,* 47, 66.
10. Patricia Kennedy Lawford, ed., *That Shining Hour* (n.p., 1969), 45–46.
11. John Kelso, in the *Boston Post,* April 12, 1953.
12. *Congressional Record,* May 14, 1953, 5078–5080. It was the *London Sunday Express* of April 19, 1953.
13. Senate Permanent Subcommittee on Investigations, *Control of Trade with the Soviet Bloc: Hearings,* pt. 1, 83 Cong., 1 Sess. (March 30–31, 1953), 29.
14. *Boston Post,* April 12, 1953.
15. F. D. Flanagan to RFK, April 2, 1953, RFK Papers.
16. LaVern Duffy, in interview by author, January 23, 1976.
17. Senate Permanent Subcommittee on Investigations, *Control of Trade with the Soviet Bloc: Hearings,* pt. 2, 83 Cong., 1 Sess. (May 4 and 20, 1953), 110, 125–126, 142.
18. *New York Journal-American,* May 6, 1953.
19. *Congressional Record,* May 19, 1953, 6448–6456.
20. Permanent Subcommittee on Investigations, *Control of Trade: Hearings,* pt. 2, 146.
21. Sherman Adams, *Firsthand Report* (New York: Popular Library reprint, 1962), 143.
22. *Boston Traveler,* May 26, 1953; *New York Times,* May 26, 1953; Cohn, *McCarthy,* 69–70.
23. Permanent Subcommittee on Investigations, *Control of Trade: Interim Report,* 83 Cong., 1 Sess. (1953), 13, 18.
24. *New York Times,* July 19, 1953.
25. *Washington Star,* August 26, 1954.
26. F. P. Carr to RFK, July 24, 1953, RFK Papers.
27. R. E. Thompson and Hortense Myers, *Robert F. Kennedy: The Brother Within* (New York: 1962), 112, 120–121; Robert F. Kennedy, *The Enemy Within* (New York: Popular Library reprint, 1960), 170, 291.
28. Stein and Plimpton, *American Journey,* 50.
29. Rovere, *Senator Joe McCarthy,* 51.
30. Thompson and Myers, *Robert F. Kennedy,* 121.
31. Kenneth O'Donnell, in recorded interview by Jean Stein, October 8, 1968, Stein Papers; Stein and Plimpton, *American Journey,* 49.
32. William McC. Blair, Jr., in recorded interview by Jean Stein, September 5, 1968, 2, Stein Papers.
33. Stein and Plimpton, *American Journey,* 50.
34. RFK to McCarthy, July 29, 1953, Symington to RFK, July 31, 1953, Jackson to RFK, July 31, 1953, RFK Papers.
35. Edward M. Kennedy, ed., *The Fruitful Bough* (n.p., 1965), 126.
36. RFK, memorandum, December 2, 1953, JPK Papers.
37. RFK, memorandum, November 16, 1953, JPK Papers.
38. K. LeMoyne Billings, in recorded interview by Jean Stein, n.d., 5, Stein Papers.
39. O'Brien, *No Final Victories,* 46.
40. Billings, in Stein interview; Billings, in interview by author, July 8, 1975.
41. *New York Times,* February 16, 1954.
42. RFK to the editor of the *Times,* February 17, 1954; copy to author, March 2, 1954, RFK Papers.
43. Sorensen, *Kennedy Legacy,* 36.
44. Herbert Hoover to RFK, February 19, 1954, Hoover Papers.
45. M. A. Jones to Louis B. Nichols, "Robert Francis Kennedy; Request to Meet the Director," July 20, 1955, RFK/FBI/FOIA release.
46. Charles E. Potter, *Days of Shame* (New York, 1965), 42.
47. Rovere, *Senator Joe McCarthy,* 37.

48. RFK to Hoover, n.d. [February 1954], Hoover Papers.
49. Potter, *Days of Shame,* 107.
50. Senate Permanent Subcommittee on Investigations, *Army Signal Corps—Subversion and Espionage: Hearings,* pt. 10, 83 Cong., 2 Sess. (March 11, 1954), 452–453.
51. Ibid., 458, 462.
52. Jones to Nichols, "Kennedy, Request to Meet Director."
53. RFK, in recorded interview by Anthony Lewis, December 4, 1964, IV, 23, RFK Papers.
54. John Kelso, in the *Boston Post,* April 4, 1954.
55. Cohn, *McCarthy,* 71. Jackson's interrogation is in Senate Special Subcommittee on Investigations, *Special Senate Investigation on Charges and Countercharges Involving: Secretary of the Army Robert T. Stevens, John G. Adams, H. Struve Hensel and Senator Joe McCarthy, Roy M. Cohn, and Francis P. Carr. Hearing,* pt. 63, 83 Cong., 2 Sess. (June 11, 1954), 2613–2617.
56. Michael Straight, *Trial by Television* (Boston, 1954), 192.
57. *New York Times,* June 12, 1954; *New York Daily News,* June 12, 1954.
58. LaVern Duffy, in interview by author, January 23, 1976.
59. Senate Special Subcommittee on Investigations, *Charges and Countercharges: Report,* 83 Cong., 2 Sess. (August 30, 1954), 88, 92, 94.
60. RFK, with James M. Landis, draft report, 229, Landis Papers.
61. "Speech Prepared for Delivery on the Senate Floor July 31, 1954," 2, 3, 5–6, JFK Papers.
62. RFK to Stuart Symington, June 1, 1957, RFK Papers.
63. Robert Griffith, *The Politics of Fear: Joseph R. McCarthy and the Senate* (Lexington, Ky., 1970), 308; Stennis to RFK, December 16, 1954, RFK Papers.
64. Welch to RFK, January 10, 1955, RFK to Welch, January 14, 1955, Welch to RFK, January 17, 1955, RFK Papers.
65. Mrs. Richard Metz to RFK, February 10, 1955, RFK to Mrs. Metz, February 15, 1955, RFK Papers.
66. Sorensen to RFK, December 8, 1954, RFK Papers; *Louisville Courier-Journal,* January 22, 1955.
67. *Louisville Courier-Journal,* January 22, 1955.
68. RFK to John L. McClellan, December 1, 1954, RFK Papers.
69. Senate Permanent Subcommittee on Investigations, *Army Personnel Actions Relating to Irving Peress: Report,* 84 Cong., 1 Sess. (July 14, 1955), 1, 35, 36, 42. Some writers—notably Victor Lasky and Ralph de Toledano—have also held Kennedy and the reconstituted committee responsible for a report of April 25, 1955, entitled *Army Signal Corps—Subversion and Espionage,* supporting the extravagant McCarthy theories about Fort Monmouth. Had they examined the report carefully, they would have noted the statement that it "was prepared for the period of the 83rd Con., 2d sess., under the chairmanship of Senator Joe McCarthy" and the disclaimer by Senators McClellan, Jackson and Symington that they could not "accept either the credit or responsibility for this report." The report was written when Kennedy was at the Hoover commission.
70. RFK to McClellan, November 23, 1954, RFK Papers.
71. RFK to Robert M. Harriss, January 31, 1955, RFK Papers.
72. See Mosely to RFK, January 20, 1955, RFK Papers. Mosely suggested that the destruction by the Customs Service of Soviet materials paid for by American research libraries "is causing great difficulties in our attempts to study Soviet developments closely."
73. RFK to Browder, March 16, 1954, RFK Papers.
74. Sylvia Berkowitz to Joseph Starobin, February 7, 1976; Starobin to the author, October 1, 1975, and February 20, 1976.
75. L. V. Boardman to A. Rosen, February 9, 1955, RFK/FBI/FOIA release.
76. James Juliana to RFK, January 28, 1955, RFK Papers. For RFK's attempt to get

the investigation going, see his letter to Charles Tracy, January 18, 1955, and Tracy's reply, January 24, in RFK Papers.

77. Jones to Nichols, "Kennedy, Request to Meet Director."
78. *New York Times,* July 22–24, 1955; *Time,* August 1 and 8, 1955; Robert J. Donovan, *Eisenhower: The Inside Story* (New York, 1956), 332–334; Charles Bartlett, "Vignettes: Khrushchev, Kennedy and Kerr," *Washington Star,* September 13, 1959; Stein and Plimpton, *American Journey,* 54; Arthur Krock, *Memoirs* (New York, 1968), 308.
79. Lord Harlech, in recorded interview by Jean Stein, April 30, 1970, 14, Stein Papers; David Hackett, in interview by author, January 27, 1975.
80. Charles Spalding, in recorded interview by L. J. Hackman, March 22, 1969, 13, RFK Oral History Program.
81. Eunice Kennedy Shriver, in recorded interview by Roberta Greene, April 29, 1971, 41–42, 44, RFK Oral History Program.
82. Krock, *Memoirs,* 344.
83. *New York Times,* April 8, 1954.
84. Walter Lippmann, "Kennedy Destroys False Hopes," *Boston Globe,* April 12, 1954.
85. John F. Kennedy, "Foreign Policy Is the People's Business," *New York Times Magazine,* August 8, 1954.
86. Jacqueline Onassis, in interview by author, June 2, 1976.
87. Charles Spalding, in interview by author, February 24, 1975; J. Onassis, in interview by author.

7. Interlude: William O. Douglas and Adlai Stevenson (*pages* 126–142)

1. Rose Fitzgerald Kennedy, in interview by author, October 23, 1975.
2. W. O. Douglas, in recorded interview by Roberta Greene, November 13, 1969, 1, 3, RFK Oral History Program.
3. Mercedes [Douglas] Eichholz, in interview by author, April 26, 1975.
4. As described by RFK in early drafts of lectures about the trip, RFK Papers.
5. RFK to Mrs. Henry Kelly, March 18, 1955, RFK Papers.
6. Frederick W. Flott, in interview by author, February 26, 1975.
7. The sources for the trip, unless otherwise noted, are: RFK's diary, letters and speech drafts in the RFK Papers; W. O. Douglas, *Russian Journey* (Garden City, N.Y., 1956); and the Flott and Eichholz interviews with the author.
8. Robert F. Kennedy, "The Soviet Brand of Colonialism," *New York Times Magazine,* April 8, 1956.
9. Douglas, in Greene interview, 7.
10. W. O. Douglas, in recorded interview by Jean Stein, n.d., 1, Stein Papers.
11. Douglas, in Greene interview, 9.
12. As remembered by Mercedes [Douglas] Eichholz, in interview by author.
13. Douglas, *Russian Journey,* 7, 238, 240.
14. RFK to David Lawrence, October 5, 1955, RFK Papers. When *U.S. News* interviewers asked him whether his views and Douglas's were the same, Kennedy answered diplomatically, "I have the greatest admiration for Justice Douglas—I would not presume to speak for him" (*U.S. News & World Report,* October 21, 1955).
15. *New York Journal-American,* September 15, 1955.
16. *New York Herald Tribune,* September 24, 1955.
17. RFK to P. W. Goetz, November 21, 1955, RFK Papers.
18. Angie Novello, in recorded interview by Jean Stein, September 17, 1968, 5–6, Stein Papers.
19. K. LeM. Billings, in recorded interview by Jean Stein, n.d., 9, Stein Papers.

20. "Lecture by the Hon. Robert F. Kennedy at Georgetown University," October 10, 1955, RFK Papers.
21. RFK to T. C. Streibert, January 23, 1956, RFK Papers.
22. Robert F. Kennedy, "The Soviet Brand of Colonialism," *New York Times Magazine,* April 8, 1956.
23. Robert F. Kennedy, "Colonialism within the Soviet Union," *Proceedings of the Fifty-Sixth Annual Meeting of the Virginia State Bar Association* (Richmond, 1956), 211; letter to *New York Times,* January 2, 1956.
24. RFK to Clive S. Gray, May 22, 1956, RFK Papers.
25. RFK, "Soviet Brand of Colonialism."
26. *New York Times,* March 19, 1956.
27. In RFK Papers.
28. Douglas, in Stein interview, 1.
29. Lord Harlech, in Stein interview, April 30, 1970, 14.
30. Interview with Robert Kennedy, "A Look Behind the Russian Smiles," *U.S. News & World Report,* October 21, 1955.
31. Mercedes [Douglas] Eichholz, in interview by author.
32. See letters to Senator McClellan from Acting Secretary of State Herbert Hoover, Jr., February 20, 1956, and Secretary of Commerce Sinclair Weeks, March 5, 1956; see also memorandum of Secretary of Defense Charles E. Wilson, March 5, 1956, in Senate Permanent Subcommittee on Investigations, *East-West Trade: Hearings,* pt. 1, app., 84 Cong., 2 Sess. (July 18, 1956), 273–284.
33. RFK, letter to editor, *American Metal Market,* April 5, 1956.
34. Permanent Subcommittee on Investigations, *East-West Trade: Hearings* (March 6, 1956), 251.
35. Ibid.: McClellan (February 15, 1956), 1; Ervin and Jackson (March 6, 1956), 203, 209.
36. Permanent Subcommittee on Investigations, *East-West Trade: Report,* 28.
37. Morse to RFK, August 2, 1956, RFK Papers.
38. RFK, in interview by John Bartlow Martin, December 7, 1966, Martin Papers.
39. RFK, in recorded interview by John Stewart, August 15, 1967, 58–60, JFK Oral History Program.
40. JPK to JFK, May 25, 1956, Sorensen Papers.
41. RFK, in Stewart interview, 51.
42. Kenneth P. O'Donnell and David F. Powers, *"Johnny, We Hardly Knew Ye"* (Boston, 1972), 118–119.
43. Author's journal, July 26, 1956.
44. Ibid., July 29, 1956.
45. O'Donnell and Powers, *"Johnny,"* 122.
46. Theodore C. Sorensen, *Kennedy* (New York, 1965), 88.
47. Kenneth O'Donnell, in interview by Jean Stein, October 8, 1968, 32–33, Stein Papers.
48. RFK to C. J. Bloch, September 5, 1956, RFK Papers.
49. O'Donnell and Powers, *"Johnny,"* 120.
50. Sorensen, *Kennedy,* 87–91; Arthur M. Schlesinger, Jr., *A Thousand Days* (Boston, 1965), 8–9; Ralph G. Martin and Ed Plaut, *Front Runner, Dark Horse* (New York, 1960), 90, 103.
51. O'Donnell, in Stein interview, 33.
52. O'Donnell and Powers, *"Johnny,"* 124.
53. Martin and Plaut, *Front Runner,* 107.
54. Ibid.
55. R. E. Thompson and Hortense Myers, *Robert F. Kennedy: The Brother Within* (New York, 1962), 184–185.
56. Jacqueline Onassis, in interview by author, June 3, 1976.
57. William McC. Blair, Jr., in recorded interview by Jean Stein, September 5, 1968,

3, 6, 8, Stein Papers; Hal Clancy, "In Politics or Investigating, Bob Kennedy Thinks Fast," *Boston Traveler,* January 11, 1961.

58. Newton N. Minow, in interview by author, August 30, 1974.
59. RFK, memorandum on Stevenson, January 25, 1957, 5–6, RFK Papers.
60. O'Donnell and Powers, *"Johnny,"* 126.
61. Harrison Salisbury, in recorded interview by Jean Stein, December 5, 1969, 2, Stein Papers.
62. RFK, memorandum on Stevenson, January 25, 1957, 1–2, RFK Papers.
63. RFK, memorandum, January 25, 1957, 5–6, RFK Papers.
64. Ibid., 4–5.
65. Ibid., 5–7.
66. Robert Kennedy, in interview with John Bartlow Martin, December 7, 1966, Martin Papers.
67. Stevenson to RFK, November 17, 1956, RFK Papers.
68. Salisbury, in Stein interview, 3.

8. Second Investigating Committee: Jimmy Hoffa (*pages* 143–176)

1. For good discussions, see John Hutchinson, *The Imperfect Union* (New York, 1970), ch. 14; and Daniel Bell, "The Scandals in Union Welfare Funds," *Fortune,* April 1954.
2. Clark Mollenhoff, *Tentacles of Power: The Story of Jimmy Hoffa* (Cleveland, 1965), 124.
3. Sam Romer, *The International Brotherhood of Teamsters* (New York, 1962), 35.
4. Murray Kempton, "The Salesman," *New York Post,* June 24, 1953.
5. *New York Times,* October 14, 1952; Mollenhoff, *Tentacles of Power,* 23.
6. Robert F. Kennedy, *The Enemy Within* (New York: Popular Library reprint, 1960), 16–17.
7. Romer, *Teamsters,* 6–8.
8. Edward Levinson, *Labor on the March* (New York, 1938), 13.
9. James R. Hoffa, *The Trials of Jimmy Hoffa: An Autobiography,* as told to Donald I. Rogers (Chicago, 1970), 105, 107–108.
10. B. J. Widick, *Labor Today* (Boston, 1964), 151.
11. John Bartlow Martin, *Jimmy Hoffa's Hot* (New York: Fawcett World, Crest, 1959), 31. This work, based in considerable part on interviews with Hoffa and Kennedy, is the paperback reprint of Martin's indispensable series "The Struggle to Get Hoffa," *Saturday Evening Post,* June 27–August 8, 1959. The paperback title was imposed by the publisher over the author's vigorous protest. For reasons of convenience I will cite the book—as Martin, *Hoffa*—rather than the magazine pieces. Mr. Martin has also made available to me the original manuscript of the *Post* series; this was considerably cut for publication. It will be cited as Martin, "Hoffa."
12. Ralph James and Estelle James, *Hoffa and the Teamsters* (Princeton, N.J., 1965), 114–116.
13. Martin, *Hoffa,* 24.
14. Paul Jacobs, *The State of the Unions* (New York, 1963), 48.
15. As conceded by Hoffa, *Trials,* 136; James R. Hoffa, *Hoffa: The Real Story,* as told to Oscar Fraley (New York, 1975), 65. Nevertheless Lewis was the labor leader Hoffa most admired; see Martin, "Hoffa," 147–148.
16. Martin, "Hoffa," 145.
17. Jacobs, *State of the Unions,* 56.
18. Carmine Bellino, in interview by author, February 3, 1976.
19. RFK, *Enemy Within,* 20.
20. Edwin Guthman, *We Band of Brothers* (New York, 1971), 1, 4–7.

21. Ibid., 9–10.
22. RFK, *Enemy Within*, 15; Nathan W. Shefferman, *The Man in the Middle* (Garden City, N.Y., 1961), 1–3.
23. Jean Kennedy Smith, in interview by author, September 15, 1975.
24. Mercedes [Douglas] Eichholz, in interview by author, April 26, 1975.
25. J. C. Goulden, *Meany* (New York, 1972), 233–235.
26. Ibid., 235.
27. John L. McClellan, *Crime without Punishment* (New York, 1962), 14.
28. RFK, memorandum, January 9, 1957, 1, RFK Papers.
29. RFK, memorandum, January 7, 1957, 1, RFK Papers.
30. RFK, *Enemy Within*, 33; Mollenhoff, *Tentacles of Power*, 146.
31. Ralph G. Martin and Ed Plaut, *Front Runner, Dark Horse* (New York, 1960), 191.
32. Martin, "Hoffa," 9.
33. Angie Novello, in recorded interview by Jean Stein, September 27, 1968, 2, Stein Papers.
34. Kenneth P. O'Donnell and David Powers, *"Johnny, We Hardly Knew Ye"* (Boston, 1972), 132–133.
35. John Bartlow Martin to author, October 19, 1975.
36. Pierre Salinger, *With Kennedy* (Garden City, N.Y., 1966), 16–18; Salinger, *Je suis un Américain: Conversations avec Philippe Labro* (Paris, 1975), 126–135; Salinger, in recorded interview by Theodore H. White, July 19, 1965, 2–9, JFK Oral History Program.
37. RFK, *Enemy Within*, 96.
38. Pierre Salinger, in recorded interview by L. J. Hackman, May 26, 1969, 22, RFK Oral History Program.
39. Walter Sheridan, in recorded interview by Jean Stein, July 23, 1968, 1–2, Stein Papers; Sheridan, *The Fall and Rise of Jimmy Hoffa* (New York, 1972), 33.
40. H. W. Flannery, "The *Other* Kennedy," *Ave Maria*, August 31, 1957; Martin, "Hoffa," 11.
41. Martin to author, October 19, 1975.
42. RFK, notes for close-up in *Life* [1957], 5, JPK Papers. There were 34 assistant counsels and investigators deployed on field investigations, reinforced by an average of 35 to 45 accountants and investigators from the General Accounting Office. Senate Select Committee on Improper Activities in the Labor or Management Field, *Final Report*, 86 Cong., 2 Sess. (March 31, 1960), 869.
43. Sheridan, in Stein interview, 1, 3–4.
44. LaVern Duffy, in interview by author, January 23, 1976.
45. McClellan, *Crime without Punishment*, 69–76.
46. RFK, in interview by Kenneth Brodney (Newhouse Newspaper Feature Syndicate), July 2, 1957, 11, 19, 22, JPK Papers.
47. Jean Stein and George Plimpton, eds., *American Journey* (New York, 1970), 55.
48. Ibid., 54.
49. Guthman, *We Band of Brothers*, 57.
50. Joseph A. Loftus, review of Robert F. Kennedy's *The Enemy Within*, *New York Times Book Review*, February 28, 1960.
51. John Seigenthaler, in recorded interview by W. A. Geoghegan [July 1964], 1–12, 15, JFK Oral History Program; Seigenthaler, in recorded interview by Jean Stein, August 27, 1968, 1–5, Stein Papers.
52. RFK, *Enemy Within*, 29–30; Martin, "Hoffa," 43.
53. RFK, *Enemy Within*, 38.
54. Lahey to RFK, postmarked March 28, 1957, JPK Papers.
55. Goulden, *Meany*, 240.
56. *Cleveland Press*, March 6, 1957.
57. George M. Belknap to RFK, March 8, 1957, JPK Papers.

58. Mrs. W. D. Goode, Jr., to JFK, March 8, 1957, JPK Papers.
59. JPK to RFK, March 14, 1957, enclosing letter from Sargent Shriver, n.d., JPK Papers; *Chattanooga Times,* March 26, 1957.
60. Paul F. Healy, "Investigator in a Hurry," *Sign,* August 1957.
61. *New York Herald Tribune,* March 17, 1957.
62. *Toledo Blade,* March 3, 1957.
63. *Kansas City Star,* March 24, 1957.
64. *Louisville Courier-Journal,* March 24, 1957.
65. RFK, notes for *Life* close-up, 6.
66. K. LeM. Billings, in recorded interview by Jean Stein, n.d., 8, Stein Papers.
67. RFK, handwritten note, October 11 [1957], RFK Papers.
68. Mollenhoff to RFK, December 23, 1957, RFK Papers.
69. Paul O'Neil, "The No. 2 Man in Washington," *Life,* January 26, 1962.
70. RFK, notes for *Life* close-up, 3, 4.
71. *New York Herald Tribune,* August 13, 1957; S. P. Friedman, *The Magnificent Kennedy Women* (New York: Monarch reprint, 1964), 74; Lester David, *Ethel* (New York: Dell reprint, 1972), 87–88.
72. RFK, memorandum, September 8, 1958, RFK Papers. Cheyfitz evidently denied the story; see RFK, *Enemy Within,* 64, though this reference does not explain in full lurid detail what Cheyfitz was denying.
73. *New York Herald Tribune,* March 17, 1959.
74. RFK, handwritten note, April 27, 1957, RFK Papers.
75. RFK, handwritten note, December 15, 1957, RFK Papers.
76. Sheridan, *Fall and Rise,* 32.
77. RFK, *Enemy Within,* 44.
78. Ibid.
79. Ibid.
80. Martin, "Hoffa," 53.
81. Cheasty to RFK, May 3, 1957, RFK Papers.
82. Martin, *Hoffa,* 7.
83. RFK, *Enemy Within,* 48; Martin, *Hoffa,* 8. In reconstructing this dinner, I have relied on Kennedy's own accounts in contemporaneous notes and in his book; on Martin (*Hoffa,* 8–9; "Hoffa," 4–7), who interviewed both Kennedy and Hoffa shortly afterward; and on Mollenhoff (*Tentacles of Power,* 148–149), who interviewed Kennedy. The account in the first of Hoffa's autobiographies (*Trials,* 150) is exceedingly brief. His second autobiography is hopelessly unreliable. Hoffa, or his collaborator, describes an earlier meeting when, allegedly, Kennedy, Salinger and Bellino invaded Hoffa's Detroit office in the summer of 1956 and were humiliated by him. This is wholly imagined, though it may have been inspired by the visit of Salinger and Bellino to Detroit in the summer of 1957. As for the dinner, the second autobiography says that Kennedy ordered Cheyfitz from the room, asked Hoffa a series of personal questions, was worsted by him in Indian hand wrestling and did not even stay for dinner (*Hoffa: The Real Story,* 95–99). Hoffa claimed none of these things in his earlier autobiography. Most are refuted by other evidence.
84. February 21, 1957, RFK Papers.
85. Martin, *Hoffa,* 20–21; RFK, *Enemy Within,* 60–62; Mollenhoff, *Tentacles of Power,* 154–155. Hoffa's pushup crack was recorded by Kennedy in a handwritten note, RFK Papers.
86. Edward Bennett Williams, in interview by author, January 23, 1976.
87. Mollenhoff, *Tentacles of Power,* 202.
88. RFK, *Enemy Within,* 62–64.
89. Edward Bennett Williams, *One Man's Freedom* (New York, 1962), 221; Mollenhoff, *Tentacles of Power,* 198–207.
90. Novello, in Stein interview, 3; Mollenhoff, *Tentacles of Power,* 213–214.

91. Novello, in Stein interview, 3.

92. Senate Select Committee on Improper Activities in the Labor or Management Field (hereafter cited as Senate Select Committee), *Investigation of Improper Activities in the Labor or Management Field: Hearings,* 85 Cong., 1 Sess. (July 31, 1957), 3595–3596.

93. Martin, *Hoffa,* 35–36; Salinger, *With Kennedy,* 22–23; Bellino, in interview by author, February 3, 1976; Pierre Salinger, in interview by author, November 13, 1975.

94. Martin, *Hoffa,* 49.

95. Senate Select Committee, *Hearings* (August 21, 1957), 5107–5108.

96. Ibid., 5109.

97. See the stories by Joseph Loftus, *New York Times,* August 21–24, 1957.

98. Senate Select Committee, *Hearings* (August 23, 1957), 52.

99. Martin, *Hoffa,* 60.

100. RFK, handwritten note, September 2 [1957], RFK Papers.

101. RFK, handwritten note, October 11 [1957], RFK Papers.

102. Martin, *Hoffa,* 61.

103. RFK, *Enemy Within,* 67–68.

104. Martin, *Hoffa,* 69.

105. RFK, memorandum, April 5, 1958, 4, RFK Papers.

106. Martin, *Hoffa,* 87.

107. RFK, *Enemy Within,* 77.

108. RFK, handwritten note, September 13 [1958], RFK Papers.

109. Martin, "Hoffa," 554.

110. Ibid., 731–732; RFK, *Enemy Within,* 157–158; Senate Select Committee, *Hearings,* 85 Cong., 2 Sess. (September 18, 1958), 15230–15231.

111. Martin, "Hoffa," 733.

112. Martin, *Hoffa,* 88.

113. RFK, handwritten note, December 19 [1958], RFK Papers.

114. Mollenhoff, *Tentacles of Power,* 325.

115. *International Teamster,* February 1959.

116. Angie Novello, in interview by author, December 11, 1975.

117. Hal Clancy, "Tough? Sensitive? Dedicated?—Depends on Whom You Ask," *Boston Traveler,* January 9, 1961.

118. Martin, "Hoffa," 137.

119. Martin, *Hoffa,* 11.

120. Martin to author, October 19, 1975.

121. Martin, *Hoffa,* 12.

122. Salinger, *With Kennedy,* 19.

123. Edward Bennett Williams, in recorded interview by Jean Stein, January 9, 1970, 9–10, Stein Papers.

124. Martin, "Hoffa," 142.

125. Hoffa, *Real Story,* 107, 115.

126. RFK, *Enemy Within,* 78.

127. Victor Lasky, *Robert F. Kennedy: The Myth and the Man* (New York: Pocket Book reprint, 1971), 119.

128. Novello, Bellino and Duffy, in interviews by author.

129. Hoffa, *Real Story,* 105.

130. Ibid., 117.

131. Stein and Plimpton, *American Journey,* 56–57.

132. RFK, handwritten note, January 15 [1959], RFK Papers.

133. Senate Select Committee, *Final Report,* 86 Cong., 2 Sess. (March 28, 1960), 570–731; RFK, *Enemy Within,* 158–159.

134. Ibid., 159.

135. Jacobs, *State of the Unions,* 50; see also Daniel Bell, "The Myth of Crime Waves," in *The End of Ideology* (New York: Collier reprint, 1962), 167–168.

136. Martin, "Hoffa," 749–750.

137. Senate Select Committee, *Hearings,* 85 Cong., 2 Sess. (August 20, 1958), 14061–14062.

138. RFK, *Enemy Within,* 238–240.

139. Senate Select Committee, *Final Report,* 514–569. For a summary of the Glimco file, see Hutchinson, *Imperfect Union,* 249–251.

140. R. S. Anson, *"They've Killed the President"* (New York, 1973), 227–228.

141. Sheridan, *Fall and Rise,* 17–18; RFK, *Enemy Within,* 87–89.

142. Senate Select Committee, *Hearings,* 86 Cong., 1 Sess. (February 20, 1959), 17042.

143. Donald R. Cressey, *Theft of the Nation* (New York: Harper & Row, Colophon reprint, 1969), 112, 189.

144. Senate Select Committee, *Hearings,* 86 Cong., 1 Sess. (June 9, 1959), 18672–18681.

145. The congressman was Roland Victor Libonati; Sheridan, *Fall and Rise,* 361–364; Cressey, *Theft of the Nation,* 271–272.

146. J. Edgar Hoover spoke of "Giancana's close relationship with Frank Sinatra" in a memorandum of May 10, 1962. Senate Select Committee to Study Governmental Operations with respect to Intelligence Activities, *Interim Report: Alleged Assassination Plots Involving Foreign Leaders,* 94 Cong., 1 Sess. (November 20, 1975), 133. See also Peter Lawford with Steve Dunleavy, "Peter Lawford Tells," *Star* (New York), February 17, 1976.

147. Cressey, *Theft of the Nation,* 220.

148. Sheridan, *Fall and Rise,* 28, 115, 282, 284; "Provenzano Comeback Reported," *New York Times,* December 6, 1975.

149. "Hoffa's Teamsters," *Life,* May 25, 1959.

150. James and James, *Hoffa and the Teamsters,* 66.

151. Senate Select Committee, *Hearings,* 85 Cong., 2 Sess. (September 16, 1958), 15092.

152. RFK, *Enemy Within,* 78.

153. Martin, "Hoffa," 749.

154. I take these terms from the fascinating study by Dwight C. Smith, Jr., *The Mafia Mystique* (New York, 1975), 89, 117, 322.

155. Walter Lippmann, "The Underworld, Our Secret Servant," *Forum,* January 1931.

156. Smith, *Mafia Mystique,* 121–122.

157. Burton Turkus and Sid Feder, *Murder, Inc.* (New York, 1951), 63.

158. RFK, *Enemy Within,* 228.

159. Senate Select Committee, *Final Report,* 488.

160. Mafiology is as murky a field as Kremlinology. The true believers include Estes Kefauver, *Crime in America* (Garden City, N.Y., 1951); President's Commission on Law Enforcement and Administration of Justice, *The Challenge of Crime in a Free Society* (Washington, 1967), especially 192–196; Cressey, *Theft of the Nation;* Peter Maas, *The Valachi Papers* (New York, 1968); Nicholas Gage, *The Mafia Is Not an Equal Opportunity Employer* (New York, 1971); and J. Edgar Hoover (later pronouncements). The skeptics include J. Edgar Hoover (early pronouncements); Turkus and Feder, *Murder, Inc.;* W. H. Moore, *The Kefauver Committee and the Politics of Crime, 1950–1952* (Columbia, Mo., 1974); Daniel Bell, "The Myth of the Cosa Nostra," *New Leader,* December 23, 1963; Murray Kempton, "Crime Does Not Pay," *New York Review of Books,* September 11, 1969; Eric Hobsbawm, "The American Mafia," *Listener,* November 20, 1969; F. A. J. Ianni, *A Family Business* (New York, 1972); J. L. Albini, *The American Mafia: Genesis of a Legend* (New York, 1972); Smith, *Mafia Mystique.* For what it is worth, I find the skeptics more persuasive. It is interesting to note that the gangster films of the early thirties—*Scarface* and *Little Caesar,* for example—do not depict their Italian protagonists as inhabiting the sentimental mythic realm later celebrated by Mario Puzo and Francis Ford Coppola in *The Godfather.* It may be that in the

end publicity created an American Mafia. What hood could resist the fearsome prestige the myth makers were wishing on him?

161. RFK, *Enemy Within*, 229.
162. RFK, in recorded interview by Anthony Lewis, December 4, 1964, IV, 22, JFK Oral History Program.
163. Ronald W. May, "Organized Crime and Disorganized Cops," *Nation*, June 27, 1959.
164. Angie Novello, in interview by author, December 11, 1975.
165. RFK, memorandum, May 29, 1958, RFK Papers.
166. May, "Organized Crime and Disorganized Cops."
167. RFK, *Enemy Within*, 253.
168. Quoted in *Newsweek*, August 18, 1975. He made a similar remark to John Bartlow Martin, in "Hoffa," 749.

9. The Second Investigating Committee: Walter Reuther (*pages* 177–200)

1. Senate Select Committee on Improper Activities in the Labor or Management Field (hereafter cited as Senate Select Committee), *Investigation of Improper Activities in the Labor or Management Field: Hearings*, 85 Cong., 2 Sess. (August 20, 1957), 4963–4964.
2. Clark Mollenhoff, *Tentacles of Power* (Cleveland, 1965), 257–260.
3. *Newsweek*, July 22, 1957.
4. *Meet the Press*, April 28, 1957.
5. RFK, in interview by Kenneth Brodney, Newhouse Newspaper Feature Syndicate, July 2, 1957, 18, JPK Papers.
6. Charles Bartlett, "Vignettes: Khrushchev, Kennedy and Kerr," *Washington Star*, September 13, 1959.
7. LaVern Duffy, in interview by author, January 23, 1976.
8. Robert F. Kennedy, *The Enemy Within* (New York: Popular Library reprint, 1960), 285–286.
9. Ibid., 287.
10. Pierre Salinger, in interview by author, November 13, 1975.
11. Arthur Watkins, *Enough Rope* (Englewood Cliffs, N.J., 1969), 192.
12. Richard Rovere, "The Last Days of Joe McCarthy," *Esquire*, August 1958.
13. RFK, memorandum, March 5, 1957, RFK Papers.
14. Ibid.
15. Robert E. Thompson and Hortense Myers, *Robert F. Kennedy: The Brother Within* (New York, 1962), 121.
16. Edwin Guthman, *We Band of Brothers* (New York, 1971), 24–25.
17. K. LeM. Billings, in recorded interview with Jean Stein, n.d., 7, Stein Papers.
18. RFK, handwritten note, May 4 [1957], RFK Papers.
19. Ibid.
20. *New York Times*, May 4, 1957.
21. RFK, *Enemy Within*, 254–255.
22. *Newsweek*, July 22, 1957.
23. Mundt, memorandum, July 15, 1957, RFK Papers.
24. RFK, *Enemy Within*, 257.
25. Ibid., 256; *Newsweek*, July 29, 1957; also *Newsweek* piece with RFK annotations, RFK Papers.
26. RFK, handwritten memorandum, October 11 [1957], RFK Papers.
27. RFK, *Enemy Within*, 259.
28. Frank Cormier and W. J. Eaton, *Reuther* (Englewood Cliffs, N.J., 1970), 344.
29. Senate Select Committee, *Hearings*, 85 Cong., 2 Sess. (March 29, 1958), 10165.

30. "Republicans Size Up Reuther's Union," *U.S. News & World Report*, February 29, 1960.
31. Jack Conway, in recorded interview by L. J. Hackman, April 10, 1972, 15–16, RFK Oral History Program.
32. RFK, *Enemy Within*, 260; Conway, in Hackman interview, 19.
33. RFK, *Enemy Within*, 261–262.
34. See W. H. Uphoff, *Kohler on Strike: Thirty Years of Conflict* (Boston, 1966), 106–107. For an opposing view, see Sylvester Petro, *Power Unlimited: The Corruption of Union Leadership* (New York, 1959), esp. ch. 4–5.
35. Senate Select Committee, *Hearings*, 85 Cong., 2 Sess. (March 26, 1958), 9962.
36. RFK, *Enemy Within*, 262–266.
37. Ibid., 254.
38. RFK, memorandum, January 8, 1958, 1–2, RFK Papers.
39. RFK, memorandum, February 22, 1958, 5, RFK Papers.
40. *U.S. News & World Report*, April 4, 1958.
41. Conway, in Hackman interview, 31–33.
42. The original letter appeared in the YPSL organ, *The Challenge*, in July 1934; Victor Reuther, *The Brothers Reuther* (Boston, 1976), ch. 17. See also RFK, memorandum, February 22, 1958, 1–4, RFK Papers; Cormier and Eaton, *Reuther*, 140.
43. RFK, memorandum, February 22, 1958, 5, memorandum, March 1, 1958, 1–2; RFK, *Enemy Within*, 275–276; Senate Select Committee, *Hearings*, 85 Cong., 2 Sess. (February 26, 1958), 8330.
44. Conway, in Hackman interview, 15–16.
45. Senate Select Committee, *Hearings*, 85 Cong., 2 Sess. (February 28, 1958), 8520.
46. RFK, memorandum, March 8, 1958, 2, RFK Papers.
47. Senate Select Committee, *Hearings*, 85 Cong., 2 Sess. (March 4, 1958), 8666.
48. Ibid. (March 19, 1958), 9525.
49. RFK, *Enemy Within*, 278.
50. RFK, memorandum, April 5, 1958, 6, RFK Papers.
51. Rauh to author, October 16, 1975.
52. RFK, *Enemy Within*, 279.
53. RFK, memorandum, March 1, 1958, 3, RFK Papers.
54. Rauh to author, October 16, 1975.
55. RFK, *Enemy Within*, 280.
56. RFK, memorandum, February 22, 1958, 1, RFK Papers.
57. RFK, *Enemy Within*, 282.
58. RFK, memorandum, April 5, 1958, 3.
59. Conway, in Hackman interview, 21.
60. John T. Dunlop, "The Public Interest in International Affairs of Unions," address before the American Bar Association, July 12, 1957 (mimeographed), 4–5.
61. RFK, *Enemy Within*, ch. 11.
62. Walter Sheridan, *The Fall and Rise of Jimmy Hoffa* (New York, 1972), 33. Shefferman gives a benign picture of his activities in *The Man in the Middle* (Garden City, N.Y., 1961).
63. Sheridan, *Fall and Rise*, 33, 50; Senate Select Committee, *Interim Report*, 85 Cong., 2 Sess. (March 24, 1958), 297–300; Daniel Bell, "Nathan Shefferman, Union Buster," *Fortune*, February 1958; Sheridan, in recorded interview by Jean Stein, July 23, 1968, 4, Stein Papers; Sheridan, in recorded interview by Roberta Greene, March 23, 1970, 34, RFK Oral History Program; Pierre Salinger, in recorded interview by L. J. Hackman, April 18, 1970, 73, RFK Oral History Program; Salinger, *Je suis un Américain* (Paris, 1957), 158.
64. RFK, *Enemy Within*, 207–209.
65. *New York Times*, November 2, 1957.
66. Warner Bloomberg, Jr., et al., "The State of the Unions," *New Republic*, June 22, 1959.

67. Goldberg to RFK, February 17, 1960, RFK Papers.
68. RFK, memorandum, March 20, 1959, RFK Papers.
69. Robert F. Kennedy, "An Urgent Reform Plan," *Life,* June 1, 1959.
70. RFK, handwritten note, September 28 [1958], RFK Papers.
71. Donald R. Larrabee, "Crooks Exposed, Not Prosecuted," *New Bedford Standard-Times,* October 4, 1959.
72. William G. Hundley, in recorded interview by J. A. Oesterle, December 9, 1970, 7–8, RFK Oral History Program.
73. RFK to Charles J. Lewin, August 1, 1959, RFK Papers.
74. RFK, memorandum, January 8, 1958, 3, RFK Papers.
75. RFK, memorandum, February 22, 1958, 4, RFK Papers.
76. RFK to Bowles, August 12, 1959, Bowles Papers.
77. *Newsweek,* August 10, 1959.
78. RFK to McClellan, September 10, 1959, RFK Papers.
79. Senate Select Committee, *Final Report,* 86 Cong., 2 Sess. (March 31, 1960), 868–869.
80. Walter Sheridan, in recorded interview by Roberta Greene, April 7, 1970, 7, 30–31, RFK Oral History Program.
81. RFK, *Enemy Within,* 284.
82. Felix Frankfurter, "Hands Off the Investigations," *New Republic,* May 21, 1924.
83. 273 U.S. 135.
84. Philip B. Kurland, "The Watergate Inquiry, 1973," in *Congress Investigates, 1972–1974,* ed. Arthur M. Schlesinger, Jr., and Roger Bruns (New York, 1975), 474.
85. Hugo Black, "Inside a Senate Investigation," *Harper's,* February 1936.
86. RFK, *Enemy Within,* 295–296.
87. *Watkins* v. *U.S.,* 354 U.S. 178.
88. RFK, *Enemy Within,* 161.
89. Pierre Salinger, in recorded interview by Theodore H. White, July 19, 1965, 10–11, JFK Oral History Program.
90. RFK, *Enemy Within,* 292.
91. John Bartlow Martin, "The Struggle to Get Hoffa," uncut manuscript, 3–12; Carmine Bellino, in interview by author, February 3, 1976.
92. Walter Sheridan, in recorded interview by Roberta Greene, March 23, 1970, 56–57, RFK Oral History Program.
93. RFK, *Enemy Within,* 175.
94. Martin to author, October 19, 1975.
95. Porter to RFK, August 23, 1957, RFK Papers.
96. Dan Wakefield, "Bob," *Esquire,* April 1962.
97. Victor Lasky, *Robert F. Kennedy: The Myth and the Man* (New York: Pocket Book reprint, 1971), 127.
98. James R. Hoffa, *The Trials of Jimmy Hoffa: An Autobiography,* as told to Donald I. Rogers (Chicago, 1970), 167.
99. Alexander M. Bickel, "Robert F. Kennedy: The Case Against Him for Attorney General," *New Republic,* January 9, 1961. See also Bickel, in recorded interview by Jean Stein, May 14, 1970, 2–3, Stein Papers.
100. Bickel, "Robert F. Kennedy."
101. Edward Bennett Williams, in interview by author, January 23, 1976.
102. RFK, handwritten note, November 2 [1957], RFK Papers.
103. Senate Select Committee, *Final Report,* 86 Cong., 2 Sess. (March 31, 1960), 868.
104. RFK, *Enemy Within,* 297–300.
105. Bickel, "Robert F. Kennedy."
106. John Seigenthaler, in recorded interview by W. A. Geoghegan [July 1964], 41–49, JFK Oral History Program.
107. Beaverbrook to RFK, May 11, 1961, Beaverbrook Papers.

108. RFK, speech at Notre Dame University, February 22, 1958, 1, RFK Papers.
109. RFK, *Enemy Within,* 307.
110. Murray Kempton, in recorded interview by Jean Stein, October 27, 1969, 3, Stein Papers.
111. Kempton, in interview by author, December 10, 1975.
112. RFK, *Enemy Within,* 261.
113. Walter Reuther, in recorded interview by Jean Stein, October 14, 1968, 4–5, Stein Papers.
114. Victor Reuther, in interview by author, August 10, 1971.
115. Peter Maas, "Robert Kennedy Speaks Out," *Look,* March 28, 1961.
116. *San Francisco Monitor,* July 19, 1957.
117. Kempton, in Stein interview, 4.
118. Murray Kempton, "The Uncommitted," *Progressive,* September 1960.

10. 1960 (*pages* 201–231)

1. Theodore C. Sorensen, *Kennedy* (New York, 1965), 35, 117.
2. RFK, memorandum to Theodore H. White on the manuscript of *The Making of a President, 1960,* March 23, 1961, RFK Papers.
3. David Hackett, in recorded interview by John Douglas, July 22, 1970, 13–14, RFK Oral History Program.
4. Pierre Salinger, in recorded interview by Theodore H. White, July 19, 1965, 28, JFK Oral History Program; Salinger, *With Kennedy* (Garden City, N.Y., 1966), 30.
5. Paul B. Fay, Jr., *The Pleasure of His Company* (New York, 1966), 6–7.
6. Fred Dutton, in recorded interview by L. J. Hackman, November 18, 1969, 15–16, RFK Oral History Program.
7. Harris Wofford, in recorded interview by Jean Stein, October 3, 1968, 7, Stein Papers.
8. Barrett Prettyman, Jr., in recorded interview by L. J. Hackman, June 5, 1969, 57, RFK Oral History Program.
9. Kenneth P. O'Donnell and David Powers, *"Johnny, We Hardly Knew Ye"* (Boston, 1972), 151.
10. Author's journal, March 25–27, 1960.
11. *Peoria Journal-Star,* February 14, 1960.
12. Joseph Alsop, in recorded interview by Roberta Greene, June 10, 1971, 55, RFK Oral History Program.
13. O'Donnell and Powers, *"Johnny,"* 157.
14. Hubert H. Humphrey, *The Education of a Public Man* (Garden City, N.Y., 1976), 208.
15. Ibid., 208.
16. Patrick Lucey, in recorded interview by L. D. Epstein, August 1, 1964, 37–38, JFK Oral History Program.
17. Jerry Bruno and Jeff Greenfield, *The Advance Man* (New York: Bantam reprint, 1972), 28, 35.
18. Jean Stein and George Plimpton, eds., *American Journey* (New York, 1970), 70.
19. Ibid., 69.
20. Joseph Dolan, in recorded interview by L. J. Hackman, April 10, 1970, 56–57, RFK Oral History Program; Stein and Plimpton, *American Journey,* 69.
21. Humphrey, *Education of a Public Man,* 208.
22. *National Review,* December 16, 1961.
23. Franklin Wallick, "I Remember Hubert," *United Auto Workers Washington Report,* January 16, 1978.
24. Lawrence F. O'Brien, *No Final Victories* (Garden City, N.Y., 1964), 65.

25. Walter Cronkite, in recorded interview by Jean Stein, December 2, 1969, 7, Stein Papers.
26. Minutes of "Meeting re West Virginia Primary—April 8, 1960," RFK Papers.
27. O'Donnell and Powers, *"Johnny,"* 161.
28. Minutes of meeting, April 8, 1960.
29. O'Donnell and Powers, *"Johnny,"* 166–167.
30. Salinger, in White interview, 59.
31. William Walton, in recorded interview by Jean Stein, September 22, 1968, 4, Stein Papers.
32. Franklin D. Roosevelt, Jr., in interview by author, February 12, 1975.
33. Charles Spalding, in recorded interview by L. J. Hackman, March 22, 1969, 31, RFK Oral History Program.
34. D. E. Koskoff, *Joseph P. Kennedy* (Englewood Cliffs, N.J., 1974), 399, 596; James MacGregor Burns, *John Kennedy* (New York, 1960), 196.
35. Fay, *Pleasure of His Company,* 9.
36. *Newsweek,* September 12, 1960.
37. Jeffrey Potter, *Men, Money and Magic: The Story of Dorothy Schiff* (New York, 1976), 261.
38. Rose Kennedy, in interview by author, May 25, 1976.
39. Franklin D. Roosevelt, Jr., in recorded interview by Jean Stein, December 9, 1969, 3–5, Stein Papers.
40. Ibid., 5.
41. O'Brien, *No Final Victories,* 68.
42. Humphrey, *Education of a Public Man,* 216–217.
43. Walter Lippmann to JFK, January 22, 1960, Lippmann Papers.
44. Sorensen, *Kennedy,* 141.
45. O'Brien, *No Final Victories,* 72.
46. Ibid., 73.
47. Victor Lasky, *J. F. K.: The Man and the Myth* (New York, 1963), 344.
48. Humphrey, *Education of a Public Man,* 475.
49. Theodore White, in interview by author, July 5, 1976.
50. O'Donnell and Powers, *"Johnny,"* 171.
51. Author's journal, May 14, 1960.
52. John Bartlow Martin, *Adlai Stevenson and the World* (New York, 1977), 499.
53. Author's journal, May 22, 1960.
54. Ibid., May 29, 1960.
55. Ibid., June 16, 1960.
56. Ibid.
57. RFK to author, June 17, 1960, Schlesinger Papers.
58. Theodore C. Sorensen, "Election of 1960," in *History of American Presidential Election,* ed. Arthur M. Schlesinger, Jr. (New York, 1971), vol. 4, 3460.
59. RFK, in recorded interview by author, February 27, 1965, 32–33, JFK Oral History Program.
60. Peter Lisagor, in recorded interview by R. J. Grele, April 22, 1966, 25, JFK Oral History Program.
61. *New York Times,* July 14, 1960.
62. John Seigenthaler, in recorded interview by W. A. Geoghegan [July 1964], 92–93, JFK Oral History Program.
63. Joseph Tydings, in recorded interview by Roberta Greene, May 3, 1971, 6, RFK Oral History Program.
64. Author's journal, July 14, 1960.
65. The Graham memorandum was subsequently printed by Theodore H. White as an appendix to *The Making of the President, 1964* (New York, 1965).
66. These and subsequent RFK quotations are from RFK, in recorded interview by author, February 27, 1965, JFK Oral History Program.

67. Jack Conway, in recorded interview by L. J. Hackman, April 10, 1972, 66–67, RFK Oral History Program.
68. Author's journal, June 12, 1960.
69. Clark Clifford, in recorded interview by L. J. Hackman, December 16, 1974, 23, JFK Oral History Program; Nancy Dickerson, *Among Those Present* (New York: Ballantine reprint, 1977), 47.
70. John Seigenthaler, in recorded interview by R. J. Grele, February 21, 1966, 30–31, JFK Oral History Program.
71. Jack Conway, in interview by L. J. Hackman, April 11, 1972, 2, RFK Oral History Program.
72. Edwin Guthman, *We Band of Brothers* (New York, 1971), 75.
73. O'Donnell and Powers, *"Johnny,"* 189.
74. Evelyn Lincoln, *Kennedy and Johnson* (New York, 1968), 92–93.
75. James H. Rowe, Jr., in interview by author, August 16, 1964.
76. O'Donnell and Powers, *"Johnny,"* 191–193.
77. Conway, in Hackman interview, 2–3.
78. RFK, in recorded interview by John Bartlow Martin, April 13, 1964, II, 5, JFK Oral History Program.
79. Ibid., 9.
80. Bobby Baker, with Larry King, *Wheeling and Dealing: Confessions of a Capitol Hill Operator* (New York, 1978), 113. Rowe, in interview by author.
81. Charles Spalding, in recorded interview by Jean Stein, January 22, 1970, 2, Stein Papers.
82. Charles Bartlett, in recorded interview by Jean Stein, January 9, 1970, 11, Stein Papers; John Seigenthaler, in Geoghegan interview [July 1964], 73.
83. Bartlett, in Stein interview, 14.
84. Theodore H. White, *The Making of the President, 1960* (New York, 1961), 383.
85. John Seigenthaler, in recorded interview by L. J. Hackman, July 1, 1970, 88, RFK Oral History Program.
86. Author's journal, July 15, 1960.
87. O'Donnell and Powers, *"Johnny,"* 199.
88. *Time,* October 10, 1960.
89. Richard Wade, in recorded interview by Roberta Greene, December 13, 1973, 9–10, 20.
90. Ralph Horton, Jr., in recorded interview by Joseph Dolan, June 1, 1964, 29, JFK Oral History Program.
91. Tydings, in Greene interview, 7–10.
92. Joan Braden, in recorded interview by D. J. O'Brien, October 11, 1969, 82, RFK Oral History Program.
93. Ralph de Toledano, *RFK: The Man Who Would Be President* (New York: New American Library, Signet reprint, 1967), 169.
94. Norman Mailer, *The Presidential Papers* (New York, 1963), 36.
95. Hugh Sidey, "Brother on the Spot," in *The Kennedy Circle,* ed. Lester Tanzer (New York, 1961), 209.
96. As reported by Kennedy immediately afterward to Seigenthaler; Seigenthaler, in Grele interview, 168–169.
97. Merle Miller, ed., *Plain Speaking* (New York: Berkley reprint, 1974), 438.
98. Stewart Alsop, "Kennedy's Magic Formula," *Saturday Evening Post,* August 13, 1960.
99. Sidey, "Brother on the Spot," 207.
100. RFK, memorandum, February 14, 1959, RFK Papers.
101. Theodore Sorensen to RFK, December 14, 1959, RFK Papers.
102. RFK, "Georgia and Virginia," memorandum for the files, November 16, 1959, RFK Papers.
103. Author's journal, May 14, 1960.

104. RFK to JFK, June 24, 1960, JFK Papers.
105. Harris Wofford, in interview by Jean Stein, October 3, 1968, 4, Stein Papers.
106. Theodore H. White, 1960 convention notes, White Papers.
107. Author's journal, July 11, 1960; Stein and Plimpton, *American Journey,* 90.
108. Carl M. Brauer, *John F. Kennedy and the Second Reconstruction* (New York, 1977), 53.
109. John A. Williams, *The King God Didn't Save* (New York: Pocket Book reprint, 1971), 27.
110. This account is based on: Seigenthaler to the author, November 9, 1976; Wofford, in Stein interview, 9–20; Wofford, in recorded interview by Berl Bernhard, November 29, 1965, 24–28, JFK Oral History Program; Wofford's Christmas letter (mimeographed), January 7, 1964; and Seigenthaler, in Grele interview, 108–111.
111. J. K. Galbraith, *Ambassador's Journal* (Boston, 1969), 6.
112. Martin Luther King, Jr., "It's a Difficult Thing to Teach a President," *Look,* November 17, 1964; David L. Lewis, *King: A Critical Biography* (New York: Penguin, Pelican reprint, 1971), 129.
113. Brauer, *Kennedy and the Second Reconstruction,* 48.
114. Wofford, Christmas letter.
115. Murray Kempton, "His Brother's Keeper," *New York Post,* November 10, 1960.
116. *Atlanta Constitution,* September 10, 1960.
117. George McGovern, in recorded interview by Jean Stein, September 25, 1969, 1–2, Stein Papers; McGovern, in recorded interview by L. J. Hackman, July 16, 1970, 3–4, RFK Oral History Program.
118. *Time,* October 10, 1960.
119. Arthur Edson, "Bobby—Washington's No. 2 Man," AP feature for release April 14, 1963.
120. *Time,* October 10, 1960; Sidey, "Brother on the Spot," 209.
121. A thought I passed on to John Kennedy in a letter of August 30, 1960, Schlesinger Papers.
122. Wofford, Christmas letter; as amended by Theodore H. White, in interview by author, February 8, 1978.
123. Pierre Salinger, *With Kennedy* (Garden City, 1966), 51.
124. Jack Conway, in recorded interview by L. J. Hackman, April 11, 1972, 21–22, RFK Oral History Program.
125. Kempton, "His Brother's Keeper."
126. Churchill to JFK, November 11, 1960, JFK Papers.

11. To the Department of Justice (*pages 232–255*)

1. RFK, in recorded interview by John Bartlow Martin, February 29, 1964, 1, JFK Oral History Program.
2. John F. Kennedy, *A Compendium of Speeches, Statements, and Remarks Delivered During His Service in the Congress of the United States* (Washington, 1964), 1108.
3. Robert A. Lovett, in recorded interview by Dorothy Fosdick, July 20, 1964, 9, JFK Oral History Program.
4. RFK, memorandum, February 9, 1961, 10–11, RFK Papers.
5. Chester Bowles, *Promises to Keep* (New York, 1971), 299–300.
6. See W. A. Harriman and Elie Abel, *Special Envoy to Churchill and Stalin, 1941–1946* (New York, 1975), 78–105.
7. Author's journal, December 1, 1960.
8. Arthur M. Schlesinger, Jr., *A Thousand Days* (Boston, 1965), 149.
9. RFK, memorandum, 1–2.

10. Roswell Gilpatric, in recorded interview by D. J. O'Brien, May 5, 1970, 6, JFK Oral History Program.
11. RFK, in Martin interview, 12–13.
12. RFK, memorandum, 9.
13. Ibid., 5–6.
14. Ibid., 2–5.
15. Ibid., 13.
16. Dorothy Goldberg, *A Private View of a Public Life* (New York, 1975), 5.
17. RFK, in recorded interview by author, February 27, 1965, 53, JFK Oral History Program.
18. RFK, memorandum, 6–7, 12.
19. Author's journal, December 1, 1960.
20. Schlesinger, *Thousand Days,* 142–143, 162.
21. RFK, in interview by author, 50.
22. Author's journal, June 15, 1960.
23. RFK, memorandum, 7.
24. Hugh Sidey, "Brother on the Spot," in *The Kennedy Circle,* ed. Lester Tanzer (Washington, 1961), 186.
25. RFK, memorandum, 7; RFK, in interview by author, 49.
26. William O. Douglas, in recorded interview by Roberta Greene, November 13, 1969, 13–14, RFK Oral History Program; Douglas, in recorded interview by John Stewart, November 9, 1967, 13, JFK Oral History Program.
27. RFK, Martin interview, 21.
28. Drew Pearson to RFK, December 5, 1960, RFK Papers, 47–48.
29. RFK, in interview by author, 47–49.
30. Paul B. Fay, Jr., *The Pleasure of His Company* (New York, 1966), 11.
31. Clark Clifford, in recorded interview by L. J. Hackman, December 16, 1974, 65, JFK Oral History Program.
32. *New York Times,* November 23, 1960.
33. Author's journal, December 1, 1960.
34. RFK, in interview by author, 49.
35. William C. Sullivan, in interview by author, July 26, 1976.
36. Victor Navasky, *Kennedy Justice* (New York, 1971), 4.
37. W. O. Douglas, in introduction to Robert E. Thompson and Hortense Myers, *Robert F. Kennedy: The Brother Within* (New York, 1962). In 1969 Douglas recalled it somewhat differently: "In the end, I urged him to do it, but I was trying to get him to think through what he wanted to do with his life and that maybe this was a turning point" (Douglas, in Greene interview, 13).
38. Sidey, "Brother on the Spot," 186.
39. John Seigenthaler, in recorded interview by R. J. Grele, February 22, 1966, 182, JFK Oral History Program.
40. RFK, in interview by author, 49.
41. Seigenthaler, in Grele interview, 183–201.
42. Peter Maas, "Robert Kennedy Speaks Out," *Look,* March 28, 1961.
43. RFK, memorandum, 7.
44. RFK, in recorded interview by Anthony Lewis, December 4, 1964, I, 14, JFK Oral History Program.
45. RFK, memorandum, 8.
46. Ibid., 9.
47. Ralph de Toledano, *RFK: The Man Who Would Be President* (New York: New American Library, Signet reprint, 1968), 178.
48. Alexander M. Bickel, "Robert F. Kennedy: The Case Against Him for Attorney General," *New Republic,* January 9, 1961.
49. Booth Mooney, *LBJ: An Irreverent Chronicle* (New York, 1976), 50.

50. For a sketch, see Charlotte Hays, "South of the Line of Succession," *Washington Post,* December 30, 1973.
51. RFK, in Lewis interview, I, 20–21.
52. Bobby Baker, with Larry King, *Wheeling and Dealing: Confessions of a Capitol Hill Operator* (New York, 1978), 120–121.
53. RFK, memorandum, 13.
54. Ibid.
55. Senate Judiciary Committee, *Robert F. Kennedy: Attorney-General-Designate, Hearing,* 87 Cong., 1 Sess. (January 13, 1961), 4–5, 30.
56. Ibid., 15.
57. Ibid., 22.
58. Ibid., 34.
59. *New York Times,* January 14, 1961.
60. Maas, "Robert Kennedy Speaks Out."
61. William Manchester, *Portrait of a President* (Boston, 1962), 60.
62. *San Francisco News,* July 12, 1957.
63. RFK, in Martin interview, 35–36.
64. Maas, "Robert Kennedy Speaks Out."
65. Alexander M. Bickel, in recorded interview by Jean Stein, May 14, 1970, 4, Stein Papers.
66. *Berlingske Tidende,* February 3, 1963; translation in RFK Papers.
67. Roy Wilkins, in recorded interview by Jean Stein, May 12, 1970, Stein Papers.
68. Arthur Edson, "Bobby—Washington's No. 2 Man," AP feature for release April 14, 1963.
69. Ovid Demaris, *The Director* (New York, 1975), 137.
70. Edward V. Bander to author, March 17, 1977.
71. Ramsey Clark, in recorded interview by L. J. Hackman, June 29, 1970, 35, RFK Oral History Program.
72. Robert Morgenthau, in recorded interview by Jean Stein, November 21, 1969, 1, Stein Papers.
73. Louis Oberdorfer, in recorded interview by Roberta Greene, February 5, 1970, 18, RFK Oral History Program.
74. John Seigenthaler, in recorded interview by R. J. Grele, February 22, 1966, 219, JFK Oral History Program.
75. Nicholas Katzenbach, in recorded interview by Anthony Lewis, November 16, 1964, 42, JFK Oral History Program.
76. Norbert Schlei, in recorded interview by John Stewart, February 20–21, 1968, 21, JFK Oral History Program.
77. Archibald Cox to author, January 3, 1977.
78. Victor Navasky, *Kennedy Justice* (New York, 1971), 182. This brilliant if sometimes overschematic book is indispensable for an understanding of Robert Kennedy as Attorney General. I have drawn heavily on it.
79. William Orrick, in recorded interview by L. J. Hackman, April 13, 1970, 63, RFK Oral History Program.
80. Louis Oberdorfer, in interview by author, December 23, 1976.
81. John Douglas, in recorded interview by L. J. Hackman, June 16, 1969, 17, 27, RFK Oral History Program.
82. Nicholas Katzenbach, in recorded interview by Jean Stein, August 7, 1968, 17, Stein Papers.
83. Clark, in Hackman interview, 34.
84. Edwin Guthman, *We Band of Brothers* (New York, 1971), 88.
85. Angie Novello to RFK, November 4, 1963, RFK Papers.
86. Paul O'Neill, "The No. 2 Man in Washington," *Life,* January 26, 1962.
87. Douglas, in Hackman interview, 16.
88. Morgenthau, in Stein interview, 1.

89. Patrick Anderson, "Robert's Character," *Esquire,* April 1965.
90. Joseph Dolan, in recorded interview by L. J. Hackman, April 11, 1970, 220, RFK Oral History Program.
91. Navasky, *Kennedy Justice,* 354.
92. RFK to Evelyn Ewright, October 11, 1962, RFK Papers.
93. RFK, memorandum to assistant attorneys general, October 23, 1961, RFK Papers.
94. Navasky, *Kennedy Justice,* 355.
95. Ibid.
96. Jean Stein and George Plimpton, eds., *American Journey* (New York, 1970), 78.
97. Guthman, *We Band of Brothers,* 206.
98. Navasky, *Kennedy Justice,* 48.
99. Orrick, in Hackman interview, 27.
100. Clark, in Hackman interview, 9.
101. Guthman, *We Band of Brothers,* 86.

12. The Pursuit of Justice: J. Edgar Hoover (*pages* 256–271)

1. Victor Navasky, *Kennedy Justice* (New York, 1971), 8.
2. A. T. Mason, *Harlan Fiske Stone: Pillar of the Law* (New York, 1956), 152.
3. Max Lowenthal, *The Federal Bureau of Investigation* (New York, 1950), 298.
4. Mason, *Harlan Fiske Stone,* 153.
5. Fred J. Cook, "The FBI," *Nation,* October 18, 1958.
6. Senate Select Committee to Study Governmental Operations with respect to Intelligence Activities (hereafter cited as Church committee), *Hearings,* vol. 6, *Federal Bureau of Investigation,* 94 Cong., 2 Sess. (1976), 35, 409–415.
7. Church committee, *Final Report,* bk. II, *Intelligence Activities and the Rights of Americans,* 94 Cong., 2 Sess. (1976), 44.
8. George E. Allen, "J. Edgar Hoover Off-Duty," *Congressional Record,* October 13, 1972, S18165.
9. See interview with Allen in Ovid Demaris, "The Private Life of J. Edgar Hoover," *Esquire,* September 1975.
10. William C. Sullivan, "Personal Observations and Recommendations on Privacy," in *Privacy in a Free Society,* Final Report, Annual Chief Justice Warren Conference on Advocacy in the United States, June 1974, 94.
11. Demaris, "Private Life of Hoover."
12. W. W. Turner, *Hoover's FBI* (New York: Dell reprint, 1971), 29–30, 65.
13. Joseph L. Schott, *No Left Turns* (New York, 1975), 5–6, 130, 137, passim; William C. Sullivan, in interview by author, July 26, 1976; Ovid Demaris, *The Director* (New York, 1975), 81–82, 220.
14. W. C. Sullivan to J. E. Hoover, August 28, 1971, Sullivan Papers.
15. Schott, *No Left Turns,* 42, 249–250.
16. Turner, *Hoover's FBI,* xi.
17. Ibid., 4.
18. Roy Cohn, "Could He Walk on Water?" *Esquire,* November 1972.
19. W. C. Sullivan to Hoover, October 6, 1971, Sullivan Papers.
20. Demaris, *Director,* 77.
21. W. C. Sullivan, in interview by Jack Nelson of the *Los Angeles Times,* May 15, 1973; Frank J. Donner, "Hoover's Legacy," *Nation,* June 1, 1974.
22. Walter Pincus, "The Bureau's Budget," in *Investigating the FBI,* ed. Pat Watters and Stephen Gillers (New York, 1973), 70.
23. Dean Rusk, in testimony before the Senate Foreign Relations Committee, July 23, 1974; quoted in Church committee, *Final Report,* bk. III, *Supplementary*

Detailed Staff Reports on Intelligence Activities and the Rights of Americans, 94 Cong., 2 Sess. (1976), 469–470.

24. Clarence M. Kelley on CBS program *Face the Nation,* August 8, 1976.

25. W. C. Sullivan to C. D. DeLoach, July 19, 1966, in Church committee, *Hearings,* vol. 6, 357.

26. W. C. Sullivan, in interview by author, July 26, 1976. The situation changed, Sullivan added (in a letter to me of October 1, 1977), when Ramsey Clark became Attorney General.

27. Church committee, *Final Report,* bk. II, 284.

28. *Olmstead* v. *United States,* 277 U.S. 438 (1928).

29. *Nardone* v. *United States,* 302 U.S. 379 (1937); *Nardone* v. *United States,* 308 U.S. 338 (1939).

30. FDR to Thomas H. Eliot, February 21, 1941, Roosevelt Papers.

31. Joseph Lash, *Roosevelt and Churchill, 1939–1941* (New York, 1976), 119.

32. FDR to Robert H. Jackson, May 21, 1940, Roosevelt Papers.

33. FDR to Eliot.

34. R. H. Jackson to Congressman Hatton Sumners, March 19, 1941, in Church committee, *Final Report,* bk. III, 280.

35. Francis Biddle, *In Brief Authority* (New York, 1962), 187.

36. Demaris, *Director,* 127.

37. Elsey to Truman, February 2, 1950, in Church committee, *Final Report,* bk. III, 283.

38. Brownell to Hoover, May 22, 1954, in Church committee, *Final Report,* bk. III, 296–297.

39. Sullivan, in interview by author.

40. RFK, in recorded interview by Anthony Lewis, December 4, 1964, IV, 22, JFK Oral History Program; RFK, in recorded interview by John Bartlow Martin, February 29, 1964, 51, JFK Oral History Program.

41. RFK, in Lewis interview, IV, 33–35.

42. Nicholas Katzenbach, in recorded interview by L. J. Hackman, October 8, 1969, 40, RFK Oral History Program.

43. RFK, in Lewis interview, IV, 35–36.

44. Author's journal, October 17, 1961.

45. Ibid., March 13, 1962.

46. William Manchester, *The Death of a President* (New York, 1967), 119.

47. Benjamin C. Bradlee, *Conversations with Kennedy* (New York, 1975), 228.

48. Demaris, *Director,* 288.

49. Biddle, *In Brief Authority,* 259.

50. Clark Clifford, in recorded interview by L. J. Hackman, February 4, 1975, 44, JFK Oral History Program.

51. Demaris, *Director,* 189–190.

52. RFK, in Lewis interview, V, 13; Demaris, *Director,* 185–186.

53. RFK, in Lewis interview, IV, 35.

54. Hoover, note on H. L. Edwards to John P. Mohr, "Attorney General's Effort to Get Into Bureau Gymnasium," February 1, 1961, RFK/FBI/FOIA release.

55. Schott, *No Left Turns,* 192–193.

56. Demaris, *Director,* 147.

57. Walter Sheridan, in recorded interview by Jean Stein, July 23, 1968, 7, Stein Papers.

58. Sullivan, in interview by author.

59. Edwin Guthman, *We Band of Brothers* (New York, 1971), 261.

60. Sullivan, in interview by author; Turner, *Hoover's FBI,* 89.

61. Ralph de Toledano, *J. Edgar Hoover: The Man in His Time* (New York: Manor Books reprint, 1974), 307.

62. Navasky, *Kennedy Justice,* 35.

63. William Barry, in recorded interview by Roberta Greene, October 22, 1969, 69, RFK Oral History Program.

64. Toledano, *J. Edgar Hoover,* 291.

65. Sullivan, in interview by author.

66. S. J. Ungar, *FBI* (Boston, 1976), 276.

67. John Seigenthaler, in recorded interview by R. J. Grele, February 23, 1966, 352, JFK Oral History Program.

68. Hoover to RFK, February 22, 1963, RFK Papers.

69. Turner, *Hoover's FBI,* 43.

70. William Barry, in recorded interview by Jean Stein, April 1970, 11, Stein Papers.

71. RFK, in Lewis interview, V, 13.

72. RFK, in recorded interview by John Bartlow Martin, April 13, 1964, I, 34, 36, JFK Oral History Program.

13. The Pursuit of Justice: The Mob (*pages 272–297*)

1. It is on this point, I take it, that I disagree most sharply with Victor Navasky's analysis of the contest; but I want to express again my debt to the insight and information in his valuable *Kennedy Justice* (New York, 1971).

2. Hoover to RFK, January 10, 1961, in Senate Select Committee to Study Governmental Operations with respect to Intelligence Activities (hereafter cited as Church committee), *Hearings,* vol. 6, *Federal Bureau of Investigation,* 94 Cong., 2 Sess. (1976), 822.

3. Church committee, *Hearings,* vol. 6, 58–59; W. C. Sullivan to J. E. Hoover, October 6, 1971, Sullivan Papers.

4. As told by Henry Brandon, in author's journal, December 4, 1961. When Brandon subsequently quoted the Attorney General in the *London Sunday Times* as saying that half the membership of the CPUSA consisted of FBI agents, an outraged patriot sent the clipping to Hoover. "It was good of you to make this item available to me," Hoover quickly replied, enclosing five statements expressing his own views of the Communist threat. See exchange in RFK/FBI/FOIA release, March 5, 8, 1962.

5. Transcript of interview in RFK Papers [1961].

6. I owe this interesting intelligence to the Freedom of Information Act, under which I received copies of: Hoover's notation on a memorandum to L. B. Nicholas, July 21, 1950; his instruction to the FBI Boston office, October 28, 1954; and his notation on a memorandum of June 15, 1962.

7. RFK, in speech given at the University of Georgia Law School; *New York Times,* May 7, 1961.

8. RFK, statement before the Senate Government Operations Committee, September 25, 1963 (mimeographed), 3, 23, RFK Papers.

9. D. P. Moynihan, "The Private Government of Crime," *Reporter,* July 6, 1961.

10. William W. Turner could find only one; Turner, *Hoover's FBI* (New York: Dell reprint, 1971), 152.

11. William C. Sullivan, in interview by author, July 26, 1976; Navasky, *Kennedy Justice,* 44.

12. Peter Maas, *The Valachi Papers* (New York: Bantam reprint, 1969), 28.

13. Ovid Demaris, *The Director* (New York, 1975), 141.

14. Ibid., 141–142; Pat Watters and Stephen Gillers, eds., *Investigating the FBI* (New York, 1973), 207.

15. Gerald Goettel, "Why the Crime Syndicates Can't Be Touched," *Harper's,* November 1960.

16. Turner, *Hoover's FBI,* 157. Emphasis added.

17. "Interview with J. Edgar Hoover," *U.S. News & World Report,* December 21, 1964.
18. Navasky, *Kennedy Justice,* 33–34.
19. Ralph de Toledano, *J. Edgar Hoover* (New York: Manor Books reprint, 1974), 263.
20. Ibid., 313.
21. S. J. Ungar, *FBI* (Boston, 1976), 391.
22. Kennedy's figure in 1963 ("Robert Kennedy Speaks His Mind," *U.S. News & World Report,* January 28, 1963). Navasky lists twenty-seven (*Kennedy Justice,* 50). Probably Kennedy left out the CIA.
23. Toledano, *J. Edgar Hoover,* 306–307.
24. RFK, in recorded interview by Anthony Lewis, December 4, 1964, IV, 30, 32, JFK Oral History Program.
25. Peter Maas, *The Valachi Papers* (New York: Bantam reprint, 1969), 54–55.
26. Navasky, *Kennedy Justice,* 32.
27. RFK, in Lewis interview, IV, 27–28.
28. William H. Hundley, in recorded interview by J. A. Oesterle, February 22, 1971, 129, 144–145, RFK Oral History Program.
29. *FBI Law Enforcement Bulletin,* September 1963.
30. RFK, in recorded interview by John Bartlow Martin, April 13, 1964, I, 35, JFK Oral History Program.
31. Navasky, *Kennedy Justice,* 32.
32. RFK, in Martin interview, I, 31.
33. Peter Maas, "Robert Kennedy Speaks Out," *Look,* March 28, 1961.
34. There are several accounts of this meeting: William Orrick, in recorded interview by L. J. Hackman, April 14, 1970, 269–271, RFK Oral History Program; Joseph Dolan, in recorded interview by L. J. Hackman, July 18, 1970, 268, RFK Oral History Program; Ramsey Clark, in recorded interview by L. J. Hackman, July 20, 1970, 117–119, RFK Oral History Program.
35. RFK, in Martin interview, I, 37; Theodore C. Sorensen, *The Kennedy Legacy* (New York, 1969), 242.
36. Nicholas Katzenbach, in recorded interview by L. J. Hackman, October 8, 1969, 54–55, RFK Oral History Program.
37. See Robert F. Kennedy, "Attorney General's Opinion on Wiretaps," *New York Times Magazine,* June 3, 1962.
38. Alexander M. Bickel, in recorded interview by Jean Stein, May 14, 1970, 5, Stein Papers.
39. *On Lee* v. *United States,* 343 U.S. 747, 760–761. For a convenient summary of the criticism, see the American Civil Liberties Union report *The Wiretapping Problem Today* (March 1962).
40. In 1968 the Omnibus Crime Control and Safe Streets Act attempted to establish standards for wiretapping.
41. Church committee, *Final Report,* bk. III, *Supplementary Detailed Staff Reports on Intelligence Activities and the Rights of Americans,* 94 Cong., 2 Sess. (1976), 301.
42. Katzenbach, in Hackman interview, 58.
43. RFK, in Martin interview, I, 38.
44. Toledano, *J. Edgar Hoover,* 316.
45. Church committee, *Hearings,* vol. 6, 166.
46. Evans to RFK, February 17, 1966, in Toledano, *J. Edgar Hoover,* 318–319.
47. Church committee, *Hearings,* vol. 6, 200.
48. Church committee, *Final Report,* bk. III, 329–330.
49. Toledano, *J. Edgar Hoover,* 317.
50. Demaris, *Director,* 146.
51. Sullivan, in interview by author.

52. William Hundley, in interview by author, August 4, 1976.
53. Edwin Guthman, *We Band of Brothers* (New York, 1971), 263.
54. Navasky, *Kennedy Justice,* 88–89.
55. Frank Mankiewicz, in recorded interview by L. J. Hackman, September 9, 1969, 21–22, RFK Oral History Program.
56. Navasky, *Kennedy Justice,* 91.
57. Hundley, in interview by author.
58. Katzenbach, in Hackman interview, 41.
59. Victor Lasky, *Robert F. Kennedy: The Myth and the Man* (New York: Pocket Book reprint, 1971), 428.
60. G. Robert Blakey to RFK, December 14, 1966, RFK Papers.
61. Church committee, *Final Report,* bk. III, 368.
62. Ibid., 368–369.
63. Toledano, *J. Edgar Hoover,* 319.
64. Joseph W. Schott, *No Left Turns* (New York, 1975), 194.
65. Guthman, *We Band of Brothers,* 263–264.
66. Hundley, in interview by author; Hundley, in Oesterle interview, 45–46.
67. Katzenbach, in Hackman interview, 53.
68. Navasky, *Kennedy Justice,* 32.
69. Burke Marshall, "Can the FBI Rebuild Itself?" *Washington Post,* July 1, 1973.
70. John Douglas to RFK, December 27, 1966, RFK Papers.
71. Demaris, *Director,* 229.
72. Dolan, in Hackman interview, 287, 290, 291.
73. Demaris, *Director,* 145–146; Hundley, in Oesterle interview, 37–38.
74. Katzenbach, in Hackman interview, 41.
75. RFK, in Lewis interview, IV, 26.
76. J. Edgar Hoover, "The FBI's War on Organized Crime," *U.S. News & World Report,* April 18, 1966.
77. "Interview with J. Edgar Hoover," *U.S. News & World Report,* December 21, 1964.
78. And 677 in 1964. For statistics, see *Congressional Record,* March 11, 1969, S2642.
79. This letter, and another from Hunter on the same subject, were printed by Drew Pearson in the *Washington Post,* January 4, 1961; see Walter Sheridan, *The Fall and Rise of Jimmy Hoffa* (New York, 1972), 158–159, 165–166.
80. *New York Daily News,* December 21, 1960.
81. Navasky, *Kennedy Justice,* 413.
82. Sheridan, *Fall and Rise of Hoffa,* 193.
83. Ibid., 281.
84. Ibid., 217.
85. Ibid., 276–278.
86. Ibid., 280.
87. *Detroit Sunday News,* August 1, 1976.
88. Sheridan, *Fall and Rise of Hoffa,* 528.
89. *New York Times,* October 10, 1975.
90. Ralph James and Estelle James, *Hoffa and the Teamsters* (Princeton, 1965), 62.
91. Sheridan, *Fall and Rise of Hoffa,* 283, 459.
92. Ibid., 293, 460.
93. Ibid., 459.
94. Robert H. Jackson, "The Federal Prosecutor," *Journal of the American Judicature Society,* June 1940.
95. Navasky, *Kennedy Justice,* 417.
96. Ibid., 435–436.
97. Mortimer M. Caplin, "Special Racketeer Investigations," February 24, 1961, Johnson Papers; Navasky, *Kennedy Justice,* 49, 56, 60.

98. Maas, "Robert Kennedy Speaks Out."
99. Navasky, *Kennedy Justice,* 56–61; Louis Oberdorfer, in interview by author, December 29, 1976.
100. In congressional testimony in 1967, quoted by Herman Schwartz, "Six Years of Tapping and Bugging," *Civil Liberties Review,* Summer 1974.
101. Navasky, *Kennedy Justice,* 410.
102. Herbert Hoover, *Memoirs . . . The Cabinet and the Presidency, 1920–1933* (New York, 1952), 276–277.
103. Elmer L. Irey with William J. Slocum, *The Tax Dodgers* (New York, 1948), 26, 35–36.

14. The Pursuit of Justice: Civil Rights (*pages* 298–329)

1. Peter Maas, "Robert Kennedy Speaks Out," *Look,* March 22, 1961.
2. Edwin Guthman, *We Band of Brothers* (New York, 1971), 181.
3. Harris Wofford, in recorded interview by Berl Bernhard, November 29, 1965, 10–11, JFK Oral History Program.
4. Senate Commerce Committee, *The Speeches of Senator John F. Kennedy: Presidential Campaign of 1960,* 87 Cong., 1 Sess. (1961), 432, 576.
5. Harris Wofford, "Memorandum to President-Elect Kennedy on Civil Rights—1961," December 30, 1960, RFK Papers; Wofford to RFK, "On the Civil Rights Division," January 12, 1961, RFK Papers.
6. Carl M. Brauer, *John F. Kennedy and the Second Reconstruction* (New York, 1977), 66–67.
7. Martin Luther King, Jr., "It's a Difficult Thing to Teach a President," *Look,* November 17, 1964.
8. RFK, in recorded interview by Anthony Lewis, December 4, 1964, II, 4, 9, JFK Oral History Program. Burke Marshall also participated in the civil rights interviews on that date.
9. RFK, in recorded interview by John Bartlow Martin, February 29, 1964, 54, JFK Oral History Program.
10. John Seigenthaler, in recorded interview by R. J. Grele, February 22, 1966, 210, JFK Oral History Program.
11. Guthman, *We Band of Brothers,* 95–96.
12. RFK, memorandum, February 9, 1961, RFK Papers.
13. Burke Marshall, in recorded interview by Jean Stein, October 6, 1968, 2–3, Stein Papers.
14. RFK and Burke Marshall, in Lewis interview, II, 5.
15. Nicholas Katzenbach, in recorded interview by Anthony Lewis, November 16, 1964, 34–35, JFK Oral History Program.
16. John Seigenthaler, in recorded interview by R. J. Grele, February 23, 1966, 360–361, JFK Oral History Program.
17. Guthman, *We Band of Brothers,* 103–104.
18. RFK to the Board of Governors, Metropolitan Club, April 11 and September 19, 1961, RFK Papers; RFK to author, December 21, 1961, RFK Papers.
19. RFK, in Lewis interview, V, 22–23.
20. Alexander M. Bickel, *Politics and the Warren Court* (New York, 1972), 58–59.
21. Wofford to RFK, January 12, 1961, RFK Papers.
22. John T. Elliff, "Aspects of Federal Civil Rights Enforcement: The Justice Department and the FBI, 1939–1964," *Perspectives,* vol. 5 (1971), 621.
23. Victor Reuther, *The Brothers Reuther* (Boston, 1976), 281.
24. Elliff, "Civil Rights Enforcement," 643–647.
25. *To Secure These Rights: Report of the President's Committee on Civil Rights* (Washington, 1947), 123.

26. S. J. Ungar, *FBI* (Boston, 1976), 408.
27. William Sullivan, in interview by author, July 26, 1976; Senate Select Committee to Study Governmental Operations with respect to Intelligence Activities (hereafter cited as Church committee), *Hearings,* vol. 6, *Federal Bureau of Investigation,* 94 Cong., 1 Sess. (1975), 33.
28. Hoover, in interview by Dean Fischer, *Time,* December 14, 1970; see also interview by Ken Clawson, *Washington Post,* November 17, 1970.
29. James Wechsler, "The FBI's Failure in the South," *Progressive,* December 1963.
30. Elliff, "Civil Rights Enforcement," 650–651.
31. John Doar and Dorothy Landsberg, "The Performance of the FBI in Investigating Violations of Federal Laws Protecting the Right to Vote—1960–1967" (1971), in Church committee, *Hearings,* vol. 6, esp. 895–896, 903–904, 928; Arlie Schardt, "Civil Rights: Too Much, Too Late," in *Investigating the FBI,* ed. Pat Watters and Stephen Gillers (Garden City, N.Y., 1973), 184; Alan Lichtman, "The Federal Assault Against Voting Discrimination in the Deep South, 1957–1967," *Journal of Negro History,* October 1969, 352.
32. RFK, in Lewis interview, V, 22–23.
33. RFK to Black, n.d. [March 1961], Black Papers. The paper was the *Shades Valley Sun,* March 2, 1961. Black replied that the editorial had probably been written by his friend Charles Feidelson (Black to RFK, March 28, 1961, Black Papers).
34. The text of the Law Day speech was printed in the *New York Times,* May 7, 1961.
35. Brauer, *Kennedy and the Second Reconstruction,* 98.
36. Nicholas Katzenbach, in recorded interview by Jean Stein, September 27, 1968, 2, Stein Papers.
37. Howell Raines, *My Soul Is Rested* (New York, 1977), 337.
38. Brauer, *Kennedy and the Second Reconstruction,* 152–153, 343.
39. Peter Maas, "Robert Kennedy Speaks Out," *Look,* March 28, 1961.
40. Seigenthaler, in Grele interview, February 23, 1966, 334.
41. *New York Times,* May 7, 1961.
42. *Boynton* v. *Virginia,* 364 U.S. 454 (1960).
43. Guthman, *We Band of Brothers,* 167; Rowe's testimony before Church committee, *Hearings,* vol. 6, 117.
44. Gary Thomas Rowe, Jr., *My Undercover Years with the Ku Klux Klan* (New York, 1976), 39–44; Church committee, *Hearings,* vol. 6, 127.
45. RFK, in Lewis interview, II, 7.
46. Maas, "Robert Kennedy Speaks Out."
47. Harris Wofford, in recorded interview by Jean Stein, October 3, 1968, 19, Stein Papers.
48. Seigenthaler, in Grele interview, February 22, 1966, 305–309.
49. RFK, in Lewis interview, II, 23.
50. Seigenthaler, in Grele interview, February 22, 1966, 314–324.
51. Guthman, *We Band of Brothers,* 171.
52. Ungar, *FBI,* 410; Victor Navasky, *Kennedy Justice* (New York, 1971), 22.
53. Jean Stein and George Plimpton, eds., *American Journey* (New York, 1970), 103.
54. Seigenthaler, in Grele interview, February 22, 1966, 325–333.
55. Raines, *My Soul Is Rested,* 309.
56. Brauer, *Kennedy and the Second Reconstruction,* 102.
57. Raines, *My Soul Is Rested,* 308–309.
58. Edwin Guthman in Pierre Salinger et al., eds., *An Honorable Profession* (Garden City, N.Y., 1968), 20–21.
59. RFK in Lewis interview, II, 20, 21; Guthman, *We Band of Brothers,* 178.
60. John Lewis, in recorded interview by Jean Stein, November 26, 1968, 3, Stein Papers.
61. William Orrick, in recorded interview by L. J. Hackman, April 14, 1970, 249–253, RFK Oral History Program.

62. RFK, in Lewis interview, III, 12–13.
63. August Meier and Elliott Rudwick, *CORE: A Study in the Civil Rights Movement, 1942–1968* (New York, 1973), 139.
64. John Maguire, in recorded interview by Jean Stein, October 17, 1969, 9, Stein Papers.
65. Raines, *My Soul Is Rested,* 123, 277.
66. RFK, in Lewis interview, III, 11.
67. Ibid.
68. Guthman, *We Band of Brothers,* 154–155.
69. Stein and Plimpton, *American Journey,* 96; Guthman, *We Band of Brothers,* 175.
70. Anthony Lewis and the *New York Times, Portrait of a Decade* (New York, 1964), 118.
71. Brauer, *Kennedy and the Second Reconstruction,* 119.
72. RFK, in Lewis interview, I, 21.
73. Elliff, "Civil Rights Enforcement," 651–652.
74. Doar and Landsberg, "Performance of the FBI," 905–906.
75. RFK, "Civil Liberties: Against the Rule of Force," address to Ansonia Independent Democratic Club, October 8, 1964, RFK Papers.
76. Burke Marshall, *Federalism and Civil Rights* (New York, 1964), 9.
77. Ibid., 11–12.
78. Raines, *My Soul Is Rested,* 228.
79. Vincent Harding, in recorded interview by Jean Stein, December 9, 1969, 4, Stein Papers.
80. RFK, in Lewis interview, III, 25.
81. Raines, *My Soul Is Rested,* 228.
82. Howard Zinn, *SNCC: The New Abolitionists* (Boston: Beacon reprint, 1965), 58–59.
83. James Forman, *The Making of Black Revolutionaries* (New York, 1972), 264.
84. Meier and Rudwick, *CORE,* 175.
85. Martin Luther King, Jr., "Dear Friend" fund-raising letter, November 11, 1961, Schlesinger Papers.
86. RFK, in Lewis interview, III, 27.
87. Forman, *Making of Black Revolutionaries,* 265–266.
88. Miriam Feingold, "Chronicling the 'Movement,'" *Reviews in American History,* March 1974, 155.
89. Samuel Lubell, "It's Bobby Who Roils Dixie," *Detroit Free Press,* July 13, 1961.
90. Marshall, *Federalism and Civil Rights,* 46–48.
91. RFK, in foreword to Marshall, *Federalism and Civil Rights,* viii.
92. Lichtman, "Federal Assault," 359.
93. Brauer, *Kennedy and the Second Reconstruction,* 158.
94. Burke Marshall to R. H. Barrett, January 3, 1964, Marshall Papers.
95. Thurgood Marshall, in recorded interview by Berl Bernhard, April 7, 1964, 22–24, JFK Oral History Program.
96. RFK, in Marshall, *Federalism and Civil Rights,* ix.
97. Brauer, *Kennedy and the Second Reconstruction,* 167.
98. Burke Marshall, "Equitable Remedies as Instruments of Social Change," speech at New York University, November 14, 1964, Marshall Papers.
99. R. H. Jackson, *The Supreme Court in the American System of Government* (Cambridge, Mass., 1955), 70–72.
100. Bickel, *Politics and the Warren Court,* 112–113.
101. Marshall, *Federalism and Civil Rights,* 81.
102. Marshall, "Equitable Remedies."
103. Pat Watters and Reese Cleghorn, *Climbing Jacob's Ladder: The Arrival of Negroes in Southern Politics* (New York, 1967), 231.
104. Walter Lord, *The Past That Would Not Die* (New York, 1965), 247.

105. RFK, in Lewis interview, III, 15–17.
106. Marshall, *Federalism and Civil Rights,* 31.
107. Wilkins to JFK, June 22, 1961, JFK Papers. The telegram is annotated: "Discussed with him."
108. RFK, in Lewis interview, III, 38; IV, 7.
109. Robert Sherrill, *Gothic Politics in the Deep South* (New York: Ballantine reprint, 1969), 212.
110. RFK, in recorded interview by John Bartlow Martin, May 14, 1964, I, 10, JFK Oral History Program.
111. RFK phone messages, June 1962, RFK Papers.
112. RFK, in Martin interview, I, 10.
113. See "Judicial Performance in the Fifth Circuit," *Yale Law Journal,* November 1963, n. 87. The Clarke County situation is well described by one of the government attorneys in Gerald M. Stern, "Judge William Harold Cox and the Right to Vote in Clarke County, Mississippi," in *Southern Justice,* ed. Leon Friedman (New York, 1965).
114. W. H. Cox to J. C. McLaurin, February 14, 1963, RFK Papers.
115. Cox to John Doar, October 16, 1963, RFK Papers.
116. RFK to Cox, November 18, 1963, RFK Papers.
117. *New York Times,* March 9, 1964.
118. Leon Jaworski to Burke Marshall, March 23, 1964, Marshall Papers.
119. "Judicial Performance," n. 71.
120. Marshall, *Federalism and Civil Rights,* 6.
121. Navasky, *Kennedy Justice,* 112.
122. Ibid., 251.
123. RFK to Mrs. Franklin D. Roosevelt, May 22, 1962, RFK Papers.
124. Navasky, *Kennedy Justice,* 270.
125. Mary J. Curzan, "A Case Study in the Selection of Federal Judges in the Fifth Circuit, 1953–1963." This Yale Ph.D. dissertation draws on confidential interviews and is available only in summary. It is discussed in Brauer, *Kennedy and the Second Reconstruction,* 123, 340; and in Navasky, *Kennedy Justice,* 269–270. Brauer points out that Kennedy's integrationist judges were largely appointed in the upper and western south, and that the somewhat rigid Curzan criteria had the curious result of classifying Judge Frank Johnson as a segregationist.
126. RFK, in Lewis interview, VI, 35.
127. Martin Luther King, Jr., "Equality Now," *Nation,* February 4, 1961.
128. Archibald C. Cox, address before the Associated Harvard Alumni, *Harvard Today,* June 1975.
129. John F. Kennedy, *Public Papers . . . 1961* (Washington, 1962), 256.
130. William S. White, *The Professional* (Boston, 1964), 228.
131. Evelyn Lincoln, *Kennedy and Johnson* (New York, 1968), 182.
132. John Seigenthaler, in recorded interview by L. J. Hackman, June 5, 1970, 26, RFK Oral History Program.
133. Brauer, *Kennedy and the Second Reconstruction,* 82.
134. RFK, in Lewis interview, IV, 23, 27.
135. "Interview of Attorney General by Bob Spivack . . . May 18, 1962," 11, RFK Papers.
136. Berl Bernhard, in interview by author, August 23, 1965.
137. Theodore M. Hesburgh, in recorded interview by Joseph E. O'Connor, March 27, 1966, 21, 23, JFK Oral History Program.
138. Ibid., 8–9.
139. Harris Wofford, in recorded interview by L. J. Hackman, February 3, 1969, 147, RFK Oral History Program.
140. RFK, in Lewis interview, VI, 38–39.
141. Hesburgh, in O'Connor interview, 20.

142. Martin Luther King, Jr., "Fumbling on the New Frontier," *Nation,* March 3, 1962.
143. Robert C. Weaver, in recorded interview by Daniel Patrick Moynihan, October 1, 1964, 210, JFK Oral History Program.
144. Wilkins to Dungan, November 19, 1962, JFK Papers.
145. Loren Miller, "Farewell to Liberals: A Negro View," *Nation,* October 20, 1962.
146. Bayard Rustin, "The Meaning of the March on Washington," *Liberation,* October 1963.
147. Meier and Rudwick, *CORE,* 180.
148. Forman, *Making of Black Revolutionaries,* 265, 546.
149. King, "It's Difficult to Teach a President."
150. Arthur Edson, Associated Press story on Robert Kennedy, April 14, 1963, RFK Papers; Clarence Mitchell, in recorded interview by John Stewart, February 1967, 46, JFK Oral History Program.
151. Marshall, in Bernhard interview, April 7, 1964, 16.
152. Stein and Plimpton, *American Journey,* 111.
153. Harris Wofford, in interview by L. J. Hackman, May 22, 1968, 63, RFK Oral History Program.

15. The Pursuit of Justice: Ross Barnett and George Wallace (*pages* 330–356)

1. Loren Miller, "Farewell to Liberals: A Negro View," *Nation,* October 20, 1962.
2. Alexis de Tocqueville, *The Old Regime and the French Revolution,* ch. 4.
3. On *Meet the Press,* May 26, 1963; James Meredith, *Three Years in Mississippi* (Bloomington, Ind., 1966), 294.
4. John Bowers, "James Meredith at Columbia Law," *New York Herald Tribune,* April 3, 1966.
5. Walter Lord, *The Past That Would Not Die* (New York, 1965), 139.
6. Author's journal, September 17, 1962.
7. Transcript of conversation between RFK and Governor Ross Barnett, 12:20 P.M., September 25, 1962, Burke Marshall Papers.
8. RFK, in recorded interview by Anthony Lewis, December 4, 1964, VII, 6, JFK Oral History Program.
9. Edwin Guthman, *We Band of Brothers* (New York, 1971), 189; Lord, *Past That Would Not Die,* ch. 7; C. M. Brauer, *John F. Kennedy and the Second Reconstruction* (New York, 1977), ch. 7.
10. Guthman, *We Band of Brothers,* 189.
11. RFK, in Lewis interview, VII, 9–10.
12. Author's journal, September 28, 1962.
13. Ibid., September 29, 1962.
14. Transcript of conversation between JFK and Barnett, 2:30 P.M., September 29, 1962, Burke Marshall Papers.
15. Author's journal, September 29, 1962.
16. Norbert Schlei, in recorded interview by John Stewart, February 20–21, 1968.
17. Transcript of conversation between RFK and Barnett, 12:45 P.M., September 30, 1962, Burke Marshall Papers.
18. RFK, in Lewis interview, VII, 11.
19. Budd Schulberg, "R.F.K.—Harbinger of Hope," *Playboy,* January 1969.
20. Nicholas Katzenbach, in recorded interview by Anthony Lewis, November 29, 1964, 15–16, JFK Oral History Program.
21. Guthman, *We Band of Brothers,* 201; RFK, in Lewis interview, VIII, 5.
22. Meredith, *Three Years in Mississippi,* 194.
23. John F. Kennedy, *Public Papers . . . 1962* (Washington, 1963), 728.

24. Guthman, *We Band of Brothers,* 204–205.
25. Katzenbach, in Lewis interview, 30.
26. RFK, in Lewis interview, VII, 14, 17.
27. Lord, *Past That Would Not Die,* 3–4.
28. RFK, in Lewis interview, VII, 12.
29. Theodore C. Sorensen, *Kennedy* (New York, 1965), 487.
30. RFK, in Lewis interview, VII, 23.
31. Burke Marshall, *Federalism and Civil Rights* (New York, 1965), 68.
32. RFK, in Lewis interview, VII, 22, 25.
33. Lord, *Past That Would Not Die,* 231.
34. James Meredith to RFK, September 5, 1963, RFK Papers.
35. Guthman, *We Band of Brothers,* 205.
36. Ibid., 181.
37. John F. Kennedy, *Profiles in Courage* (New York, 1956), ch. 6.
38. RFK, in Lewis interview, VII, 10.
39. John F. Kennedy, *Public Papers . . . 1961* (Washington, 1962), 19.
40. James W. Silver, *Mississippi: The Closed Society* (New York, 1964), 144.
41. RFK to H. M. Ray, April 16, 1963, RFK Papers.
42. Guthman, *We Band of Brothers,* 188.
43. Ralph Dungan relaying the message from Rusk to JFK, October 3, 1962, JFK Papers.
44. Howard P. Jones to RFK, October 25, 1962, RFK Papers.
45. Arthur M. Schlesinger, Jr., *A Thousand Days* (Boston, 1965), 948.
46. William Goldsmith, *The Growth of Presidential Power* (New York, 1974), iii, 1665.
47. Martin Luther King, Jr., "It's a Difficult Thing to Teach a President," *Look,* November 17, 1964.
48. Martin Luther King, Jr., "Bold Design for a New South," *Nation,* March 30, 1963.
49. John F. Kennedy, *Public Papers . . . 1963* (Washington, 1964), 222.
50. King, "Bold Design for New South."
51. Burke Marshall to Leslie Dunbar, February 26, 1963, Marshall Papers.
52. RFK, in recorded interview by Anthony Lewis, December 22, 1964, 4, JFK Oral History Program.
53. Jean Stein and George Plimpton, eds., *American Journey* (New York, 1970), 114.
54. *Atlanta Inquirer,* April 14, 1962; D. W. Matthews and J. R. Prothro, *Negroes and the New Southern Politics* (New York, 1966), 240.
55. Martin Luther King, Jr., *Why We Can't Wait* (New York: New American Library, Signet reprint, 1964), 80–81.
56. Coretta King, *My Life with Martin Luther King, Jr.* (New York, 1970), 239–241.
57. King, *Why We Can't Wait,* 97.
58. Stein and Plimpton, *American Journey,* 118.
59. Alan F. Westin and Barry Mahoney, *The Trial of Martin Luther King* (New York, 1974), 149.
60. King, *Why We Can't Wait,* 103.
61. Stein and Plimpton, *American Journey,* 119.
62. David L. Lewis, *King: A Critical Biography* (New York: Penguin Books, Pelican reprint, 1971), 199.
63. Andrew Young, in recorded interview by Jean Stein, September 9, 1968, 4, Stein Papers.
64. Lewis, *King,* 202.
65. Matthews and Prothro, *Negroes,* 240.
66. King, *Why We Can't Wait,* 103.
67. Young, in Stein interview, 3; Stein and Plimpton, *American Journey,* 117–118.
68. Michael Dorman, *We Shall Overcome* (New York: Dell reprint, 1965), 197.
69. The *New Yorker* piece was incorporated in James Baldwin, *The Fire Next Time* (New York, 1963); the quotation is from p. 63.

70. RFK, in Lewis interview, December 22, 1964, 64.
71. James Baldwin, in recorded interview by Jean Stein, February 7, 1970, 1, Stein Papers.
72. Burke Marshall, in recorded interview by Jean Stein, October 6, 1968, 31.
73. August Meier and Elliott Rudwick, *CORE: A Study in the Civil Rights Movement, 1942–1968* (New York, 1975), 116, 143, 298, 408.
74. RFK, in recorded interview by Anthony Lewis, December 6, 1964, I, 7, JFK Oral History Program.
75. Baldwin, in Stein interview, 2–3.
76. Ibid., 4.
77. Kenneth B. Clark, in recorded interview by Jean Stein, January 30, 1970, 3, Stein Papers; James Wechsler, "RFK and Baldwin," *New York Post,* May 28, 1963.
78. Lena Horne and Richard Schickel, *Lena* (New York: New American Library, Signet reprint, 1966), 210.
79. Clark, in Stein interview, 4.
80. RFK, in Lewis interview, December 22, 1964, I, 68.
81. Kenneth B. Clark, in interview by author, September 9, 1976.
82. Horne and Schickel, *Lena,* 209.
83. *Meet the Press,* May 26, 1963; Meredith, *Three Years in Mississippi,* 299.
84. Wechsler, "RFK and Baldwin."
85. RFK, in Lewis interview, December 22, 1964, I, 67.
86. Author's journal, May 27, 1963; RFK, in recorded interview by John Bartlow Martin, April 30, 1964, III, 35, JFK Oral History Program.
87. Wechsler, "RFK and Baldwin."
88. Author's journal, May 27, 1963.
89. James Baldwin, Malcolm X, Martin Luther King talk with Kenneth B. Clark, in *The Negro Protest* (Boston, 1963), 3.
90. RFK, in Martin interview, III, 35–36.
91. Clark, in interview by author.
92. Committee on Equal Employment Opportunity, Minutes of the Seventh Meeting, May 29, 1963, Lyndon Johnson Papers.
93. Committee on Equal Employment Opportunity, Transcript of Eighth Meeting, July 18, 1963, 33–38; Jack Conway, in recorded interview by L. J. Hackman, April 11, 1972, 83, RFK Oral History Program; William V. Shannon, *The Heir Apparent* (New York, 1967), 49.
94. RFK, in Lewis interview, December 4, 1964, IV, 26.
95. RFK, memorandum, July 16, 1963, RFK Papers.
96. RFK, in Lewis interview, December 4, 1964, VI, 7.
97. Marshall Frady, *Wallace* (New York, 1968), 133, 142.
98. "Playboy Interview: Martin Luther King," *Playboy,* January 1965.
99. Brooks Hays to JFK, November 30, 1962, reporting on conversation with Sparkman, RFK Papers.
100. JFK to RFK, November 30, 1962, RFK Papers.
101. RFK, in Lewis interview, December 6, 1964, I, 42.
102. The observer was Benjamin Muse; Carl M. Brauer, *John F. Kennedy and the Second Reconstruction* (New York, 1977), 141.
103. RFK, in Lewis interview, December 6, 1964, I, 19–20.
104. The quotations are from "Transcript of Conversation between Attorney General Robert F. Kennedy and Governor Wallace, Montgomery, Alabama, April 25, 1963," RFK Papers. See also Frady, *Wallace,* 150–169.
105. JFK, *Public Papers . . . 1963,* 408.
106. Pierre Salinger, "Memorandum of Conversation between President Kennedy and Governor George Wallace . . . May 18, 1963," JFK Papers.
107. Burke Marshall, "Memorandum to the Members of the Cabinet re: University of Alabama," May 21, 1963, Marshall Papers.

108. RFK, in Lewis interview, December 1964, I, 30–31.
109. Ibid., 31–33.
110. Ibid., 36.
111. RFK to Frances Battle, June 11, 1963, RFK Papers.
112. Guthman, *We Band of Brothers,* 214–216; Sorensen, *Kennedy,* 492. There is also valuable material in Robert Drew's cinema verité film *Crisis—Behind a Presidential Commitment* (ABC News—Drew Associates, 1963).
113. Howell Raines, *My Soul Is Rested* (New York, 1977), 331, 341.
114. Frady, *Wallace,* 169–170; Guthman, *We Band of Brothers,* 214–217; *New York Times,* June 12, 1963; Dorman, *We Shall Overcome,* 335–365.
115. RFK, in Lewis interview, December 6, 1964, I, 43.
116. Robert Sherrill, *Gothic Politics in the Old South* (New York, Ballantine reprint, 1969), 331–332.
117. Robert F. Kennedy, Jr., *Judge Frank M. Johnson: A Study in Integrity* (New York, 1978), ch. 15.
118. RFK to David Kennedy and to Michael Kennedy, June 11, 1963, RFK Papers.

16. The Pursuit of Justice: Martin Luther King (*pages* 357–382)

1. RFK, in recorded interview by Anthony Lewis, December 4, 1964, VIII, 25; and December 6, 1964, II, 3, 5, JFK Oral History Program.
2. RFK, in Lewis interview, December 6, 1964, II, 7–9; RFK, in recorded interview by John Bartlow Martin, April 30, 1964, III, 39–40, JFK Oral History Program.
3. John F. Kennedy, *Public Papers . . . 1963* (Washington, 1964), 469.
4. James Meredith, *Three Years in Mississippi* (Bloomington, Ind., 1966), 310; Jack Mendelsohn, *The Martyrs* (New York, 1966), 78–80; article on Doar in *Milwaukee Sentinel,* August 12, 1963.
5. Charles Evers, in recorded interview by Jean Stein, n.d. [1968], 4, Stein Papers.
6. Charles Evers, "For Robert F. Kennedy," *New York Post,* October 23, 1964.
7. John Lewis, in recorded interview by Jean Stein, September 9, 1968, 1–3, Stein Papers.
8. William J. vanden Heuvel, in recorded interview by Jean Stein, November 10, 1968, 1–5, Stein Papers; Anthony Lewis and the *New York Times, Portrait of a Decade* (New York, 1964), 298–300.
9. Jack Newfield, *Robert Kennedy* (New York, 1969), 22–23.
10. RFK, in Lewis interview, December 22, 1964, 80–81.
11. Kennedy, *Public Papers . . . 1963,* 469.
12. Luther Hodges, in recorded interview by D. B. Jacobs, May 18, 1964, 92, JFK Oral History Program.
13. Victor Navasky, *Kennedy Justice* (New York, 1971), 99.
14. RFK, in Lewis interview, December 22, 1964, 4; December 4, 1964, VI, 19, VIII, 14.
15. For the background of the bill, see, from the administration's viewpoint, Norbert Schlei, in recorded interview by John Stewart, February 20–21, 1968, 52 ff., JFK Oral History Program; and Nicholas Katzenbach, in recorded interview by Anthony Lewis, November 16, 1964, 42 ff., JFK Oral History Program. From the viewpoint of the civil rights leadership, see Joseph Rauh, unpublished manuscript on the fight for the 1964 civil rights bill, Rauh Papers.
16. Marshall, in Lewis interview with RFK, December 4, 1964, 27.
17. Norbert Schlei to RFK, "Comments of the Vice President on the Civil Rights Legislative Proposals," June 4, 1963, RFK Papers; Schlei, in Stewart interview, 47–49.
18. Bobby Baker to Mike Mansfield, June 27, 1963, JFK Papers.
19. RFK, in Lewis interview, December 22, 1964, 5.

20. RFK, in Lewis interview, December 4, 1964, VIII, 24; and December 6, I, 3.
21. RFK, in Lewis interview, December 6, 1964, I, 52–53.
22. Burke Marshall, in recorded interview by Jean Stein, October 5, 1969, 4, Stein Papers.
23. RFK, in Lewis interview, December 6, 1964, I, 9–10.
24. Marshall, in Stein interview, October 6, 1968, 27–28.
25. Jean Stein and George Plimpton, eds., *American Journey* (New York, 1970), 123–124.
26. Joseph Rauh, unpublished manuscript, 4.
27. Rauh, "Memorandum Concerning Administration's Civil Rights Bill as Background for Meeting of Pro-Civil-Rights Groups on July 2, 1963," RFK Papers.
28. Jervis Anderson, *A. Philip Randolph: A Political Portrait* (New York, 1973), 323–325.
29. Author's journal, June 22, 1963.
30. I describe the meeting at length in *A Thousand Days* (Boston, 1965), 969–971.
31. Author's journal, June 22, 1963.
32. Joseph Rauh, in recorded interview by C. T. Morrissey, December 23, 1965, 103–104, JFK Oral History Program.
33. Martin Luther King, Jr., "It's a Difficult Thing to Teach a President," *Look,* November 17, 1964.
34. Walter Reuther, in recorded interview by Jean Stein, October 24, 1968, 12–13, Stein Papers; John Douglas, in recorded interview by L. J. Hackman, May 5, 1970, 2–3; Jack Conway, in recorded interview by L. J. Hackman, December 29, 1972, 8–9; Alan Raywid, in recorded interview by Roberta W. Greene, August 15, 1974, 34–35, RFK Oral History Program.
35. For details, see Douglas, in Hackman interview, and Raywid, in Greene interview.
36. Author's journal, August 15, 1963.
37. The original text may be found in Joanne Grant, *Black Protest: History, Documents and Analyses* (New York, 1968), 375–377.
38. Reuther, in Stein interview, 14.
39. James Forman, *The Making of Black Revolutionaries* (New York, 1972), 332, 335.
40. Ibid., 335–336.
41. Malcolm X, *Autobiography* (New York: Grove reprint, 1966), 280–281.
42. John A. Williams, *This Is My Country Too* (New York: New American Library, Signet reprint, 1966), 149.
43. Bayard Rustin, "The Washington March—a 10-Year Perspective," *Crisis,* September 1973.
44. Senate Select Committee to Study Governmental Operations with respect to Intelligence Activities (hereafter cited as Church committee), *Final Report,* bk. III, *Supplementary Detailed Staff Reports on Intelligence Activities and the Rights of Americans,* 94 Cong., 2 Sess. (1976), 105–109.
45. William Sullivan, in interview by author, July 26, 1976.
46. Quoted in Department of Justice, "Report of . . . Task Force to Review the FBI Martin Luther King, Jr., Security Assassination Investigation," January 11, 1977 (mimeographed), 165–166, 172.
47. Ibid., 113, 123.
48. Church committee, *Final Report,* bk. III, 82, 87–91.
49. Hoover to RFK, April 20, 1962, RFK Papers.
50. Don Oberdorfer, "King Adviser Says FBI 'Used' Him," *Washington Post,* December 15, 1975.
51. Senate Judiciary Committee, Internal Security Subcommittee, Levison Hearing, April 30, 1962, transcript in RFK Papers.
52. Stanley Levison, in interview by author, August 3, 1976.
53. Coretta Scott King, *My Life with Martin Luther King, Jr.* (New York, 1969), 345.

54. Church committee, *Final Report,* bk. III, 95–96; King to O'Dell, July 3, 1963, in Navasky, *Criminal Justice,* 143–144.
55. Church committee, *Final Report,* bk. III, 88.
56. Burke Marshall, in interview by author, August 1, 1976.
57. Levison, in interview by author.
58. Harris Wofford, in recorded interview by L. J. Hackman, February 3, 1969, 143, RFK Oral History Program.
59. John Seigenthaler, in recorded interview by R. J. Grele, February 22, 1966, 336–338, JFK Oral History Program.
60. RFK, in Lewis interview, December 4, 1964, VI, 2.
61. Church committee, *Hearings,* vol. 6, *Federal Bureau of Investigation,* 94 Cong., 1 Sess. (1975), 208.
62. Levison, in interview by author.
63. Department of Justice, "Report of Task Force to Review King," 125.
64. Church committee, *Hearings,* vol. 6, 170.
65. Sullivan, in interview by author.
66. Oberdorfer, *Washington Post,* December 15, 1975. See also David L. Lewis, *King: A Critical Biography* (New York: Penguin Books, Pelican reprint, 1957), 357: "Attorney Stanley Levison . . . advised Martin that his Vietnam position would bankrupt the organization."
67. Marshall, in interview by author; Carl Rowan, "King's 'Communist Adviser,' " *New York Post,* December 19, 1975.
68. Edward Jay Epstein, *Legend: The Secret World of Lee Harvey Oswald* (New York, 1978), 20, 263–264.
69. For accounts of the Kennedy meeting as reported by King to Young, see Leon Howell, "An Interview with Andrew Young," *Christianity and Crisis,* February 16, 1976; Howell Raines, *My Soul Is Rested* (New York, 1977), 430–431; Ovid Demaris, *The Director* (New York, 1975), 210; Church committee, *Final Report,* bk. III, 97.
70. Levison, in interview by author.
71. Howell, "Interview with Young"; Levison, in interview by author.
72. JFK, *Public Papers . . . 1963,* 574.
73. RFK to Senator Mike Monroney, July 23, 1963, RFK Papers. Identical letters went to a number of senators.
74. Sullivan, in interview by author.
75. Victor Navasky, "The Government and Martin Luther King," *Atlantic Monthly,* November 1970.
76. Church committee, *Final Report,* bk. III, 101–102.
77. David Wise, *The American Police State* (New York, 1976), 301.
78. *New York Times,* June 20 and 21, 1969.
79. So Evans told the Bureau; see Church committee, *Final Report,* bk. III, 103.
80. Rowan, "King's 'Communist Adviser.' "
81. Wise, *American Police State,* 301.
82. Howell, "Interview with Young."
83. Martin Luther King, Jr., *Why We Can't Wait* (New York: New American Library, Signet reprint, 1964), 147.
84. Levison, in interview by author.
85. Ibid.
86. Church committee, *Final Report,* bk. III, 132; Department of Justice, "Report of Task Force to Review King," 120, 176.
87. Nicholas Katzenbach, in recorded interview by L. J. Hackman, October 8, 1969, 61, RFK Oral History Program.
88. Sullivan, in interview by author.
89. Church committee, *Final Report,* bk. III, 143, 146.
90. RFK, in Lewis interview, December 4, 1964, VI, 7–8.

91. Church committee, *Final Report*, bk. III, 133.
92. Ibid., 108, 136–137.
93. Ibid., 137.
94. Ibid., 83.
95. *Time*, December 14, 1970.
96. *U.S. News & World Report*, December 7, 1964.
97. Church committee, *Final Report*, bk. III, 158–160.
98. Howell Raines, *My Soul Is Rested*, 428.
99. Howell, "Interview with Young."
100. Church committee, *Hearings*, vol. 6, 210.
101. Hugh Sidey, "L.B.J., Hoover and Domestic Spying," *Time*, February 10, 1975.
102. Church committee, *Final Report*, bk. III, 154.
103. Katzenbach, in Hackman interview, 69–70.
104. Kenneth Clark, in interview by author, September 9, 1976.
105. Church committee, *Final Report*, bk. III, 163–168; Howell, "Interview with Young."
106. Sullivan, in interview by author.
107. *Time*, December 14, 1970.
108. RFK, statement before the Senate Commerce Committee, July 1, 1963 (Department of Justice release), 14, RFK Papers.
109. Katzenbach, in Lewis interview, 63.
110. RFK, in Lewis interview, December 22, 1964, 15, 17.
111. RFK, statement before Senate Judiciary Committee, July 18, 1963 (Department of Justice release), 23–24, RFK Papers.
112. For a good account, see Dick Dabney, *A Good Man: The Life of Sam J. Ervin* (Boston, 1976), 210–217; also, Senate Judiciary Committee, *Hearings: Civil Rights —The President's Program*, 88 Cong., 2 Sess. (July–September 1963), passim.
113. Navasky, *Kennedy Justice*, 96–97.

17. The Politics of Justice (*pages* 383–407)

1. Peter Maas, "Robert Kennedy Speaks Out," *Look*, March 28, 1961.
2. Ramsey Clark, in interview by author, March 15, 1977.
3. Ovid Demaris, *The Director* (New York, 1975), 284; Courtney Evans to A. H. Belmont, "Re: Paul Corbin," February 1, 1962, RFK/FBI/FOIA release.
4. Hubert Humphrey to John Bailey, May 22, 1961, RFK Papers.
5. Author's journal, June 2, 1963.
6. Ibid., May 2, 1962.
7. RFK to John Bailey, July 19, 1961, RFK Papers.
8. Donald M. Wilson, in recorded interview by James Greenfield, September 2, 1964, 31, JFK Oral History Program.
9. Author's journal, September 18, 1962. See also Joseph Dolan, in recorded interview by L. J. Hackman, July 18, 1970, 299, RFK Oral History Program; John English, in recorded interview by Roberta Greene, November 3, 1969, 18–19, RFK Oral History Program.
10. Frank O'Connor, in recorded interview by Roberta Greene, June 19, 1970, 8–9, 16–18, RFK Oral History Program. Edwin Weisl, Lyndon Johnson's man in New York, reported to the Johnson White House in 1964 after a talk with Buckley, "In the last state election Attorney General Kennedy induced Buckley, against his better judgment, to support Henry [sic] Morgenthau, Jr., for Governor" (E. L. Weisl to Walter Jenkins, January 28, 1964, Johnson Papers).
11. RFK, in recorded interview by John Bartlow Martin, April 13, 1964, II, 61–62, JFK Oral History Program.

12. Milton Gwirtzman, in recorded interview by Roberta Greene, December 23, 1971, 6–9, RFK Oral History Program.
13. Author's journal, September 18, 1962.
14. RFK, in recorded interview by Anthony Lewis, December 22, 1964, 10–11, JFK Oral History Program.
15. Benjamin C. Bradlee, *Conversations with Kennedy* (New York, 1975), 71.
16. George McGovern, in recorded interview by L. J. Hackman, July 16, 1970, 13–17, RFK Oral History Program.
17. Joseph Dolan, in recorded interview by L. J. Hackman, July 18, 1970, 227, RFK Oral History Program.
18. Ibid., 326.
19. Robert Morgenthau, in letter to *New Yorker,* April 19, 1971.
20. J. C. Goulden, *The Benchwarmers: The Private World of the Powerful Federal Judges* (New York: Ballantine reprint, 1976), 68.
21. Ibid., 70; H. W. Chase, *Federal Judges: The Appointing Process* (Minneapolis, Minn., 1972), 119.
22. RFK, in Lewis interview, December 4, 1964, IV, 1–2.
23. See the summary in a confidential report of the House Judiciary Committee, "Investigation of Judicial Behavior in the Tenth Circuit United States Court of Appeals," April 30, 1968, in Goulden, *Benchwarmers,* 255–256, 416.
24. Bobby Baker, with Larry King, *Wheeling and Dealing: Confessions of a Capitol Hill Operator* (New York, 1978), 84.
25. RFK, in Lewis interview, December 4, 1964, IV, 2; RFK, in Martin interview, April 13, 1964, I, 40.
26. RFK, in Lewis interview, December 4, 1964, IV, 2–5; Victor Navasky, *Kennedy Justice* (New York, 1971), 252–253.
27. Goulden, *Benchwarmers,* 68.
28. Ramsey Clark, in recorded interview by L. J. Hackman, July 7, 1970, 66–68, RFK Oral History Program; Navasky, *Kennedy Justice,* 262–263.
29. Clark, in Hackman interview, 71–74, 79; Navasky, *Kennedy Justice,* 263.
30. Author's journal, July 28, 1961.
31. Ibid., August 1, 1961.
32. Anthony Lewis, in recorded interview by L. J. Hackman, July 23, 1970, 28, RFK Oral History Program.
33. Nicholas Katzenbach, in recorded interview by Anthony Lewis, November 16, 1964, 78, JFK Oral History Program.
34. RFK, in Lewis interview, December 4, 1964, IV, 12–14; RFK, in Martin interview, April 13, 1964, I, 43; Archibald Cox, in interview by author, October 29, 1976.
35. Clark Clifford, in recorded interview by L. J. Hackman, February 4, 1975, 13–14, JFK Oral History Program; RFK, in Lewis interview, December 4, 1964, IV, 14–15; Katzenbach, in Lewis interview, 66.
36. Author's journal, March 31, 1962.
37. RFK, in Lewis interview, December 4, 1964, IV, 14.
38. For accounts, see Katzenbach, in Lewis interview, 56–71; and Joseph Dolan, in recorded interview by Charles Morrissey, December 4, 1964, 98–102, JFK Oral History Program.
39. Kenneth O'Donnell and David Powers with Joe McCarthy, *"Johnny, We Hardly Knew Ye"* (Boston, 1972), 280.
40. Katzenbach, in Lewis interview, 71.
41. Author's journal, March 31, 1962.
42. Ibid., April 1, 1962.
43. RFK, memorandum, September 11, 1962, RFK Papers.
44. Dorothy Goldberg, *A Private View of a Public Life* (New York, 1975), 128.
45. Felix Frankfurter, in recorded interview by Charles McLaughlin, June 10, 1964, 52, JFK Oral History Program.

46. Author's journal, May 8, 1963.
47. Ibid., August 31, 1962.
48. John F. Kennedy, *Public Papers . . . 1961* (Washington, 1962), 19.
49. Raoul Berger, *Executive Privilege: A Constitutional Myth* (Cambridge, Mass., 1974), 239–240.
50. Clark Mollenhoff, *Washington Cover-Up* (Garden City, N.Y., 1962), 179–185.
51. *Meet the Press,* September 24, 1961, vol. 5, no. 37, 7.
52. Byron White to JFK, "Executive Privilege," February 6, 1962, RFK Papers. Emphasis added.
53. Clark Mollenhoff, *Despoilers of Democracy* (Garden City, N.Y., 1965), 21.
54. JFK to Porter Hardy, May 1, 1962, JFK Papers.
55. Berger, *Executive Privilege,* 240.
56. Ibid., 252.
57. Ronald Goldfarb, "Politics at the Justice Department," in *Conspiracy,* ed. John C. Raines (New York, 1974), 119–120.
58. RFK, in Martin interview, April 30, 1964, II, 17.
59. John Seigenthaler, in recorded interview by R. J. Grele, February 22, 1966, 268–269, JFK Oral History Program.
60. William Hundley, in recorded interview by J. A. Oesterle, February 17, 1971, 30–32, RFK Oral History Program.
61. Navasky, *Kennedy Justice,* 368–369.
62. Seigenthaler, in Grele interview, 270.
63. Hundley, in Oesterle interview, 31–32.
64. Ibid., 30.
65. Ibid.; Hundley, in interview by author, August 4, 1976.
66. Walter Sheridan, in recorded interview by Roberta Greene, May 1, 1970, 55–56, RFK Oral History Program.
67. Seigenthaler, in Grele interview, 266–268; Navasky, *Kennedy Justice,* 372–378.
68. John Douglas, in recorded interview by L. J. Hackman, June 11, 1970, 30, RFK Oral History Program.
69. RFK, memorandum, August 4, 1964, 3, RFK Papers; RFK, in Martin interview, April 30, 1964, III, 9–10
70. Eric F. Goldman, *The Tragedy of Lyndon Johnson* (New York, 1969), 83.
71. RFK, memorandum, February 22, 1961, 2–3, RFK Papers; Hundley, Oesterle interview, December 9, 1970, 20.
72. RFK, memorandum, 3.
73. John Kennedy, in whatever mood of truth or teasing, told such a story to Joseph Alsop. No one then in the Department of Justice with whom I discussed the story had heard of it.
74. RFK, in Martin interview, February 29, 1964, 49–50.
75. RFK, in Martin interview, April 30, 1964, II, 14–15.
76. Ibid., II, 19; Brock Brower, *Other Loyalties* (New York, 1968), 98.
77. Jean Stein and George Plimpton, eds., *American Journey* (New York, 1970), 79–80.
78. RFK, in Martin interview, April 30, 1964, II, 18.
79. Igor Cassini, *I'd Do It All Over Again* (New York, 1977), 228–229.
80. Bradlee, *Conversations with Kennedy,* 170.
81. Stein and Plimpton, *American Journey,* 79, 81.
82. Peter Maas, in recorded interview by Jean Stein, September 15, 1969, 11, Stein Papers.
83. Justin Feldman, in recorded interview by Roberta Greene, October 23, 1969, 48, RFK Oral History Program.
84. Navasky, *Kennedy Justice,* 378.
85. Feldman, in Greene interview, 58–59; Navasky, *Kennedy Justice,* 388. The judge was Sylvester J. Ryan.

86. Feldman, in Greene interview, 61–66. For different language but the same points, see Navasky, *Kennedy Justice*, 389.
87. RFK, to David Lawrence, September 3, 1963, RFK Papers.
88. RFK, in Martin interview, April 30, 1964, II, 21.

18. Justice and Poverty (*pages* 408–434)

1. Robert F. Kennedy, *The Pursuit of Justice* (New York, Perennial Press reprint, 1964), 9.
2. RFK, address at Marquette University, June 7, 1964, RFK Papers.
3. Kennedy, *Pursuit of Justice*, 9, 84. Emphasis added.
4. Peter Maas, "Robert Kennedy Speaks Out," *Look,* March 28, 1961.
5. Kennedy, *Pursuit of Justice*, 82.
6. Ramsey Clark, *Crime in America* (New York, Pocket Books reprint, 1971), 282–283.
7. *Gideon* v. *Wainwright,* 372 U.S. 335 (1963); Kennedy, *Pursuit of Justice,* 82.
8. Hoover, notation on UPI excerpt from UPI ticker, November 6, 1961; Hoover, notation on Courtney Evans to A. H. Belmont, "Travels of the Attorney General, June 25–30, 1962," July 3, 1962; both in RFK/FBI/FIOA release.
9. Victor Navasky, *Kennedy Justice* (New York, 1971), 10.
10. RFK, in recorded interview by John Bartlow Martin, April 30, 1964, II, 22–23, JFK Oral History Program.
11. James V. Bennett, *I Chose Prison* (New York, 1970), 183–184.
12. Patricia Kennedy Lawford, ed., *That Shining Hour* (n.p., 1969), 56.
13. So Robert Kennedy told me on December 21, 1962; noted in my journal of that date.
14. RFK, in Martin interview, April 30, 1964, I, 38–39.
15. Anthony Lewis, "A Tribute to Robert Francis Kennedy," delivered at unveiling of RFK portrait, Justice Department, July 22, 1975.
16. Navasky, *Kennedy Justice,* 38. For background on the case, see also James Wechsler, "Persecution," *New York Post,* November 28, 1962; and author to RFK, December 18, 1962, RFK Papers.
17. John Douglas, in recorded interview by L. J. Hackman, June 11, 1970, 31–32, RFK Oral History Program.
18. Abba Schwartz to author, memorandum, n.d. [1976], with supporting material from 1963. There is no point in identifying the scholar.
19. Francis Biddle to RFK, January 8, 1962; RFK to Biddle, January 22, 1962, RFK Papers.
20. Archibald Cox, in interview by author, October 29, 1976.
21. Burke Marshall, in recorded interview by Jean Stein, October 6, 1968, 24, Stein Papers.
22. RFK, in Martin interview, April 30, 1964, III, 31.
23. *Baltimore Sun,* July 23, 1928; reprinted in H. L. Mencken, *A Carnival of Buncombe* (New York, 1956), 160.
24. J. R. Moskin, "The Revolt against Rural Rule," *Look,* January 15, 1963.
25. John F. Kennedy, "The Shame of the States," *New York Times Magazine,* May 18, 1958.
26. Anthony Lewis, "Legislative Apportionment and the Federal Courts," *Harvard Law Review,* April 1958.
27. For useful discussions, see R. G. Dixon, Jr., *Democratic Representation: Reapportionment in Law and Politics* (New York, 1968), esp. ch. 6 and 177–178; R. C. Cortner, *The Apportionment Cases* (New York: Norton reprint, 1972), esp. ch. 5; and Royce Hanson, *The Political Thicket* (Englewood Cliffs, N.J., 1966), esp. ch. 3.

28. *New York Times,* March 28, 1962.

29. John F. Kennedy, *Public Papers . . . 1962* (Washington, 1963), 274.

30. *New York Times,* March 28, 1962.

31. Robert B. McKay, *Reapportionment: The Law and Politics of Equal Representation* (New York, 1970), 84.

32. Archibald Cox to RFK, December 20, 1962, RFK Papers.

33. These are in the RFK Papers.

34. James Clayton in the *Washington Post;* see Navasky, *Kennedy Justice,* 277.

35. RFK, "Gray v. Sanders. Notes for Oral Argument," RFK Papers.

36. Navasky, *Kennedy Justice,* 278.

37. Joseph Dolan, in recorded interview by L. J. Hackman, July 19, 1970, 402–403, RFK Oral History Program.

38. *Gray* v. *Sanders,* 372 U.S. 368, 381 (1963).

39. Navasky, *Kennedy Justice,* 303.

40. Cox to RFK, "Reapportionment Cases in Supreme Court," August 21, 1963, RFK Papers.

41. Cox to RFK, August 21, 1963, RFK Papers. See also Cox to RFK, "Reapportionment Cases," September 5, 1963, RFK Papers.

42. Navasky, *Kennedy Justice,* 316.

43. Cox, in interview by author, October 29, 1976.

44. RFK, in recorded interview by Anthony Lewis, December 22, 1964, 54–55, JFK Oral History Program.

45. Archibald C. Cox, *The Role of the Supreme Court in American Government* (New York, 1976), 29.

46. See Ward E. Y. Elliott, *The Rise of Guardian Democracy: The Supreme Court Role in Voting Rights Disputes, 1845–1969* (Cambridge, Mass., 1974), esp. 218–236, 266, 273; and David Brady and Douglas Edmonds, "One Man, One Vote—So What?" *Trans-Action,* March 1967.

47. Cox, in interview by author.

48. Peter Maas, "Robert Kennedy Speaks Out," *Look,* March 28, 1961.

49. Lee Loevinger, in recorded interview by R. J. Grele, May 13, 1966, 6, JFK Oral History Program.

50. John Seigenthaler, in recorded interview by R. J. Grele, February 22, 1966, 276, JFK Oral History Program.

51. Hobart Rowen, *The Free Enterprisers: Kennedy, Johnson and the Business Establishment* (New York, 1964), 81.

52. Ramsey Clark, in recorded interview by L. J. Hackman, June 29, 1970, 26, RFK Oral History Program.

53. Loevinger, in Grele interview, 9–10.

54. William Orrick, in recorded interview by L. J. Hackman, April 14, 1970, 282, RFK Oral History Program.

55. Edwin Guthman, *We Band of Brothers* (New York, 1971), 237–238.

56. W. W. Rostow, *The Diffusion of Power, 1957–1972* (New York, 1972), 122.

57. Roger Blough, *The Washington Embrace of Business* (New York, 1975), 93–94. For general background, see Rostow, *Diffusion of Power,* chs. 13–15; and W. J. Barber, "The Kennedy Years: Purposeful Pedagogy," in *Exhortation and Controls: The Search for a Wage-Price Policy, 1945–1971,* ed. C. D. Goodwin (Washington, 1975), 135–191.

58. Roger Blough, "My Side of the Steel Story," *Look,* January 29, 1963.

59. Dorothy Goldberg, *A Private View of a Public Life* (New York, 1975), 112.

60. David McDonald, in recorded interview by Charles T. Morrissey, February 15, 1966, 15, JFK Oral History Program.

61. RFK, "Some Notes on the Steel Increase," April 20, 1962, 1–2, RFK Papers.

62. Grant McConnell, *Steel and the Presidency—1962* (New York, 1963), 89.

63. Guthman, *We Band of Brothers,* 233.

64. RFK, in recorded interview by John Bartlow Martin, April 13, 1964, I, 35, JFK Oral History Program.
65. Ovid Demaris, *The Director* (New York, 1975), 288.
66. Douglas Dillon, in recorded interview by L. J. Hackman, June 18, 1970, 20–21, RFK Oral History Program.
67. RFK, in Martin interview, April 13, 1964, III, 5, 7–8, JFK Oral History Program.
68. *New York Times,* April 23, 1962.
69. Clark Clifford, in recorded interview by L. J. Hackman, February 4, 1975, 33, JFK Oral History Program.
70. RFK, "Some Notes on the Steel Increase," 5–6.
71. Blough, *Washington Embrace of Business,* 100–101.
72. Loevinger, in Grele interview, 19.
73. RFK, in Martin interview, April 30, 1964, I, 44.
74. "Interview with Robert Kennedy," *U.S. News & World Report,* January 28, 1963.
75. Author's journal, June 19, 1962.
76. Cox, in interview by author.
77. Ibid.
78. *Christian Science Monitor,* April 16, 1962.
79. *Wall Street Journal,* April 19, 1962.
80. Charles Reich, "Another Such Victory," *New Republic,* April 30, 1962.
81. Kennedy, *Public Papers . . . 1962,* 895.
82. RFK, in Martin interview, April 13, 1964, III, 5, 8.
83. William Goldsmith, *The Growth of Presidential Power* (New York, 1974), vol. 3, 1687.
84. Hugh Sidey, *A Very Personal Presidency: Lyndon Johnson in the White House* (New York, 1968), 71.
85. RFK, address at G.I. Forum, Chicago, August 23, 1963, 4–5, RFK Papers.
86. Joseph Dolan, in recorded interview by L. J. Hackman, July 18, 1970, 249, RFK Oral History Program.
87. Ramsey Clark, in recorded interview by L. J. Hackman, June 29, 1970, 37–38, RFK Oral History Program.
88. Clark, in Hackman interview, 48–50.
89. RFK, address before National Congress of American Indians, Bismarck, North Dakota, September 13, 1963, RFK Papers; RFK, commencement address, Trinity College, Hartford, Conn., June 2, 1963, RFK Papers.
90. Clark, in Hackman interview, 49.
91. Jack Newfield, *Robert Kennedy* (New York, 1969), 18.
92. Navasky, *Kennedy Justice,* 17.
93. Department of Justice release, "Text of Attorney General Robert F. Kennedy's Statement," April 6, 1961.
94. Richard Blumenthal, "The Bureaucracy: Antipoverty and the Community Action Program," in *American Political Institutions and Public Policy,* ed. A. P. Sindler (Boston, 1969), 134. Blumenthal's essay, derived from a Harvard honors thesis, draws extensively on unpublished interviews and is an essential source. Another invaluable work, Daniel Knapp and Kenneth Polk, *Scouting the War on Poverty: Social Reform Politics in the Kennedy Administration* (Lexington, Mass., 1971), is based on the files of the President's Committee on Juvenile Delinquency. Peter Marris and Martin Rein, *Dilemmas of Social Reform: Poverty and Community Action in the United States,* 2d ed. (Chicago, 1973), is a probing analysis and evaluation. See also L. A. Ferman, ed., "Evaluating the War on Poverty," *Annals of the American Academy of Political and Social Science,* September 1969, especially the papers by R. H. Davidson, L. B. Rubin, Sanford Kravitz and F. K. Kolodner. I am also indebted for helpful comment to communications from Richard Boone (January 8, 1977), Lloyd Ohlin (January 14, 1977), William B. Cannon and Leonard J. Duhl (August 19, 1977).

95. Recorded transcript of conference sponsored by the Kennedy Library and Brandeis University, "The Federal Government and Urban Poverty," pt. 3, 30.

96. Richard A. Cloward and Lloyd Ohlin, *Delinquency and Opportunity: A Theory of Delinquent Gangs* (New York, 1960), 108–113, 124–127, 211.

97. See Daniel Patrick Moynihan, *Maximum Feasible Misunderstanding: Community Action in the War on Poverty* (New York, 1969), 170.

98. See Marris and Rein, *Dilemmas of Social Reform,* 132.

99. Blumenthal, "Bureaucracy," 133.

100. David Hackett, in interview by author, January 27, 1975.

101. David Hackett to RFK, November 8, 1963, RFK Papers.

102. Kenneth B. Clark, "Community Action and the Social Program of the 1960s," in *Toward New Human Rights: The Social Policies of the Kennedy and Johnson Administrations,* ed. David C. Warner (Austin, Tex., 1977), 99; see also Kenneth B. Clark, *Dark Ghetto: Dilemmas of Social Power* (New York, 1965).

103. Lloyd Ohlin to author, January 14, 1977.

104. Knapp and Polk, *Scouting the War on Poverty,* 75–77, 127.

105. See the account in Guthman, *We Band of Brothers,* 226–227.

106. Wesley Barthelmes, in recorded interview by Roberta Greene, June 5, 1969, 155–158, RFK Oral History Program.

107. Eunice Kennedy Shriver, in recorded interview by John Stewart, May 7, 1968, 26–27, JFK Oral History Program.

108. Richard Boone, in recorded interview by Jean Stein, September 20, 1968, 2–3, Stein Papers.

109. RFK, testimony before the Labor Subcommittee of the House Committee on Education and Labor; see Kennedy, *Pursuit of Justice,* 26–33.

110. RFK to LBJ, "Racial Violence in Urban Centers," August 5, 1964, RFK Papers.

111. E. Barrett Prettyman, Jr., in recorded interview by L. J. Hackman, June 5, 1969, 17–20, RFK Oral History Program.

112. Patrick Anderson, "Robert's Character," *Esquire,* April 1965.

113. Kenneth B. Clark and Jeanette Hopkins, *A Relevant War against Poverty: A Study of Community Action Programs and Observable Social Change* (New York, 1969), 4.

114. Arthur M. Schlesinger, Jr., *A Thousand Days* (Boston, 1965), 1011.

115. Boone, in Stein interview, 4.

116. Leonard Duhl, in recorded interview by Jean Stein, August 19, 1968, 3–4, Stein Papers.

19. The Kennedys and the Cold War (*pages 435–461*)

1. Kenneth P. O'Donnell and David F. Powers, *"Johnny, We Hardly Knew Ye"* (Boston, 1972), 278.

2. John F. Kennedy, *A Compendium of Speeches, Statements, and Remarks Delivered During His Service in the Congress of the United States,* Senate Document 79, 88 Cong., 2 Sess. (Washington, 1964), 710.

3. John F. Kennedy, *The Strategy of Peace* (New York, 1960), 81, 132–133.

4. The article appeared in *Foreign Affairs,* April 1960. Chester Bowles, in recorded interview by R. R. R. Brooks, February 2, 1965, 7, JFK Oral History Program.

5. Charles Spalding, in recorded interview by John Stewart, March 14, 1968, 5, JFK Oral History Program.

6. Joseph P. Kennedy, "A Foreign Policy for America" [1956], 2, 6, 9, JPK Papers. The article was never published, perhaps because Joseph Kennedy feared to complicate his son's political career.

7. Kennedy, *Strategy of Peace,* 7, 10–12.

8. Ibid., ch. 1.

9. RFK, in recorded interview by author, February 27, 1965, 57, JFK Oral History Program.

10. JFK to G. F. Kennan, February 13, 1958; see George F. Kennan, in recorded interview by Louis Fischer, March 23, 1965, 5–6, JFK Oral History Program.

11. JFK to Kennan, January 21, 1959; see Kennan, in Fischer interview, 11–12.

12. Author's journal, May 29, 1960.

13. Ibid., May 22, 1960.

14. John F. Kennedy, review of *Deterrent or Defense* by B. H. Liddell Hart, *Saturday Review,* September 3, 1960.

15. Kennedy, *Strategy of Peace,* 7.

16. "Deterrence and Survival in the Nuclear Age," reprinted by Joint Committee on Defense Production, 94 Cong., 2 Sess. (1976); see esp. 26–27.

17. Edgar M. Bottome, *The Missile Gap* (Rutherford, N.J., 1971), 93.

18. Henry A. Kissinger, *The Necessity for Choice: Prospects of American Foreign Policy* (New York, 1960), 1.

19. Kennan to JFK, August 17, 1960, JFK to Kennan, October 30, 1960, Kennan, in Fischer interview, 21–26.

20. Adlai Stevenson, report, November 7, 1960, pt. 2, 1, Schlesinger Papers.

21. Stevenson to Theodore Sorensen, December 30, 1960, Sorensen Papers.

22. N. S. Khrushchev, *Khrushchev Remembers: The Last Testament,* ed. Strobe Talbott (Boston, 1974), 489–490.

23. RFK to Dean Rusk, December 18, 1960, RFK Papers.

24. Kennan, in Fischer interview, 29–32.

25. N. S. Khrushchev, "For New Victories of the World Communist Movement," at the meeting of party organizations of the Higher Party School, the Academy of Social Sciences and the Institute of Marxism-Leninism, Moscow, January 6, 1961.

26. State Department, "Analysis of Moscow Conference 'Statement' and Khrushchev Speech of January 6," January 25, 1961, RFK Papers.

27. L. C. Gardner, Arthur M. Schlesinger, Jr., and Hans Morgenthau, *The Origins of the Cold War* (Lexington, Ky., 1970), 98.

28. RFK, in recorded interview by John Bartlow Martin, April 13, 1964, II, 22, JFK Oral History Program.

29. John F. Kennedy, *Public Papers . . . 1961* (Washington, 1962), 1–3.

30. *New York Times,* January 21, 1961.

31. Eleanor Roosevelt to JFK, January 24 [1961], JFK Papers.

32. JFK, in a speech at the University of Washington, Seattle, November 16, 1961; see JFK, *Public Papers . . . 1961,* 726.

33. See especially his speech in Berkeley, California, March 23, 1962; John F. Kennedy, *Public Papers . . . 1962* (Washington, 1963), 263–266.

34. John F. Kennedy, *Public Papers . . . 1963* (Washington, 1964), 462.

35. For an able account of these issues, see R. A. Aliano, *American Defense Policy from Eisenhower to Kennedy: The Politics of Changing Military Requirements, 1957–1961* (Athens, Ohio, 1975).

36. Bottome, *Missile Gap,* 179–184.

37. A. C. Enthoven and K. W. Smith, *How Much Is Enough? Shaping the Defense Program, 1961–1969* (New York: Harper Colophon reprint, 1972), 195.

38. Roswell Gilpatric, in recorded interview by D. J. O'Brien, June 30, 1970, 71, JFK Oral History Program.

39. Robert S. McNamara, *The Essence of Security: Reflections in Office* (New York, 1968), 58.

40. JFK, *Compendium of Speeches,* 929.

41. Maxwell Taylor, *The Uncertain Trumpet* (New York, 1960), 24.

42. See Bernard Brodie's brilliant *War and Politics* (New York, 1973), 126.

43. Author's journal, April 5, 1961.

44. Dean Acheson, in recorded interview by Lucius Battle, April 27, 1964, 12, 20, JFK Oral History Program.
45. Author's journal, May 10, 1961.
46. RFK, in recorded interview by author, February 27, 1965, 28, JFK Oral History Program.
47. John F. Kennedy, *The Strategy of Peace* (New York, 1960), 212.
48. JFK, *Public Papers . . . 1961,* 533–540.
49. RFK, dictated August 1, 1961, RFK Papers.
50. RFK, in Martin interview, April 13, 1964, I, 12.
51. L. C. McHugh, "Ethics at the Shelter Doorway," *America,* September 30, 1961.
52. Author's journal, November 24, 1961.
53. A. D. Sakharov, *Sakharov Speaks,* ed. Harrison Salisbury (New York, 1974), 33.
54. RFK, dictated September 1, 1961, RFK Papers.
55. Ibid.
56. Arthur M. Schlesinger, Jr., *A Thousand Days* (Boston, 1965), 398.
57. O'Donnell and Powers, *"Johnny, We Hardly Knew Ye,"* 299.
58. Author's journal, September 5, 1961.
59. Ibid., August 30, 1961.
60. RFK, dictated August 1, 1961, RFK Papers.
61. Author's journal, September 5, 1961.
62. Paul Blanshard, *Personal and Controversial: An Autobiography* (Boston, 1973), 243.
63. Barry Goldwater, *Why Not Victory?* (New York: Macfadden reprint, 1963), 16, 97, 118, 120, 122.
64. James Wechsler, "JFK (Contd.)," *New York Post,* September 22, 1961.
65. R. M. Slusser, *The Berlin Crisis of 1961* (Baltimore, Md., 1973). It is pathetic that Soviet historians are denied any opportunity to write honest contemporary history. In the absence of Soviet evidence, western historians have no alternative to speculation.
66. Ibid., x.
67. Theodore C. Sorensen, *Kennedy* (New York, 1965), 552.
68. JFK, *Public Papers . . . 1961,* 726–727.
69. JFK, *Compendium of Speeches,* 927–928.
70. Peter Lisagor, in recorded interview by R. J. Grele, May 12, 1966, 56, JFK Oral History Program.
71. RFK, in Martin interview, February 29, 1964, 28–31; also a subsequent interview on Adlai Stevenson, December 7, 1966, Martin Papers; also interview by author, February 27, 1965, 5, 13.
72. Averell Harriman, in recorded interview by author, June 6, 1965, 133–134, JFK Oral History Program.
73. David Halberstam, in recorded interview by Jean Stein, May 2, 1970, 5, Stein Papers.
74. John Kenneth Galbraith, in recorded interview by Jean Stein, July 30, 1968, 5, Stein Papers.
75. W. W. Attwood, *The Reds and the Blacks* (New York, 1967), 325.
76. Roswell Gilpatric, in recorded interview by D. J. O'Brien, August 12, 1970, 102, JFK Oral History Program.
77. Patrick Anderson, "Robert's Character," *Esquire,* April 1965.
78. RFK to Dean Rusk, May 16, 1963, RFK Papers. The editorial appeared on May 4, 1963.
79. Abba Schwartz, *The Open Society* (New York, 1968), 25.
80. Ibid., 4, 34.
81. Ibid., 40–44.
82. Angie Novello to Harold Reis, April 8, 1964, RFK Papers.
83. Schwartz, *Open Society,* 47–50.

84. William O. Douglas, in recorded interview by Roberta Greene, November 13, 1969, 18, RFK Oral History Program; Douglas, in recorded interview by Jean Stein, n.d., 1, Stein Papers.

85. *Kent* v. *Dulles,* 357 U.S. 118 (1958).

86. Schwartz, *Open Society,* ch. 5.

87. Ibid.; *Aptheker* v. *Secretary of State,* 348 U.S. 500 (1964).

88. Schwartz, *Open Society,* 28.

89. Galbraith to JFK, August 15, 1961, JFK Papers.

90. Chester Bowles to Adlai Stevenson, July 23, 1961, Bowles Papers.

91. RFK to JFK, August 15, 1961, RFK Papers.

92. RFK, in interview by author, February 27, 1965, 11–13.

93. Harriman, in interview by author, June 6, 1965, 80–82.

94. William Orrick, in recorded interview by L. J. Hackman, April 13, 1970, 154–155, RFK Oral History Program.

95. John Seigenthaler, in recorded interview by L. J. Hackman, June 5, 1970, 59, RFK Oral History Program.

96. Orrick, in Hackman interview, 162.

97. Donald Wilson, in recorded interview by W. W. Moss, March 13, 1972, 85, JFK Oral History Program.

98. RFK to JFK, May 30, 1962, RFK Papers.

99. See John F. Campbell's characterization in his generally intelligent book *The Foreign Affairs Fudge Factory* (New York, 1971), 54–59. For an account of the argument, see Schlesinger, *Thousand Days,* 875–881.

100. J. P. Davies, Jr., *Foreign and Other Affairs* (New York, 1964), 198.

101. Philip Bonsal, "Open Letter to an Author," *Foreign Service Journal,* February 1967.

102. Philip L. Graham to JFK, December 15, 1962, JFK Papers.

103. Orrick, in Hackman interview, 158–159.

104. RFK, in Martin interview, April 13, 1964, I, 19–20.

105. Eric Hobsbawm, "Why America Lost the Vietnam War," *Listener,* May 18, 1972.

106. R. J. Walton, *Cold War and Counter-Revolution: The Foreign Policy of John F. Kennedy* (New York, 1972), 233. See also Louise FitzSimons, *The Kennedy Doctrine* (New York, 1972).

107. Khrushchev, *Last Testament,* 491, 495.

20. The CIA and Counterinsurgency (*pages* 462–487)

1. RFK, memorandum, dictated June 1, 1961, RFK Papers.

2. Ibid.

3. Edwin Guthman, *We Band of Brothers* (New York, 1971), 113.

4. RFK, handwritten notes after Cuba Study Group meetings of May 1 and 11, 1961, RFK Papers.

5. Cuba Study Group, May 19, 1961, RFK Papers.

6. RFK, in recorded interview by John Bartlow Martin, March 1, 1964, II, 9, JFK Oral History Program.

7. Maxwell Taylor, in recorded interview by L. J. Hackman, October 22, 1969, 2, RFK Oral History Program.

8. "Conclusions of the Cuba Study Group," June 13, 1961, Schlesinger Papers; Maxwell Taylor, *Swords and Plowshares* (New York, 1972), ch. 14.

9. Taylor, *Swords and Plowshares,* 186.

10. RFK, in Martin interview, March 1, 1964, II, 33.

11. Taylor, in Hackman interview, 26.

12. Maxwell Taylor, in *That Shining Hour,* ed. Patricia Kennedy Lawford (n.p., 1969), 81–82.

13. Taylor, in Hackman interview, 16.
14. Taylor, *Swords and Plowshares,* 205.
15. Roswell Gilpatric, in recorded interview by D. J. O'Brien, August 12, 1970, 117, JFK Oral History Program.
16. Jerry Bruno, *The Advance Man* (New York: Bantam reprint, 1972), 20.
17. RFK, in recorded interview by Anthony Lewis, December 4, 1964, VII, 25, JFK Oral History Program.
18. *New York Times,* February 1, 1962.
19. Gilpatric, in O'Brien interview, June 30, 1970, 69, and August 12, 1970, 112, 116.
20. Paul B. Fay, Jr., *The Pleasure of His Company* (New York, 1966), 190.
21. John F. Kennedy, *Public Papers . . . 1961* (Washington, 1962), 735.
22. Joseph Rauh, in interview by author, October 26, 1976.
23. The full text is reprinted in Victor Reuther, *The Brothers Reuther* (Boston, 1976), 491–500.
24. See, for example, William E. Mallett, *The Reuther Memorandum: Its Applications and Implications* (n.p., Liberty Lobby, 1963).
25. Charles U. Daly, in recorded interview by C. T. Morrissey, April 5, 1966, 11–13, JFK Oral History Program.
26. For a critique, see Fred W. Friendly, *The Good Guys, the Bad Guys and the First Amendment* (New York, 1976), esp. ch. 3.
27. Author's journal, April 18, 1961.
28. RFK, in Martin interview, March 1, 1964, II, 13. See Haynes Johnson, *The Bay of Pigs* (New York, 1964), 75.
29. RFK, in handwritten notes after Cuba Study Group meetings of May 24 and June 11, 1961, RFK Papers.
30. Johnson, *Bay of Pigs,* 75–77, 222.
31. E. Howard Hunt, *Give Us This Day* (New York: Popular Library reprint, 1973), 188–189.
32. Fay, *Pleasure of His Company,* 188.
33. Tom Wicker, in interview by author, July 8, 1975. The *New York Times* was doing a series on the CIA.
34. Senate Select Committee to Study Governmental Operations with respect to Intelligence Activities (hereafter cited as Church committee), *Interim Report: Alleged Assassination Plots Involving Foreign Leaders,* 94 Cong., 1 Sess. (1975), 92.
35. Hunt, *Give Us This Day,* 38.
36. Cuba Study Group, May 19, 1961, RFK Papers.
37. Howard Hunt, "The Azalea Trail Guide to CIA," *National Review,* April 29, 1977.
38. Cuba Study Group, May 11, 1961, RFK Papers.
39. David Bruce and Robert Lovett, "Covert Operations," report to President's Board of Consultants on Foreign Intelligence Activities [1956], RFK Papers.
40. President's Board of Consultants on Foreign Intelligence Activities (hereafter cited as PBCFIA), report to President Eisenhower, December 20, 1956, RFK Papers.
41. William Manchester, *Portrait of a President* (Boston, 1962), 35.
42. PBCFIA, report to the Special Assistant for National Security, February 12, 1957, RFK Papers.
43. Joseph B. Smith, *Portrait of a Cold Warrior* (New York, 1976), 229–230, 240.
44. Howard P. Jones, *Indonesia: The Possible Dream* (New York, 1971), 143, 145.
45. In addition to J. B. Smith and H. P. Jones, see ch. 8 of David Wise and Thomas B. Ross, *The Invisible Government* (New York: Bantam reprint, 1965); and Ray S. Cline, *Secrets, Spies and Scholars* (Washington, 1976), 181–183.
46. White House meeting of PBCFIA with Eisenhower, December 16, 1958, RFK Papers.

47. Church committee, *Final Report,* bk. I, *Foreign and Military Intelligence,* 94 Cong., 2 Sess. (1976), 52.

48. Cuba Study Group, May 11, 1961, RFK Papers.

49. PBCFIA, report to Eisenhower, January 5, 1961, RFK Papers.

50. Cuba Study Group, May 11, 1961, RFK Papers.

51. Robert Lovett, in recorded interview by Dorothy Fosdick, August 17, 1964, 5, JFK Oral History Program.

52. Interview with Clark Clifford, in *Christian Science Monitor,* July 24, 1975; Clifford, in recorded interview by L. J. Hackman, December 17, 1974, 10, JFK Oral History Program.

53. Deborah Shapley, "Foreign Intelligence Advisory Board: A Lesson in Citizen Oversight?" *Science,* March 12, 1976.

54. Clifford, in Hackman interview, February 4, 1975, 43.

55. RFK, in Martin interview, March 1, 1964, II, 27–29.

56. Cuba Study Group, memorandum no. 4, "A Mechanism for the Planning and Coordination of Cold War Strategy," June 13, 1961, Schlesinger Papers.

57. This point is well made by Charles A. Cannon in an unpublished paper, "John F. Kennedy's 'Proving Ground of Democracy in Asia,'" read at the American Historical Association convention, December 29, 1975 (see esp. p. 6).

58. W. W. Rostow, "Guerrilla Warfare in Underdeveloped Areas," in *The Guerrilla —and How to Fight Him,* ed. T. N. Greene (New York, 1962), 55–58.

59. Special Group (Counterinsurgency), "Memorandum for the Record . . . the Special Group (CI) from January 18, 1962, to November 21, 1963," May 13, 1964, RFK Papers.

60. JFK, *Public Papers . . . 1961,* 232.

61. E. G. Lansdale, *In the Midst of Wars: An American's Mission to Southeast Asia* (New York, 1972), 84, 99.

62. E. G. Lansdale, in interview by author, December 30, 1976.

63. Lansdale, *In the Midst of Wars,* ix, 372–373, 376.

64. E. G. Lansdale, "Vietnam: Do We Understand Revolution," *Foreign Affairs,* October 1964.

65. Michael Forrestal, in interview by author, January 27, 1977.

66. Special Group (CI), "U.S. Overseas Internal Defense Policy," September 1962, RFK Papers.

67. Robert F. Kennedy, *To Seek a Newer World* (Garden City, N.Y., 1967), 116–117. Emphasis added.

68. Taylor, in Hackman interview, October 22, 1969, 21; Joint Chiefs of Staff (JCS) to Secretary of Defense, "Joint Counterinsurgency Concept and Doctrinal Guidance," April 5, 1962, RFK Papers.

69. Department of the Army, *U.S. Army Counterinsurgency Forces,* Field Manual no. 31-22, November 12, 1963; esp. appendix 2, "Examples of Civil Action," 96–97.

70. John Bartlow Martin, *U.S. Policy in the Caribbean* (Boulder, Colo., 1978), 364.

71. Herbert L. Matthews, *Return to Cuba* (Stanford University, n.d. [1964]), 15.

72. For a good account, see Maurice Halperin, *The Rise and Decline of Fidel Castro* (Berkeley, 1972), chs. 28–29. Since I had some harsh words about the author in *A Thousand Days,* may I say here that *The Rise and Decline of Fidel Castro* is a detached, incisive and valuable work.

73. *New York Times,* October 17, 1963.

74. John F. Kennedy, *Public Papers . . . 1963* (Washington, 1964), 184.

75. Romulo Betancourt, "The Venezuelan Miracle," *Reporter,* August 13, 1964.

76. Betancourt, "The Venezuelan Miracle"; Halperin, *Rise and Decline of Castro,* 318, 337–344.

77. Gilpatric, in O'Brien interview, August 12, 1970, 40.

78. C. V. Clifton, "Hail to the Chief!" *Army,* January 1964.

79. JCS to Special Group (CI), June 25, 1963, RFK Papers.
80. Robert F. Kennedy, *The Enemy Within* (New York: Popular Library reprint, 1960), 306.
81. Averell Harriman, in recorded interview by L. J. Hackman, March 13, 1970, 10, RFK Oral History Program.
82. W. V. Shannon, *The Heir Apparent* (New York, 1967), 50.
83. George Ball, in recorded interview by Jean Stein, n.d. [1968], 9, Stein Papers.
84. Ably discussed in D. S. Blaufarb, *The Counterinsurgency Era: U.S. Doctrine and Performance, 1950 to the Present* (New York, 1977), esp. 86–87, 289–292, 303–304.
85. Charles Maechling, Jr., "Our Internal Defense Policy: A Reappraisal," *Foreign Service Journal*, January 1969.
86. R. W. Komer to McGeorge Bundy, April 10, 1962, JFK Papers.
87. Quoted by Eqbal Ahmad, "The Theory and Fallacies of Counterinsurgency," *Nation*, August 2, 1971.
88. Peter De Vries, *I Hear America Swinging* (Boston, 1976).
89. Michael Forrestal, in recorded interview by Jean Stein, n.d. [1968], 5, Stein Papers.
90. RFK, in Martin interview, April 13, 1964, II, 50.
91. Taylor, in Hackman interview, 25.
92. Ralph Dungan to RFK, January 17, 1963, RFK Papers.

21. The Cuban Connection: I (*pages* 488–520)

1. Maxwell Taylor, *Swords and Plowshares* (New York, 1972), 181.
2. Kenneth P. O'Donnell and David F. Powers, *"Johnny, We Hardly Knew Ye"* (Boston, 1972), 274–275.
3. RFK, in recorded interview by John Bartlow Martin, April 30, 1964, III, 17, JFK Oral History Program.
4. The account of the Tractors for Freedom Committee is drawn from Milton Eisenhower, *The Wine Is Bitter* (Garden City, N.Y., 1963), chs. 15–16; Haynes Johnson, *The Bay of Pigs* (New York, 1964), bk. 4, ch. 3; and Victor Reuther, *The Brothers Reuther* (Boston, 1976), 440–445.
5. Johnson, *Bay of Pigs*, 273–275.
6. Author's journal, April 5, 1962.
7. Alvaro Sanchez, Jr., "Policy Memorandum," May 2, 1962, RFK Papers.
8. Johnson, *Bay of Pigs*, 303.
9. A transaction well described in Donovan's book *Strangers on a Bridge: The Case of Colonel Abel* (New York, 1964).
10. James B. Donovan, *Challenges: Reflections of a Lawyer-at-Large* (New York, 1967), 91.
11. RFK, memorandum dictated September 11, 1962, RFK Papers.
12. RFK to Kenneth O'Donnell for the President, April 19, 1961, RFK Papers.
13. RFK, memorandum dictated June 1, 1961, RFK Papers.
14. Chester Bowles, in recorded interview by R. R. R. Brooks, February 2, 1965, 33, JFK Oral History Program.
15. Senate Select Committee to Study Governmental Operations with respect to Intelligence Activities (hereafter cited as Church committee), *Interim Report: Alleged Assassination Plots Involving Foreign Leaders*, 94 Cong., 1 Sess. (1975), 142.
16. RFK, memorandum, June 1, 1961.
17. Author's journal, May 4–5, 1961.
18. RFK, memorandum, June 1, 1961.

19. Richard M. Nixon, "Cuba, Castro and John F. Kennedy," *Reader's Digest,* November 1964.
20. Mike Mansfield to JFK, May 1, 1961, JFK Papers.
21. Maxwell Taylor, in recorded interview by L. J. Hackman, October 22, 1969, 10, RFK Oral History Program.
22. Office of Legal Counsel, Department of Justice, "Constitutional and Legal Basis for So-Called Covert Activities of the Central Intelligence Agency," January 17, 1962, quoted in Church committee, *Final Report,* bk. I, *Foreign and Military Intelligence,* 94 Cong., 2 Sess. (1975), 36–37, 497. Emphasis added.
23. RFK to John McCone, January 19, 1962, RFK Papers.
24. Church committee, *Assassination Plots,* 148.
25. Schlesinger to Richard Goodwin, July 8, 1961, Schlesinger Papers.
26. Goodwin to JFK, September 6, 1961, Schlesinger Papers.
27. The White House meeting was described by the assistant to the head of the CIA unit working on Cuban operations. Bissell himself could not recall such a meeting, though he agreed in essence with the spirit of the instruction. Church committee, *Assassination Plots,* 141.
28. Goodwin to JFK, November 1, 1961, in Church committee, *Assassination Plots,* 139.
29. RFK, handwritten notes, November 7, 1961, RFK Papers.
30. Church committee, *Assassination Plots,* 140–141.
31. JFK to the Secretary of State, et al., November 30, 1961, in Church committee, *Assassination Plots,* 139.
32. Taylor, in Hackman interview, 11.
33. Church committee, *Assassination Plots,* 141.
34. Ibid., 142–143.
35. Ibid., 146–147.
36. According to one CIA source, it cost $100 million; J. B. Smith, *Portrait of a Cold Warrior* (New York, 1976), 367. For a useful, though incomplete and occasionally inaccurate, account of the Miami operation, see Taylor Branch and George Crile III, "The Kennedy Vendetta," *Harper's,* August 1975.
37. Church committee, *Assassination Plots,* 146, 159.
38. Ramón Barquin, review of *Give Us This Day* by E. Howard Hunt, *Society,* July/August 1975.
39. E. Howard Hunt, *Give Us This Day* (New York: Popular Library reprint, 1973), 219–220.
40. David C. Martin, "The CIA's 'Loaded Gun,'" *Washington Post,* October 10, 1976; W. A. Corson, *Armies of Ignorance* (New York, 1977), 287–288.
41. Edward G. Lansdale, in interview by author, December 30, 1976.
42. Church committee, *Assassination Plots,* 144–146.
43. Branch and Crile, "Kennedy Vendetta."
44. Church committee, *Assassination Plots,* 146.
45. Ibid., 145–146.
46. Branch and Crile, "Kennedy Vendetta."
47. RFK, in recorded interview by John Bartlow Martin, April 30, 1964, III, 23, JFK Oral History Program.
48. Lansdale, in interview by author.
49. Hunt, *Give Us This Day,* 219.
50. Taylor, in Hackman interview, 12; Lansdale, in interview by author.
51. Martin, "CIA's 'Loaded Gun.'"
52. RFK to Maxwell Taylor, message dictated over telephone, August 9, 1962, RFK Papers.
53. Church committee, *Assassination Plots,* 147.
54. Edward Lansdale to RFK, October 15, 1962, RFK Papers.

55. Church committee, *Final Report*, bk. IV, *Supplementary Detailed Staff Reports on Foreign and Military Intelligence*, 94 Cong., 2 Sess. (1976), 128–131.
56. Church committee, *Assassination Plots*, 72–73.
57. Paul Meskil, "CIA Sent Bedmate to Kill Castro in '60," *New York Daily News*, June 13, 1976. Fiorini supported the Lorenz story. Later they fell out.
58. Nicholas Gage, *The Mafia Is Not an Equal Opportunity Employer* (New York, 1971), 64–65; Paul Meskil, "How U.S. Made Unholy Alliance with the Mafia," *New York Daily News*, April 23, 1975; R. S. Anson, "The CIA and the Mafia," *New Times*, May 30, 1975; and Anson, "Jack, Judy, Sam & Johnny," *New Times*, January 23, 1976.
59. Nicholas M. Horrock, "Maheu Says He Recruited Man for C.I.A. in Poison Plot," *New York Times*, July 31, 1975; Church committee, *Assassination Plots*, 307.
60. Church committee, *Assassination Plots*, 91, 97.
61. Ibid., 76–79, 126–131.
62. For Ruby's Cuba visits see *New York Daily News*, July 4, 1976, and W. S. Malone, "The Secret Life of Jack Ruby," *New Times*, January 23, 1978.
63. For this and other evidence pointing to the thesis that Trafficante was a double agent, see George Crile III, "The Mafia, the CIA and Castro," *Washington Post*, May 16, 1976.
64. The friend was Joseph Shimon. Church committee, *Assassination Plots*, 79, 82.
65. Ibid., 79–82.
66. Ibid., 83, 181–188.
67. Ibid., 83–85.
68. Ibid., 85–86.
69. Ibid., 15–16, 52–62.
70. Ibid., 65.
71. Ibid., 109–113.
72. Nixon, "Cuba, Castro and John F. Kennedy."
73. Philip Bonsal, *Cuba, Castro and the United States* (Pittsburgh, 1971), 93–94, 135, 174.
74. Hunt, *Give Us This Day*, 40.
75. Ehrlichman's notes were published in appendix 3 of the House Judiciary Committee's impeachment hearings; see Aaron Latham, "A Few Words About the 37th President," *New York*, July 28, 1975.
76. Corson, *Armies of Ignorance*, 345.
77. Church committee, *Assassination Plots*, 117–121.
78. *Boston Globe*, March 13, 1975.
79. Church committee, *Assassination Plots*, 148–150, 313.
80. Ibid., 136–137.
81. JFK to Gamal Abdel Nasser, March 2, 1961, in Mohammad Heikal, *The Cairo Documents* (Garden City, N.Y., 1973), 194–195.
82. RFK, notes dictated June 1, 1961, RFK Papers.
83. Church committee, *Assassination Plots*, 195–211; Richard Goodwin, "The Record of JFK and Political Assassinations," *Boston Globe*, November 24, 1975.
84. Arthur M. Schlesinger, Jr., *A Thousand Days* (Boston, 1965), 769.
85. Goodwin, "Record of JFK"; Church committee, *Assassination Plots*, 212–213; George Lardner, Jr., "JFK Rejected Trujillo Slaying, Aide Says," *Washington Post*, July 19, 1975.
86. RFK, notes dictated June 1, 1961.
87. Church committee, *Assassination Plots*, 138–139; Tad Szulc, "Cuba on Our Mind," *Esquire*, February 1974.
88. George Lardner, Jr., "Fear of Retaliation Curbed Anti-Castro Plots," *Washington Post*, July 21, 1975.
89. John F. Kennedy, *Public Papers . . . 1961* (Washington, 1962), 725.
90. George Smathers, in recorded interview by Donald M. Wilson, March 31, 1964,

6–7, 10–11, JFK Oral History Program; Jack Anderson, "Questions in the Closet," *New York Post,* January 19, 1971.

91. Church committee, *Assassination Plots,* 126–131.
92. Ibid., 131–134.
93. Richard Goodwin, in interview by author, June 11, 1977; also Tad Szulc, "The Politics of Assassination," *New York,* June 23, 1975.
94. Jack Anderson, "Washington Merry-Go-Round," for release March 3, 1967.
95. See Judith Exner, *My Story,* as told to Ovid Demaris (New York, 1977).
96. Church committee, *Assassination Plots,* 129.
97. Ibid., 129–130.
98. The first two sentences are from William Hundley, in interview by author, August 4, 1976; the third, from a story by Nicholas Gage, *New York Times,* April 13, 1976.
99. Giancana's intermediary was Charles English. See Nicholas Gage, quoting an FBI report, "Ex-Aides Say Justice Department Rejected a Sinatra Inquiry," *New York Times,* April 14, 1976.
100. Nicholas Gage, "Two Mafiosi Linked to CIA Treated Leniently by U.S.," *New York Times,* April 13, 1976.
101. "Peter Lawford Tells," *Star* (New York), February 17, 1976.
102. The report is summarized in Gage, *Mafia Is Not an Equal Opportunity Employer,* ch. 5.
103. "Peter Lawford Tells."
104. Author's journal, October 28, 1963.
105. See Gage piece, *New York Times,* April 14, 1976.
106. Hundley, in interview by author.
107. *New York Times,* April 16, 1976.
108. Church committee, *Assassination Plots,* 133.
109. Ibid., 133, 151, 153–155.
110. Ibid., 164–167.
111. See, e.g., Branch and Crile, "The Kennedy Vendetta."
112. Church committee, *Assassination Plots,* 120, 157, 159.

22. Robert Kennedy and the Missile Crisis (*pages 521–555*)

1. Pierre Salinger, *With Kennedy* (Garden City, N.Y., 1966), 198.
2. Benjamin C. Bradlee, *Conversations with Kennedy* (New York, 1975), 194.
3. James W. Symington, *The Stately Game* (New York, 1971), 144.
4. RFK, handwritten notes, November 7, 1961, RFK Papers.
5. RFK, memorandum dictated May 29, 1962, RFK Papers.
6. RFK, memorandum dictated July 21, 1962, RFK Papers.
7. RFK, in recorded interview by John Bartlow Martin, March 1, 1964, I, 40, 47, JFK Oral History Program.
8. RFK, in Martin interview, April 13, 1964, I, 9.
9. RFK, in Martin interview, March 1, 1964, I, 45.
10. RFK, memorandum dictated May 29, 1962, RFK Papers.
11. RFK to JFK, June 19, 1962, RFK Papers.
12. RFK to McGeorge Bundy, July 11, 1962, RFK Papers.
13. RFK, in Martin interview, March 1, 1964, I, 46.
14. Salinger, *With Kennedy,* 200.
15. Article by N. Karev in *Za Rubezhom,* June 9, 1962; reported in aerogram from American embassy, Moscow, June 19, 1962, RFK Papers.
16. Salinger, *With Kennedy,* 209.
17. RFK, in Martin interview, April 30, 1964, I, 10.

18. Llewellyn Thompson, in recorded interview by Elizabeth Donahue, March 25, 1964, 4, JFK Oral History Program.

19. RFK, memorandum dictated July 21, 1962, RFK Papers; RFK, Martin interview, April 30, 1964, I, 9.

20. Jean Daniel in *L'Express,* December 14, 1963; Daniel, "Unofficial Envoy," *New Republic,* December 14, 1963; Daniel, *Le Temps qui reste* (Paris, 1973), 159–160; N. S. Khrushchev, *Khrushchev Remembers: The Last Testament* (Boston, 1974), 511; Claude Julien in *Le Monde,* March 22, 1963.

21. N. S. Khrushchev, *Khrushchev Remembers* (Boston, 1970), 493–494.

22. Graham T. Allison, *Essence of Decision: Explaining the Cuban Missile Crisis* (Boston, 1971), 49.

23. Herbert L. Matthews, *Fidel Castro* (New York, 1969), 225.

24. Daniel, "Unofficial Envoy."

25. Khrushchev, *Khrushchev Remembers,* 494.

26. RFK, memorandum dictated September 11, 1962, RFK Papers.

27. Minutes of White House meeting, September 4, 1962, RFK Papers.

28. Louise FitzSimons, *The Kennedy Doctrine* (New York, 1972), 138; Clare Boothe Luce, "Cuba and the Unfaced Truth," *Life,* October 5, 1962; Hugh Thomas, *Cuba or the Pursuit of Freedom* (London, 1971), 1399–1400; Richard Rovere, "Washington Letter," *New Yorker,* October 10, 1962.

29. Robert F. Kennedy, *Thirteen Days: A Memoir of the Cuban Missile Crisis* (New York, 1971 ed., with afterword by Richard E. Neustadt and Graham T. Allison), 2.

30. I owe this story to R. Harris Smith, who turned it up in the course of his research on a biography of Allen W. Dulles (R. Harris Smith to author, December 22, 1973).

31. John F. Kennedy, *Public Papers . . . 1962* (Washington, 1963), 807, 897–898.

32. White House meeting, October 16, 1962, RFK Papers.

33. In *Thirteen Days* (9) he writes that he passed the note to the President. In a contemporaneous memorandum dictated October 31, 1962, in the RFK Papers, he said that he passed it to Sorensen. Perhaps Sorensen, who put Kennedy's manuscript in final shape for publication, made the change in an excess of modesty.

34. Maxwell Taylor, *Swords and Plowshares* (New York, 1972), 268.

35. RFK, handwritten notes, October 31, 1962, RFK Papers.

36. RFK, in interview by author, February 27, 1965, 6, JFK Oral History Program.

37. RFK, memorandum dictated November 30, 1962, RFK Papers.

38. Joseph Dolan, in recorded interview by L. J. Hackman, April 11, 1970, 1, RFK Oral History Program.

39. RFK, *Thirteen Days,* 15.

40. Ibid., 17.

41. Roswell Gilpatric, in recorded interview by D. J. O'Brien, May 27, 1970, 55, JFK Oral History Program.

42. "No Yearning to be Loved—Dean Acheson talks to Kenneth Harris," *Listener,* April 8, 1971.

43. Dean Acheson, "Dean Acheson's Version of Robert Kennedy's Version of the Cuban Missile Affair," *Esquire,* February 1969.

44. Leonard C. Meeker, memorandum of October 19, 1962, meeting of the Executive Committee of the National Security Council, 5, Schlesinger Papers. Meeker, an able and incorruptible public servant, was later ambassador to Rumania. We had worked together in the OSS during the Second World War.

45. RFK, memorandum dictated October 31, 1962, RFK Papers.

46. Meeker, memorandum, 5–6.

47. RFK, *Thirteen Days,* 16.

48. Meeker, memorandum, 7.

49. RFK, memorandum, October 31, 1962.

50. Jean Stein and George Plimpton, eds., *American Journey* (New York, 1970), 136–137.
51. U. Alexis Johnson, in recorded interview by William Brubeck, n.d. [1964], 45, JFK Oral History Program.
52. Minutes of National Security Council (NSC) meeting, 2:30–5:10 P.M., October 20, 1962, RFK Papers.
53. Theodore C. Sorensen, *Kennedy* (New York, 1965), 694.
54. Minutes of NSC.
55. Robert McNamara, in interview for David Wolper's television special on Robert Kennedy, October 23, 1969.
56. RFK, memoranda dictated October 31 and November 15, 1962, RFK Papers.
57. Taylor, *Swords and Plowshares,* 271.
58. Gilpatric, in O'Brien interview, August 12, 1970, 116.
59. Kenneth O'Donnell and David F. Powers, *"Johnny, We Hardly Knew Ye"* (Boston, 1972), 318.
60. R. J. Walton, *Cold War and Counterrevolution* (New York, 1972), 103, 116.
61. In addition to Walton, see, e.g., FitzSimons, *Kennedy Doctrine,* ch. 5; Ronald Steel, "Endgame," in *Imperialists and Other Heroes* (New York: Random House, Vintage reprint, 1973), 115–136; I. F. Stone, "What If Khrushchev Hadn't Backed Down?" in *In a Time of Torment* (New York, 1967), 18–27; Barton J. Bernstein, "The Cuban Missile Crisis," in *Reflections on the Cold War,* ed. L. H. Miller and R. W. Pruessen (Philadelphia, 1974), 108–142; Barton J. Bernstein, " 'Courage and Commitment': The Missiles of October," *Foreign Service Journal,* December 1975.
62. McGeorge Bundy, on *Issues and Answers,* October 14, 1962.
63. Bernstein, "Cuban Missile Crisis," 137.
64. RFK, *Thirteen Days,* 45.
65. Walton, *Cold War and Counterrevolution,* 122.
66. Bohlen to JFK, October 18, 1962, in Charles E. Bohlen, *Witness to History, 1929–1969* (New York, 1973), 491.
67. Theodore Sorensen, memorandum, October 18, 1962, RFK Papers.
68. Sorensen, memorandum, October 20, 1962, RFK Papers.
69. RFK to JFK, October 24, 1962, RFK Papers.
70. Edwin Guthman, *We Band of Brothers* (New York, 1971), 126.
71. RFK, handwritten notes on White House meeting of October 24, 1962, RFK Papers. This passage, somewhat rewritten and polished, appeared in RFK, *Thirteen Days,* 48–49.
72. RFK, *Thirteen Days,* 48–49.
73. Theodore Sorensen, draft, October 18, 1962, RFK Papers.
74. Meeker, memorandum, 10.
75. Minutes of NSC.
76. RFK, in interview by John Bartlow Martin, December 7, 1966, Martin Papers.
77. Minutes of NSC.
78. O'Donnell and Powers, *"Johnny,"* 322.
79. Minutes of NSC.
80. O'Donnell and Powers, *"Johnny,"* 323.
81. RFK, memorandum, November 15, 1962.
82. Author's journal, October 22, 1962.
83. RFK, *Thirteen Days,* 28.
84. Harold Macmillan, *At the End of the Day, 1961–1963* (New York, 1973), 210–211.
85. Stone, *In a Time of Torment,* 21–22.
86. O'Donnell and Powers, *"Johnny,"* 310.
87. Ronald Steel, *Imperialists and Other Heroes,* 135; Bernstein, " 'Courage and Commitment.' "
88. Sorensen, *Kennedy,* 711.

89. Macmillan, *End of the Day*, 199.

90. RFK, notes on White House meeting, October 24, 1962.

91. Michel Tatu, *Power in the Kremlin: From Khrushchev to Kosygin* (New York, 1969), 263.

92. Khrushchev to JFK, October 25, 1962. The final text is reprinted in *The Dynamics of World Power: A Documentary History of United States Foreign Policy, 1945–1973*, ed. Arthur M. Schlesinger, Jr., vol. 3, *Eastern Europe and the Soviet Union*, ed. Walter La Feber (New York, 1973), 699–703.

93. Macmillan, *End of the Day*, 211.

94. Khrushchev, *Last Testament*, 512.

95. RFK, *Thirteen Days*, 74.

96. Macmillan, *End of the Day*, 187, 212–213, 217; Macmillan, in interview by Robert McKenzie, "The Cuba Crisis," *Listener*, October 11, 1973.

97. Henry Kissinger, "Reflections on Cuba," *Reporter*, November 22, 1962.

98. Elie Abel, *The Missile Crisis* (New York: Bantam reprint, 1966), 168.

99. RFK, memorandum, November 15, 1962, RFK Papers.

100. Abel, *Missile Crisis*, 174.

101. Executive Committee of National Security Council, minutes, October 23, 1962, RFK Papers.

102. RFK, *Thirteen Days*, 75–76.

103. Allison, *Essence of Decision*, 225, 227.

104. RFK, *Thirteen Days*, 79.

105. Ibid., 79–81.

106. RFK to Dean Rusk, October 30, 1962, RFK Papers; and Anatoly Gromyko, "Diplomatic Efforts of the USSR to Liquidate the Crisis," *Voprosy Istorii*, August 1971 (Gromyko cites Soviet Foreign Ministry Archives). This was the second of two articles; the first, "Concoction of the Caribbean Crisis by the U.S. Government," ran in July 1971. The Gromyko series, a characteristic piece of Soviet "history," is noteworthy for the fact that the name N. S. Khrushchev nowhere appears.

107. So Dobrynin said to Averell Harriman in Hobe Sound, Florida, in the winter of 1969, as described by Harriman to me.

108. Khrushchev, *Last Testament*, 498.

109. Douglas Dillon, in recorded interview by L. J. Hackman, June 18, 1970, 13, RFK Oral History Program.

110. Abram Chayes, *The Cuban Missile Crisis: International Crises and the Role of Law* (New York, 1974), 98.

111. Robert McNamara to JFK, April 25 [1963], JFK Papers; Jupiter missiles were also removed from Italy.

112. Curtis E. LeMay, *America Is in Danger* (New York, 1968), 200.

113. Thomas, *Cuba or the Pursuit of Freedom*, 1414.

114. Lee Lockwood, *Castro's Cuba, Cuba's Fidel* (New York, 1967), 200.

115. A point I adapt from K. S. Karol, *Guerrillas in Power: The Course of the Cuban Revolution* (New York, 1970).

116. Author's journal, October 29, 1962.

117. Bradlee, *Conversations with Kennedy*, 1122.

118. Author's journal, October 30, 1962.

119. RFK, in recorded interview by John Bartlow Martin, May 14, 1964, II, 1, RFK Oral History Program.

120. RFK, memorandum dictated November 30, 1962, RFK Papers.

121. James B. Donovan, *Challenges* (New York, 1967), 100.

122. Abel, *Missile Crisis*, 190–191.

123. Sorensen, *Kennedy*, 720.

124. RFK, memorandum dictated November 15, 1962, RFK Papers.

125. RFK, memorandum dictated November 14, 1962, RFK Papers.

126. RFK, memorandum, November 30, 1962.
127. In RFK Papers.
128. RFK, memorandum, November 30, 1962.
129. Ibid.
130. RFK to Bolshakov, March 7, 1963; photocopy in RFK Papers. Alsop's column was in the *Washington Post,* November 5, 1962.
131. Fidel Castro, in interview with Claude Julien, *Le Monde,* March 22, 1963.
132. Bernstein, " 'Courage and Commitment.' "
133. Robert McNamara to JFK, April 17, 1963, "Could the Defense Budget Be Cut to $43 Billion Without Weakening the Security of the United States?" JFK Papers.
134. Sorensen, *Kennedy,* 705.
135. Abel, *Missile Crisis,* 180.
136. RFK, *Thirteen Days,* 104–105.
137. Ibid., 106.
138. Tatu, *Power in the Kremlin,* 422.
139. Lord Harlech, in recorded interview by Jean Stein, April 30, 1970, 11, Stein Papers.
140. See Graham T. Allison, "Cuban Missiles and Kennedy Macho," *Washington Monthly,* October 1972.
141. Abel, *Missile Crisis,* 162.
142. Richard Nixon, "Cuba, Castro, and John F. Kennedy," *Reader's Digest,* November 1964.
143. Playboy Interview, *Playboy,* March 1977.
144. Khrushchev, *Khrushchev Remembers,* 500; *Last Testament,* 513–514.
145. Matthews, *Fidel Castro,* 225.
146. George S. McGovern, *Cuban Realities: May 1975,* report to the Committee on Foreign Relations, 94 Cong., 1 Sess. (1975), 14.
147. Robert McNamara, statement for release April 14 [1968], RFK Papers.
148. Adlai Stevenson to RFK, December 22, 1962, RFK Papers.
149. Khrushchev, *Khrushchev Remembers,* 500.
150. "Harold Macmillan and Lord Harlech Discuss with Robert MacNeil the Cuban Missile Crisis of 1962," *Listener,* January 30, 1969.
151. O'Donnell and Powers, *"Johnny,"* 283.
152. Stein and Plimpton, *American Journey,* 139.

23. The Cuban Connection: II (*pages 557–583*)

1. RFK, in recorded interview by John Bartlow Martin, April 30, 1964, III, 22–23, JFK Oral History Program; Senate Select Committee to Study Governmental Operations with respect to Intelligence Activities (hereafter cited as Church committee), *Interim Report: Alleged Assassination Plots Involving Foreign Leaders,* 94 Cong., 1 Sess. (1975), 148.
2. E. G. Lansdale to Special Group (Augmented), November 14, 1962, RFK Papers; Lansdale, in interview by author, December 30, 1976.
3. Maxwell Taylor, in recorded interview by L. J. Hackman, October 22, 1969, 9, RFK Oral History Program.
4. Lansdale, in interview by author.
5. John Nolan, in recorded interview by Frank DeRosa, April 25, 1967, 6, JFK Oral History Program.
6. Edwin Guthman, *We Band of Brothers* (New York, 1971), 131–132; Haynes Johnson, *The Bay of Pigs* (New York, 1964), 321.
7. Joseph Dolan, in recorded interview by Frank DeRosa, July 8, 1964, 2–3, JFK Oral History Program.

8. Victor Navasky, *Kennedy Justice* (New York, 1971), 335.

9. Lloyd N. Cutler, in recorded interview by Frank DeRosa, June 22, 1964, 23, JFK Oral History Program.

10. Robert F. Shea, in recorded interview by Frank DeRosa, July 1, 1963, 24–25, JFK Oral History Program.

11. Barrett Prettyman, "The Cuban Prisoner Exchange," n.d. [1963], 3, Prettyman Papers.

12. Ibid., 21.

13. Nolan, in DeRosa interview, 7–9.

14. Prettyman, "Cuban Prisoner Exchange," 34.

15. Kenneth O'Donnell and David Powers, *"Johnny, We Hardly Knew Ye"* (Boston, 1972), 275–276.

16. Richard Cardinal Cushing, in recorded interview by Jean Stein, n.d., 3, Stein Papers.

17. Dolan, in DeRosa interview, 6.

18. O'Donnell and Powers, *"Johnny,"* 276–277.

19. John F. Kennedy, *Public Papers . . . 1962* (Washington, 1963), 911–912.

20. *Newsweek,* January 7, 1963.

21. Church committee, *Assassination Plots,* 173.

22. Sterling Cottrell to McGeorge Bundy, January 22, 1963, RFK Papers.

23. Robert Hurwich, in recorded interview by John Plank, April 24–May 4, 1964, 151, JFK Oral History Program.

24. RFK to JFK, March 14, 1963, RFK Papers.

25. Bundy to Acting Director of Central Intelligence, March 14, 1963; RFK to JFK, March 26, 1963, RFK Papers.

26. Sir Herbert Marchant, "Cuba on the Brink—II," *London Sunday Telegraph,* October 22, 1967.

27. Roger Hilsman, *To Move a Nation* (Garden City, N.Y., 1967), 226; *New York Times,* April 21, 1963; George McCully, "Keating and the Debate Concerning the Soviet Buildup in Cuba," n.d. [September 1964], RFK Papers.

28. Benjamin C. Bradlee, *Conversations with Kennedy* (New York, 1975), 132–133.

29. Marquis Childs, *Witness to Power* (New York, 1975), 180.

30. RFK, handwritten notes, March 29, 1963, RFK Papers.

31. Church committee, *Final Report,* bk. V, The Investigation of the Assassination of President John F. Kennedy: Performance of the Intelligence Agencies, 94 Cong., 2 Sess. (1976), 11–13.

32. Church committee, *Assassination Plots,* 173.

33. McGeorge Bundy to RFK, May 16, 1963, RFK Papers.

34. Nolan, in DeRosa interview, 11–12.

35. Ibid., 22–26.

36. Lee Lockwood, *Castro's Cuba, Cuba's Fidel* (New York, 1967), 80.

37. M. C. Miskovsky to McCone, April 13, 1963, RFK Papers.

38. John Nolan to RFK, n.d. [April 1963], RFK Papers.

39. Nolan, in DeRosa interview, 10–13.

40. James B. Donovan, *Challenges* (New York, 1967), 92.

41. Ibid., 85.

42. Church committee, *Assassination Plots,* 172.

43. Ibid., 172–173, 337.

44. Ibid., 173.

45. McGeorge Bundy, in interview by author, July 18, 1977.

46. Church committee, *Assassination Plots,* 173, 337.

47. General Krulak appears under thin disguise as General Tartak in B. E. Ayer's account, *The War That Never Was* (Indianapolis, 1976), 15, 52–53. His CIA experience deeply upset Ayers; it broke up his marriage, created an impassioned identification with the Cubans and led to his resignation from both the Agency

and the Army when interest passed in 1964 from Cuba to Vietnam. His book is at times highly emotional, though ordinarily prosaic when describing covert operations.

48. Dick Russell, "Little Havana's Reign of Terror," *New Times,* October 29, 1976.
49. Church committee, *Assassination of President Kennedy,* 12–13.
50. RFK, in Martin interview, III, 19, 24.
51. J. H. Crimmins to RFK, June 24, 1963, RFK Papers.
52. McGeorge Bundy to RFK, n.d. [soon after July 12, 1963], enclosing memorandum from CIA/Miami on Hendrix, RFK Papers.
53. John McCone to RFK, July 20, 1963, enclosing report provided by J. M. Bosch of a conversation with Somoza.
54. Memorandum of conversation between J. H. Crimmins, Felipe Rivero and Paulino Sierra, August 17, 1963, RFK Papers.
55. U.S. ambassador, Nicaragua, to Thomas Mann, April 3, 1964, Mann to ambassador, April 7, 1964, RFK Papers.
56. Church committee, *Assassination Plots,* 171.
57. Hugh Thomas, *Cuba* (London, 1971), 1286–1287; George Crile III, "The Riddle of AM LASH," *Washington Post,* May 2, 1976.
58. Church committee, *Assassination Plots,* 87; Church committee, *Assassination of President Kennedy,* 13–14.
59. Church committee, *Assassination of President Kennedy,* 14; Johnson, *Bay of Pigs,* 354.
60. Church committee, *Assassination of President Kennedy,* 17, 74–75; Church committee, *Assassination Plots,* 174.
61. Church committee, *Assassination Plots,* 88–89; Church committee, *Assassination of President Kennedy,* 17–19.
62. Church committee, *Assassination Plots,* 89–90; Church committee, *Assassination of President Kennedy,* 78–79. Tad Szulc believes that Howard Hunt may have been the CIA officer working with Cubela and Artime in this period (Szulc, *Compulsive Spy: The Strange Career of E. Howard Hunt* [New York, 1974], 90–97).
63. Thomas, *Cuba,* 1070.
64. Statement from office of Senator George McGovern, July 30, 1975; Church committee, *Assassination Plots,* 71.
65. The FBI deleted the words "in place" before sending copies of Morgan's deposition to the Attorney General, the Secret Service and the White House. For some reason no copy went to the CIA. Church committee, *Assassination of President Kennedy,* 83–85. For further detail, see Ronald Kessler and Laurence Stern, "Slain Mobster Claimed Cuban Link to JFK Death," *Washington Post,* August 22, 1976.
66. Jack Anderson, "Did Castro Arrange for Mob to Kill Kennedy," *Washington Post,* March 24, 1977.
67. Nicholas Gage, "Mafia Said to Have Slain Rosselli Because of His Senate Testimony," *New York Times,* February 25, 1977.
68. George Crile III, "The Mafia, the CIA and Castro," *Washington Post,* May 16, 1976.
69. RFK, in Martin interview, III, 18.
70. Author's journal, December 13, 1963; notes taken by Richard Goodwin on meeting that day, Goodwin Papers.
71. Abba Schwartz, *The Open Society* (New York, 1968), ch. 5.
72. Ball to Rusk, December 13, 1963, RFK Papers.
73. RFK, in Martin interview, III, 18.
74. William Attwood, *The Reds and the Blacks* (New York, 1967), 142.
75. Church committee, *Assassination of President Kennedy,* 20.
76. William Attwood, "Memorandum on Cuba," September 18, 1963, RFK Papers.
77. Attwood, *Reds and Blacks,* 142.

78. Church committee, *Assassination Plots,* 173–174.
79. Attwood, *Reds and Blacks,* 143.
80. RFK, in Martin interview, III, 18–19.
81. Church committee, *Assassination Plots,* 174.
82. Jean Daniel, *Le Temps qui reste* (Paris, 1973), 149–152; Jean Daniel, "Unofficial Envoy," *New Republic,* December 14, 1963.
83. State Department, American Republics Division, "The Future of Cuba," November 7, 1963, RFK Papers.
84. McGeorge Bundy, memorandum re Attwood-Vallejo talks, November 12, 1963.
85. Attwood, *Reds and Blacks,* 144.
86. John F. Kennedy, *Public Papers . . . 1963* (Washington, 1964), 875–876.
87. Attwood, *Reds and Blacks,* 144; Church committee, *Assassination Plots,* 174.
88. Daniel, *Temps,* 158–162; Daniel, "Unofficial Envoy"; Daniel, "When Castro Heard the News," *New Republic,* December 7, 1963.
89. Daniel, *Temps,* 163–164; "When Castro Heard the News."
90. Author's journal, December 4, 1963.
91. Ibid., December 23, 1963.
92. Attwood, *Reds and Blacks,* 146.
93. Frank Mankiewicz and Kirby Jones, *With Fidel* (Chicago, 1975), 164, 166.
94. Maurice Halperin, *The Rise and Decline of Fidel Castro* (Berkeley, 1972), 344.
95. Hurwich, in Plank interview, 104–106.
96. Richard Helms to RFK, June 26, 1963, RFK Papers.
97. William Manchester, *The Death of a President* (New York, 1967), 46.
98. After John Kennedy's death, Bosch printed up his letter as a brochure with pictures (Russell, "Little Havana"). See also "Miami, Haven for Terror," *Nation,* March 19, 1977.
99. George Crile III, "Our Heritage—the Exile Cuban Terrorists," *Washington Post,* November 7, 1976.

24. Missions to the Third World (*pages* 584–609)

1. David Halberstam, *The Unfinished Odyssey of Robert Kennedy* (New York, 1968), 145–146.
2. Felix Houphouët-Boigny and Robert Kennedy, memorandum of conversation, August 7, 1961, RFK Papers.
3. Clark Mollenhoff, in recorded interview by Jean Stein, July 25, 1968, 17–18, Stein Papers.
4. RFK to JFK, September 5, 1961, RFK Papers.
5. Walt W. Rostow, *The Diffusion of Power* (New York, 1972), 202–203. I cheerfully yield to Rostow's memory of the presidential comment in preference to the version—"the hot breath of his disapproval"—in *A Thousand Days* (Boston, 1965), 573. Robert Kennedy himself had a variant memory: "He made some remark about [my] cross little face looking over his shoulder while he was doing this." RFK, recorded interview by John Bartlow Martin, April 13, 1964, II, 2, JFK Oral History Program.
6. RFK to JFK, December 7, 1961, RFK Papers.
7. RFK, in Martin interview, April 13, 1964, II, 2–3.
8. Author to RFK, July 1, 1963; Robert McNamara to Dean Rusk, July 11, 1963, RFK Papers.
9. Wayne Fredericks, in interview by author, January 10, 1977.
10. RFK to McGeorge Bundy, November 20, 1963, RFK Papers.
11. RFK, in Martin interview, April 13, 1964, II, 51–52. Ball recalled the memorandum as saying: "God watches every sparrow that may fall, but I don't see why we

have to compete in that league." George Ball, in recorded interview by Jean Stein, n.d. [1968], 12, Stein Papers.

12. John Kenneth Galbraith, *Ambassador's Journal* (Boston, 1969), 303.
13. Anthony Lewis, "A Tribute to Robert Francis Kennedy," address at unveiling of RFK portrait, Department of Justice, March 14, 1975 (Washington, 1975).
14. Robert F. Kennedy, "Our Generation, Our World, Our Future," address at Nihon University, Tokyo, February 6, 1962, RFK Papers.
15. Robert F. Kennedy, *Just Friends and Brave Enemies* (New York, 1962), 53.
16. Edwin Reischauer, in recorded interview by D. J. O'Brien, April 25, 1969, 21, JFK Oral History Program.
17. RFK, *Just Friends*, 59.
18. John Seigenthaler, in recorded interview by R. J. Grele, February 23, 1966, 412, JFK Oral History Program.
19. American embassy, Tokyo, "Visit of Attorney General to Japan, February 4–10, 1962," February 28, 1962, RFK Papers.
20. RFK, *Just Friends*, 61.
21. Ibid., 66.
22. Seigenthaler, in Grele interview, 388.
23. Events at Waseda as observed by the Attorney General's interpreter, in "Visit of Attorney General to Japan," RFK Papers.
24. Reischauer to Rusk, February 8, 1962, RFK Papers.
25. Reischauer, in O'Brien interview, 22.
26. Ibid., 21.
27. "Visit of Attorney General."
28. Seigenthaler, in Grele interview, 389.
29. "Visit of Attorney General."
30. "Kennedy's Kansai Trip," *Nihon Kezai*, February 12, 1962.
31. R. A. Mlynarchik to David Osborn, February 13, 1962, RFK Papers.
32. "Visit of Attorney General."
33. Reischauer, in O'Brien interview, 13–14.
34. Roger Hilsman, *To Move a Nation* (Garden City, N.Y., 1967), 363.
35. RFK, *Just Friends*, 113–114.
36. Ibid., 114–117; Howard Jones to Rusk, February 18, 1962, containing Kennedy's Mexican War heresy as transcribed in the tape recording of the meeting, RFK Papers.
37. Jones to Rusk, February 14 and February 22, 1962, RFK Papers.
38. N. S. Khrushchev, *Khrushchev Remembers: The Last Testament* (Boston, 1974), 312–322; RFK, *Just Friends*, 100.
39. RFK, in Martin interview, April 13, 1964, II, 33.
40. Howard P. Jones, in recorded interview by D. J. O'Brien, June 23, 1969–April 9, 1970, 41, JFK Oral History Program.
41. Khrushchev, *Last Testament*, 323.
42. Howard P. Jones, *Indonesia: The Impossible Dream* (New York, 1971), 197, 199, 203.
43. W. Averell Harriman, in recorded interview by author, June 6, 1965, 16–17, JFK Oral History Program.
44. McGeorge Bundy to RFK, February 5, 1962, RFK Papers.
45. Howard Jones to Rusk, February 14, 1962, RFK Papers.
46. RFK to JFK and Rusk, February 14, 1962, RFK Papers.
47. RFK to Bundy, July 24, 1962, memorandum on conversation with Subandrio, July 20, 1962, RFK Papers.
48. Jones to RFK, May 3, 1962, RFK Papers.
49. Jones to Rusk, August 16, 1962, JFK Papers.
50. RFK to Mrs. William C. Battle, June 11, 1963, RFK Papers.
51. Khrushchev, *Last Testament*, 327.

52. Cindy Adams, *Sukarno: An Autobiography as Told to Cindy Adams* (Indianapolis, 1965), 271.

53. RFK, in Martin interview, April 13, 1964, II, 30.

54. Seigenthaler, in Grele interview, 399–408; RFK, in Martin interview, April 13, 1964, II, 35–37.

55. Jones, in O'Brien interview, 41.

56. Adams, *Sukarno,* 271.

57. Allen Pope to RFK, July 11, 1962, RFK Papers.

58. Galbraith, *Ambassador's Journal,* 305.

59. Author's journal, February 21, 1962.

60. Willy Brandt, *Begegnungen und Einsichten* (1976), as reported in the *New York Times,* August 18, 1976.

61. RFK, *Just Friends,* 153–161.

62. Author's journal, February 23, 1962.

63. RFK to JFK, "From Extensive Notes Made during My Discussion with Chancellor Adenauer," March 16, 1962, RFK Papers; RFK, *Just Friends,* 166–168.

64. RFK, in Martin interview, April 13, 1964, II, 41.

65. Anthony Lewis, in recorded interview by L. J. Hackman, July 23, 1970, 18, RFK Oral History Program.

66. For an extended discussion, see Arthur M. Schlesinger, Jr., "The Alliance for Progress: A Retrospective," in *Latin America: The Search for a New International Role,* ed. R. G. Hellman and H. J. Rosenbaum (New York, 1975), 57–92. The quotations are from Lawrence Harrison, "Waking from the Pan American Dream," *Foreign Policy,* Winter 1971–72, 1969; and Suzanne Bodenheimer, "Dependency and Imperialism: The Roots of Latin American Underdevelopment," in *Readings in U.S. Imperialism,* ed. E. T. Fann and D. C. Hodges (Boston, 1971), 177.

67. Eduardo Frei, "Urgencies in Latin America: The Alliance That Lost Its Way," *Foreign Affairs,* April 1967, 437–438, 442.

68. Richard Goodwin, "Our Stake in a Big Awakening," *Life,* April 14, 1967.

69. John F. Kennedy, *Public Papers . . . 1962* (Washington, 1963), 223.

70. William D. Rogers, *The Twilight Struggle: The Alliance for Progress and the Politics of Development in Latin America* (New York, 1967), 218–219.

71. Jerome Levinson and Juan De Onis, *The Alliance That Lost Its Way: A Critical Report on the Alliance for Progress* (Chicago, 1970), 71.

72. A. F. Lowenthal, "United States Policy Toward Latin America: 'Liberal,' 'Radical,' and 'Bureaucratic' Perspectives," *Latin American Research Review,* Fall 1973, 17.

73. Jean Daniel, "Unofficial Envoy," *New Republic,* December 14, 1963.

74. Frank Mankiewicz and Kirby Jones, *With Fidel* (Chicago, 1975), 200–202.

75. Herbert L. Matthews, *Return to Cuba* (Stanford University, n.d. [1964]), 15.

76. Daniel, "Unofficial Envoy."

77. Luis Muñoz-Marin, address before the AFL-CIO National Conference on Community Service, Chicago, May 3, 1962, 6 (mimeographed).

78. Ibid., 8.

79. JFK, *Public Papers . . . 1962,* 231, 495, 883.

80. John F. Kennedy, *Public Papers . . . 1961* (Washington, 1962), 172.

81. John F. Kennedy, *Public Papers . . . 1963* (Washington, 1964), 873–875.

82. Roberto Campos, in recorded interview by John E. Reilly, May 29–30, 1964, JFK Oral History Program.

83. Lincoln Gordon, in interview by author, October 17, 1974.

84. Gordon, in interview by author; Campos, in Reilly interview, 26.

85. Campos, in Reilly interview, 24–25.

86. Ibid., 33.

87. Gordon, in interview by author.

88. Ibid.
89. Ethel Kennedy to RFK, December 17, 1962, RFK Papers.
90. U.S. embassy, Brazil, memorandum of conversation of talk among Robert Kennedy, João Goulart and Lincoln Gordon, 11:15 A.M.–2:30 P.M., December 17, 1962, RFK Papers.
91. Campos, in Reilly interview, 45.
92. Gordon, in interview by author.
93. RFK, in Martin interview, April 30, 1964, I, 37.
94. RFK, in Martin interview, April 13, 1964, I, 51.
95. Robert F. Kennedy, *The Pursuit of Justice* (New York: Harper & Row, Perennial Library reprint, 1964), 116–117.

25. The Brothers: II (*pages* 610–629)

1. Richard N. Goodwin, "The Art of Assuming Power," *New York Times Magazine,* December 26, 1976.
2. John F. Kennedy, *Public Papers . . . 1962* (Washington, 1963), 889.
3. John F. Kennedy, foreword to Theodore C. Sorensen, *Decision-Making in the White House* (New York, 1963), xii.
4. Jean Stein and George Plimpton, eds. *American Journey* (New York, 1970), 161, 163–164.
5. Art Buchwald, in recorded interview by Roberta Greene, March 12, 1969, 11, RFK Oral History Program.
6. Edwin Guthman, *We Band of Brothers* (New York, 1971), 241–243; Pierre Salinger, *With Kennedy* (New York, 1966), 239–247.
7. David Brinkley to RFK, February 11, 1963, RFK Papers.
8. *Time,* December 29, 1961.
9. *Boston Record,* May 9, 1957.
10. John Seigenthaler, in recorded interview by W. A. Geoghegan, n.d. [July 1964], 94, JFK Oral History Program.
11. R. J. Whalen, *The Founding Father* (New York, 1964), 452.
12. Hugh Sidey, *John F. Kennedy, President* (New York, 1963), 21.
13. Stephen Smith, in interview by author, March 5, 1976.
14. Charles Spalding, in recorded interview by John Stewart, March 14, 1968, 102, JFK Oral History Program.
15. Rita Dallas with Jeanira Ratcliffe, *The Kennedy Case* (New York: Popular Library reprint, 1973), 71–72, 146.
16. Dallas, *Kennedy Case,* 36, 83.
17. Ibid., 119, 122.
18. Benjamin C. Bradlee, *Conversations with Kennedy* (New York, 1975), 167–170.
19. Dallas, *Kennedy Case,* 109, 141, 167.
20. RFK, in recorded interview by John Bartlow Martin, April 13, 1964, II, 20, JFK Oral History Program.
21. Peter Edelman, in recorded interview by L. J. Hackman, December 12, 1969, 58–59, RFK Oral History Program.
22. Author's journal, April 10, 1963.
23. RFK to Randolph Churchill, April 24, 1963, RFK Papers.
24. Author's journal, September 11, 1963.
25. Adlai Stevenson to Mary Lasker, May 21, 1962, in a forthcoming volume of Stevenson's letters, edited by Walter Johnson, to whose courtesy I am indebted for this letter.
26. Author's journal, August 6, 1962.
27. Buchwald, in Greene interview, 10.
28. John Glenn, in recorded interview by Roberta Greene, June 26, 1969, 5–6, RFK

Oral History Program; Glenn, in recorded interview by Jean Stein, July 1, 1968, 1–2, 15–16, Stein Papers.

29. Rose Kennedy to RFK, October 4, 1961, RFK Papers.

30. RFK to author, July 25, 1963, Schlesinger Papers.

31. Stein and Plimpton, *American Journey*, 166–167.

32. Ramsey Clark, in interview by author, March 15, 1977.

33. Peter Maas, in recorded interview by Jean Stein, September 15, 1969, 4, Stein Papers.

34. Anthony Lewis, "A Tribute to Robert Francis Kennedy," address at the unveiling of RFK portrait, Department of Justice, March 14, 1975 (Washington, 1975).

35. Kenneth O'Donnell and David F. Powers, *"Johnny, We Hardly Knew Ye"* (Boston, 1972), 94.

36. Michael Forrestal, in recorded interview by Jean Stein, n.d. [1968], 13, Stein Papers.

37. RFK to author, June 4, 1962, Schlesinger Papers.

38. O'Donnell and Powers, *"Johnny,"* 282.

39. Gore Vidal, "The Best Man, 1968," *Esquire,* March 1963.

40. Interview with Gore Vidal, *Penthouse,* April 1975.

41. Anaïs Nin, *Diary,* vol. 4, *1944–1947,* ed. Gunther Stuhlman (New York, 1971), 105, 142.

42. *Penthouse* interview.

43. John English, in recorded interview by Roberta Greene, November 3, 1969, 4, 6, RFK Oral History Program.

44. Author's journal, November 12, 1961.

45. Budd Schulberg, "RFK—Harbinger of Hope," *Playboy,* January 1969.

46. Margaret Laing, *The Next Kennedy* (New York, 1968), 17.

47. Theodore C. Sorensen, *The Kennedy Legacy* (New York, 1969), 78.

48. RFK to JFK, April 3, 1963, RFK Papers.

49. Norman Cousins, *The Improbable Triumvirate* (New York, 1972), 114.

50. Author's journal, October 11, 1963. See O'Donnell and Powers, *"Johnny,"* 381.

51. Y. I. Nosenko, "Under the Eye of the KGB—a Former Police Chief Looks Back," *Listener,* May 22, 1975.

52. RFK, in Martin interview, May 14, 1964, I, 18.

53. RFK, in Martin interview, April 30, 1964, I, 3.

54. RFK, in Martin interview, December 7, 1966, Martin Papers.

55. George F. Kennan, in recorded interview by Louis Fischer, March 23, 1965, 95–96, JFK Oral History Program.

56. Mansfield, UPI interview by Mike Feinsilber, *Buffalo Evening News,* September 16, 1976.

57. O'Donnell and Powers, *"Johnny,"* 278.

58. RFK to JFK, March 14, 1963, RFK Papers.

59. RFK to JFK, November 12, 1963, RFK Papers. RFK had been reading Herbert Agar's *The Price of Union.*

60. RFK, memorandum dictated February 13, 1961, RFK Papers.

61. Stein and Plimpton, *American Journey,* 127.

62. Chester Bowles, in recorded interview by R. R. R. Brooks, February 2, 1965, 17, JFK Oral History Program.

63. Bradlee, *Conversations with Kennedy,* 142–143.

64. Robert McNamara, in interview for David Wolper's television special on Robert Kennedy, October 23, 1969.

65. Goodwin, "Art of Assuming Power."

66. Author's journal, December 16, 1963.

67. Pearl S. Buck, *The Kennedy Women: A Personal Appraisal* (New York, 1970), 83.

68. Charles Spalding, in recorded interview by L. J. Hackman, March 22, 1969, 41, RFK Oral History Program.

69. Roy Jenkins, *Nine Men of Power* (London, 1974), 215–216.
70. Roy Jenkins, *Nine Men of Power* (London, 1974), 215–216; Tom Wicker, in recorded interview by Jean Stein, November 25, 1969, 7, Stein Papers.
71. Stein and Plimpton, *American Journey*, 129; Spalding, in Stewart interview, 7–8.
72. RFK, in Martin interview, April 13, 1964, I, 57.
73. Quoted by Ted Lewis, *New York Daily News*, June 6, 1968.
74. O'Donnell, *"Johnny,"* 278.
75. Stein and Plimpton, *American Journey*, 128.
76. Benjamin C. Bradlee, in recorded interview by Jean Stein, October 18, 1968, 3, Stein Papers.
77. John F. Kennedy, *Public Papers . . . 1962* (Washington, 1963), 259. This characteristic Irish American mood was classically expressed by George M. Cohan in his sardonic threnody "Life's a Very Funny Proposition After All."
78. Richard Neustadt, in recorded interview by Jean Stein, October 9, 1968, 3, Stein Papers.
79. *Newsweek,* March 18, 1963.
80. Roy Wilkins, in recorded interview by Berl Bernhard, August 13, 1964, 14, JFK Oral History Program.
81. As told me by Lord Harlech. Lord Longford eventually wrote a perceptive biography of Kennedy, but found little enough to say about the influence of Catholicism; see Lord Longford, *Kennedy* (London, 1976), 203–204.
82. Tom Wicker, *Kennedy without Tears* (New York, 1964), 61.

26. Corridors of Grief (*pages* 630–648)

1. RFK, in recorded interview by John Bartlow Martin, May 14, 1964, I, 28, JFK Oral History Program; RFK, in recorded interview by Anthony Lewis, December 4, 1964, I, 15–16, JFK Oral History Program.
2. RFK, in Martin interview, May 14, 1964, I, 27.
3. RFK, in Martin interview, April 30, 1964, I, 21; RFK, in Lewis interview, December 4, 1964, I, 17. He also discussed his Romney concern with Paul Fay but warned him not to talk about it (Fay, *The Pleasure of His Company* [New York, 1966], 259).
4. RFK, in Martin interview, May 14, 1964, I, 24.
5. Ibid.
6. Stephen Smith to the President et al., November 13, 1963, RFK Papers; Kenneth O'Donnell and David F. Powers, *"Johnny, We Hardly Knew Ye"* (Boston, 1972), 386–387.
7. Theodore H. White, *The Making of the President, 1964* (New York, 1965), 28.
8. Leonard Baker, *The Johnson Eclipse* (New York, 1966), 105–106.
9. Benjamin C. Bradlee, *Conversations with Kennedy* (New York, 1975), 217–218.
10. O'Donnell and Powers, *"Johnny,"* 5.
11. RFK, in Martin interviews, April 30, 1964, I, 5, May 14, 1964, I, 21.
12. Evelyn Lincoln, *Kennedy and Johnson* (New York, 1968), 205.
13. Sam Houston Johnson, *My Brother Lyndon* (New York, 1970), 117.
14. RFK, in Martin interview, May 14, 1964, I, 25.
15. Ibid., April 13, 1964, I, 59–60.
16. G. H. Gallup, ed., *The Gallup Poll: Public Opinion, 1935–1971* (New York, 1972), vol. 3, 1800, 1845, 1850.
17. RFK, in Martin interview, May 14, 1964, I, 25.
18. Marquis Childs, *Witness to Power* (New York, 1975), 164–165.
19. Patrick Anderson, "Robert's Character," *Esquire,* April 1965.
20. John Douglas, in recorded interview by L. J. Hackman, June 16, 1969, 20, RFK Oral History Program.

21. Ramsey Clark, in recorded interview by L. J. Hackman, July 20, 1970, 8–11, RFK Oral History Program.

22. RFK, in recorded interview by William Manchester, May 16, 1964, 4–5, 8.

23. This and the following account, unless otherwise specified, is drawn from Robert Morgenthau, in recorded interview by Jean Stein, April 20, 1970, 1–2, Stein Papers; RFK, in Manchester interview, 12–33, 40–45; James Wechsler, "RFK's Ordeal" (an interview with Morgenthau), *New York Post,* December 3, 1963; Bill Davidson, "A Profile in Family Courage," *Saturday Evening Post,* December 14, 1963; William Manchester, *The Death of a President* (New York, 1967), 146, 195–196.

24. Edwin Guthman, *We Band of Brothers* (New York, 1971), 244.

25. Manchester, *Death of a President,* 378.

26. Author's journal, November 23, 1963.

27. Charles Spalding, in recorded interview by Jean Stein, January 22, 1970, 18–19, Stein Papers.

28. RFK, in Manchester interview, 46–47, 54–56.

29. Ibid., 63–65.

30. Ibid., 61.

31. Author's journal, November 25, 1963.

32. RFK Papers.

33. Author's journal, November 23, 1963.

34. Bradlee, *Conversations with Kennedy,* 243.

35. K. LeMoyne Billings, in recorded interview by Jean Stein, n.d. [1968], 18, Stein Papers.

36. John Seigenthaler, in recorded interview by L. J. Hackman, June 5, 1970, 31, RFK Oral History Program.

37. Pierre Salinger, in recorded interview by L. J. Hackman, May 26, 1969, 2, RFK Oral History Program.

38. Seigenthaler, in Hackman interview, 15.

39. Helen Keyes, in recorded interview by Jean Stein, October 9, 1968, 22, Stein Papers.

40. Mary Bailey Gimbel, in recorded interview by Jean Stein, n.d. [1968], 23, Stein Papers.

41. John Bartlow Martin, *Overtaken by Events* (Garden City, N.Y., 1966), 632.

42. Jean Stein and George Plimpton, eds., *American Journey* (New York, 1970), 146–147; Guthman, *We Band of Brothers,* 247.

43. Anderson, "Robert's Character."

44. Charles Spalding, in recorded interview by Jean Stein, January 22, 1970, 19, Stein Papers.

45. Nicholas Katzenbach, in recorded interview by L. J. Hackman, October 8, 1969, 75, RFK Oral History Program.

46. Edward Jay Epstein, *Legend: The Secret World of Lee Harvey Oswald* (New York, 1968), 15–17.

47. Senate Select Committee to Study Governmental Operations with respect to Intelligence Activities (Church committee), *Final Report,* bk. V, *The Investigation of the Assassination of President John F. Kennedy: Performance of the Intelligence Agencies,* 94 Cong., 2 Sess. (1976), 23, 33.

48. Vivian Cadden, "The Murder of President Kennedy," *McCall's,* March 1977.

49. Author's journal, December 9, 1963.

50. Walter Sheridan, in recorded interview by Roberta Greene, May 1, 1970, 3–4, RFK Oral History Program; Sheridan, *The Fall and Rise of Jimmy Hoffa* (New York, 1972), 300, 356, 408. The letter writer, Frank Chavez, Secretary-Treasurer of Local 901, was later murdered by one of his own bodyguards.

51. Author's journal, October 30, 1966.

52. Frank Mankiewicz, in recorded interview by L. J. Hackman, October 2, 1969, 69, RFK Oral History Program.

53. Anthony Lewis, "What Not to Do," *New York Times,* September 25, 1975.

54. The ballad was about Owen Roe O'Neill. Robert Kennedy quoted it at a St. Patrick's Day banquet in Scranton, Pennsylvania, in March 1964 (and elsewhere).

55. Handwritten notes [1964], RFK Papers.

56. Jacqueline Onassis, in recorded interview by author, June 2, 1976, 9.

57. I am indebted to Mary Bailey Gimbel for lending me one of Robert Kennedy's copies, dog-eared and heavily marked, of *The Greek Way.* He used the Norton Library paperback edition (1964) and always kept a copy in his dispatch case. The quotations are from 52, 53, 109, 116, 147, 158, 166.

58. Author's journal, August 14, 1966.

59. RFK to Angie Novello, n.d. [June 1967], RFK Papers.

60. Jeff Greenfield, in recorded interview by Roberta Greene, December 10, 1969, 99–100, RFK Oral History Program.

61. W. H. Auden, "The Christian Tragic Hero," *New York Times Book Review,* December 16, 1945.

62. "Favorite Quotations of John F. Kennedy and Robert F. Kennedy," under "Miscellaneous," RFK Papers. This was a loose-leaf volume, kept by Angie Novello under various headings and used by RFK for sustenance when he had to give a speech or write an article. He used the last three sentences in the third Camus quote as the epigraph for his own book *To Seek a Newer World* (New York, 1967), curiously omitting, however, the word *believer* in the last sentence.

63. Rita Dallas, *The Kennedy Case* (New York: Popular Library reprint, 1973), 259, 264.

27. Stranger in a Strange Land (*pages* 649–674)

1. Benjamin C. Bradlee, *Conversations with Kennedy* (New York, 1975), 194.

2. Doris Kearns, *Lyndon Johnson and the American Dream* (New York, 1976), 164.

3. Repeated by Johnson in a backgrounder on July 25, 1964, in Jack Valenti, *A Very Human President* (New York, 1975), 306.

4. Ralph Dungan, relaying message from Rusk to JFK, October 3, 1962, JFK Papers.

5. Charles Spalding, in recorded interview by Jean Stein, January 22, 1970, 8–9, Stein Papers.

6. Bobby Baker, with Larry King, *Wheeling and Dealing: Confessions of a Capitol Hill Operator* (New York, 1978), 244.

7. American Bar Association, Special Committee on Election Reform, "Symposium on the Vice-Presidency," *Fordham Law Review,* February 1977, 750. For some reason the ABA, wrong again, insists on the usage Vice-President. The title has no hyphen in the Constitution.

8. Evelyn Lincoln, *Kennedy and Johnson* (New York, 1968), 151, 153.

9. Kenneth P. O'Donnell and David F. Powers, *"Johnny, We Hardly Knew Ye"* (Boston, 1972), 8.

10. Lincoln, *Kennedy and Johnson,* 161, 186.

11. Bill Moyers, in television interview with David Susskind, October 13, 1974; Daniel Patrick Moynihan, interview, *Playboy,* March 1977.

12. Kearns, *Johnson,* 164.

13. O'Donnell and Powers, *"Johnny,"* 6; Baker, *Wheeling and Dealing,* 126.

14. Lyndon B. Johnson, *The Vantage Point* (New York, 1971), 539.

15. Spalding, in Stein interview, 13–14.

16. John Seigenthaler, in recorded interview by W. A. Geoghegan, n.d. [July 1964], 60–61, JFK Oral History Program; Seigenthaler, in recorded interview by L. J.

Hackman, June 5, 1970, 60–61; Seigenthaler to RFK, January 28, 1963, RFK Papers.

17. RFK, in recorded interview by author, February 27, 1965, 37, 42–43, JFK Oral History Program.

18. Ramsey Clark, in recorded interview by L. J. Hackman, July 7, 1970, 93, RFK Oral History Program.

19. Nicholas Katzenbach, in recorded interview by L. J. Hackman, October 8, 1969, 30, RFK Oral History Program.

20. RFK, in interview by author, 37.

21. Pierre Salinger, in recorded interview by L. J. Hackman, May 26, 1969, 13, RFK Oral History Program.

22. O'Donnell and Powers, *"Johnny,"* 6.

23. Michael Janeway, "LBJ and the Kennedys," *Atlantic Monthly,* February 1972.

24. Helen Thomas, *Deadline: White House* (New York, 1975), 121.

25. Kearns, *Johnson,* esp. ch. 1 and author's postscript; also 17, 201.

26. Hubert Humphrey, *The Education of a Public Man* (New York, 1976), 307.

27. Memoranda by James Wechsler, November 27, 1963, and Joseph P. Lash, November 27, 1963, Wechsler Papers; memorandum by Dorothy Schiff, in Jeffrey Potter, *Men, Money and Magic: The Story of Dorothy Schiff* (New York, 1976), 280–281.

28. John Adams, of course; emphasis added; J. D. Feerick, *The Twenty-Fifth Amendment* (New York, 1976), 31.

29. Kearns, *Johnson,* 170.

30. Jim Bishop, *The Day Kennedy Was Shot* (New York: Bantam reprint, 1969), 350. Bishop and Robert Kennedy, it should be added, were old foes in consequence of pro-Hoffa articles Bishop had written in 1959.

31. RFK, in recorded interview by William Manchester, May 16, 1964, 26, RFK Papers.

32. RFK, in recorded interview by John Bartlow Martin, February 29, 1964, 30, JFK Oral History Program; RFK, in interview by author, 42.

33. RFK, in Martin interview, May 14, 1964, I, 30, JFK Oral History Program.

34. RFK, in Manchester interview, 50–51; Evelyn Lincoln's account to me, author's journal, March 25, 1964.

35. RFK, in Manchester interview, 51–53.

36. William Manchester, *The Death of a President* (New York, 1967), 477–478.

37. RFK, in Manchester interview, 70–71.

38. Author's journal, November 27, 1963.

39. RFK, in Manchester interview, 71–72.

40. LBJ to RFK, January 1, 1964, RFK to LBJ, January 3, 1964, RFK Papers.

41. Joseph L. Schott, *No Left Turns* (New York, 1975), 204–205.

42. Joseph Dolan, in recorded interview by L. J. Hackman, July 18, 1970, 296, RFK Oral History Program.

43. Author's journal, December 5, 1963.

44. RFK, in recorded interview by Anthony Lewis, December 4, 1964, IV, 38–40, JFK Oral History Program.

45. RFK, in Martin interview, April 13, 1964, I, 33.

46. RFK, in Lewis interview, December 4, 1964, V, 9; Kennedy made similar statements in a memorandum dictated August 6, 1964, RFK Papers.

47. RFK, in Lewis interview, December 4, 1964, V, 19–20.

48. Ken W. Clawson, "Praises Mitchell as 'Very Human': FBI's Hoover Scores Ramsey Clark, RFK," *Washington Post,* November 17, 1970.

49. Ralph de Toledano, *J. Edgar Hoover* (New York; Manor reprint, 1974), 301–302.

50. Tom Wicker, *JFK and LBJ* (Baltimore: Penguin reprint, 1970), 196.

51. Author's journal, December 13, 1963.

52. Ibid.; Richard N. Goodwin, "The Structure Itself Must Change," *Rolling Stone,* June 6, 1974.

53. Author's journal, December 14, 1963.
54. Author to RFK, December 15, 1963, RFK Papers.
55. Author's journal, December 23, 1963.
56. Walter Sheridan, in recorded interview by Roberta Greene, May 1, 1970, 4, RFK Oral History Program.
57. Howard P. Jones, *Indonesia: The Impossible Dream* (New York, 1971), 289.
58. Roger Hilsman, *To Move a Nation* (Garden City, N.Y., 1967), 393.
59. Jones, *Indonesia,* 295–297.
60. Ibid., 300.
61. McGeorge Bundy, in recorded interview by William W. Moss, January 12, 1972, 23, RFK Oral History Program.
62. Michael Forrestal to RFK, January 9, 1964, RFK Papers.
63. "Background Guidance on Attorney General's Visit to the Far East," January 10, 1964, RFK Papers.
64. Forrestal, in interview by author, January 27, 1977.
65. D. L. Osborn to State Department, February 14, 1964, RFK Papers; *New York Times,* January 19, 1964; Edwin Guthman, *We Band of Brothers* (New York, 1971), 248–249.
66. Jones, *Indonesia,* 301.
67. Forrestal to William Bundy, May 8, 1964, RFK Papers.
68. Cindy Adams, *My Friend the Dictator* (Indianapolis, 1967), 78.
69. Forrestal, in recorded interview by Jean Stein, [n.d., 1968], 12, Stein Papers; Forrestal, in interview by author.
70. Tunku Abdul Rahman to RFK, January 30, 1964, RFK Papers.
71. Guthman, *We Band of Brothers,* 251; Theodore H. White, *The Making of the President, 1964* (New York, 1965), 261.
72. Murray Kempton, "Pure Irish: Robert F. Kennedy," *New Republic,* February 15, 1964.
73. RFK, in Martin interviews, March 1, 1964, II, 21, May 14, 1964, II, 17.
74. "Spectrum of Courses of Action with Respect to Cuba," February 21, 1964, RFK Papers.
75. RFK, in Martin interview, May 14, 1964, I, 34; Johnson, *Vantage Point,* 184–187.
76. RFK, in Martin interview, May 14, 1964, I, 34–37; author's journal, March 11, 1964.
77. Adam Walinsky, in recorded interview by Thomas Johnston, November 25, 1969, 2–3, RFK Oral History Program; Jean Stein and George Plimpton, eds., *American Journey* (New York, 1970), 277–278. Muste was in fact seventy-nine years old.
78. Katzenbach, in Hackman interview, 15–16.
79. Kempton, "Pure Irish."
80. Murray Kempton, in recorded interview by Jean Stein, March 28, 1970, 3, Stein Papers.
81. Angie Novello, in interview by author, December 11, 1975.
82. Kenneth O'Donnell, in recorded interview by L. J. Hackman, May 6, 1969, 37, RFK Oral History Program.
83. William Hundley, in interview by author, August 4, 1976.
84. "The Federal Government and Urban Poverty," conference sponsored by the Kennedy Library and Brandeis University, June 16–17, 1973, transcript, vol. 3, 48. This is an indispensable source for the evolution of the war against poverty. I am also grateful to several participants for their kindness in letting me see unpublished papers: to William B. Cannon for the relevant portion of his manuscript "The Dangerous Abuse of the Middle Class"; to Richard W. Boone for "Reflections on Citizen Participation and the Economic Opportunity Act," a paper delivered on May 7, 1970; to Leonard J. Duhl for "Some Origins of the Poverty Program," a paper of April 6, 1967. These accounts are necessary to supplement and correct the arresting version provided by D. P. Moynihan in *Maximum Feasible Misunderstanding* (New York, 1969).

85. Cannon, "Dangerous Abuse," VI–16.

86. Johnson, *Vantage Point*, 74–75.

87. Richard Blumenthal, "The Bureaucracy: Antipoverty and the Community Action Program," in *American Political Institutions and Public Policy*, ed. A. P. Sindler, (Boston, 1969), 145–146.

88. Cannon, "Dangerous Abuse," VI–35.

89. Moynihan, *Maximum Feasible Misunderstanding*, 82; Adam Yarmolinsky, "The Beginnings of OEO," in *On Fighting Poverty*, ed. J. L. Sundquist (New York, 1969), 36.

90. Kenneth B. Clark and Jeanette Hopkins, *A Relevant War against Poverty: A Study of Community Action Programs and Observable Social Change* (New York, 1969), 4.

91. "The Federal Government and Urban Poverty," recorded transcript of conference sponsored by the Kennedy Library and Brandeis University, vol. 5, 8.

92. Richard Boone, in recorded interview by Jean Stein, September 20, 1968, 6, Stein Papers; Boone, "Reflections," 7–8; Cannon, "Dangerous Abuse," VI–46.

93. J. C. Donovan, *The Politics of Poverty* (New York, 1967), 35. Emphasis added.

94. *Atlanta Constitution*, May 27, May 28, 1964; *Robert F. Kennedy: Apostle of Change*, ed. Douglas Ross (New York: Pocket Book reprint, 1968), 74.

95. John Doar and Dorothy Landsberg, "The Performance of the FBI in Investigating Violations of Federal Laws Protecting the Right to Vote—1960–1967" (1971) in Senate Select Committee to Study Governmental Operations with respect to Intelligence Activities (hereafter cited as Church committee), *Hearings*, vol. 6, *Federal Bureau of Investigation*, 94 Cong., 1 Sess. (1975), 929.

96. Haywood Burns, "The Federal Government and Civil Rights," in *Southern Justice*, ed. Leon Friedman (New York, 1965), 235; Pat Watters and Reese Cleghorn, *Climbing Jacob's Ladder* (New York, 1967), 139.

97. *Newsweek*, November 30, 1964.

98. Martin Luther King, Jr., "Hammer of Civil Rights," *Nation*, March 9, 1964.

99. Sally Belfrage, *Freedom Summer* (New York, 1965), 15.

100. James Wechsler, "The FBI's Failure in the South," *Progressive*, December 1963.

101. RFK, in Lewis interview, December 4, 1964, V, 21.

102. RFK to LBJ, June 5, 1964, Johnson Papers.

103. Church committee, *Final Report*, bk. III, *Supplementary Detailed Staff Reports on Intelligence Activities and the Rights of Americans*, 94 Cong., 2 Sess. (1976), 7–8.

104. Ibid., 65–66.

105. Hoover to McGeorge Bundy, July 25, 1961, in Church committee, *Final Report*, bk. II, *Intelligence Activities and the Rights of Americans*, 94 Cong., 2 Sess. (1976), 282.

106. Richard D. Cotter, "Notes toward a Definition of National Security," *Washington Monthly*, December 1975.

107. Sullivan, in interview by author, July 26, 1976; Ovid Demaris, *The Director* (New York, 1975), 326.

108. Gary Thomas Rowe, Jr., *My Undercover Years with the Ku Klux Klan* (New York, 1976), 53–54.

109. "Interview with J. Edgar Hoover," *U.S. News & World Report*, December 21, 1964.

110. Hoover to Katzenbach, September 2, 1965, Church committee, *Hearings*, vol. 6, 513–514; see also memorandum of December 19, 1967, 518–527, and *New York Times*, November 12, 1977. Deletions in the Church committee version of the September memorandum are supplied in Jack Nelson, "Will the Real KKK Please Stand Up?" *New York Post*, August 16, 1975, and in J. J. Berman and M. H. Halperin, eds., *The Abuses of the Intelligence Agencies* (Washington, 1975), 20. See also Church committee, *Final Report*, bk. III, 251–252; Sullivan, in inter-

view by author; Harry Overstreet and Bonaro Overstreet, *The FBI in Our Open Society* (New York, 1969), 303.

111. For a listing, see Doar and Landsberg, "Performance of the FBI," in Church committee, *Hearings,* vol. 6, 938–940.

112. Demaris, *Director,* 327; Sullivan to author, October 1, 1977.

113. For the case against informers, see Frank Donner, "Political Informers," in *Investigating the FBI,* ed. Pat Watters and Stephen Gillers (Garden City, N.Y., 1973), 338–365, and Vern Countryman on 367–368; also Robert McAfee Brown, in *Conspiracy,* ed. John C. Raines (New York, 1975), intro.

114. Bernard Fensterwald thus denigrated Sam Baron. For Fensterwald's exchange with Kennedy, see Senate Subcommittee on Administrative Practice and Procedures, *Hearings: On Invasions of Privacy (Governmental Agencies),* 89 Cong., 1 Sess., (March 3, 1965), 274.

115. *Dennis* v. *United States,* 183 F. 2nd 201, 224 (1950).

116. *Hoffa* v. *United States,* 385 U.S. 293 (1966).

117. Church committee, *Final Report,* bk. III, 243–244.

118. Ibid., 240.

119. Rowe, *Undercover Years,* 175.

120. Burke Marshall, "The Issues on Trial," in Raines, *Conspiracy,* 157–158.

121. Kearns, *Johnson,* 191.

122. RFK, in Lewis interview, December 22, 1964, 24, 26–27.

123. Kearns, *Johnson,* 183.

124. Victor Reuther, *The Brothers Reuther* (Boston, 1976), 430.

125. Walter Fauntroy, in recorded interview by Jean Stein, November 11, 1969, 13–14, Stein Papers.

28. The Vice Presidency (*pages* 675–695)

1. I am indebted to the Johnson Library for searching its records to the above effect.

2. Liz Carpenter, *Ruffles and Flourishes* (New York: Pocket Book reprint, 1971), 265–266.

3. Pierre Salinger, in recorded interview by L. J. Hackman, May 26, 1969, 16–17.

4. Doris Kearns, *Lyndon Johnson and the American Dream* (New York, 1976), 200.

5. Eric Goldman, *The Tragedy of Lyndon Johnson* (New York, 1969), 78–79.

6. Kenneth O'Donnell, in recorded interview by L. J. Hackman, April 3, 1969, 62–63, RFK Oral History Program.

7. Murray Kempton, "Pure Irish: Robert F. Kennedy," *New Republic,* February 15, 1964.

8. Ibid.

9. Walter Heller to LBJ, January 9, 1964, RFK Papers.

10. RFK, in recorded interview by John Bartlow Martin, May 14, 1964, I, 33, JFK Oral History Program.

11. Richard Goodwin, notes, March 1964, Goodwin Papers.

12. RFK, in Martin interview, I, 40.

13. McGeorge Bundy, in recorded interview by William W. Moss, January 12, 1972, 25, RFK Oral History Program.

14. Goldman, *Tragedy of Johnson,* 19.

15. RFK, in Martin interview, II, 4.

16. Ibid., I, 33.

17. Author's journal, March 19, 1964; author to RFK, March 20, 1964, RFK Papers.

18. Author's journal, March 25, 1964.

19. Tom Wicker, *JFK and LBJ* (Baltimore: Pelican reprint, 1970), 230.

20. Lyndon B. Johnson, *The Vantage Point* (New York, 1971), 92–94.

21. Kenneth P. O'Donnell and David F. Powers, *"Johnny, We Hardly Knew Ye"* (Boston, 1972), 391.
22. Sam Houston Johnson, *My Brother Lyndon* (New York, 1969), 159.
23. Joseph Dolan to RFK, December 3, 1963, RFK Papers. The Michigan committeewoman was Mildred Jeffrey.
24. Author's journal, December 5, 1963.
25. Kennedy sent the letter over to his brother Edward wih a scribble: "Will you talk to him?" Peter Crotty to RFK, February 13, 1964, RFK to EMK, February 21, 1964, RFK Papers.
26. William Dunfey, in recorded interview by L. J. Hackman, December 15, 1971, 68–72, RFK Oral History Program.
27. Edwin Guthman, *We Band of Brothers* (New York, 1971), 254.
28. John Seigenthaler, in recorded interview by L. J. Hackman, June 5, 1970, 36, 45–46, RFK Oral History Program.
29. Joseph Dolan, in recorded interview by L. J. Hackman, April 10, 1970, 57, RFK Oral History Program.
30. Dunfey, in Hackman interview, 66–67.
31. O'Donnell, in Hackman interview, May 6, 1969, 71; Seigenthaler, in Hackman interview, 36; RFK, in Martin interview, I, 31–32.
32. Guthman, *We Band of Brothers,* 254.
33. Ibid., 254–256.
34. Ibid., 256–257, 270.
35. Author's journal, January 22, 1964.
36. George H. Gallup, ed., *The Gallup Poll: Public Opinion, 1935–1971* (New York, 1972), vol. 3, 1874–1875.
37. See Arthur M. Schlesinger, Jr., "On the Presidential Succession," *Political Science Quarterly,* Fall 1974.
38. Quoted in Ovid Demaris, *The Director* (New York, 1975), 170.
39. Charles Spalding, in recorded interview by L. J. Hackman, March 22, 1969, 68, RFK Oral History Program.
40. RFK, in Martin interview, II, 8–17.
41. Burton Hersh, *The Education of Edward Kennedy* (New York, 1972), 200–202.
42. Walter Sheridan, in recorded interview by Roberta Greene, May 1, 1970, 12, RFK Oral History Program.
43. Hersh, *Education,* 202.
44. William V. Shannon, "Said Robert Kennedy, 'Maybe We're All Doomed Anyway,'" *New York Times Magazine,* June 16, 1968.
45. Susan Wilson, "A Guide to Travelling with the Robert F. Kennedys," ms. in the author's possession, 4–5.
46. RFK, press conference, Berlin, June 26, 1964, transcript in RFK Papers.
47. John Moors Cabot to assistant secretary of state for European affairs, June 24, 1964, RFK Papers.
48. Guthman, *We Band of Brothers,* 275.
49. John Moors Cabot, in recorded interview by W. W. Moss, January 27, 1971, 22, JFK Oral History Program; William V. Shannon, *The Heir Apparent* (New York, 1967), 12.
50. Cabot, in Moss interview, 22.
51. Joseph Kraft, in recorded interview by Roberta Greene, March 7, 1970, 18, RFK Oral History Program; Shannon, *Heir Apparent,* 12.
52. Cabot, in Moss interview, 22.
53. Ibid., 23; RFK notes on conversation with Jozef Winiewicz, June 29, 1964, RFK Papers.
54. RFK, notes on conversation with Stefan Cardinal Wyszynski, June 30, 1964, RFK Papers.
55. Translation of article by Daniel Passent in RFK Papers.

56. Cabot, in Moss interview, 21.
57. Cabot to Harriman, July 2, 1964, RFK Papers.
58. Lee Stull to Harriman, July 6, 1964, RFK Papers.
59. Guthman, *We Band of Brothers*, 278.
60. Kearns, *Johnson*, 199–200.
61. Johnson, *My Brother Lyndon*, 161.
62. O'Donnell, in Hackman interview, April 3, 1969, 32–33; O'Donnell and Powers, *"Johnny,"* 393–394.
63. Benjamin Bradlee, in recorded interview by Jean Stein, October 18, 1968, 1–2, Stein Papers; Margaret Laing, *The Next Kennedy* (New York, 1968), 7.
64. *Newsweek,* July 6, 1964; Benjamin C. Bradlee, *Conversations with Kennedy* (New York, 1975), 24.
65. Author's journal, July 21, 1964.
66. Hubert Humphrey, *The Education of a Public Man* (Garden City, N.Y., 1976), 297–298.
67. Author's journal, June 9, July 23, 1964.
68. Jack Tarver to LBJ, July 26, 1964, Johnson Papers.
69. Johnson, *My Brother Lyndon,* 165.
70. Author's journal, July 23, 1964.
71. O'Donnell and Powers, *"Johnny,"* 396–397.
72. Guthman, *We Band of Brothers,* 280.
73. O'Donnell, in Hackman interview, May 6, 1969, 18.
74. Johnson, *Vantage Point,* 100, 576–577.
75. RFK, memorandum dictated August 4–6, 1964, RFK Papers.
76. Jack Valenti, *A Very Human President* (New York, 1975), 148.
77. Guthman, *We Band of Brothers,* 282.
78. O'Donnell and Powers, *"Johnny,"* 397; see Lawrence O'Brien, *No Final Victories* (Garden City, N.Y., 1974), 175.
79. RFK, memorandum.
80. Bundy, in Moss interview, 27.
81. RFK to Bundy, August 26, 1964, RFK Papers.
82. RFK, memorandum.
83. Richard Harwood and Haynes Johnson, *Lyndon* (New York, 1973), 73–74; David Wise, *The Politics of Lying* (New York, 1973), 294; Johnson, *My Brother Lyndon,* 167; Theodore H. White, *The Making of the President, 1964* (New York, 1965), 263–265; Guthman, *We Band of Brothers,* 281; RFK, memorandum.
84. RFK, memorandum.
85. Author's journal, August 2, 1964.
86. Clark Clifford, in recorded interview by L. J. Hackman, February 4, 1975, 39–41, JFK Oral History Program.
87. For details see: Senate Select Committee to Study Governmental Operations with respect to Intelligence Activities (hereafter cited as Church committee), *Final Report,* bk. III, *Supplementary Detailed Staff Reports on Intelligence Activities and the Rights of Americans,* 94 Cong., 2 Sess. (1976), 346–347; Church committee, *Hearings,* vol. 6, *Federal Bureau of Investigation,* 94 Cong., 1 Sess. (1975), 495–496; David Wise, *The American Police State* (New York, 1976), 287–288; Demaris, *Director,* 286.
88. Testimony of Leo T. Clark, *Washington Post,* January 26, 1975.
89. Sanford J. Ungar, *FBI* (Boston, 1975), 289.
90. William Barry, in recorded interview by Roberta Greene, October 22, 1969, 75, RFK Oral History Program.
91. Church committee, *Hearings,* vol. 6, 495–496, 509–510.
92. Seigenthaler, in Hackman interview, July 1, 1970, 95.
93. Humphrey, *Education,* 301–302.
94. O'Donnell and Powers, *"Johnny,"* 400.

95. Seigenthaler, in Hackman interview, July 1, 1970, 103–110.
96. Ibid., 113.

29. To the Senate (*pages* 696–720)

1. RFK to Peter Lisagor, August 17, 1964, RFK Papers.
2. John F. Kraft to Stephen Smith, August 20, 1964, Smith Papers.
3. Author's journal, August 2, 1964.
4. Author to RFK, August 5, 1964, RFK Papers.
5. Jack English, in recorded interview by Roberta Greene, November 25, 1969, 13, RFK Oral History Program.
6. Liz Carpenter to Johnson, memorandum reporting a telephone message from Harriman, August 9, 1964, Johnson Papers.
7. Stevenson to Marietta Tree, August 10, 1964, in John Bartlow Martin, *Adlai Stevenson and the World* (Garden City, N.Y., 1977), 812.
8. Stevenson to Mary Lasker, August 14, 1964, in Martin, *Stevenson,* 813.
9. Jeffrey Potter, *Men, Money and Magic* (New York, 1976), 290.
10. Gerald Gardner, *Robert Kennedy in New York* (New York, 1965), 82.
11. Author to Stephen Smith, September 15, 1964, Smith Papers.
12. Francis Biddle to the editor, *New York Times,* August 24, 1964, copy in RFK Papers.
13. See advertisements in *New York Times,* November 1, 2, 1964.
14. *New York Times,* October 27, 1964.
15. Justin Feldman, in recorded interview by Roberta Greene, November 26, 1969, 97, RFK Oral History Program.
16. Thomas Johnston, in recorded interview by L. J. Hackman, October 27, 1969, 198–199, RFK Oral History Program.
17. Guthman, *We Band of Brothers* (New York, 1971), 295; Gardner, *Kennedy,* 74–75.
18. Gardner, *Kennedy,* 44, 63.
19. Guthman, *We Band of Brothers,* 294.
20. Feldman, in Greene interview, 101.
21. Paul Corbin, in recorded interview by Jean Stein, n.d. [1968], 4, Stein Papers.
22. Douglas to RFK, October 8, 1964, Smith Papers.
23. John Douglas, in recorded interview by L. J. Hackman, June 16, 1969, 24–26, RFK Oral History Program.
24. Associated Press dispatch from Rochester, October 6, 1964.
25. Kraft to Smith, October 6, 8, 1964, RFK Papers.
26. *New York World-Telegram,* October 8, 1964.
27. Jean Stein and George Plimpton, eds., *American Journey* (New York, 1970), 180; Guthman, *We Band of Brothers,* 307–308.
28. Charles Evers, "For Robert Kennedy," *New York Post,* October 23, 1964.
29. *New York Times,* October 22, 1964.
30. Douglas Robinson, "Kennedy in Trouble with Italian-Americans," *New York Times,* October 13, 1964.
31. William Haddad to Stephen Smith, September 26, 1964, Smith Papers.
32. Neil Sheehan, "Keating Reported Gaining among Democratic and Liberal Jews," *New York Times,* October 3, 1964.
33. David Halberstam, "Keating Sees Cartel 'Deal,'" *New York Times,* September 21, 1964; Homer Bigart, "Kennedy Assails Keating Tactics," *New York Times,* September 23, 1964.
34. *Congressional Record,* March 4, 1963, 3333–3334. See also Guthman, *We Band of Brothers,* 101–102, 300–303; Victor Navasky, *Kennedy Justice* (New York, 1971), 349–352.

35. William Orrick, in recorded interview by L. J. Hackman, April 13, 1970, 128, RFK Oral History Program.

36. *New York Times,* September 23, 1964.

37. [James Stevenson], "Campaigning," in "The Talk of the Town," *New Yorker,* October 24, 1964.

38. Guthman, *We Band of Brothers,* 301.

39. *Newsweek,* November 16, 1964.

40. Mailer wrote his endorsement "A Vote for Bobby K." for the *Village Voice.* It is reprinted in Norman Mailer, *The Idol and the Octopus* (New York: Dell reprint, 1968), 242–245. The references to John Kennedy are from the same book, 112, 173.

41. Rita Dallas, *The Kennedy Case* (New York: Popular Library reprint, 1973), 288–289.

42. Gardner, *Kennedy,* 5, 9.

43. For accounts of RFK and television in the 1964 campaign, see Terry Smith, "Bobby's Image," *Esquire,* April 1965; George Lois, *George, Be Careful* (New York, 1972), 107–112; Fred Papert, in recorded interview by Roberta Greene, March 21, 1973, esp. 10–21, RFK Oral History Program; William vanden Heuvel and Milton Gwirtzman, *On His Own: RFK, 1964–1968* (Garden City, N.Y., 1970), 44; transcript of Columbia University appearance, RFK Papers.

44. *New York Times,* October 16, 1964.

45. Richard Wade, in recorded interview by Roberta Greene, December 13, 1973, 41–42, RFK Oral History Program.

46. Author's journal, October 30, 1966.

47. *New York Daily News,* October 19, 1964.

48. Kraft to Smith, October 28, 29, 30, 1964, Smith Papers.

49. *New York Times,* October 19, 1964.

50. Gardner, *Kennedy,* 93.

51. *New York Times,* October 28, 30, 1964; vanden Heuvel and Gwirtzman, *On His Own,* 49–52. For the FCPC executive director's version, see Bruce Felknor, *Dirty Politics* (New York, 1966), 175–196.

52. Harry Golden, "The Bobby Twins Revisited," *Esquire,* June 1965.

53. Murray Kempton, "Another Empty Chair," *New York World-Telegram,* October 28, 1964; Frank Borsky, "I Ran the Keating Obstacle Course," *New York Daily News,* October 28, 1964; Homer Bigart, "Keating vs. Kennedy: A Near Debate," *New York Times,* October 28, 1964; vanden Heuvel and Gwirtzman, *On His Own,* 52–54; Guthman, *We Band of Brothers,* 308–311.

54. Nancy Dickerson, *Among Those Present* (New York: Ballantine reprint, 1977), 149.

55. Stein and Plimpton, *American Journey,* 182.

56. Wes Barthelmes, in recorded interview by Roberta Greene, May 20, 1969, 6, RFK Oral History Program.

57. Ibid., 3.

58. Frank Mankiewicz, in recorded interview by L. J. Hackman, August 12, 1969, 42, RFK Oral History Program.

59. Mankiewicz, in Hackman interview, July 10, 1969, 49; Joseph Dolan, in recorded interview by L. J. Hackman, April 11, 1970, 115, RFK Oral History Program; Barthelmes, in Greene interview, May 20, 1969, 11; Peter Edelman, in recorded interview by L. J. Hackman, July 15, 1969, 117, RFK Oral History Program.

60. Dolan, in Hackman interview, April 10, 1970, 11, 17.

61. Adam Walinsky, in recorded interview by Thomas Johnston, November 29, 1969, 34, RFK Oral History Program.

62. Walinsky, in Johnston interview, November 30, 1969, II, 2.

63. Barthelmes, in Greene interview, May 20, 1969, 7; June 5, 1969, 170.

64. Walinsky, in Johnston interview, November 29, 1969, 32; November 30, 1969 (2), 16, 25.
65. Martin Arnold, *New York Times,* June 7, 1968.
66. Walinsky, in Johnston interview, November 30, 1969, 54.
67. Remarks to Western New York Publishers Association, Painted Post, N.Y., October 9, 1965, RFK Papers.
68. Author's journal, January 19, 1965.
69. Nick Thimmesch and William Johnson, *Robert Kennedy at 40* (New York, 1965), 244; Walinsky, in Johnston interview, November 30, 1969, 53–57.
70. Barthelmes, in Greene interview, 14.
71. Edelman, in Hackman interview, January 3, 1970, 28.
72. Jacob Javits, in recorded interview by William vanden Heuvel, June 19, 1970, 11, RFK Oral History Program.
73. Javits, in recorded interview by Roberta Greene, June 7, 1973, 7, RFK Oral History Program.
74. *New York Times,* January 4, 1965; William V. Shannon, *The Heir Apparent* (New York, 1967), 75.
75. Vanden Heuvel and Gwirtzman, *On His Own,* 64.
76. Stein and Plimpton, *American Journey,* 182–183.
77. Vanden Heuvel and Gwirtzman, *On His Own,* 64.
78. Dolan, in Hackman interview, July 19, 1970, 414.
79. N.d., RFK Papers.
80. Fred Harris, *Potomac Fever* (New York, 1977), 119, 124, 126.
81. George McGovern, in recorded interview by L. J. Hackman, July 16, 1970, 19–20, 34.
82. Confidential source.
83. Fred Harris, in recorded interview by Roberta Greene, July 29, 1970, 5, RFK Oral History Program.
84. Jack Newfield, *Robert Kennedy* (New York, 1969), 58.
85. RFK to Byrd, August 8, 1965, RFK Papers.
86. RFK to Murphy, August 22, 1966, RFK Papers.
87. Shannon, *Heir Apparent,* 78–79.
88. Thus Meg Greenfield in the pro-Johnson *Reporter,* December 15, 1966, and elsewhere.
89. Harris, in Greene interview, 2.
90. Joseph Tydings, in recorded interview by Jean Stein, December 1969, 4–5, Stein Papers.
91. David Burke, in recorded interview by Jean Stein, October 17, 1968, 3–4, Stein Papers.
92. Javits, in vanden Heuvel interview, 14–15.
93. Richard Reeves, "Kennedy: 2 Years after His Election," *New York Times,* November 14, 1966.
94. RFK to LBJ, September 2, 1964, RFK Papers.
95. Burton Hersh, *The Education of Edward Kennedy* (New York, 1972), 233.
96. Milton Gwirtzman, in recorded interview by Roberta Greene, February 10, 1972, 28–29, RFK Oral History Program.
97. William C. Sullivan, in interview by author, July 26, 1976.
98. Harold W. Chase, *Federal Judges: The Appointing Process* (Minneapolis, 1972), 174.
99. Joseph Tydings, in recorded interview by Roberta Greene, September 29, 1971, 38–39, RFK Oral History Program.
100. Gwirtzman, in Greene interview, 43–44.
101. All letters in Johnson Papers.
102. Dolan, in Hackman interview, 33–34.
103. Clark to Watson, May 31, 1966, Johnson Papers. Actually Kennedy had consid-

ered Mansfield for judicial appointment when he was Attorney General and endorsed him now; Dolan, in Hackman interview, April 10, 1970, 37.

104. Javits, in vanden Heuvel interview, 12, 14.
105. Reeves, "Kennedy."
106. Roger Wilkins, in recorded interview by Jean Stein, n.d. [1968], 10–11, Stein Papers.
107. Harris, *Potomac Fever*, 105.
108. Robert S. Allen and Paul Scott in the *Birmingham News*, June 10, 1966.
109. Walter Mondale, in recorded interview by Roberta Greene, May 17, 1973, 19, RFK Oral History Program.
110. Harris, in Greene interview, 3.
111. Kenneth O'Donnell, in recorded interview by L. J. Hackman, April 3, 1969, 3, RFK Oral History Program.
112. McGovern, in Hackman interview, 32.
113. Barthelmes, in Greene interview, 27.
114. Mankiewicz, in Hackman interview, August 12, 1969, 5.
115. Donald Riegle with Trevor Armbrister, *O Congress* (New York: Popular Library reprint, 1972), 144.
116. Author's journal, January 19, 1965.
117. RFK to Lewis, n.d. [summer 1965], RFK Papers.
118. Margaret Laing, *The Next Kennedy* (New York, 1968), 31.

30. The Foreign Policy Breach: Latin America (*pages* 721–733)

1. William D. Rogers, *The Twilight Struggle: The Alliance for Progress and the Politics of Development in Latin America* (New York, 1967), 226.
2. Jerome Levinson and Juan De Onis, *The Alliance That Lost Its Way* (Chicago, 1970), 72–73.
3. Teodoro Moscoso, lecture 3 at Mills College, February 1965 (mimeographed), 12.
4. Quoted by Richard Goodwin, "Our Stake in a Big Awakening," *Life*, April 14, 1967.
5. Juscelino Kubitschek, "L'Alliance pour le progrès," *Historia*, hors série 33 (1973), 151.
6. Quoted by Evelyn Lincoln, *Kennedy and Johnson* (New York, 1968), 188.
7. Eric Goldman, *The Tragedy of Lyndon Johnson* (New York, 1969), 382.
8. Author's journal, April 30–May 2, 1965.
9. *Congressional Record*, May 6, 1965, 9761–9762.
10. Author's journal, July 16, 1965.
11. *Congressional Record*, June 23, 1965, 14566–14568.
12. Richard Goodwin, in interview by author, January 22, 1974. Since he had already cut another significant part of the draft because it had been leaked to Reston of the *Times*, the UN ended up with thin fare.
13. Valenti to LBJ, September 14, 1965, Johnson Papers.
14. Adam Walinsky, in recorded interview by L. J. Hackman, May 22, 1972, 21–25, RFK Oral History Program; Frank Mankiewicz, in recorded interview by Jean Stein, September 21, 1968, 4–8, Stein Papers; Mankiewicz, in recorded interview by L. J. Hackman, June 26, 1969, 5–8; Frank Mankiewicz and Tom Braden, "U.S. on Wrong Side in Dispute with Peru," column released March 13, 1969.
15. John Nolan, in recorded interview by Jean Stein, August 8, 1968, 12–14, Stein Papers.
16. William vanden Heuvel, "Notes on RFK South American Trip (2)," 8–12, vanden Heuvel Papers; *New York Times*, November 14, 1965.
17. Vanden Heuvel, "Notes," 12–17; William vanden Heuvel and Milton Gwirtzman, *On His Own* (Garden City, N.Y., 1970), 166–167.

18. Walinsky, in Hackman interview, 34.
19. Vanden Heuvel and Gwirtzman, *On His Own,* 166; Peter Collier and David Horowitz, *The Rockefellers: An American Dynasty* (New York, 1976), 417.
20. Andrew J. Glass, "The Compulsive Candidate," *Saturday Evening Post,* April 23, 1966.
21. Transcript, "Senator Robert F. Kennedy . . . Conversation with Students in Hotel in Concepción," vanden Heuvel Papers; Glass, "Compulsive Candidate."
22. Martin Arnold, in recorded interview by Jean Stein, December 5, 1969, 9, Stein Papers. See also his account in *New York Times,* November 17, 1965.
23. John Seigenthaler, in recorded interview by Jean Stein, May 15, 1970, 27.
24. Vanden Heuvel and Gwirtzman, *On His Own,* 167–168; Glass, "Compulsive Candidate."
25. Arnold, in Stein interview, 16.
26. Margaret Laing, *The Next Kennedy* (New York, 1968), 291–292.
27. *New York Times,* November 19, 1965.
28. Robert Hopkins to author, December 1, 1965.
29. Arnold, in Stein interview, 21; William vanden Heuvel, in recorded interview by Jean Stein, February 28, 1970, 9, Stein Papers; Mildred Sage, in interview by author, June 9, 1977.
30. Angie Novello, in recorded interview by Jean Stein, September 27, 1968, 8, Stein Papers.
31. *New York Times,* November 23, 1965.
32. Glass, "Compulsive Candidate."
33. Ibid.; vanden Heuvel and Gwirtzman, *On His Own,* 175.
34. Sage, in interview by author.
35. Patricia Kennedy Lawford, ed., *That Shining Hour* (n.p., 1969), 67.
36. Sage, in interview by author.
37. Glass, "Compulsive Candidate."
38. "Impressions of RFK South American Tour," Johnson Papers. The anonymous author was in Lima when Kennedy arrived.
39. Glass, "Compulsive Candidate."
40. Jean Stein and George Plimpton, eds., *American Journey* (New York, 1970), 153.
41. Lincoln Gordon, in interview by author, October 14, 1974.
42. Paulo de Castro, "Robert Kennedy," *Correio da Manha* (Rio de Janeiro), November 23, 1965.
43. Walinsky, in Hackman interview, 31, 47–48.
44. *Meet the Press,* IX, 43 (December 5, 1965).
45. Theodore C. Sorensen, *The Kennedy Legacy* (New York, 1969), 174.
46. Moyers to RFK, May 30, 1966, RFK Papers.
47. *Congressional Record,* May 9, 1966, 9609–9620, May 10, 1966, 9705–9716.

31. Vietnam Legacy (*pages* 734–756)

1. RFK, in recorded interview by John Bartlow Martin, April 13, 1964, I, 22, JFK Oral History Program.
2. Jann Wenner, in interview with Daniel Ellsberg, *Rolling Stone,* December 6, 1973.
3. JFK before the American Friends of Vietnam, Washington, June 1, 1956, *Vital Speeches,* August 1, 1956.
4. U.S. Department of Defense, *The Pentagon Papers,* Senator Gravel Edition (Boston, 1971), vol. 1, 626.
5. Clark Clifford, "Memorandum on Conference between President Eisenhower and President-elect Kennedy and Their Chief Advisers on January 19, 1961," 3. The emphasis is in the original.

6. Macmillan to Eisenhower, April 9, 1961, copy transmitted by the British ambassador to JFK, April 9, 1961, JFK Papers.
7. RFK, memorandum dictated June 1, 1961, 3, RFK Papers.
8. Author's journal, May 14, 1962.
9. RFK, memorandum, 3.
10. *New York Times,* April 9, 1961.
11. *Pentagon Papers,* vol. 2, 8, 49.
12. Roswell Gilpatric, in recorded interview by D. J. O'Brien, May 5, 1970, 19, JFK Oral History Program.
13. RFK, memorandum dictated August 1, 1961, 1, RFK Papers.
14. Alexis Johnson, in recorded interview by William Brubeck, n.d. [1964], 33–34, JFK Oral History Program.
15. Maxwell Taylor, in recorded interview by L. J. Hackman, November 13, 1969, 47.
16. Arthur Krock, *In the Nation: 1932–1966* (New York, 1966), 324–325, 447.
17. Maxwell Taylor, *Swords and Plowshares* (Washington, 1972), 219, 225–226.
18. Taylor, in Hackman interview, 43.
19. *Pentagon Papers,* vol. 2, 92–93, 98, 108.
20. Taylor, in Hackman interview, 47.
21. Author's journal, November 13, 1961.
22. J. K. Galbraith, in interview by author, June 23, 1977.
23. William Bundy was the deputy assistant secretary of defense for international security affairs. I am indebted to Mr. Bundy for letting me read his valuable unpublished manuscript on United States policy in East Asia during the Kennedy-Johnson years. The quotation is taken from ch. 4.
24. George Ball, in interview by author, June 15, 1977.
25. *New York Times,* December 12, 1961.
26. Ibid., December 20, 1961.
27. Ibid., October 27, 1961.
28. Directorate for Information Operations, Department of Defense, March 22, 1972. See chart in R. H. Fifield, *Americans in Southeast Asia: The Roots of Commitment* (New York, 1973), 276.
29. Roger Hilsman, *To Move a Nation* (Garden City, N.Y., 1967), 426.
30. Roger Hilsman and Michael Forrestal, "A Report on South Vietnam," n.d. [January 1963], RFK Papers.
31. *Newsweek,* May 25, 1970.
32. *Pentagon Papers,* vol. 2, 123.
33. Robert Shaplen, "The Cult of Diem," *New York Times Magazine,* May 14, 1972.
34. Edward G. Lansdale, in interview by author, December 30, 1976.
35. Hilsman, *To Move a Nation,* 419, 439.
36. Michael Forrestal to Robert W. Komer, June 2, 1971, copy in Schlesinger Papers. This instinct was clearly expressed in General Lemnitzer's memorandum on "Counterinsurgency Operations in South Vietnam" to General Taylor, October 12, 1961 (*Pentagon Papers,* vol. 2, 650–651).
37. Roger Hilsman, in recorded interview by D. J. O'Brien, August 14, 1970, 20, RFK Oral History Program.
38. Charles Maechling, Jr., review of *Anatomy of Error* by Henry Brandon, *Foreign Service Journal,* March 1970.
39. Roswell Gilpatric, in interview by D. J. O'Brien, August 12, 1970, 1, RFK Oral History Program.
40. John F. Kennedy, *Public Papers . . . 1962* (Washington, 1963), 137, 228.
41. *Pentagon Papers,* vol. 2, 670–671.
42. Ball to McGeorge Bundy, May 1, 1962, Bundy to JFK, May 1, 1962, JFK Papers.
43. *Pentagon Papers,* vol. 2, 175–181.
44. Gilpatric, in O'Brien interview, August 12, 1970, 1; Ellsberg, in *Rolling Stone* interview.

45. *Viet Nam and Southeast Asia: Report of Senator Mike Mansfield, Senator J. Caleb Boggs, Senator Claiborne Pell, Senator Benjamin Smith to the Committee on Foreign Relations,* 88 Cong., 1 Sess. (February 24, 1963), 8.

46. Kenneth O'Donnell and David F. Powers, *"Johnny, We Hardly Knew Ye"* (Boston, 1972).

47. Henry Brandon, *Anatomy of Error* (London, 1970), 30.

48. John F. Kennedy, *Public Papers . . . 1963* (Washington, 1964), 244, 569, 652.

49. Louis Harris, *The Anguish of Change* (New York, 1973), 54.

50. Chalmers M. Roberts, *First Rough Draft* (New York, 1973), 195–196. Roberts was the very well informed diplomatic correspondent of the *Washington Post.*

51. O'Donnell and Powers, *"Johnny,"* 16.

52. *Washington Post,* August 3, 1970; Jack Anderson, "The Roots of Our Vietnam Involvement," *Washington Post,* May 4, 1975.

53. JFK, *Public Papers . . . 1963,* 652.

54. RFK, in Martin interview, April 30, 1964, II, 34.

55. *New York Times,* February 19, 1962.

56. Forrestal to RFK, November 7, 1962, RFK Papers.

57. RFK, in Martin interview, March 1, 1964, II, 13, 16–17.

58. RFK, in recorded interview by author, February 27, 1965, 8, JFK Oral History Program.

59. National Security Council meeting, August 28, 1963, RFK Papers.

60. Gilpatric, in O'Brien interview, May 5, 1970, 31.

61. RFK, in Martin interview, April 30, 1964, II, 34.

62. Charles Bartlett, in recorded interview by Jean Stein, January 9, 1970, 20, Stein Papers.

63. Michael Forrestal, in recorded interview by Jean Stein, n.d. [1968], 6, Stein Papers.

64. Hilsman, *To Move a Nation,* 501.

65. *Pentagon Papers,* vol. 2, 738.

66. Lodge to Rusk, September 11, 1963, RFK Papers.

67. RFK, in interview by author, 25–26; RFK, in Martin interviews, April 13, 1964, I, 62, April 30, 1964, II, 38.

68. See, e.g., the cable of September 17, 1963, *Pentagon Papers,* vol. 2, 743–745.

69. RFK, in Martin interview, April 30, 1964, II, 39.

70. Ibid., III, 3.

71. Brandon, *Anatomy of Error,* 30.

72. Bundy manuscript, ch. 9.

73. *Pentagon Papers,* vol. 2, 756. Emphasis added.

74. Taylor, *Swords and Plowshares,* 296–297.

75. Michael Forrestal, in interview by author, July 13, 1977. See also Averell Harriman, in recorded interview by author, June 6, 1965, 83–85, JFK Oral History Program.

76. O'Donnell and Powers, *"Johnny,"* 17.

77. JFK, *Public Papers . . . 1963,* 846.

78. *Pentagon Papers,* vol. 2, 170. See also the valuable analysis by Peter Dale Scott, "Vietnamization and the Drama of the Pentagon Papers" *Pentagon Papers* (Boston, 1972), vol. 5, esp. 224.

79. O'Donnell and Powers, *"Johnny,"* 18.

80. JFK, *Public Papers . . . 1963,* 421.

81. Hilsman, in O'Brien interview, 21; letter to *New York Times,* August 8, 1970.

82. Ellsberg, *Rolling Stone* interview; see also William vanden Heuvel and Milton Gwirtzman, *On His Own* (Garden City, N.Y., 1970), 243.

83. Shaplen, "Cult of Diem."

84. Bui Kien Thanh, "Mandarins of Vietnam," *International History Magazine,* January 1974.

85. Michael Forrestal, in interview by author.
86. Mieczyslaw Maneli, *War of the Vanquished* (New York, 1971), 146.
87. Maneli, *War,* 121–122; Maneli, "Vietnam '63 and Now," *New York Times,* January 27, 1975; Maneli, in interview by author, June 24, 1977.
88. Maneli, "Vietnam '63."
89. Maneli, *War,* 127, 134–135.
90. Ibid., 141–142.
91. Ibid., 141.
92. Maneli, in interview by author.
93. Bundy manuscript, ch. 9.
94. Arthur M. Schlesinger, Jr., *A Thousand Days* (Boston, 1965), 874.
95. JFK, *Public Papers . . . 1963,* 652.
96. The visitor was George T. Altman. See Altman's letter in the *Nation,* June 21, 1975.
97. *New York Times,* November 3, 1963.
98. Schlesinger, *Thousand Days,* 871.
99. National Security Council meeting, 4:20 P.M., October 29, 1963, RFK Papers.
100. *Pentagon Papers,* vol. 2, 789, 792.
101. Henry Cabot Lodge, *The Storm Has Many Eyes* (New York, 1973), 210.
102. Taylor, *Swords and Plowshares,* 301.
103. Schlesinger, *Thousand Days,* 997–998.
104. Lodge to JFK, November 6, 1963, RFK Papers.
105. Brandon, *Anatomy of Error,* 30.
106. Forrestal on an NBC show, in Roberts, *First Rough Draft,* 221.
107. *Boston Globe,* June 24, 1973.
108. Pierre Salinger, *Je suis un Américain* (Paris, 1975), 239.
109. Fifield, *Americans in Southeast Asia,* 276.
110. James M. Gavin, "We Can Get Out of Vietnam," *Saturday Evening Post,* February 24, 1968.
111. Mieczyslaw Maneli, "Encounters with John F. Kennedy and Discussions on 'Democratic Socialism,' Polish Policy, and Vietnam" (unpublished paper), 24.

32. The Breach Widens: Vietnam (*pages* 757–776)

1. LBJ to JFK, May 23, 1961, JFK Papers.
2. U.S. Department of Defense, *The Pentagon Papers,* Senator Gravel Edition (Boston, 1971), vol. 2, 743.
3. Hubert Humphrey, *The Education of a Public Man* (Garden City, N.Y., 1976), 265.
4. Tom Wicker, *JFK and LBJ* (Baltimore: Penguin reprint, 1970), 205.
5. Bill Moyers, "Flashbacks," *Newsweek,* February 10, 1975.
6. Lyndon B. Johnson, *The Vantage Point* (New York, 1971), 45. Emphasis added.
7. John F. Kennedy, *Public Papers . . . 1963* (Washington, 1964), 569.
8. *Pentagon Papers,* vol. 3, 18.
9. *Pentagon Papers,* vol. 2, 171, 191.
10. Rusk to Lodge, December 6, 1963, Johnson Papers.
11. *New York Times,* January 2, 1964.
12. *Pentagon Papers,* vol. 2, 197–198.
13. Mieczyslaw Maneli, in interview by author, June 22, 1977.
14. Franz Schurman, P. D. Scott and Reginald Zelnick, *The Politics of Escalation in Vietnam* (Boston, 1966), 26.
15. McGeorge Bundy, ms. on U.S. policy in East Asia during the Kennedy-Johnson years, ch. 12.

16. RFK, in recorded interview by John Bartlow Martin, April 30, 1964, II, 30–31, RFK Oral History Program.

17. Sherman Kent for the Board of National Estimates, "Would the Loss of South Vietnam and Laos Precipitate a 'Domino Effect' in the Far East?" June 9, 1964; Mansfield to Johnson, June 9, 1964; RFK Papers.

18. RFK to LBJ, n.d. [June 11, 1964], Johnson Papers.

19. Jack Valenti, *A Very Human President* (New York, 1975), 141.

20. Transcript, Columbia University appearance, RFK Papers.

21. F. M. Kail, *What Washington Said: Administration Rhetoric and the Vietnam War* (New York, 1973), 104–105, 182.

22. Chester Cooper, "Fateful Day in Vietnam," *Washington Post,* February 11, 1975; see also Cooper, *The Lost Crusade* (New York, 1970), 256–260.

23. Charles Maechling, Jr., review of *Anatomy of Error* by Henry Brandon, *Foreign Service Journal,* March 1970.

24. Johnson, *Vantage Point,* 136.

25. Author's journal, May 6, 1965.

26. *Congressional Record,* May 6, 1965, 9760–9761.

27. Adam Walinsky, in recorded interview by Jean Stein, February 7, 1970, 9, Stein Papers.

28. RFK, advance text of commencement address at International Police Academy, July 9, 1965.

29. Marvin Watson to LBJ, July 8, 1965, Johnson Papers.

30. Fred Harris, in recorded interview by Roberta Greene, July 29, 1970, 3, RFK Oral History Program.

31. Bill Moyers, in recorded interview by Jean Stein, May 23, 1970, 2, Stein Papers.

32. Cherif Guellal, in recorded interview by Jean Stein, October 18, 1968, 1–7; Guellal, in interview by author, January 1, 1978.

33. Joseph Kraft, in recorded interview by Jean Stein, May 3, 1970, 6, Stein Papers; Kraft, in recorded interview by Roberta Greene, March 7, 1970, 37, RFK Oral History Program.

34. Guellal, in Stein interview, 12.

35. *Time,* October 22, 1965.

36. *New York Times,* October 29, 1965.

37. Transcript of RFK press conference, Los Angeles, November 5, 1965, RFK Papers.

38. *New York Daily News,* November 10, 1965.

39. *Chicago Tribune,* November 12, 1965.

40. Victor Lasky, *R.F.K.: The Myth and the Man* (New York: Pocket Books reprint, 1971), 302.

41. Adam Walinsky, in recorded interview by Thomas Johnston, November 30, 1969, 4, RFK Oral History Program.

42. Jack Newfield, *Robert Kennedy* (New York, 1969), 71; A. C. Brackman, *The Communist Collapse in Indonesia* (New York, 1969), 122.

43. *Congressional Record,* January 29, 1966. The editorial was from the *Washington Daily News,* January 28, 1966.

44. Author's journal, March 13, 1966.

45. David Kraslow and S. H. Loory, *The Secret Search for Peace in Vietnam* (New York, 1968), 132–133.

46. Stephen Schlesinger, "RFK–Hickory Hill," December 19, 1965.

47. See the still furious article by General Wallace M. Greene, "The Bombing 'Pause': Formula for Failure," *Air Force Magazine,* April 1976.

48. Author's journal, January 6, 1966.

49. RFK to LBJ, n.d. [January 1966], Johnson Papers.

50. LBJ to RFK, January 27, 1966, Johnson Papers.

51. McGovern to RFK, January 26, 1966, RFK Papers.

52. *Congressional Record,* January 31, 1966, 1602–1603.
53. Robert F. Kennedy, statement on Vietnam, February 19, 1966, RFK Papers.
54. *New York Times,* February 22, 1966.
55. McGeorge Bundy to David Ginsburg, March 13, 1967, Johnson Papers.
56. Draft in RFK Papers.
57. Bundy to RFK, February 21, RFK to Bundy, February 24, 1966, RFK Papers.
58. Unsigned memorandum to LBJ reporting conversation with Governor Connally, February 21, 1966, Johnson Papers.
59. *Chicago Tribune,* February 21, 1966.
60. Murray Kempton, "The Message Delivered," *New York World-Telegram,* February 23, 1966.
61. Moyers to LBJ, February 22, 1966, Johnson Papers; Patrick Anderson, *The President's Men* (New York, 1968), 346–347; William vanden Heuvel and Milton Gwirtzman, *On His Own* (Garden City, N.Y., 1970), 220–223.
62. David E. Lilienthal, *Journals,* vol. 6, *Creativity and Conflict, 1964–1967* (New York, 1967), 206.
63. Author's journal, February 27, 1966.
64. RFK, on *Face the Nation,* February 27, 1966.
65. RFK to Humphrey, January 27, 1966, RFK Papers.
66. RFK to Humphrey (handwritten), February 24, 1966, RFK Papers.
67. RFK, in Martin interview, May 14, 1964, II, 24.
68. Humphrey, on *Issues and Answers,* February 27, 1966.
69. Author's journal, February 27, 1966.
70. Vanden Heuvel and Gwirtzman, *On His Own,* 222.
71. *Congressional Record,* April 27, 1966, 9041.
72. See "RFK-Humor" file in Mankiewicz Papers.
73. Author's journal, July 20, 1966.
74. Ibid., July 24, 1966.
75. Ibid., August 7, 1966.
76. Spock to RFK, September 21, 1966, with RFK handwritten notes, RFK Papers.
77. *I. F. Stone's Weekly,* October 24, 1966.
78. Doris Kearns, *Lyndon Johnson and the American Dream* (New York, 1976), 251–252.
79. George Reedy, *The Twilight of the Presidency* (New York, 1970), 11.
80. Chester Bowles, *Promises to Keep* (New York, 1971), 535.
81. Kearns, *Johnson,* 316–317. I have taken the liberty of restoring a sentence that appeared in the manuscript but not in the book.
82. Richard Goodwin, in interview by author, June 11, 1977.
83. Author's journal, December 14, 1966.
84. Frank Mankiewicz, in recorded interview by L. J. Hackman, August 12, 1969, 3–4, RFK Oral History Program.
85. Kearns, *Johnson,* 253, 259.

33. The Breach Widens: South Africa, New York (*pages* 777–792)

1. RFK, handwritten first draft of South Africa article, 5, RFK Papers.
2. Wayne Fredericks, in interview by author, January 10, 1977.
3. *Manchester Union-Leader,* November 11, 1965.
4. Fredericks, in interview by author.
5. *New York Times,* May 28, 1966.
6. RFK draft, 6.
7. South Africa Department of Information, May 25, 1966. For this and other quotations I am indebted to a manuscript by Lawrence Ralston, "The Senator and the Republic: Robert Kennedy and the Many Ways of Looking at South

Africa," vanden Heuvel Papers, and for clippings in the notebook kept by Thomas Johnston, Johnston Papers.

8. Thomas Johnston, in recorded interview by Jean Stein, October 19, 1969, 2, Stein Papers.

9. Thomas Johnston, in interview by author, June 21, 1977.

10. Ralston ms.

11. Robert F. Kennedy, "Suppose God Is Black," *Look,* August 23, 1966.

12. *Cape Times,* June 7, 1966.

13. Adam Walinsky, in recorded interview by L. J. Hackman, May 22, 1972, 88–89, RFK Oral History Program.

14. The full texts of Kennedy's South African speeches are to be found in a pamphlet published after his trip by the *Rand Daily Mail* entitled "Robert Kennedy in South Africa." The Day of Affirmation speech is on 7–12.

15. *Cape Times,* June 7, 1966.

16. Frank Taylor, "In South Africa, a Kennedy Turns Jeers to Cheers," *National Observer* (New York), June 13, 1966.

17. Ralston ms.

18. *Cape Times,* June 8, 1966.

19. RFK, "Suppose God Is Black."

20. Ralston ms.

21. Johnston, in interview by author.

22. Walinsky, in Hackman interview, 98–99.

23. Johnston, in Stein interview, 7.

24. RFK, handwritten notes, RFK Papers; RFK, "Suppose God Is Black."

25. William vanden Heuvel and Milton Gwirtzman, *On His Own* (Garden City, N.Y., 1970), 160.

26. "Robert Kennedy in South Africa," 29–31.

27. Ralston ms.

28. Quoted by Frank Taylor, *National Observer,* June 13, 1966.

29. Johnston, in interview by author.

30. Anthony Delius, "Daylight from Outside World—Why Kennedy Visit Made Such a Stir," *Cape Times,* June 10, 1966.

31. *Rand Daily Mail,* June 9, 1966.

32. American Embassy Country Team to State Department, July 26, 1966, RFK Papers.

33. Alan Paton, "Waiting for Robert: The Kennedy Visit," *Contact,* July 1966.

34. [James Stevenson], "Kennedy in Africa," in "The Talk of the Town," *New Yorker,* July 9, 1966.

35. *Cape Argus,* June 10, 1966.

36. *New York Times,* June 13, 1966.

37. *Cape Argus,* June 9, 1966.

38. RFK notes, RFK Papers.

39. Walinsky, in Hackman interview, 110.

40. RFK notes; RFK, "Suppose God Is Black."

41. Bowles to RFK, July 26, 1966, RFK to Galbraith, August 1, 1966, RFK Papers.

42. Walinsky, in Hackman interview, 117–118.

43. Joseph Kraft, "New York Safari," *Washington Post,* June 8, 1966.

44. [Stevenson], "Kennedy in Africa."

45. RFK, in recorded interview by John Stewart, August 15, 1967, 59–60, JFK Oral History Program.

46. John Burns, in recorded interview by Roberta Greene, November 25, 1969–February 25, 1970, 19, 66, RFK Oral History Program.

47. Fred Dutton to RFK, April 6, 1966, RFK Papers.

48. Richard Goodwin, a 1967 jotting; in interview by author, June 11, 1977.

49. Jack Newfield, *Robert Kennedy* (New York, 1969), 142.

50. To Albert H. Blumenthal, Ronnie Eldridge, Jack Newfield, Arthur M. Schlesinger, Jr., and others.

51. Marvin Watson to LBJ, June 6, 1966, Johnson Papers.

52. Vanden Heuvel and Gwirtzman, *On His Own*, 134.

53. William V. Shannon, *The Heir Apparent* (New York, 1967), 168–171; Newfield, *Kennedy*, 151–152; vanden Heuvel and Gwirtzman, *On His Own*, 138–139.

54. Newfield, *Kennedy*, 154.

55. Vanden Heuvel and Gwirtzman, *On His Own*, 140.

56. Samuel Silverman, in recorded interview by Roberta Greene, September 3, 1969, 2–4, RFK Oral History Program; Silverman, in recorded interview by Jean Stein, July 18, 1968, 2–3, Stein Papers.

57. Ronnie Eldridge, in recorded interview by Roberta Greene, April 21–July 13, 1970, 92; RFK Oral History Program.

58. Milton Gwirtzman, in recorded interview by Roberta Greene, February 10, 1972, 68, RFK Oral History Program.

59. Alfred Connable and Edward Silberfarb, *Tigers of Tammany* (New York, 1967), 358.

60. Penn Kimball, *Bobby Kennedy and the New Politics* (Englewood Cliffs, N.J., 1968), 102.

61. Silverman, in Stein interview, 9, in Greene interview, 10–11; vanden Heuvel and Gwirtzman, *On His Own*, 143; Kimball, *Bobby Kennedy*, 87; author's journal, June 23, 1966.

62. Author's journal, June 23, 1966.

63. Silverman, in Stein interview, 14; in Greene interview, 8.

64. Newfield, *Kennedy*, 155.

65. Justin Feldman, in recorded interview by Roberta Greene, February 4, 1970, 190, RFK Oral History Program.

66. Frank O'Connor, in recorded interview by Roberta Greene, June 19, 1970, 34, RFK Oral History Program.

67. Eugene Nickerson, in recorded interview by Roberta Greene, November 30, 1971, 12–13, RFK Oral History Program.

68. Jack English, in recorded interview by Roberta Greene, November 25, 1969, 44, RFK Oral History Program.

69. John Burns, in Greene interview, 267–268.

70. Author's journal, July 31, 1966.

71. English, in Greene interview, 47.

72. O'Connor, in Greene interview, 71, 74, 75.

73. Ibid., 69–71.

74. Vanden Heuvel and Gwirtzman, *On His Own*, 201.

75. Wilson to Robert Kintner, August 26, 1966, Johnson Papers.

76. In a piece of September 1966, reprinted in Jack Newfield, *Bread and Roses Too* (New York, 1971), 167, 169.

77. Newfield, *Kennedy*, 23.

78. Ibid., 24.

79. Ralph Blumenfeld, "Hugh Carey," *New York Post*, January 23, 1975.

80. Newfield, *Kennedy*, 24–25.

81. Ibid., 24–27.

34. Time of Troubles (*pages* 793–811)

1. For Gallup polls in August 1966 and early January 1967, see G. H. Gallup, ed., *The Gallup Poll: Public Opinion 1935–1971* (New York, 1972), vol. 3, 2023, 2046. The quotation is from the August 21 release. Harris polled to the same effect in November 1966.

2. Author's journal, October 30, 1966.

3. Victor Navasky, *Kennedy Justice* (New York, 1971), 357–358.

4. RFK to Katzenbach, July 13, 1966, RFK Papers.

5. Richard Goodwin, in interview by author, June 11, 1977.

6. *Washington Post,* December 18, 1966.

7. Henry Hall Wilson to LBJ, December 13, 1966, Johnson Papers.

8. "RFK-Humor" file, Mankiewicz Papers.

9. William Manchester, *Controversy* (Boston, 1976), 12.

10. The full text may be found in John Corry, *The Manchester Affair* (New York, 1967), 29–31.

11. Author to RFK, William Manchester and Evan Thomas, April 24, 1966, Schlesinger Papers.

12. Edwin Guthman, *We Band of Brothers* (New York, 1971), 313; Salinger to RFK, September 15, 1966, RFK Papers.

13. Manchester, *Controversy,* 20.

14. Ibid., 19.

15. Ibid., 45.

16. Evan Thomas, in recorded interview by Jean Stein, November 6, 1969, 2, Stein Papers.

17. Corry, *Manchester,* 97.

18. Manchester, *Controversy,* 4.

19. Corry, *Manchester,* 163.

20. Frank Mankiewicz, in recorded interview by L. J. Hackman, October 2, 1969, 25, RFK Oral History Program.

21. Corry, *Manchester,* 206–207.

22. For further reflections on this theme, see Arthur M. Schlesinger, Jr., "On the Writing of Contemporary History," *Atlantic Monthly,* March 1967.

23. RFK to Katharine Graham, n.d. [1966–67], RFK Papers.

24. Corry, *Manchester,* 199.

25. Mankiewicz, in Hackman interview, October 2, 1969, 46.

26. Murray Kempton, in recorded interview by Jean Stein, October 27, 1969, 13, Stein Papers.

27. Louis Oberdorfer, in recorded interview by Roberta Greene, February 12, 1970, 45–46, RFK Oral History Program; Lester David, *Ethel* (New York: Dell reprint, 1972), 99.

28. *Washington Post,* October 24, 25, 1966.

29. Jack Newfield, *Robert Kennedy* (New York, 1969), 128.

30. In vanden Heuvel papers.

31. William vanden Heuvel and Milton Gwirtzman, *On His Own* (Garden City, N.Y., 1970), 228–230.

32. Peter Osnos, "Kennedy Acclaimed on Oxford Visit," *Washington Post,* January 29, 1967.

33. Memorandum of conversation, RFK and François Mitterand, January 30, 1967, RFK Papers.

34. Memorandum of conversation, RFK and Couve de Murville, January 30, 1967, RFK Papers.

35. Memorandum of conversation, RFK and André Malraux, January 30, 1967, RFK Papers.

36. William vanden Heuvel, in recorded interview by Jean Stein, February 28, 1970, 2–3, Stein Papers.

37. Memorandum of conversation, RFK and Charles de Gaulle, January 31, 1967, RFK Papers.

38. Memorandum of conversation, RFK and Étienne Manac'h, January 31, 1967, RFK Papers.

39. David Kraslow and S. H. Loory, *The Secret Search for Peace in Vietnam* (New York: Random House, Vintage reprint, 1968), 177–178.

40. Memorandum of conversation, RFK and Kurt Georg Kiesinger, February 2, 1967, RFK Papers.

41. Memorandum of conversation, RFK and Willy Brandt, February 2, 1967, RFK Papers.

42. Memorandum of conversation, RFK and Amintore Fanfani, February 3, 1967, RFK Papers.

43. Memorandum of conversation, RFK and Giuseppe Saragat, February 3, 1967, RFK Papers.

44. Memorandum of conversation, RFK and Pope Paul VI, February 4, 1967, RFK Papers.

45. Kraslow and Loory, *Secret Search*, 201–203; vanden Heuvel and Gwirtzman, *On His Own*, 287; David Wise, *The Politics of Lying* (New York, 1973), 80, 369.

46. Chester L. Cooper, *The Lost Crusade* (New York, 1970), 503.

47. Rostow to LBJ, January 28, 1967, Johnson Papers.

48. Wise, *Politics of Lying*, 79–80, based on interviews with the relevant State Department people.

49. Mankiewicz, in Hackman interview, August 12, 1969, 62.

50. Ibid., 71.

51. Ibid., 6, 70–75; Mankiewicz, in recorded interview by Jean Stein, April 13, 1970, 1–6, Stein Papers; Peter Edelman, in recorded interview by L. J. Hackman, July 15, 1969, 65–70; Newfield, *Kennedy*, 131–132; Kraslow and Loory, *Secret Search*, 202–204.

52. *Time*, March 17, 1967. For Rostow's categorical denial of the SOB story and its withdrawal by Hugh Sidey of *Time*, see Denis O'Brien, *Murderers and Other Friendly People* (New York, 1973), 258, 262.

53. Guthman, *We Band of Brothers*, 315.

54. Mankiewicz, in Hackman interview, August 12, 1969, 82.

55. *New York Times*, October 16, 1967.

56. Ibid.

57. Newfield, *Kennedy*, 135–136; Jean Stein and George Plimpton, eds., *American Journey* (New York, 1970), 211–212.

58. W. C. Westmoreland, *A Soldier Reports* (Garden City, N.Y., 1976), 224.

59. Victor Lasky, *Robert F. Kennedy: The Myth and the Man* (New York: Pocket Books reprint, 1971), 469.

60. Dick Schaap, *R.F.K.* (New York: New American Library, Signet reprint, 1968), 22.

61. Newfield, *Kennedy*, 133.

62. Author, in recorded interview by Jean Stein, July 11, 1968, 7–8, Stein Papers.

63. John Burns, in recorded interview by Roberta Greene, November 25, 1969–February 25, 1970, 22, RFK Oral History Program.

64. Schaap, *R.F.K.*, 17–24. Schaap spent March 2 with the Kennedys.

65. Vanden Heuvel and Gwirtzman, *On His Own*, 254.

66. Schaap, *R.F.K.*, 27.

67. Bowles to Humphrey, May 25, 1967, Bowles Papers.

68. John Galloway, ed., *The Kennedys and Vietnam* (New York: Facts on File, 1971), 89.

69. *Congressional Record*, March 2, 1967, S2995–S3000.

70. Schaap, *R.F.K.*, 35.

71. Galloway, *Kennedys*, 97.

72. William Dunfey, in recorded interview by L. J. Hackman, December 15, 1971, 85, RFK Oral History Program; Lasky, *Robert F. Kennedy*, 471–472.

73. Fred Harris, in recorded interview by Roberta Greene, July 29, 1970, 7–8, RFK Oral History Program; Harris, *Potomac Fever* (New York, 1977), 147–148.

74. On *Meet the Press,* March 17, 1968.

75. Author's journal, April 18, 1967.

76. *Congressional Record,* April 25, 1967, 10617–10618.

77. Author's journal, April 26, 1967.

78. W. W. Rostow, *The Diffusion of Power, 1955–1972* (New York, 1972), 480, citing Albert H. Cantril, *The American People, Viet-Nam and the Presidency* (Washington, D.C.: American Political Science Association, 1970), 5.

79. *New York Post,* January 28, 1967.

80. *Washington Post,* November 14, 1966.

81. *Newsweek,* March 13, 1967.

82. RFK, remarks at Democratic State Committee Dinner, New York, June 3, 1967, RFK Papers.

83. Peter Maas, in recorded interview by Jean Stein, September 15, 1969, 14, Stein Papers.

84. Author's journal, April 18, 1967.

85. Ibid., May 20, 1967.

35. Tribune of the Underclass (*pages* 812–835)

1. "Favorite Quotations of John F. Kennedy and Robert F. Kennedy" (commonplace book), under "Miscellaneous," RFK Papers. The quotation, unattributed in the commonplace book, is from Keats's *Fall of Hyperion,* canto 1, l. 147. I am indebted to Emily Morison Beck, the editor of *Bartlett's Familiar Quotations,* for this identification.

2. Jack Valenti, *A Very Human President* (New York, 1975), 150.

3. Interview, Washington, D.C., June 5, 1963, in *Robert F. Kennedy: Apostle for Change,* ed. Douglas Ross (New York: Pocket Books reprint, 1968), 56. This is the best compilation of Kennedy's speeches and statements.

4. RFK to LBJ, "Racial Violence in Urban Centers," August 5, 1964, RFK Papers.

5. RFK, in recorded interview by Anthony Lewis, December 4, 1964, VII, 1–2, RFK Oral History Program.

6. John Seigenthaler, in recorded interview by L. J. Hackman, June 5, 1970, 50, RFK Oral History Program.

7. Author's journal, March 23, 1966.

8. Ralph Blumenfeld, "Bobby and Ike Clash over Riots," *New York Post,* August 18, 1965.

9. Richard Rovere, in interview by author, December 4, 1976.

10. Speech before National Council of Christians and Jews, April 28, 1965, in Ross, *Robert F. Kennedy,* 78.

11. RFK, address to Independent Order of Odd Fellows, Spring Valley, New York, August 18, 1965, RFK Papers.

12. Blumenfeld, "Bobby and Ike Clash."

13. Address to Third Annual WGHO Human Relations Award Dinner, Ellenville, New York, April 19, 1966, RFK Papers.

14. Memorandum of conversation, RFK and Pope Paul VI, February 4, 1967, RFK Papers.

15. Ralph Blumenfeld, "RFK Says Rights Leaders Must Share Riot Blame," *New York Post,* August 19, 1965.

16. Nick Kotz and Mary Lynn Kotz, *A Passion for Equality: George A. Wiley and the Movement* (New York, 1977), 253.

17. Martin Luther King, Jr., "Let Justice Roll Down," *Nation,* March 15, 1965.

18. *New York Post,* August 18, 1965.

19. Pat Watters, *Down to Now* (New York, 1971), 135.

20. Louis Lomax, "When 'Nonviolence' Meets 'Black Power,'" in *Martin Luther King, Jr.: A Profile,* ed. C. Eric Lincoln (New York, 1970), 170.
21. Andrew Young to William vanden Heuvel, May 14, 1969, vanden Heuvel Papers.
22. Pete Hamill, in recorded interview by Jean Stein, November 16, 1968, 17–18, Stein Papers.
23. John C. Donovan, *The Politics of Poverty* (New York, 1967), 74–78; Ross, *Robert F. Kennedy,* 146.
24. For RFK's attitude toward welfare, see "Dialogue: Robert Kennedy and Oscar Lewis," *Redbook,* September 1967; Ross, *Robert F. Kennedy,* ch. 6 and esp. his statement of May 19, 1968, "Solutions to the Problems of Welfare," on 551–558.
25. Kotz and Kotz, *Passion for Equality,* 249.
26. Adam Walinsky, in recorded interview by L. J. Hackman, May 22, 1972, 60.
27. Ross, *Robert F. Kennedy,* 555–556.
28. Peter Edelman, in recorded interview by L. J. Hackman, July 29, 1969, 227–230, RFK Oral History Program.
29. *Congressional Record,* October 2, 1974, S17987.
30. RFK, "Federal Role in Urban Affairs," statement before the Subcommittee on Executive Reorganization, August 15, 1966; reprinted in *Congressional Record,* January 23, 1967, esp. S667.
31. RFK, address to Day Care Council, RFK Papers.
32. RFK, address to Federation of Jewish Philanthropies, New York, January 20, 1966, RFK Papers.
33. RFK, "Federal Role in Urban Affairs," S667.
34. Robert F. Kennedy, "Crisis in Our Cities," *Critic,* October–November 1967.
35. Robert F. Kennedy, *To Seek a Newer World* (Garden City, N.Y., 1967), 21, 37.
36. RFK, "A Program for the Urban Crisis," in Ross, *Robert F. Kennedy,* 579.
37. Campaign statement, Binghamton, New York, September 8, 1964; text in Ross, *Robert F. Kennedy,* 61–62.
38. RFK, address to Borough President's Conference of Community Leaders, January 21, 1966, RFK Papers.
39. RFK, "Federal Role in Urban Affairs," S669–S670.
40. I take this analysis, and much that follows, from the illuminating recorded interview of Thomas Johnston by L. J. Hackman, January 21, 1970, esp. 247–250, RFK Oral History Program; supplemented by my interview with Johnston, June 21, 1977.
41. Michael Harrington, "The South Bronx Shall Rise Again," *New York,* April 3, 1978.
42. Johnston, in Hackman interview, 251–252; Bedford-Stuyvesant Restoration Corporation and Bedford-Stuyvesant D & S Corporation, *Annual Report,* 1968.
43. Johnston, in Hackman interview, 254.
44. Jack Newfield, *Robert Kennedy* (New York, 1969), 94.
45. Johnston, in interview by author; in Hackman interview, 254–255.
46. Johnston, in Hackman interview, 377–378, 389–390.
47. Johnston, in interview by author.
48. David E. Lilienthal, *Journals,* vol. 6, *Creativity and Conflict, 1964–1967* (New York, 1976), 302.
49. Benno Schmidt, in recorded interview by Roberta Greene, July 17, 1969, 1, 10–11, RFK Oral History Program.
50. Lilienthal, *Journals,* vol. 6, 444.
51. John Doar, in recorded interview by Jean Stein, July 31, 1968, 6, 13, Stein Papers.
52. Harrington, "The South Bronx Shall Rise Again."
53. Ross, *Robert F. Kennedy,* 581.
54. Newfield, *Kennedy,* 105.

55. Kenneth Clark, in recorded interview by Jean Stein, January 30, 1970, 9, Stein Papers.

56. In interview with Clive Barnes, *New York Times,* August 30, 1968.

57. Ronald B. Taylor, *Chavez and the Farm Workers* (Boston, 1975), 11–12.

58. Walter Reuther, in recorded interview by Jean Stein, October 24, 1968, 6–7, Stein Papers; Victor Reuther, *The Brothers Reuther* (Boston, 1976), 368–369.

59. Peter Edelman, in recorded interview by Jean Stein, March 6, 1969, 6, Stein Papers.

60. Jack Conway, in recorded interview by Jean Stein, August 21, 1968, 5, Stein Papers.

61. William vanden Heuvel and Milton Gwirtzman, *On His Own* (Garden City, N.Y., 1970), 102.

62. Taylor, *Chavez,* 160–167; Jacques Levy, *Cesar Chavez: Autobiography of La Causa* (New York, 1975), 204–205; vanden Heuvel and Gwirtzman, *On His Own,* 103.

63. Cesar Chavez, in recorded interview by Jean Stein, August 24, 1968, 2, Stein Papers; Chavez, in recorded interview by D. J. O'Brien, January 28, 1970, 7, RFK Oral History Program; Peter Matthiessen, *Sal Si Puedes: Cesar Chavez and the New American Revolution* (New York: Dell, Laurel reprint, 1973), 174–175.

64. Levy, *Cesar Chavez,* 449.

65. Chavez, in O'Brien interview, 1–2.

66. Dolores Huerta, in recorded interview by Jean Stein, September 8, 1968, 1–2, Stein Papers.

67. Edelman, in Hackman interview, July 15, 1969, 127; Edelman, in Stein interview, 8.

68. Jack Newfield in Patricia Kennedy Lawford, ed., *That Shining Hour* (n.p., 1969), 137–138; Newfield, *Kennedy,* 82–83; Jerry Bruno and Jeff Greenfield, *The Advance Man* (New York: Bantam reprint, 1972), 105–106.

69. Fred Harris, in recorded interview by Roberta Greene, July 29, 1970, 7, RFK Oral History Program.

70. Quoted by Fred Harris, *Congressional Record,* July 30, 1968, S9711.

71. Edelman, in Stein interview, 12; vanden Heuvel and Gwirtzman, *On His Own,* 108.

72. Steve Bell on ABC, June 9, 1968, reprinted in *An Honorable Profession,* ed. Pierre Salinger (Garden City, N.Y., 1968), 135.

73. Gertrude Claflin to Ethel Kennedy, June 6, 1968, in Salinger, *Honorable Profession,* 71.

74. Vine Deloria, Jr., *Custer Died for Your Sins: An Indian Manifesto* (New York: Avon reprint, 1969), 192, 272.

75. Nick Kotz, *Let Them Eat Promises* (New York: Doubleday, Anchor reprint, 1971), 3–4.

76. Carr, in O'Brien interview, 13.

77. Charles Evers, in recorded interview by Jean Stein, n.d. [1968], 17, Stein Papers.

78. Ibid.

79. Ibid., 18; Kotz, *Promises,* 2.

80. *New Orleans Times-Picayune,* June 9, 1968.

81. Roger Wilkins, in recorded interview by Jean Stein, n.d. [1968], 16, Stein Papers.

82. Edelman (who was present), in Stein interview, 9.

83. Gilbert A. Steiner, *The State of Welfare* (Washington, D.C., 1971), 222.

84. Califano to LBJ, April 17, 1967, Johnson Papers.

85. Steiner, *State of Welfare,* 223.

86. Daniel Patrick Moynihan, *The Politics of a Guaranteed Income* (New York, 1973), 118.

87. Joseph Califano, in recorded interview by Jean Stein, September 21, 1968, 5, Stein Papers.

88. Kotz, *Promises*, 8–9.
89. Robert Coles, in recorded interview by Jean Stein, August 2, 1968, 5–6, Stein Papers.
90. Kotz, *Promises*, 70–74, 77, 141, 170.
91. Ibid., 176–177, 179.
92. Daniel Patrick Moynihan, "The Democrats, Kennedy and the Murder of Dr. King," *Commentary*, May 1968.
93. José Torres, in recorded interview by Jean Stein, August 6, 1968, 2–4.
94. Lyndon B. Johnson, *The Vantage Point* (New York, 1971), 167–172.
95. Harry McPherson, *A Political Education* (Boston, 1972), 359–361.
96. Frank Mankiewicz, in recorded interview by L. J. Hackman, August 12, 1969, 87; Frank Mankiewicz and Tom Braden, *Washington Post*, February 24, 1970; Johnston, in interview by author.
97. *Meet the Press*, August 6, 1967.
98. RFK, "Crisis in Our Cities."
99. Chavez, in Stein interview, 2; in O'Brien interview, 16.
100. Quoted by Anthony Lewis, "A Tribute to Robert Francis Kennedy," Washington, July 22, 1975.
101. Robert Coles, in Stein interview, 2, 3, 9, 11, 16; Jean Stein and George Plimpton, eds., *American Journey* (New York, 1970), 278–279.
102. Newfield, *Kennedy*, 46.
103. Murray Kempton, "The Monument," *New York Post*, December 2, 1966.
104. *Meet the Press*, August 6, 1967.

36. Images (*pages* 836–857)

1. Andrew Kopkind in the *New Republic*, quoted by Penn Kimball, *Bobby Kennedy and the New Politics* (New York, 1968), 70.
2. Ralph Waldo Emerson, "Heroism," in *Essays*.
3. Roger Baldwin, in interview with author, May 15, 1975.
4. Margaret Laing, *The Next Kennedy* (New York, 1968), 32.
5. Jean Stein and George Plimpton, eds., *American Journey* (New York, 1970), 193.
6. Murray Kempton, "Pure Irish: Robert F. Kennedy," *New Republic*, February 15, 1964.
7. Wes Barthelmes, in recorded interview by Roberta Greene, May 20, 1969, 72, RFK Oral History Program.
8. Richard N. Goodwin, "A Day," *McCall's*, June 1970.
9. Allard Lowenstein, memorandum on Robert Kennedy, n.d. [summer 1967], kindly made available to me by Mr. Lowenstein.
10. "RFK-Humor" file, Mankiewicz Papers.
11. Julius Duscha, "Kennedy Man of Hour at ADA Dinner in N.Y.," *Washington Post*, January 28, 1966.
12. Dick Schaap, *R.F.K.* (New York: New American Library, Signet reprint, 1968), 121.
13. Franklin D. Roosevelt, Jr., in recorded interview by Jean Stein, December 9, 1969, 10, Stein Papers.
14. RFK, on the *Today* show, NBC, January 11, 1967, transcript in RFK Papers.
15. RFK, address to Americans for Democratic Action, February 27, 1967, RFK Papers.
16. Jack Newfield, *Robert Kennedy* (New York, 1969), 63.
17. Stein and Plimpton, *American Journey*, 185.
18. Barthelmes, in Greene interview, June 5, 1969, 171.
19. Shirley MacLaine, in recorded interview by Jean Stein, August 26, 1968, 2, Stein Papers.

20. Quoted by Milton Viorst, "The Skeptics," *Esquire,* November 1968.

21. Robert Scheer, "A Political Portrait of Robert Kennedy," *Ramparts,* February 1967; Scheer, in recorded interview by Jean Stein, September 6, 1969, 10–12, Stein Papers; Stein and Plimpton, *American Journey,* 196.

22. Fred Dutton to RFK, December 8, 1966, RFK Papers.

23. Gerald W. Johnson, "Whose Waterloo?" *New Republic,* February 10, 1968.

24. James Wechsler, "Robert F. Kennedy: A Case of Mistaken Identity," *Progressive,* June–July 1965.

25. *Village Voice,* February 2, 1967, and on occasion thereafter.

26. The Ellinger and Barthelmes quotations are from Viorst, "The Skeptics"; the Meany quotation is from Joseph C. Goulden, *Meany* (New York, 1972), 361.

27. John Nolan, in recorded interview by Roberta Greene, August 12, 1970, 57–58, RFK Oral History Program.

28. Herbert Hoover to JFK, April 10, 1948, Hoover Papers. For an overserious account, see G. W. Domhoff, *The Bohemian Grove and Other Retreats: A Study in Ruling-Class Cohesiveness* (New York, 1974).

29. William Orrick, in recorded interview by L. J. Hackman, April 14, 1970, 264–265, RFK Oral History Program.

30. Douglas Dillon, in recorded interview by L. J. Hackman, June 18, 1970, 39, RFK Oral History Program.

31. Frank A. Capell, *Robert F. Kennedy, Emerging American Dictator* (Zarephath, N.J., 1968), 4, 18.

32. Joseph B. Smith, *Portrait of a Cold Warrior* (New York, 1976), 399–400.

33. Finis Farr, *Fair Enough: The Life of Westbrook Pegler* (New Rochelle, N.Y., 1975), 221.

34. Jeffrey Potter, *Men, Money and Magic* (New York, 1976), 299.

35. Margaret Laing, *The Next Kennedy* (New York, 1968), 33.

36. Bruce Biossat, in *An Honorable Profession,* ed. Pierre Salinger (Garden City, N.Y., 1968), 144.

37. Theodore H. White, "The Wearing Last Weeks and a Precious Last Day," *Life,* June 21, 1968.

38. Emerson, "Intellect."

39. Benton to author, May 9, 1968, Schlesinger Papers.

40. Remarks in *In Memory of Robert Francis Kennedy: A Service . . . Memorial Church, Harvard University* (Cambridge, Mass., 1968), 6.

41. Joseph Alsop to James Stevenson, *New Yorker,* June 15, 1967.

42. Salinger, *Honorable Profession,* 121.

43. Excerpt from interview used in "The Journey of Robert F. Kennedy," David Wolper television production, aired February 17, 1970.

44. Author's journal, November 15, 1966.

45. Stein and Plimpton, *American Journey,* 164–165.

46. Art Buchwald, in recorded interview by Roberta Greene, March 12, 1969, 3, RFK Oral History Program.

47. Edward Bennett Williams to RFK, August 7, 1967, RFK Papers.

48. Rose Kennedy to RFK, November 16, 1967, RFK Papers.

49. Cynthia Stone to RFK, November 10, 1964, RFK Papers.

50. Robert F. Kennedy, "Our Climb Up Mt. Kennedy," *Life,* April 9, 1965; Robert F. Kennedy, "A Peak Worthy of the President," *National Geographic,* July 1965.

51. Rita Dallas, *The Kennedy Case* (New York: Popular Library reprint, 1973), 276.

52. James W. Whittaker, "The First Ascent," *National Geographic,* July 1965; RFK articles in *National Geographic* and *Life;* Whittaker in Patricia Kennedy Lawford, ed., *That Shining Hour* (n.p., 1969), 217; "Where Are They Now?" *Newsweek,* March 30, 1970.

53. See the reaction of the Explorers Club of New York as reported by Laing, *Next Kennedy,* 272.

54. Unidentified news ticker, RFK Papers.
55. George Plimpton, in recorded interview by Jean Stein, September 4, 1968, 6, Stein Papers.
56. See the account by Barrett Prettyman, who was along, in Lawford, *Shining Hour,* 204–207; and story by Ward Just, *Washington Post,* September 2, 1965.
57. Charles Spalding, in recorded interview by L. J. Hackman, March 22, 1969, 66, RFK Oral History Program; Lawford, *Shining Hour,* 216.
58. John Glenn, in recorded interview by Roberta Greene, June 26, 1969, 15, RFK Oral History Program.
59. Lawford, *Shining Hour,* 191.
60. Goodwin, "A Day."
61. James Dickey interview, *Paris Review,* Spring 1976.
62. Emerson, "Heroism."
63. Robert F. Kennedy, foreword to memorial edition of John F. Kennedy, *Profiles in Courage* (New York: Harper & Row, Perennial Library reprint, 1964), ix.
64. "Favorite Quotations of John F. Kennedy and Robert F. Kennedy," under "Miscellaneous," RFK Papers.
65. Kenneth P. O'Donnell and David F. Powers, *"Johnny, We Hardly Knew Ye"* (Boston, 1972), 14.
66. Stein and Plimpton, *American Journey,* 167.
67. Goodwin, "A Day."
68. Ibid.
69. Theodore C. Sorensen, *The Kennedy Legacy* (New York, 1969), 37.
70. Stephen Schlesinger, notes, autumn 1967.
71. The phrase is from *The Education of Henry Adams,* ch. 21.
72. As recalled by Jack Newfield in recorded interview, with Ronnie Eldridge, by Jean Stein, n.d. [1968], 17, Stein Papers.
73. Philip Roth, in recorded interview, with William Styron, by Jean Stein, November 13, 1969, 6, Stein Papers.
74. William Styron, in recorded interview, with Philip Roth, by Jean Stein, November 13, 1969, 6, Stein Papers.
75. James Baldwin, in interview by author, October 29, 1976.
76. Stein and Plimpton, *American Journey,* 168–169, 199.
77. Saul Bellow, *Humboldt's Gift* (New York, 1975), 113.
78. Norman Mailer, *Miami and the Siege of Chicago* (New York: New American Library, Signet reprint, 1968), 93, 200–201.
79. James Stevenson, in recorded interview by Jean Stein, November 13, 1969, 2–4, Stein Papers; Carter Burden, in recorded interview by Roberta Greene, February 13, 1974, 26–27, RFK Oral History Program.
80. [James Stevenson], "The Talk of the Town," *New Yorker,* June 15, 1968.
81. Stephen Schlesinger, notes on dinner, autumn 1967.
82. Thomas Johnston, in recorded interview by L. J. Hackman, February 9, 1970, 7, RFK Oral History Program.
83. Yevgeny Yevtushenko, "Under the Skin of the Statue of Liberty," *New York Times Magazine,* February 1970.
84. Author's journal, May 5, 1967.
85. Stein and Plimpton, *American Journey,* 188.
86. It is reprinted in Salinger, *Honorable Profession,* 122.
87. Allen Ginsberg, in recorded interview by Jean Stein, January 22, 1970, 6, 11–13; as amended by Mr. Ginsberg in a letter to me, August 1977. Peter Edelman, in recorded interview by Jean Stein, February 13, 1970, 2–6, Stein Papers; Stein and Plimpton, *American Journey,* 186–188.
88. Robert Lowell to RFK, February 25, 1967, RFK Papers.
89. Stein and Plimpton, *American Journey,* 36, 192–193.

90. Robert Lowell, "Robert Kennedy 1925–1968," *Notebook,* rev. ed. (New York, 1970), 197–198.

37. The Dilemma (*pages 858–878*)

1. *Washington Post,* October 1, 1967.
2. Louis Harris, *The Anguish of Change* (New York, 1973), 203.
3. The Defense Department statistics can be conveniently found in R. H. Fifield, *Americans in Southeast Asia* (New York, 1973), 274–276, and in H. Y. Schandler, *The Unmaking of a President: Lyndon Johnson and Vietnam* (Princeton, 1967), 32.
4. *Face the Nation,* November 26, 1967.
5. Author's journal, February 19, 1968.
6. Schandler, *Unmaking of a President,* 56, 61.
7. Doris Kearns, *Lyndon Johnson and the American Dream* (New York, 1976), 320–321.
8. Author's journal, November 29, 1967.
9. Ibid., December 7, 1967.
10. John Galloway, ed., *The Kennedys and Vietnam* (New York: *Facts on File,* 1971), 101–102.
11. *Face the Nation,* November 26, 1967.
12. Jack Newfield, *Robert Kennedy* (New York, 1969), 177. The story of Lowenstein's guerrilla movement, and indeed the whole political history of 1968, has been well told. For general treatments, see Theodore H. White, *The Making of the President, 1968* (New York, 1969); Lewis Chester, Godfrey Hodgson and Bruce Page, *An American Melodrama: The Presidential Campaign of 1968* (New York, 1969); David English and the staff of the *London Daily Express, Divided They Stand* (Englewood Cliffs, N.J., 1969); Norman Mailer, *Miami and the Siege of Chicago* (New York: Signet reprint, 1968).

    For the Kennedy viewpoint, see David Halberstam, *The Unfinished Odyssey of Robert Kennedy* (New York, 1968); Jules Witcover, *85 Days: The Last Campaign of Robert Kennedy* (New York, 1969); and the relevant parts of Newfield, *Kennedy,* and William vanden Heuvel and Milton Gwirtzman, *On His Own* (Garden City, N.Y., 1970).

    For the McCarthy viewpoint, see Eugene J. McCarthy, *The Year of the People* (New York, 1969); Abigail McCarthy, *Private Faces, Public Places* (Philadelphia: Curtis reprint, 1972); Jeremy Larner, *Nobody Knows: Reflections on the McCarthy Campaign of 1968* (New York, 1970); Richard T. Stout, *People* (New York, 1970); Ben Stavis, *We Were the Campaign* (Boston, 1969); Arthur Herzog, *McCarthy for President* (New York, 1969).
13. Author's journal, September 15, 1967.
14. Newfield's account in *Kennedy* (185–186) generally corresponds to my own notes and recollections. He forgets, however, that he and Lowenstein arrived with Loeb and did not find him there on arrival (in fact, they all drove out in Loeb's car); and he is incorrect in suggesting that Loeb was pro-Johnson. See also author's journal, September 23, 1967; Loeb to author, October 21, 1974; Loeb, in recorded interview by L. J. Hackman, May 25, 1972, 5–6, RFK Oral History Program.
15. George McGovern, in recorded interview by L. J. Hackman, July 16, 1970, 38, RFK Oral History Program.
16. Ibid., 47–48; see also George McGovern, *Grassroots* (New York, 1978), 111.
17. Stout, *People,* 59–60.
18. *Congressional Record,* October 17, 1967, S14894–S14897.
19. McGovern, in Hackman interview, 44–46.

20. Author's journal, October 19, 1967.
21. Kenneth O'Donnell and David Powers, *"Johnny, We Hardly Knew Ye"* (Boston, 1972), 186.
22. Kenneth O'Donnell, in recorded interview by L. J. Hackman, April 3, 1969, 26, RFK Oral History Program.
23. Abigail McCarthy, *Private Faces, Public Places,* 242.
24. Eugene McCarthy, *Year of the People,* 129; McCarthy, in interview with *Boston Globe,* December 22, 1968.
25. Theodore C. Sorensen, *The Kennedy Legacy* (New York, 1969), 129.
26. McCarthy, *Year of the People,* 131.
27. See, for example, the discussion of McCarthy in his second Senate term in Stout, *People,* 105–108, and in Herzog, *McCarthy,* 59–61.
28. J. K. Galbraith, in recorded interview by Jean Stein, September 19, 1969, 4, Stein Papers.
29. O'Donnell, in Hackman interview, 26.
30. Galbraith, in Stein interview, 4.
31. See Eugene McCarthy's eulogy of Kennedy in Herzog, *McCarthy,* 58.
32. McCarthy, *Year of the People,* 51.
33. O'Donnell, in Hackman interview, 28.
34. Joseph Dolan, in recorded interview by L. J. Hackman, April 10, 1970, 76, RFK Oral History Program.
35. Pierre Salinger, in recorded interview by L. J. Hackman, May 26, 1969, 51, RFK Oral History Program.
36. O'Donnell, in Hackman interview, 7.
37. Goodwin to RFK, n.d. [autumn 1967], RFK Papers.
38. Dutton to RFK, November 3, 1967, RFK Papers.
39. Author to RFK, November 3, 1967, RFK Papers.
40. Author's journal, November 5, 1967.
41. O'Donnell, in Hackman interview, 6.
42. Joseph Kraft, in recorded interview by Jean Stein, September 7, 1968, 24–25, Stein Papers; Kraft, in recorded interview by Roberta Greene, March 7, 1970, 65, RFK Oral History Program.
43. Author's journal, November 29, 1967.
44. Witcover, *85 Days,* 35.
45. RFK to Lewis, November 29, 1967, RFK Papers.
46. Author's journal, December 10, 1967.
47. Roche to LBJ, December 4, 1967, Johnson Papers.
48. David E. Lilienthal, *Journals,* vol. 6, *Creativity and Conflict* (New York, 1976), 529.
49. Califano to LBJ, December 8, 1967, Johnson Papers.
50. Rowe to LBJ, January 16, 1968, Johnson Papers.
51. Roche to LBJ, January 26, 1968, Johnson Papers.
52. Thomas Johnston, in recorded interview by L. J. Hackman, May 6, 1969, 57, RFK Oral History Program.
53. *Village Voice,* December 28, 1967.
54. Newfield, *Kennedy,* 196.
55. *Newsweek,* January 29, 1968.
56. Halberstam, *Unfinished Odyssey,* 58–59.
57. Benno Schmidt, in recorded interview by Roberta Greene, July 17, 1969, 31, RFK Oral History Program.
58. Dolan, in Hackman interview, 106–107.
59. Rowe, memorandum.
60. Jack English, in recorded interview by Roberta Greene, December 19, 1969, 19, RFK Oral History Program.
61. Author's journal, January 19, 1968.

62. *Congressional Record,* July 30, 1968, 39717.

63. McGovern, in Stein interview, 4.

64. Justin Feldman, in recorded interview by Roberta Greene, February 4, 1970, 147, RFK Oral History Program.

65. Author's journal, January 29, 1968.

66. Ibid., January 17, 1968.

67. Ibid.

68. Newfield, *Kennedy,* 200–203.

69. G. H. Gallup, ed., *The Gallup Poll, 1935–1971* (New York, 1972), vol. 3, 2104.

70. Harris, *Anguish of Change,* 207.

71. Quoted by A. J. Reichley, "He's Running Himself out of the Race," *Fortune,* March 1968.

72. Jeffrey Potter, *Men, Money and Magic* (New York, 1976), 308–309.

73. Frank Burns, in recorded interview by L. J. Hackman, April 17, 1970, 16, RFK Oral History Program.

74. English, in Greene interview, 23.

75. Author's journal, January 25, 1968.

76. Schmidt, in Greene interview, 33–36; author's journal, January 25, 1968.

77. Vanden Heuvel and Gwirtzman, *On His Own,* 293–294.

78. Adam Walinsky, in recorded interview by Jean Stein, February 7, 1970, 4, Stein Papers.

79. Dolan, in Hackman interview, April 11, 1970, 127.

80. Peter Edelman, in recorded interview by L. J. Hackman, July 15, 1969, 18, RFK Oral History Program.

81. Jean Stein and George Plimpton, eds., *American Journey* (New York, 1970), 223–224; Allard Lowenstein, in interview by author, February 26, 1973; Newfield, *Kennedy,* 204.

38. The Decision (*pages* 879–895)

1. *New York Times,* January 2, 1968.

2. RFK, address at Book and Author Luncheon, Chicago, February 8, 1968, RFK Papers.

3. Adam Walinsky, in recorded interview by Jean Stein, February 7, 1970, 5, Stein Papers.

4. RFK, Book and Author address.

5. G. H. Gallup, ed., *The Gallup Poll: Public Opinion, 1935–1971* (New York, 1972), vol. 3, 2106.

6. Author's journal, February 12, 1968.

7. As he told Jack Anderson, "Daniel Ellsberg," *Washington Post,* September 28, 1975.

8. *Congressional Record,* March 7, 1968, 5647–5648.

9. William Walton, in recorded interview by Roberta Greene, May 14, 1970, 45–46, RFK Oral History Program.

10. Rowland Evans, in recorded interview by Roberta Greene, July 30, 1970, 61, RFK Oral History Program.

11. Thomas J. Watson, Jr., in recorded interview by Roberta Greene, January 6, 1970, 21, RFK Oral History Program.

12. Quoted by Murray Kempton, "The Emperor's Kid Brother," *Esquire,* July 1968.

13. Murray Kempton, "The Monument," *New York Post,* December 2, 1966.

14. Joseph Dolan, in recorded interview by L. J. Hackman, April 11, 1970, 122, RFK Oral History Program.

15. Author's journal, February 7, 1968.

16. Arthur Herzog, *McCarthy for President* (New York, 1969), 104.

17. Jack Newfield, *Robert Kennedy* (New York, 1969), 208.
18. Robert F. Kennedy, " 'Things Fall Apart; the Center Cannot Hold . . .' " *New York Times,* February 10, 1968.
19. Lawrence F. O'Brien, *No Final Victories* (Garden City, N.Y., 1974), 217.
20. Goodwin to RFK, "Conversation with TK on Feb. 13," n.d., RFK Papers.
21. D. P. Moynihan, *The Politics of a Guaranteed Income* (New York, 1973), 100. Moynihan's account is poetically correct, though Johnson in fact had the report analyzed and dismissed its recommendations on budgetary grounds; see the irritable account in Lyndon B. Johnson, *The Vantage Point* (New York, 1971), 172–173.
22. Jules Witcover, *85 Days: The Last Campaign of Robert Kennedy* (New York, 1969), 53.
23. Newfield, *Kennedy,* 211–212.
24. John Seigenthaler, in recorded interview by Jean Stein, May 15, 1970, 51, Stein Papers.
25. Jean Stein and George Plimpton, eds., *American Journey* (New York, 1970), 281–283.
26. Peter Matthiessen, *Sal Si Puedes* (New York: Dell, Laurel reprint, 1973), 176.
27. Peter Edelman, in recorded interview by Jean Stein, March 6, 1969, 20, Stein Papers.
28. Author's journal, March 10, 1968.
29. Witcover, *85 Days,* 57.
30. William vanden Heuvel and Milton Gwirtzman, *On His Own* (Garden City, N.Y., 1970), 302–303.
31. Author's journal, March 11, 1968.
32. Ibid., March 12, 1968.
33. Ibid.
34. RFK to Anthony Lewis, March 13, 1968, RFK Papers.
35. Author's journal, March 13, 1968.
36. Newfield, *Kennedy,* 218–219.
37. Richard T. Stout, *People* (New York, 1969), 185.
38. Author's journal, March 13, 1968.
39. Ibid.
40. Ibid.
41. Theodore C. Sorensen, *The Kennedy Legacy* (New York, 1969), 137.
42. Dolan, in Hackman interview, 164.
43. "Transcript of telephone conversation between DeVier Pierson at the White House and Ted Sorensen at Senator Robert F. Kennedy's office," March 14, 1968, Johnson Papers.
44. Clark Clifford, memorandum of conversation with Senator Robert F. Kennedy and Theodore C. Sorensen, March 14, 1968, Johnson Papers.
45. George McGovern, in recorded interview by L. J. Hackman, July 16, 1970, 52–56, RFK Oral History Program; McGovern, in recorded interview by Jean Stein, September 25, 1968, 5–6, Stein Papers; Stewart Udall, in recorded interview by Jean Stein, July 26, 1968, 9–11, Stein Papers (as edited by Mr. Udall in a letter to me, August 26, 1977); George McGovern, *Grassroots* (New York, 1978), 112.
46. Clifford, memorandum.
47. Statement by RFK, March 17, 1968, RFK Papers.
48. Newfield, *Kennedy,* 224–225.
49. Everything in this section, unless otherwise specified, is from author's journal, March 16, 1968.
50. George Stevens, Jr., in recorded interview by Roberta Greene, April 10, 1969, 69–70, RFK Oral History Program.
51. Fred Dutton, in recorded interview by Jean Stein, July 26, 1968, 13, Stein Papers.

52. Abigail McCarthy, *Private Faces, Public Places* (Philadelphia: Curtis reprint, 1972), 368–374; Herzog, *McCarthy,* 108–109; Blair Clark, in recorded interview by Jean Stein, November 26, 1969, 4–7, Stein Papers.
53. Jeff Greenfield, in recorded interview by Jean Stein, July 30, 1968, 22, Stein Papers.
54. Author's journal, April 2, 1968.

39. The Journey Begins (*pages* 896–914)

1. Eisenhower to Robert Cutler, March 26, 1968, *New York Post,* March 21, 1975.
2. Richard J. Whalen, *Catch the Falling Flag* (Boston, 1972), 96–97.
3. Mike Manatos to LBJ, March 16, 1968, Johnson Papers.
4. Ibid., March 19, 1968.
5. Sam Houston Johnson, *My Brother Lyndon* (New York, 1969), 242.
6. Jack Newfield, *Robert Kennedy* (New York, 1969), 226.
7. *New York Times,* March 24, 1968.
8. *Washington Post,* June 2, 1968.
9. J. K. Galbraith, "Robert F. Kennedy," *ADA World,* July 1968.
10. Richard T. Stout, *People* (New York, 1969), 186.
11. Milton Viorst, "The Skeptics," *Esquire,* November 1968.
12. *Meet the Press,* March 17, 1968.
13. Jimmy Breslin, "With Kennedy in Kansas," *New York Post,* March 18, 1968.
14. Jimmy Breslin, "Last Year in Manhattan (Kansas)," *New York Post,* June 9, 1969.
15. RFK, Alfred M. Landon Lecture, Manhattan, Kansas, March 18, 1968, RFK Papers.
16. Newfield, *Kennedy,* 234.
17. Breslin, "Last Year."
18. Newfield, *Kennedy,* 236.
19. Jules Witcover, *85 Days: The Last Campaign of Robert Kennedy* (New York, 1969), 109–110.
20. Author to RFK, March 27, 1968.
21. Witcover, *85 Days,* 119.
22. Richard Harwood, "Crowd Madness and Kennedy Strategy," *Washington Post,* March 28, 1968.
23. Ibid.
24. Newfield, *Kennedy,* 230.
25. Helen Dudar, "The Perilous Campaign," *New York Post,* June 5, 1968.
26. *New York Times,* March 25, 1968; Jimmy Breslin, " 'Daley Means the Ball Game,' Bobby Says," *Chicago Sun Times,* March 26, 1968.
27. Breslin, " 'Daley Means the Ball Game.' "
28. Dun Gifford, in recorded interview by Jean Stein, August 7, 1968, 39–40, Stein Papers.
29. Jack Gallivan, in recorded interview by Jean Stein, n.d. [1968], 9–10, Stein Papers.
30. Witcover, *85 Days,* 114.
31. Alan King, in recorded interview by Jean Stein, May 1970, 5, Stein Papers.
32. G. H. Gallup, ed., *The Gallup Poll: Public Opinion, 1935–1971* (New York, 1972), vol. 3, 2112.
33. *Newsweek,* April 1, 1968.
34. Lyndon B. Johnson, *The Vantage Point* (New York, 1971), 538.
35. McPherson to LBJ, March 22, 1968, Johnson Papers.
36. "Report of the Department of Justice Task Force to Review the FBI Martin Luther King, Jr., Security and Assassination Investigations," January 11, 1977, 131.
37. Townsend Hoopes, *The Limits of Intervention,* rev. ed. (New York, 1973), 206.

38. James Rowe to LBJ, March 19, 1968, Johnson Papers.

39. Walt W. Rostow, *The Diffusion of Power* (New York, 1972), 521.

40. Harry McPherson, *A Political Education* (Boston, 1972), 428.

41. Joseph Califano, *A Presidential Nation* (New York, 1975), 211; Califano, in interview by author, July 25, 1971.

42. George Christian, *The President Steps Down* (New York, 1970), 259.

43. Lady Bird Johnson, *A White House Diary* (New York: Dell reprint, 1971), 706.

44. Johnson, *Vantage Point,* 425.

45. Doris Kearns, *Lyndon Johnson and the American Dream* (New York, 1976), 342.

46. Ibid., 28–29, 32, 343. Emphasis added.

47. Bobby Baker, with Larry King, *Wheeling and Dealing: Confessions of a Capitol Hill Operator* (New York, 1978), 103, also 32–33; Lawrence O'Brien, *No Final Victories* (Garden City, N.Y., 1974), 229.

48. William Barry, in recorded interview by Jean Stein, April 1970, 24, Stein Papers.

49. Witcover, *85 Days,* 126–127.

50. Author's journal, March 31, 1968.

51. Witcover, *85 Days,* 132.

52. Whalen, *Falling Flag,* 145.

53. Abigail McCarthy, *Private Faces, Public Places* (Curtis reprint, 1972), 257.

54. Johnson, *My Brother Lyndon,* 251–252.

55. Ibid.

56. The memorandum of the conversation in Johnson, *Vantage Point,* 539–542, differs in immaterial respects from "Notes on Meeting of the President with Senator Robert Kennedy, April 3, 1968," in Johnson Papers. Sorensen's recollections are in Theodore C. Sorensen, *The Kennedy Legacy* (New York, 1969), 146–147, and, with more detail, in Sorensen, in recorded interview by L. J. Hackman, March 21, 1969, 57–58.

57. Hubert Humphrey, *The Education of a Public Man* (Garden City, N.Y., 1976), 361.

58. W. W. Rostow, memorandum of conversation with the President, the Vice President, Charles Murphy, April 3, 1968, Johnson Papers.

59. Author's journal, April 4, 1968.

60. Jeremy Larner, *Nobody Knows: Reflections on the McCarthy Campaign of 1968* (New York, 1970), 63–64. Emphasis added.

61. Author's journal, March 19, 1968.

62. Jon Bradshaw, "Richard Goodwin: The Good, the Bad, and the Ugly," *New York Times,* August 18, 1975.

63. Author's journal, March 19, 1968.

64. Ibid., April 3, 1968.

65. Johnston to RFK, April 20, 1968, Schlesinger Papers.

66. Fred Dutton, in recorded interview by L. J. Hackman, November 18, 1969, 49, RFK Oral History Program.

67. Witcover, *85 Days,* 134.

68. Author's journal, April 3, 1968.

69. Robert S. Bird, "Robert F. Kennedy: At Home with the Heir Apparent," *Saturday Evening Post,* August 26, 1967.

70. *Meet the Press,* March 17, 1968.

71. Lewis Chester, et al., *An American Melodrama* (New York, 1969), 145.

72. Pierre Salinger, ed., *An Honorable Profession* (Garden City, N.Y., 1968), 125.

73. Victor Reuther, in interview by author, August 10, 1971; see also Frank Cormier and W. J. Eaton, *Reuther* (Englewood Cliffs, N.J., 1970), 391.

74. Walter Fauntroy, in recorded interview by Jean Stein, November 11, 1969, 25, Stein Papers.

75. Peter Edelman, in recorded interview by L. J. Hackman, July 29, 1969, 263, RFK Oral History Program.

76. Stanley Levison, in recorded interview by Jean Stein, November 21, 1962, 2, Stein Papers.
77. John Lewis, in recorded interview by Jean Stein, September 9, 1968, 5, Stein Papers.
78. Walter Sheridan, in recorded interview by Roberta Greene, August 5, 1969, 6, RFK Oral History Program.
79. John J. Lindsay, in recorded interview by Jean Stein, September 6, 1968, 10, Stein Papers; Walter Sheridan to author, October 17, 1977.
80. Lindsay, in Stein interview, 10–11; Lindsay to author, September 10, 1977.
81. William Barry, in recorded interview by Roberta Greene, March 20, 1969, 39, RFK Oral History Program.
82. Frank Mankiewicz, in recorded interview by Jean Stein, September 21, 1968, 26, Stein Papers; Adam Walinsky, in recorded interview by Jean Stein, September 20, 1968, 25, Stein Papers.
83. Jean Stein and George Plimpton, eds., *American Journey* (New York, 1970), 256.
84. Remarks by Senator Robert F. Kennedy on the death of the Reverend Martin Luther King, rally in Indianapolis, Indiana, April 4, 1968.

40. The Long Day Wanes (*pages* 915–942)

1. Coretta Scott King, *My Life with Martin Luther King, Jr.* (London, 1970), 333–334.
2. Coretta Scott King, in recorded interview by Jean Stein, November 18, 1969, 1–2, Stein Papers.
3. John Lewis, in recorded interview by Jean Stein, September 9, 1968, 7, Stein Papers; William vanden Heuvel and Milton Gwirtzman, *On His Own* (Garden City, N.Y., 1970), 338.
4. Jeff Greenfield, in recorded interview by Roberta Greene, December 10, 1969, 96–99, RFK Oral History Program.
5. RFK, speech at Cleveland City Club, April 5, 1968, RFK Papers.
6. Jean Stein and George Plimpton, eds., *American Journey* (New York, 1970), 261.
7. Ibid., 258.
8. Roy Jenkins, *Nine Men of Power* (London, 1974), 208.
9. Jimmy Breslin, "Back to Earth," *New York Post,* December 27, 1968.
10. Author's journal, April 10, 1968.
11. Stein and Plimpton, *American Journey,* 260–261.
12. Ibid., 259–260.
13. Andrew Young, in recorded interview by Jean Stein, September 9, 1968, 12–13, Stein Papers; Joseph Lelyveld, "Our New Voice at the U.N.," *New York Times Magazine,* February 6, 1977.
14. Ralph Abernathy, in "R.F.K.," Metromedia Broadcast, June 6, 1969.
15. Stein and Plimpton, *American Journey,* 261.
16. RFK to Katzenbach, February 12, 1968, Katzenbach to RFK, February 16, 1968, RFK Papers.
17. Nicholas Katzenbach, in recorded interview by Jean Stein, September 27, 1968, 20, Stein Papers.
18. John Bartlow Martin to RFK, n.d. [April 1968], RFK Papers.
19. Martin to RFK, March 29, 1968, RFK Papers.
20. Martin, "RFK Notes [on the 1968 campaign]," June 28, 1968, 11–12, Martin Papers.
21. Fred Dutton, in recorded interview by L. J. Hackman, November 18, 1969, 52, RFK Oral History Program.
22. *New York Times,* April 28, 1968.
23. Martin, "RFK Notes," 26.

24. Barry Stavis, *We Were the Campaign* (Boston, 1969), 67–68.
25. Stein and Plimpton, *American Journey,* 248.
26. Martin, "RFK Notes," 36–37.
27. David Halberstam, "Travels with Bobby Kennedy," *Harper's,* July 1968.
28. Thomas B. Congdon, Jr., "Robert F. Kennedy, 1925–1968," *Saturday Evening Post,* June 29, 1968.
29. RFK, remarks at Indiana University Medical School, Indianapolis, April 26, 1968, RFK Papers.
30. Jules Witcover, *85 Days: The Last Campaign of Robert Kennedy* (New York, 1969), 165.
31. David Halberstam, *The Unfinished Odyssey of Robert Kennedy* (New York, 1968), 121.
32. RFK, remarks at Valparaiso University, April 29, 1968, RFK Papers.
33. Jack Newfield, *Robert Kennedy* (New York, 1969), 256–257.
34. Quoted in vanden Heuvel and Gwirtzman, *On His Own,* 345–347.
35. Martin, "RFK Notes," 36.
36. Newfield, *Kennedy,* 265.
37. Richard Stout, *People* (New York, 1970), 237.
38. Lewis Chester, et al., *An American Melodrama* (New York, 1969), 146.
39. Stein and Plimpton, *American Journey,* 196–197.
40. Vanden Heuvel and Gwirtzman, *On His Own,* 359–361.
41. [James Stevenson], "Notes and Comment," in "The Talk of the Town," *New Yorker,* June 15, 1968.
42. James Stevenson, in recorded interview by Jean Stein, November 13, 1969, 9, Stein Papers.
43. Rita Dallas, *The Kennedy Case* (New York: Popular Library reprint, 1973), 301–304; Theodore C. Sorensen, *The Kennedy Legacy* (New York, 1969), 25–26.
44. *Washington Post,* April 30, 1968.
45. "Free" [Abbie Hoffman], *Revolution for the Hell of It* (New York, 1968), 104.
46. Marshall McLuhan, "All of the Candidates Are Asleep," *Saturday Evening Post,* August 10, 1968.
47. Hal Higon, "Kennedy in the Midwest," *Chicago Tribune Magazine,* August 25, 1968.
48. Joseph Alsop, "Robert Kennedy on the Stump," *Washington Post,* May 16, 1968.
49. Ibid.
50. Stewart Alsop, "Bobby's Red Guards," *Saturday Evening Post,* May 4, 1968.
51. John Douglas, "Robert Kennedy and the Qualities of Personal Leadership," speech at Loyola University, Chicago, October 31, 1968, 9.
52. Halberstam, *Unfinished Odyssey,* 185.
53. Congdon, "Kennedy"; Witcover, *85 Days,* 160–163.
54. Jeff Greenfield, in recorded interview by Jean Stein, July 30, 1968, 18, Stein Papers; Greenfield, in recorded interview by Roberta Greene, January 5, 1970, 123–124, RFK Oral History Program.
55. Newfield, *Kennedy,* 261.
56. Halberstam, *Unfinished Odyssey,* 172.
57. Peter Edelman, in recorded interview by L. J. Hackman, August 5, 1969, 343, RFK Oral History Program; Theodore H. White, *The Making of the President, 1968* (New York, 1969), 171–172.
58. Newfield, *Kennedy,* 259.
59. Witcover, *85 Days,* 192.
60. Ibid., 191.
61. Greenfield, in Greene interview, 125.
62. Witcover, *85 Days,* 193–194.
63. Helen Dudar, "The Perilous Campaign," *New York Post,* June 5, 1968; Witcover, *85 Days,* 194.

64. John Glenn, in recorded interview by Roberta Greene, June 30, 1969, 40, RFK Oral History Program.
65. Edelman, in Hackman interview, 346.
66. Witcover, *85 Days,* 197.
67. Ibid., 198.
68. Eugene McCarthy, "Speaking Out," *Saturday Evening Post,* January 4, 1964.
69. In a eulogy of Humphrey, "Tragedy of Valor and Love," from the *Austin Daily Texan,* reprinted in *Congressional Record,* January 31, 1978, E274.
70. Newfield, *Kennedy,* 253.
71. Stein and Plimpton, *American Journey,* 286–287.
72. Richard Harwood, remarks at RFK Journalism Award's luncheon, Washington, D.C., May 14, 1976.
73. Abigail McCarthy, *Private Faces, Public Places* (Philadelphia: Curtis reprint, 1972), 373.
74. Robert Coles, "Ordinary Hopes, Ordinary Fears," in *Conspiracy: The Implications of the Harrisburg Trial for the Democratic Tradition,* ed. J. C. Raines (New York, 1974), 99–100.
75. Alexander M. Bickel, "Robert Kennedy as History," *New Republic,* July 5, 1969.
76. Paul Cowan, "Wallace in Yankeeland," *Village Voice,* July 18, 1968.
77. Jack Newfield, "A Look at Kennedy," mimeographed, n.d. [spring 1968].
78. Homer Bigart, "Negroes Are Cool to McCarthy as He Opens Indiana Campaign," *New York Times,* April 19, 1968.
79. A. McCarthy, *Private Faces,* 381.
80. Eugene McCarthy, in interview with *Boston Globe* Washington staff, *Boston Globe,* December 24, 1968.
81. Abigail McCarthy, "The McCarthy Campaign," *Atlantic Monthly,* August 1970.
82. Norman Mailer, *Miami and the Siege of Chicago* (New York: New American Library, Signet reprint, 1968), 92–93, 99.
83. *Salem* (Oreg.) *Statesman,* May 22, 1968.
84. Jeremy Larner, *Nobody Knows* (New York, 1970), 93.
85. Ibid., 76–77; Larner, "Nobody Knows . . . Part II," *Harper's,* May 1969.
86. Eugene J. McCarthy, "Why I'm Battling LBJ," *Look,* February 6, 1968.
87. *London Sunday Times,* August 18, 1968.
88. Eugene J. McCarthy, *The Year of the People* (Garden City, N.Y., 1969), 295.
89. McCarthy, speech in Cleveland, June 18, 1968, in *Washington Post,* June 19, 1968; *New York Daily News,* June 19, 1968.
90. Stavis, *We Were the Campaign,* 52, 134.
91. David Halberstam, "Travels with Bobby Kennedy," *Harper's,* July 1968.
92. Richard Harwood, "McCarthy and Kennedy: Philosopher vs. Evangelist," *Washington Post,* May 26, 1968.
93. Stein and Plimpton, *American Journey,* 257.
94. A. McCarthy, *Private Faces,* 397.
95. Halberstam, "Travels with Kennedy."
96. White, *Making of the President, 1968,* 79.
97. *Washington Post,* May 26, 1968.
98. Stavis, *We Were the Campaign,* 32.
99. Larner, *Nobody Knows,* 36.
100. Stavis, *We Were the Campaign,* 135.
101. Larner, *Nobody Knows,* 33.
102. Ibid., 33, 79–81, 144.
103. Stavis, *We Were the Campaign,* 51.
104. Larner, *Nobody Knows,* 76.
105. Ibid.
106. Halberstam, "Travels with Kennedy."
107. Jack Newfield, "The Arrogance of Class," *Village Voice,* May 2, 1968.

108. Author's journal, May 27, 1968.
109. Stein and Plimpton, *American Journey,* 269–270.
110. Elizabeth Hardwick, in recorded interview by Jean Stein, September 18, 1968, 4, Stein Papers, edited by Miss Hardwick in a letter of September 4, 1977.
111. William Manchester, "RFK: Not at All a Brute," *Baltimore Sun,* April 26, 1968.
112. Jacqueline Kennedy to William Manchester, June 17, 1968. I am indebted to Mr. Manchester for this letter.
113. Alexander M. Bickel, "The Kennedy Cause," *New Republic,* July 20, 1968.
114. "Free," *Revolution,* 104.
115. Nick Kotz and Mary Lynn Kotz, *A Passion for Equality: George A. Wiley and the Movement* (New York, 1977), 255.
116. Michael Harrington, *Fragments of the Century* (New York, 1973), 237–238, 243.
117. Charles Quinn, in recorded interview by Jean Stein, October 19, 1968, 15, Stein Papers.
118. Stein and Plimpton, *American Journey,* 319.
119. Witcover, *85 Days,* 224.
120. L. K. Obst, *The Sixties* (New York, 1977), 254.
121. Congdon, "Kennedy."
122. Stein and Plimpton, *American Journey,* 293; Newfield, *Kennedy,* 286.
123. Romain Gary, *White Dog* (New York, 1970), 192–196; Gary, in interview by Henry Raymont, *New York Times,* August 21, 1968; Pierre Salinger, *Je suis un Américain* (Paris, 1975), 247, 309–310; Stein and Plimpton, *American Journey,* 293–294.
124. Witcover, *85 Days,* 114.
125. William Barry, in recorded interview by Roberta Greene, March 19, 1969, 5–6, 9, RFK Oral History Program.
126. Barry, in Greene interview, March 20, 1969, 47.
127. Jack Eberhardt, in recorded interview by Jean Stein, August 23, 1968, 1, Stein Papers.
128. Stein and Plimpton, *American Journey,* 294–295; Quinn, in Stein interview, 19.
129. Warren Rogers and Stanley Trettick, "RFK," *Look,* July 9, 1968.
130. Dudar, "Perilous Campaign."
131. Walter Sheridan, in recorded interview by Roberta Greene, August 5, 1969, 90, RFK Oral History Program.
132. Barry, in Greene interview, 23.

41. To Sail Beyond . . . the Western Stars, Until I Die (*pages* 943–956)

1. Jean Stein and George Plimpton, eds., *American Journey* (New York, 1970), 273–274.
2. Jeremy Larner, *Nobody Knows* (New York, 1970), 91.
3. Eugene McCarthy, interview with *Boston Globe* Washington staff, *Boston Globe,* December 24, 1968.
4. See Eugene McCarthy, *The Year of the People* (Garden City, N.Y., 1969), 118–124.
5. Arthur Herzog, *McCarthy for President* (New York, 1969), 158.
6. *San Francisco Chronicle,* May 31, 1968.
7. *New York Times,* May 5, 1968.
8. Herzog, *McCarthy,* 158.
9. Frank Mankiewicz, in recorded interview by L. J. Hackman, September 30, 1969, 60–61, RFK Oral History Program.
10. McCarthy, *Year of the People,* 143.
11. Barry Stavis, *We Were the Campaign* (Boston, 1969), 62.

12. McCarthy, *Year of the People,* 143.

13. Ibid., 124. Emphasis added.

14. Larner, *Nobody Knows,* 94–97.

15. Lewis Chester, et al., *American Melodrama* (New York, 1969), 304.

16. Richard Stout, *People* (New York, 1970), 260; Jules Witcover, *85 Days: The Last Campaign of Robert Kennedy* (New York, 1969), 216–217.

17. Larner, *Nobody Knows,* 97.

18. Edith Green, in recorded interview by Roberta Greene, February 27, 1974, 2, RFK Oral History Program.

19. William vanden Heuvel and Milton Gwirtzman, *On His Own* (Garden City, N.Y., 1970), 367.

20. Joseph Kraft, in recorded interview by Roberta Greene, March 7, 1970, 72, RFK Oral History Program.

21. Ralph Friedman, "The Disenchanted Suburbia," *Nation,* May 8, 1972.

22. Pierre Salinger, in recorded interview by L. J. Hackman, April 18, 1970, 55, RFK Oral History Program.

23. Witcover, *85 Days,* 206.

24. Larner, *Nobody Knows,* 101–102.

25. M. S. Devorkin, "Kennedy Campaigning in Primary States" (B.S. thesis, Massachusetts Institute of Technology, June 1969), 114.

26. Witcover, *85 Days,* 221–222.

27. RFK, press conference statement, Los Angeles, May 29, 1968, RFK Papers.

28. Janet Auchincloss to RFK, n.d. [May 31, 1968], RFK Papers.

29. William Orrick, in recorded interview by L. J. Hackman, April 14, 1970, 258, RFK Oral History Program.

30. Walter Sheridan, in interview by Roberta Greene, August 13, 1969, 62, RFK Oral History Program; vanden Heuvel and Gwirtzman, *On His Own,* 104.

31. Author's journal, May 30, 1968.

32. Fred Dutton, in recorded interview by Jean Stein, July 26, 1968, 59.

33. Stein and Plimpton, *American Journey,* 305.

34. Curtis Lee Baker (Black Jesus), in recorded interview by Jean Stein, December 4, 1969, 5–6, Stein Papers.

35. John Seigenthaler, in recorded interview by Jean Stein, August 27, 1968, 38, Stein Papers.

36. Dutton, in Stein interview, 62.

37. Baker, in Stein interview, 7–8.

38. Hector Lopez, in recorded interview by Jean Stein, October 6, 1969, 6, Stein Papers.

39. Willie Brown, in recorded interview by Jean Stein, August 17, 1968, 6, Stein Papers.

40. Lopez, in Stein interview, 15.

41. Herzog, *McCarthy,* 177.

42. Larner, *Nobody Knows,* 111.

43. Author's journal, June 1, 1968.

44. Frank Mankiewicz, in recorded interview by L. J. Hackman, December 16, 1969, 53.

45. Herzog, *McCarthy,* 179.

46. Andreas Teuber; Stein and Plimpton, *American Journey,* 311.

47. Ibid., 309–310.

48. Stout, *People,* 271–272.

49. Stein and Plimpton, *American Journey,* 312.

50. *New York Times,* June 2, 1968.

51. Mankiewicz, in Hackman interview, December 16, 1969, 54.

52. Chester, *American Melodrama,* 345.

53. Larner, *Nobody Knows,* 117.

54. Ibid.

55. Herzog, *McCarthy,* 187.

56. Theodore H. White, "The Wearing Last Weeks and a Precious Last Day," *Life,* June 21, 1968; Richard N. Goodwin, "A Day," *McCall's,* June 1970.

57. R. B. Kaiser, *"R.F.K. Must Die"* (New York, 1970), 15.

58. George McGovern, in recorded interview by Jean Stein, September 25, 1968, 12, Stein Papers.

59. Hackett's estimate, misdated June 4, 1968, is in vanden Heuvel and Gwirtzman, *On His Own,* 390–392.

60. Richard N. Goodwin, "A Sentimental Tribute"; I quote here the original version rather than the one published as "A Day" in *McCall's.*

61. J. K. Galbraith, in recorded interview by Jean Stein, July 30, 1968, 14, Stein Papers.

62. Justin Feldman, in recorded interview by Roberta Greene, February 4, 1970, 160–162, RFK Oral History Program.

63. Budd Schulberg, "R.F.K.–Harbinger of Hope," *Playboy,* January 1969.

64. Salinger, *Je suis un Américain* (Paris, 1975), 312.

65. Goodwin, "A Day."

66. Witcover, *85 Days,* 262; Jack Newfield, *Robert Kennedy* (New York, 1969), 298.

67. Larner, *Nobody Knows,* 121.

68. Author's journal, June 6, 1968.

69. Mankiewicz, in Hackman interview, October 2, 1969, 56.

70. Gloria Steinem, "Link between the New Politics and the Old," *Saturday Review,* August 2, 1969.

71. Newfield, *Kennedy,* 303–304.

72. Author's journal, June 8, 1968.

73. Lady Bird Johnson, *A White House Diary* (New York: Dell reprint, 1971), 756.

Index

Dulles, Allen W. (*cont'd*)
465, 467, 471, 472, 473, 478; and
Indonesia, 476; and political assassi-
nation, 506; death, 514; and Warren
Commission, 519, 642
Dulles, John Foster, 106, 124, 127,
435, 445, 453, 460, 601
Dunfey, William, 680
Dungan, Ralph, 328, 487, 579 n, 677,
727
Dunlop, John, 188
Dunn, John (Cockeyed), 171
Durban, RFK in, 780
Dutton, Fred, 202, 238, 688, 771, 785,
811, 892; on RFK, 841; and ques-
tion of RFK as presidential candi-
date, 866, 869, 873, 882, 883, 889;
in RFK's campaign, 908, 909, 910,
920, 930, 953
Dylan, Bob, 808

Eastland, James O., 244, 245, 372; and
RFK, 301, 312, 314, 332, 712; and
judicial appointments, 320, 321; and
Levison hearing, 369, 371
Eberhardt, Jack, 942
Economic Opportunity Act, 668, 823
Edelman, Peter, 855, 909 n; on RFK,
615; in RFK's Senate campaign,
699; on RFK's Senate staff, 707,
710; and guaranteed minimum income, 817, 818; and migrant workers, 825, 827; and poverty in Mississippi, 829; in RFK's presidential
campaign, 877, 928
Eden, Anthony, 885
Educational desegregation, 299, 306,
319, 330–341, 351–356, 359, 361,
819
Edwards, Sheffield, 502 n
Egypt, 77, 474
Ehrlichman, John D., 507
Eisenhower, Dwight D., 100, 107, 108,
112, 123, 191, 240; and U-2 incident, 212; sends troops to Little
Rock, 299; and civil rights, 303,
326; and judicial appointments, 323,
388 n; and executive privilege, 395;
and Sherman Adams, 401, 402–403;
and pardon process, 410; and summit talks, 437; and Gaither committee, 438; relations with Soviet
Union, 439, 461; and national
security, 443; and Southeast Asia,

442, 735; and travel restrictions,
453, 455; and Cuban invasion plan,
463, 467; and CIA, 474, 475, 476,
477, 502 n; and political assassina-
tion, 506, 508, 509; and Dominican
Republic, 511, 512; trip to Japan
canceled, 588; at JFK's funeral,
639; sends troops to Lebanon,
756 n; on Watts riot, 814; on RFK,
896
Eisenhower, John, 506
Eisenhower, Mamie, 403 n
Eisenhower, Milton, 489
Eldridge, Ronnie, 697, 785, 787
Electoral college votes (1960), 230 n
Electrical Workers (AFL), 172
Electronic surveillance, 262–265, 275,
295, 296. *See also* Bugging; Wire-
tapping
Ellender, Allen, 245
Ellinger, Don, 841
Elliott, Robert, 322
Elliott, William Yandell, 68–69
Ellison, Ralph, 938
Ellsberg, Daniel, 743, 745 n, 751, 880
Elsey, George, 264
Emerson, Ralph Waldo, 792, 836, 843,
848, 898
Emerson, Rupert, 69
Emmet, Robert, 80
Employment opportunities, 325, 349–
350, 361, 384–385, 817–818. *See
also* Civil rights; Committee on
Equal Employment Opportunity
Enemy Within, The (RFK), 158 n,
175, 197–198, 243, 485, 838; pro-
posal to film, 273
England: Kennedys' visits to, 10–11,
799; JPK as ambassador to, 26–30,
34–37; support of, by Americans,
33; aid to, 38 n, 39, 40, 51; hatred
of, 76, 78, 79, 81; and China trade,
105, 107; and Indonesia, 661–662
English, John, 621, 697, 789, 873
Epstein, Edward Jay, 371, 642;
*Legend: The Secret World of Lee
Harvey Oswald,* 579 n, 642 n
Equal Employment Opportunity. *See*
Committee on Equal Employment
Opportunity
Ernst, Morris, 258
Ervin, Sam, 119, 135, 149, 178, 185,
186, 245, 324, 381, 382
Esquire, 620, 622
Esterline, J. D., 474, 477, 496